Air Law

Cases & Materials

Editor-in-Chief:
Joseph J. Vacek, J.D.

Editors:
Brett D. Venhuizen, J.D.
William D. Watson, J.D.
Douglas M. Marshall, J.D.
Ernest E. Anderson, J.D.

KENDALL/HUNT PUBLISHING COMPANY
4050 Westmark Drive   Dubuque, Iowa 52002

Table of Contents

About the Editors

Joseph J. Vacek, J.D.

Joseph Vacek is an Assistant Professor of Aviation at the University of North Dakota. In addition to Aviation Law, he teaches many other undergraduate, graduate, and honors classes related to transportation, including space law, air transportation, environmental issues, alternative transportation, and other aviation courses. Professor Vacek researches in the area of transportation law and policy. Additionally, Professor Vacek practices law, is an active instructor pilot, and serves as the faculty advisor to the UND Aerobatic Team.

Ernest E. Anderson, J.D.

Ernest Anderson is an Assistant Professor of Aviation at the University of North Dakota, where he teaches Aviation Law. Prior to that, he served as an attorney for the Federal Aviation Administration for twelve years, where he represented the FAA's Flight Standards, Medical, and Security program offices in litigation with the National Transportation Safety Board and Department of Transportation. Professor Anderson spent six years on active duty with the Marine Corps as a helicopter pilot, and eighteen years in the Marine and Army Reserve. Professor Anderson holds a commercial pilot's license with helicopter, single, and multi-engine airplane ratings.

Douglas Marshall, J.D.

Douglas Marshall is an Associate Professor at the University of North Dakota. He teaches undergraduate and graduate courses in the Aviation Department, and researches in the area of Unmanned Aerial Systems. Professor Marshall served as General Counsel and President of Pacific Coast Airlines, representing the airline in various regulatory, enforcement, and contractual matters before the FAA and NTSB. Professor Marshall was admitted to the bar association of the U.S. Supreme Court, the Ninth Circuit of Appeals, and all California state and federal courts.

Brett D. Venhuizen, J.D.

Brett D. Venhuizen, J.D. is an Associate Professor of Aeronautical Science at Embry-Riddle Aeronautical University, where he teaches Aviation Law and Private Pilot Operations. Professor Venhuizen holds both a Bachelor's of Science and a Juris Doctor degree from the University of South Dakota. An active pilot and flight instructor since 1990, he has previous experience as a corporate and charter pilot. Prior to joining the faculty at ERAU, Professor Venhuizen was a faculty member at the University of North Dakota. He also maintains a law practice representing pilots and other certificate holders in FAA enforcement proceedings.

William Watson, J.D.

William Watson is an Assistant Professor of Aviation at the University of North Dakota. He teaches Aviation Law, Helicopter Aerodynamics, and Aviation Safety Management in the graduate school. Professor Watson researches in the area of Unmanned Aerial Systems. Prior to his tenure at UND, Professor Watson was a Deputy Attorney General for the state of California, practiced Aviation Law in Los Angeles, California, and piloted helicopters for the U.S. Army.

Introduction

This casebook is designed to introduce readers to aviation law in the context of an advanced undergraduate level class, graduate studies course, or law school special topics class. Aviation law a distinct subject area with its own history, vocabulary, and bodies of statutory and case law. Yet it also borrows heavily from other areas of law. To ensure all users of this casebook get the most value and information from it, the book is arranged so that it can be studied from front to back, in order, giving readers unfamiliar with law, except for a basic understanding of civics, a working knowledge of the discipline of aviation law. It also may be used piecemeal, to delve deeper into the details of aviation law by students already well versed in law, politics, or public policy.

Part I of this book should prepare readers with little or no formal legal training to understand the principles on which aviation law cases are decided. First, readers are introduced to the history of law, legal research, and the U.S. legal system. Because the U.S. legal system relies heavily on precedent, or cases that have been already decided, a working knowledge of the major areas of law that affect aviation law is necessary. Those major areas of law are introduced in Part I as well. They include constitutional law, administrative law and federal regulation of aviation, FAA enforcement, property law, contract law, tort law, international law, and criminal law. Astute readers will note that the rest of this casebook, Part II through IX, is divided into those major areas, in that order. From each of those areas come many different principles that together shape the discipline of aviation law.

Finally, the wide margins are purposeful to facilitate taking notes. Since the study of law is language-intensive, it may help you understand the cases better and simplify later studying to write notes and questions in the margins.

I. History of Law

Entire treatises have been written on the history of law, but to be well-versed in the issues contemporary to aviation law does not require one to be able to trace the entire history of every branch of the law. However, full understanding of any discipline is incomplete until one is familiar enough with its history to see from where it came and to where it is going. To that end, the history of law in the context of aviation law starts with the notion that almost every aspect of our society is influenced by law, and generally always has been, starting at the beginning of human civilization.

A. Law as Power

At its most basic level, law is power. Whoever has the guns holds power over those who don't. Of course, history shows that law based purely on individual power is unstable: someone else with even bigger guns inevitably comes along and seizes power. When entire societies amass resources, the power of those societies may last longer, but without some enforceable, stable system of rules or social norms any government that manages to emerge will be overthrown fairly regularly.

Although the United States is not ruled by people with guns, some legal theorists argue that our current system of laws is merely the will of those in power, cloaked in eloquently worded disguise from the mouths of judges. To some extent, they are right. Federal judges hold lifetime tenure during good behavior, and are thus somewhat insulated from public pressure. Thus, a judge could wholly ignore social trends and the will of the people and instead adhere to ancient legal doctrine and make rulings that seem racist, unreasonable, or out of touch. The argument continues: Judges are typically old, white males, whose job it is to maintain the status quo of their profession and other old, white men, ignoring the needs and desires of a far more diverse and populous majority.

On the other hand, because judges are indeed somewhat insulated from public pressure, judges have the weighty and important job of saving society from itself. Political winds shift rapidly, and unchecked majority action can result in crushing discrimination for unpopular or political minority groups. At its best, judges and the legal system balance the wishes of the majority with the rights of the minority, using those same ancient legal doctrines and precedent to wield the power of fairness and justice.

B. Natural Law

Although it is easy to see examples of law at work in most situations present and past, the question of its origin arises. The theory of Natural Law posits that justice and fairness exist naturally, and people merely discover and apply them. The Bill of Rights, for example, describes Natural Law in application to persons in the United States—the framers didn't actually create new human rights, they just transcribed them. The source of Natural law has been debated, with two camps generally divided on the issue. The religious camp believes that some higher power or being other than humans created law and handed it down, and the nonreligious camp maintains that natural laws exist like other physical laws do—never created, never destroyed, but present nonetheless. Either way, the theory had a significant effect on the drafters of the U.S. Declaration of Independence and the framers of the U.S. Constitution, and on the judges that heard and decided disputes at that time. The philosophies of several noted thinkers, namely, Thomas Aquinas, Thomas Hobbs, and John Locke all incorporated natural law, and have heavily influenced the jurisprudence of the United States.

C. Legal Positivism

Standing in opposition to Natural Law, the theory of Legal Positivism holds that a law's validity is unconnected with natural morality or justice. A law merely is what it is. If a law is recognized and obeyed by those it governs as well as by those in power, then it is valid, regardless of the result. Slavery, by way of example, was legal in the early years of U.S. history, and was upheld by the courts for many years, despite the obvious ethical problems presented. So Legal Positivism describes what the law is, whereas Natural Law attempts to determine what the law should be.

D. Legal Realism

Legal Realism can be thought of as the next step from Natural Law and Legal Positivism. Recognition that laws are influenced by human behavior, regardless of their source, and are therefore subject to human viewpoints, biases, and imperfections is the core tenet of the theory. Although the theory has lost some of its popularity from its zenith approximately fifty years ago, most emerging legal and jurisprudential theories incorporate some form of Legal Realism while arguing for a particular result, such as ethical norming or restorative justice.

E. Functions of Law

No matter the theory, law in practice sets social norms, bringing stability, predictability, and fairness to society. Without stability and predictability, no person or group of people would be willing to establish long-term relationships outside immediate family or trade for goods or services. And without some assurance that tomorrow will not be radically different from today, motivation to improve one's own life would lack.

Of course, dispute resolution is the corollary to social norms. Even in a society with fairly homogeneous norms some variation will exist, and fair, predictable resolution of those disputes promotes stability. When disputes are resolved predictably and fairly by those in power, people are willing to be subject to that power. If, on the other hand, power is exercised arbitrarily and unfairly, people won't know when or if they will be punished tomorrow for something they did today, and will work to overthrow those in power.

Law acts as a social negative feedback mechanism in its dispute resolution role. Stable legal systems counterweight forces of radical change or social upheaval by examining and relying on precedent. Successful resolution of a past dispute should lend itself to successful resolution of similar disputes in the future, all things being equal. But since all things are not equal and beliefs, social mores, and perceptions change with time and location, resolution of a present dispute may require departure from precedent. Departure from precedent is inherently destabilizing, and therefore courts depart from precedent only when it would be more unfair to adhere to it.

Although adherence to precedent in law slows adaptation and change and sometimes frustrates parties in court, doing so regulates and dampens the swings of public opinion, protecting society from destabilization.

F. U.S. Legal System

The U.S. legal system is based on common law, or judge-made law, from early British court decisions. Although the founders of our nation specifically rejected most of the governmental systems of Britain, the legal doctrines were imported almost wholesale with little changes, merely because they existed and were useful for solving disputes. One legal doctrine imported with the rest of common law that is particularly important is the doctrine of stare decisis, which means that courts will stand by cases they have already decided. Thus, any prior case law that is related to a new case will affect the decision a judge will make.

The U.S. legal system is multilayered and complicated. The best way to break it down is to divide it into two main parts—the federal system and the state system. The federal system was established by the Constitution, which provides for a uniform, centralized government with specific powers but reserves the majority of governmental power to individual states. Of course, the federal legal system is only one branch of the federal government, the others being the legislative and executive branches. While the legislative branch makes law and the executive enforces it, the legal (or judicial) branch interprets the law.
In the federal system, any issues that require all of the states' cooperation, such as interstate trade, coining money, or maintaining a military will fall under federal jurisdiction.

Federal courts interpret matters of federal law, and the U.S. Supreme Court has final authority. Generally, a conflict will be litigated in a federal district court near the place of the conflict. If either party is dissatisfied with the court's decision, an appeal to a circuit court of appeal (of which there are twelve) may follow. If different courts of appeal decide similar matters differently, the Supreme Court may decide to hear the matter to resolve the difference.

The second main part of the U.S. legal system is made up of all fifty state court systems. State governments are free to structure their own governmental systems the way they see fit, as long as they don't run afoul of the U.S. Constitution. Generally, state governments mirror the federal system, with three political branches and similar court structures. However, some are different. Louisiana, for example, does not subscribe to common law, instead relying on French Napoleonic code.

Matters of state law are resolved in state courts, but sometimes legal issues involve both federal and state law. For example, aviation is federally regulated, but sometimes state laws affect airplanes. In that case, a federal court generally has jurisdiction (the authority to hear the case), but may apply federal or state law, or resolve any inconsistency between them. Generally, if a state law is inconsistent with a federal law, the federal law preempts (takes precedence over) the inconsistent state law.

As a final matter, both federal and state courts hear two kinds of disputes—civil and criminal. A civil dispute is a dispute between two or more people, while a criminal matter is a dispute between one person (the accused) and the government. Civil matters are tried to the "preponderance of the evidence" standard, meaning that one side need only show they are slightly more right than the other side to win.

A civil case starts with a dispute between two or more people. One party serves the other with a document called a "summons," which is merely a notice that a civil lawsuit has been started. If that person doesn't respond to the summons or defend his or her position, he or she will lose by default. The court will generally hold a hearing where the parties will present the basic facts of their cases, and the court will order the parties to try to resolve their dispute by negotiation, and will also set a timetable for discovery, where the parties will gather facts and answer questions posed by the other side.

After discovery and negotiations are complete, if the parties have not resolved the dispute by themselves, the court will hold a trial, where both sides present their version of the case and argue for a result. The judge or a jury will then decide the case and either party may appeal the decision if it seems unfair.

Criminal matters are treated differently, and will be treated in more detail below, in section E7. But briefly, the government must prove "beyond a reasonable doubt" that the accused has violated a law before punishing that person.

Different vocabulary applies to civil and criminal disputes: Civilly, a person is "liable" for doing something wrong, whereas criminally, a person is "guilty."

G. Legal Citation and the Language of Law

1. Legal Citation

Lawyers and legal scholars use a unique shorthand language to identify legal precedent and use it in support of their arguments or points. Since law is based on precedent, it is important to be able to efficiently demonstrate how precedent supports one's position. Unlike other disciplines where a list of references following the text is sufficient citation, each sentence that carries legal implications must be cited in legal citation.

Immediately following such a sentence making a legal argument or point is a "citation sentence." It is a separate sentence, written in legal citation shorthand, that indicates to the reader where to find the source for that particular argument or point.

Most cases heard by courts of appeal are published and recorded in print, because of the great weight placed upon legal precedent. Conversely, most cases disposed of by the trial court are not published because trial court decisions do not set precedent. The system that has been devised to catalog all the important appellate cases divides the United States up by geographic area.

The court systems of the United States—federal and state—from top to bottom are slightly different from each other structurally, as described above. Luckily, however, the citation system used to find the cases is fairly uniform. The citation sentence starts with the case name, followed by a volume number, followed by the court identifier, and then a page number. Here is an example:

United States v. Louisiana, 389 U.S. 155 (1967).

Deciphered, that example citation means "the parties to the case were the United States and Louisiana, and the text of the opinion is found in volume 389 of the U.S. Supreme Court Reporter, page 155." Each circuit court of appeals has a unique number, and state or specialty courts also have unique identifiers. The date of decision usually follows in parenthesis, along with other identifying information.

Once you have that citation information, you can go to any law library or online legal search engine and find the argument or point referenced by the writer.

2. The Language of Law

Cases may be difficult to read, at first. Along with many unfamiliar terms, they are typically organized and structured differently than other things non-lawyers read.

Regarding unfamiliar terms, a good legal dictionary will assist you in understanding legal jargon in cases. Good legal dictionaries are available both in print and online.

Reading cases can be confusing if you don't know what to look for. Remember, if legal precedent exists for a dispute, the parties probably will not end up in court, because a known resolution for their dispute already exists in that other, similar suit. So when a case is published, either no other cases have facts like it (which is usually the case) or the law has changed.

When reading new cases, lawyers look for and annotate certain sections of the case. Those sections are the facts, the issue, the rule, the court's analysis, the conclusion, and any dissent. Also, lawyers usually write a short note at the top of the case summarizing it in a few words and identifying the implication of the case. Here is what those sections mean:

Facts:
The case will tell a story, a short summary of the events that led the parties to court. Since it is a summary, many of the facts are not there, and the facts are usually slanted towards the winner of the case.

Issue:
The issue of the case is the legal reason the parties are in court. The issue may be narrow or broad, but it is the question the court is resolving in the case. Sometimes the court will state exactly what the issue is, other times it is more difficult to find.

Rule:
The rule of the case is the legal principle the court uses to decide the issue. The rule may be borrowed verbatim from precedent, the court may modify precedent, or the court may invent a completely new rule to decide a novel issue.

Analysis:
The court applies the rule of the case to the facts before it in its analysis. In analysis, the court will discuss the merits of the case, fairness, justice, and compare other cases that may have come out differently than the one at hand. Depending on the complexity and ramifications of the case, the analysis may be short, or it may be long and involved. The court's analysis answers the question: "Why is the court ruling the way it is?"

Conclusion:
The conclusion is the result of the case. It is much less important than the other sections of the case. Usually, the conclusion is one or two words at the end of the case.

Dissent:
The dissent, if there is one, follows the conclusion of the case. Although dissents have no precedential value, they do offer some reasons and arguments why the analysis of the court may be incorrect or challenged.

Implication:
The implication of the case is usually a reformulation and broadening of the rule of the case. The rule of the case applies only to the facts of the case, but the implication of the case answers the question: "How does this case impact what I do?"

Unfortunately, cases are not all written in the neat format given above (some are, and they are delightful to read). You will need to pick apart the cases you read, looking for those sections and identifying them. It takes a lot of effort at first, but as you become proficient at recognizing the sections, the cases you read will be much more understandable.

Since the U.S. legal system relies on precedent, using common law as the foundation for building new legal doctrines, an introduction to the major areas of law that influence aviation law is necessary to fully understand the cases in this book. Please note that these sections are merely introductions to small parts of the law in the United States. Do not rely on them for answers to legal questions you may have—these sections are very brief summaries of some of the law that applies to aviation.

1. Constitutional Law

Constitutional law deals primarily with balancing power between the various branches of government. Secondarily, it has a large impact on the government's role in citizens' lives. The U.S. Constitution is not specific, for the most part. There are several exceptions, namely Article I, Section 8, which gives Congress seventeen specific powers, but generally the Judiciary must interpret whether one branch of government has overstepped its boundaries or not. When the Judiciary is interpreting the Constitution, it abides by several limitations, some of which are constitutionally imposed and some that are self-imposed.

First, courts may not give advisory opinions. There must be an actual case or controversy before a court may hear the matter. This is a constitutional limitation, given in Article III, Section 2. Second, courts follow what is termed the "strict necessity policy," which means that even if the court has jurisdiction and the authority to decide a constitutional issue, it will only decide the issue if it is necessary for the case. In other words, courts frequently decline to address constitutional issues if the case can be decided on other issues.

There are a few additional jurisprudential limitations, as well. Courts will not hear cases if there is a constitutional assignment of power to another branch of government; if there are no existing rules of law to judge the case by; if the court would have to make a policy decision before it decided the case; if the court would interfere with another branch's authority; if it is more important that the different branches don't disagree; and if the different branches would end up with different answers to the same question. Obviously, these doctrines are more complicated and involved than we have time to discuss here, but they illustrate the edges of the body of constitutional law.

Although separation of power is essential for our model of government to work, most citizens experience constitutional law in the context of regulation of commerce and in exercising their individual rights.

Article I, Section 8, Clause 3 of the U.S. Constitution gives Congress the power to regulate commerce with foreign nations, among the states, and with the Indian tribes. This is a vast area of constitutional law, and where most federal regulation gets its legitimacy. Generally, if goods of a certain industry cross state lines in interstate commerce, then the federal government has the constitutional authority to regulate that industry. Aviation is a prime example of federal regulation. Because airplanes regularly cross state lines in interstate commerce and because air navigation should not depend on an individual state's political whims, federal regulation of aviation is appropriate.

Individual rights stem from the Bill of Rights, the first ten amendments to the U.S. Constitution. The Bill of Rights was later added to the Constitution as a compromise to convince all of the states to ratify it. The drafters of the Constitution thought it wasn't necessary, because the government itself was ideally structured to contain those same rights. Today, it is clear that the Bill of Rights was a fortuitous compromise, since many civil rights are still being fully fleshed out in court.

When courts examine any laws affecting civil rights, such as free speech or voting regulations, the laws are judged according to one of three levels of scrutiny. The first, Rational Basis Scrutiny, is a fairly low hurdle. To pass constitutional muster under Rational Basis, the law must merely be rationally related to a legitimate governmental interest. This standard is fairly easy for the government to meet, and therefore it applies only to socioeconomic legislation that minimally affects individual rights.

The second level of scrutiny is Intermediate Scrutiny. Unfortunately, this standard is not well developed yet. It is something more than Rational Basis, but less than the highest level of scrutiny. Laws impacting a woman's right to obtain an abortion are subject to Intermediate Scrutiny, where the standard is that the law may not place an "undue burden" on the person seeking to exercise that individual right. Laws affecting an individual's right to die are also judged under Intermediate Scrutiny.

The highest level of constitutional scrutiny is Strict Scrutiny. Laws affecting fundamental constitutional rights, such as speech, liberty, religion, marriage, divorce, child bearing and child rearing, racial discrimination, voting, etc. must be narrowly tailored to fit a compelling governmental interest. This is a very difficult level of constitutional scrutiny, and consequently almost no legislation affecting fundamental constitutional rights passes Strict Scrutiny.

Some specific areas of constitutional law impacting individual rights that merit mentioning are Equal Protection and Free Speech. Equal Protection stems from the Fourteenth Amendment, Section 1, and mandates that everyone shall be treated equally under the law. Therefore, any law that contains a disadvantaging "suspect" classification (race, gender, religion, ethnicity, or any other uncontrollable trait), an otherwise neutral law that was enacted with the purpose of disadvantaging a group, or any neutral law that was enacted for a neutral purpose that is administered in a purposefully discriminatory manner violates Equal Protection and is unconstitutional. Affirmative action is an area rife with Equal Protection claims. Affirmative action is a non-merit-based system of selection, generally based on race, but also including things like veteran's preference, legacy appointments, athletic scholarships, and nepotism. Although affirmative action laws are usually enacted with the best of intentions, they are subject to strict scrutiny and have been struck down every time.

Free speech is a continually evolving area of constitutional law. Although the First Amendment prohibits the government from "abridging the freedom of speech," it can be limited according to time, place, and manner. The classic example is the notion that a person may not shout "fire" in a crowded theatre and expect not to be punished for the resulting panic and injuries by claiming freedom of speech. Likewise, certain kinds of speech fall outside the protection of the First Amendment and are subject to regulation. They include hate speech, incitement, and commercial speech. Hate speech is speech intended to degrade, intimidate, or incite violence or prejudicial action against a person or group of people based on their race, gender, age, ethnicity, nationality, or other innate characteristics. Although people in a democratic society must develop a tolerance to other, differing opinions, speech that goes beyond the boundaries of civilized discourse and into the realm of hate speech is not protected by the First Amendment and is subject to regulation and punishment.

Incitement is also unprotected speech, and is punishable by law. Incitement means speech that is intended to encourage others to commit a crime. The general rule is that the speech must incite a group to immediate violent action for it to fall outside constitutional protection. Questioning or challenging governmental power is fundamental to democracy in the United States, so the line where rousing political speech becomes incitement is not clear, and courts are regularly called upon to balance citizens' rights to free speech with governmental calls for regulation and punishment.

Finally, commercial speech may be regulated in excess of what the First Amendment would allow for individual political speech. Commercial speech is done with the intent of making a profit, and as such usually includes an argument for the listening audience to buy a product. Unregulated commercial speech tends to overstate, overpromise, and deceive, due to its economic nature. Therefore, the government may regulate commercial speech (as it does via Truth-in-Advertising laws, for example) to protect consumers, and not violate the First Amendment in doing so.

2. Administrative Law and Regulation

Administrative agencies make up the "fourth branch" of government. Although not an officially enumerated branch of government under the Constitution itself, administrative agencies do the majority of the work of the federal government. There are several hundred administrative agencies in the federal government, ranging the alphabet and regulating almost every conceivable industry.

Since administrative agencies do not have a constitutional delegation of power, the question arises as to where they do get their power to make and enforce laws. The answer is that Congress enacted the Administrative Procedure Act (APA) in 1946, essentially acknowledging that they didn't have the knowledge or expertise to regulate in every industry. Congress delegated its legislative power to specific agencies regulating in specific industries, like the Federal Aviation Administration does for the aviation industry.

Not only did Congress delegate its legislative power to administrative agencies, but the APA also gave agencies the power to enforce the rules they made—adjudication. However, enforcing laws is constitutionally delegated to the executive branch of government. This would seem to be a problematic situation, administrative agencies consolidating power that two separate branches would ordinarily have. This dilemma is solved by the judiciary. All rules made and enforced by administrative agencies are subject to judicial oversight. Of course, an appeals process must be followed in the event of a dispute, but the end result is that all agency actions are explicitly or implicitly authorized by Congress and are subject to judicial review.

Since administrative agencies are experts in their particular regulatory field, when courts become involved in the appeals process they scrutinize agency adjudications less so than they would court cases. When a person appeals an administrative law judge's decision, the appeals court applies the "arbitrary and capricious" standard to the appeal. The arbitrary and capricious standard means that the decision will be upheld unless the administrative judge's decision was unreasonable or was made without consideration of the facts or circumstances. This standard is very deferential to the administrative law judge's decision, as is the case in most courts of appeal.

When administrative agencies make rules, they must do so following a procedure set out by the APA. The APA requires an agency to make rules either formally or informally. Formal rulemaking is akin to a congressional hearing, with recorded testimony, questions under oath, and formal fact-finding. Informal rulemaking, which is done the majority of the time, is much simpler. The agency merely publishes a "notice of proposed rulemaking" in the Federal Register, allows for public comment in an adequate "notice and comment" period, and considers all of those comments in their final rule.

Another way administrative agencies make rules is by adjudication. Like the courts, an agency may interpret what a rule or regulation means by judicial process. The major difference between agency adjudications and court decisions is that agency adjudications have no precedential value. Of course, most agencies try to make consistent adjudications to promote stability in the industries they regulate, but agency decisions are not bound by the principle of stare decisis, as courts of law are.

3. Property Law

At its most basic, property law deals with peoples' rights to own and use land and "chattels" (legal terminology for "things"). Property itself is based on possession, but in a different sense than the common but incorrect "finders keepers" theory. The right to possess property is called "holding title to" the property. Once title to property is held by a person, there are few ways that possession and title are relinquished.

To illustrate the ways in which possession of property can change (other than buying or selling it), imagine you are walking on a beach. You stumble upon an old, broken bicycle with a sign on it that says "free." That bicycle is legally abandoned property, and you now own it because you possess it. Since the original owner voluntarily relinquished his title to the property, your property rights trump everyone else's, including the original owner's. The bicycle was essentially a gift to whoever wanted it. This illustrates the concept of "abandoned property."

Next, imagine you are walking along the same beach, and you stumble over a lump in the sand. Upon investigation, you uncover a shiny new bicycle that had tipped over and become covered with wind-blown sand. This is "lost" property, since it is new and the original owner probably didn't abandon it, but lost it because of the wind and sand. You now possess the bicycle, but it isn't truly yours. You do have more rights to it (finders keepers) than anyone other than the original owner, but you also have a duty to make reasonable efforts to find the original owner and return the bicycle, because title to the bicycle still resides with the original owner. If it is impossible to find the original owner, then the bicycle does indeed become yours. This example illustrates the concept of "lost property."

For the third example, you are now the owner of a used airplane. While it is at the shop getting a new radio, the mechanic discovers a huge wad of cash in one of the fuel tanks. You are delighted, since the cash would more than pay off the loan for the airplane. However, the cash is technically "mislaid property," since the person who hid it there probably did so deliberately, but now can't remember where it is (or isn't telling). Unfortunately for you, the cash doesn't belong to you, the title-holder of the airplane, nor does it belong to the mechanic who found it. The property belongs to the owner of the premises (the shop, in this example) until the true owner can be found. This odd legal result is from the legal concept of "mislaid property."

These three examples deal with title to tangible, personal property. Ownership of land is treated a bit differently, since you can't "lose" land. You can, however, abandon it. If you own land and don't take care of it, you can lose it through the legal concept called "adverse possession." Adverse possession occurs if someone else "squats" on your land or uses it without your permission for a period of time, and you don't do anything. Ownership and title to the land will then pass to the user of the land. Because you didn't exercise your rights to it and remove the squatter, you would lose your ownership rights. That result is an equitable result that encourages people to make good use of their land.

To protect your property from illegitimate claims against it, you have the option to record the title of the property you own with a local or federal office in most circumstances, thereby establishing a record of proof that you indeed are the owner of the property.

Back to "chattels" or personal property: if you loan someone your car, park your airplane in someone else's hanger, or if someone steals your computer, a legal relationship called a "bailment" results. A bailment occurs whenever someone else possesses your property temporarily. Depending on the reason for the bailment, the duty of care the person holding your property (the "bailee") owes you varies. If the bailment was solely for your benefit (like free parking), the bailee owes you a very slight duty of care. If the bailment was for mutual benefit (example: rented storage), the bailee owes you a reasonable duty of care. If the bailment was solely for the bailee's benefit (e.g. theft), the bailee owes you a very high duty of care.

Other issues in property law that relate to aviation are land use and zoning, environmental regulation, and tax implications. Those areas will be covered in detail in the cases in the Property Law section of this book.

4. Contract Law

A contract is merely a legally enforceable promise. Many promises are not legally enforceable. For example, if I promised to give you $100 if I felt like it, that is not an enforceable contract, because it is an illusory promise. I don't have to give you $100 if I don't feel like it, so you have no way of enforcing the promise.

Likewise, some activities are illegal to contract for, such as sex, illegal drugs, or criminal acts. But for the most part, most things are legal to contract for, and you probably do it all the time.

A contract can be broken down into a series of legally defined steps: First, an offer is made. The offer is valid if a buyer could say "I accept" and make a contract. Therefore, an offer depends on how specific it is, and the past history of the parties to the deal.

Second, the offer must be accepted. The buyer may accept by either a return promise or by doing something. If I offer to pay $20 to the first person who washes my car, I am looking for a clean car, not a return promise. The acceptance must mirror the offer. Also, the buyer must notify the seller of the acceptance, or it will not be valid.

Third, there must be "consideration." Consideration is a legal term that relates to the things being bargained for. If I agree to sell you my bicycle for $100, the bicycle and the $100 together make up the consideration of the contract. A contract without consideration is illusory, like the example in the first paragraph showed. Technically, consideration exists only when a promise is followed by a return promise, an action, or a promise not to act (forbearance).

Finally, the parties to a contract must mutually assent to the contract for it to be valid. Neither party can be drunk, under duress, or a minor in a valid contract.

Those elements make up a valid contract. Notice a valid contract does not have to be in writing. Certain contracts must be written (contracts for land, for more than $500 in value, or long-term promises, to name a few), but generally oral contracts are valid. Once a valid contract is formed, if either party breaches or fails to perform the contract, the injured party may sue and demand money or performance of the contract, in certain circumstances.

People sometimes make bad decisions and attempt to break a contract. First, you may merely breach the contract by refusing to perform. If you do this, however, you may be sued and have to pay money. Second, you may argue that the contract wasn't fair. Unless there was fraud or some other bad influence, courts generally won't let you out of a contract merely because it was a bad deal. Third, you may get out of a contract if the other party breaches first. For example, if you hire someone to clean your house for $100, you don't have to pay if no one shows up to clean your house. Even though there was a valid contract, the other party's nonperformance releases you from your duty to perform your part of the contract.

Seldom are contract disputes so simple, though. If the parties to a contract disagree over what the contract means, they can ask a court to decide for them. However, courts are hesitant to insert themselves into a dispute, so they will generally look at the following things to decide contract disputes: First, a court will look at the contract itself and try to decide the dispute using only what is contained in the contract (the "four corners" rule). Second, the court will look at the relationship between the parties, including any past dealings they have had with each other. Finally, the court will consider the meaning of certain language used in the particular industry (trade usage).

As mentioned above, if one party has breached its part of the contract, the court can order it to pay the injured party the amount in the contract, plus any other incidental damages, like the cost of finding replacement goods, for example. The only time courts will order a party to perform a contract is for a land sale. That is because forcing a party to perform a labor contract, for example, is tantamount to slavery, and is prohibited by the Constitution.

5. Tort Law

A tort is a civil wrong. The law of torts developed from the philosophy that it is just to compensate people for injuries done to them. Thus, tort law is liability based on fault. Tort law provides several benefits to society: It provides a peaceful method to right wrongs; it deters wrongful conduct; and it encourages socially responsible behavior, and restores injured people to their original condition (as much as possible).

There are four main categories of torts: intentional torts, negligence, strict liability torts, and "other" torts. Intentional torts are wrongs done with intent and then some action. Some examples are assault, battery, false imprisonment, trespass, and conversion (civil theft). All those torts require the tortfeasor (the person doing the bad action) to intend to act. There is no requirement that the intent be to cause harm, but merely to act. For example, if I throw a rock at you in anger, I need not intend that the rock hit you—just that I intended to throw it. If it does indeed hit you, I have committed the tort of battery. If I miss, I still have committed a tort—assault.

The second major category of tort law is negligence. Negligence is essentially carelessness, but there are four elements of negligence that must be present for the tort of negligence to attach. They are (1) duty, (2) breach, (3) causation, and (4) damage. Everyone is under some kind of duty, all the time. It may vary with the circumstances, but generally you are under a duty to use reasonable care in everything you do. If you accidentally hurt someone, the question of whether you acted as a reasonable person would have acted under the same circumstances will arise. At other times, you are held to a higher standard of care—while acting as the pilot of an aircraft, for example, you are held to a much higher standard of care than a non-pilot passenger.

Breaching the duty of care is merely the failure to act as a reasonable person would act.

Causation has two parts to it, legal (or but-for) causation, and proximate (or foreseeable) causation. Legal causation, the first part, is determined by examining whether the breach of the duty of care caused the damages—i.e., the accident wouldn't have happened but for your negligence. Proximate cause addresses the issue of whether your actions were too remote to have realistically caused the accident. Here is an example that illustrates this: A mother is pushing her baby in a stroller along a street, when two cars crash into each other a few blocks up the road. The noise startles the mother, who trips and falls into traffic with her stroller, with the unfortunate result of her baby being injured. The car accident a few blocks away was the legal cause of the baby's injury, but it was too far removed to be foreseeable. The drivers of the accident cars could not be held liable for the baby's injuries on the principle of forseeability.

Finally, for negligence to attach there must be some kind of damage. Damage can be physical or economic, and courts will award injured parties with monetary compensation, to attempt to make the injured party whole; punitive fines to punish a tortfeasor who knew better but failed to use due care; and nominal money awards to prove a legal point. The kind and amount of compensation depends on the facts of the case in front of the court.

Included within the sphere of negligence are two "shortcuts" to proving negligent acts that don't require each element to be proven. The first is called "negligence per se." Negligence per se is negligence as a matter of law. A good example of this is a speeding ticket. By speeding, you are breaching your duty to drive carefully, as a reasonable person would drive, and so the police officer need not argue that you had a duty to drive with due care and that you breached that duty. The fact that you were speeding proves those points as a matter of law.

The second shortcut is a legal doctrine called "res ipsa loquiter," which is Latin for "the thing speaks for itself." Essentially, res ipsa stands for the proposition that bad things don't just happen by themselves, and that any given accident wouldn't happen without the negligence of the tortfeasor. An example of this is a very old English case where a person was walking down the street and a barrel of flour rolled out of a factory window and killed him. Flour barrels don't just roll out of windows by themselves, and no one else had caused the barrel to roll out, so the flour factory was held negligent under the theory of res ipsa loquiter.

The third main category of tort law is strict liability. Normally, tort law is liability based on fault, but there are some activities where no matter how careful you are, if someone is injured you are automatically liable, even if you used the utmost care. Blasting, for example, is deemed an "ultra-hazardous activity" and strict liability attaches. Interestingly, aviation used to be classified as an ultra-hazardous activity until around

WWII, and some segments of aviation still are, such as experimental or test aircraft, and private space flight.

The fourth main category of tort law encompasses all other torts that don't fit into the previous three categories. This "junk drawer" of torts includes vicarious liability, products liability, and defamation, among others. Vicarious liability occurs when one person is liable for the torts of another person. For example, if you are working as a server at a restaurant and you assault a customer, the customer can sue both you and the restaurant under the theory of vicarious liability. Vicarious liability can occur outside employee/employer situations as well. If you are going on a road trip with some friends, you may be liable for someone else's bad driving that caused an accident. If you all have a common purpose for the road trip and are all in agreement, have equal control, and share the costs of the trip, each person in the car can be liable for an accident under the "joint enterprise" theory of vicarious liability.

Products liability is essentially strict liability applied to the manufacturers of goods. If someone manufactures a defective product that causes injury to a user or reasonably foreseeable misuser, the manufacturer is strictly liable for the injury. The various theories of products liability include design flaws, manufacturing flaws, and failure to warn. The strict liability of manufacturers is why you see warning labels that seem obvious, like "Warning-sharp edge!" on a new kitchen knife, for example.

Defamation is the final tort in the junk drawer, and can be either slander (spoken words), libel (printed material), or invasion of privacy. It is very hard to prove defamation, and truth is an absolute defense. Because we live in a society where free speech is valued over almost everything else, proving someone defamed you is extremely difficult.

All of the above torts have a myriad of defenses available to them. We shall start with the most common defense of consent. If you consent to an act that would otherwise be a tort, no tort has occurred. For example, if you play football, you have impliedly consented to the tort of battery, since tackling and rough plays are part of football. On the other hand, if you are playing ping-pong, you probably haven't consented to being tackled.

Self-defense and defense of others is another good defense to several torts. If someone is trying to hurt you, you have the legal right to protect yourself (or someone with you) by responding with appropriate force. Generally, the "equivalence rule" applies to self-defense. This means you may respond with the same force (not necessarily the same weapon, though). If someone threatens you with a knife and you fear for your life, using a gun in self-defense if probably appropriate. However, if a small child calls you names and you respond by brandishing a gun, you have probably responded with unreasonable force, and you may be liable for a tort yourself.

Protection of your property is another situation where force may be used, but never deadly force. The value of human life is always deemed to be greater than the value of property. However, you may use reasonable force to stop a thief from taking your property, and you may chase the same thief to retrieve your property, but it must be fresh pursuit.

Several other defenses exist, notably necessity, meaning that you had to choose between the lesser of two evils. But if you damage someone else's property while protecting your life or property, you must compensate that person for the damages.

Finally, a defense to negligence is negligence itself. This is the doctrine of comparative negligence, where each party's negligence will be compared and assigned a percentage of the fault, accordingly.

6. International Law

International law deals with the relationships of sovereign nations. Since there is no world police force or world court, international laws cannot be made and enforced like domestic laws.

International law consists mostly of treaties, but there are two major principles of international law that most nations recognize: The first, "jus cogens," means compelling laws, which are norms that no nation may deviate lawfully from. An example of a principle of jus cogens is torture. No nation may lawfully permit torture under international law. Of course, some nations do use torture, but again, there is no "world court" that has the jurisdiction to step in and stop the practice.

The second principle of international law is customary law, which is merely common knowledge or practice. This principle is held in high regard but is rather inelegant, since there is no easy way to quantify or qualify what common knowledge or practices are valid, international laws. Slavery, for example, and trade in human beings used to be a legitimate practice, but now the majority of the international community has condemned the practice.

Both of these major principles (and several other principles) affect the major vehicle of international law—treaty. A treaty is merely an agreement between two sovereign nations. A treaty can be compared to a contract, but it is not enforceable like a contract is.

Generally, treaties are held in high esteem by courts worldwide, and treaties have the same effect as validly enacted laws. But what happens when a treaty and a domestic law conflict? In the United States, any treaty that conflicts with the Constitution is void. However, most treaties are subsumed into federal law, in the sense that the president and U.S. Congress have the power to make, modify, or repeal them. Therefore, if an international treaty conflicts with a federal law, the treaty will preempt the federal law, but must stop short of affecting constitutional rights.

In order to make or ratify a treaty in the United States, the president must do so with two-thirds of the Senate's approval under Article II of the U.S. Constitution, which is a "supermajority" not required for regular domestic legislation.

"Breaking" a treaty is generally more of a political act than a legal process. Because foreign courts do not have jurisdiction to enforce a treaty with the United States and U.S. courts may not inject themselves into foreign legal systems, when sovereign nations decide to ignore a treaty agreement, the only recourse is generally political or economic sanctions against that nation.

Finally, U.S. courts are jealous protectors of the power the Constitution gives them, and generally will not allow principles of international law to intrude upon valid domestic law, unless the treaty expressly provides for it.

7. Criminal Law

The body of criminal law deals with the rights of society as a whole and determines what conduct is punishable, and what those punishments are for individuals who violate proscribed conduct. Any proscribed conduct must be clearly enumerated by statute—there is no "common law" in criminal law, unlike tort law, for example.

Generally, criminal conduct requires a "guilty mind," or mens rea, plus some criminal act. Unfortunately, there is no standardized federal criminal law, and since there is no common criminal law, the body of criminal law is made up of a hodgepodge of state and federal statutes, which are sometimes inconsistent with each other.

To gain a better understanding of how the criminal system works, an overview of the steps from the commission of the crime to the final appeal is in order.

First, a crime is committed and reported. Then the police investigate the crime. Investigation can be simple or complicated, depending on the crime. If an officer stops you for speeding, for example, the investigation is essentially complete when you receive a traffic ticket. For a Class A Homicide, the investigation may take years. Regardless of the nature of the offense, all investigations are subject to constitutional limitations of the Fourth Amendment, which prohibits unreasonable searches and seizures, and requires the police to have probable cause before they can detain, question, or search you.

Following investigation, the arrest is made. Most arrests are made without a warrant, which is appropriate if the officer witnesses the crime. For an arrest to be made significantly after the crime is committed, the police must obtain a warrant from a judge first.

After the arrest, the suspect (all persons arrested are presumed innocent until proven guilty beyond reasonable doubt) is taken to the police station, "booked," and is either held in jail or released on bail until appearing in court. Following that, there is generally further investigation by the police, and perhaps other court appearances. It is only at this time in the process that the suspect must be given *Miranda* warnings of the right to remain silent and the right to counsel. The police do not need to give an arrestee or suspect *Miranda* warnings unless the person is both in police custody and being questioned.

Generally, if questioning leads to more investigation and evidence, the state prosecuting attorney will charge the suspect, now the "defendant" with a crime or crimes, and the matter proceeds to trial.

In trial, the defendant has the right to remain silent, to cross-examine the state's evidence and witnesses, to present his or her own witnesses, and/or to make arguments to the judge and jury. During and after trial, the defendant or the defendant's lawyer will make various motions and arguments to exclude evidence that would show the defendant's guilt.

Meanwhile, the prosecutor attempts to prove each element of the crime beyond a reasonable doubt. If the prosecutor is unable to prove each element beyond reasonable doubt, the defendant is deemed to be not guilty, and is set free, even if it seems more than likely that he or she committed the crime. "The criminal is to go free, because the constable has blundered" was the way this was phrased by the famous jurist Benjamin Cardozo. This legal philosophy results from the American notion that it is better for ninety-nine guilty criminals go free than for one innocent person to be convicted and punished.

A defendant judged to be guilty may appeal once as a matter of right and thereafter only for good cause. On the same note, if the state loses its case it may appeal under certain limited circumstances, abiding by the Fifth Amendment's prohibition on being tried twice for the same crime.

Even though the particular criminal laws may vary from state to state, constitutional protections and fairly uniform principles of criminal law apply to all the states. Criminal conduct is usually based on the intent of the defendant. Conduct may be purposeful, knowing, reckless, or negligent. Punishments are most severe for conduct that is purposefully wrong, and less so for criminally negligent behavior.

The most active area in criminal law is Fourth Amendment law— defining the intersection of police behavior with your constitutional rights to be free of unwanted searches and seizures by police. Generally, if the police violate your Fourth Amendment rights, your remedy lies with the "exclusionary rule." The exclusionary rule is unique to the U.S. legal system, and operates to exclude evidence obtained illegally by police from being used in court, with some exceptions. Without evidence, a jury probably cannot find someone to be guilty beyond a reasonable doubt.

The Fourth Amendment also prohibits searches and seizures without a search warrant, but a number of exceptions have developed. First, if you consent to a search, police need not obtain a search warrant. Second, if contraband is in plain view, police may seize it without a search warrant. Third, "open fields" may be searched without a warrant, because no one has any reasonable expectation of privacy in publicly accessible areas. Fourth, if police are acting under "exigent circumstances," like responding to an emergency, they may seize contraband if they encounter it while responding to the emergency. Fifth, individuals in motor vehicles have a lesser expectation of privacy than in their homes, and a motor vehicle may be searched with less than probable cause—police need only a reasonable suspicion of criminal activity or contraband to search a vehicle. Sixth, police may search a lawfully arrested person without a search warrant, to prevent destruction of evidence or harm to the officer. Seventh, persons crossing borders or boarding aircraft have a reduced expectation of privacy, and may be searched without a warrant in the name of public safety. There are several more minor exceptions, but you can see that the Fourth Amendment is more complicated than it appears at first read.

Criminal law, especially the law related to Fourth Amendment searches and seizures, is constantly evolving. People's constitutional rights are continually balanced with the rights of society as a whole.

A. *Origins*

The Declaration of Independence

July 4, 1776

When in the Course of human events it becomes necessary for one people to dissolve the political bands which have connected them with another and to assume among the powers of the earth, the separate and equal station to which the Laws of Nature and of Nature's God entitle them, a decent respect to the opinions of mankind requires that they should declare the causes which impel them to the separation.

We hold these truths to be self-evident, that all men are created equal, that they are endowed by their Creator with certain unalienable Rights, that among these are Life, Liberty and the pursuit of Happiness. — That to secure these rights, Governments are instituted among Men, deriving their just powers from the consent of the governed, — That whenever any Form of Government becomes destructive of these ends, it is the Right of the People to alter or to abolish it, and to institute new Government, laying its foundation on such principles and organizing its powers in such form, as to them shall seem most likely to effect their Safety and Happiness. Prudence, indeed, will dictate that Governments long established should not be changed for light and transient causes; and accordingly all experience hath shewn that mankind are more disposed to suffer, while evils are sufferable than to right themselves by abolishing the forms to which they are accustomed. But when a long train of abuses and usurpations, pursuing invariably the same Object evinces a design to reduce them under absolute Despotism, it is their right, it is their duty, to throw off such Government, and to provide new Guards for their future security. — Such has been the patient sufferance of these Colonies; and such is now the necessity which constrains them to alter their former Systems of Government. The history of the present King of Great Britain is a history of repeated injuries and usurpations, all having in direct object the establishment of an absolute Tyranny over these States. To prove this, let Facts be submitted to a candid world.

He has refused his Assent to Laws, the most wholesome and necessary for the public good.

He has forbidden his Governors to pass Laws of immediate and pressing importance, unless suspended in their operation till his Assent should be obtained; and when so suspended, he has utterly neglected to attend to them.

He has refused to pass other Laws for the accommodation of large districts of people, unless those people would relinquish the right of Representation in the Legislature, a right inestimable to them and formidable to tyrants only.

He has called together legislative bodies at places unusual, uncomfortable, and distant from the depository of their Public Records, for the sole purpose of fatiguing them into compliance with his measures.

He has dissolved Representative Houses repeatedly, for opposing with manly firmness his invasions on the rights of the people.

He has refused for a long time, after such dissolutions, to cause others to be elected, whereby the Legislative Powers, incapable of Annihilation, have returned to the People at large for their exercise; the State remaining in the mean time exposed to all the dangers of invasion from without, and convulsions within.

He has endeavoured to prevent the population of these States; for that purpose obstructing the Laws for Naturalization of Foreigners; refusing to pass others to encourage their migrations hither, and raising the conditions of new Appropriations of Lands.

He has obstructed the Administration of Justice by refusing his Assent to Laws for establishing Judiciary Powers.

He has made Judges dependent on his Will alone for the tenure of their offices, and the amount and payment of their salaries.

He has erected a multitude of New Offices, and sent hither swarms of Officers to harass our people and eat out their substance.

He has kept among us, in times of peace, Standing Armies without the Consent of our legislatures.

He has affected to render the Military independent of and superior to the Civil Power.

He has combined with others to subject us to a jurisdiction foreign to our constitution, and unacknowledged by our laws; giving his Assent to their Acts of pretended Legislation:

For quartering large bodies of armed troops among us:

For protecting them, by a mock Trial from punishment for any Murders which they should commit on the Inhabitants of these States:

For cutting off our Trade with all parts of the world:

For imposing Taxes on us without our Consent:

For depriving us in many cases, of the benefit of Trial by Jury:

For transporting us beyond Seas to be tried for pretended offences:

For abolishing the free System of English Laws in a neighboring Province, establishing therein an Arbitrary government, and enlarging its Boundaries so as to render it at once an example and fit instrument for introducing the same absolute rule into these Colonies

For taking away our Charters, abolishing our most valuable Laws and altering fundamentally the Forms of our Governments:

For suspending our own Legislatures, and declaring themselves invested with power to legislate for us in all cases whatsoever.

He has abdicated Government here, by declaring us out of his Protection and waging War against us.

He has plundered our seas, ravaged our coasts, burnt our towns, and destroyed the lives of our people.

He is at this time transporting large Armies of foreign Mercenaries to complete the works of death, desolation, and tyranny, already begun with circumstances of Cruelty & Perfidy scarcely paralleled in the most barbarous ages, and totally unworthy the Head of a civilized nation.

He has constrained our fellow Citizens taken Captive on the high Seas to bear Arms against their Country, to become the executioners of their friends and Brethren, or to fall themselves by their Hands.

He has excited domestic insurrections amongst us, and has endeavored to bring on the inhabitants of our frontiers, the merciless Indian Savages whose known rule of warfare, is an undistinguished destruction of all ages, sexes and conditions.

In every stage of these Oppressions We have Petitioned for Redress in the most humble terms: Our repeated Petitions have been answered only by repeated injury. A Prince, whose character is thus marked by every act which may define a Tyrant, is unfit to be the ruler of a free people.

Nor have We been wanting in attentions to our British brethren. We have warned them from time to time of attempts by their legislature to extend an unwarrantable jurisdiction over us. We have reminded them of the circumstances of our emigration and settlement here. We have appealed to their native justice and magnanimity, and we have conjured them by the ties of our common kindred to disavow these usurpations, which would inevitably interrupt our connections and correspondence. They too have been deaf to the voice of justice and of consanguinity. We must, therefore, acquiesce in the necessity, which denounces our Separation, and hold them, as we hold the rest of mankind, Enemies in War, in Peace Friends.

We, therefore, the Representatives of the united States of America, in General Congress, Assembled, appealing to the Supreme Judge of the world for the rectitude of our intentions, do, in the Name, and by Authority of the good People of these Colonies, solemnly publish and declare, That these united Colonies are, and of Right ought to be Free and Independent States, that they are Absolved from all Allegiance to the British Crown, and that all political connection between them and the State of Great Britain, is and ought to be totally dissolved; and that as Free and Independent States, they have full Power to levy War, conclude Peace, contract Alliances, establish Commerce, and to do all other Acts and Things which Independent States may of right do. — And for the support of this Declaration, with a firm reliance on the protection of Divine Providence, we mutually pledge to each other our Lives, our Fortunes, and our sacred Honor.

The Constitution of the United States

September, 1787

We the People of the United States, in Order to form a more perfect Union, establish Justice, insure domestic Tranquility, provide for the common defense, promote the general Welfare, and secure the Blessings of Liberty to ourselves and our Posterity, do ordain and establish this Constitution for the United States of America.

Article. I.

Section. 1. All legislative Powers herein granted shall be vested in a Congress of the United States, which shall consist of a Senate and House of Representatives.

Section. 2. The House of Representatives shall be composed of Members chosen every second Year by the People of the several States, and the Electors in each State shall have the Qualifications requisite for Electors of the most numerous Branch of the State Legislature.

No Person shall be a Representative who shall not have attained to the Age of twenty five Years, and been seven Years a Citizen of the United States, and who shall not, when elected, be an Inhabitant of that State in which he shall be chosen.

Representatives and direct Taxes shall be apportioned among the several States which may be included within this Union, according to their respective Numbers, which shall be determined by adding to the whole Number of free Persons, including those bound to Service for a Term of Years, and excluding Indians not taxed, three fifths of all other Persons [Modified by Amendment XIV]. The actual Enumeration shall be made within three Years after the first Meeting of the Congress of the United States, and within every subsequent Term of ten Years, in such Manner as they shall by Law direct. The Number of Representatives shall not exceed one for every thirty Thousand, but each State shall have at Least one Representative; and until such enumeration shall be made, the State of New Hampshire shall be entitled to chuse three, Massachusetts eight, Rhode-Island and Providence Plantations one, Connecticut five, New-York six, New Jersey four, Pennsylvania eight, Delaware one, Maryland six, Virginia ten, North Carolina five, South Carolina five, and Georgia three.

When vacancies happen in the Representation from any State, the Executive Authority thereof shall issue Writs of Election to fill such Vacancies.

The House of Representatives shall choose their Speaker and other Officers; and shall have the sole Power of Impeachment.

Section. 3. The Senate of the United States shall be composed of two Senators from each State, *chosen by the Legislature thereof* [Modified by Amendment XVII], for six Years; and each Senator shall have one Vote.

Immediately after they shall be assembled in Consequence of the first Election, they shall be divided as equally as may be into three Classes. The Seats of the Senators of the first Class shall be vacated at the Expiration of the second Year, of the second Class at the Expiration of the fourth Year, and of the third Class at the Expiration of the sixth Year, so that one third may be chosen every second Year; *and if Vacancies happen by Resignation, or otherwise, during the Recess of the Legislature of any State, the Executive thereof may make temporary Appointments until the next Meeting of the Legislature, which shall then fill such Vacancies* [Modified by Amendment XVII].

No Person shall be a Senator who shall not have attained to the Age of thirty Years, and been nine Years a Citizen of the United States, and who shall not, when elected, be an Inhabitant of that State for which he shall be chosen.

The Vice President of the United States shall be President of the Senate, but shall have no Vote, unless they be equally divided.

The Senate shall chuse their other Officers, and also a President pro tempore, in the Absence of the Vice President, or when he shall exercise the Office of President of the United States.

The Senate shall have the sole Power to try all Impeachments. When sitting for that Purpose, they shall be on Oath or Affirmation. When the President of the United States is tried, the Chief Justice shall preside: And no Person shall be convicted without the Concurrence of two thirds of the Members present.

Judgment in Cases of Impeachment shall not extend further than to removal from Office, and disqualification to hold and enjoy any Office of honor, Trust or Profit under the United States: but the Party convicted shall nevertheless be liable and subject to Indictment, Trial, Judgment and Punishment, according to Law.

Section. 4. The Times, Places and Manner of holding Elections for Senators and Representatives, shall be prescribed in each State by the Legislature thereof; but the Congress may at any time by Law make or alter such Regulations, except as to the Places of choosing Senators.

The Congress shall assemble at least once in every Year, *and such Meeting shall be on the first Monday in December* [Modified by Amendment XX], unless they shall by Law appoint a different Day.

Section. 5. Each House shall be the Judge of the Elections, Returns and Qualifications of its own Members, and a Majority of each shall constitute a Quorum to do Business; but a smaller Number may adjourn from day to day, and may be authorized to compel the Attendance of absent Members, in such Manner, and under such Penalties as each House may provide.

Each House may determine the Rules of its Proceedings, punish its Members for disorderly Behavior, and, with the Concurrence of two thirds, expel a Member.

Each House shall keep a Journal of its Proceedings, and from time to time publish the same, excepting such Parts as may in their Judgment require Secrecy; and the Yeas and Nays of the Members of either House on any question shall, at the Desire of one fifth of those Present, be entered on the Journal.

Neither House, during the Session of Congress, shall, without the Consent of the other, adjourn for more than three days, nor to any other Place than that in which the two Houses shall be sitting.

Section. 6. The Senators and Representatives shall receive a Compensation for their Services, to be ascertained by Law, and paid out of the Treasury of the United States. They shall in all Cases, except Treason, Felony and Breach of the Peace, be privileged from Arrest during their Attendance at the Session of their respective Houses, and in going to and returning from the same; and for any Speech or Debate in either House, they shall not be questioned in any other Place.

No Senator or Representative shall, during the Time for which he was elected, be appointed to any civil Office under the Authority of the United States, which shall have been created, or the Emoluments whereof shall have been increased during such time; and no Person holding any Office under the United States, shall be a Member of either House during his Continuance in Office.

Section. 7. All Bills for raising Revenue shall originate in the House of Representatives; but the Senate may propose or concur with Amendments as on other Bills.

Every Bill which shall have passed the House of Representatives and the Senate, shall, before it become a Law, be presented to the President of the United States; If he approve he shall sign it, but if not he shall return it, with his Objections to that House in which it shall have originated, who shall enter the Objections at large on their Journal, and proceed to reconsider it. If after such Reconsideration two thirds of that House shall agree to pass the Bill, it shall be sent, together with the Objections, to the other House, by which it shall likewise be reconsidered, and if approved by two thirds of that House, it shall become a Law. But in all such Cases the Votes of both Houses shall be determined by yeas and Nays, and the Names of the Persons voting for and against the Bill shall be entered on the Journal of each House respectively. If any Bill shall not be returned by the President within ten Days (Sundays excepted) after it shall have been presented to him, the Same shall be a Law, in like Manner as if he had signed it, unless the Congress by their Adjournment prevent its Return, in which Case it shall not be a Law.

Every Order, Resolution, or Vote to which the Concurrence of the Senate and House of Representatives may be necessary (except on a question of Adjournment) shall be presented to the President of the

United States; and before the Same shall take Effect, shall be approved by him, or being disapproved by him, shall be repassed by two thirds of the Senate and House of Representatives, according to the Rules and Limitations prescribed in the Case of a Bill.

Section. 8. The Congress shall have Power To lay and collect Taxes, Duties, Imposts and Excises, to pay the Debts and provide for the common Defense and general Welfare of the United States; but all Duties, Imposts and Excises shall be uniform throughout the United States;

To borrow Money on the credit of the United States;

To regulate Commerce with foreign Nations, and among the several States, and with the Indian Tribes;

To establish an uniform Rule of Naturalization, and uniform Laws on the subject of Bankruptcies throughout the United States;

To coin Money, regulate the Value thereof, and of foreign Coin, and fix the Standard of Weights and Measures;

To provide for the Punishment of counterfeiting the Securities and current Coin of the United States;

To establish Post Offices and post Roads;

To promote the Progress of Science and useful Arts, by securing for limited Times to Authors and Inventors the exclusive Right to their respective Writings and Discoveries;

To constitute Tribunals inferior to the supreme Court;

To define and punish Piracies and Felonies committed on the high Seas, and Offences against the Law of Nations;

To declare War, grant Letters of Marque and Reprisal, and make Rules concerning Captures on Land and Water;

To raise and support Armies, but no Appropriation of Money to that Use shall be for a longer Term than two Years;

To provide and maintain a Navy;

To make Rules for the Government and Regulation of the land and naval Forces;

To provide for calling forth the Militia to execute the Laws of the Union, suppress Insurrections and repel Invasions;

To provide for organizing, arming, and disciplining, the Militia, and for governing such Part of them as may be employed in the Service of the

United States, reserving to the States respectively, the Appointment of the Officers, and the Authority of training the Militia according to the discipline prescribed by Congress;

To exercise exclusive Legislation in all Cases whatsoever, over such District (not exceeding ten Miles square) as may, by Cession of particular States, and the Acceptance of Congress, become the Seat of the Government of the United States, and to exercise like Authority over all Places purchased by the Consent of the Legislature of the State in which the Same shall be, for the Erection of Forts, Magazines, Arsenals, dock-Yards, and other needful Buildings; — And

To make all Laws which shall be necessary and proper for carrying into Execution the foregoing Powers, and all other Powers vested by this Constitution in the Government of the United States, or in any Department or Officer thereof.

Section. 9. The Migration or Importation of such Persons as any of the States now existing shall think proper to admit, shall not be prohibited by the Congress prior to the Year one thousand eight hundred and eight, but a Tax or duty may be imposed on such Importation, not exceeding ten dollars for each Person.

The Privilege of the Writ of Habeas Corpus shall not be suspended, unless when in Cases of Rebellion or Invasion the public Safety may require it.

No Bill of Attainder or ex post facto Law shall be passed.

No Capitation, or other direct, Tax shall be laid, unless in Proportion to the Census or Enumeration herein before directed to be taken.

No Tax or Duty shall be laid on Articles exported from any State.

No Preference shall be given by any Regulation of Commerce or Revenue to the Ports of one State over those of another; nor shall Vessels bound to, or from, one State, be obliged to enter, clear, or pay Duties in another.

No Money shall be drawn from the Treasury, but in Consequence of Appropriations made by Law; and a regular Statement and Account of the Receipts and Expenditures of all public Money shall be published from time to time.

No Title of Nobility shall be granted by the United States: And no Person holding any Office of Profit or Trust under them, shall, without the Consent of the Congress, accept of any present, Emolument, Office, or Title, of any kind whatever, from any King, Prince, or foreign State.

Section. 10. No State shall enter into any Treaty, Alliance, or Confederation; grant Letters of Marque and Reprisal; coin Money; emit Bills of Credit; make any Thing but gold and silver Coin a Tender in Payment of Debts; pass any Bill of Attainder, ex post facto Law, or

Law impairing the Obligation of Contracts, or grant any Title of Nobility.

No State shall, without the Consent of the Congress, lay any Imposts or Duties on Imports or Exports, except what may be absolutely necessary for executing it's inspection Laws; and the net Produce of all Duties and Imposts, laid by any State on Imports or Exports, shall be for the Use of the Treasury of the United States; and all such Laws shall be subject to the Revision and Control of the Congress.

No State shall, without the Consent of Congress, lay any Duty of Tonnage, keep Troops, or Ships of War in time of Peace, enter into any Agreement or Compact with another State, or with a foreign Power, or engage in War, unless actually invaded, or in such imminent Danger as will not admit of delay.

Article. II.

Section. 1. The executive Power shall be vested in a President of the United States of America. He shall hold his Office during the Term of four Years, and, together with the Vice President, chosen for the same Term, be elected, as follows:

Each State shall appoint, in such Manner as the Legislature thereof may direct, a Number of Electors, equal to the whole Number of Senators and Representatives to which the State may be entitled in the Congress: but no Senator or Representative, or Person holding an Office of Trust or Profit under the United States, shall be appointed an Elector.

The Electors shall meet in their respective States, and vote by Ballot for two Persons, of whom one at least shall not be an Inhabitant of the same State with themselves. And they shall make a List of all the Persons voted for, and of the Number of Votes for each; which List they shall sign and certify, and transmit sealed to the Seat of the Government of the United States, directed to the President of the Senate. The President of the Senate shall, in the Presence of the Senate and House of Representatives, open all the Certificates, and the Votes shall then be counted. The Person having the greatest Number of Votes shall be the President, if such Number be a Majority of the whole Number of Electors appointed; and if there be more than one who have such Majority, and have an equal Number of Votes, then the House of Representatives shall immediately chuse by Ballot one of them for President; and if no Person have a Majority, then from the five highest on the List the said House shall in like Manner chuse the President. But in chusing the President, the Votes shall be taken by States, the Representation from each State having one Vote; a quorum for this Purpose shall consist of a Member or Members from two thirds of the States, and a Majority of all the States shall be necessary to a Choice. In every Case, after the Choice of the President, the Person having the greatest Number of Votes of the Electors shall be the Vice President. But if there should remain two or more who have equal Votes, the Senate shall chuse from them by Ballot the Vice President [Modified by Amendment XII].

The Congress may determine the Time of chusing the Electors, and the Day on which they shall give their Votes; which Day shall be the same throughout the United States.

No Person except a natural born Citizen, or a Citizen of the United States, at the time of the Adoption of this Constitution, shall be eligible to the Office of President; neither shall any Person be eligible to that Office who shall not have attained to the Age of thirty five Years, and been fourteen Years a Resident within the United States.

In Case of the Removal of the President from Office, or of his Death, Resignation, or Inability to discharge the Powers and Duties of the said Office, the Same shall devolve on the Vice President, and the Congress may by Law provide for the Case of Removal, Death, Resignation or Inability, both of the President and Vice President, declaring what Officer shall then act as President, and such Officer shall act accordingly, until the Disability be removed, or a President shall be elected [Modified by Amendment XXV].

The President shall, at stated Times, receive for his Services, a Compensation, which shall neither be increased nor diminished during the Period for which he shall have been elected, and he shall not receive within that Period any other Emolument from the United States, or any of them.

Before he enter on the Execution of his Office, he shall take the following Oath or Affirmation: — "I do solemnly swear (or affirm) that I will faithfully execute the Office of President of the United States, and will to the best of my Ability, preserve, protect and defend the Constitution of the United States."

Section. 2. The President shall be Commander in Chief of the Army and Navy of the United States, and of the Militia of the several States, when called into the actual Service of the United States; he may require the Opinion, in writing, of the principal Officer in each of the executive Departments, upon any Subject relating to the Duties of their respective Offices, and he shall have Power to grant Reprieves and Pardons for Offences against the United States, except in Cases of Impeachment.

He shall have Power, by and with the Advice and Consent of the Senate, to make Treaties, provided two thirds of the Senators present concur; and he shall nominate, and by and with the Advice and Consent of the Senate, shall appoint Ambassadors, other public Ministers and Consuls, Judges of the supreme Court, and all other Officers of the United States, whose Appointments are not herein otherwise provided for, and which shall be established by Law: but the Congress may by Law vest the Appointment of such inferior Officers, as they think proper, in the President alone, in the Courts of Law, or in the Heads of Departments.

The President shall have Power to fill up all Vacancies that may happen during the Recess of the Senate, by granting Commissions which shall expire at the End of their next Session.

Section. 3. He shall from time to time give to the Congress Information of the State of the Union, and recommend to their Consideration such Measures as he shall judge necessary and expedient; he may, on extraordinary Occasions, convene both Houses, or either of them, and in Case of Disagreement between them, with Respect to the Time of Adjournment, he may adjourn them to such Time as he shall think proper; he shall receive Ambassadors and other public Ministers; he shall take Care that the Laws be faithfully executed, and shall Commission all the Officers of the United States.

Section. 4. The President, Vice President and all civil Officers of the United States, shall be removed from Office on Impeachment for, and Conviction of, Treason, Bribery, or other high Crimes and Misdemeanors.

Article. III.

Section. 1. The judicial Power of the United States shall be vested in one supreme Court, and in such inferior Courts as the Congress may from time to time ordain and establish. The Judges, both of the supreme and inferior Courts, shall hold their Offices during good Behaviour, and shall, at stated Times, receive for their Services a Compensation, which shall not be diminished during their Continuance in Office.

Section. 2. The judicial Power shall extend to all Cases, in Law and Equity, arising under this Constitution, the Laws of the United States, and Treaties made, or which shall be made, under their Authority; — to all Cases affecting Ambassadors, other public Ministers and Consuls; — to all Cases of admiralty and maritime Jurisdiction; — to Controversies to which the United States shall be a Party; — to Controversies between two or more States; — *between a State and Citizens of another State* [Modified by Amendment XI]; — between Citizens of different States; — between Citizens of the same State claiming Lands under Grants of different States, and between a State, or the Citizens thereof, and foreign States, Citizens or Subjects.

In all Cases affecting Ambassadors, other public Ministers and Consuls, and those in which a State shall be Party, the supreme Court shall have original Jurisdiction. In all the other Cases before mentioned, the supreme Court shall have appellate Jurisdiction, both as to Law and Fact, with such Exceptions, and under such Regulations as the Congress shall make.

The Trial of all Crimes, except in Cases of Impeachment, shall be by Jury; and such Trial shall be held in the State where the said Crimes shall have been committed; but when not committed within any State, the Trial shall be at such Place or Places as the Congress may by Law have directed.

Section. 3. Treason against the United States shall consist only in levying War against them, or in adhering to their Enemies, giving them Aid and Comfort. No Person shall be convicted of Treason unless on the Testimony of two Witnesses to the same overt Act, or on Confession in open Court.

The Congress shall have Power to declare the Punishment of Treason, but no Attainder of Treason shall work Corruption of Blood, or Forfeiture except during the Life of the Person attainted.

Article. IV.

Section. 1. Full Faith and Credit shall be given in each State to the public Acts, Records, and judicial Proceedings of every other State. And the Congress may by general Laws prescribe the Manner in which such Acts, Records and Proceedings shall be proved, and the Effect thereof.

Section. 2. The Citizens of each State shall be entitled to all Privileges and Immunities of Citizens in the several States.

A Person charged in any State with Treason, Felony, or other Crime, who shall flee from Justice, and be found in another State, shall on Demand of the executive Authority of the State from which he fled, be delivered up, to be removed to the State having Jurisdiction of the Crime.

No Person held to Service or Labour in one State, under the Laws thereof, escaping into another, shall, in Consequence of any Law or Regulation therein, be discharged from such Service or Labour, but shall be delivered up on Claim of the Party to whom such Service or Labour may be due [Modified by Amendment XIII].

Section. 3. New States may be admitted by the Congress into this Union; but no new State shall be formed or erected within the Jurisdiction of any other State; nor any State be formed by the Junction of two or more States, or Parts of States, without the Consent of the Legislatures of the States concerned as well as of the Congress.

The Congress shall have Power to dispose of and make all needful Rules and Regulations respecting the Territory or other Property belonging to the United States; and nothing in this Constitution shall be so construed as to Prejudice any Claims of the United States, or of any particular State.

Section. 4. The United States shall guarantee to every State in this Union a Republican Form of Government, and shall protect each of them against Invasion; and on Application of the Legislature, or of the Executive (when the Legislature cannot be convened), against domestic Violence.

Article. V.

The Congress, whenever two thirds of both Houses shall deem it necessary, shall propose Amendments to this Constitution, or, on the Application of the Legislatures of two thirds of the several States, shall call a Convention for proposing Amendments, which, in either Case, shall be valid to all Intents and Purposes, as Part of this Constitution, when ratified by the Legislatures of three fourths of the several States, or by Conventions in three fourths thereof, as the one or the other Mode of Ratification may be proposed by the Congress; Provided that no Amendment which may be made prior to the Year One thousand eight hundred and eight shall in any Manner affect the first and fourth Clauses in the Ninth Section of the first Article; *and that no State, without its Consent, shall be deprived of its equal Suffrage in the Senate* [Possibly abrogated by Amendment XVII].

Article. VI.

All Debts contracted and Engagements entered into, before the Adoption of this Constitution, shall be as valid against the United States under this Constitution, as under the Confederation.

This Constitution, and the Laws of the United States which shall be made in Pursuance thereof; and all Treaties made, or which shall be made, under the Authority of the United States, shall be the supreme Law of the Land; and the Judges in every State shall be bound thereby, any Thing in the Constitution or Laws of any State to the Contrary notwithstanding.

The Senators and Representatives before mentioned, and the Members of the several State Legislatures, and all executive and judicial Officers, both of the United States and of the several States, shall be bound by Oath or Affirmation, to support this Constitution; but no religious Test shall ever be required as a Qualification to any Office or public Trust under the United States.

Article. VII.

The Ratification of the Conventions of nine States, shall be sufficient for the Establishment of this Constitution between the States so ratifying the Same.

Amendments

to the

Constitution of the United States

Amendment I (1791)

Congress shall make no law respecting an establishment of religion, or prohibiting the free exercise thereof; or abridging the freedom of speech, or of the press; or the right of the people peaceably to assemble, and to petition the government for a redress of grievances.

Amendment II (1791)

A well regulated militia, being necessary to the security of a free state, the right of the people to keep and bear arms, shall not be infringed.

Amendment III (1791)

No soldier shall, in time of peace be quartered in any house, without the consent of the owner, nor in time of war, but in a manner to be prescribed by law.

Amendment IV (1791)

The right of the people to be secure in their persons, houses, papers, and effects, against unreasonable searches and seizures, shall not be violated, and no warrants shall issue, but upon probable cause, supported by oath or affirmation, and particularly describing the place to be searched, and the persons or things to be seized.

Amendment V (1791)

No person shall be held to answer for a capital, or otherwise infamous crime, unless on a presentment or indictment of a grand jury, except in cases arising in the land or naval forces, or in the militia, when in actual service in time of war or public danger; nor shall any person be subject for the same offense to be twice put in jeopardy of life or limb; nor shall be compelled in any criminal case to be a witness against himself, nor be deprived of life, liberty, or property, without due process of law; nor shall private property be taken for public use, without just compensation.

Amendment VI (1791)

In all criminal prosecutions, the accused shall enjoy the right to a speedy and public trial, by an impartial jury of the state and district wherein the crime shall have been committed, which district shall have been previously ascertained by law, and to be informed of the nature and cause of the accusation; to be confronted with the witnesses against him; to have compulsory process for obtaining witnesses in his favor, and to have the assistance of counsel for his defense.

Amendment VII (1791)

In suits at common law, where the value in controversy shall exceed twenty dollars, the right of trial by jury shall be preserved, and no fact tried by a jury, shall be otherwise reexamined in any court of the United States, than according to the rules of the common law.

Amendment VIII (1791)

Excessive bail shall not be required, nor excessive fines imposed, nor cruel and unusual punishments inflicted.

Amendment IX (1791)

The enumeration in the Constitution, of certain rights, shall not be construed to deny or disparage others retained by the people.

Amendment X (1791)

The powers not delegated to the United States by the Constitution, nor prohibited by it to the states, are reserved to the states respectively, or to the people.

Amendment XI (1798)

The judicial power of the United States shall not be construed to extend to any suit in law or equity, commenced or prosecuted against one of the United States by citizens of another state, or by citizens or subjects of any foreign state.

Amendment XII (1804)

The electors shall meet in their respective states and vote by ballot for President and Vice-President, one of whom, at least, shall not be an inhabitant of the same state with themselves; they shall name in their ballots the person voted for as President, and in distinct ballots the person voted for as Vice-President, and they shall make distinct lists of all persons voted for as President, and of all persons voted for as Vice-President, and of the number of votes for each, which lists they shall sign and certify, and transmit sealed to the seat of the government of the United States, directed to the President of the Senate;--The President of the Senate shall, in the presence of the Senate and House of Representatives, open all the certificates and the votes shall then be counted;--the person having the greatest number of votes for President, shall be the President, if such number be a majority of the whole number of electors appointed; and if no person have such majority, then from the persons having the highest numbers not exceeding three on the list of those voted for as President, the House of Representatives shall choose immediately, by ballot, the President. But in choosing the President, the votes shall be taken by states, the representation from each state having one vote; a quorum for this purpose shall consist of a member or members from two-thirds of the states, and a majority of all the states shall be necessary to a choice. And if the House of Representatives shall not choose a President whenever the right of choice shall devolve upon them, before the fourth day of March next following, then the Vice-President shall act as President, as in the case of the death or other constitutional disability of the President. The person having the greatest number of votes as Vice-President, shall be the Vice-President, if such number be a majority of the whole number of electors appointed, and if no person have a majority, then from the two highest numbers on the list, the Senate shall choose the Vice-President; a quorum for the purpose shall consist of two-thirds of the whole number of Senators, and a majority of the whole number shall be necessary to a choice. But no person constitutionally ineligible to the office of President shall be eligible to that of Vice-President of the United States.

Amendment XIII (1865)

Section 1.

Neither slavery nor involuntary servitude, except as a punishment for crime whereof the party shall have been duly convicted, shall exist within the United States, or any place subject to their jurisdiction.

Section 2.

Congress shall have power to enforce this article by appropriate legislation.

Amendment XIV (1868)

Section 1.

All persons born or naturalized in the United States, and subject to the jurisdiction thereof, are citizens of the United States and of the state wherein they reside. No state shall make or enforce any law which shall abridge the privileges or immunities of citizens of the United States; nor shall any state deprive any person of life, liberty, or property, without due process of law; nor deny to any person within its jurisdiction the equal protection of the laws.

Section 2.

Representatives shall be apportioned among the several states according to their respective numbers, counting the whole number of persons in each state, excluding Indians not taxed. But when the right to vote at any election for the choice of electors for President and Vice President of the United States, Representatives in Congress, the executive and judicial officers of a state, or the members of the legislature thereof, is denied to any of the male inhabitants of such state, being twenty-one years of age, and citizens of the United States, or in any way abridged, except for participation in rebellion, or other crime, the basis of representation therein shall be reduced in the proportion which the number of such male citizens shall bear to the whole number of male citizens twenty-one years of age in such state.

Section 3.

No person shall be a Senator or Representative in Congress, or elector of President and Vice President, or hold any office, civil or military, under the United States, or under any state, who, having previously taken an oath, as a member of Congress, or as an officer of the United States, or as a member of any state legislature, or as an executive or judicial officer of any state, to support the Constitution of the United States, shall have engaged in insurrection or rebellion against the same, or given aid or comfort to the enemies thereof. But Congress may by a vote of two-thirds of each House, remove such disability.

Section 4.

The validity of the public debt of the United States, authorized by law, including debts incurred for payment of pensions and bounties for services in suppressing insurrection or rebellion, shall not be questioned. But neither the United States nor any state shall assume or pay any debt or obligation incurred in aid of insurrection or rebellion against the United States, or any claim for the loss or emancipation of any slave; but all such debts, obligations and claims shall be held illegal and void.

Section 5.

The Congress shall have power to enforce, by appropriate legislation, the provisions of this article.

Amendment XV (1870)

Section 1.

The right of citizens of the United States to vote shall not be denied or abridged by the United States or by any state on account of race, color, or previous condition of servitude.

Section 2.

The Congress shall have power to enforce this article by appropriate legislation.

Amendment XVI (1913)

The Congress shall have power to lay and collect taxes on incomes, from whatever source derived, without apportionment among the several states, and without regard to any census of enumeration.

Amendment XVII (1913)

The Senate of the United States shall be composed of two Senators from each state, elected by the people thereof, for six years; and each Senator shall have one vote. The electors in each state shall have the qualifications requisite for electors of the most numerous branch of the state legislatures.

When vacancies happen in the representation of any state in the Senate, the executive authority of such state shall issue writs of election to fill such vacancies: Provided, that the legislature of any state may empower the executive thereof to make temporary appointments until the people fill the vacancies by election as the legislature may direct.

This amendment shall not be so construed as to affect the election or term of any Senator chosen before it becomes valid as part of the Constitution.

Amendment XVIII (1919)

Section 1.

After one year from the ratification of this article the manufacture, sale, or transportation of intoxicating liquors within, the importation thereof into, or the exportation thereof from the United States and all territory subject to the jurisdiction thereof for beverage purposes is hereby prohibited.

Section 2.

The Congress and the several states shall have concurrent power to enforce this article by appropriate legislation.

Section 3.

This article shall be inoperative unless it shall have been ratified as an amendment to the Constitution by the legislatures of the several states, as provided in the Constitution, within seven years from the date of the submission hereof to the states by the Congress.

Amendment XIX (1920)

The right of citizens of the United States to vote shall not be denied or abridged by the United States or by any state on account of sex.

Congress shall have power to enforce this article by appropriate legislation.

Amendment XX (1933)

Section 1.

The terms of the President and Vice President shall end at noon on the 20th day of January, and the terms of Senators and Representatives at noon on the 3d day of January, of the years in which such terms would have ended if this article had not been ratified; and the terms of their successors shall then begin.

Section 2.

The Congress shall assemble at least once in every year, and such meeting shall begin at noon on the 3d day of January, unless they shall by law appoint a different day.

Section 3.

If, at the time fixed for the beginning of the term of the President, the President elect shall have died, the Vice President elect shall become President. If a President shall not have been chosen before the time fixed for the beginning of his term, or if the President elect shall have failed to qualify, then the Vice President elect shall act as President until a President shall have qualified; and the Congress may by law provide for the case wherein neither a President elect nor a Vice President elect shall have qualified, declaring who shall then act as President, or the manner in which one who is to act shall be selected, and such person shall act accordingly until a President or Vice President shall have qualified.

Section 4.

The Congress may by law provide for the case of the death of any of the persons from whom the House of Representatives may choose a President whenever the right of choice shall have devolved upon them, and for the case of the death of any of the persons from whom the Senate may choose a Vice President whenever the right of choice shall have devolved upon them.

Section 5.

Sections 1 and 2 shall take effect on the 15th day of October following the ratification of this article.

Section 6.

This article shall be inoperative unless it shall have been ratified as an amendment to the Constitution by the legislatures of three-fourths of the several states within seven years from the date of its submission.

Amendment XXI (1933)

Section 1.

The eighteenth article of amendment to the Constitution of the United States is hereby repealed.

Section 2.

The transportation or importation into any state, territory, or possession of the United States for delivery or use therein of intoxicating liquors, in violation of the laws thereof, is hereby prohibited.

Section 3.

This article shall be inoperative unless it shall have been ratified as an amendment to the Constitution by conventions in the several states, as provided in the Constitution, within seven years from the date of the submission hereof to the states by the Congress.

Amendment XXII (1951)

Section 1.

No person shall be elected to the office of the President more than twice, and no person who has held the office of President, or acted as President, for more than two years of a term to which some other person was elected President shall be elected to the office of the President more than once. But this article shall not apply to any person holding the office of President when this article was proposed by the Congress, and shall not prevent any person who may be holding the office of President, or acting as President, during the term within which this article becomes operative from holding the office of President or acting as President during the remainder of such term.

Section 2.

This article shall be inoperative unless it shall have been ratified as an amendment to the Constitution by the legislatures of three-fourths of the several states within seven years from the date of its submission to the states by the Congress.

Amendment XXIII (1961)

Section 1.

The District constituting the seat of government of the United States shall appoint in such manner as the Congress may direct:

A number of electors of President and Vice President equal to the whole number of Senators and Representatives in Congress to which the District would be entitled if it were a state, but in no event more than the least populous state; they shall be in addition to those appointed by the states, but they shall be considered, for the purposes of the election of President and Vice President, to be electors appointed by a state; and they shall meet in the District and perform such duties as provided by the twelfth article of amendment.

Section 2.

The Congress shall have power to enforce this article by appropriate legislation.

Amendment XXIV (1964)

Section 1.

The right of citizens of the United States to vote in any primary or other election for President or Vice President, for electors for President or Vice President, or for Senator or Representative in Congress, shall not be denied or abridged by the United States or any state by reason of failure to pay any poll tax or other tax.

Section 2.

The Congress shall have power to enforce this article by appropriate legislation.

Amendment XXV (1967)

Section 1.

In case of the removal of the President from office or of his death or resignation, the Vice President shall become President.

Section 2.

Whenever there is a vacancy in the office of the Vice President, the President shall nominate a Vice President who shall take office upon confirmation by a majority vote of both Houses of Congress.

Section 3.

Whenever the President transmits to the President pro tempore of the Senate and the Speaker of the House of Representatives his written declaration that he is unable to discharge the powers and duties of his office, and until he transmits to them a written declaration to the contrary, such powers and duties shall be discharged by the Vice President as Acting President.

Section 4.

Whenever the Vice President and a majority of either the principal officers of the executive departments or of such other body as Congress may by law provide, transmit to the President pro tempore of the Senate and the Speaker of the House of Representatives their written declaration that the President is unable to discharge the powers and duties of his office, the Vice President shall immediately assume the powers and duties of the office as Acting President.

Thereafter, when the President transmits to the President pro tempore of the Senate and the Speaker of the House of Representatives his written declaration that no inability exists, he shall resume the powers and duties of his office unless the Vice President and a majority of either the principal officers of the executive department or of such other body as Congress may by law provide, transmit within four days to the President pro tempore of the Senate and the Speaker of the House of Representatives their written declaration that the President is unable to discharge the powers and duties of his office. Thereupon Congress shall decide the issue, assembling within forty-eight hours for that purpose if not in session. If the Congress, within twenty-one days after receipt of the latter written declaration, or, if Congress is not in session, within twenty-one days after Congress is required to assemble, determines by two-thirds vote of both Houses that the President is unable to discharge the powers and duties of his office, the Vice President shall continue to discharge the same as Acting President; otherwise, the President shall resume the powers and duties of his office.

Amendment XXVI (1971)

Section 1.

The right of citizens of the United States, who are 18 years of age or older, to vote, shall not be denied or abridged by the United States or any state on account of age.

Section 2.

The Congress shall have the power to enforce this article by appropriate legislation.

Amendment XXVII (1992)

No law varying the compensation for the services of the Senators and Representatives shall take effect until an election of Representatives shall have intervened.

WILLIAM MARBURY v. JAMES MADISON, SECRETARY OF STATE OF THE UNITED STATES.

SUPREME COURT OF THE UNITED STATES

5 U.S. 137

February 24, 1803

[Background information: John Adams, the outgoing president of the United States, had nominated several "midnight judges" to fill vacant positions to ensure his political legacy. The nominations were sealed with wax and affixed to the official commissions, and the only thing left was for the new Secretary of State to deliver the sealed commissions to the waiting judges-to-be. However, the incoming president, Thomas Jefferson, directed his new Secretary of State, James Madison, to lock them in a drawer. That way Jefferson could fill the vacant judicial positions with his own political allies. William Marbury, one of the nominated "midnight judges" sued Madison, demanding his sealed commission. The case was brought directly to the US Supreme Court. – JJV, ed.]

Opinion of the court.

At the last term on the affidavits then read and filed with the clerk, a rule was granted in this case, requiring the secretary of state to show cause why a mandamus should not issue, directing him to deliver to William Marbury his commission as a justice of the peace of the county of Washington, in the district of Columbia.

No cause has been shown, and the present motion is for a mandamus. The peculiar delicacy of this case, the novelty of some of its circumstances, and the real difficulty attending the points which occur in it, require a complete exposition of the principles, on which the opinion to be given by the court, is founded.

These principles have been, on the side of the applicant, very ably argued at the bar. In rendering the opinion of the court, there will be some departure in form, though not in substance, from the points stated in that argument.

In the order in which the court has viewed this subject, the following questions have been considered and decided.

1st. Has the applicant a right to the commission he demands?

2dly. If he has a right, and that right has been violated, do the laws of his country afford him a remedy?

3dly. If they do afford him a remedy, is it a mandamus issuing from this court?

[Regarding the 1st issue, Marshall concluded that Marbury was indeed entitled to his sealed commission, since it had been signed by the president and sealed by the Secretary of State (who happened to be Marshall himself, before he was appointed to the Supreme Court!). As

43

for the 2nd issue, Marshall decided that since Madison's failure to deliver the commission was in fact illegal and not just political maneuvering, and therefore was within the Court's jurisdiction. –JJV, ed.]

This, then, is a plain case for a mandamus, either to deliver the commission, or a copy of it from the record; and it only remains to be enquired,

Whether it can issue from this court.

The act to establish the judicial courts of the United States authorizes the supreme court "to issue writs of mandamus, in cases warranted by the principles and usages of law, to any courts appointed, or persons holding office, under the authority of the United States."

[The Congress had passed the Judiciary Act on Sept. 24, 1789. It read, in part, as follows:

> *SEC. 13. And be it further enacted, That the Supreme Court shall have exclusive jurisdiction of all controversies of a civil nature, where a state is a party, except between a state and its citizens; and except also between a state and citizens of other states, or aliens, in which latter case it shall have original but not exclusive jurisdiction. And shall have exclusively all such jurisdiction of suits or proceedings against ambassadors, or other public ministers, or their domestics, or domestic servants, as a court of law can have or exercise consistently with the law of nations; and original, but not exclusive jurisdiction of all suits brought by ambassadors, or other public ministers, or in which a consul, or vice consul, shall be a party. And the trial of issues in fact in the Supreme Court, in all actions at law against citizens of the United States, shall be by jury. The Supreme Court shall also have appellate jurisdiction from the circuit courts and courts of the several states, in the cases herein after specially provided for; and shall have power to issue writs of prohibition to the district courts, when proceeding as courts of admiralty and maritime jurisdiction, and writs of mandamus, in cases warranted by the principles and usages of law, to any courts appointed, or persons holding office, under the authority of the United States.*]

The secretary of state, being a person holding an office under the authority of the United States, is precisely within the letter of the description; and if this court is not authorized to issue a writ of mandamus to such an officer, it must be because the law is unconstitutional, and therefore absolutely incapable of conferring the authority, and assigning the duties which its words purport to confer and assign.

The constitution vests the whole judicial power of the United States in one supreme court, and such inferior courts as congress shall, from time to time, ordain and establish. This power is expressly extended to all cases arising under the laws of the United States; and consequently, in some form, may be exercised over the present case; because the right claimed is given by a law of the United States.

In the distribution of this power it is declared that "the supreme court shall have original jurisdiction in all cases affecting ambassadors, other public ministers and consuls, and those in which a state shall be a party. In all other cases, the supreme court shall have appellate jurisdiction."

It has been insisted, at the bar, that as the original grant of jurisdiction, to the supreme and inferior courts, is general, and the clause, assigning original jurisdiction to the supreme court, contains no negative or restrictive words; the power remains to the legislature, to assign original jurisdiction to that court in other cases than those specified in the article which has been recited; provided those cases belong to the judicial power of the United States.

If it had been intended to leave it to the discretion of the legislature to apportion the judicial power between the supreme and inferior courts according to the will of that body, it would certainly have been useless to have proceeded further than to have defined the judicial powers, and the tribunals in which it should be vested. The subsequent part of the section is mere surplusage, is entirely without meaning, if such is to be the construction. If congress remains at liberty to give this court appellate jurisdiction, where the constitution has declared their jurisdiction shall be original; and original jurisdiction where the constitution has declared it shall be appellate; the distribution of jurisdiction, made in the constitution, is form without substance.

Affirmative words are often, in their operation, negative of other objects than those affirmed; and in this case, a negative or exclusive sense must be given to them or they have no operation at all.

It cannot be presumed that any clause in the constitution is intended to be without effect; and therefore such a construction is inadmissible, unless the words require it.

If the solicitude of the convention, respecting our peace with foreign powers, induced a provision that the supreme court should take original jurisdiction in cases which might be supposed to affect them; yet the clause would have proceeded no further than to provide for such cases, if no further restriction on the powers of congress had been intended. That they should have appellate jurisdiction in all other cases, with such exceptions as congress might make, is no restriction; unless the words be deemed exclusive of original jurisdiction.

When an instrument organizing fundamentally a judicial system, divides it into one supreme, and so many inferior courts as the legislature may ordain and establish; then enumerates its powers, and proceeds so far to distribute them, as to define the jurisdiction of the supreme court by declaring the cases in which it shall take original jurisdiction, and that in others it shall take appellate jurisdiction; the plain import of the words seems to be, that in one class of cases its jurisdiction is original, and not appellate; in the other it is appellate, and not original. If any other construction would render the clause inoperative, that is an additional reason for rejecting such other construction, and for adhering to their obvious meaning.

To enable this court then to issue a mandamus, it must be shown to be an exercise of appellate jurisdiction, or to be necessary to enable them to exercise appellate jurisdiction.

It has been stated at the bar that the appellate jurisdiction may be exercised in a variety of forms, and that if it be the will of the legislature that a mandamus should be used for that purpose, that will must be obeyed. This is true, yet the jurisdiction must be appellate, not original.

It is the essential criterion of appellate jurisdiction, that it revises and corrects the proceedings in a cause already instituted, and does not create that cause. Although, therefore, a mandamus may be directed to courts, yet to issue such a writ to an officer for the delivery of a paper, is in effect the same as to sustain an original action for that paper, and therefore seems not to belong to appellate, but to original jurisdiction. Neither is it necessary in such a case as this, to enable the court to exercise its appellate jurisdiction.

The authority, therefore, given to the supreme court, by the act establishing the judicial courts of the United States, to issue writs of mandamus to public officers, appears not to be warranted by the constitution; and it becomes necessary to enquire whether a jurisdiction, so conferred, can be exercised.

The question, whether an act, repugnant to the constitution, can become the law of the land, is a question deeply interesting to the United States; but, happily, not of an intricacy proportioned to its interest. It seems only necessary to recognize certain principles, supposed to have been long and well established, to decide it.

That the people have an original right to establish, for their future government, such principles as, in their opinion, shall most conduce to their own happiness, is the basis, on which the whole American fabric has been erected. The exercise of this original right is a very great exertion; nor can it, nor ought it to be frequently repeated. The principles, therefore, so established, are deemed fundamental. And as the authority, from which they proceed, is supreme, and can seldom act, they are designed to be permanent.

This original and supreme will organizes the government, and assigns, to different departments, their respective powers. It may either stop here; or establish certain limits not to be transcended by those departments.

The government of the United States is of the latter description. The powers of the legislature are defined, and limited; and that those limits may not be mistaken, or forgotten, the constitution is written. To what purpose are powers limited, and to what purpose is that limitation committed to writing, if these limits may, at any time, be passed by those intended to be restrained? The distinction, between a government with limited and unlimited powers, is abolished, if those limits do not confine the persons on whom they are imposed, and if acts prohibited and acts allowed, are of equal obligation. It is a proposition too plain to be contested, that the constitution controls any legislative act repugnant to it; or, that the legislature may alter the constitution by an ordinary act.

Between these alternatives there is no middle ground. The constitution is either a superior, paramount law, unchangeable by ordinary means, or it is on a level with ordinary legislative acts, and like other acts, is alterable when the legislature shall please to alter it.

If the former part of the alternative be true, then a legislative act contrary to the constitution is not law: if the latter part be true, then written constitutions are absurd attempts, on the part of the people, to limit a power, in its own nature illimitable.

Certainly all those who have framed written constitutions contemplate them as forming the fundamental and paramount law of the nation, and consequently the theory of every such government must be, that an act of the legislature, repugnant to the constitution, is void.

This theory is essentially attached to a written constitution, and is consequently to be considered, by this court, as one of the fundamental principles of our society. It is not therefore to be lost sight of in the further consideration of this subject.

If an act of the legislature, repugnant to the constitution, is void, does it, notwithstanding its invalidity, bind the courts, and oblige them to give it effect? Or, in other words, though it be not law, does it constitute a rule as operative as if it was a law? This would be to overthrow in fact what was established in theory; and would seem, at first view, an absurdity too gross to be insisted on. It shall, however, receive a more attentive consideration.

It is emphatically the province and duty of the judicial department to say what the law is. Those who apply the rule to particular cases, must of necessity expound and interpret that rule. If two laws conflict with each other, the courts must decide on the operation of each.

So if a law be in opposition to the constitution; if both the law and the constitution apply to a particular case, so that the court must either decide that case conformably to the law, disregarding the constitution; or conformably to the constitution, disregarding the law; the court must determine which of these conflicting rules governs the case. This is of the very essence of judicial duty.

If then the courts are to regard the constitution; and the constitution is superior to any ordinary act of the legislature; the constitution, and not such ordinary act, must govern the case to which they both apply.

Those then who controvert the principle that the constitution is to be considered, in court, as a paramount law, are reduced to the necessity of maintaining that courts must close their eyes on the constitution, and see only the law.

This doctrine would subvert the very foundation of all written constitutions. It would declare that an act, which, according to the principles and theory of our government, is entirely void; is yet, in practice, completely obligatory. It would declare, that if the legislature shall do what is expressly forbidden, such act, notwithstanding the express prohibition, is in reality effectual. It would be giving to the legislature a practical and real omnipotence, with the same breath which professes to restrict their powers within narrow limits. It is prescribing limits, and declaring that those limits may be passed at pleasure.

That it thus reduces to nothing what we have deemed the greatest improvement on political institutions -- a written constitution -- would of itself be sufficient, in America, where written constitutions have been viewed with so much reverence, for rejecting the construction. But the peculiar expressions of the constitution of the United States furnish additional arguments in favor of its rejection.

The judicial power of the United States is extended to all cases arising under the constitution.

Could it be the intention of those who gave this power, to say that, in using it, the constitution should not be looked into? That a case arising under the constitution should be decided without examining the instrument under which it arises?

This is too extravagant to be maintained.

In some cases then, the constitution must be looked into by the judges. And if they can open it at all, what part of it are they forbidden to read, or to obey?

There are many other parts of the constitution which serve to illustrate this subject.

It is declared that "no tax or duty shall be laid on articles exported from any state." Suppose a duty on the export of cotton, of tobacco, or of flour; and a suit instituted to recover it. Ought judgment to be rendered in such a case? Ought the judges to close their eyes on the constitution, and only see the law?

The constitution declares that "no bill of attainder or ex post facto law shall be passed."

If, however, such a bill should be passed and a person should be prosecuted under it; must the court condemn to death those victims whom the constitution endeavors to preserve?

"No person," says the constitution, "shall be convicted of treason unless on the testimony of two witnesses to the fame overt act, or on confession in open court."

Here the language of the constitution is addressed especially to the courts. It prescribes, directly for them, a rule of evidence not to be departed from. If the legislature should change that rule, and declare one witness, or a confession out of court, sufficient for conviction, must the constitutional principle yield to the legislative act?

From these, and many other selections which might be made, it is apparent, that the framers of the constitution contemplated that instrument, as a rule for the government of courts, as well as of the legislature.

Why otherwise does it direct the judges to take an oath to support it? This oath certainly applies, in an especial manner, to their conduct in their official character. How immoral to impose it on them, if they were to be used as the instruments, and the knowing instruments, for violating what they swear to support!

The oath of office, too, imposed by the legislature, is completely demonstrative of the legislative opinion on the subject. It is in these words, "I do solemnly swear that I will administer justice without respect to persons, and do equal right to the poor and to the rich; and that I will faithfully and impartially discharge all the duties incumbent on me as   according to the best of my abilities and understanding, agreeably to the constitution, and laws of the United States."

Why does a judge swear to discharge his duties agreeably to the constitution of the United States, if that constitution forms no rule for his government? If it is closed upon him, and cannot be inspected by him?

If such be the real state of things, this is worse than solemn mockery. To prescribe, or to take this oath, becomes equally a crime.

It is also not entirely unworthy of observation, that in declaring what shall be the supreme law of the land, the constitution itself is first mentioned; and not the laws of the United States generally, but those only which shall be made in pursuance of the constitution, have that rank.

Thus, the particular phraseology of the constitution of the United States confirms and strengthens the principle, supposed to be essential to all written constitutions, that a law repugnant to the constitution is void; and that courts, as well as other departments, are bound by that instrument.

The rule must be discharged.

GIDEON v. WAINWRIGHT, CORRECTIONS DIRECTOR

SUPREME COURT OF THE UNITED STATES

372 U.S. 335

March,1963

MR. JUSTICE BLACK delivered the opinion of the Court.

Petitioner was charged in a Florida state court with having broken and entered a poolroom with intent to commit a misdemeanor. This offense is a felony under Florida law. Appearing in court without funds and without a lawyer, petitioner asked the court to appoint counsel for him, whereupon the following colloquy took place:

"The COURT: Mr. Gideon, I am sorry, but I cannot appoint Counsel to represent you in this case. Under the laws of the State of Florida, the only time the Court can appoint Counsel to represent a Defendant is when that person is charged with a capital offense. I am sorry, but I will have to deny your request to appoint Counsel to defend you in this case.

"The DEFENDANT: The United States Supreme Court says I am entitled to be represented by Counsel."

Put to trial before a jury, Gideon conducted his defense about as well as could be expected from a layman. He made an opening statement to the jury, cross-examined the State's witnesses, presented witnesses in his own defense, declined to testify himself, and made a short argument "emphasizing his innocence to the charge contained in the Information filed in this case." The jury returned a verdict of guilty, and petitioner was sentenced to serve five years in the state prison. Later, petitioner filed in the Florida Supreme Court this habeas corpus petition attacking his conviction and sentence on the ground that the trial court's refusal to appoint counsel for him denied him rights "guaranteed by the Constitution and the *Bill of Rights* by the United States Government." [1] Treating the petition for habeas corpus as properly before it, the State Supreme Court, "upon consideration thereof" but without an opinion, denied all relief. Since 1942, when *Betts v. Brady, 316 U.S. 455*, was decided by a divided Court, the problem of a defendant's federal constitutional right to counsel in a state court has been a continuing source of controversy and litigation in both state and federal courts. [2] To give this problem another review here, we granted certiorari. *370 U.S. 908*. Since Gideon was proceeding *in forma pauperis*, we appointed counsel to represent him and requested both sides to discuss in their briefs and oral arguments the following: "Should this Court's holding in *Betts v. Brady, 316 U.S. 455*, be reconsidered?"

1 Later in the petition for habeas corpus, signed and apparently prepared by petitioner himself, he stated, "I, Clarence Earl

Gideon, claim that I was denied the rights of the *4th, 5th* and *14th amendments* of the *Bill of Rights*."

2 Of the many such cases to reach this Court, recent examples are *Carnley v. Cochran, 369 U.S. 506 (1962)*; *Hudson v. North Carolina, 363 U.S. 697 (1960)*; *Moore v. Michigan, 355 U.S. 155 (1957)*. Illustrative cases in the state courts are *Artrip v. State, 136 So. 2d 574 (Ct. App. Ala. 1962)*; *Shaffer v. Warden, 211 Md. 635, 126 A. 2d 573 (1956)*. For examples of commentary, see Allen, The Supreme Court, Federalism, and State Systems of Criminal Justice, 8 De Paul L. Rev. 213 (1959); Kamisar, The Right to Counsel and the *Fourteenth Amendment*: A Dialogue on "The Most Pervasive Right" of an Accused, 30 U. of Chi. L. Rev. 1 (1962); The Right to Counsel, 45 Minn. L. Rev. 693 (1961).

I.

The facts upon which Betts claimed that he had been unconstitutionally denied the right to have counsel appointed to assist him are strikingly like the facts upon which Gideon here bases his federal constitutional claim. Betts was indicted for robbery in a Maryland state court. On arraignment, he told the trial judge of his lack of funds to hire a lawyer and asked the court to appoint one for him. Betts was advised that it was not the practice in that county to appoint counsel for indigent defendants except in murder and rape cases. He then pleaded not guilty, had witnesses summoned, cross-examined the State's witnesses, examined his own, and chose not to testify himself. He was found guilty by the judge, sitting without a jury, and sentenced to eight years in prison. Like Gideon, Betts sought release by habeas corpus, alleging that he had been denied the right to assistance of counsel in violation of the *Fourteenth Amendment*. Betts was denied any relief, and on review this Court affirmed. It was held that a refusal to appoint counsel for an indigent defendant charged with a felony did not necessarily violate the *Due Process Clause of the Fourteenth Amendment*, which for reasons given the Court deemed to be the only applicable federal constitutional provision. The Court said:

"Asserted denial [of due process] is to be tested by an appraisal of the totality of facts in a given case. That which may, in one setting, constitute a denial of fundamental fairness, shocking to the universal sense of justice, may, in other circumstances, and in the light of other considerations, fall short of such denial." *316 U.S., at 462.*

Treating due process as "a concept less rigid and more fluid than those envisaged in other specific and particular provisions of the *Bill of Rights*," the Court held that refusal to appoint counsel under the particular facts and circumstances in the *Betts* case was not so "offensive to the common and fundamental ideas of fairness" as to amount to a denial of due process. Since the facts and circumstances of the two cases are so nearly indistinguishable, we think the *Betts* v. *Brady* holding if left standing would require us to reject Gideon's claim that the Constitution guarantees him the assistance of counsel. Upon full reconsideration we conclude that *Betts* v. *Brady* should be overruled.

II.

The *Sixth Amendment* provides, "In all criminal prosecutions, the accused shall enjoy the right . . . to have the Assistance of Counsel for his defense." We have construed this to mean that in federal courts counsel must be provided for defendants unable to employ counsel unless the right is competently and intelligently waived. [3] Betts argued that this right is extended to indigent defendants in state courts by the *Fourteenth Amendment*. In response the Court stated that, while the *Sixth Amendment* laid down "no rule for the conduct of the States, the question recurs whether the constraint laid by the Amendment upon the national courts expresses a rule so fundamental and essential to a fair trial, and so, to due process of law, that it is made obligatory upon the States by the *Fourteenth Amendment*." *316 U.S., at 465*. In order to decide whether the *Sixth Amendment's* guarantee of counsel is of this fundamental nature, the Court in *Betts* set out and considered "relevant data on the subject . . . afforded by constitutional and statutory provisions subsisting in the colonies and the States prior to the inclusion of the *Bill of Rights* in the national Constitution, and in the constitutional, legislative, and judicial history of the States to the present date." *316 U.S., at 465*. On the basis of this historical data the Court concluded that "appointment of counsel is not a fundamental right, essential to a fair trial." *316 U.S., at 471*. It was for this reason the *Betts* Court refused to accept the contention that the *Sixth Amendment's* guarantee of counsel for indigent federal defendants was extended to or, in the words of that Court, "made obligatory upon the States by the *Fourteenth Amendment*." Plainly, had the Court concluded that appointment of counsel for an indigent criminal defendant was "a fundamental right, essential to a fair trial," it would have held that the *Fourteenth Amendment* requires appointment of counsel in a state court, just as the *Sixth Amendment* requires in a federal court.

[Here the court reviews several past decisions that conflict with the instant ruling, like *Betts*]. –JJV, ed.

In light of these and many other prior decisions of this Court, it is not surprising that the *Betts* Court, when faced with the contention that "one charged with crime, who is unable to obtain counsel, must be furnished counsel by the State," conceded that "expressions in the opinions of this court lend color to the argument . . . ." *316 U.S., at 462-463*. The fact is that in deciding as it did -- that "appointment of counsel is not a fundamental right, essential to a fair trial" -- the Court in *Betts* v. *Brady* made an abrupt break with its own well-considered precedents. In returning to these old precedents, sounder we believe than the new, we but restore constitutional principles established to achieve a fair system of justice. Not only these precedents but also reason and reflection require us to recognize that in our adversary system of criminal justice, any person haled into court, who is too poor to hire a lawyer, cannot be assured a fair trial unless counsel is provided for him. This seems to us to be an obvious truth. Governments, both state and federal, quite properly spend vast sums of money to establish machinery to try defendants accused of crime. Lawyers to prosecute are everywhere deemed essential to protect the public's interest in an orderly society. Similarly, there are few defendants charged with crime, few indeed, who fail to hire the best lawyers they can get to prepare and present their defenses. That government hires lawyers to prosecute and defendants who have the money hire lawyers to defend are the strongest indications of the widespread belief that lawyers in criminal courts are necessities, not luxuries. The right of one charged with crime to counsel may not be deemed fundamental and essential to fair trials in some countries, but it is in ours. From the very beginning, our state and national constitutions and laws have laid great emphasis on procedural and substantive safeguards designed to assure fair trials before impartial tribunals in which every defendant stands equal before the law. This noble ideal cannot be realized if the poor man charged with crime has to face his accusers without a lawyer to assist him. A defendant's need for a lawyer is nowhere better stated than in the moving words of Mr. Justice Sutherland in *Powell* v. *Alabama*:

"The right to be heard would be, in many cases, of little avail if it did not comprehend the right to be heard by counsel. Even the intelligent and educated layman has small and sometimes no skill in the science of law. If charged with crime, he is incapable, generally, of determining for himself whether the indictment is good or bad. He is unfamiliar with the rules of evidence. Left without the aid of counsel he may be put on trial without a proper charge, and convicted upon incompetent evidence, or evidence irrelevant to the issue or otherwise inadmissible. He lacks both the skill and knowledge adequately to prepare his defense, even though he have a perfect one. He requires the guiding hand of counsel at every step in the proceedings against him. Without it, though he be not guilty, he faces the danger of conviction because he does not know how to establish his innocence." *287 U.S., at 68-69*.

The Court in *Betts* v. *Brady* departed from the sound wisdom upon which the Court's holding in *Powell* v. *Alabama* rested. Florida, supported by two other States, has asked that *Betts* v. *Brady* be left intact. Twenty-two States, as friends of the Court, argue that *Betts* was "an anachronism when handed down" and that it should now be overruled. We agree.

The judgment is reversed and the cause is remanded to the Supreme Court of Florida for further action not inconsistent with this opinion.

Reversed.

[Justice DOUGLAS's joinder and Justices CLARK and HARLAN's concurrence are omitted].—JJV, ed.

UNITED STATES v. CAUSBY ET UX.

SUPREME COURT OF THE UNITED STATES

328 U.S. 256

May, 1946

MR. JUSTICE DOUGLAS delivered the opinion of the Court.

This is a case of first impression. The problem presented is whether respondents' property was taken, within the meaning of the *Fifth Amendment*, by frequent and regular flights of army and navy aircraft over respondents' land at low altitudes. The Court of Claims held that there was a taking and entered judgment for respondents, one judge dissenting. *104 Ct. Cls. 342, 60 F.Supp. 751*. The case is here on a petition for a writ of certiorari which we granted because of the importance of the question presented.

Respondents own 2.8 acres near an airport outside of Greensboro, North Carolina. It has on it a dwelling house, and also various outbuildings which were mainly used for raising chickens. The end of the airport's northwest-southeast runway is 2,220 feet from respondents' barn and 2,275 feet from their house. The path of glide to this runway passes directly over the property -- which is 100 feet wide and 1,200 feet long. The 30 to 1 safe glide angle approved by the Civil Aeronautics Authority passes over this property at 83 feet, which is 67 feet above the house, 63 feet above the barn and 18 feet above the highest tree. The use by the United States of this airport is pursuant to a lease executed in May, 1942, for a term commencing June 1, 1942 and ending June 30, 1942, with a provision for renewals until June 30, 1967, or six months after the end of the national emergency, whichever is the earlier.

Various aircraft of the United States use this airport -- bombers, transports and fighters. The direction of the prevailing wind determines when a particular runway is used. The northwest-southeast runway in question is used about four per cent of the time in taking off and about seven per cent of the time in landing. Since the United States began operations in May, 1942, its four-motored heavy bombers, other planes of the heavier type, and its fighter planes have frequently passed over respondents' land and buildings in considerable numbers and rather close together. They come close enough at times to appear barely to miss the tops of the trees and at times so close to the tops of the trees as to blow the old leaves off. The noise is startling. And at night the glare from the planes brightly lights up the place. As a result of the noise, respondents had to give up their chicken business. As many as six to ten of their chickens were killed in one day by flying into the walls from fright. The total chickens lost in that manner was about 150. Production also fell off. The result was the destruction of the use of the property as a commercial chicken farm. Respondents are frequently deprived of their sleep and the family has become nervous and frightened. Although there have been no airplane accidents on respondents' property, there have been several accidents near the airport and close to respondents' place. These are the essential facts found by the Court of Claims. On the basis of these facts, it found that respondents' property had depreciated in value. It held that the United

States had taken an easement over the property on June 1, 1942, and that the value of the property destroyed and the easement taken was $ 2,000.

I. The United States relies on the Air Commerce Act of 1926, 44 Stat. 568, 49 U. S. C. § 171, as amended by the Civil Aeronautics Act of 1938, 52 Stat. 973, 49 U. S. C. § 401. Under those statutes the United States has "complete and exclusive national sovereignty in the air space" over this country. 49 U. S. C. § 176 (a). They grant any citizen of the United States "a public right of freedom of transit in air commerce [4] through the navigable air space of the United States." 49 U. S. C. § 403. And "navigable air space" is defined as "airspace above the minimum safe altitudes of flight prescribed by the Civil Aeronautics Authority." 49 U. S. C. § 180. And it is provided that "such navigable airspace shall be subject to a public right of freedom of interstate and foreign air navigation. " *Id* . It is, therefore, argued that since these flights were within the minimum safe altitudes of flight which had been prescribed, they were an exercise of the declared right of travel through the airspace. The United States concludes that when flights are made within the navigable airspace without any physical invasion of the property of the landowners, there has been no taking of property. It says that at most there was merely incidental damage occurring as a consequence of authorized air navigation. It also argues that the landowner does not own superadjacent airspace which he has not subjected to possession by the erection of structures or other occupancy. Moreover, it is argued that even if the United States took airspace owned by respondents, no compensable damage was shown. Any damages are said to be merely consequential for which no compensation may be obtained under the *Fifth Amendment*.

It is ancient doctrine that at common law ownership of the land extended to the periphery of the universe -- *Cujus est solum ejus est usque ad coelum*. But that doctrine has no place in the modern world. The air is a public highway, as Congress has declared. Were that not true, every transcontinental flight would subject the operator to countless trespass suits. Common sense revolts at the idea. To recognize such private claims to the airspace would clog these highways, seriously interfere with their control and development in the public interest, and transfer into private ownership that to which only the public has a just claim.

But that general principle does not control the present case. For the United States conceded on oral argument that if the flights over respondents' property rendered it uninhabitable, there would be a taking compensable under the *Fifth Amendment*. It is the owner's loss, not the taker's gain, which is the measure of the value of the property taken. *United States v. Miller, 317 U.S. 369*. Market value fairly determined is the normal measure of the recovery. *Id*. And that value may reflect the use to which the land could readily be converted, as well as the existing use. *United States v. Powelson, 319 U.S. 266, 275*, and cases cited. If, by reason of the frequency and altitude of the flights, respondents could not use this land for any purpose, their loss would be complete. It would be as complete as if the United States had entered upon the surface of the land and taken exclusive possession of it.

We agree that in those circumstances there would be a taking. Though it would be only an easement of flight which was taken, that easement, if permanent and not merely temporary, normally would be the equivalent of a fee interest. It would be a definite exercise of complete dominion and control over the surface of the land. The fact that the planes never touched the surface would be as irrelevant as the absence in this day of the feudal livery of seisin on the transfer of real estate. The owner's right to possess and exploit the land -- that is to say, his beneficial ownership of it -- would be destroyed. It would not be a case of incidental damages arising from a legalized nuisance such as was involved in *Richards v. Washington Terminal Co., 233 U.S. 546*. In that case, property owners whose lands adjoined a railroad line were denied recovery for damages resulting from the noise, vibrations, smoke and the like, incidental to the operations of the trains. In the supposed case, the line of flight is over the land. And the land is appropriated as directly and completely as if it were used for the runways themselves.

There is no material difference between the supposed case and the present one, except that here enjoyment and use of the land are not completely destroyed. But that does not seem to us to be controlling. The path of glide for airplanes might reduce a valuable factory site to grazing land, an orchard to a vegetable patch, a residential section to a wheat field. Some value would remain. But the use of the airspace immediately above the land would limit the utility of the land and cause a diminution in its value. That was the philosophy of *Portsmouth Co.* v. *United States, 260 U.S. 327*. In that case the petition alleged that the United States erected a fort on nearby land, established a battery and a fire control station there, and fired guns over petitioner's land. The Court, speaking through Mr. Justice Holmes, reversed the Court of Claims, which dismissed the petition on a demurrer, holding that "the specific facts set forth would warrant a finding that a servitude has been imposed." *260 U.S. p. 330*. And see *Delta Air Corp.* v. *Kersey, 193 Ga. 862, 20 S. E. 2d 245*. Cf. *United States* v. *357.25 Acres of Land, 55 F.Supp. 461*.

The fact that the path of glide taken by the planes was that approved by the Civil Aeronautics Authority does not change the result. The navigable airspace which Congress has placed in the public domain is "airspace above the minimum safe altitudes of flight prescribed by the Civil Aeronautics Authority." 49 U. S. C. § 180. If that agency prescribed 83 feet as the minimum safe altitude, then we would have presented the question of the validity of the regulation. But nothing of the sort has been done. The path of glide governs the method of operating -- of landing or taking off. The altitude required for that operation is not the minimum safe altitude of flight which is the downward reach of the navigable airspace. The minimum prescribed by the Authority is 500 feet during the day and 1,000 feet at night for air carriers (Civil Air Regulations, Pt. 61, §§ 61.7400, 61.7401, Code Fed. Reg. Cum. Supp., Tit. 14, ch. 1), and from 300 feet to 1,000 feet for other aircraft, depending on the type of plane and the character of the terrain. *Id.*, Pt. 60, §§ 60.350-60.3505, Fed. Reg. Cum. Supp., *supra*. Hence, the flights in question were not within the navigable airspace which Congress placed within the public domain. If any airspace needed for landing or taking off were included, flights which were so close to the land as to render it uninhabitable would be immune. But the United States concedes, as we have said, that in that event there would be a taking. Thus, it is apparent that the path of glide is not the minimum safe altitude of flight within the meaning of the statute. The Civil Aeronautics Authority has, of course, the power to prescribe air traffic rules. But Congress has defined navigable airspace only in terms of one of them -- the minimum safe altitudes of flight.

We have said that the airspace is a public highway. Yet it is obvious that if the landowner is to have full enjoyment of the land, he must have exclusive control of the immediate reaches of the enveloping atmosphere. Otherwise buildings could not be erected, trees could not be planted, and even fences could not be run. The principle is recognized when the law gives a remedy in case overhanging structures are erected on adjoining land. The landowner owns at least as much of the space above the ground as he can occupy or use in connection with the land. See *Hinman v. Pacific Air Transport, 84 F.2d 755.*The fact that he does not occupy it in a physical sense -- by the erection of buildings and the like -- is not material. As we have said, the flight of airplanes, which skim the surface but do not touch it, is as much an appropriation of the use of the land as a more conventional entry upon it. We would not doubt that, if the United States erected an elevated railway over respondents' land at the precise altitude where its planes now fly, there would be a partial taking, even though none of the supports of the structure rested on the land. The reason is that there would be an intrusion so immediate and direct as to subtract from the owner's full enjoyment of the property and to limit his exploitation of it. While the owner does not in any physical manner occupy that stratum of airspace or make use of it in the conventional sense, he does use it in somewhat the same sense that space left between buildings for the purpose of light and air is used. The superadjacent airspace at this low altitude is so close to the land that continuous invasions of it affect the use of the surface of the land itself. We think that the landowner, as an incident to his ownership, has a claim to it and that invasions of it are in the same category as invasions of the surface.

In this case, as in *Portsmouth Co. v. United States, supra*, the damages were not merely consequential. They were the product of a direct invasion of respondents' domain. As stated in *United States v. Cress, 243 U.S. 316, 328*, ". . . it is the character of the invasion, not the amount of damage resulting from it, so long as the damage is substantial, that determines the question whether it is a taking."

We said in *United States v. Powelson, supra, p. 279*, that while the meaning of "property" as used in the *Fifth Amendment* was a federal question, "it will normally obtain its content by reference to local law." If we look to North Carolina law, we reach the same result. Sovereignty in the airspace rests in the State "except where granted to and assumed by the United States." Gen. Stats. 1943, *§ 63-11*. The flight of aircraft is lawful "unless at such a low altitude as to interfere with the then existing use to which the land or water, or the space over the land or water, is put by the owner, or unless so conducted as to be imminently dangerous to persons or property lawfully on the land or water beneath." *Id., § 63-13*. Subject to that right of flight, "ownership of the space above the lands and waters of this State is declared to be vested in the several owners of the surface beneath . . ." *Id., § 63-12*. Our holding that there was an invasion of respondents' property is thus not inconsistent with the local law governing a landowner's claim to the immediate reaches of the superadjacent airspace.

The airplane is part of the modern environment of life, and the inconveniences which it causes are normally not compensable under the *Fifth Amendment*. The airspace, apart from the immediate reaches above the land, is part of the public domain. We need not determine at this time what those precise limits are. Flights over private land are not a taking, unless they are so low and so frequent as to be a direct and immediate interference with the enjoyment and use of the land. We need not speculate on that phase of the present case. For the findings of the Court of Claims plainly establish that there was a diminution in value of the property and that the frequent, low-level flights were the direct and immediate cause. We agree with the Court of Claims that a servitude has been imposed upon the land.

II. By § 145 (1) of the Judicial Code, *28 U. S. C. § 250 (1)*, the Court of Claims has jurisdiction to hear and determine "All claims (except for pensions) founded upon the Constitution of the United States or . . . upon any contract, express or implied, with the Government of the United States . . ."

We need not decide whether repeated trespasses might give rise to an implied contract. Cf. *Portsmouth Co. v. United States, supra.* If there is a taking, the claim is "founded upon the Constitution" and within the jurisdiction of the Court of Claims to hear and determine. See *Hollister v. Benedict Mfg. Co., 113 U.S. 59, 67*; *Hurley v. Kincaid, 285 U.S. 95, 104*; *Yearsley v. Ross Construction Co., 309 U.S. 18, 21*. Thus, the jurisdiction of the Court of Claims in this case is clear.

III. The Court of Claims held, as we have noted, that an easement was taken. But the findings of fact contain no precise description as to its nature. It is not described in terms of frequency of flight, permissible altitude, or type of airplane. Nor is there a finding as to whether the easement taken was temporary or permanent. Yet an accurate description of the property taken is essential, since that interest vests in the United States. *United States v. Cress, supra, 328-329* and cases cited. It is true that the Court of Claims stated in its opinion that the easement taken was permanent. But the deficiency in findings cannot be rectified by statements in the opinion. *United States v. Esnault-Pelterie, 299 U.S. 201, 205-206*; *United States v. Seminole Nation, 299 U.S. 417, 422*. Findings of fact on every "material issue" are a statutory requirement. *53 Stat. 752, 28 U. S. C. § 288*. The importance of findings of fact based on evidence is emphasized here by the Court of Claims' treatment of the nature of the easement. It stated in its opinion that the easement was permanent because the United States "no doubt intended to make some sort of arrangement whereby it could use the airport for its military planes whenever it had occasion to do so." That sounds more like conjecture rather than a conclusion from evidence; and if so, it would not be a proper foundation for liability of the United States. We do not stop to examine the evidence to determine whether it would support such a finding, if made. For that is not our function. *United States v. Esnault-Pelterie, supra, p. 206*.

Since on this record it is not clear whether the easement taken is a permanent or a temporary one, it would be premature for us to consider whether the amount of the award made by the Court of Claims was proper.

The judgment is reversed and the cause is remanded to the Court of Claims so that it may make the necessary findings in conformity with this opinion.

Reversed.

MR. JUSTICE BLACK, dissenting.

The *Fifth Amendment* provides that "private property" shall not "be taken for public use without just compensation." The Court holds today that the Government has "taken" respondents' property by repeatedly flying Army bombers directly above respondents' land at a height of eighty-three feet where the light and noise from these planes caused respondents to lose sleep and their chickens to be killed. Since the effect of the Court's decision is to limit, by the imposition of relatively absolute constitutional barriers, possible future adjustments through legislation and regulation which might become necessary with the growth of air transportation, and since in my view the Constitution does not contain such barriers, I dissent.

The following is a brief statement of the background and of the events that the Court's opinion terms a "taking" within the meaning of the *Fifth Amendment*: Since 1928 there has been an airfield some eight miles from Greensboro, North Carolina. In April, 1942, this airport was taken over by the Greensboro-High Point Municipal Airport Authority and it has since then operated as a municipal airport. In 1942 the Government, by contract, obtained the right to use the field "concurrently, jointly, and in common" with other users. Years before, in 1934, respondents had bought their property, located more than one-third of a mile from the airport. Private planes from the airport flew over their land and farm buildings from 1934 to 1942 and are still doing so. But though these planes disturbed respondents to some extent, Army bombers, which started to fly over the land in 1942 at a height of eighty-three feet, disturbed them more because they were larger, came over more frequently, made a louder noise, and at night a greater glare was caused by their lights. This noise and glare disturbed respondents' sleep, frightened them, and made them nervous. The noise and light also frightened respondents' chickens so much that many of them flew against buildings and were killed.

The Court's opinion seems to indicate that the mere flying of planes through the column of air directly above respondents' land does not constitute a "taking." Consequently, it appears to be noise and glare, to the extent and under the circumstances shown here, which make the Government a seizer of private property. But the allegation of noise and glare resulting in damages, constitutes at best an action in tort where there might be recovery if the noise and light constituted a nuisance, a violation of a statute, or were the result of negligence. [2] But the Government has not consented to be sued in the Court of Claims except in actions based on express or implied contract. And there is no implied contract here, unless by reason of the noise and glare caused by the bombers the Government can be said to have "taken" respondents' property in a constitutional sense. The concept of taking property as used in the Constitution has heretofore never been given so sweeping a meaning. The Court's opinion presents no case where a man who makes noise or shines light onto his neighbor's property has been ejected from that property for wrongfully taking possession of it. Nor would anyone take seriously a claim that noisy automobiles passing on a highway are taking wrongful possession of the homes located thereon, or that a city elevated train which greatly interferes with the sleep of those who live next to it wrongfully takes their property. Even the one case in this Court which in considering the sufficiency of a complaint gave the most elastic meaning to the phrase "private property be taken" as used in the *Fifth Amendment*, did not go so far. *Portsmouth Co.* v. *United States, 260 U.S. 327.* I am not willing, nor do I think the Constitution and the decisions authorize me, to extend that phrase so as to guarantee an absolute constitutional right to relief not subject to legislative change, which is based on averments that at best show mere torts committed by government agents while flying over land. The future adjustment of the rights and remedies of property owners, which might be found necessary because of the flight of planes at safe altitudes, should, especially in view of the imminent expansion of air navigation, be left where I think the Constitution left it, with Congress.

Nor do I reach a different conclusion because of the fact that the particular circumstance which under the Court's opinion makes the tort here absolutely actionable, is the passing of planes through a column of air at an elevation of eighty-three feet directly over respondents' property. It is inconceivable to me that the Constitution guarantees that the airspace of this Nation needed for air navigation is owned by the particular persons who happen to own the land beneath to the same degree as they own the surface below. [1] No rigid constitutional rule, in my judgment, commands that the air must be considered as marked off into separate compartments by imaginary metes and bounds in order to synchronize air ownership with land ownership. I think that the Constitution entrusts Congress with full power to control all navigable airspace. Congress has already acted under that power. It has by statute, 44 Stat. 568, 52 Stat. 973, provided that "the United States of America is . . . to possess and exercise complete and exclusive national sovereignty in the air space above the United States . . ." This was done under the assumption that the *Commerce Clause of the Constitution* gave Congress the same plenary power to control navigable airspace as its plenary power over navigable waters. H. Rep. No. 572, 69th Cong., 1st Sess., p. 10; H. Rep. No. 1162, 69th Cong., 1st Sess., p. 14; see *United States v. Commodore Park, 324 U.S. 386.* To make sure that the airspace used for air navigation would remain free, Congress further declared that "navigable airspace shall be subject to a public right of freedom of interstate and foreign air navigation," and finally stated emphatically that there exists "a public right of freedom of transit . . . through the navigable air space of the United States." Congress thus declared that the air is free, not subject to private ownership, and not subject to delimitation by the courts. Congress and those acting under its authority were the only ones who had power to control and regulate the flight of planes. "Navigable airspace" was defined as "airspace above the minimum safe altitudes of flight prescribed by the Civil Aeronautics Authority . . ." 49 U. S. C. § 180. Thus, Congress has given the Civil Aeronautics Authority exclusive power to determine what is navigable airspace subject to its exclusive control. This power derives specifically from the Section which authorizes the Authority to prescribe "air traffic rules governing the flight of, and for the navigation, protection, and identification of, aircraft, including rules as to safe altitudes of flight and rules for the prevention of collisions between aircraft, and between aircraft and land or water vehicles." Here there was no showing that the bombers flying over respondents' land violated any rule or regulation of the Civil Aeronautics Authority. Yet, unless we hold the Act unconstitutional, at least such a showing would be necessary before the courts could act without interfering with the exclusive authority which Congress gave to the administrative agency. Not even a showing that the Authority has not acted would be sufficient. For in that event, were the courts to have any authority to act in this case at all, they should stay their hand till the Authority has acted.

The broad provisions of the congressional statute cannot properly be circumscribed by making a distinction, as the Court's opinion does, between rules of safe altitude of flight while on the level of cross-country flight and rules of safe altitude during landing and taking off. First, such a distinction cannot be maintained from the practical standpoint. It is unlikely that Congress intended that the Authority prescribe safe altitudes for planes making cross-country flights, while at the same time it left the more hazardous landing and take-off operations unregulated. The legislative history, moreover, clearly shows that the Authority's power to prescribe air traffic rules includes the power to make rules governing landing and take-off. Nor is the Court justified in ignoring that history by labeling rules of safe altitude while on the level of cross-country flight as rules prescribing the safe altitude proper and rules governing take-off and landing as rules of operation. For the Conference Report explicitly states that such distinctions were purposely eliminated from the original House Bill in order that the Section on air traffic rules "might be given the broadest possible construction by the . . . [Civil Aeronautics Authority] and the courts." In construing the statute narrowly, the Court thwarts the intent of Congress. A proper broad construction, such as Congress commanded, would not permit the Court to decide what it has today without declaring the Act of Congress unconstitutional. I think the Act given the broad construction intended is constitutional.

No greater confusion could be brought about in the coming age of air transportation than that which would result were courts by constitutional interpretation to hamper Congress in its efforts to keep the air free. Old concepts of private ownership of land should not be introduced into the field of air regulation. I have no doubt that Congress will, if not handicapped by judicial interpretations of the Constitution, preserve the freedom of the air, and at the same time, satisfy the just claims of aggrieved persons. The noise of newer, larger, and more powerful planes may grow louder and louder and disturb people more and more. But the solution of the problems precipitated by these technological advances and new ways of living cannot come about through the application of rigid constitutional restraints formulated and enforced by the courts. What adjustments may have to be made, only the future can reveal. It seems certain, however, that courts do not possess the techniques or the personnel to consider and act upon the complex combinations of factors entering into the problems. The contribution of courts must be made through the awarding of damages for injuries suffered from the flying of planes, or by the granting of injunctions to prohibit their flying. When these two simple remedial devices are elevated to a constitutional level under the *Fifth Amendment*, as the Court today seems to have done, they can stand as obstacles to better adapted techniques that might be offered by experienced experts and accepted by Congress. Today's opinion is, I fear, an opening wedge for an unwarranted judicial interference with the power of Congress to develop solutions for new and vital national problems. In my opinion this case should be reversed on the ground that there has been no "taking" in the constitutional sense.

MR. JUSTICE BURTON joins in this dissent.

GRIGGS v. ALLEGHENY COUNTY

SUPREME COURT OF THE UNITED STATES

369 U.S. 84

March, 1962

MR. JUSTICE DOUGLAS delivered the opinion of the Court.

This case is here on a petition for a writ of certiorari to the Supreme Court of Pennsylvania which we granted (*366 U.S. 943*) because its decision (*402 Pa. 411, 168 A. 2d 123*) seemed to be in conflict with *United States v. Causby, 328 U.S. 256*. The question is whether respondent has taken an air easement over petitioner's property for which it must pay just compensation as required by the *Fourteenth Amendment*. *Chicago, B. & Q. R. Co.* v. *Chicago, 166 U.S. 226, 241*. The Court of Common Pleas, pursuant to customary Pennsylvania procedure, appointed a Board of Viewers to determine whether there had been a "taking" and, if so, the amount of compensation due. The Board of Viewers met upon the property; it held a hearing, and in its report found that there had been a "taking" by respondent of an air easement over petitioner's property and that the compensation payable (damages suffered) was $ 12,690. The Court of Common Pleas dismissed the exceptions of each party to the Board's report. On appeal, the Supreme Court of Pennsylvania decided, by a divided vote, that if there were a "taking" in the constitutional sense, the respondent was not liable.

Respondent owns and maintains the Greater Pittsburgh Airport on land which it purchased to provide airport and air-transport facilities. The airport was designed for public use in conformity with the rules and regulations of the Civil Aeronautics Administration within the scope of the National Airport Plan provided for in *49 U. S. C. § 1101 et seq.* By this Act the federal Administrator is authorized and directed to prepare and continually revise a "national plan for the development of public airports." § 1102 (a). For this purpose he is authorized to make grants to "sponsors" for airport development. §§ 1103, 1104. Provision is made for apportionment of grants for this purpose among the States. § 1105. The applications for projects must follow the standards prescribed by the Administrator. § 1108.

It is provided in § 1108 (d) that: "No project shall be approved by the Administrator with respect to any airport unless a public agency holds good title, satisfactory to the Administrator, to the landing area of such airport or the site therefor, or gives assurance satisfactory to the Administrator that such title will be acquired." The United States agrees to share from 50% to 75% of the "allowable project costs," depending, so far as material here, on the class and location of the airport. § 1109.

Allowable costs payable by the Federal Government include "costs of acquiring land or interests therein or easements through or other interests in air space . . . ." *§ 1112 (a)(2)*.

Respondent executed three agreements with the Administrator of Civil Aeronautics in which it agreed, among other things, to abide by and adhere to the Rules and Regulations of C. A. A. and to "maintain a master plan of the airport," including "approach areas." It was provided that the "airport approach standards to be followed in this connection shall be those established by the Administrator"; and it was also agreed that respondent "will acquire such easements or other interests in lands and air space as may be necessary to perform the covenants of this paragraph." The "master plan" laid out and submitted by respondent included the required "approach areas"; and that "master plan" was approved. One "approach area" was to the northeast runway. As designed and approved, it passed over petitioner's home which is 3,250 feet from the end of that runway. The elevation at the end of that runway is 1,150.50 feet above sea level; the door sill at petitioner's residence, 1,183.64 feet; the top of petitioner's chimney, 1,219.64 feet. The slope gradient of the approach area is as 40 is to 3,250 feet or 81 feet, which leaves a clearance of 11.36 feet between the bottom of the glide angle and petitioner's chimney.

The airlines that use the airport are lessees of respondent; and the leases give them, among other things, the right "to land" and "take off." No flights were in violation of the regulations of C. A. A.; nor were any flights lower than necessary for a safe landing or take-off. The planes taking off from the northeast runway observed regular flight patterns ranging from 30 feet to 300 feet over petitioner's residence; and on let-down they were within 53 feet to 153 feet.

On take-off the noise of the planes is comparable "to the noise of a riveting machine or steam hammer." On the let-down the planes make a noise comparable "to that of a noisy factory." The Board of Viewers found that "The low altitude flights over plaintiff's property caused the plaintiff and occupants of his property to become nervous and distraught, eventually causing their removal therefrom as undesirable and unbearable for their residential use." Judge Bell, dissenting below, accurately summarized the uncontroverted facts as follows:

"Regular and almost continuous daily flights, often several minutes apart, have been made by a number of airlines directly over and very, very close to plaintiff's residence. During these flights it was often impossible for people in the house to converse or to talk on the telephone. The plaintiff and the members of his household (depending on the flight which in turn sometimes depended on the wind) were frequently unable to sleep even with ear plugs and sleeping pills; they would frequently be awakened by the flight and the noise of the planes; the windows of their home would frequently rattle and at times plaster fell down from the walls and ceilings; their health was affected and impaired, and they sometimes were compelled to sleep elsewhere. Moreover, their house was so close to the runways or path of glide that as the spokesman for the members of the Airlines Pilot Association admitted 'If we had engine failure we would have no course but to plow into your house.'" *402 Pa. 411, 422, 168 A. 2d 123, 128-129.*

We start with *United States v. Causby, supra,* which held that the United States by low flights of its military planes over a chicken farm made the property unusable for that purpose and that therefore there had been a "taking," in the constitutional sense, of an air easement for which compensation must be made. At the time of the *Causby* case, Congress had placed the navigable airspace in the public domain, defining it as "airspace above the minimum safe altitudes of flight prescribed" by the C. A. A. 44 Stat. 574. We held that the path of the glide or flight for landing or taking off was not the downward reach of the "navigable airspace." *328 U.S., at 264*. Following the decision in the *Causby* case, Congress redefined "navigable airspace" to mean "airspace above the minimum altitudes of flight prescribed by regulations issued under this chapter, and shall include airspace needed to insure safety in take-off and landing of aircraft." 72 Stat. 739, 49 U. S. C. § 1301 (24). By the present regulations [1] the "minimum safe altitudes" within the meaning of the statute are defined, so far as relevant here, as heights of 500 feet or 1,000 feet, "except where necessary for take-off or landing." But as we said in the *Causby* case, the use of land presupposes the use of some of the airspace above it. *328 U.S., at 264*. Otherwise no home could be built, no tree planted, no fence constructed, no chimney erected. An invasion of the "superadjacent airspace" will often "affect the use of the surface of the land itself." *328 U.S., at 265*.

It is argued that though there was a "taking," someone other than respondent was the taker -- the airlines or the C. A. A. acting as an authorized representative of the United States. We think, however, that respondent, which was the promoter, owner, and lessor of the airport, was in these circumstances the one who took the air easement in the constitutional sense. Respondent decided, subject to the approval of the C. A. A., where the airport would be built, what runways it would need, their direction and length, and what land and navigation easements would be needed. The Federal Government takes nothing; it is the local authority which decides to build an airport *vel non*, and where it is to be located. We see no difference between its responsibility for the air easements necessary for operation of the airport and its responsibility for the land on which the runways were built. Nor did the Congress when it designed the legislation for a National Airport Plan. For, as we have already noted, Congress provided in 49 U. S. C. § 1109 for the payment to the owners of airports, whose plans were approved by the Administrator, of a share of "the allowable project costs," including the "costs of acquiring land or interests therein or easements through or other interests in air space." *§ 1112 (a)(2)*. A county that designed and constructed a bridge would not have a usable facility unless it had at least an easement over the land necessary for the approaches to the bridge. Why should one who designs, constructs, and uses an airport be in a more favorable position so far as the *Fourteenth Amendment* is concerned? That the instant "taking" was "for public use" is not debatable. For respondent agreed with the C. A. A. that it would operate the airport "for the use and benefit of the public," that it would operate it "on fair and reasonable terms and without unjust discrimination," and that it would not allow any carrier to acquire "any exclusive right" to its use.

The glide path for the northeast runway is as necessary for the operation of the airport as is a surface right of way for operation of a bridge, or as is the land for the operation of a dam. See *United States v. Virginia Electric Co., 365 U.S. 624, 630*. As stated by the Supreme Court of Washington in *Ackerman v. Port of Seattle, 55 Wash. 2d 401, 413, 348 P. 2d 664, 671*, ". . . an adequate approach way is as necessary a part of an airport as is the ground on which the airstrip, itself, is constructed . . . ." Without the "approach areas," an airport is indeed not operable. Respondent in designing it had to acquire some private property. Our conclusion is that by constitutional standards it did not acquire enough.

Reversed.

MR. JUSTICE BLACK, with whom MR. JUSTICE FRANKFURTER concurs, dissenting.

In *United States* v. *Causby,* the Court held that by flying its military aircraft frequently on low landing and takeoff flights over Causby's chicken farm the United States had so disturbed the peace of the occupants and so frightened the chickens that it had "taken" a flight easement from Causby for which it was required to pay "just compensation" under the *Fifth Amendment.* Today the Court holds that similar low landing and takeoff flights, making petitioner Griggs' property "undesirable and unbearable for . . . residential use," constitute a "taking" of airspace over Griggs' property -- not, however, by the owner and operator of the planes as in *Causby*, but by Allegheny County, the owner and operator of the Greater Pittsburgh Airport to and from which the planes fly. Although I dissented in *Causby* because I did not believe that the individual aircraft flights "took" property in the constitutional sense merely by going over it and because I believed that the complexities of adjusting atmospheric property rights to the air age could best be handled by Congress, I agree with the Court that the noise, vibrations and fear caused by constant and extremely low overflights in this case have so interfered with the use and enjoyment of petitioner's property as to amount to a "taking" of it under the *Causby* holding. I cannot agree, however, that it was the County of Allegheny that did the "taking." I think that the United States, not the Greater Pittsburgh Airport, has "taken" the airspace over Griggs' property necessary for flight. [2] While the County did design the plan for the airport, including the arrangement of its takeoff and approach areas, in order to comply with federal requirements it did so under the supervision of and subject to the approval of the Civil Aeronautics Administrator of the United States.

Congress has over the years adopted a comprehensive plan for national and international air commerce, regulating in minute detail virtually every aspect of air transit -- from construction and planning of ground facilities to safety and methods of flight operations. As part of this overall scheme of development, Congress in 1938 declared that the United States has "complete and exclusive national sovereignty in the air space above the United States" and that every citizen has "a public right of freedom of transit in air commerce through the navigable air space of the United States." Although in *Causby* the Court held that under the then existing laws and regulations the airspace used in landing and takeoff was not part of the "navigable airspace" as to which all have a right of free transit, Congress has since, in 1958, enacted a new law, as part of a regulatory scheme even more comprehensive than those before it, making it clear that the "airspace needed to insure safety in take-off and landing of aircraft" is "navigable airspace." Thus Congress has not only appropriated the airspace necessary for planes to fly at high altitudes throughout the country but has also provided the low altitude airspace essential for those same planes to approach and take off from airports. These airspaces are so much under the control of the Federal Government that every takeoff from and every landing at airports such as the Greater Pittsburgh Airport is made under the direct signal and supervisory control of some federal agent.

In reaching its conclusion, however, the Court emphasizes the fact that highway bridges require approaches. Of course they do. But if the United States Highway Department purchases the approaches to a bridge, the bridge owner need not. The same is true where Congress has, as here, appropriated the airspace necessary to approach the Pittsburgh airport as well as all the other airports in the country. Despite this, however, the Court somehow finds a congressional intent to shift the burden of acquiring flight airspace to the local communities in *49 U. S. C. § 1112*, which authorizes reimbursement to local communities for "necessary" acquisitions of "easements through or other interests in air space." But this is no different from the bridge-approach argument. Merely because local communities might eventually be reimbursed for the acquisition of necessary easements does not mean that local communities must acquire easements that the United States has already acquired. And where Congress has already declared airspace *free* to all -- a fact not denied by the Court -- pretty clearly it need not again be acquired by an airport. The "necessary" easements for which Congress authorized reimbursement in *§ 1112* were those "easements through or other interests in air space" necessary for the clearing and protecting of "aerial approaches" from physical "airport hazards" -- a duty explicitly placed on the local communities by the statute (§ 1110) and by their contract with the Government. There is no such duty on the local community to acquire flight airspace. Having taken the airspace over Griggs' private property for a public use, it is the United States which owes just compensation.

The construction of the Greater Pittsburgh Airport was financed in large part by funds supplied by the United States as part of its plan to induce localities like Allegheny County to assist in setting up a national and international air-transportation system. The Court's imposition of liability on Allegheny County, however, goes a long way toward defeating that plan because of the greatly increased financial burdens (how great one can only guess) which will hereafter fall on all the cities and counties which till now have given or may hereafter give support to the national program. I do not believe that Congress ever intended any such frustration of its own purpose.

Nor do I believe that Congress intended the wholly inequitable and unjust saddling of the entire financial burden of this part of the national program on the people of local communities like Allegheny County. The planes that take off and land at the Greater Pittsburgh Airport wind their rapid way through space not for the peculiar benefit of the citizens of Allegheny County but as part of a great, reliable transportation system of immense advantage to the whole Nation in time of peace and war. Just as it would be unfair to require petitioner and others who suffer serious and peculiar injuries by reason of these transportation flights to bear an unfair proportion of the burdens of air commerce, so it would be unfair to make Allegheny County bear expenses wholly out of proportion to the advantages it can receive from the national transportation system. I can see no justification at all for throwing this monkey wrench into Congress' finely tuned national transit mechanism. I would affirm the state court's judgment holding that the County of Allegheny has not "taken" petitioner's property.

ARCHIE J. SNEED v. COUNTY OF RIVERSIDE ET AL.,

COURT OF APPEAL OF CALIFORNIA, FOURTH APPELLATE DISTRICT

218 Cal. App. 2d 205

July, 1963

Plaintiff has appealed from a judgment of dismissal entered after demurrers were sustained to the first amended supplemental complaint without leave to amend.

The first amended supplemental complaint (hereinafter called complaint) seeks to establish a cause of action in inverse condemnation against defendant County of Riverside, with the proceeds of such action belonging to plaintiff and not to defendants James Minor and Jessie F. Minor (hereinafter called Minor).

(1) The only question is whether the court erred in sustaining a demurrer to the complaint. For that purpose the allegations of the complaint must be accepted as true. (*Gogerty v. Coachella Valley Jr. College Dist., 57 Cal.2d 727, 730 [21 Cal.Rptr. 806, 371 P.2d 582].*) We have concluded the complaint sets forth a cause of action.

In substance the complaint states that plaintiff owned 234 1/2 acres of improved real property adjacent to Ryan Airport which is owned, operated and maintained by Riverside County; pursuant to the authority given counties by *Government Code sections 50485- 50485.14,* on February 10, 1958 the Riverside County Board of Supervisors adopted Ordinance No. 448, which was an "Ordinance of the County of Riverside establishing airport operating areas and regulating height standards and limits therein."

(2) Plaintiff claims that by reason of the ordinance the county took from him an air navigation easement over approximately 60 acres of his property, the easement ranging from 4 feet in height at that part of the property closest to the airport to a height of 75 feet farthest away, all within the "Glide Angle of the Clear Zone and Approach Zone." In his closing brief plaintiff asserts the 4 feet mentioned above is wrong and instead the minimum distance above his property at the beginning of the easement is 3 inches. Whether the minimum figure is 3 inches, 4 feet, or 24 feet as claimed by respondent county, is a question of fact to be determined in trial.

The property over which the ordinance is effective has a railroad on one side, a highway on the other, a road on the third side, and the fourth side is 10 feet from the airport runway. It is alleged that large numbers of aircraft have used the airport since the ordinance was adopted; the intent and purpose of the ordinance was to obtain for the county and for all parties using the airport a flight easement at all levels above the "Glide Angle of the Clear Zone and Approach Zone" ranging from 4 feet to 75 feet above plaintiff's land.

Plaintiff's property was a thoroughbred race horse breeding and training farm, certain improvement structures of which exceed the height permitted by the ordinance.

It is claimed the fair market value of the property was reduced from $ 550,000 before the ordinance was passed to $ 225,000 afterwards. Plaintiff filed his claim and it was rejected by the Board of Supervisors of Riverside County.

After suit was begun plaintiff sold the property to defendants Minor who knew of the lawsuit and orally agreed the proceeds should be plaintiff's property. Defendants do not question or argue this subject matter in their briefs.

The basic controversy is whether the Riverside County Ordinance is in reality a height limit ordinance authorized under the police power or whether it takes an air easement over plaintiff's property without payment of compensation therefor.

Article I, section 14 of the California Constitution provides: "Private property shall not be taken or damaged for public use without just compensation having first been made to, or paid into court for, the owner. . . ."

The Code of Civil Procedure sections 1239.2 and 1239.4 authorizes counties to acquire airspace or air easements through eminent domain proceedings, in airspace above property if the taking of such is necessary to protect the approaches to airports.

The Airport Approaches Zoning Law, *Government Code sections 50485- 50485.14*, defines and authorizes the elimination of airport hazards, to "be accomplished, *to the extent legally possible*, by exercise of the police power. . . ." (*Gov. Code, § 50485.2*.) (Italics ours.)

Section 50485.13 provides: "In any case in which: . . . (b) the approach protection necessary cannot, *because of constitutional limitations*, be provided by airport zoning regulations under this article . . . the . . . county within which the property . . . is located, or the . . . county owning the airport or served by it may acquire, by purchase, grant, or condemnation in the manner provided by the law under which a . . . county is authorized to acquire real property for public purposes, such air right, air navigation easement, or other estate or interest in the property or nonconforming structure or use in question as may be necessary to effectuate the purposes of this article." (Italics ours.)

Ordinance No. 448 of Riverside County, which is attached to the complaint as an exhibit, describes itself as the "Airport Approaches Zoning Ordinance," and states that it is adopted pursuant to the Airport Approaches Zoning Law recited in the Government Code, *supra*.

Section 8 of Ordinance No. 448 provides in part: "Nothing in this ordinance shall be construed as depriving any person who shall suffer damages by reason of the use of airspace adjacent to or over his property by aircraft of bringing an appropriate notice for such damages."

In summary, the zoning law and the zoning ordinance permit elimination of airport hazards in approaches to airports through the exercise of the police power "to the extent legally possible" (*Gov. Code, § 50485.2*); where "constitutional limitations" prevent the necessary approach protection under the police power, the necessary property right may be acquired by purchase, grant, or condemnation in the manner provided by law.

While height restriction zoning has long been recognized as a valid exercise of the police power, there has been a reluctance to extend this method to the protection of approaches to airports; instead, air easements with payment of compensation appear to be the more acceptable, although not undisputed, method of protecting approach zones. (See 13 Hastings L.J. 397, *Airport Zoning and Height Restriction*.)

(3) We believe there is a distinction between the commonly accepted and traditional height restriction zoning regulations of buildings and zoning of airport approaches in that the latter contemplates actual use of the airspace zoned, by aircraft, whereas in the building cases there is no invasion or trespass to the area above the restricted zone.

(4) In his complaint plaintiff seeks to set forth two bases upon which he is entitled to compensation, (1) upon an easement obtained through the ordinance, and (2) on the ground that large numbers of aircraft take off and land, fly at low altitudes over plaintiff's property pursuant to instructions from the employees of defendant county. We believe that a cause of action has been stated on each ground.

In *Griggs v. Allegheny County, 369 U.S. 84*, the court held the operator of an airport was liable, under certain circumstances, for the taking of an easement of flight over property necessary for the use of airplanes in landing and taking off from the airport. The circumstances of that case involved actual interference with the livability of residential quarters near the end of the runway.

Johnson v. Airport Authority of City of Omaha, 173 Neb. 801 was an action brought by the airport authority to condemn airspaces over lands in the vicinity of an airport and to condemn obstructions within the designated airspaces. The action was brought pursuant to statutory provisions relating to the taking and damaging of private property for public use. The lowest portion of the easement was 26 feet over plaintiff's property; two trees were taken which extended above the 26-foot limit, and in another phase of the case was the "incorporeal taking above that height of the right of use and occupancy in the landing and taking off of aircraft." (P. 429.)

The right to condemn and take was not questioned in the case; the airport authority conceded damages for the taking of the trees, but contended damages sustained by the incorporeal taking were not compensable. The court stated at page 431 [115 N.W.2d], "The legal authorities are in substantial accord in the view that a taking of real property in the establishment of an avigation easement which reduces the value of that to which the easement attaches entitles the owner to damages in the amount of the difference in value before and after the taking. See, *United States v. Causby, 328 U.S. 256*; *Griggs v. County of Allegheny, 369 U.S. 84*.)

" . . . .

" . . . all of the decisions previously cited herein from the United States courts clearly declare that damage to the value of land caused by navigation within an avigation easement amounts to a taking within the meaning of the Fifth Amendment."

(5) A temporary invasion of airspace by aircraft over land of another is privileged so long as it does not unreasonably interfere with

persons or property on the land. (*La Com v. Pacific Gas & Elec. Co., 132 Cal.App.2d 114 P.2d 894, 48 A.L.R.2d 1455].)*

See also *Thornburg v. Port of Portland, 233 Ore. 178 [376 P.2d 100]* and *Ackerman v. Port of Seattle, 55 Wn.2d 400 [348 P.2d 664].* In the *Ackerman* case the court stated:

"One of the fundamental principles involved in this action is the ownership of private property and the right to the free use and enjoyment thereof. Another basic principle is the authority of the government (always subject to constitutional safeguards) to regulate the use and utilization of private property for the promotion of the public welfare. At times, as in the instant litigation, these principles are in conflict, and the courts are called upon to resolve the resulting problem in human and legal relationships. In doing so, the courts constantly emphasize the concepts of (1) 'regulation' under the police power, and (2) 'constitutional taking or damaging' under the eminent domain power. When restrictions upon the ownership of private property fall into the category of 'proper exercise of the police power', they, validly, may be imposed without payment of compensation. The difficulty arises in deciding whether a restriction is an exercise of the police power or an exercise of the eminent domain power. When private property rights are actually destroyed through the governmental action, then police power rules are *usually* applicable. See *State ex rel. Miller v. Cain (1952) 40 Wn.2d 216 [242 P.2d 505]*. But, when private property rights are taken from the individual and are conferred upon the public for public use, eminent domain principles are applicable. See, generally, *Conger v. Pierce County (1921) 116 Wash. 27.*

"In this connection it is well to recall the words of Justice Holmes in *Pennsylvania Coal Co. v. Mahon (1922), 260 U.S. 393, 415, 416:*

"'. . . The protection of private property in the Fifth Amendment presupposes that it is wanted for public use, but provides that it shall not be taken for such use without compensation. A similar assumption is made in the decisions upon the Fourteenth Amendment. [Citing case.] When this seemingly absolute protection is found to be qualified by the police power, the natural tendency of human nature is to extend the qualification more and more until at last private property disappears. But that cannot be accomplished in this way under the Constitution of the United States.

"'. . . *We are in danger of forgetting that a strong public desire to improve the public condition is not enough to warrant achieving the desire by a shorter cut than the constitutional way of paying for the change. . . .*' (Emphasis supplied.)" (Pp. 668-669.)

The court held in *Ackerman, supra*, that the "alleged continuing and frequent low flights over the appellants' land amount to a taking of an air easement for the purpose of flying airplanes over the land" and that the port, which did not operate the planes, but operated the airport, was liable for the alleged taking.

In *Jensen v. United States (Ct. Cl.) 305 F.2d 444*, plaintiffs sued in four related cases for just compensation for the taking of avigation easements over their properties. The government did not deny a taking occurred and conceded if the claims were not barred by limitations it was proper for the court to allow compensation for the taking. The facts indicated it was clear the flights directly and immediately interfered with the use and enjoyment of plaintiffs' properties; there was noise intensity as well as frequent low level flights by large airplanes. (See also *Aaron v. United States (Ct. Cl.) 311 F.2d 798*.)

The minority view in the United States is expressed in the case of *Harrell's Candy Kitchen, Inc. v. Sarasota-Manatee Airport Authority (Fla.) 111 So.2d 439*.

(6)   Defendants contend plaintiff failed to exhaust his administrative remedies as a prerequisite to judicial relief; that he should have sought a permit from the Planning Commission with respect to nonconforming uses or variances under section 7 of Ordinance No. 448; and cite *Dunham v. City of Westminster, 202 Cal.App.2d 245*, as authority for the point that administrative remedies must be exhausted. In the *Dunham* case a city building department refused to file an application for a building permit unless plaintiffs dedicated and agreed to improve a portion of their property for street purposes, or were relieved from same by obtaining a variance; plaintiffs asserted the ordinance was unconstitutional; this court held plaintiffs had not exhausted their administrative remedies. In the instant case, however, the situation is different in that it is not the plaintiff who has sought or obtained a change from what existed before, but the county which has invaded the alleged property rights of plaintiff, and in response thereto plaintiff does not challenge the constitutionality of the ordinance but merely seeks damages in inverse condemnation as provided in section 8 of the ordinance.

Judgment reversed.

DONALD SMITH v. COUNTY OF SANTA BARBARA

Court of Appeal of California, Second Appellate District, Division Two

243 Cal. App. 2d 126

June, 1966

Appellants Donald Smith and Wayne Bates appeal from a judgment dismissing their suit for inverse condemnation (*Cal. Const., art. I, § 14*) against respondent County of Santa Barbara (County) and City of Santa Maria. The judgment was entered after the court sustained respondent's demurrer to appellants' second amended complaint without leave to amend. There does not appear to be any ruling or judgment in favor of the City of Santa Maria, although it is a party to the second amended complaint. It is not a party to this appeal.

Appellants allege that: they owned a parcel of realty consisting of approximately 87 acres within the County of Santa Barbara; in January 1960, with the approval of the county they filed a subdivision map for family residences covering one portion of the parcel; thereafter they prepared another such map for a second portion of the property which was again approved by the county; the Committee of the Santa Maria Public Airport acted as agent for the two defendants, indicated that it wished to negotiate an exchange of appellants' land for land owned by the airport committee because (1) the committee anticipated acquisition of appellants' land for expansion of the airport and (2) to avoid future damage claims against the airport by future residents who might inhabit the projected subdivision; the committee represented that it would try to obtain a removal of U.S. government interests in the airport land to effectuate the exchange for appellants' land, but that the committee never contacted the U.S. government; appellants refrained from filing their second subdivision map believing that the exchange would be effected, but when negotiations broke down, it was too late to file the second map; appellants' requests to the county for an extension of time in which to file the second map were denied for the stated reason that the county was apprehensive of future damage claims by future residents on the property and the possibility of future expansion of the airport; the highest and best use of the land was for residential property and the actions of the defendants rendered appellants property worthless for such use; the action of the defendants was arbitrary, discriminatory, unreasonable and oppressive; and that from 1959 to date the county has received and granted approximately 30 requests for extension of time for filing subdivision maps, appellants' request being the only denial.

Appellants further allege that on or about April 1, 1963, the county "rezoned all of [appellants'] property, and the surrounding area to a new and different zoning, to wit: Design Industrial. . . . That the reasons given by [the county] for changing the zoning of [appellants' land and the surrounding area were] the same as those given for refusing the extension of time to record said Final Map." County's action rendered appellants' property worthless for its highest and best use; and that as a consequence appellants' property was taken or damaged without just compensation in violation of *article I, section 14 of the California Constitution*. Appellants pray for one million dollars in damages.

On appeal, appellants concentrate on the validity of the zoning change effected by the county on April 1, 1963.

It should be noted at the outset that appellants fail to allege that the property was rendered valueless by the rezoning. The allegation is that the denial of the extension of time for filing the subdivision map "has rendered said property worthless for development to its highest and best use as aforesaid," and that the rezoning of the property "rendered plaintiffs' property virtually worthless *as set forth herein*." (Italics added.) As we have noted, the phrase "highest and best use" refers to residential use. Nothing in the allegation indicates that the property is not valuable as "Design Industrial" property, as the new zoning category is called.

(1) Assuming, as we must, the truth of the allegations, the practical question at bench is whether county could validly enact a zoning ordinance which depreciated the value of appellants' property.

Appellants reach that question by conceding the accepted principle that if the facts upon which a zoning ordinance is predicated are fairly debatable, courts will not disturb a legislative determination. They contend, however, that such legislative determination may not be unreasonable, oppressive or discriminatory and that the admitted facts at bench show that the zoning ordinance here involved was all three. We do not agree.

Appellants rely on *Kissinger v. City of Los Angeles, 161 Cal.App.2d 454 [327 P.2d 10]*. In that case, the court struck down a zoning ordinance restricting the use of plaintiff's land situated near an airport. The ordinance constituted what is known as "spot zoning." Kissinger's land was the only property affected. The property surrounding Kissinger's land was no different in character or use. Shortly before the zoning ordinance passed, a motion was passed by the city council requesting the Board of Airport Commissioners to consider condemning Kissinger's property for airport purposes "on a basis of its present value as vacant land," although the evidence revealed that Kissinger had already commenced building apartments on the property in conformity with the then existing zoning restrictions. The city gave many public welfare reasons for the spot zoning ordinance, but these reasons were undermined by the fact that they were as applicable to properties surrounding Kissinger's land. Kissinger's property was the only property condemned for airport use.

The court held that the wisdom of an ordinance is not subject to judicial scrutiny, and that any reasonable justification will sustain it; (*Johnston v. City of Claremont, 49 Cal.2d 826, 838-839; Lockard v. City of Los Angeles, 33 Cal.2d 453, 461-463*), but that a zoning ordinance may be struck down if it is unreasonable, oppressive or discriminatory. It said a zoning ordinance may not be used as a device to take property for public use without the payment of compensation. [citations omitted].

In *Kissinger*, however, a most obvious mainstay of the court's decision was its finding that the ordinance which was subjected to attack had not even been passed in the lawfully prescribed manner, and that therefore it was devoid of any force and effect. In a word, the Los

Angeles City Council had abused the legislative discretion vested in it, by entirely ignoring certain procedural limitations imposed upon it by the city charter (*Kissinger* v. *City of Los Angeles*, pp. 463-465.)

There are no procedural defects in the enactment of the ordinance in the case at bench, at least none are called to our attention.

Further, in the case at bench, appellants do not allege that the county rezoned their property solely for the purpose of depressing its value prior to condemnation; they allege only that this was something the defendants "took into consideration." Appellants, to the contrary, allege directly that the primary reason the county denied their request for an extension of time to file a second map and for rezoning the property as "Design Industrial" was to prevent future damage claims by prospective residents of appellants' property, if it were zoned as residential. The expressed reason given by the county alleged by appellants is implicit with the admission that private citizens residing near the airport would be so harassed and annoyed by the operation of the airport that they would suffer damages. Such a reason, in our opinion, justifies the passage of the zoning ordinance.

In *Wilkins v. City of San Bernardino, 29 Cal.2d 332*, the court said at pages 338-339 [*175 P.2d 542*]: "[The] mere fact that some hardship is experienced is not material, since 'Every exercise of the police power is apt to affect adversely the property interest of somebody.' [Citation.] It is implicit in the theory of police power that an individual cannot complain of incidental injury, if the power is exercised for proper purposes of public health, safety, morals and general welfare, and if there is no arbitrary and unreasonable application in the particular case.

"Where it is claimed that the ordinance is unreasonable as applied to plaintiff's property, . . . it is incumbent on plaintiff to produce sufficient evidence from which the court can make such findings as to the physical facts involved as were justified in concluding, *as a matter of law* [italics added], that the ordinance is unreasonable and invalid. It is not sufficient for him to show that it will be more profitable to him to make other use of his property, or that such other use will not cause injury to the public, but he must show an abuse of discretion on the part of the zoning authorities and that there has been an unreasonable and unwarranted exercise of the police power. [Citation.] Every intendment is in favor of the validity of the exercise of police power, and, even though a court might differ from the determination of the legislative body, if there is a reasonable basis for the belief that the establishment of a strictly residential district has substantial relation to the public health, safety, morals or general welfare, the zoning measure will be deemed to be within the purview of the police power [citations]."

(2) We note also that this case differs from the *Kissinger* decision in that there is no allegation that the zoning affected only those lands which were to be purchased for public use. There are no allegations of spot-zoning. Indeed, the allegation is that the county rezoned all of appellants' property "and the surrounding area." Nor do appellants allege, as was the fact in *Kissinger*, that the zoning was restricted to properties to be condemned. In the absence of such allegations, we must presume that the purposes underlying the passage of the ordinance were valid and constitutional. (*Longridge Estates v. City of Los Angeles, 183 Cal.App.2d 533, 539.*)

(3) Appellants also rely on *Bank of America v. Town of Atherton, 60 Cal.App.2d 268*. The court in that case stated at page 273:

"The courts have held . . . that zoning is the deprivation, for the public good, of certain uses by owners of property to which their property might otherwise be put (*Gilbert v. Stockton Port Dist., 7 Cal.2d 384*) and that if the use is so far restricted and the value depreciated that it can be said that the regulation goes too far, it will be deemed a taking of the property, in which event the ordinance becomes invalid and unconstitutional, because the taking is without due process of law."

Atherton, too, was decided on demurrer on the procedural point that the administrator did not have capacity to sue. The cause was reversed on the ground that the administrator could sue and in discussing the allegations of the complaint which it, of course, accepted as true, the court uses the language excerpted.

In the case at bench, there are no comparable allegations. Here, the allegation is that the land is worthless for residential use. Industrial use may or may not make the land worth more. The exercise of police power is not unreasonable, oppressive or discriminatory because it changes the use to which land can be put. Assuming *arguendo* depreciation in value, such a result does not make the ordinance unreasonable, oppressive and discriminatory. Valid exercise of the police power frequently has such a result. [citations omitted].

Appellants urge that county abused its discretion in refusing to permit filing of the second map. They acknowledge, however, that *Business and Professions Code, section 11554*, relating to the extension of time within which to file final subdivision maps grants the county broad discretion in this regard.

Since we have upheld the rezoning ordinance, we are unable to see how appellants were in any way harmed by the refusal of the county to accept their second map proposing a residential subdivision of property which had been zoned exclusively for industry.

The judgment is affirmed.

BOARD OF AIRPORT COMMISSIONERS OF THE CITY OF LOS ANGELES. v. JEWS FOR JESUS, INC.

SUPREME COURT OF THE UNITED STATES

482 U.S. 569

June, 1987

JUSTICE O'CONNOR delivered the opinion of the Court.

The issue presented in this case is whether a resolution banning all "*First Amendment* activities" at Los Angeles International Airport (LAX) violates the *First Amendment*.

I

On July 13, 1983, the Board of Airport Commissioners (Board) adopted Resolution No. 13787, which provides in pertinent part:

"NOW, THEREFORE, BE IT RESOLVED by the Board of Airport Commissioners that the Central Terminal Area at Los Angeles International Airport is not open for *First Amendment* activities by any individual and/or entity;

. . . .

"BE IT FURTHER RESOLVED that after the effective date of this Resolution, if any individual and/or entity seeks to engage in *First Amendment* activities within the Central Terminal Area at Los Angeles International Airport, said individual and/or entity shall be deemed to be acting in contravention of the stated policy of the Board of Airport Commissioners in reference to the uses permitted within the Central Terminal Area at Los Angeles International Airport; and

"BE IT FURTHER RESOLVED that if any individual or entity engages in *First Amendment* activities within the Central Terminal Area at Los Angeles International Airport, the City Attorney of the City of Los Angeles is directed to institute appropriate litigation against such individual and/or entity to ensure compliance with this Policy statement of the Board of Airport Commissioners . . . ." App. 4a-5a.

Respondent Jews for Jesus, Inc., is a nonprofit religious corporation. On July 6, 1984, Alan Howard Snyder, a minister of the Gospel for Jews for Jesus, was stopped by a Department of Airports peace officer while distributing free religious literature on a pedestrian walkway in the Central Terminal Area at LAX. The officer showed Snyder a copy of the resolution, explained that Snyder's activities violated the resolution, and requested that Snyder leave LAX. The officer warned Snyder that the city would take legal action against him if he refused to leave as requested. *Id.*, at 19a-20a. Snyder stopped distributing the leaflets and left the airport terminal. *Id.*, at 20a.

Jews for Jesus and Snyder then filed this action in the District Court for the Central District of California, challenging the constitutionality of the resolution under both the California and Federal Constitutions. First, respondents contended that the resolution was facially unconstitutional under *Art. I, § 2, of the California Constitution* and the *First Amendment to the United States Constitution* because it bans all speech in a public forum. Second, they alleged that the resolution had been applied to Jews for Jesus in a discriminatory manner. Finally, respondents urged that the resolution was unconstitutionally vague and overbroad.

When the case came before the District Court for trial, the parties orally stipulated to the facts, and the District Court treated the trial briefs as cross-motions for summary judgment. The District Court held that the Central Terminal Area was a traditional public forum under federal law, and that the resolution was facially unconstitutional under the United States Constitution. The District Court declined to reach the other issues raised by Jews for Jesus, and did not address the constitutionality of the resolution under the California Constitution. The Court of Appeals for the Ninth Circuit affirmed. *785 F.2d 791 (1986)*. Relying on *Rosen v. Port of Portland, 641 F.2d 1243 (CA9 1981)*, and *Kuszynski v. Oakland, 479 F.2d 1130 (CA9 1973)*, the Court of Appeals concluded that "an airport complex is a traditional public forum," *785 F.2d, at 795*, and held that the resolution was unconstitutional on its face under the Federal Constitution. We granted certiorari, *479 U.S. 812 (1986)*, and now affirm, but on different grounds.

II

In balancing the government's interest in limiting the use of its property against the interests of those who wish to use the property for expressive activity, the Court has identified three types of fora: the traditional public forum, the public forum created by government designation, and the nonpublic forum. *Perry Ed. Assn.* v. *Perry Local Educators' Assn., 460 U.S. 37, 45-46 (1983)*. The proper *First Amendment* analysis differs depending on whether the area in question falls in one category rather than another. In a traditional public forum or a public forum by government designation, we have held that *First Amendment* protections are subject to heightened scrutiny:

"In these quintessential public forums, the government may not prohibit all communicative activity. For the State to enforce a content-based exclusion it must show that its regulation is necessary to serve a compelling state interest and that it is narrowly drawn to achieve that end. . . . The State may also enforce regulations of the time, place, and manner of expression which are content-neutral, are narrowly tailored to serve a significant government interest, and leave open ample alternative channels of communication." *Id., at 45*.

We have further held, however, that access to a nonpublic forum may be restricted by government regulation as long as the regulation "is reasonable and not an effort to suppress expression merely because officials oppose the speaker's view." *Id., at 46*.

The petitioners contend that LAX is neither a traditional public forum nor a public forum by government designation, and accordingly argue that the latter standard governing access to a nonpublic forum is appropriate. The respondents, in turn, argue that LAX is a public forum subject only to reasonable time, place, or manner restrictions. Moreover, at least one commentator contends that *Perry* does not control a case such as this in which the respondents already have access to the airport, and therefore concludes that this case is analogous to *Tinker v. Des Moines School Dist., 393 U.S. 503 (1969)*. See Laycock, Equal Access and Moments of Silence: The Equal Status of Religious Speech by Private Speakers, *81 NW. U. L. Rev. 1, 48 (1986)*. Because we conclude that the resolution is facially unconstitutional under the the *First Amendment* overbreadth doctrine regardless of the proper standard, we need not decide whether LAX is indeed a public forum, or whether the *Perry* standard is applicable when access to a nonpublic forum is not restricted.

Under the *First Amendment* overbreadth doctrine, an individual whose own speech or conduct may be prohibited is permitted to challenge a statute on its face "because it also threatens others not before the court -- those who desire to engage in legally protected expression but who may refrain from doing so rather than risk prosecution or undertake to have the law declared partially invalid." *Brockett v. Spokane Arcades, Inc., 472 U.S. 491, 503 (1985)*. A statute may be invalidated on its face, however, only if the overbreadth is "substantial." *Houston* v. *Hill, ante*, at 458-459; *New York v. Ferber, 458 U.S. 747, 769 (1982)*; *Broadrick v. Oklahoma, 413 U.S. 601, 615 (1973)*. The requirement that the overbreadth be substantial arose from our recognition that application of the overbreadth doctrine is, "manifestly, strong medicine," *Broadrick v. Oklahoma, supra, at 613*, and that "there must be a realistic danger that the statute itself will significantly compromise recognized *First Amendment* protections of parties not before the Court for it to be facially challenged on overbreadth grounds." *City Council of Los Angeles v. Taxpayers for Vincent, 466 U.S. 789, 801 (1984)*.

On its face, the resolution at issue in this case reaches the universe of expressive activity, and, by prohibiting *all* protected expression, purports to create a virtual "*First Amendment* Free Zone" at LAX. The resolution does not merely regulate expressive activity in the Central Terminal Area that might create problems such as congestion or the disruption of the activities of those who use LAX. Instead, the resolution expansively states that LAX "is not open for *First Amendment* activities by any individual and/or entity," and that "any individual and/or entity [who] seeks to engage in *First Amendment* activities within the Central Terminal Area . . . shall be deemed to be acting in contravention of the stated policy of the Board of Airport Commissioners." App. 4a-5a. The resolution therefore does not merely reach the activity of respondents at LAX; it prohibits even talking and reading, or the wearing of campaign buttons or symbolic clothing. Under such a sweeping ban, virtually every individual who enters LAX may be found to violate the resolution by engaging in some "*First Amendment* activit[y]." We think it obvious that such a ban cannot be justified even if LAX were a nonpublic forum because no conceivable governmental interest would justify such an absolute prohibition of speech.

Additionally, we find no apparent saving construction of the resolution. The resolution expressly applies to all "*First Amendment* activities," and the words of the resolution simply leave no room for a narrowing construction. In the past the Court sometimes has used either abstention or certification when, as here, the state courts have not had the opportunity to give the statute under challenge a definite construction. See, *e. g., Babbitt v. Farm Workers, 442 U.S. 289 (1979)*.

79

Neither option, however, is appropriate in this case because California has no certification procedure, and the resolution is not "fairly subject to an interpretation which will render unnecessary or substantially modify the federal constitutional question." *Harmon v. Forssenius, 380 U.S. 528, 535 (1965)*. The difficulties in adopting a limiting construction of the resolution are not unlike those found in *Baggett v. Bullitt, 377 U.S. 360 (1964)*. At issue in *Baggett* was the constitutionality of several statutes requiring loyalty oaths. The *Baggett* Court concluded that abstention would serve no purpose given the lack of any limiting construction, and held the statutes unconstitutional on their face under the *First Amendment* overbreadth doctrine. We observed that the challenged loyalty oath was not "open to one or a few interpretations, but to an indefinite number," and concluded that "it is fictional to believe that anything less than extensive adjudications, under the impact of a variety of factual situations, would bring the oath within the bounds of permissible constitutional certainty." *Id., at 378*. Here too, it is difficult to imagine that the resolution could be limited by anything less than a series of adjudications, and the chilling effect of the resolution on protected speech in the meantime would make such a case-by-case adjudication intolerable.

The petitioners suggest that the resolution is not substantially overbroad because it is intended to reach only expressive activity unrelated to airport-related purposes. Such a limiting construction, however, is of little assistance in substantially reducing the overbreadth of the resolution. Much nondisruptive speech -- such as the wearing of a T-shirt or button that contains a political message -- may not be "airport related," but is still protected speech even in a nonpublic forum. See *Cohen v. California, 403 U.S. 15 (1971)*. Moreover, the vagueness of this suggested construction itself presents serious constitutional difficulty. The line between airport-related speech and nonairport-related speech is, at best, murky. The petitioners, for example, suggest that an individual who reads a newspaper or converses with a neighbor at LAX is engaged in permitted "airport-related" activity because reading or conversing permits the traveling public to "pass the time." Reply Brief for Petitioners 12. We presume, however, that petitioners would not so categorize the activities of a member of a religious or political organization who decides to "pass the time" by distributing leaflets to fellow travelers. In essence, the result of this vague limiting construction would be to give LAX officials alone the power to decide in the first instance whether a given activity is airport related. Such a law that "confers on police a virtually unrestrained power to arrest and charge persons with a violation" of the resolution is unconstitutional because "the opportunity for abuse, especially where a statute has received a virtually open-ended interpretation, is self-evident." *Lewis v. City of New Orleans, 415 U.S. 130, 135-136 (1974)* (POWELL, J., concurring); see also *Houston v. Hill, ante*, at 465; *Kolender v. Lawson, 461 U.S. 352, 358 (1983)*.

We conclude that the resolution is substantially overbroad, and is not fairly subject to a limiting construction. Accordingly, we hold that the resolution violates the *First Amendment*. The judgment of the Court of Appeals is

Affirmed.

[concurrence by Justice White omitted].

PARK SHUTTLE N FLY, INC. v. NORFOLK
AIRPORT AUTHORITY, NORFOLK
INTERNATIONAL AIRPORT.

UNITED STATES DISTRICT COURT FOR THE
EASTERN DISTRICT OF VIRGINIA, NORFOLK
DIVISION

352 F. Supp. 2d 688

December, 2004

The Court held a bench trial in the above-captioned matter on September 9, 2004. Having conducted a trial and thoroughly reviewed the evidence, arguments, and records in this case, the Court finds that this case is ripe for decision. For the reasons stated below, the Court awards judgment for the DEFENDANT.

I. PROCEDURAL HISTORY AND FACTUAL FINDINGS

A. Procedural History

The Plaintiff, Park Shuttle N Fly, Inc. ("Park Shuttle"), brought suit on June 30, 2003 alleging that the Defendant, Norfolk Airport Authority ("Authority"), had imposed an invalid privilege fee upon it for its use of the airport's facilities. The complaint alleged violations of the *Due Process, Equal Protection*, and the *Commerce clauses of the United States Constitution*. The complaint stemmed from an Authority regulation imposed in May 2003 that required off-airport parking operators to pay a fee of 8% of the operators' gross monthly revenue for the privilege of accessing airport property to pick up or discharge customers. The Plaintiff alleged that this fee was different from the lump sum fee that other courtesy vehicle operators were required to pay, including hotels, taxis, and limousine services, among others. It also alleged that the amount of fee the Authority imposed was an "arbitrary, discriminatory, and artificial classification" that imposed an undue burden on interstate commerce and violated the *due process* and *equal protection clauses of the Constitution*. (Pl. Compl. at P11).

The Defendant filed a Motion to Dismiss on August 18, 2003 on the grounds that Plaintiff's complaint failed to state a claim upon which relief can be granted under *Federal Rule of Civil Procedure 12(b)(6)*, and in the alternative for Summary Judgment on the *Commerce Clause* claim. On February 6, 2004 this Court granted Defendant's Motion to Dismiss Plaintiff's *Equal Protection* claim which alleged that Park Shuttle was treated differently than hotels, and the *Due Process* Claim. It denied Defendant's Motion to Dismiss the challenge to the amount of user fee charged and to the prohibition of Park Shuttle to pick up passengers which do not have prior arrangements with the company. It also denied the Motion to Dismiss and Summary Judgment on the *Commerce Clause* claim.

The Court also made several findings that are relevant to the analysis here. The Court found that the revenues Plaintiff paid to Defendant constitute a usage fee rather than a state-imposed tax. *Park*

Shuttle N Fly, Inc. v. Norfolk Airport Auth., 2004 U.S. Dist. LEXIS 28116, No. 2:03cv461, at 7 (February 6, 2004). In addition, the Court found that state law allows the Authority to impose usage fees of some kind, thus establishing a legitimate purpose for the regulation.

After the Court's decision, the Plaintiff filed its First Amended Complaint for Declaratory Judgment, Preliminary Injunction, Permanent Injunction and Other Relief ("Pl. Am. Compl."). The Amended Complaint reiterated the initial allegations regarding the *Equal Protection, Due Process,* and *Commerce Clause* claims, and added a claim alleging a violation of Free Speech and Equal Protection. The Plaintiff newly alleged that Defendant denied Plaintiff the opportunity to advertise in the concourses of the airport terminals, while other commercial entities were allowed to advertise.

B. Factual Findings

1. Stipulated Facts

The Plaintiff, Park Shuttle is a duly organized and existing Virginia corporation engaged in the business of operating a parking lot in close proximity to the Norfolk International Airport ("Airport"), which parking lot is used by persons traveling in interstate commerce by using the flight facilities at said Airport. (Final Pre-Trial Order at P1). The Norfolk Airport Authority ("Authority") is a political subdivision of the Commonwealth of Virginia and is an independent body that owns and operates the Airport pursuant to state law and the Code and Charter of the City of Norfolk. For purposes of this litigation, the Authority operates in its proprietary capacity and not in its governmental or regulatory capacity. (Final Pre-Trial Order at P2). The Authority is governed by a Board of Commissioners (the "Board"), which oversees the general operation and management of the Airport. At all relevant times, the Chairman of the Board is and has been Richard D. Roberts. As Chairman of the Board, Mr. Roberts is familiar with the overall operational, business, and financial aspects of the Airport and the Authority. Mr. Roberts presides at its meetings and activities. The other members of the Board are: Peter G. Decker, Jr., Esquire; Louis F. Ryan, Esquire; Thomas P. Host, III; Dr. Harold J. Cobb, Jr.; Robert D. Jack, Jr.; Gus J. James, II, Esquire; Robert T. Taylor; and Howard M. Webb, Sr. (Final Pre-Trial Order at P3). At all material times, the Executive Director of the Authority is and has been Kenneth R. Scott. As Executive Director, Mr. Scott is the highest-ranking employee and officer of the Authority. Mr. Scott reports to the Board. Mr. Scott is responsible for all day-to-day operations and management of the Airport, as well as strategic and financial planning. (Final Pre-Trial Order at P4).

The Airport is served by major airlines, including American, Continental, Delta, Northwest, Southwest, United, US Airways, or their subsidiaries and affiliates. From 1998 through 2002, on average, approximately 3,079,470 passengers flew into and out of the Airport per year. This figure does not include people who come to the Airport to meet passengers or for other purposes. With the exception of 2001 (during which the September 11 terrorist attacks occurred), the number of passengers has increased every year. (Final Pre-Trial Order at P6). All passengers arriving at and departing from said Airport use automotive surface transportation for purposes of ingress and egress to and from the Airport facilities. (Final Pre-Trial Order at P7). Automotive surface transportation at the Airport, other than personal automobiles, consists of common carrier buses, limousines, taxi cabs, shuttles, and vehicles commonly denominated as "courtesy vehicles", which pick up and discharge customers of hotels, parking lots, motels, and car rental agencies. (Final Pre-Trial Order at P8).

A substantial portion of the traveling passengers using the facilities of the Airport reach the facilities by driving their automobiles or by taking limousines, taxi cabs, shuttles and courtesy vehicles. (Final Pre-Trial Order at P9). The Authority owns and operates the parking facilities located on Airport property. There are three parking lots and three parking garages on the Airport, containing a total of approximately 6,800 spaces. (Final Pre-Trial Order at P10).

At present, Park Shuttle operates the only known off-Airport parking facility. The Park Shuttle lot is located on Military Highway, approximately 1.5 miles from the main entrance to the Airport. (Final Pre-Trial Order at P11). The travelers who park their automobiles off the Airport on Park Shuttle's facility are then provided transportation to and from Park Shuttle's parking lot and the Airport by means of Park Shuttle's courtesy vehicles. Plaintiff's courtesy vehicles also transport its customers' luggage and drop off Park Shuttle's customers and luggage at the appropriate check-in and baggage check-in facility. The Authority's parking facility provides no such transportation of customers' luggage to the appropriate airline terminal. (Final Pre-Trial Order at P12). On an annual basis, more than 90% of Park Shuttle's revenues are generated from customers who are parking on Park Shuttle's property for the purpose of accessing the Airport and thereby traveling in interstate commerce. If the Airport did not exist, Plaintiff would have too few, if any, customers to operate its parking facility. (Final Pre-Trial Order at P13). Hotels located near the Airport provide courtesy vehicles to transport customers to the Airport. (Final Pre-Trial Order at P14).

On May 22, 2003, at its regularly scheduled meeting, the Board of Commissioners of the Authority adopted the Resolution Establishing Regulations and Fees for Off-Airport Public Parking Operators at Norfolk International Airport ("Resolution"). (Final Pre-Trial Order at P15). The Resolution provides, among other things, that all off-Airport parking operators shall pay a fee of 8% of the operator's gross monthly revenue derived from its customers who are transported to or from the Airport (the "Privilege Fee") for the privilege of accessing Airport property to pick up or discharge customers. The Resolution went into effect on July 1, 2003. (Final Pre-Trial Order at P16). At present, the Privilege Fee does not apply to vehicles operated by hotels, or to limos, taxi cabs or any other private or public vans transporting passengers to the Airport. Rather, such other businesses pay a different permit fee. (Final Pre-Trial Order at P17). The Authority has imposed a privilege fee of 8% of gross revenues for off-Airport rental car companies. At present, all rental car companies are located on the Airport and pay fees pursuant to concession agreements with the Authority. However, the Privilege Fee would apply to vehicles operated by an off-Airport rental car company in the event such a company were to open for business. (Final Pre-Trial Order at P18). The Authority does not require itself to pay a percentage of its gross revenue as required by the Authority of Park Shuttle. (Final Pre-Trial Order at P19).

In establishing the Privilege Fee, the Authority considered several factors, including, among others, the following: a) under federal law, and under mandates from the Federal Aviation Administration ("FAA") imposed pursuant to such law, the Airport is required to be self-sustaining. These requirements are also contained in the FAA Grant Assurances by which the Authority is bound. Thus, the Authority must maximize revenue in order to comply with these federal mandates; b) in order to attract airlines and maintain service, the Airport's rates and charges to airlines must be competitive; c) the Authority's expenses to operate the Airport have been increasing every year for the past five years. From fiscal year 1998-1999 through fiscal year 2002-2003, the Authority's expenses increased by approximately 7.6% annually. (The Authority fiscal year runs from July 1 through June 30.) The projected expenses for fiscal year 2003-2004 are expected to increase 42% over fiscal year 2002-2003; d) the predominant reasons for the increases in the Authority's expenses are the expansion of the Airport to accommodate the increasing volume of passengers and the additional security measures required as a result of the terrorist attacks of September 11, 2001. The Authority's only enterprise is the Airport; it does not have other businesses to offset such increased expenses; e) the Authority elected to impose the Privilege Fee in the form of a percentage of gross revenue because an increase in the receipts of an off-Airport parking operator corresponds to increased use of the Airport's facilities by the off-Airport parking operator; f) in selecting the 8% figure for the Privilege Fee, the Authority found that it was within the range charged by other airport operators, some of whom charge as much as 10%; g) the information on other airports was obtained from a survey entitled "2002 Ground Transportation Vehicle Fees Paid to Airports" compiled by the Airport Ground Transportation Association ("AGTA"), under the supervision of Ray Mundy, Ph.D., of the University of Missouri at St. Louis Center for Transportation Studies. The survey reveals that at least 16 airports across the United States charge percentage-based fees ranging from 4% to 10% to off-airport parking operators; h) the AGTA is a national organization comprised of major airport operators, ground transportation service providers, and manufacturers of ground transportation vehicles; i) also, in 2000, the Authority commissioned Leigh Fisher Associates, an airport management consulting firm, to study the types of fees charged to off-airport parking operators. The Leigh Fisher study also concluded that the range of fees charged by other airports was from 4% to 10%; j) in addition, the Authority considered that the vast majority, if not all, of Park Shuttle's customers are derived from the Airport; k) the Authority considered that Park Shuttle's marketing and advertising efforts, on their face, attempt to connect Park Shuttle with the Airport. For example, Park Shuttle's roadside billboard and the sign at its facility feature the phrase "Airport Valet Parking." Likewise, Park Shuttle's newspaper advertisements use the words "Airport Parking;" 1) Park Shuttle has chosen to inextricably link itself to the Airport and has obtained its customers from the Airport; m) Park Shuttle not only uses the actual Airport roads, but Park Shuttle also benefits from the Airport as a whole in terms of its customer base and revenue source; n) other businesses such as hotels, limousines, and taxis, have other sources of revenue. For example, hotels exist primarily to provide lodging and conference services, and transportation between the hotels and the Airport is generally complimentary; o) the Authority does not provide the services offered by these other businesses, while the Authority does provide Airport parking; p) Park Shuttle's business is materially different from hotels, motels, taxicabs and limousine operators in that Park Shuttle's primary purpose is to provide parking, while the other businesses have primary purposes other than parking; q) other businesses such as hotels enhance the flow of passengers through the Airport by hosting conferences and by providing lodging for travelers. Off-airport parking operators such as Park Shuttle have the opposite effect: they compete directly with the Authority; r) at present, the Authority has excess parking capacity on average of at least 2000 spaces per day; s) in deciding to impose the Privilege Fee, the Authority also considered its need to retire debts incurred in connection with the operation and maintenance of the Airport; t) those who use the Airport for commercial purposes, such as off-Airport parking operators, cause the Authority to incur costs associated with maintaining and securing the terminals, gates, roadways, and other facilities used by such businesses. The Authority believes that such commercial users should pay for the privilege of using the Airport for commercial purposes and for the market generated by the Airport's existence and continuing operation. (Final Pre-Trial Order at P20).

Prior to adopting the Resolution imposing the Privilege Fee, the Authority provided written notice to those who would be affected, including Park Shuttle, and conducted a public hearing at a meeting of the Board's Ground Transportation Committee. In response to the notice, Park Shuttle's out-of-state counsel sent a letter to the Authority outlining various legal challenges and objections to the Privilege Fee. (Final Pre-Trial Order at P21). Mr. Ben Gordon and another Park Shuttle representative, Ms. Janet Ayers, were invited to and appeared at a meeting held on May 13, 2003 by the Board's Ground Transportation Committee. At this meeting, the Ground Transportation Committee, chaired by Mr. Peter G. Decker, Jr., received and considered the comments presented by Mr. Gordon and Ms. Ayers. (Final Pre-Trial Order at P22). The Ground Transportation Committee discussed the issue and voted unanimously to recommend the imposition of the Privilege Fee to the full Board. The Board adopted the Resolution upon the recommendation of the Ground Transportation Committee after due consideration of all the facts stated above. (Final Pre-Trial Order at P23).

Peter B. Mandle is an expert in the field of airport management. Mr. Mandle has more than 25 years of experience in traffic engineering and transportation planning, with emphasis on airport grounds transportation, parking, airport access and circulation, and other airport management-related areas. Mr. Mandle is employed by Leigh Fisher Associates. Mr. Mandle is generally familiar with operations of airports in the United States and the commercial grounds transportation management and business practices at such airports. (Final Pre-Trial Order at P24). Mr. Mandle evaluated the Privilege Fee imposed by the Authority and the circumstances under which it was enacted. Mr. Mandle also analyzed off-airport parking fees charged by other airports. Mr. Mandle's research and analysis of the foregoing is contained in a report title "Evaluation of Off-Airport Parking Lot Privilege Fees", dates June 10, 2004 (the "Mandle Report"). (Final Pre-Trial Order at P25).

The fees charged by airports to commercial ground transportation operators fall into four general categories: privilege fees; cost-recover fees; monthly or annual fees; and other fees, such as those based on vehicle size or waiting time. (Final Pre-Trial Order at P26). Approximately 21 U.S. airports require that operators of off-airport parking facilities pay a privilege fee. As shown in Table 1 of the Mandle Report, these airports range in size from those serving fewer than 500,000 originating airline passengers to those which serve over 11 million originating airport passengers. (Final Pre-Trial Order at P27). As shown in Table 1 of the Mandle Report, the privilege fees range from 1% to 10% of gross receipts, with twelve airports charging 8% or higher. All of the 21 airports that charge off-airport parking operators privilege fees charge them as a percentage of gross receipts. (Final Pre-Trial Order at P28).

The factors typically considered by airport managers in assessing a privilege fee on off-airport parking operators are: the fees charged other companies, such as rental car companies, providing transportation services; the amount of off-airport parking lot privilege fees charged at other airports; and the amount of fees charged other airport concessionaires. (Final Pre-Trial Order at P29). As stated in Table 2 of the Mandle Report, eight of the airports similar in size to the Airport considered fees charged by other airports as a factor in establishing the off-airport parking privilege fee. (Final Pre-Trial Order at P30).

From time to time, various commercial enterprises purchase and pay for advertising space in the Airport terminal and passenger concourses in the Airport facility. (Final Pre-Trial Order at P31). In September 2000, Park Shuttle made application to the Authority for permission to place commercial advertising in the passenger concourses of said Airport. (Final Pre-Trial Order at P32). On September 29, 2000, Park Shuttle received a letter from Kenneth Scott, the Authority's Executive Director, stating that the Airport would not allow Park Shuttle any advertising in the passenger terminal area. However, Mr. Scott indicated that Park Shuttle could have a listing and a telephone line on the Reservation Board in the Baggage Claim Lobby. (Final Pre-Trial Order at P33). In January 2004, Park Shuttle again made application, through Interspace Airport Advertising Co., to place Park Shuttle's advertising in the Airport terminal. (Final Pre-Trial Order at P34). On February 6, 2004, Park Shuttle received a letter from Mr. Scott denying the application of Park Shuttle to advertise in the concourses of the terminal. (Final Pre-Trial Order at P35).

The Airport is not a public forum for purposes of restrictions on speech under the *First Amendment*. (Final Pre-Trial Order at P36). The advertisement that Park Shuttle desires to place in the airport does not express any particular political or social viewpoint or idea. (Final Pre-Trial Order at P37). In seeking to advertise on the airport premises, Park Shuttle's intent is to attract more customers to its parking lot. (Final Pre-Trial Order at P38).

2. Additional Trial Factual Findings

The Defendant has a legitimate business interest to protect its sources of income. Park Shuttle is a direct competitor with the Authority. The Defendant decided to impose a privilege fee based on information from an AGTA study, the Leigh Fisher study regarding off-airport parking fees, and similar airport administrators. A privilege fee is a fee based upon the benefits a company receives from the entire existence of the airport. It differs from a permit fee or cost-recovery fee that is imposed for courtesy vehicles. The privilege fee is not based on any estimate of Plaintiff's actual use of the airport or any of the Authority's facilities, or on Defendant's lost revenue due to Plaintiff's business. It is greatly in excess of the fees imposed on hotel shuttle vans and taxicabs that provide transportation to or from the airport. The privilege fee is within the range of 4-10% that the Leigh Fisher study identified for establishing a privilege fee. The privilege fees imposed at other airports for off-airport parking companies also fall within this range. Instead of a privilege fee, many airports charge off-airport parking companies an annual permit fee or have standard fees unrelated to the companies' revenue. The particular characteristics of an airport have some bearing on the type and amount of fee imposed based on the relative benefits conferred by the airport and the parking operators. At the Norfolk International Airport, the Authority is currently able to meet the parking needs of its customers.

The advertisement cases for which the Plaintiff sought access are in the main concourses of the airport, and contain paid advertisements by commercial companies, including some of the hotels that offer courtesy vehicle services to the airport. The principal purpose of the advertising display cases is to generate revenue for the Authority. (Tr. at 69.) In this case, applications were submitted in 2000 and 2004 to Mr. Scott to place advertisements. The Authority's procedure was to have the Board approve any prospective advertiser, and then approve any prospective advertisements to be placed within the airport. (Tr. at 69.) The Board delegated preliminary decision-making authority to Mr. Scott, but generally the advertising was coordinated by Interspace Airport Advertising Company. (Tr. at 70.) The Board did not have any written policy regarding advertising on the airline concourses.

Based on what he considered a general policy direction from the Board, Mr. Scott rejected Plaintiff's requests. (Tr. at 35.) Generally, he interpreted that policy to disallow any offensive advertisement, tobacco or alcohol ads, and to disallow any advertising for companies in competition with the Authority or the airlines present at the Norfolk International Airport. For example, airlines that do not service the Norfolk International Airport are not allowed to place advertisements at the airport. (Tr. at 37.) The Authority policy also applies to off-airport rental car companies, and thus Mr. Scott inferred that the policy would also likely apply for an off-airport parking company such as Park Shuttle. The purpose of this restriction was to avoid diversion of revenue from the airport or concessions within it. The Plaintiff's request to advertise in the airport concourse was denied because Plaintiff is a direct competitor and the airport provides comparable parking facilities. Defendant's sole reason for denying Plaintiff's advertisement was to protect its market share. (Tr. at 94.)

The Authority has an appeal process by which a prospective advertiser can appeal an initial rejection decision. (Tr. at 36.) Park Shuttle did not appeal Mr. Scott's decision, nor were they notified of the appeal process. (Tr. at 104.) After the second application to advertise was rejected, counsel for Park Shuttle made a written request for an explanation for the rejection of the application. Mr. Scott did not consider Park Shuttle's counsel's letter to be an appeal, and Park Shuttle did not get a response.

II. CONCLUSIONS OF LAW

A plaintiff alleging a violation of Equal Protection under the *Fourteenth Amendment* must first show that the government treated it differently than other individuals or groups. If the government action neither discriminates based on a suspect classification nor impinges a fundamental right, the Defendant must assert a legitimate purpose for treating the Plaintiff different from other similarly situated individuals or groups. *Kimel v. Fla. Bd. of Regents, 528 U.S. 62, 84, 145 L. Ed. 2d 522, 120 S. Ct. 631 (2000).* For a mere economic regulation, the government need only show a rational basis for its action. *Williamson v. Lee Optical Co., 348 U.S. 483, 489, 99 L. Ed. 563, 75 S. Ct. 461 (1955).* The Plaintiff bears the ultimate burden of proving that the government's disparate treatment was so unrelated to the proffered purpose that it was irrational. *Mass. Bd. of Ret. v. Murgia, 427 U.S. 307, 314, 49 L. Ed. 2d 520, 96 S. Ct. 2562 (1976)*; *Eldridge v. Bouchard, 645 F. Supp. 749, 755 (W.D. Va. 1986).*

The *Commerce Clause* prohibits a state from enacting any regulation that places an undue burden on interstate commerce. *U.S. CONST. ART. I, SECT. 8., CL. 3.* The actions of the state are treated as correct, unless they are proven to be unreasonable and arbitrary. *Hendrick v. Maryland, 235 U.S. 610, 624, 59 L. Ed. 385, 35 S. Ct. 140 (1915).* A government fee is reasonable if it (1) is based on some fair approximation of use of the facilities, (2) is not excessive in relation to the benefits conferred, and (3) does not discriminate against interstate commerce. *Evansville-Vanderburgh Airport Auth. Dist. v. Delta Airlines, Inc., 405 U.S. 707, 716-17, 31 L. Ed. 2d 620, 92 S. Ct. 1349 (1972).*

The *First Amendment* generally prohibits certain government restrictions on speech. *U.S. CONST. AMEND. I*; *Gitlow v. New York, 268 U.S. 652, 666, 69 L. Ed. 1138, 45 S. Ct. 625 (1925).* Regulations restricting speech on government property must be analyzed using the public forum doctrine. If the property is a traditional public forum or a designated public forum, a content based regulation must "serve a compelling state interest" and be "narrowly drawn to achieve that end." *Perry Educ. Ass'n v. Perry Local Educators' Ass'n, 460 U.S. 37, 45-46, 74 L. Ed. 2d 794, 103 S. Ct. 948 (1983).* In a non-public forum, the regulation must be reasonable and not just an attempt to suppress the prospective speaker's point of view. *Id.* Speech on government property is subject to a lower level of *First Amendment* scrutiny when the government is acting in a proprietary rather than regulatory manner. *United States v. Kokinda, 497 U.S. 720, 725, 111 L. Ed. 2d 571, 110 S. Ct. 3115 (1990).* Regulations restricting commercial speech must be analyzed according to the doctrine established by *Central Hudson.* A regulation on commercial speech is valid if: 1) the speech concerns lawful activity and is not misleading, 2) the asserted governmental interest is substantial, 3) the regulation directly advances the governmental interest asserted, and 4) it is not more extensive than is necessary to serve that interest. *Central Hudson Gas & Elec. Corp. v. Public Serv. Comm'n, 447 U.S. 557, 566, 65 L. Ed. 2d 341, 100 S. Ct. 2343 (1980).*

III. ANALYSIS

A. Equal Protection

Plaintiff asserts varying equal protection violations. First, the Plaintiff alleges that the imposed privilege fee unconstitutionally discriminates against Park Shuttle because the type and amount of rate charged differs from the rate charged to every other type of courtesy vehicle company. The Defendant claims that it has legitimate reasons for imposing a type of privilege fee different from the fee imposed on other courtesy vehicle companies. The Court previously found that at least one legitimate basis for Defendant's classification did exist, protecting a source of its income. Park Shuttle's parking business does take away revenue that would otherwise go to the Authority, whereas hotels are in a completely different business. *Park Shuttle N Fly, Inc. v. Norfolk Airport Auth.*, No. 03cv461 (E.D. Va. Feb. 6, 2004) (order partially granting Motion to Dismiss). Thus, the Authority can legitimately classify Park Shuttle differently because it is a revenue generating entity that can act to protect its source of revenue. The question currently before the Court is whether the amount of the privilege fee imposed on Park Shuttle is related to that legitimate government objective. *See id.*

The Plaintiff argues that the 8% privilege fee is arbitrary, not based on any determination of the revenue lost by the airport, and not based on Park Shuttle's actual use of the Authority's facilities. The Defendant contends that the 8% privilege fee was determined in several, non-arbitrary ways. First, the Authority, led by Mr. Scott, contacted directors at other airports including the Raleigh-Durham airport, and the Columbus, Ohio airport to determine what type of payment structure they used. (Tr. at 60.) He was informed that the Raleigh-Durham airport imposes a 10% privilege fee, and the Columbus airport a 7-8% fee for off-Airport parking services. (Tr. at 62.)

Second, Mr. Scott relied on information provided by Leigh Fisher, an airport management consulting firm. In 2000, the Authority contacted the firm requesting information regarding the types of fees charged to off-airport parking operators. (Ex. 10). Leigh Fisher responded that there were three types of fees applicable to off-airport parking facilities: permit fees, cost-recovery fees, or privilege fees. (Tr. at 128.) Mr. Peter Mandle, an expert consultant from Leigh Fisher, testified that a permit fee usually applies to commercial vehicles such as taxis or limousines, and it is an annual or monthly fee based on obtaining a license. Each commercial operator is required to pay such a fee. A cost-recovery fee applies to commercial vehicles and is a fee to reimburse the airport for the cost of building, operating, or maintaining facilities used by those vehicles. Cost-recovery fees can be assessed per vehicle, per operator, per vehicle trip, per passenger, or another measure of the actual use of the airport facilities. A privilege fee is assessed for the privilege of doing business on airport property and from the benefits a company or vehicle operator derives from the presence of the entire airport. Leigh Fisher also reported that the privilege fees charged at other airports range from 4% to 10% for off-airport parking businesses. (Ex. 10).

Third, Mr. Scott testified that he determined the fee based on the 2002 Airport Ground Transportation Association ("AGTA") study regarding ground transportation vehicle fees paid to airports. (Tr. at 58.) The study surveyed various airports around the country, and tabulated the information regarding fees imposed for on and off airport rental car companies, on and off airport parking operators, as well as fees for other commercial vehicles such as taxis and limousines. (Ex. 33). Finally, in determining what type and amount of fee to impose, Mr. Scott also considered the fact that off-airport rental car companies were previously charged an 8% privilege fee for their use of the airport.

The Court finds that the privilege fee imposed on Park Shuttle is substantial in comparison to other commercial vehicle operators. For the months of July through December 2003, Park Shuttle paid an average of $ 2,269.09 per month as a privilege fee. Similarly, it paid an average of $ 2,137.84 for the first five months of 2004. Taxicabs, in comparison, are charged a fee of $ 15 per month to pick up passengers at the airport, and they must be registered in Norfolk. There is no charge to drop off passengers. (Ex. 19). The Authority also provides taxis with a holding area for operators to park and wait for customers. (Tr. at 16-17.) Limousines are not charged a fee to pick up passengers at the airport, but they must have a pre-arranged agreement with the customer. (Ex. 19). Hotels are charged an annual permit fee of $ 180 per year to pick up customers who call to be picked up at the airport. (Tr. at 21.)

To find that this type of governmental action violated the *Equal Protection Clause*, the Court must determine that officials reasonably could not have believed that the action was rationally related to a legitimate governmental interest. *Front Royal & Warren County Indus. Park Corp. v. Town of Front Royal, 135 F.3d 275, 290 (4th Cir.1998)*; *Star Scientific v. Beales, 278 F.3d 339, 351 (4th Cir. 2002)*. Park Shuttle must therefore show that no reasonable official could have believed that the amount of the privilege was rationally related to the purpose of protecting the Authority's revenue. The Plaintiff has not met this burden. The Defendant, Norfolk Airport Authority, concedes that the fee imposed on Park Shuttle exceeds that imposed on other commercial vehicle operators, and concedes that it bears no relationship to either the cost of building or maintaining the airport or its roadway facilities. It is also irrelevant that the fee was not necessarily imposed due to lost revenue from parking, but instead due to increased security costs. The privilege fee is nevertheless rationally related to the legitimate purpose of protecting its revenue because the Authority has a right to charge commercial operators for the benefit and use of its facilities, and the amount of the fee is rational.

Park Shuttle generates more than 90% of its revenue from customers that access the airport. (Final Pre-Trial Order at P13). The vast majority of its business, therefore, is a direct result of the existence and operation of the airport. A benefit of this nature is specifically the type contemplated by the percentage based privilege fee. As Mr. Mandle testified, the privilege fee is designed to exact payment when a company benefits from the existence of the entire airport, as Plaintiff does here. Plaintiff concedes that without the airport, it would have too few customers to operate the parking facility. (Final Pre-Trial Order at P13).

Defendants conducted a reasonable inquiry into procedures used by other similar airports, and confirmed these results by the Leigh Fisher firm. (Tr. at 55.) It then established a fee squarely within the range suggested by Leigh Fisher, and comparable to other airports. (Ex. 33). The privilege fee structure is used in airports around the country for commercial businesses similar to Plaintiff's. Of the fifty-two airports surveyed in the 2002 AGTA study that charge off-airport parking fees, seventeen charged by percentage of gross revenue, and thirty-five either imposed no fee or charged using other methods. All of the airports using percentage-based fees had rates between the 4 and 10% indicated by Leigh Fisher.

The Defendant's rate also accounts for the relative benefits the Plaintiff and the Authority receive. Courts have upheld similar percentage-based fee structures based on an entity's comparison of the relative benefits it receives from various entities. *See Alamo Rent-A-Car, Inc. v. Sarasota-Manatee Airport, 825 F.2d 367, 371-72 (11th Cir. 1987)* (finding privilege fee charged to off-airport rental car company constitutional). The AGTA did not include a consideration of the relative benefits of an off-airport parking facility, but such information is very relevant to decisions based on what fees to charge particular entities.

The Norfolk International Airport has approximately 6,800 parking spaces, and expects to be able to meet the parking demands of its customers for several years. (Tr. at 52.) It, therefore, does not currently have a particular need for off-airport parking services. Other airports that do have such a need based on limited parking facilities at the airport likely have a greater need for such companies. These airports derive a greater benefit from off-airport parking entities than does Defendant, and thus may vary the fees based on entirely different criteria. In addition, under the percentage based fee, increased revenue from Park Shuttle corresponds with increased usage of the airport, and thus Plaintiff pays more for the increased benefits it receives. The Authority does not have to show that the fee is the same as other airports, nor must it justify why some of Plaintiff's revenue is not exempted from the fee structure. It must merely show that the fee is rational based on the relative benefits and detriments it derives based on the operation of Plaintiff's business. *See Alamo Rent-A-Car, 825 F.2d at 372.*

Park Shuttle has presented no evidence on benefits it provides to the Authority, whereas the Authority shows that Park Shuttle derives enormous benefits from the airport. Almost all of its revenue is generated because of the airport, and the Authority can constitutionally impose a different fee as a result. *See Williamson, 348 U.S. at 489; Allied Stores v. Bowers, 358 U.S. 522, 526-27, 3 L. Ed. 2d 480, 79 S. Ct. 437, 82 Ohio Law Abs. 312 (1959)* (finding states can vary the rates of taxes and fees based on legitimate classifications). Thus, even though Plaintiff is charged a much higher rate for essentially the same use of the airport, the Defendant's determination of relative benefits from Plaintiff as compared to similar commercial operators justifies the discrepancy, especially given the wide latitude governmental entities enjoy in determining the type and amount of fees charged for their services. *See City of New Orleans v. Dukes, 427 U.S. 297, 303, 49 L. Ed. 2d 511, 96 S. Ct. 2513 (1976).* It is therefore rational for Defendant to charge a different, percentage-based fee to companies such as Park

Shuttle that operate almost exclusively to supplement the airport's existing services.

Second, the Plaintiff raises an Equal Protection challenge to Defendant's advertising policy which disallows Park Shuttle to place advertisements in the main concourses where other advertisements are located. Because Plaintiff's proposed advertisements are purely commercial, the Court will apply the rational basis test. *City of New Orleans, 427 U.S. at 303* ("When economic or commercial legislation is challenged under the *equal protection clause*, the state defendant needs only to demonstrate that the regulation is rationally related to a legitimate state interest."); *Norfolk Fed'n of Bus. Dist. v. Dep't of Hous. and Urban Dev., 932 F.Supp. 730, 738 n. 4 (E.D. Va. 1996)*. Having found that Defendant has a legitimate business interest in classifying Plaintiff differently, the Court must only consider whether the restriction is rationally related to that interest. Here, again, Defendant classifies Plaintiff as a competing entity, and therefore prohibits the commercial advertisements. In a commercial arena, where the government is acting as a proprietor, it is reasonable for the government entity to discriminate against its competitors in establishing regulations. The Authority is rationally distinguishing Plaintiff in an attempt to maximize its profits at the airport which serves the public, and the Court cannot consider the economic fairness to Plaintiff if the classification is rational. *See Nat'l Paint & Coatings Ass'n. v. City of Chicago, 45 F.3d 1124, 1127 (7th Cir 1995)*. The Court finds that Defendant's rejection of Plaintiff's advertisements is therefore rationally related to its legitimate interest of generating and protecting revenue. Plaintiff's Equal Protection claim, therefore, fails.

B. *Commerce Clause*

The Plaintiff alleges that the Norfolk Airport Authority's privilege fee unconstitutionally interferes with interstate commerce by forcing airline passengers to pay additional fees. The Court has determined that the Authority's fee requirement is a user fee rather than a tax imposed upon Plaintiff. As such, the Court uses the analysis from *Evansville-Vanderburgh Airport Auth. Dist. v. Delta Airlines, Inc. 405 U.S. 707, 31 L. Ed. 2d 620, 92 S. Ct. 1349 (1972)*. A state may exact reasonable compensation for the use of those engaged in interstate commerce. *Id. at 712* (quoting *Hendrick v. Maryland, 235 U.S. 610, 59 L. Ed. 385, 35 S. Ct. 140 (1915))*. A fee is reasonable if it is based on some fair approximation of the use of the facilities, it is not excessive in relation to the benefits conferred, and it does not discriminate against interstate commerce. *Northwest Airlines v. County of Kent, Michigan, 510 U.S. 355, 369, 127 L. Ed. 2d 183, 114 S. Ct. 855 (1994)*; *Evansville-Vanderburgh, 405 U.S. at 716*.

The Plaintiff claims that the Authority's fee is not based on any fair approximation of the use of the facilities involved. Park Shuttle argues that its use of the airport is limited to the access roads and driveways of the airport, and that it should not be charged based on its use of the entire airport. The Defendant responds that Plaintiff benefits from the entire existence of the airport and uses its passengers who by extension use the entire airport. Defendant's argument is consistent with arguments made in other federal courts considering the constitutionality of similar fees. *See Alamo Rent-A-Car v. Sarasota-Manatee Airport Auth., 906 F.2d 516, 519 (11th Cir. 1990)* ("*Alamo II*").

The user fee is unquestionably inexact. Plaintiff is charged an 8% privilege fee regardless of how many customers park each month to access the airport. The fee also applies regardless of how many trips Plaintiff actually makes to the airport to pick up or drop off passengers. It also applies regardless of how many passengers use each parking spot at the facility, and how long each passenger parks the car. Thus, Defendant receives the same amount from Plaintiff whether one passenger parks one car for ten days and Park Shuttle makes a total of two trips to the airport, or whether ten passengers park ten cars for one day each and Park Shuttle makes twenty separate trips to the airport. At the same time, the hotels are charged the same, exponentially lower rate regardless of how many customers arrive via the airport, and how many trips their shuttle buses make to the airport. But, the user fee is not required to be exact, it just cannot be "manifestly disproportionate to the services rendered." *Commonwealth Edison Co. v. Montana, 453 U.S. 609, 620-23 n. 12, 69 L. Ed. 2d 884, 101 S. Ct. 2946 (1981).*

According to Park Shuttle's financial statements, it paid a total of $ 11,500.27 to the Defendant for the last six months of 2003. The Plaintiff has presented no information about the number of trips it made to the airport throughout those six months. The Plaintiff does, indicate, however, that over 90% of its revenue is generated by customers who seek access to the airport. The Plaintiff therefore gains enormous benefits from the existence of the airport and from passengers using its facilities. As long as a user fee is "based on some fair approximation of use or privilege for use, . .. and is neither discriminatory against interstate commerce nor excessive in comparison with the governmental benefit conferred, it will pass constitutional muster, even though some other formula might reflect more exactly the relative use of the state facilities by individual users." *Alamo II, 906 F.2d at 519* (quoting *Evansville-Vanderburgh, 405 U.S. at 716-17*). Although the user fee is not based upon an approximation of use, it is based on an approximation of Plaintiff's privilege for use of the facilities. In addition, though it may be deemed excessive in comparison with other commercial vehicle operators, the fee is not excessive when compared to the benefit the Authority confers. The Defendant allows Plaintiff access to its facility to directly compete with Defendant's own parking facilities, and earn revenue that would otherwise go to Defendant. Plaintiff may argue that some customers prefer the door-to-door service offered by Park Shuttle, but it cannot refute the enormous benefits it receives because of the Defendant, and because of the access Defendant allows to its facilities. The Court therefore finds that the privilege fee is not excessive in comparison with the government benefit conferred, and is based on a fair approximation of Plaintiff's privilege for use of the airport.

Finally, the regulation does not discriminate against interstate commerce. The regulation imposes a percentage fee without respect to the destination of airport customers. As such, it meets the requirements of *Evansville-Vanderburgh,* and does not unconstitutionally violate the Commerce Clause.

C. Freedom of Speech

The Plaintiff alleges that the Norfolk Airport Authority unconstitutionally violates Park Shuttle's rights under the *First Amendment* by disallowing it to advertise on the airport concourse while other companies are allowed to advertise. The Norfolk International Airport terminals contain advertisement spaces on which various companies pay to place advertisements. The Authority controls access to these advertisement spaces and refuses to allow Plaintiff to place advertisements on the spaces because it considers Park Shuttle to be a competitor.

Where a plaintiff challenges a regulation of commercial speech on government property, the Court must determine how to apply the Supreme Court's two different free speech doctrines. In considering such a case, the United States Court of Appeals for the Fourth Circuit applied the first prong of the *Central Hudson* test to determine whether the commercial speech is granted any *First Amendment* protection, and then applied the *Perry* public forum analysis. *Shopco Distrib. Co., Inc. v. Commanding General of Marine Corps Base, Camp Lejeune, North Carolina, 885 F.2d 167, 171 (4th Cir. 1989)* (applying commercial speech doctrine only to determine whether the speech concerned lawful activity and was not misleading, then applying public forum doctrine). This analysis is comparable to the analyses used by other courts. In cases considering both speech in airports, and commercial speech in similar public facilities, most courts apply the public forum doctrine. *See Air Line Pilots Ass'n Int'l v. Dep't of Aviation, 45 F.3d 1144 (7th Cir. 1995)*; *Lebron v. AMTRAK, 69 F.3d 650 (2d Cir. 1995)*; *Change the Climate, Inc. v. Mass. Bay Transp. Auth., 214 F. Supp. 2d 125 (D. Mass. 2002)*; *Capital Leasing of Ohio, Inc. v. Columbus Mun. Airport Auth., 13 F. Supp. 2d 640, 659 (S.D. Ohio 1998)*. Other courts have relied exclusively upon the commercial speech doctrine, however. *See New York Magazine v. Metro. Transp. Auth., 136 F.3d 123, 130 (2d Cir. 1998)*(applying commercial speech doctrine); *Am. Future Sys., Inc. v. Penn. State Univ., 752 F.2d 854, 862-62 (3d Cir. 1984)* (applying commercial speech doctrine because college dorm room didn't qualify as either a public forum or non-public forum).

Using the analysis from *Shopco Distributing,* the Court must first determine if the commercial speech concerned lawful activity and was not misleading. *885 F.2d at 171.* Neither the Plaintiff nor Defendant has argued that Plaintiff's proposed advertisement was misleading or concerned unlawful activity. The Court therefore finds that the proposed speech does fall under the *First Amendment* protections for commercial speech. *See Central Hudson, 447 U.S. at 566.* The Court must next apply the *First Amendment* doctrine concerning speech on government property.

To scrutinize government regulation of speech on government property using the public forum doctrine, the Court must first determine what property is sought to be used for the prohibited speech. If a speaker seeks only limited access to a public facility, the relevant forum is that property for which access is sought. *Cornelius v. NAACP Legal Def. & Educ. Fund, Inc., 473 U.S. 788, 801, 87 L. Ed. 2d 567, 105 S. Ct. 3439 (1985)*; *Air Line Pilots, 45 F.3d at 1151.* In *Air Line Pilots,* the court drew a distinction between a diorama display case and the greater airport terminal that would be used for the distribution of literature. *45 F.3d at 1153* (citing *Lehman v. City of Shaker Heights, 418 U.S. 298, 41 L. Ed. 2d 770, 94 S. Ct. 2714 (1974)* and *Planned Parenthood Ass'n v. Chicago Transit Auth., 767 F.2d 1225, 1231 (7th Cir. 1985)* (considering only the advertising system of the Chicago Transit Authority)). Similar to the facts in *Lehman* and *Air Line Pilots,*

Plaintiff seeks limited access to the public property, *Lehman, 418 U.S. at 301-02*; *Air Line Pilots, 45 F.3d at 1151*, so the relevant forum is just the advertising display cases. In considering prohibited speech involving public transportation facilities, other courts have similarly limited their inquiry to a consideration of only the space in which the prohibited speech was to occur. *See Amtrak, 69 F.3d at 655-56*; *Hubbard Broad., Inc. v. Metro. Sports Facilities Comm'n, 797 F.2d 552, 555-56 (8th Cir. 1986)*; *Change the Climate, 214 F. Supp. 2d 125. But see, U.S. Southwest Africa/Namibia Trade & Cultural Council v. United States, 228 U.S. App. D.C. 191, 708 F.2d 760, 764-66 (D.C. Cir. 1983)*(considering airport as a whole rather than just the advertising spaces). Since the Plaintiff here seeks only to place a commercial advertisement on the advertising boards, the Court concludes that the terminal advertising space is the relevant forum to consider.

Secondly, the Court must classify the public facility where the speech is purportedly being restricted either as a public forum, a limited or designated public forum, or a non-public forum. *Perry, 460 U.S. at 44*. Courts have generally found that an airport terminal is not a public forum. *Int'l Soc'y for Krishna Consciousness v. Lee, 505 U.S. 672, 120 L. Ed. 2d 541, 112 S. Ct. 2701 (1992)*; *Jamison v. City of St. Louis, 828 F.2d 1280, 1283 (8th Cir.1987)*; *Gannett Satellite Info. Network, Inc. v. Berger, 894 F.2d 61, 64-65 (3d Cir. 1990)*. The parties here have stipulated that the airport is not a public forum for purposes of restrictions on speech under the *First Amendment*, (Final Pre-Trial Order at P36), but they are silent as to whether it is a designated public forum. However, the relevant inquiry is whether the advertisement space, not the entire airport, constitutes a public forum, a designated public forum, or a non-public forum.

A public forum is government property that has "as a principal purpose ... the free exchange of ideas," such as a park, or sidewalk. *Cornelius, 473 U.S. at 800*. To determine whether certain property is a public forum, the Court considers: 1) the physical characteristics of the place, 2) the function of the property, and 3) the degree of incompatibility between the challenged speech and the normal activities of the place. *Lehman, 418 U.S. at 303-04*. The advertisement spaces are clearly not a public forum. Their principal purpose is to generate revenue, rather than to promote the free exchange of ideas.

On the other hand, a designated public forum is property that the government "has opened for use by the public as a place for expressive activity." *Perry, 460 U.S. at 46*. City auditoriums and public theaters are common examples of designated public fora. *Gannett Satellite Information Network, Inc. v. Berger, 716 F. Supp. 140, at 148*. To determine if the space qualifies as a designated public forum, the Court must look at the government's intent in establishing and maintaining the advertising space. *Cornelius, 473 U.S. at 802*. To determine intent, the Court looks at the policy and practice of the government with respect to the property, and then the nature of the property and its compatibility with expressive activity. *Air Line Pilots, 45 F.3d at 1152* (citing *Cornelius, 473 U.S. at 802*). In addition, the government must intend to create a public forum by "intentionally opening a nontraditional forum for public discourse." *Krishna Consciousness, 505 U.S. at 680* (citing *Cornelius, 473 U.S. at 802*).

The advertisement spaces are in the main concourses of the airport, and contain advertisements by a variety of commercial companies, including some of the hotels that offer courtesy vehicle services to the airport. The principal purpose of the advertising display cases is to generate revenue for the Authority. (Tr. at 69.) There is no evidence that the current advertisement space is geared towards promoting any particular type of business or venture, or aimed at any particular type of traveler.

Furthermore, there is no evidence that the Authority has intended to make the space available for public expression, as is required to find that it is a designated public forum. *See Krishna Consciousness, 505 U.S. at 680*; *New York Magazine, 136 F.3d at 130* (finding that advertising spaces on outside of MTA buses was designated public forum because MTA accepts political and commercial advertisements); *Lebron v. WMATA, 749 F.2d 893, 896 (D.C. Cir.1984)*. Neither party provided any evidence that the advertising space had ever been used for non-commercial purposes such as for public service announcements or political advertisements. Every indication is that the Authority uses the advertising space to generate revenue and promote business both within the airport and peripherally to passengers using the airport. The fact that they disallow advertisements from competing airlines and parking facilities supports the finding that the advertising spaces are not open for public expression and are not intended as such. *See Ark. Educ. Television Comm'n v. Forbes, 523 U.S. 666, 679, 140 L. Ed. 2d 875, 118 S. Ct. 1633 (1998)* ("[a] designated public forum is not created when the government allows selective access for individual speakers rather than general access for a class of speakers.").

The Court therefore finds that the advertisement space within the airport terminals is not a "designated public forum" because the Authority has not made it available for public expression, and instead limits its use to commercial ventures. The Court's finding is also supported by the Authority's role in this speech-related venture. When the government is engaged in commerce related to the challenged fora, that inquiry is relevant to the classification of such fora. *United States v. Laton, 352 F.3d 286, 293 (6th Cir. 2003)*. Thus, if the government is acting as a commercial participant, rather than as a regulator, the public space is not likely a public forum. *See Lehman, 418 U.S. at 303* (holding that a municipal vehicle is not a public forum because "the city is engaged in commerce" and the advertising space is a commercial venture); *Krishna Consciousness, 505 U.S. at 678 (1992)* (finding that government acts as a proprietor when it owns and operates an airport); *United States v. Kokinda, 497 U.S. 720, 725, 111 L. Ed. 2d 571, 110 S. Ct. 3115 (1990)*. Governmental bodies that operate airports are generally regarded as a market participant, and the parties here have stipulated that the Authority is acting in a proprietary fashion in operating the airport. *See e.g., Four T's, Inc. v. Little Rock Mun. Airport Comm'n, 108 F.3d 909, 912 (8th Cir.1997)*; *Air Line Pilots, 45 F.3d 1144*; *Capital Leasing, 13 F. Supp. 2d at 658*. The revenue-generating purpose of the advertisement space further supports the fact that the government is acting in its proprietary capacity with regards to the challenged speech. Since the Authority is acting in its proprietary function, its regulations are subject to less *First Amendment* scrutiny.

The Court concludes that the advertisement space is a non-public forum. "In a nonpublic forum the government may restrict expression 'based on subject matter and speaker identity so long as the distinctions drawn are reasonable in light of the purpose served by the forum and are viewpoint neutral.'" *Change the Climate, 214 F. Supp. 2d at 132* (quoting *Cornelius, 473 U.S. 788, at 806*). Under Authority procedures, the Board was to approve any prospective advertiser, and then any prospective advertisements to be placed within the airport. (Tr. at 69.) The regulation in question here prohibits the Plaintiff, and similar competing businesses from advertising in the airport terminal. The distinction is therefore made based upon the identity of the speakers. The Plaintiff's parking business competes with the Authority's parking lots and thus they are disallowed from placing any advertisement promoting their business. Defendant merely seeks to protect the sources of its income, which includes its parking lots. The Court has already found this to be a legitimate purpose. *See Park Shuttle N Fly*, No. 03cv461, at 12. Thus, as long as the regulation is reasonable in light of that purpose, it meets constitutional standards.

The Defendant's restrictions on Plaintiff's advertisements are reasonable given its purpose to generate revenue. Each person that parks at Plaintiff's facilities for the purposes of accessing the airport could potentially park in the airport's lots and generate direct revenue for the Authority. The Authority generates substantially more revenue from customers parking in its lots than it does from the privilege fees that Park Shuttle pays for its customers. It promotes this interest by disallowing Plaintiff to advertise on its property. Further, since the regulation applies to purely commercial speech, the Authority has more freedom than it would for a similar noncommercial advertisement. *See Metromedia, Inc. v. City of San Diego, 453 U.S. 490, 514, 69 L. Ed. 2d 800, 101 S. Ct. 2882 (1981)* ("although the city may distinguish between the relative value of different categories of commercial speech, the city does not have the same range of choice in the area of noncommercial speech ...") (citing *Carey v. Brown, 447 U.S. 455, 462, 65 L. Ed. 2d 263, 100 S. Ct. 2286 (1980)*). The Defendant operates the airport and must be financially self-sufficient, and the Court finds that it is reasonable to impose restrictions regulating commercial advertising towards competitors such as Plaintiff on airport property.

The Plaintiff has failed to meet its burden of proving that Defendant's content based restrictions in this non-public forum violate the *First Amendment*. The Court declines to consider whether Defendant's "guidelines" are unconstitutionally vague because the parties have not raised the issue. The Court does, however, limit its holding to the Plaintiff in this matter because the parties have stipulated that Plaintiff directly competes with the Authority. (Final Pre-Trial Order P20q).

IV. CONCLUSION

The Court finds that Defendant's regulation is constitutionally valid as it satisfies the requirements of both the *Equal Protection Clause* and the *Commerce Clause*. In addition, Defendant's policy regarding advertising is constitutional and does not violate the *First Amendment*. For the reasons stated above, the Court awards judgment to the DEFENDANT.

IT IS SO ORDERED.

DISTRICT OF COLUMBIA, ET AL., PETITIONERS v. DICK
ANTHONY HELLER

No. 07-290

SUPREME COURT OF THE UNITED STATES

June, 2008

[Note—the full body of this opinion (more than 100 pages long) has been omitted in the interest of brevity. Please re-read the text of the Second Amendment before you read this opinion.] –JJV, ed.

SYLLABUS

District of Columbia law bans handgun possession by making it a crime to carry an unregistered firearm and prohibiting the registration of handguns; provides separately that no person may carry an unlicensed handgun, but authorizes the police chief to issue 1-year licenses; and requires residents to keep lawfully owned firearms unloaded and dissembled or bound by a trigger lock or similar device. Respondent Heller, a D. C. special policeman, applied to register a handgun he wished to keep at home, but the District refused. He filed this suit seeking, on *Second Amendment* grounds, to enjoin the city from enforcing the bar on handgun registration, the licensing requirement insofar as it prohibits carrying an unlicensed firearm in the home, and the trigger-lock requirement insofar as it prohibits the use of functional firearms in the home. The District Court dismissed the suit, but the D. C. Circuit reversed, holding that the *Second Amendment* protects an individual's right to possess firearms and that the city's total ban on handguns, as well as its requirement that firearms in the home be kept nonfunctional even when necessary for self-defense, violated that right.

Held:

1. The *Second Amendment* protects an individual right to possess a firearm unconnected with service in a militia, and to use that arm for traditionally lawful purposes, such as self-defense within the home.

(a) The Amendment's prefatory clause announces a purpose, but does not limit or expand the scope of the second part, the operative clause. The operative clause's text and history demonstrate that it connotes an individual right to keep and bear arms.

(b) The prefatory clause comports with the Court's interpretation of the operative clause. The "militia" comprised all males physically capable of acting in concert for the common defense. The Antifederalists feared that the Federal Government would disarm the people in order to disable this citizens' militia, enabling a politicized standing army or a select militia to rule. The response was to deny Congress power to abridge the ancient right of individuals to keep and bear arms, so that the ideal of a citizens' militia would be preserved.

(c) The Court's interpretation is confirmed by analogous arms-bearing rights in state constitutions that preceded and immediately followed the *Second Amendment*.

(d) The *Second Amendment's* drafting history, while of dubious interpretive worth, reveals three state *Second Amendment* proposals that unequivocally referred to an individual right to bear arms.

(e) Interpretation of the *Second Amendment* by scholars, courts and legislators, from immediately after its ratification through the late 19th century also supports the Court's conclusion.

(f) None of the Court's precedents forecloses the Court's interpretation. Neither *United States v. Cruikshank, 92 U.S. 542, 553, 23 L. Ed. 588,* nor *Presser v. Illinois, 116 U.S. 252, 264-265, 6 S. Ct. 580, 29 L. Ed. 615,* refutes the individual-rights interpretation. *United States v. Miller, 307 U.S. 174, 59 S. Ct. 816, 83 L. Ed. 1206, 1939-1 C.B. 373,* does not limit the right to keep and bear arms to militia purposes, but rather limits the type of weapon to which the right applies to those used by the militia, *i.e.,* those in common use for lawful purposes.

2. Like most rights, the *Second Amendment* right is not unlimited. It is not a right to keep and carry any weapon whatsoever in any manner whatsoever and for whatever purpose: For example, concealed weapons prohibitions have been upheld under the Amendment or state analogues. The Court's opinion should not be taken to cast doubt on longstanding prohibitions on the possession of firearms by felons and the mentally ill, or laws forbidding the carrying of firearms in sensitive places such as schools and government buildings, or laws imposing conditions and qualifications on the commercial sale of arms. *Miller's* holding that the sorts of weapons protected are those "in common use at the time" finds support in the historical tradition of prohibiting the carrying of dangerous and unusual weapons.

3. The handgun ban and the trigger-lock requirement (as applied to self-defense) violate the *Second Amendment.* The District's total ban on handgun possession in the home amounts to a prohibition on an entire class of "arms" that Americans overwhelmingly choose for the lawful purpose of self-defense. Under any of the standards of scrutiny the Court has applied to enumerated constitutional rights, this prohibition--in the place where the importance of the lawful defense of self, family, and property is most acute--would fail constitutional muster. Similarly, the requirement that any lawful firearm in the home be disassembled or bound by a trigger lock makes it impossible for citizens to use arms for the core lawful purpose of self-defense and is hence unconstitutional. Because Heller conceded at oral argument that the D. C. licensing law is permissible if it is not enforced arbitrarily and capriciously, the Court assumes that a license will satisfy his prayer for relief and does not address the licensing requirement. Assuming he is not disqualified from exercising *Second Amendment* rights, the District must permit Heller to register his handgun and must issue him a license to carry it in the home.

III. ADMINISTRATIVE LAW & FEDERAL REGULATION OF AVIATION

A. Preemption and Rulemaking

VIOLA ROGERS, GUARDIAN ET AL v. RAY GARDNER FLYING SERVICE, INC. ET AL.

UNITED STATES COURT OF APPEALS FOR THE FIFTH CIRCUIT

435 F.2d 1389

November, 1970

[Note: this case deals with the doctrine of preemption. Preemption means that federal law will trump conflicting state law in certain circumstances. This case deals with preemption under the Federal Tort Claim Act (FTCA). The FTCA, 28 U.S.C. 1346 et. seq., provides that "the district courts shall have original jurisdiction [over] civil actions or claims against the United States [of less than $10,000 that are based on the Constitution or federal law.] --JJV, ed.

OPINION

SIMPSON, Circuit Juddge:

This appeal requires us once more to examine the amorphous subject of federal pre-emption. The precise question is whether Title 49, U.S.C. Section 1301(26) (reprinted below) preempts the Oklahoma law of bailments as it bears upon the liability of an owner-lessor of an airplane for the negligent acts of a non-agent operator -lessee.

> "§ 1301. *Definitions*
>
> > As used in this chapter, unless the context otherwise requires --
> >
> > (26) 'Operation of aircraft' or 'operate aircraft' means the use of aircraft, for the purpose of air navigation and includes the navigation of aircraft. Any person who causes or authorizes the operation of aircraft, whether with or without the right of legal control (in the capacity of owner, lessee, or otherwise) of the aircraft, shall be deemed to be engaged in the operation of aircraft within the meaning of this chapter."

This is a wrongful death action arising out of the crash of a private plane on January 2, 1967, in Oklahoma. Federal jurisdiction is based on diversity of citizenship. Gordon Hunter, a citizen of Texas, was pilot of the plane. The other occupants were his wife, Johnnie R. Hunter, and her sister, Ella Dunn. All three were killed in the crash, which occurred near Ardmore, Oklahoma, on a return trip to Wichita Falls, Texas, from Arkansas. Hunter was a member of the United States Air Force stationed in and a resident of Wichita Falls. The plaintiffs-appellees, Mr. and Mrs. Rogers, are Arkansas citizens, the parents of Mrs. Hunter and Mrs. Dunn. Mr. and Mrs. Rogers sued individually and Mrs. Rogers asserted a separate claim as guardian of the minor children of Mrs. Hunter by a previous marriage.

The defendants below, appellants here, are Ray Gardner Flying Service, Incorporated, a fixed base operator in Wichita Falls, and Ray Gardner, the president of the corporation, individually. The plane was owned by Les Wilson and had been leased by Wilson to the corporate defendant, which in turn rented it to Hunter under oral agreement.

Appellees alleged that Hunter was negligent in the operation of the plane, and that such negligence was the proximate cause of the accident in which all occupants of the plane perished. They did not contend that the appellants exercised any control over the operation of the plane, that appellants were present in the plane, or that Hunter was their agent. Neither do they allege that the plane was negligently inspected or was rented while in a defective condition, or that the appellants were in any other manner negligent. The single thrust of the claim asserted against the appellants was that by operation of Title 49 U.S.C. § 1301(26) the defendants became vicariously liable for the negligence of the operator Hunter, and that this affords the basis for a wrongful death action under the law of Oklahoma.

The controlling issue was raised before the district court by a defense motion for summary judgment. The district court denied the motion, holding that Title 49 U.S.C. § 1301(26) "does not provide the source for establishing owner and lessee responsibility for the negligence of the pilot, the cause of action being created by the Oklahoma wrongful death statute". The district judge certified that her order involved a controlling question of law to which there was substantial ground for difference of opinion, and that appeal therefrom might materially advance the ultimate termination of the litigation. A panel of this Court allowed the appeal, under Title *28 U.S.C. Section 1292(b)*.

The Oklahoma wrongful death statute, *12 Okla. Stats. Ann. § 1053*, (reprinted below) provides that the defendant is liable only if the deceased might have maintained an action against the defendant for the same act or omission. However, Oklahoma decisions would not allow a cause of action against the defendants below. The Oklahoma Supreme Court has expressly held that the negligence of the bailee of an airplane may not be imputed to the bailor. *Spartan Aircraft Company v. Jamison, 181 Okla. 645, 75 P.2d 1096 (1938)*. See also *Randolph v. Schuth, 185 Okla. 204, 90 P.2d 880 (1939)*.

> "§ 1053. Death -- Action for
>
>> "When the death of one is caused by the wrongful act or omission of another, the personal representative of the former may maintain an action therefor against the latter, or his personal representative if he is also deceased, if the former might have maintained an action had he lived, against the latter, or his representative, for an injury for the same act or omission. The action must be commenced within two years. The damages must inure to the exclusive benefit

of the surviving spouse and children, if any, or next of kin; to be distributed in the same manner as personal property of the deceased."

Appellees apparently concede that no cause of action accrued to them under the Oklahoma law of bailments; they maintain, rather, that Title 49 U.S.C. § 1301(26), forms the basis for a cause of action under the Oklahoma wrongful death statute. They point out that this section of the Federal Aviation Act of 1958 provides that anyone who authorizes the operation of aircraft in the capacity of an owner or lessee or otherwise is deemed to be engaged in the operation of aircraft as defined in the statute. Also, Title 49 U.S.C. § 1430 provides:

"(a) It shall be unlawful --

(5) For any person to operate aircraft in air commerce in violation of any other rule, regulation, or certificate of the Administrator under this subchapter."

An agency regulation states that "No person may operate an aircraft in a careless manner so as to endanger the life or property of another ". *14 C.F.R. § 91.9*. The interweaving of these statutory sections and agency rules leads the appellees to the conclusion that if they can prove that the pilot was operating the airplane in a careless and negligent manner, then this declared unlawful conduct is imputed to the defendants by law under the provisions of Title 49 U.S.C. § 1301(26).

In 1948, the following section was added to the Act [now Title 49 U.S.C. *S* 1404]:

"No person having a security interest in, or security title to, any civil aircraft, aircraft engine, or propeller under a contract of conditional sale, equipment trust, chattel or corporate mortgage, or other instrument of similar nature, and no lessor of any such aircraft, aircraft engine, or propeller under a bona fide lease of thirty days or more, shall be liable by reason of such interest or title, or by reason of his interest as lessor or owner of the aircraft, aircraft engine, or propeller so leased, for any injury to or death of persons, or damage to or loss of property, on the surface of the earth (whether on land or water) caused by such aircraft, aircraft engine, or propeller, or by the ascent, descent, or flight of such aircraft, aircraft engine, or propeller or by the dropping or falling of an object therefrom, unless such aircraft, aircraft engine, or propeller is in the actual possession or control of such person at the time of such injury, death, damage, or loss."

The House Committee Report on the amendment, as the reason for exempting security holders and certain lessors, stated:

"Provisions of present Federal and State law might be construed to impose upon persons who are owners of aircraft for security purposes only, or who are lessors of aircraft, liability for damages caused by the operation of such aircraft even though they have no control over the operation of the aircraft. This bill would remove this doubt by providing clearly that such persons have no liability under such circumstances." U.S. Congressional Code Service, 1948, 80th Congress, 2nd Session, p. 1836; House Report, No. 2091, 80th Congress, 2nd Session.

The appellees rely on these statutes as evidence of their claim that Congress purposefully considered the question of pre -empting state laws on bailment of airplanes and concluded that only those persons exempted by Section 1404 should not be held liable as operators. They reason that Congress clearly intended to preempt state law and to protect the public from the negligence and financial irresponsibility of pilots by imposing vicarious liability upon one who allows his aircraft to be flown by another. Appellees argue that it is sound public policy to place the responsibility for negligence upon the parties in a position to control the use of airplanes and upon those who generally are more likely to be financially responsible.

Appellees contend that we have in fact endorsed their view of the applicable law in the case of *Hays v. Morgan, 221 F.2d 481, 5* Cir. They also cite *Sosa v. Young Flying Service, S.D. Tex. 1967, 277 F. Supp. 554; Lamasters v. Snodgrass, 248 Iowa 1377, 85 N.W.2d 622 (1957); Hoebee v. Howe, 98 N.H. 168, 97 A.2d 223 (1953)*, as supporting their position.

We do not question that under its *commerce clause* powers Congress could pre -empt state law with regard to the liability for injuries resulting from air crashes. But we are not convinced that in this instance Congress has clearly indicated any such intent to supersede state laws of bailments as related to the operation of aircraft. See *Double-Eagle Lubricants, Incorporated v. State of Texas, N.D. Tex. 1965, 248 F. Supp. 515*, appeal dismissed *384 U.S. 434, 86 S. Ct. 1601, 16 L. Ed. 2d 670*, and the cases cited therein. If Congress had any such intent toward pre-emption in this area it was fully capable of making that intent clear directly and not by indirection requiring the circuitous reasoning plaintiffs find themselves driven to employ. In our judgment, what Congress did intend was to subject the classes of persons named in Title 49, Sec. 1301(26), equally with pilots to the rules, regulations, and penalties provided *in the Federal Aviation Act*. Several courts have in fact concluded that civil remedies for damages as a means of enforcing the act were not envisioned by Congress. *Yelinek v. Worley, E.D. Va. 1968, 284 F. Supp. 679; Moungey v. Brandt, W.D. Wis. 1966, 250 F. Supp. 445; Southeastern Aviation, Incorporated v. Hurd, 209 Tenn. 639, 355 S.W.2d 436 (1962)*, appeal dismissed *371 U.S. 21, 83 S. Ct. 120, 9 L. Ed. 2d 96 (1962)*.

We have been cited no case and we have found none from our independent research in which this precise subject has been before any of the Courts of Appeal. However, the issue was treated in depth by Chief Judge Arraj of the District of Colorado in Rosdail v. Western Aviation, Incorporated, 969, *297 F. Supp. 681*. That court stated:

"We disagree, however, that Congress intended to alter common law principles with a definitional section of a regulatory scheme. The Federal Aviation Program regulates the licensing, inspection and registration of aircraft and airmen. It makes no provision for its application to tort liability and in fact provides that nothing in the Program shall abridge or alter the remedies now existing at common law or by statute. 49 U.S.C. § 1506. Responsibility placed upon owners and lessors by § 1301(26) arises merely in the context of violations of the Program and regulations promulgated pursuant thereunder. Furthermore, responsibility is in the nature of express civil and criminal penalties as provided for in §§ 1471, 1472 and 1474 of the Program." (*297 F. Supp. at 684-685*).

Appellees' reliance upon our earlier decision in *Hays, 221 F.2d 481, page 6,* is a mistake. In *Hays* the State of Mississippi had expressly incorporated the language of the Federal Aviation Act into the law of that state. Code Miss. 1942, Sec. 7536-26(9) and 7536-12, and we were hence interpreting state law. It is one thing to say that the words of a state statute impose vicarious liability on the owners and lessors of an airplane. When those same words embodied in a federal statute are relied upon to widen state tort liability it is necessary additionally to consider federal-state comity and the requirement that Congress clearly manifest an intention to exercise fully its power under the *commerce clause*.

The *Lamasters* and *Hoebee* cases, supra, were likewise cases where state laws patterned after the Federal Aviation Act were being interpreted. Only *Sosa, 277 F. Supp. 554,* involved an interpretation of the Federal Aviation Act. That decision appears to us to be based upon the same incorrect reading of *Hays* successfully urged by appellees upon the court below.

We are not unsettled by the 1948 amendment, Title 49 U.S.C. § 1404. That section excludes certain persons from liability for injuries *on the surface of the earth*. On its face it was enacted to facilitate financing of the purchase of aircraft by providing that those holding security interests would not be liable for injuries caused by falling planes or the parts thereof. This provision appears *clearly* and forthrightly to preempt any contrary state law which might subject holders of security interests to liability for injuries so incurred. If the Congressional intent was as clearly stated with regard to Title 49 U.S.C. § 1301(26) our task would be correspondingly simpler. In the absence of similar clear manifestation of Congressional intent we find nothing in Title 49 U.S.C. § 1404 which supports construction of Title 49 U.S.C. § 1301(26) so as to preempt state law.

With leave of court the appellees have filed with the Court a post-submission brief in which it is urged that the recent opinion of the Supreme Court of the United States in *Moragne v. State Marine Lines, Incorporated, 398 U.S. 375, 385, 90 S. Ct. 1772, 26 L. Ed. 2d 339 (1970)* bears upon this case. In *Moragne*, a longshoreman was killed while working aboard a vessel on navigable waters within the State of Florida. His widow brought an action against the owners of the vessel in a state court to recover damages for wrongful death and for the pain and suffering experienced by the decedent prior to his death. The claims were based upon unseaworthiness of the vessel and negligence. After removal of the case to the federal district court, the vessel owner moved for dismissal of the wrongful death claim on the grounds that maritime law provided no recovery for wrongful death within a state's territorial waters, and that the unseaworthiness was not a basis for liability under the Florida Wrongful Death Act. The district court dismissed the complaint and this Court affirmed after the Supreme Court of Florida answered our certified question by holding that the Florida Death by Wrongful Act statute does not allow recovery for wrongful death based upon unseaworthiness. The Supreme Court reversed, overruling *The Harrisburg, 119 U.S. 199, 30 L. Ed. 358, 7 S. Ct. 140 (1886)*, and holding that a wrongful death action may be brought under general federal maritime law for violation of maritime duty even in the absence of a cause of action under state statute.

Appellees attempt to analogize this decision with the instant case by urging that they may now bring this wrongful death action for alleged breach of federally declared aviation standards even in the absence of a cause of action under Oklahoma law.

Appellants' counter-argument quickly reaches the flaw in appellees' analogy to maritime law. The Constitution of the United States extends the judicial power of the federal courts to admiralty and maritime cases, and the federal courts have therefore been obliged to fashion a general maritime law in the absence of federal statute. Article III, Section 2, Clause 1; *American Insurance Company v. Canter, 26 U.S. (1 Pet) 511, 545-6, 7 L. Ed. 242 (1828)*. State legislation which conflicts with general maritime law or federal statute is invalid. See Gilmore and Black. The Law of Admiralty, Sections 1-16, 1-17.

Conversely, the *commerce clause* as interpreted by the courts has left state sovereignty unimpaired except where Congress has clearly indicated an intent to supersede state law. *Rice v. Santa Fe Elevator Corporation, supra*, footnote 7, *Napier v. Atlantic Coast Line Railroad Company, 272 U.S. 605, 47 S. Ct. 207, 71 L. Ed. 432 (1926)*; *Double-Eagle Lubricants, supra*. The difference is clearly expressed by appellants' reply to the supplemental brief:

> "Under this constitutional grant, the federal courts, except insofar as precluded by Congressional enactment or inhibited by stare decisis, are free to recognize and apply a judge-made cause of action for wrongful death in an admiralty case as was done in *Moragne*. The Constitution, however, has not granted the federal courts any comparable power to fashion their own common law remedies in tort cases arising in the airways."

It becomes clear that the development of the power of the federal government under these two constitutional provisions has been strikingly dissimilar. A clear mandate has been recognized in the maritime area for the establishment of uniform federal law, whereas the delicate problem of federal-state relations has resulted in a more stringent rule that federal preemption under the *commerce clause* will not be presumed in the absence of a clear indication of the intent of Congress. The analogy to the *Moragne* holding fails to withstand analysis.

The judgment of the district court is reversed. The cause is remanded with directions to enter summary judgment in favor of the defendants-appellants.

MANAGEMENT ACTIVITIES, INC. v. UNITED STATES OF AMERICA.

UNITED STATES DISTRICT COURT FOR THE CENTRAL DISTRICT OF CALIFORNIA

21 F. Supp. 2d 1157

September, 1998

I. INTRODUCTION

This litigation arises from an aircraft accident at John Wayne Airport, Santa Ana, California, on December 15, 1993, at 1733:18 Pacific Standard Time, involving an Israel Aircraft Industries Westwind II business jet ("Westwind"), Federal Aviation Administration ("FAA") registration number N309CK. At 0700 hours on the day of the accident, the Westwind departed Long Beach Airport to begin a multileg operation. After several intervening stops during the day, the aircraft arrived at Brackett Field, located in the northeast area of the Los Angeles basin, north of Pomona, California. In late afternoon, the Westwind crew prepared for the short 35-mile flight from Brackett Field to John Wayne Airport. They filed an Instrument Flight Rules ("IFR") flight plan, and obtained an instrument clearance from air traffic control ("ATC"). The Westwind was attempting to fly a visual approach to Runway 19-Right (19R) when it encountered wake turbulence from a preceding United Airlines Boeing 757 ("Boeing 757"), lost control, and crashed approximately 3.2 miles short of the runway. Both pilots and all three passengers aboard the Westwind sustained fatal injuries in the crash.

The Westwind was owned by Management Activities, Inc. ("MAI"), Long Beach, California, and jointly operated by MAI and Martin Aviation ("Martin"), Santa Ana, California, pursuant to a joint venture agreement. Martin is located at John Wayne Airport and is known in the aviation industry as a fixed-base operator.

The flight was an air-taxi passenger flight, operating under the provisions of 14 C.F.R. Part 135, and was transporting three corporate executives as passengers (Richard Snyder, Philip West and Jack Sims). The Westwind was flown by two professional pilots: Captain Stephen Barkin and Co-pilot John McDaniel. Mr. Barkin was employed by MAI and was acting within the scope and course of his employment. Mr. McDaniel was employed by Martin and was acting within the scope and course of his employment. In addition, both pilots held an airline transport pilot certificate, the highest pilot rating issued by the FAA, and were qualified to serve as Captain of the Westwind.

In the three months leading up to the crash, both Mr. Barkin and Mr. McDaniel had piloted the Westwind on numerous occasions into John Wayne Airport. Both pilots were very familiar with the Westwind aircraft and with John Wayne Airport.

[procedural history omitted]

III. DISCUSSION

A. LIABILITY OF FAA HEADQUARTERS

1. Discretionary Function Doctrine

The United States moves for summary adjudication of negligence claims against the Federal Aviation Administration ("FAA") Headquarters, arguing that those claims are barred by the discretionary function exception to the Federal Tort Claims Act. Pursuant to *Federal Rule of Civil Procedure 78* and Central District of California Local Civil Rule 7.11, the Court dispensed with formal oral argument on the motion, and the Court took the motion under submission. The Court and counsel discussed the motion, on the record, during a number of in-chambers conferences during trial. After careful review, considering all pertinent papers on file, the arguments, and materials presented by the parties, the Court hereby GRANTS summary adjudication in favor of the United States on claims of FAA Headquarters negligence. The Court finds that the discretionary function exception to the Federal Tort Claims Act shields the United States from liability for alleged negligence on behalf of FAA Headquarters.

The discretionary function exception is applicable only to the claims alleging FAA Headquarters' negligence. Pursuant to Central District Local Rule 9.8 and this Court's Order Re: Preparation for Pre-trial Conference, the Parties lodged a Joint Pre-trial Conference Order. The local rules state that the Pre-trial Conference Order shall control the subsequent course of the action and supersedes the pleadings. The first five claims in the Pre-trial Conference Order address negligence at the FAA Headquarters' level and state in pertinent part:

1. The FAA failed to warn the aviation community of known dangers of B-757 wake turbulence;

2. The FAA negligently failed to change the wake turbulence classification and separation standards as it committed to do in 1990;

3. The FAA failed to follow its commitment to update advisory and educational materials to alert pilots of the known dangers;

4. The FAA was negligent per se in violating *49 U.S.C. § 44505* and failing to develop systems and procedures to address the known hazards created by the B-757; and

5. The FAA was negligent per se in violating its own Order 1000.1A which required that the agency assume to implement safety improvements before incidents occur.

[Summary Judgment discussion omitted]

3. Discretionary Function Exception

The FTCA authorizes suits in tort against the federal government in cases where a private citizen would be liable for the same tortious conduct. *28 U.S.C. §§ 2671-2680*. Likewise, the FTCA grants jurisdiction for district courts to hear such suits. *28 U.S.C. § 1346*.

The discretionary function exception is a qualification on the federal government's general waiver of sovereign immunity for tort claims and is explicitly codified within the Federal Tort Claims Act ("FTCA"). The exception is an outgrowth of the doctrine of separation of powers, which is integral to the orderly operation of the federal government. *See Plaut v. Spendthrift Farm, Inc., 514 U.S. 211, 131 L. Ed. 2d 328, 115 S. Ct. 1447 (1995)*. In waiving sovereign immunity, Congress needed to guard against unnecessary judicial meddling in legislative and executive policy decisions. The discretionary function exception delineates the boundary between Congress' willingness to impose tort liability upon the United States and its desire to shield certain activities from private causes of action. *United States v. S.A. Empresa de Viacao aerea Rio Grandense (Varig Airlines), 467 U.S. 797, 808, 81 L. Ed. 2d 660, 104 S. Ct. 2755 (1984)*.

Pursuant to the exception, the government retains sovereign immunity from suit for "any claim . . . based upon the exercise or performance or the failure to exercise or perform a discretionary function or duty on the part of a federal agency or an employee of the Government, whether or not the discretion involved be abused." *28 U.S.C. § 2680(a)*.

a. Test for Applying the Discretionary Function Exception

The Supreme Court has formulated a two-step procedure to guide courts in determining whether conduct falls within the discretionary function exception. *Berkovitz v. United States, 486 U.S. 531, 536, 100 L. Ed. 2d 531, 108 S. Ct. 1954 (1988)*. First, a court must consider whether the challenged conduct is a matter of judgment or choice, or whether the conduct is specifically prescribed by a federal statute, regulation or policy. *Id.* The Ninth Circuit requires that a plaintiff show that the government violated a specific and mandatory standard for the discretionary function exception to be deemed inapplicable. *Kennewick Irrigation Dist. v. United States, 880 F.2d 1018, 1027 (9th Cir. 1989)*.

Second, if the challenged conduct involves a matter of judgment, a court "must determine whether that judgment is the kind that the discretionary function was designed to shield." *Id.* Under the second step of the procedure, the discretionary function exception protects from liability government decisions and actions based on decisions grounded in social, economic and political policy. *486 U.S. at 537*.

4. Claims For Alleged Headquarters FAA Negligence

Title *49 U.S.C. § 44505* requires the FAA administrator to maintain a "safe and efficient" air traffic control system. Plaintiffs assert that the FAA did not do so because of its failure to warn of B757 wake hazards and failure to modify Instrument Flight Rules ("IFR") approach separation standards. The first question is whether a statute or regulation mandates that the FAA give such a warning or make the proposed change to separation standards. *See Berkowitz, 486 U.S. at 536*.

At the time of the accident, the FAA had a specifically prescribed policy of providing wake vortex information and training, and policy for setting separation standards. However, no specific directive required the FAA to take the particular actions proposed by Plaintiffs. The mere presence of a statute will not deprive the federal agent of discretion and "[a] general statutory duty to promote safety would not be sufficient..." *Kennewick, 880 F.2d at 1026-27*. The statute cited by the Plaintiffs in the pretrial order is not a mandatory directive that commands specific conduct. *49 U.S.C. § 44505*. Likewise, the language of FAA Order 1000.1A sets forth general policy and an organizational mission statement, but does not mandate particularized conduct. The Supreme Court has held that the FAA's statutory duty to promote safety is broad and discretionary. *See Varig*, 467 U.S. at 808. Thus, the FAA's decision not to warn of B757 wake turbulence was a matter of judgment under the first step of *Berkowitz*.

Second, the Court must consider whether the decision not to warn was of the type grounded in social, political or economic policy. The issue is not whether the government agency or official actually balanced social, economic or political considerations, but whether the actions "are susceptible to policy analysis." *United States v. Gaubert, 499 U.S. 315, 326, 113 L. Ed. 2d 335, 111 S. Ct. 1267 (1991)*.

In the present case, Plaintiff contends that the FAA should have warned of the alleged extraordinary turbulence, educated air traffic controllers, and altered the IFR separation standards. The prioritization of aviation risks to emphasize and guard against is clearly the type of decision that is a matter of FAA policy. In the field of aviation there is an infinite number of potential risks. The FAA has the responsibility of determining how to allocate its resources to best operate the air traffic system. Furthermore, the FAA is charged with operating a system that is both "safe and efficient." *49 U.S.C. § 44505*.

It is theoretically and practically impossible for the FAA to maximize both safety and efficiency. The agency could maximize either one, or the other. In many circumstances, the interests of safety and efficiency conflict. Therefore, the Court construes the statute to require the FAA to balance these two goals. In deciding not to take the actions proposed in Plaintiff's five claims against Headquarters FAA, the FAA officials exercised discretion on a matter that is susceptible to policy analysis.

In *ARA Leisure Services v. United States, 831 F.2d 193 (9th Cir. 1987)*, a tour bus operated by a subsidiary of ARA Leisure Services went off a road in Denali National Park and rolled over, killing five passengers and injuring twenty-five others. In assessing the government's liability, the court found that the decision to design and construct the road without guardrails was grounded in social and political policy even though the rails served a safety function. *ARA Leisure Services, 831 F.2d at 195 (9th Cir. 1987)*. See *Dalehite v. United States, 346 U.S. 15, 38-42, 97 L. Ed. 1427, 73 S. Ct. 956 (1953)* (holding that alleged negligence in manufacture of fertilizer fell within exception because manufacturer followed specifications and plans adopted as policy matter with exercise of expert judgment). However, the Court did not agree that the failure to maintain the road in safe condition was a decision grounded in social, economic, or political policies since (1) there was no clear link between Park Service road policies and the condition of the road, and (2) Park Service maintenance work was not the kind of regulatory activity that the Supreme Court singled out in *Varig Airlines, 467 U.S. 797, 104 S. Ct. 2755, 81 L. Ed. 2d 660 (1984). ARA Leisure Services, 831 F.2d at 195*.

In this case, no such distinction can be made. All of the alleged omissions by Headquarters involved decisions that involve policy considerations. Unlike the situation in *ARA Leisure Services*, the question of what to do about possible B757 hazards necessarily involves both policy and safety in each discretionary decision. The road safety rails and road surface maintenance are distinct. Because of the high degree of integration and regulation in licensing, training, controlling traffic, and certifying aircraft, aviation safety decisions are not so easily isolated policy decisions that have political, economic, and social ramifications. Therefore, all of the claims against Headquarters involve decisions that are protected by the discretionary function exception.

Failure To Warn of Specific Known Dangers From B757 Wake Vortex

Plaintiff argues that the discretionary function exception to the FTCA does not apply because the failure to warn of B757 wake turbulence was a matter of safety, not a matter of policy. Plaintiff contends that the first claim against Headquarters, that the FAA failed to warn the aviation community of known dangers of B757 wake turbulence, is simply a matter of safety and is not shielded by the discretionary function exception.

The Ninth Circuit has held that a decision not to warn of a specific, known hazard for which the acting agency is responsible is not the kind of broader social, economic, or political policy decision that the discretionary function exception is intended to protect. *Sutton v. Earles, 26 F.3d 903, 910 (9th Cir. 1994)*. The FAA could not simply acknowledge a potential threat and do nothing more without impacting social, economic, and political policy concerns. Once the FAA warned of the threat the FAA would have to take some sort of corrective action. While the simple act of warning the aviation community may or may not fall within the exception, the ensuing corrective actions that would follow are necessarily policy decisions.

In *Sutton v. Earles* a pleasure boat collided with a Navy mooring buoy, killing a number of passengers and injuring others. The Navy failed to enforce statutory permit requirements for private vessels in the Navy waterway, failed to illuminate the hazardous buoy, and failed to post the speed limit. *Id.* The Ninth Circuit held that the omissions with regard to the speed limit and illumination were not protected by the discretionary function exception because they were not economic, social, or political policy decisions of the type that Congress intended to protect.

But the Ninth Circuit found that the Navy's decision not to dedicate resources to enforcing the permit requirement fell within the discretionary function exception. In addition to the economics of managing the permit system, the Navy would have faced the political fallout from forcing local boaters to comply. The court likened the Navy's decision to that of FAA's decision to conduct "spot-checks" instead of comprehensive checks when certifying aircraft. *Id. at 909* (citing *Varig Airlines, 467 U.S. 797 (1984)*). In *Varig Airlines*, the Supreme Court stated that the discretionary function exception "plainly was intended to encompass the discretionary acts of the Government acting in its role as regulator of the conduct of private individuals." *Id. at 813*. The Court added, "When an agency determines the extent to which it will supervise the safety procedures of private individuals, it is exercising discretionary regulatory authority of the most basic kind." *Id. at 819-20*.

When the allegations of failure to warn implicate the balancing of permissible social, economic, and political policies, the discretionary function exception applies. *See Dalehite v. United States, 346 U.S. 15,*

36, 97 L. Ed. 1427, 73 S. Ct. 956 (1953). The FAA's decision not to warn, or to merely wait to warn, of the alleged dangers of the B757 was inextricably linked to other matters of policy that involve social, economic, and political implications.

In *Sutton v. Earles*, the Navy could have posted the speed limit, and illuminated the buoy, without enforcing the permit requirement. However, in running a coherent air traffic system, the FAA's decision to acknowledge and warn of a hazard cannot be separated from the necessary remedial actions that must follow. The FAA could not simply hang a sign in the sky warning of potential B757 hazards. In different circumstances, failing to warn of a known dangerous condition is separate and distinct from failing to correct the known dangerous condition.

For instance, in *Faber v. United States, 56 F.3d 1122 (9th Cir. 1995)*, the plaintiff was rendered quadriplegic when he dove from a waterfall in the Coronado National Forest. Reversing the trial court's summary judgment for the United States based on the discretionary function exception, the Ninth Circuit held that "a failure to warn involves considerations of safety, not public policy." *Id. at 1125.* The court pointed out that the question of adequate warning does not typically relate to broad public policy. *Id.* In *Faber*, the Defendant Forest Service was subject to a "June 1986 plan [which] focused on solving specific known safety hazards through the implementation of three unambiguous directives." *Id. at 1127.* Under the plan, the Forest Service had no discretion to balance considerations. Under the plan, the Forest Service had posted signs to warn of some dangers, but failed to post a sign at the waterfall, which had been identified as a significant danger to park patrons.

The present case is unlike *Faber* in that *Faber* dealt with a natural condition, for which it would be impossible or absurd to take remedial action. Whereas, for the FAA, which tightly regulates the behavior of those operating in the air traffic system, the decision to warn is inseparable from the decision to remedy.

Based on the foregoing, The Court finds that the alleged negligent actions or inaction on the part of Headquarters FAA was a matter of judgment and a matter of policy such that the discretionary function exception shields the United States from liability. Accordingly, the Court hereby GRANTS summary adjudication in favor of the United States on the claims alleging Headquarters FAA negligence.

IV. LIABILITY OF AIR TRAFFIC CONTROLLERS

A. FINDINGS OF FACT

[discussion on aircraft speed omitted]

b. SEQUENCING

The Plaintiffs allege that the ATC were negligent in failing to sequence the United to follow the Westwind. However, the Court adopts the following findings of fact submitted by defendants, finding the ATC were not negligent in sequencing the Westwind to follow the United.

Mr. Whitaker was sequencing the Westwind behind United Airlines Flight 103, a Boeing 757. The United flight had been instructed to reduce its speed to 170 knots. The two airliners preceding

United 103 to Runway 19R (Alpha Air and Eagle Air) had also been instructed to reduce their speed to 170 knots. This reflects the principle of "compatible speeds," in which a series of aircraft are all slowed to the same speed, so that they may follow each other at a fixed spacing.

At 1728:55, Mr. Whitaker instructed United 103 to descend to 3,000 feet from 5,000 feet. As the United Captain testified, there was nothing unusual about the sequence of events on downwind whereby United 103 was first slowed and then descended. In fact, that is the preference of airline pilots, since it is difficult to execute both maneuvers simultaneously. In addition, if United 103 had been cleared to a lower altitude earlier, it would not necessarily have been any lower when intercepting the final approach course, since it is United's policy for "anti-noise" reasons to stay as high as possible while flying visual approaches.

At 1729:43, Mr. Whitaker instructed the Westwind to turn left to a 100-degree heading. The Westwind responded, "Okay, left turn to one zero zero, charlie kilo." This vector was designed to turn the Westwind away from United 103. This would maintain the applicable IFR separation distance of three miles between the Westwind and United 103 in case the Westwind was unable to accept the anticipated visual approach.

Mr. Whitaker's issuance of the 100-degree vector to the Westwind was proper. There was no requirement, as argued by plaintiffs, that Mr. Whitaker include in the vector a statement that this would be a "vector across the ILS final approach course." The Westwind was being vectored for a visual approach, and the statement at issue applies only to vectors for an ILS approach.

There was also no requirement for Mr. Whitaker to state the "purpose" of the vector at the time he issued the 100-degree vector to the Westwind pilots (e.g., "vectors for a visual approach to Runway 19-R,"). A vector normally includes a statement of its purpose, but in this case Mr. Whitaker was busy with several higher-priority duties. Mr. Whitaker gave the Westwind pilots their heading, issued important control communications to United 103 and an America West Boeing 737 (radio callsign "Cactus 667"), then turned back to the Westwind a fraction of a minute later to point out United 103 and issue the visual approach clearance.

Mr. Whitaker used good judgment in prioritizing his actions while sequencing several arriving airplanes, pursuant to the "duty priority" section of the ATC Handbook. There was no deviation from proper procedure in the issuance of the 100-degree vector.

United 103, under the command of by Captain Paul Martin, was flying a typical, normal visual approach to John Wayne Airport. This consisted of approaching from the southwest over the ocean, crossing the shoreline on "downwind" leg at 5000 feet, descending and slowing on downwind, and executing a visual approach. The headings, vectors, speed reductions, and altitudes of the flight of United 103 were all typical and normal. In good weather conditions, pilots always expect visual approaches. Almost every aircraft arriving at John Wayne Airport that night was issued a visual approach clearance.

Although the visual approach of United 103 was steep, it was neither abnormal nor dangerous. On a visual approach, aircraft

113

normally descend at angles significantly above the three degree "glideslope" that is part of the Instrument Landing System (ILS) approach used in bad weather. United Airlines' company policy (not required by the FARs) is for pilots to establish a "stabilized approach" by the time they reach 500 feet above ground level (approximately two miles from the runway). This does not require that they be on the three degree ILS glideslope, but that they be stabilized and not descending more than 1000 feet per minute.

The flight path of United 103 did not violate another controller's airspace without prior coordination, as argued by plaintiffs. United 103 descended through 3,200 feet to 3,000, while turning from base to final, in an area indicated on the "Tustin sector" airspace chart as having a maximum sector altitude of 3,000. The overlying airspace (4,000 feet and above) is normally the responsibility of the "Maverick" sector.

As Mr. Whitaker explained, he had been given control of Cactus 667, the America West 737 approaching from the east at 5,100 feet. According to the facility Standard Operating Practice ("SOP"), Mr. Whitaker in the Tustin sector automatically takes control of Cactus 667 for the descent, and thus controls all the airspace in front of Cactus 667, all the way to the ground. If other traffic had not been in the way, Mr. Whitaker could have cleared Cactus 667 for the visual approach from 5,100 feet, and Cactus 667 could have descended all the way down to the airport without any inter-sector coordination.

Because Mr. Whitaker had control of Cactus 667 for the descent, he also had control of the airspace in front of and below Cactus 667, which included the "3,200 to 3,000" flight path of United that is the subject of criticism. Therefore, Mr. Whitaker had control of this airspace, and he did not need any coordination for United 103 to fly its approach. Indeed, any such coordination would require Mr. Whitaker to coordinate with himself, an absurd proposition. Mr. Whitaker could also see on his radar screen that there was no conflicting traffic anywhere near United 103 in its descent.

c. INFORMATION PROVIDED TO PILOTS BY THE AIR TRAFFIC CONTROLLERS

The Plaintiffs allege the ATC were negligent by providing inaccurate/ incomplete information to the Westwind pilots with regard to the United and wake turbulence warnings. However, the Court adopts the following findings of fact submitted by defendants.

At 1730:05, the approach controller stated, "Westwind nine charlie kilo, you're following a United Boeing jet, on base, two o'clock, four miles, southeast bound, four thousand, descending." The Westwind responded, "In sight, charlie kilo." The purpose of this "point out" transmission was to tell the Westwind pilots where to look to see the United jet. It gave adequate information about the location, altitude, heading, and intentions of the United aircraft. The identification as a "United Boeing jet" was a correct and adequate description, pursuant to the ATC Handbook, which requires that an airliner be identified by "manufacturer's name [e.g. Boeing] or model." A description of the aircraft as a "Boeing" alone would have been adequate.

Mr. Whitaker went further in his description by adding that it was a "United" aircraft, and that it was a "jet" aircraft. This description would put a reasonable Westwind pilot on notice that he was following a much larger aircraft with a potentially dangerous wake.

Informing the Westwind pilots that the United Boeing jet was "on base" told them that United 103 was flying the "base leg" of the traffic pattern. This meant to the Westwind crew that the United Boeing Jet was flying roughly perpendicular to the Westwind's flight path and that it would turn right and proceed on final approach to land at John Wayne Airport.

The statement that the United Boeing Jet was on base "southeast bound" added further useful information. United 103 was in a turn to a heading of 130 degrees, which is southeast. It is standard practice for controllers, when a plane is turning, to point out that plane to other pilots by stating the heading "being turned to." Pilots and controllers alike understand this concept.

At 1730:12, Mr. Whitaker stated, "Westwind nine charlie kilo, follow that traffic, cleared visual approach, runway one niner right, reduce speed to follow, he's slowing through a hundred and seventy [knots]." This clearly meant that the United Boeing Jet would soon be *slower* than 170 knots. At 1730:18, the Westwind responded, "Okay, we're cleared for the visual, we'll follow that traffic at our three o'clock, and we're cleared for the visual, one niner right, slowin' to one seventy."

From an air traffic control perspective, Mr. Whitaker's "point out" of United and the subsequent visual approach clearance to the Westwind was proper and gave the pilots all necessary information. Mr. Whitaker had every reason to believe that the pilots would execute a normal visual approach thereafter, and advise him if there were any problems.

At the time Mr. Whitaker issued the Westwind its visual approach clearance, the Westwind was in an excellent position, from the controller's perspective, for the visual approach. The Westwind was approximately four miles from United; the Westwind had been assigned the same speed as United (170 knots); the Westwind was level at 4000 feet while United 103 was descending through 3,900 feet; and the Westwind was in a turn to 100 degrees (taking it away from United 103).

The pilots' acceptance of a visual approach clearance to "follow" a preceding aircraft constitutes an acknowledgment that the pilots will maintain a safe interval or spacing behind the preceding aircraft, and that they accept responsibility for their own wake turbulence separation. The acceptance of a visual approach clearance cancels all previous ATC assignments of heading, altitude and speed, transferring these elements to the control of the pilots. This shift in responsibility was testified to by both pilot witnesses and ATC witnesses.

The pilots' acceptance of a visual approach clearance also eliminates any responsibility of the controllers to apply in-flight IFR separation (in this case, the 3 mile minimum between the Westwind and United 103). The pilot on a visual approach may maneuver his aircraft at his discretion, following the preceding aircraft as closely as he deems appropriate in order to provide his own separation and wake turbulence avoidance.

A Mitre Corporation study of visual approaches nationwide revealed that pilots typically "close up" to a distance of between 1.9 and 2.1 miles behind the lead aircraft while flying visual approaches. In this context, the two-mile spacing that the Westwind pilots chose to provide for the last two minutes of the flight was absolutely normal and unremarkable from the controllers' perspective.

The only applicable ATC separation criterion for aircraft on a visual approach is "runway separation," applied by the tower controller. This provides that at the time the second aircraft is over the landing threshold, the first aircraft must have cleared the runway. If the runway is not clear, the tower must issue a "go around" instruction.

After accepting the visual approach clearance, it was the responsibility of the Westwind crew to maneuver their aircraft at their discretion for a safe approach and landing. A reasonable Westwind pilot, instructed to follow a "United Boeing Jet," would be very concerned about potential wake turbulence affecting his much smaller aircraft.

The description of United 103 as a "United Boeing Jet" was adequate to alert a reasonable Westwind pilot to the presence of major, hazardous wake turbulence. Whether the United was a 737, 757, 767, or 747, was irrelevant: each of these aircraft creates a wake that is very hazardous to a Westwind. A reasonable Westwind pilot would give a "wide berth" to avoid the "danger zone" behind and below the United jet.

Pilots are trained that wake turbulence can be a serious hazard to aircraft, especially to a small aircraft such as the Westwind in trail of a large aircraft such as an airliner. The characteristics of wake turbulence are described in detail in the AIM. The main duty of the Westwind crew while on the visual approach was to stay safely above the wake of the preceding United Boeing jet. To do this, pilots should visualize the location of the preceding aircraft's flight path, and ensure that their flight path remains above it.

One commonly used pilot technique to visualize flight paths was described by visibility and pilot expert Warren DeHaan. The technique involves drawing an imaginary line from your aircraft to the runway threshold, and looking to see whether the preceding aircraft is above or below this line. This can be done even before the preceding aircraft intercepts the final approach course (e.g., when the preceding aircraft is approaching on a base leg from the side). If the preceding aircraft is above the line at any time, pilots should be aware of potential danger, and apply appropriate wake avoidance techniques. Whatever technique the pilots may choose to apply, they are responsible for ensuring that their flight path remains safely above that of any preceding larger aircraft.

Among the options available to the Westwind pilots to avoid wake turbulence were: (1) maintaining adequate altitude, by not starting their descent from 4000 feet until they were safely above the flight path of United 103, then descending above its flight path and landing beyond its touchdown point; (2) continuing the turn to 100 degrees and then turning back towards the runway, and doing "s-turns" or other maneuvers to increase their spacing behind United 103; and (3) providing ample lateral separation from United 103. Preferably, all three techniques would be applied in combination. All of these options involve only normal, routine piloting maneuvers. If these measures did not suffice, the pilots had the option at any time of executing a "go around" and making a second approach.

In fact, the Westwind pilots did none of the above. Instead, (1) they descended precipitously (at a greater "rate of descent" than United 103) until they reached an altitude *under* its flight path; (2) they turned immediately straight towards the runway, following directly behind United 103 on the final approach course, instead of flying an offset path or "s-turning"; and (3) they did not slow expeditiously (by extending speed brakes, landing gear, and flaps). As pilot expert Joseph Lintzenich explained, the Westwind crew flew an approach profile that included all the elements necessary for a demonstration of how intentionally to encounter (rather than to avoid) the United's wake. They essentially did everything wrong.

Proper altitude control alone would have prevented a wake encounter, since wake turbulence only moves downward from the preceding aircraft, and staying above its flight path guarantees safety. In essence, the Westwind initially should have stayed level or descended gradually; then, when the Westwind was positioned safely well above United 103's flight path, the Westwind should have descended more steeply. Instead, the Westwind pilots did the opposite: they descended steeply at first, putting themselves below United 103's flight path, and then later descended more gradually.

Although plaintiff's visibility expert Dr. Arthur Ginsburg and pilot expert Donald Lykins testified that it was extremely difficult for the Westwind pilots to determine their flight path relative to United 103, these opinions are contradicted by the Westwind crew's own words.

The Westwind was equipped with a "cockpit voice recorder" which recorded the voices of the two pilots. A transcript of this recording (the "CVR transcript") was prepared by the National Transportation Safety Board.

The CVR Transcript reveals several comments indicating that the crew did observe United 103's flight path, and *did* realize that they were flying into danger:

-- "He's [United 103] pretty close" (1730:26);

-- "He's a little high too on the approach" (1731:53);

-- "I think we'll run this a dot high given where he's at . . . (1732:13)

-- "Yeah we might still get a little wake turbulence there" (1732:17)

-- "I don't know, looks kinda close" (1732:34)

-- "Yeah it's close but I think we'll be okay" (1732:35).

As intra-cockpit communications, none of these statements could be heard by the air traffic controllers. The crew did not communicate any of their doubts or concerns to the controllers. None of the controllers knew or had any reason to know of the flight path observations and concerns being discussed by the pilots.

Even the *last* of these communications ("Yeah it's close . . . .") was made approximately 43 seconds before the accident (1732:35 to 1733:18). Therefore, the Westwind crew had ample time to have executed a safe "go around," even at this late point, and thereby to have avoided the accident.

At 1730:42, the approach controller radioed: "Westwind nine charlie kilo, traffic you're following is at a hundred and fifty knots, you can s-turn as necessary to follow that traffic, contact John Wayne Tower, [frequency] one two six point eight." At 1730:49, the first officer responded: "Okay, we'll slow it up and do what we have to do, and we're switching [to the tower] . . . ." Ex. 316, at 25.

At no time did controller Whitaker believe there was any potential wake turbulence hazard for the Westwind. The ATC Handbook provides for the mandatory issuance of wake turbulence cautionary advisories only when the preceding aircraft is a "heavy" jet (which United 103 was not: both the United 757 and the Westwind were in the "large" category). For all non-heavy aircraft, the issuance of a wake turbulence cautionary advisory is appropriate only when, in the controller's opinion, wake turbulence may have an adverse effect on an aircraft. Mr. Whitaker had no reason to anticipate such a wake encounter, and he therefore did not issue a cautionary advisory. The radar targets displayed on Mr. Whitaker's radar screen always showed the Westwind at a higher altitude than United. Only the Westwind crew had the ability to compare the two flight paths; Mr. Whitaker did not.

Controller Whitaker relied on the Westwind pilots to follow the Federal Aviation Regulations (FARs), the guidance in the AIM, and good operating practices.

At 1731:04, the Westwind contacted the John Wayne Tower. On duty in the tower, manning the Local Control One position (combined with Local Control Two), was air traffic controller James Zimmerman. Mr. Zimmerman, a former United States Air Force Controller, was a full performance level controller responsible generally for issuing takeoff and landing clearances for all active runways, as well as taxiing ground traffic across those runways.

In its initial radio transmission to the tower, the Westwind pilots reported that they were "on a visual [approach] behind the, ah, I believe United." The local controller responded, "Westwind three zero nine charlie kilo, John Wayne Tower, [you're] number three behind the United, he's indicating thirty knots slower." The first officer responded, "Ah, we're slowing, three zero nine charlie kilo." There were no further communications between the Westwind and the Tower. At this time, the Westwind was at 3,400 feet and about 2.2 miles behind United 103 which was at about 2,800 feet.

At 1731:57, the Westwind pilot stated, "I'll slightly 'S' [-turn] back and forth." Despite this statement, any such "s-turns" were so minor as to be imperceptible on the radar track: the Westwind continued straight towards the runway.

At 1732:13, the captain stated, "I think I'll run this a dot high given where he's at John." The first officer responded, "You bet," in a concerned voice. Flying a "dot high" refers to flying the aircraft so that the aircraft's "glideslope" instrument depicts the aircraft's position as being one dot or gradation above the glideslope. This results in the aircraft flying an approach path that is a fraction of a degree above the standard three degree glideslope, for a height increase of approximately 30 feet per mile from the airport. Despite this statement, the Westwind descended slightly *below* the glideslope, and then moved back up to the glideslope.

The crew's reference to the "dot high" technique does reveal their strategy to deal with the anticipated wake encounter that they had been discussing. Unfortunately, they chose a flawed technique. If United 103 had been on an ILS approach, and therefore flying the three-degree ILS glideslope, the "dot high" technique could provide the Westwind with a tiny extra safety margin (the main margin would be provided by the fact that wakes descend at between 300 - 500 feet per minute). However, the "dot high" technique had no applicability to the Westwind's visual approach behind United 103 on its observed high visual approach descent.

Aircrafts on visual approaches do not fly on the three degree ILS glideslope, but normally approach at much steeper angles.

The accident occurred at approximately 1733:18. The last radar target on the Westwind was at 1733:07. At this time, the Westwind was at 1100 feet MSL, approximately 2.1 nautical miles behind United 103. The aircraft crashed approximately 3.2 nautical miles short of the runway.

Two minutes elapsed between the Westwind's last radio communication to the Tower and the accident (1731:13 to 1733:18). During this period, controller Zimmerman handled his traffic (both airborne and ground traffic), coordinated with other tower positions for runway crossings, monitored the airport and surrounding area visually, and consulted his BRITE radar scope as necessary.

Mr. Zimmerman did not observe anything unusual about the Westwind at any time before the accident. Tower controllers cannot determine flight paths of aircraft, but can only see a present-moment "snapshot" of where the aircraft is at the time of observation.

Determining the position and altitude of aircraft at night visually from the tower cab is extremely difficult. At times, this involves trying to discern whether one target is "one-quarter inch" higher than another when far away in the night sky. Moreover, the tower is offset to the side and located partly down the runway, further complicating the viewing task. This phenomenon was explained by optometrist Warren DeHaan, describing the difficult optical geometry involved in viewing aircraft lights from the tower at night. As Mr. Zimmerman periodically looked at the landing lights of various approaching aircraft, including United 103 and the Westwind, he did not observe anything out of the ordinary.

If Mr. Zimmerman had looked at the indicated altitudes of United 103 and the Westwind on his BRITE radar screen at any time that the aircraft were on his frequency, he would have observed that the Westwind was always above the altitude of United 103. This was true even though the actual flight path of the Westwind was significantly below that of United, as observed by the Westwind pilots.

Mr. Zimmerman testified that it would have been impossible for him to visualize and compare the flight paths of two aircraft such as the Westwind and United 103. To do that, he would have to observe the altitude of each aircraft as it passed a specific location, and remember that altitude for an extended period of time. This would be impossible to do while performing his other responsibilities at Local Control One and Two. At no time did controller Zimmerman believe there was any potential wake turbulence hazard for the Westwind.

The ATC Handbook provides for the mandatory issuance of wake turbulence cautionary advisories only when the preceding aircraft is a "heavy" jet (which United 103 was not). For all other aircraft, the issuance of an advisory is appropriate only when, in the controller's opinion, wake turbulence may have an adverse effect on an aircraft. Mr. Zimmerman had observed thousands of aircraft fly similar-appearing visual approaches over may years, without any incidents or complaints. Mr. Zimmerman had no reason to anticipate such a wake encounter from what he knew and observed of the flight of the Westwind, and he therefore did not issue a cautionary advisory, nor was one required.

Controller Zimmerman relied on the Westwind pilots to follow the Federal Aviation Regulations (FARs), the guidance in the AIM, and good operating practices. His one radio transmission to the Westwind provided it with all necessary and required information, and he had no reason to take any additional actions.

At no time did the controllers believe nor did they have reason to believe, that the Westwind was in a position of danger or potential danger. Moreover, at no time did either the crew of the Westwind request any assistance from ATC, report any problem or difficulty, or ask for any additional information or assistance.

For over two minutes before the accident, the Westwind pilots flew a fixed two-mile distance behind United 103. From the controllers' perspective, this spacing was normal and typical for aircraft flying a visual approach. The Westwind did not have to transition through the wake of United 103 in order to stay above its flight path on the final approach course.

Based on the ground tracks, airspeeds, and altitudes of the Westwind and United 103, and the positive radio transmissions from the Westwind pilots (*e.g.* "we'll slow it up and do what we have to do . . ."), the controllers had every right to believe, and did reasonably believe, that the crew of the Westwind would maintain a safe distance above and behind the flight path of United 103.

No controller violated or deviated from any mandatory ATC procedure, regulation, standard operating practice, letter of agreement, or other requirement. No action or inaction of any controller caused or contributed in any way to the accident.

The air traffic controllers who provided ATC services to the Westwind acted professionally, prudently, and in accordance with applicable manual provisions, practices, and procedures. Their actions in no way caused or contributed to this accident.

Robert Nietzel, plaintiffs' ATC expert on tower issues, testified to a personal practice unrelated to the conduct of a reasonable controller.

Mr. Nietzel testified that, when he was a controller, he always gave wake turbulence cautionary advisories to any aircraft following a Boeing 757. Mr. Nietzel admitted that this is not the standard provided for in the ATC Handbook. His unvarying issuance of advisories, whether or not required, sheds no light on the standards to be applied in a negligence case.

Plaintiffs' visibility expert, Arthur Ginsburg, Ph.D. testified that Mr. Whitaker should have issued to the Westwind the range and altitude of United 103 in half-mile increments. This absurd assertion would seem to require an individual air traffic controller for every airplane. Although plaintiffs' counsel promised to produce an expert witness who would testify that this was the standard, no such testimony was ever offered.

Plaintiff's ATC expert on radar issues was R.P. Burgess. Just before his retirement from the FAA, Mr. Burgess was suspended by the FAA for 12 days, removed from a supervisory position, and demoted. Mr. Burgess demonstrated his lack of credibility by opining, in response to an inquiry by the Court, that the Westwind pilots bore no responsibility for this accident, in the face of overwhelming evidence to the contrary.

B. CONCLUSIONS OF LAW

This is an action under the Federal Tort Claims Act (FTCA), *28 U.S.C. §§ 1346(b)*, 2671-2680. The Court adopts the following conclusions of law submitted by Defendants, finding the ATC were not negligent in this matter.

In this action, Plaintiffs allege operational error on the part of FAA air traffic controllers at the Ontario TRACON, Coast TRACON, and John Wayne Airport Control Tower, and further allege various errors on the part of FAA headquarters employees.

Specifically, Plaintiffs contend that the controllers were negligent in the sequencing and separation of the aircraft and in failing to provide necessary information and warnings to the Westwind crew including more detailed identification of the lead aircraft and wake turbulence warnings. The Court has subject matter jurisdiction over Plaintiffs' claims concerning controller negligence. *28 U.S.C. § 1346(b)*.

In this case, the substantive law of California controls with respect to claims of air traffic control negligence. *See 28 U.S.C. § 1346(b)*; *see also Richards v. United States, 369 U.S. 1, 7 L. Ed. 2d 492, 82 S. Ct. 585 (1962)*.

The essential elements of actionable negligence under California law are the following: (a) a legal duty to use due care; (b) a breach of such legal duty; and (c) the breach as the "substantial factor" of the resulting injury. *Sanbutch Properties, Inc. v. United States, 343 F. Supp. 611, 614 (N.D. Cal. 1972)*; *see also Rudelson v. United States, 431 F. Supp. 1101, 1107 (C.D. Cal. 1977), aff'd, 602 F.2d 1326 (9th Cir. 1979)*. Plaintiffs have the burden of proving each of these elements by a preponderance of the evidence. BAJI 2.60.

Plaintiffs have failed to meet their burden of proof in establishing ATC negligence by a preponderance of the evidence. "In airplane tort cases, general negligence law applies; however 'the standard of due care is concurrent, resting upon both the airplane pilot and ground aviation personnel. Both are responsible for safe conduct of flight.'" *Beech Aircraft Corp. v. United States, 51 F.3d 834, 838 (9th Cir. 1995)* (quoting *Spaulding v. United States, 455 F.2d 222, 226 (9th Cir. 1972))*. "While the duty in an airplane tort case is a concurrent one, resting on both air traffic controllers and pilots, 'under VFR conditions, ultimate responsibility for the safe operations of an aircraft rests with the pilot.'" *Beech Aircraft Corp., 51 F.3d at 840 (9th Cir. 1995)* (quoting *Hamilton v. United States, 497 F.2d 370, 374 (9th Cir. 1974))*.

An air taxi operator has a duty to exercise the highest degree of care in protecting his passengers from injury. *California Civil Code §§ 2100* and *2101*.

Violations of the Federal Aviation Regulations (FARs) constitute negligence as a matter of law. *Rudelson v. United States, 602 F.2d 1326 (9th Cir. 1979) United States v. Miller, 303 F.2d 703 (9th Cir. 1962), cert. denied, 371 U.S. 955, 9 L. Ed. 2d 502, 83 S. Ct. 507 (1963); Jenrette v. United States, 14 Avi. Cases (CCH) P17,798 (C.D. Cal. 1977); Hamilton v. United States, 343 F. Supp. 426 (N.D. Cal. 1971), aff'd, 497 F.2d 370 (9th Cir. 1974)*.

Under the FARs, the pilot in command is directly responsible for, and is the final authority as to the operation of his aircraft. *14 C.F.R. § 91.3(a); Hamilton v. United States, 497 F.2d 370, 374 (9th Cir. 1974), aff'g 343 F. Supp. 426 (N.D. Cal. 1971); Spaulding, 455 F.2d at 226.* The "ultimate decision is the pilot's, since . . . 'the crew knows the condition of the aircraft, its capabilities and must deal with the unusual and unexpected during flight.'" *Neff v. United States, 136 U.S. App. D.C. 273, 420 F.2d 115, 120 (D.C. Cir. 1969), cert. denied, 397 U.S. 1066, 25 L. Ed. 2d 687, 90 S. Ct. 1500 (1970)* (quoting the district court, *Neff v. United States, 282 F. Supp. 910 (D.D.C. 1968))*.

Pursuant to *14 C.F.R. § 91.3(a)*, the pilot has "final authority, even over air traffic controllers." *In re Aircrash Disaster at John F Kennedy Int'l Airport (JFK), 635 F.2d 67, 74 (2d Cir. 1980)*.

Under the FARs, pilots are prohibited from operating an aircraft in a careless or reckless manner so as to endanger the life or property of another. *14 C.F.R. § 91.9*.

The Airman's Information Manual (AIM) is an FAA publication whose purpose is to instruct pilots about basic flight information, air traffic control procedures, and general instructional information. Pilots must study and know the appropriate provisions of the AIM and FAA Advisory Circulars (ACs) pertaining to their flying activities. These documents are evidence of the standard of care among all pilots. *Dyer v. United States, 832 F.2d 1062, 1069 (9th Cir. 1987)*(citing *Muncie Aviation Corp. v. Party Doll Fleet, Inc., 519 F.2d 1178, 1180 (5th Cir. 1975))*; *In re Aircrash Disaster at JFK, 635 F.2d 67 at 75-76*.

The AIM states, in part: "When visually following a preceding aircraft, acceptance of the visual approach clearance constitutes acceptance of pilot responsibility for maintaining a safe approach interval and adequate wake turbulence separation." "A visual approach is not an Instrument Approach Procedure." "Visual approaches are initiated by ATC to reduce pilot/controller workload and expedite traffic by shortening flight paths to the airport." This paragraph also states that, "It is the pilot's responsibility to advise ATC as soon as possible if a visual approach is not desired."

The AIM further informs pilots that, "Acceptance of a visual approach clearance to visually follow a preceding aircraft is pilot acknowledgment that he will establish a safe landing interval behind the preceding aircraft if so cleared, and that he accepts responsibility for his own wake turbulence separation."

There are also numerous warnings and illustrations published in the AIM regarding the hazards of wake turbulence, including the following: "It is more difficult for aircraft with short wingspan (relative to the generating aircraft) to counter imposed roll induced by vortex flow. Pilots of short span aircraft, even of the high performance type, must be especially alert to vortex encounters." "The wake of larger aircraft requires the respect of all pilots. "Serious and even fatal GA [General Aviation] accidents are not uncommon." "AVOID THE AREA BELOW AND BEHIND THE GENERATING AIRCRAFT, ESPECIALLY AT LOW ALTITUDE WHERE EVEN A MOMENTARY WAKE ENCOUNTER COULD BE HAZARDOUS. Whether or not a "caution-wake turbulence" warning has been given, "THE PILOT IS EXPECTED TO ADJUST HIS OR HER OPERATIONS AND FLIGHT PATH AS NECESSARY TO PRECLUDE SERIOUS WAKE ENCOUNTERS."

The AIM also recommends vortex avoidance procedures for various situations. For example, "Landing behind a larger aircraft - same runway: Stay at or above the larger aircraft's final approach flight path - note its touchdown point - land beyond it." In addition, the AIM informs pilots that "the flight disciplines necessary to ensure vortex avoidance during VFR operations must be exercised by the pilot. Vortex visualization and avoidance procedures should be exercised by the pilot using the same degree of concern as in collision avoidance."

The information contained in the AIM, particularly the section concerning the nature, behavior, and danger of wake turbulence, is chargeable to all certified pilots and is evidence of the standard of care for determining whether they exercise proper wake turbulence avoidance procedures. *Dyer, 832 F.2d at 1069*; *Muncie Aviation Corp., 519 F.2d at 1181*; *Thinguldstad v. United States, 343 F. Supp. 551* (S.D. Ohio, 1972).

Professional flight crews are "charged with that knowledge which in the exercise of the highest degree of care they should have known." *American Airlines v. United States, 418 F.2d 180, 193 (5th Cir. 1969)*.

Under Visual Flight Rule (VFR) weather conditions, the pilot's duty to see and avoid other aircraft also includes the requirement that he exercise the same degree of caution to visualize and avoid wake turbulence encounters with other aircraft. 14 C.F.R. § 91.65(a); 14 C.F.R. § 91.67(a); Ex. 9001; *Wasilko v. United States, 300 F. Supp. 573 (N.D. Ohio 1967), aff'd, 412 F.2d 859 (6th Cir. 1969)*.

In clear weather conditions the pilots, not the air traffic controllers, bear the primary responsibility to visualize and avoid the hazard of wake turbulence. *Kack v. United States, 570 F.2d 754, 756 (8th Cir. 1978), aff'g, Kack v. United States, 432 F. Supp. 633 (D. Minn. 1977)*; *See* Airman's Information Manual, Para. 7-45, Ex. 9001.

Pilots have a duty to be aware of hazards of wake turbulence; to be aware of the procedures for avoidance of wake turbulence; to obtain all available information concerning the flight, including weather and wind information; to comply with authorizations, clearances, and instructions; and to operate the aircraft in a careful manner so as not to endanger the life and property of another. *Sanbutch Properties, Inc. v. United States, 343 F. Supp. at 615.*

Air traffic controllers are held to a standard of ordinary care with respect to their responsibilities, which are concurrent with the duties of pilots. *Spaulding, 455 F.2d at 226.* "It is not enough to say that the pilot and controller are concurrently responsible (for accomplishing a safe flight), they must also be concurrently liable, and one does not necessarily follow the other even if both are found negligent." *Tinkler v. United States, 700 F. Supp. 1067, 1074 (D. Kan. 1988), aff'd, 982 F.2d 1456 (10th Cir. 1992)* (quoting *Roland v. United States, 463 F. Supp. 852, 854 (S.D. Ind. 1978)); see also In re AirCrash Disaster at Boston, Massachusetts, 412 F. Supp. 959, 989 (D. Mass. 1976), aff'd sub nom. Delta Airlines, Inc. v. United States, 561 F.2d 381 (1st Cir. 1977), cert. denied, 434 U.S. 1064, 55 L. Ed. 2d 764, 98 S. Ct. 1238 (1978)* ("pilot's knowledge of his own, his crew's, and his aircraft's capabilities and limitations, is of preeminent importance in this cooperative situation. None of these matters can be known by ATC.").

The basic duties and responsibilities of controllers are set forth in the Air Traffic Control Handbook, FAA Order 7110.65H (the ATC Handbook). This is an internal agency document, and although FAA employees must be familiar with the provisions of the manual, the provisions of the Handbook are not statutes or regulations, and it does not necessarily follow that any deviation from these provisions constitutes negligence under the Federal Tort Claims Act. *Baker v. United States, 417 F. Supp. 471, 485 (W.D. Wash. 1975).*

The ATC Handbook provides guidance and procedures for controllers with respect to "visual approaches." Specifically, the ATC Handbook provides "[a] visual approach is an authorization for an aircraft on an IFR flight plan to proceed visually to the airport of intended landing; it is not an instrument approach procedure." In addition, the ATC Handbook states in relevant part that, "A vector for a visual approach may be initiated if the reported ceiling at the airport of intended landing is at least 500 feet above the MVA/MIA [minimum vectoring altitude/minimum IFR altitude] and the visibility is three miles or more." Finally, the ATC Handbook advises controllers to (1) "resolve potential conflicts with other aircraft, and ensure that the weather conditions at the airport are VFR" before issuing a clearance for a visual approach; and to (2) clear an aircraft for a visual approach when "the aircraft is to follow a preceding aircraft and the pilot reports the preceding aircraft in sight and is instructed to follow it."

The Handbook states in relevant part, "Issue cautionary information to any aircraft if in your opinion wake turbulence may have an adverse effect on it." "Because wake turbulence is unpredictable, the controller is *not responsible* for anticipating its existence or effect."

In accordance with the Handbook provisions, the first priority of an air traffic controller is separation of aircraft for collision avoidance. *In re Air Crash at Dallas/Fort Worth on August 2, 1985, 720 F. Supp. 1258, 1288 (N.D. Tex. 1981), aff'd, 919 F.2d 1079 (5th Cir.), cert. denied sub nom., Connors v. United States, 502 U.S. 899, 116 L. Ed. 2d 228, 112 S. Ct. 276 (1991).* The provision of information and warnings specified in the Handbook, such as wake turbulence advisories, is secondary to the primary duty of separation. The air traffic controller must decide, in his judgment, whether other duties permit the performance of these services. *Id.*

In addition, there is "no duty to warn a pilot of a condition of which he would ordinarily know or of which he should be aware based on his training, experience and personal observations." *Beech Aircraft Corp.*, 51 F.3d at 840 (citing *Neff v. United States 136 U.S. App. D.C. 273, 420 F.2d 115, 120-22 (D.C. Cir.), cert. denied, 397 U.S. 1066, 25 L. Ed. 2d 687, 90 S. Ct. 1500 (1969)). See also Pan American World Airways v. Port Authority of New York and New Jersey, 787 F. Supp. 312, 319 (S.D.N.Y.), rev'd on other grounds, 995 F.2d 5 (2d Cir. 1993); Crossman v. United States, 378 F. Supp. 1312, 1318 (D. Ore. 1974).*

Air traffic controllers may rely on the assumption that a pilot knows and will abide by all applicable FARs. This includes information contained in the Airman's Information Manual, FAA Advisory Circulars, and aeronautical charts. *Hensley v. United States, 728 F. Supp. 716, 722 (S.D. Fla. 1989); Associated Aviation Underwriters v. United States, 462 F. Supp. 674, 680 (N.D. Tex. 1978); In re Air Disaster at New Orleans (Moisant Field), Louisiana on March 20, 1969, 422 F. Supp. 1166, 1177-78 (W.D. Tenn.), aff'd, 544 F.2d 270 (6th Cir. 1976).*

"Moreover 'controllers are not required to foresee or anticipate the unlawful, negligent or grossly negligent acts of pilots.'" *Beech Aircraft Corp.*, 51 F.3d at 840 (quoting *In re Air Crash at Dallas/Ft. Worth Airport, 720 F. Supp. 1258, 1290 (N.D. Tex. 1989), aff'd, 919 F.2d 1079 (5th Cir.), cert. denied sub nom., Connors v. United States, 502 U.S. 899, 116 L. Ed. 2d 228, 112 S. Ct. 276 (1991)).*

Under visual meteorological conditions, "air traffic controllers expect, and have the right to expect, pilots to maintain their own in-flight separation from other aircraft and from wake turbulence." *Jenrette*, 14 Avi. Cases (CCH) at P18,000.

"It has been specifically held as a matter of law that a reasonable pilot, upon being informed that he was to follow a large jet on approach, would fly at an altitude above the descent path of the preceding airplane and controllers have a right to assume pilots will so fly." *Id.* at 18,002 (citing *Richardson v. United States, 372 F. Supp. 921 (N.D. Cal. 1974); Sanbutch Properties, 343 F. Supp. at 616.*

"Air traffic controllers have a right to expect that pilots have been trained to maintain a flight path above that of the preceding aircraft and to touch down at a point beyond the point of touchdown of the preceding aircraft." *Jenrette* at 18,000.

"Air traffic controllers cannot be expected, under VFR circumstances where the responsibility for in-flight separation belongs to the pilot and where controllers' visibility is limited by the capability of the human visual system to make distance and height judgments, to substitute their judgment for that of the pilot who is in a far superior position to make such judgments." *Id.*

"The failure to provide a wake turbulence advisory cannot be considered the proximate cause of an accident where it results from wake turbulence where the pilot knew or should have known the hazards and the procedures designed to avoid the wake turbulence." *Id.* at 17,802-17,803.

The *Jenrette* case was cited with approval by the Ninth Circuit in *Dyer, 832 F.2d at 1070.* In *Dyer,* a small aircraft crashed during an approach following the landing of a large Coast Guard helicopter. In affirming the District Court's finding that the Coast Guard's conduct was not a substantial factor in the crash of the small plane, the Ninth Circuit stated, "Even at controlled airports where air traffic controllers help direct pilots, the primary and ultimate responsibility for safe aircraft operation under visual flight rules, including wake turbulence avoidance, rests with the pilot." *Id.*, (citing *Miller v. United States, 587 F.2d 991, 995-96 (9th Cir. 1978)*; *Kack, 570 F.2d at 755-56* (controller had no special duty to warn pilot of his precariously low altitude because pilot, even though a student, had primary responsibility to avoid wake turbulence); *Jenrette,* 14 Avi. Cases (CCH) at P18,001). "The responsibility for avoiding wake turbulence is placed on the pilot under visual flight rules because the pilot is in the best position to visualize the location of the vortex trail behind large aircraft and to do whatever is necessary to avoid the hazard." *Dyer at 1070* (citing *N-500L Cases, 517 F. Supp. 825, 833 (D.P.R. 1981), aff'd, 691 F.2d 15 (1st Cir. 1982)).

"The function of avoiding wake turbulence in VFR conditions must rest with the pilot, as he is the person who can best do something about it and is in complete control of his aircraft; he is in the best position to observe the aircraft landing before him, as he has a better view of the runways, and can better correlate the totality of events with his situation." *Sanbutch Properties, 343 F. Supp. at 615.*

The Handbook does not impose an absolute duty to advise a pilot of wake turbulence when, in the controller's judgment, there was no basis for so doing. *Id.*

The failure of air traffic controllers to give a wake turbulence advisory or warning "where the air traffic personnel are fully engaged in performance of higher priority duties, cannot be the proximate cause of an accident resulting from a wake turbulence encounter where the pilot knew, or should have known, of hazards and avoidance procedures, and was on notice and aware of presence and proximity of generating aircraft." *Id.*

The AIM informs pilots that,

> Many towers are equipped with a tower radar display. The radar uses are intended to enhance the effectiveness and efficiency of the local control, or tower, position. They are not intended to provide radar services or benefits to pilots except as they may accrue through a more efficient tower operation.

In addition, this AIM contains the following notation:

> There is no controller requirement to maintain constant radar identification. In fact, such a requirement could compromise the local controller's ability to visually scan the airport and local area to meet FAA

responsibilities to the aircraft operating on the runways and within the CLASS B, C, and D SURFACE AREA. Normally, pilots will not be advised of being in radar contact since that continued status cannot be guaranteed and since the purpose of radar identification is not to establish a link for the provision of radar services.

The AIM advises pilots in capital letters:

WHEN IN COMMUNICATION WITH A TOWER CONTROLLER WHO MAY HAVE RADAR AVAILABLE, DO NOT ASSUME THAT CONSTANT RADAR MONITORING AND COMPLETE ATC SERVICES ARE BEING PROVIDED.

A controller must give his attention to all aircraft in his control area and should not focus or concentrate on one area to the exclusion of others. *Hamilton, 497 F.2d at 376.*

While the approach controller was responsible for sequencing the Westwind into the traffic pattern, the flight crew of The Westwind was responsible for selecting its own altitude, flight path, rate of descent, speed and distance behind the aircraft it was instructed to follow. *See Richardson, 372 F. Supp. at 927 (citing United States v. Wiener, 335 F.2d 379 (9th Cir. 1964), cert. denied, 379 U.S. 951, 85 S. Ct. 452, 13 L. Ed. 2d 549 (1965); United States v. Miller, 303 F.2d 703 (9th Cir. 1962), cert. denied, 371 U.S. 955, 9 L. Ed. 2d 502, 83 S. Ct. 507 (1963).*

The failure of the Westwind flight crew to maintain proper in-trail wake turbulence separation and avoidance "is an unforeseeable fact for which the [controllers] cannot be charged with responsibility." *See Richardson, 372 F. Supp. at 927.* To avoid wake turbulence, pilots are expected to maintain a flight path at or above that of the preceding aircraft, regardless of its make or model.

Whether the Westwind pilots knew they were following a Boeing 757 is immaterial; they acknowledged they were following a commercial airliner; specifically, a "United Boeing Jet." As experienced pilots, in visual contact with the United airliner, the Westwind crew either knew or should have known they (1) were following a larger aircraft; and (2) were required to fly at or above its final approach flight path. AIM para. 7-46(1).

In conclusion, this Court cannot find that the Defendant was negligent or that the conduct of the Westwind flight crew, in failing to avoid the wake turbulence from United 103, was reasonably foreseeable by *any* employee of the Defendant, or that any such employee violated a duty owed to Plaintiffs, or that any such employee's conduct was a factor, let alone a substantial contributing factor, in the accident.

[conclusion omitted]

EDWARD CHRISTENSEN, ET AL. v. HARRIS COUNTY, ET AL.

SUPREME COURT OF THE UNITED STATES

529 U.S. 576

May, 2000

JUSTICE THOMAS delivered the opinion of the Court.

Under the Fair Labor Standards Act of 1938 (FLSA), 52 Stat. 1060, as amended, *29 U.S.C. § 201 et seq. (1994 ed. and Supp. III),* States and their political subdivisions may compensate their employees for overtime by granting them compensatory time or "comp time," which entitles them to take time off work with full pay. *§ 207(o).* If the employees do not use their accumulated compensatory time, the employer is obligated to pay cash compensation under certain circumstances. *§§ 207(o)(3)-(4).* Fearing the fiscal consequences of having to pay for accrued compensatory time, Harris County adopted a policy requiring its employees to schedule time off in order to reduce the amount of accrued compensatory time. Employees of the Harris County Sheriff's Department sued, claiming that the FLSA prohibits such a policy. The Court of Appeals rejected their claim. Finding that nothing in the FLSA or its implementing regulations prohibits an employer from compelling the use of compensatory time, we affirm.

I

A

[a discussion of the Fair Labor Standards Act is omitted].

B

Petitioners are 127 deputy sheriffs employed by respondents Harris County, Texas, and its sheriff, Tommy B. Thomas (collectively, Harris County). It is undisputed that each of the petitioners individually agreed to accept compensatory time, in lieu of cash, as compensation for overtime.

As petitioners accumulated compensatory time, Harris County became concerned that it lacked the resources to pay monetary compensation to employees who worked overtime after reaching the statutory cap on compensatory time accrual and to employees who left their jobs with sizable reserves of accrued time. As a result, the county began looking for a way to reduce accumulated compensatory time. It wrote to the United States Department of Labor's Wage and Hour Division, asking "whether the Sheriff may schedule non-exempt employees to use or take compensatory time." Brief for Petitioners 18-19. The Acting Administrator of the Division replied:

"It is our position that a public employer may schedule its nonexempt employees to use their accrued FLSA compensatory time as directed if the prior agreement specifically provides such a provision . . . .

"Absent such an agreement, it is our position that neither the statute nor the regulations permit an employer to require an employee to use accrued compensatory time." Opinion Letter from Dept. of

Labor, Wage and Hour Div. (Sept. 14, 1992), 1992 WL 845100 (Opinion Letter).

After receiving the letter, Harris County implemented a policy under which the employees' supervisor sets a maximum number of compensatory hours that may be accumulated. When an employee's stock of hours approaches that maximum, the employee is advised of the maximum and is asked to take steps to reduce accumulated compensatory time. If the employee does not do so voluntarily, a supervisor may order the employee to use his compensatory time at specified times.

Petitioners sued, claiming that the county's policy violates the FLSA because § 207(o)(5) -- which requires that an employer reasonably accommodate employee requests to use compensatory time -- provides the exclusive means of utilizing accrued time in the absence of an agreement or understanding permitting some other method. The District Court agreed, granting summary judgment for petitioners and entering a declaratory judgment that the county's policy violated the FLSA. *Moreau v. Harris County, 945 F. Supp. 1067 (SD Tex. 1996).* The Court of Appeals for the Fifth Circuit reversed, holding that the FLSA did not speak to the issue and thus did not prohibit the county from implementing its compensatory time policy. *Moreau v. Harris County, 158 F.3d 241 (1998).* Judge Dennis concurred in part and dissented in part, concluding that the employer could not compel the employee to use compensatory time unless the employee agreed to such an arrangement in advance. *Id. at 247-251.* We granted certiorari because the Courts of Appeals are divided on the issue. 528 U.S. (1999).

II

Both parties, and the United States as *amicus curiae*, concede that nothing in the FLSA expressly prohibits a State or subdivision thereof from compelling employees to utilize accrued compensatory time. Petitioners and the United States, however, contend that the FLSA implicitly prohibits such a practice in the absence of an agreement or understanding authorizing compelled use. [3] Title *29 U.S.C. § 207(o)(5)* provides:

"An employee . . .

"(A) who has accrued compensatory time off . . . , and

"(B) who has requested the use of such compensatory time,

"shall be permitted by the employee's employer to use such time within a reasonable period after making the request if the use of the compensatory time does not unduly disrupt the operations of the public agency."

[discussion of the Fair Labor Standards Act omitted]

At bottom, we think the better reading of § 207(o)(5) is that it imposes a restriction upon an employer's efforts to *prohibit* the use of compensatory time when employees request to do so; that provision says nothing about restricting an employer's efforts to *require* employees to use compensatory time. Because the statute is silent on this issue and because Harris County's policy is entirely compatible

129

with *§ 207(o)(5)*, petitioners cannot, as they are required to do by *29 U.S.C. § 216(b)*, prove that Harris County has violated *§ 207*.

Our interpretation of *§ 207(o)(5)* -- one that does not prohibit employers from forcing employees to use compensatory time -- finds support in two other features of the FLSA. First, employers remain free under the FLSA to decrease the number of hours that employees work. An employer may tell the employee to take off an afternoon, a day, or even an entire week. Cf. *Barrentine v. Arkansas-Best Freight System, Inc., 450 U.S. 728, 739, 67 L. Ed. 2d 641, 101 S. Ct. 1437 (1981)* ("The FLSA was designed . . . to ensure that each employee covered by the Act . . . would be protected from the evil of overwork . . ." (internal quotation marks and emphasis omitted)). Second, the FLSA explicitly permits an employer to cash out accumulated compensatory time by paying the employee his regular hourly wage for each hour accrued. *§ 207(o)(3)(B); 29 CFR § 553.27(a) (1999)*. Thus, under the FLSA an employer is free to require an employee to take time off work, and an employer is also free to use the money it would have paid in wages to cash out accrued compensatory time. The compelled use of compensatory time challenged in this case merely involves doing both of these steps at once. It would make little sense to interpret *§ 207(o)(5)* to make the combination of the two steps unlawful when each independently is lawful.

III

In an attempt to avoid the conclusion that the FLSA does not prohibit compelled use of compensatory time, petitioners and the United States contend that we should defer to the Department of Labor's opinion letter, which takes the position that an employer may compel the use of compensatory time only if the employee has agreed in advance to such a practice. Specifically, they argue that the agency opinion letter is entitled to deference under our decision in *Chevron U.S.A. Inc. v. Natural Resources Defense Council, Inc., 467 U.S. 837, 81 L. Ed. 2d 694, 104 S. Ct. 2778 (1984)*. In *Chevron*, we held that a court must give effect to an agency's regulation containing a reasonable interpretation of an ambiguous statute. *Id. at 842-844*.

Here, however, we confront an interpretation contained in an opinion letter, not one arrived at after, for example, a formal adjudication or notice-and-comment rulemaking. Interpretations such as those in opinion letters -- like interpretations contained in policy statements, agency manuals, and enforcement guidelines, all of which lack the force of law -- do not warrant *Chevron*-style deference. [citations omitted]. As explained above, we find unpersuasive the agency's interpretation of the statute at issue in this case.

Of course, the framework of deference set forth in *Chevron* does apply to an agency interpretation contained in a regulation. But in this case the Department of Labor's regulation does not address the issue of compelled compensatory time. The regulation provides only that "the agreement or understanding [between the employer and employee] *may* include other provisions governing the preservation, use, or cashing out of compensatory time so long as these provisions are consistent with *[§ 207(o)]*." *29 CFR § 553.23(a)(2) (1999)* (emphasis added). Nothing in the regulation even arguably requires that an employer's compelled use policy *must* be included in an agreement. The text of the regulation itself indicates that its command is permissive, not mandatory.

Seeking to overcome the regulation's obvious meaning, the United States asserts that the agency's opinion letter interpreting the regulation should be given deference under our decision in *Auer v. Robbins, 519 U.S. 452, 137 L. Ed. 2d 79, 117 S. Ct. 905 (1997)*. In *Auer*, we held that an agency's interpretation of its own regulation is entitled to deference. *Id. at 461*. See also *Bowles v. Seminole Rock & Sand Co., 325 U.S. 410, 89 L. Ed. 1700, 65 S. Ct. 1215 (1945)*. But *Auer* deference is warranted only when the language of the regulation is ambiguous. The regulation in this case, however, is not ambiguous -- it is plainly permissive. To defer to the agency's position would be to permit the agency, under the guise of interpreting a regulation, to create *de facto* a new regulation. Because the regulation is not ambiguous on the issue of compelled compensatory time, *Auer* deference is unwarranted.

As we have noted, no relevant statutory provision expressly or implicitly prohibits Harris County from pursuing its policy of forcing employees to utilize their compensatory time. In its opinion letter siding with the petitioners, the Department of Labor opined that "it is our position that neither the statute nor the regulations *permit* an employer to require an employee to use accrued compensatory time." Opinion Letter (emphasis added). But this view is exactly backwards. Unless the FLSA *prohibits* respondents from adopting its policy, petitioners cannot show that Harris County has violated the FLSA. And the FLSA contains no such prohibition. The judgment of the Court of Appeals is affirmed.

It is so ordered.

[concurrence and dissent omitted]

B. *Environmental Issues*

SANTA MONICA AIRPORT ASSOCIATION, v. CITY OF SANTA MONICA.

UNITED STATES COURT OF APPEALS, NINTH CIRCUIT

659 F.2d 100

April, 1981

OPINION

A coalition of airport users challenged the City of Santa Monica's airport noise reduction ordinances in the district court. They appeal from the resulting judgment which denied most of the relief they were seeking.

After an increase in the use of jet aircraft and helicopters, the City of Santa Monica enacted several ordinances to reduce noise at the city-owned and operated airport. Section 10101 imposed a night curfew on takeoffs and landings; § 10111C prohibited certain low aircraft approaches on weekends; § 10105A2 prohibited helicopter flight training; § 10105B established a maximum single event noise exposure level (SENEL) of 100 dB. ; § 10105A1 prohibited jets at the airport and § 10105E provided a fine for any jet landings or takeoffs.

Appellants asserted the invalidity, on various grounds, of all of the above regulations. In a well-reasoned opinion, the district court found that the ordinances: (1) were not preempted by federal law; (2) did not violate grant agreements between the FAA and Santa Monica or breach any airport lease; (3) did not violate the Federal Aviation Act; and (4) that the first four ordinances did not violate the Equal Protection or *Commerce Clauses*. The district court did find, however, that the categorical ban on all jet aircraft and the penalty statute violated the Equal Protection and *Commerce Clauses*. We affirm.

Appellants contend that the ordinances in question are preempted by the comprehensive nature of federal control of civil aviation, and cite *City of Burbank v. Lockheed Air Terminal, 411 U.S. 624, 93 S. Ct. 1854, 36 L. Ed. 2d 547 (1973)*. In that case, the Supreme Court struck down on preemption grounds Burbank's jet curfew ordinance as an unauthorized extension of state police power into the federal domain. But in doing so, the court expressly left open the question of "what limits, if any, apply to a municipality as a proprietor ...." should it decide to enact similar ordinances. *411 U.S. at 635-36 n.14, 93 S. Ct. at 1860-61 n.14*. The caveat may have been thought necessary in view of the Court's earlier decision in *Griggs v. Allegheny County, 369 U.S. 84, 82 S. Ct. 531, 7 L. Ed. 2d 585*, reh. denied, *369 U.S. 857, 82 S. Ct. 931, 8 L. Ed. 2d 16 (1962)*, which held municipal airport owners liable for *Fifth Amendment* "takings" of private property resulting from unreasonable airport use with respect to neighboring lands. Municipal airport owners needed some means of limiting their liability under Griggs. Environmental quality control ordinances by municipal airport proprietors are among those means.

Appellants argue that Burbank's footnote 14 did not endorse and should not be relied upon to create a municipal-proprietor exemption from federal preemption. They contend that a municipal-proprietor exemption would render Burbank meaningless. Their argument, while overstated, has some superficial appeal. Nevertheless, the argument is not persuasive.

The Supreme Court in Burbank instructed us to "start with the assumption that the historic police powers of the states were not to be superseded by the Federal Act unless that was the clear and manifest purpose of Congress.'" *411 U.S. at 633, 93 S. Ct. at 1859*, quoting from *Rice v. Santa Fe Elevator Corp., 331 U.S. 218, 230, 67 S. Ct. 1146, 1152, 91 L. Ed. 1447 (1947)*.

The Second Circuit in *British Airways Bd. v. Port Authority of New York, 558 F.2d 75* (2nd Cir.), on remand, *437 F. Supp. 804*, mod., *564 F.2d 1002 (1977)*, and the district court in *National Aviation v. City of Hayward, Cal., 418 F. Supp. 417 (N.D.Cal.1976)*, marshal impressive excerpts from the legislative history of the Federal Aviation Acts which show that, in light of Griggs, Congress was not preempting a municipal airport proprietor's right to enact noise ordinances. See 558 F.2d at 83-84, 418 F. Supp. at 420-422. [4] But see *San Diego Etc. v. Super. Ct. for Cty. of San Diego, 67 Cal.App.3d 361, 367, 136 Cal.Rptr. 557, 561* (4th Dist.), cert. denied, *434 U.S. 859, 98 S. Ct. 184, 54 L. Ed. 2d 132 (1977)*. Because Congressional intent not to preempt all regulation by municipal-proprietors is clear, the district court correctly concluded that these ordinances were not preempted.

Appellants make two additional preemption arguments. They argue that even if there is a municipal proprietor exception for noise regulations, the 100 dB SENEL regulation is preempted. First, they contend that Santa Monica's SENEL regulation is invalid because it frustrates the United States' exclusive control over aircraft flight and management. They argue that because this SENEL measures and limits the noise created by planes taking off and landing, it is preempted by federal supremacy.

The district court rejected this argument. It concluded that SENEL was not a regulation of airspace or aircraft in flight, but instead a reasonable regulation by an airport proprietor of noise made by aircraft. The court said:

> "(A) municipal operator of an airport in my view can govern the noise levels of planes which have taken off from it both before and for a reasonable distance after the wheels have left the ground ...."

We agree.

We have held that the power of a municipal proprietor to regulate the use of its airport is not preempted by federal legislation. We further hold that the municipal proprietor exception allows the City to choose the SENEL method involved here, despite the SENEL's monitoring of noise created by planes as they are ascending or descending.

The legislative history shows that Congress intended that municipal proprietors enact reasonable regulations to establish acceptable noise levels for airfields and their environs. See, e. g.,

133

British Airways Bd. v. Port Authority of New York, 558 F.2d 75, 84-85 (2nd Cir. 1977) (and authorities cited therein). The legislative history does not suggest that Congress intended only to allow municipalities the option of excluding certain classes of aircraft. See *National Aviation v. City of Hayward, Cal., 418 F. Supp. 417, 421-24 (N.D.Cal.1976)* (upholding a 112 dB SENEL ordinance by a municipal proprietor); *British Airways, supra, 558 F.2d at 83-84*; S.Rep. No. 92-1160, 92nd Cong., 2d Sess. (1972) (reprinted in (1972) U.S. Code Cong. & Ad. News 4655; S. Rep. No. 1353, 90th Cong., 2d Sess. (1968) (reprinted in (1968) U.S. Code Cong. & Ad. News 2688, 2694). The reasonable inference, not contradicted by the legislative history, is that Congress intended to allow a municipality flexibility in fashioning its noise regulations. See *Hayward, supra, 418 F. Supp. at 425, n.13.*

There was evidence that the City's SENEL system was one of the most direct, effective and least costly methods of monitoring and regulating noise. This SENEL regulates that noise for which the City is liable. Thus, we hold that in this instance, the SENEL method used by the City does not render its otherwise proper noise regulations unlawful.

The appellants have also argued that "preemption as applied" invalidates the 100 dB SENEL ordinance. The district court summarized this claim as follows:

> "Plaintiffs say that because the SENEL system induces such (unsafe) practices within the airspace and as a part of flight (by causing pilots to attempt to "beat the box'), it amounts to a local regulation of airspace and flight which matters are within the exclusive domain of the federal government. This is essentially what is meant by the claim of "preemption as applied.' " *Santa Monica Airport Ass'n v. City of Santa Monica, 481 F. Supp. 927, 941 (C.D.Cal.1979)*, aff'd., *647 F.2d 3 (9th Cir. 1981).*

The district court rejected this argument. It noted that the SENEL ordinance did not regulate airspace or flight. It reasoned that the tendency to violate a certain law does not render the law improper or illegal. These arguments are sound. Appellants have cited no authority which convinces us that the district court was incorrect. The principles of comity and federalism militate against our invalidating a state or local regulation unless it is written in unlawful terms, or because, on its face, it is preempted. We have no warrant to strike down an ordinance merely because the public reacts to it in a manner inconsistent with federal law.

Accordingly, we reject the "preemption as applied" argument.

Other points briefed and argued by the parties were fully and correctly answered in the district court's opinion.

Affirmed.

CITY OF SOUTH LAKE TAHOE, A MUNICIPAL CORPORATION, V. TAHOE REGIONAL PLANNING AGENCY.

UNITED STATES DISTRICT COURT
FOR THE EASTERN DISTRICT OF
CALIFORNIA

664 F. Supp. 1375

June, 1987

Defendant, Tahoe Regional Planning Agency's request that the Court publish its order of April 15, 1985 granting partial summary judgment, is granted. It is further directed that the April 15, 1987 order for partial summary judgment be amended to read as follows.

Pursuant to Tahoe Regional Planning Agency's ("TRPA") motion for partial summary judgment, filed January 10, 1985, this matter came on for hearing on February 8, 1985, in the United States District Court, Eastern District of California, the Honorable Edward J. Garcia presiding. TRPA appeared through its counsel, Susan E. Scholley; intervenor People of the State of California appeared through its counsel, Kenneth R. Williams, Deputy Attorney General; plaintiff, City of South Lake Tahoe ("City"), appeared through its counsel, Michael Scott Gatske; and amicus curiae Air California appeared through its counsel, Richard M. Sherman.

The Court having considered the motion for partial summary judgment of TRPA, and having considered all the pertinent documents and evidence on file herein, as well as the arguments of counsel, and good cause appearing, the motion of TRPA for partial summary judgment as to the first cause of action of the complaint of City is hereby granted.

Summary judgment is appropriate only when no genuine issue of material fact exists and the moving party is clearly entitled to prevail as a matter of law. *Rule 56, Fed.R.Civ.P.*; and *Ybarra v. Reno Thunderbird Mobile Home Village, 723 F.2d 675 (9th Cir. 1984)*. On this motion which is addressed to the first cause of action of the City's complaint, all parties have agreed that there are no material facts genuinely at issue and that the legal issues involved are ripe for summary adjudication.

Count 1 of plaintiff's complaint raises the question of TRPA's authority to limit the number of flights to the South Lake Tahoe Airport. Plaintiff, City, is the proprietor of that airport and filed this action to contest the validity of a cease and desist order issued by TRPA on May 25, 1984. That order would limit the number of DC-9 (80) jet aircraft flights to the airport to three per day and 19 per week. The thrust of plaintiff's contention is that a general federal regulatory scheme for airline regulation preempts and precludes local non-proprietor control of an airport. See the Federal Aviation Act of 1958 (49 U.S.C. § 1301 *et seq.*); the Noise Control Act of 1972 (*42 U.S.C. § 4901 et seq.*); and more particularly the Airline Deregulation Act of 1978 (49 U.S.C. § 1301 *et seq.*); *see also City of Burbank v. Lockheed Air Terminal, 411 U.S. 624, 36 L. Ed. 2d 547, 93 S. Ct. 1854 (1973)*; and *San Diego Unified Port District v. Gianturco, 651 F.2d 1306 (9th*

Cir. 1981). However, plaintiff overlooks the fact that Congress, while generally desirous of an open sky policy, must have realized that the enactment of the Tahoe Regional Planning Compact (P.L. 96-551, 94 Stat. 3233) ("Compact") in December of 1980, after enactment of the Airline Deregulation Act of 1978 (49 U.S.C. 1301) [hereafter "ADA"], would effectively require some incidental regulation of airlines into the Tahoe Basin. Therefore, the court concludes that the Congress necessarily created, for environmental reasons, a narrow geographical exception to the open sky policy embodied, in part, by the Airline Deregulation Act, which act is a deregulation statute.

Even though the ADA includes a preemption clause prohibiting states and interstate agencies from airline regulation, that clause does not affect TRPA because TRPA's powers are derived from a federal compact ratified by Congress pursuant to *Article 1, § 10 cl.3 of the U.S. Constitution*. Thus, the Compact itself is a congressional exercise of power under the *commerce clause* and amounts to federal legislation. *Virginia v. Tennessee, 148 U.S. 503, 519-20, 37 L. Ed. 537, 13 S. Ct. 728*; and *League to Save Lake Tahoe v. BJK, 547 F.2d 1072, 1075 (9th Cir. 1976)*. Otherwise stated, the preemption provision of the ADA, 49 U.S.C. § 1305, itself a congressional enactment, does not interfere with the Congress' ability to later approve a bi-state compact such as the Tahoe Regional Planning Compact which confers the type of broad environmental regulatory powers as complained of here. Furthermore, even though the Compact and the ADA necessarily overlap, they do so only in the Tahoe Basin. The statutory scheme regulating airlines is nationwide and the reason for that national scheme is economic. The regulatory effects of the Compact on air flights occurs only in the Tahoe Basin and only for environmental purposes. Because the ADA is general and National in scope and the Compact is specific and limited to a narrow geographic location, the two federal schemes can operate concurrently without harming the effectiveness of each other.

The first cause of action of the City's complaint attacks an integral part of the statutory scheme of the Compact, namely the environmental threshold carrying capacities which the Compact mandates. Yet, the Compact shows congressional recognition of the need for strict environmental standards in the Tahoe Basin such that the Compact is actually a part of the federal regulatory scheme for noise and air pollution control. Further, the Compact allows TRPA to adopt air and water quality standards that are stricter than the federal standards. As demonstrated in *DeVeau v. Braisted, 363 U.S. 144, 80 S. Ct. 1146, 4 L. Ed. 2d 1109 (1960)*, it would be unreasonable to conclude that Congress would ratify the creation of TRPA, a bi-state agency, to establish and maintain strict environmental standards, including noise, air pollution and transportation standards, and not to give TRPA the power to regulate the number and frequency of airline flights into the Tahoe Basin, notwithstanding the preemptive language in a previously enacted federal statute concerning economic regulation (or deregulation) of airlines. Moreover, the Compact should be given effect to the extent of any conflict between the two federal schemes, because it is a congressional enactment passed later in time and, is more specific than the Airline Deregulation Act as it is limited to a very narrow geographical area.

Plaintiff's reliance on Article X, Section 5 of the Compact, to establish preemption is misplaced. That section is a general reservation clause designed to protect the jurisdiction of the Departments of the Interior and Agriculture. It was not intended to exempt the owner of the airport from the requirements of the Compact. Moreover, that clause is very similar to the reservation clause of the waterfront compact considered by the Supreme Court in *DeVeau*. The court there concluded that the clause did not defeat jurisdiction under the waterfront compact to regulate certain labor activities which were argued as being preempted by the National Labor Relations Act.

In Sum, the City's and Air Cal's § 1305 preemption argument merely focuses on a statutory restatement of the general concepts of preemption under the supremacy and *commerce clauses of the U.S. Constitution*. The arguments lack merit because the City and Air Cal ignore the role of the Congress in approving the Compact. Thus Air Cal insists in its amicus brief that two states cannot accomplish jointly what they are prohibited by federal preemption from accomplishing separately, and misses the point that the Congress (which Air Cal concedes, as it must, is empowered to set noise and pollution standards) approved the Compact calling for the strict regulation complained of here. Because of that participation by the Congress, the regulations emanating from the Compact simply do not raise problems of federal preemption.

The court is therefore left with two federally authorized regulatory schemes having very different purposes and very limited overlap. The statutes appear quite capable of being given concurrent effect. The ADA, having an economic purpose, was designed to prevent the states from stepping into the area of economic regulation of the airlines that the Congress had just vacated. The Compact was designed to restore and preserve the environment of the Lake Tahoe Basin. The only common ground of the two is geographic and perhaps incidental but is not substantive. As for this geographic overlap, the Compact is clearly more specific and enacted later in time.

For these reasons, defendant's motion for partial summary judgment must be and is granted.

IT IS SO ORDERED.

STATE OF MINNESOTA BY MINNESOTA PUBLIC LOBBY AND
BY SOUTH METRO AIRPORT ACTION COUNCIL V.
METROPOLITAN AIRPORTS COMMISSION.

SUPREME COURT OF MINNESOTA

520 N.W.2d 388

August, 1994

Heard, considered, and decided by the court en banc.

In this case, we are asked to determine whether the Minnesota
Pollution Control Agency's (MPCA) noise standards are preempted by
federal law as applied to the Metropolitan Airports Commission's
(MAC) operation of the Minneapolis-St. Paul International Airport
(MSP). Two nonprofit organizations, Minnesota Public Lobby (MPL)
and South Metro Airport Action Council (SMAAC), brought this action
in the name of the State of Minnesota seeking to require the MAC to
comply with the MPCA's noise pollution standards set forth at *Minn. R.
§§ 7010.0040-.0080* ("noise standards").

The MAC is a public corporation formed under *Minn. Stat. §§
473.601-.679* (1992). The MAC's responsibilities include the promotion
of air navigation and transportation in the state along with "minimizing
environmental impact from air navigation and transportation, and to
that end providing for noise abatement, control of airport area land use,
and other protective measures." *Minn. Stat. § 473.602, subd. 2.* The
MAC has the "use, management, operation, regulation, policing, and
control of any or all airports owned by either the city of Minneapolis or
St. Paul ..." *Minn. Stat. § 473.621, subd. 2.* The MAC can sue and be
sued, acquire rights or easements, adopt ordinances, construct and
equip new airports, manage airports, and acquire property through
eminent domain. *Minn. Stat. § 473.608.*

The noise standards, promulgated in 1974, pursuant to *Minn. Stat.
§ 116.07* (1992), define maximum permissible noise and apply to all
"persons," including public corporations, unless exempted by *Minn.
Stat. § 116.07, subd. 2a. Minn. R. § 7010.0030.* The MAC is not
exempted by *Minn. Stat. § 116.07, subd. 2a.* The standards divide land
into three "Noise Area Classifications" and create limits on noise
pollution for each classification. *Minn. R. §§ 7010.0040-.0050.* Most of
the area surrounding the MSP falls within Classification 1, which has
the strictest requirements and applies to areas where people have an
expectation of peace and quiet such as residential areas. The standards
set a maximum noise level for daytime and nighttime which may not be
exceeded for more than a certain portion of each hour. A variance may
be sought and if "the agency finds that by reason of exceptional
circumstances strict conformity with any provisions of any noise rule
would cause undue hardship, would be unreasonable, impractical, or
not feasible under the circumstances, the agency may permit a variance
..." *Minn. R. § 7010.0080.*

Respondents MPL/SMAAC commenced this declaratory judgment
action seeking an order (1) declaring that the noise standards set forth
at *Minn. R. § 7010.0040* apply to the MAC and that the MAC is in
violation of the noise standards; (2) enjoining the MAC from

continuing to violate the noise standards; and (3) compelling the MAC to implement a plan to comply with the noise standards. In its answer, the MAC admitted aircraft operations at MSP are not in compliance with the noise standards, but asserted among other defenses that the noise standards do not apply to aircraft operations at MSP by virtue of the doctrine of federal preemption.

The parties brought cross-motions for summary judgment. MPL/SMAAC argued that no factual issues existed which would preclude summary judgment in their favor because the MAC admitted being in violation of the noise standards, and therefore, the court could resolve the issue by ruling that the standards apply to the MAC. The MAC argued it was entitled to summary judgment on three grounds: (1) the issues in the case were political questions; (2) federal law preempts the noise standards; and (3) the standards cannot be enforced because they are outside the enabling legislation of the MPCA.

A hearing on the motions was held before Hennepin County District Court Judge Pamela G. Alexander. At the hearing, the Air Transport Association of America (ATA), a non-profit association of federally certified air carriers, sought and was granted permission to intervene pursuant to Minn. R. Civ. P. 24. The ATA supported the MAC's position that the MPCA noise standards as applied to aircraft operations at MSP are preempted by federal law. By order dated January 28, 1993, Judge Alexander denied MPL/SMAAC's motion, and granted the MAC's motion in its entirety holding that the noise standards were preempted by federal law because they could not be enforced "without substantially impacting operations at MSP." The district court followed the reasoning set out by the Supreme Court in *City of Burbank v. Lockheed Air Terminal, Inc., 411 U.S. 624, 36 L. Ed. 2d 547, 93 S. Ct. 1854 (1973)*, which invalidated attempts by airport non-proprietors to regulate airport noise and made clear that noise abatement regulations which impinge on aircraft operations are preempted by federal law. The district court found that the only way the MAC could comply with the standards would be to either substantially reduce aircraft operations at MSP, "convert much of South Minneapolis and Richfield to nonresidential areas," or move the airport.

The court of appeals reversed the district court and instead granted summary judgment to MPL/SMAAC declaring that the noise standards apply to the MAC. *State by Minnesota Public Lobby v. Metropolitan Airports Comm'n, 507 N.W.2d 19 (Minn. App. 1993)*. The court of appeals, interpreting *Burbank* and subsequent federal cases, concluded that a state, even though a nonproprietor, has some authority to control airport noise, although it may not enact regulations which "purport to control aircraft flight." The court of appeals stated:

> Because the state noise standards do not purport to control aircraft flight or operations and need not be so applied, they are not preempted by federal law. It is possible that enforcement of the noise standards will result in a claim that specific applications of the noise standards constitute attempts to achieve control over aircraft flight at MSP airport. No such issue is before us, however. As in *Crotti*, consideration of the validity of enforcement of the state noise control standards against MAC and MSP must await another day.

Id. at 24.

We granted the MAC's and ATA's petitions for further review. We reverse.

The issue is whether federal law preempts the MPCA's noise standards as applied to the MAC. Preemption can be express or implied, and where it is implied "congressional intent to do so must be clearly inferred, either from the extent of federal involvement or from the scope of the federal interest; and even then the state will be preempted only to the extent that state regulation 'actually conflicts' with federal law." *Forster v. R.J. Reynolds Tobacco Co., 437 N.W.2d 655, 658 (Minn. 1989).*

The Supreme Court considered whether state regulation of aircraft noise is preempted by federal law in *Burbank, 411 U.S. 624, 36 L. Ed. 2d 547, 93 S. Ct. 1854 (1973).* In *Burbank,* the city enacted an ordinance which imposed a curfew on airplane takeoffs. Although the Noise Control Act of 1972, 49 U.S.C. § 1431 (Supp. II 1970), included no express preemption provision, the Court struck down the curfew ordinance reasoning that the Noise Control Act "reaffirms and reinforces the conclusion that FAA, now in conjunction with EPA, has full control over aircraft noise, pre-empting state and local control." *Id. at 633.* The Court reasoned that "the pervasive nature of the scheme of federal regulation of aircraft noise" indicated Congressional intent to preempt the states in this area. *Id. at 633.* The Court, quoting *Northwest Airlines Inc. v. Minnesota, 322 U.S. 292, 303, 88 L. Ed. 1283, 64 S. Ct. 950 (1944),* stated:

> Federal control is intensive and exclusive. Planes do not wander about in the sky like vagrant clouds. They move only by federal permission, subject to federal inspection, in the hands of federally certified personnel and under an intricate system of federal commands. The moment a ship taxis onto a runway it is caught up in an elaborate and detailed system of controls.

Id. at 633-34. The Court realized "control of noise is of course deep-seated in the police power of the states," but read the Noise Control Act as leaving "no room for local curfews or other local controls." *Id. at 638.* "Fractionalized control of ... takeoffs and landings would severely limit the flexibility of FAA in controlling air traffic flow," and "the difficulty of scheduling flights to avoid congestion and the concomitant decrease in safety would be compounded." *Id. at 639.* Federal courts have subsequently struck down regulations of nonproprietor municipalities imposing curfews and prescribing air traffic patterns. *See Pirolo v. City of Clearwater, 711 F.2d 1006 (11th Cir. 1983); San Diego Unified Port District v. Gianturco, 651 F.2d 1306 (9th Cir. 1981).*

Despite the broad preemptive language of *Burbank,* MPL/SMAAC argue that *Burbank* did not preclude all efforts at noise control by nonproprietor municipalities. They argue that federal courts interpreting *Burbank* have approved noise standards such as the

MPCA's and have approved methods the MAC could use to comply with those standards. The MAC counters that *Burbank* makes it clear federal law preempts all state noise regulations affecting aircraft operations, and that the federal cases cited by MPL/SMAAC are distinguishable because here undisputed facts demonstrate that compliance with the standards is impossible without impinging on aircraft operations.

MPL/SMAAC contend that two California federal court decisions support its position that the MPCA's noise standards are not preempted by federal law. In *Air Transport Assoc. of America v. Crotti, 389 F. Supp. 58 (N.D. Cal. 1975)*, the federal district court considered the California Community Noise Equivalent Level (CNEL) regulations which provided for noise reduction standards and suggested methods for achieving noise reduction. The court upheld the regulations holding they were "not per se invalid as delving into and regulating a field of aircraft operation engaged in direct flight ...." *Id. at 65.* The court considered it premature to consider whether the regulations would be invalid as applied, stating:

> Whether or not the CNEL requirements and regulations are *in fact* unrealistic, arbitrary and unreasonable, and an abuse of police power constituting an unlawful burden or infringement upon any United States constitutional right of privilege held by a proprietor of an airport, or an unreasonable burden upon interstate and foreign commerce as utilized by aircraft, is not before us upon undisputed facts and must wait a future day of judgment.

Id. (emphasis in original).

In *San Diego Unified Port District v. Gianturco, 651 F.2d 1306 (9th Cir. 1981).* The California Department of Transportation (Cal Trans) attempted to impose a curfew pursuant to the CNEL regulations on aircraft flights at the San Diego International Airport operated by the San Diego Unified Port District. The Port District, which had instituted its own less restrictive curfew, sought a variance from the regulations which was granted subject to a requirement that the Port District extend its curfew two hours. *Id. at 1309.* A federal district court enjoined enforcement of the Cal Trans curfew. *San Diego Unified Port District v. Gianturco, 457 F. Supp. 283 (1978).* The Ninth Circuit affirmed holding the curfew was a direct restriction on flight and therefore preempted. *Gianturco, 651 F.2d at 1319.* MPL/SMAAC notes the Ninth Circuit distinguished between regulation of the source of airport noise and noise abatement plans that do not impinge on aircraft operations stating that "as we read *City of Burbank,* Congress has preempted only local regulation of the source of noise[;] local governments may adopt abatement plans that do not impinge on aircraft operations." *Id. at 1314.* MPL/SMAAC argue the MPCA in essence has adopted an abatement plan that does not impinge on aircraft operations and just as in *Crotti* and *Gianturco,* the MAC has means available to comply with the noise standards.

The district court correctly distinguished *Crotti* and *Gianturco* and followed *Burbank* in granting summary judgment to the MAC. It found

141

that enforcement of the noise standards would "'severely limit the flexibility of the FAA in controlling aircraft flow,'" quoting *Burbank, 411 U.S. at 639*, and recognized that although the noise standards do not expressly require any direct control of aircraft operations, the undisputed evidence demonstrates that compliance would be impossible without either substantially reducing aircraft operations, including reducing departures by 82% during the peak daytime hours, converting much of South Minneapolis, and the surrounding suburbs to nonresidential areas, or moving the airport.

The court of appeals erred by equating this case with *Crotti* in that the issue here is whether the noise standards as applied to the MAC are preempted. The *Crotti* court, having determined the regulations were not per se preempted, expressly left for another day the issue of whether the regulations were preempted as applied. The undisputed facts demonstrate the noise standards as applied to the MAC would impinge on aircraft operations.

The attorney general, in its amicus brief, argues the evidence is disputed, and the district court ignored evidence demonstrating how the MAC could comply with the noise standards. The record reveals, however, the district court correctly found the evidence presented no disputed material facts as to whether compliance with the standards was possible without impinging on aircraft operations. The evidence submitted by MPL/SMAAC lists 19 actions they contend the MAC could take to reduce noise. In submitting the list, MPL/SMAAC fail to indicate which of the actions do not impinge on aircraft operations. Further, there is nothing in the record to suggest that if any or all of the actions on the list were taken, the MAC would be brought into compliance with the noise standards without substantially reducing aircraft operations at MSP, converting the surrounding residential areas to nonresidential uses, or moving the airport.

MPL/SMAAC also argue the availability of a variance precludes a finding that the noise standards are preempted. They reason that if the MAC finds it must take an action which it cannot be legally required to take, it can simply seek a variance. That argument fails because the MAC cannot be required to seek a variance from noise standards which are preempted and thus not applicable to it.

Finally, MPL/SMAAC argue the MAC's proprietor powers provide it with a choice of methods to comply with MPCA noise standards. In a footnote in *Burbank*, the Court suggested that a municipality acting as the proprietor of an airport might have different powers to control aircraft noise than a municipality acting pursuant to its police power. *411 U.S. at 635-36, n. 14*. Subsequently, federal courts have described the power of airport proprietors to be broader than that possessed by a nonproprietor municipality, such that a proprietor, with some exceptions, "may restrict the use of its facilities on the basis of noise without running afoul of the preemption doctrine." *Gianturco, 457 F. Supp. at 291; see also National Aviation v. City of Hayward, 418 F. Supp. 417 (N.D. Cal. 1976)*. However, as MPL/SMAAC themselves admit, the MPCA cannot require an airport proprietor to use its broader proprietary powers. *See Gianturco, 457 F. Supp. at 291-92*.

We do not doubt the aircraft noise generated by MSP is a serious and unpleasant problem which interferes with the enjoyment of life and property for people living in areas affected by that noise. The problem, though, cannot be remedied with means Congress preempted. The Supreme Court has made clear states may not enact noise regulations which impinge on aircraft operations, and that is precisely what the MPCA noise standards do. The MAC's enabling legislation creates statutory responsibilities which include minimizing the environmental impact of aircraft operation and abating noise. The MAC must act on these responsibilities in balancing the needs of air carriers, travelers, and residents of areas surrounding the airport.

Because we find the noise standards to be preempted, we need not consider the MAC's other arguments in support of its summary judgment motion. Reversed.

LAKE IN THE HILLS AVIATION GROUP, INC. v. VILLAGE OF LAKE IN THE HILLS.

APPELLATE COURT OF ILLINOIS, SECOND DISTRICT

698 N.E.2d 163

June, 1998

PRESIDING JUSTICE GEIGER delivered the opinion of the court:

The defendant, Village of Lake in the Hills (Village), appeals from the December 19, 1997, order of the circuit court of McHenry County preliminarily enjoining it from taking possession of the Lake in the Hills Airport from the plaintiffs, Lake in the Hills Aviation Group, Inc., Gary Meisner, Howard Seedorf, and Gerald Finefield. On appeal, the Village argues that the entry of a preliminary injunction was improper because the plaintiffs failed to present sufficient evidence demonstrating that they were entitled to such relief. We reverse and remand.

The facts relevant to the disposition of this appeal are as follows. The Village is a municipal corporation which owns the Lake in the Hills Airport (airport). In February 1992, the Village entered into an Airport Operating Agreement (operating agreement) with Lake in the Hills Aviation Group, Inc. (the Av Group). Gary Meisner, Gerald Finefield, and Howard Seedorf each own a one-third share of the Av Group. The term of the operating agreement was from February 12, 1992, through February 11, 2004.

Under the provisions of the operating agreement, the Av Group was designated as the "operator" of the airport and took possession of the airport premises on February 12, 1992. As operator, the Av Group was required to provide certain services at the airport, including aircraft sales, aircraft maintenance, charter services, and flight training facilities. The operating agreement permitted the Av Group to provide these services directly or by subcontract. In addition, the Av Group was obligated to collect all revenues and pay all expenses associated with the operation of the airport. The operating agreement also required the Av Group to pay the Village $ 6,000 per month plus a percentage of the gross revenue it received from its operation of the airport.

Additionally, the operating agreement required the Av Group to operate the facility as a public airport at all times. The Av Group was also required to comply with all applicable municipal, federal, and state laws and regulations relating to airports. In the event that the Av Group failed to abide by the terms of the operating agreement, the Village had the right to terminate the operating agreement and to reenter the airport premises.

In 1992, the Av Group subcontracted the aircraft sales, aircraft maintenance, charter, and flight school services to various companies individually owned by Meisner, Finefield, and Seedorf. The aircraft sales service was subcontracted to Meisner Aircraft Sales, which was owned by Meisner. The aircraft maintenance service was subcontracted to Finefield Aviation, which was owned by Finefield. The charter and flight school services were subcontracted to Northern Illinois Flight Center, which was owned by Seedorf. These subcontract agreements provided for a monthly lease payment to the Av Group and were automatically renewable on a yearly basis. Although the Av Group paid the Village a percentage of these lease amounts, the Village did not receive a percentage of the gross revenues of Meisner Aircraft, Finefield Aviation, or Northern Illinois Flight Center.

On May 10, 1996, the Village was notified that the Illinois Department of Transportation (IDOT) had received a formal letter of complaint concerning the operation of the airport. The complaint had been made by Fred Shay, president of Blue Skies Flying Services (Blue Skies). Shay operated a flight school out of the airport. Shay complained that Seedorf had refused to sell him airplane fuel and had assaulted and harassed his employees. Shay also complained that the Av Group would not provide him with an agreement to operate at the airport unless he complied with certain requirements, including an EPA storm water protection permit, $ 5 million in insurance coverage, and the payment of other monthly fees.

IDOT warned the Village that, under the terms of a $ 200,000 development grant the Village had received from the state, it was required to control and operate the airport "for the rightful, fair, equal, and uniform use and benefit of the public." IDOT explained that the Village could not deny access to the airport or its facilities to any individual or company desiring to do business at the airport unless there were compelling reasons justifying such a denial. IDOT also suggested that there was a conflict of interest in permitting the primary service providers at the airport to serve in the capacity of operator. IDOT recommended that the Village create a set of operating rules and regulations and develop separate agreements, leases, or contracts for the airport operator and the various subcontractors. Although the Village apparently spoke with IDOT about these problems, it took no formal action to remedy them.

On October 9, 1996, the Village was notified that IDOT had received another complaint about the Av Group. This complaint was made by a teacher at Prospect High School who used the airport to teach his physical science and aeronautics class. Apparently, Seedorf refused to sell the teacher fuel once he began renting planes from Blue Skies. IDOT warned the Village that the airport would not be considered for further state and federal airport funding until these discriminatory practices were remedied. Under IDOT's Proposed Airport Improvement Program, the airport had previously been designated to receive $ 8.5 million in federal and state funds between 1996 and 1999.

On October 10, 1997, the Village sent the Av Group notice that it was in default on the operating agreement. The notice provided the following specific violations of the covenants contained in the operating agreement:

"1. Failing to pay the Village the applicable percentage of gross revenues received by Messrs. Seedorf, Meisner and Finefield and their business entities as 'subcontractors' of [the Av Group];

2. Arbitrarily and discriminatorily refusing to sell fuel and lease unoccupied hangar space to Blue Skies Flight Services, Inc. ... or its clients;

3. Arbitrarily and discriminatorily refusing to allow other commercial enterprises to operate at the Airport;

4. Arbitrarily and discriminatorily refusing to offer a tie-down agreement to Blue Skies on terms equally applicable to others;

5. Operating as the exclusive Fixed Base Operator at the Airport in violation of *49 U.S.C. § 40103(e)*, applicable to the Airport by reason of paragraph 10.2 of the Agreement and state grant assurances; and

6. Violating, by virtue of the foregoing actions, the FAA regulations regarding airport use ([14] C.F.R. [Pt.] 152, App. D), applicable to the Airport by reason of paragraph 10.2 of the Agreement and state grant assurances."

The notice further provided that the operating agreement would be terminated on December 10, 1997, and that the Village would re-enter the airport premises on that date.

On December 3, 1997, the Av Group, Meisner, Finefield, and Seedorf (collectively, plaintiffs) filed the instant declaratory judgment action. The plaintiffs alleged that they had fully performed their obligations under the operating agreement and that they had not breached any of its conditions or terms. The plaintiffs requested a judgment declaring them to be in compliance with the terms of the operating agreement and that the Village was not entitled to reenter the airport and remove them from the premises.

Also on December 3, 1997, the plaintiffs filed motions for the entry of a temporary restraining order and a preliminary injunction. On December 8, 1997, the trial court entered a temporary restraining order prohibiting the Village from reentering the airport to remove the Av Group and from taking possession of the premises.

On December 18, 1997, the trial court held a hearing on the motion for preliminary injunction. At the hearing, Seedorf testified that the Av Group had made every single monthly payment due to the Village under the agreement, including a monthly percentage of Av Group's gross receipts. These payments totaled over $ 500,000. He testified that the Village did not receive a percentage of the gross revenues of Meisner Aircraft, Finefield Aviation, or Northern Illinois Flight Center because they were not the "operator" of the airport. Rather, these businesses had contracted with the Av Group to provide services at the airport.

On cross-examination, Seedorf testified that any prospective businesses that wished to rent hangar space at the airport were required to execute a rental agreement. This agreement prohibited the business from conducting any commercial activity in the hangar without the express written permission of the Av Group. At no time did the Av Group ever permit any individual or business to conduct commercial activities in the airport hangars. However, Seedorf acknowledged that the Av Group waived this prohibition for Northern Illinois Flight Center. Therefore, Seedorf's business was permitted to conduct commercial activities in the airport hangars.

Seedorf also acknowledged that, on December 12, 1995, he sent Fred Shay a letter indicating that, in order for Blue Skies to operate at the airport, he would have to comply with certain requirements, including (1) the execution of a commercial operating agreement; (2) $ 5 million in liability insurance coverage; and (3) the payment of an annual $ 2,500 fee for an Illinois EPA storm water protection and pollution prevention plan. Appended to this letter were purported excerpts of a document entitled "Lake in the Hills Airport Policy." The document detailed additional monthly fees due to the Av Group for each instructor or mechanic that would be working at the airport. Similar demands were made to the other businesses that sought to operate out of the airport.

Seedorf acknowledged that these requirements had not been officially approved by the Village. He also acknowledged that none of these fees were ever paid by Meisner Aircraft, Finefield Aviation, or Northern Illinois Flight Center. Additionally, none of the plaintiffs' businesses carried $ 5 million in insurance coverage. Seedorf acknowledged that, under the terms of the operating agreement, only $ 1 million in coverage was required.

Finefield also testified at the hearing. Included in his testimony was an explanation of the content of certain conversations among Meisner, Seedorf, and Finefield at the time the operating agreement was executed. He testified that, based upon these conversations, it was his understanding that only Meisner Aircraft would be permitted to provide aircraft sales service at the airport, only Finefield Aviation would be permitted to provide maintenance services at the airport, and only Northern Illinois Flight School would be permitted to provide flight instruction.

Maureen Cousins testified that she is one of the owners of Valley Service, Inc. (Valley Air). Valley Air is an executive air charter company that has been operating at the airport since May 1995. Cousins testified that Valley Air encountered significant difficulties from Seedorf in setting up operations at the airport. Seedorf told her that the airport was private and that there was no space for commercial hangars. In an effort to commence operations at the airport, Cousins was required to speak with her attorney, IDOT, and the Village. Although she was eventually permitted to operate at the airport, she has never been given an operating agreement despite repeated attempts to obtain one. Additionally, although Valley Air has a hangar at the airport where it stores its aircraft, it has not been permitted to conduct any commercial operations out of the hangar. Cousins testified that Valley Air has continually refused to comply with Av Group's requirement that it purchase $ 5 million in insurance.

Fred Shay testified that he is the president of Blue Skies. Blue Skies is a flying school and aircraft dealership. Shay testified that his company operates out of an office outside of the airport because it has not been permitted to conduct any commercial operations out of its hangar on the airport premises. Shay explained that when he first approached Seedorf about operating at the airport, Seedorf advised him of the insurance and fee obligations described above. Shay refused to pay these fees and hired an attorney to contact the Village directly. Eventually, Shay was permitted to begin operations at the airport in February 1996. After Shay commenced operations, Seedorf refused to sell him fuel to operate his planes. On one occasion, Seedorf told Shay that the "airport was [Seedorf's]" and that "[Seedorf] could do whatever he wanted." Shay reported these incidents to IDOT. The Av Group later terminated Shay's hangar lease and commenced litigation to evict him. This litigation was later settled, and Blue Skies was permitted to continue its operations at the airport.

Lynn Hadler testified that he operates Motive Services Company, an aircraft maintenance company. Hadler has operated his business out of two hangars at the airport since 1982. In 1996, he received a notice from Av Group indicating that his lease was being terminated because he was conducting commercial activities in his hangars. The Av Group also initiated litigation against Motive Services, seeking to evict it from the airport. Once again, the litigation was settled, and Motive Services was permitted to continue its operations at the airport.

James Bildilli testified that he was the bureau chief of aviation, education, and safety for the aeronautics division at IDOT. He testified that it was improper for an airport operator to request a business to pay the fee necessary to obtain an EPA storm water permit. He also testified that $ 5 million in insurance required by the Av Group was unnecessary for the type of business that Shay was operating. In a letter to the Village, Bildilli noted that it was unsafe for Seedorf to refuse to sell fuel to the businesses at the airport, as it would require pilots to fly aircraft to other airports for the purposes of fueling. Finally, Bildilli testified that the airport was not eligible to receive federal or state funds because of the Av Group's discriminatory practices and the "exclusive rights" situation created as a result of the operating agreement.

At the close of the hearing, the trial court granted the plaintiffs' motion for a preliminary injunction. The injunction provided as follows:

"The Village ...[is] prohibited and enjoined from re-entering the airport premises of the Lake in the Hills Airport ... for the purpose of removing the plaintiffs from all publicly owned property and [is] also enjoined from taking possession of the airport premises and any property, books, records, and things associated therewith during the pendency of this cause."

The trial court also denied the Village's request that the plaintiffs be required to post a bond. The Village had argued that such a bond was necessary to protect its interests, particularly in light of the fact that it might lose $ 8.5 million in federal and state grant funds. On January 12, 1998, the Village filed a timely interlocutory appeal. On February 5, 1998, we granted IDOT leave to file an amicus brief urging reversal of the preliminary injunction.

On appeal, the Village argues that the trial court abused its discretion in granting the preliminary injunction. Specifically, the Village contends that the plaintiffs failed to prove that they have no adequate remedy at law and that they are likely to succeed on the merits of the case. The Village also argues that there is a substantial public interest in removing the Av Group from the airport premises, as the Village could potentially lose millions of dollars in federal and state funds. Finally, the Village contends that the trial court erred in refusing to require the plaintiffs to post a bond.

In order to grant preliminary injunctive relief, the trial court must find that (1) the plaintiff has demonstrated a clearly ascertained right in need of protection; (2) irreparable injury will occur without the injunction; (3) no adequate remedy at law exists; and (4) there is a probability that the plaintiff will succeed on the merits of the case. *Lindholm v. Holtz, 221 Ill. App. 3d 330, 333, 163 Ill. Dec. 706, 581 N.E.2d 860 (1991)*. It is not the purpose of a preliminary injunction to determine any controverted rights or to decide the merits of the case. *Grillo v. Sidney Wanzer & Sons, Inc., 26 Ill. App. 3d 1007, 1011, 326 N.E.2d 180 (1975)*. Rather, a preliminary injunction is granted prior to trial on the merits for the purpose of preventing a threatened wrong and to preserve the status quo with the least injury to the parties concerned. *Bojangles, Inc. v. City of Elmhurst, 39 Ill. App. 3d 19, 26, 349 N.E.2d 478 (1976)*.

The issuance of a preliminary injunction is within the sound discretion of the trial court upon a *prima facie* demonstration that there is a fair question as to the existence of the right claimed and that the circumstances lead to a reasonable belief that the moving party will be entitled to the relief sought. *City of Chicago v. Airline Canteen Service, Inc., 64 Ill. App. 3d 417, 432, 20 Ill. Dec. 897, 380 N.E.2d 1106 (1978)*. The reviewing court will not set aside the trial court's determination unless there has been a manifest abuse of discretion. *Russell v. Howe, 293 Ill. App. 3d 293, 295, 227 Ill. Dec. 894, 688 N.E.2d 375 (1997)*.

Based upon our review of the record, we do not believe that there is a probability that the plaintiffs will succeed on the merits of their declaratory judgment action. Rather, we believe that the evidence adduced at the hearing demonstrates that the plaintiffs have committed numerous violations of the operating agreement and that they have failed to operate the airport in compliance with the applicable laws and regulations. Under the express terms of the operating agreement, the plaintiffs were obligated to operate the airport for the benefit of the public and in compliance with all applicable federal and state laws and regulations relating to airports.

For example, as an airport receiving state funding, the plaintiffs were required to keep the airport open to all types of aeronautical uses and were prohibited from discriminating against others desiring to operate out of the airport. *620 ILCS 5/34* (West 1996); see also *14 C.F.R. Pt. 152, App. D (18), (19), (20) (1996)*. Indeed, state law specifically provides that "the public will not be deprived of its rightful, fair, equal and uniform use" of the airport. *620 ILCS 5/34* (West 1996); see also *49 U.S.C. § 40103(e) (1996)*. The purpose of such provisions is to prohibit monopolies and combinations in restraint of trade or commerce and to promote and encourage competition in civil aeronautics. See *Niswonger v. American Aviation, Inc., 411 F. Supp. 763, 766 (E.D. Tenn. 1975)*.

The evidence presented at the hearing demonstrates that the plaintiffs attempted to prevent other businesses from operating at the airport. The Av Group imposed numerous "minimum requirements" to operate at the airport, including fees for an EPA storm water permit and $ 5 million in insurance coverage. As noted by IDOT employee James Bildilli, many of these fees and insurance requirements were either improper or excessive. Additionally, none of these requirements had been imposed upon the operations of Meisner Aircraft, Finefield Aviation, or Northern Illinois Flight Center. The obvious result of these "requirements" was to delay and frustrate other businesses, such as

149

Blue Skies and Valley Air, from competing at the airport. Such conduct would appear to be discriminatory and violative of state and federal law. See *City of Pompano Beach v. Federal Aviation Administration, 774 F.2d 1529, 1544 (11th Cir. 1985)* (city improperly discriminated against potential airport operator by imposing unreasonable standards and lease requirements).

Additionally, as noted above, all of the hangar lease agreements executed by the Av Group contained provisions that prevented any business from conducting commercial operations within the hangars. While the plaintiffs apparently waived this prohibition for their own businesses, they vigorously enforced the prohibition against Blue Skies and Motive Services. On several occasions, the Av Group sent notices to these businesses warning them that they were operating in violation of this lease provision. Indeed, the Av Group terminated both of these leases and commenced litigation against both Blue Skies and Motive Services to evict them from the premises. Such conduct had a clear discriminatory effect and would appear to be an illegal attempt to gain exclusive control of the airport. See *Pompano Beach, 774 F.2d at 1544; Niswonger v. American Aviation, Inc., 411 F. Supp. 769, 770-71 (E.D. Tenn. 1975)*.

The plaintiffs also appear to have violated state and federal regulations by refusing to sell fuel on the airport premises. State aviation regulations specifically require that every airport must provide fuel and oil facilities. 92 Ill. Adm. Code § 14.675(c) (1996). Additionally, federal regulations require the operation and maintenance of all facilities necessary to serve the aeronautical users of an airport and prohibit the interference with the use of such facilities. 14 C.F.R. Pt. 152, App. D(22) (1996). During the hearing on the plaintiff's motion, Seedorf acknowledged that he refused to sell fuel to Shay on several occasions. According to Bildilli, such a practice was unsafe because it would force a pilot to fly an aircraft that was low on fuel.

The plaintiffs argue that they have not unreasonably prevented other businesses from operating at the airport. In support of their contention, the plaintiffs contend that Blue Skies, Motive Services, and Valley Air all successfully commenced operations at the airport and continued operations throughout the time in question. Such an argument is without merit. That plaintiffs were ultimately unsuccessful in their attempts to prevent other businesses from operating at the airport does not negate their discriminatory and illegal conduct.

Rather, the plaintiffs' failure to operate the airport in conformity with the applicable laws and regulations appears to be a clear breach of their operating agreement with the Village. Under the terms of the operating agreement, the Village would therefore be permitted to terminate the operating agreement and reenter the premises. Although we are mindful that the purpose of a preliminary injunction is to preserve the status quo between the parties and not to determine the ultimate factual issues, such relief is not warranted where there is no possibility of success on the merits. See *Ajax Engineering Corp. v. Sentry Insurance, 143 Ill. App. 3d 81, 84, 96 Ill. Dec. 668, 491 N.E.2d 947 (1986)*. Based on the record before us at the present time, the Av Group's right to the permanent relief it seeks is doubtful. We are therefore compelled to conclude that the trial court abused its discretion in entering the preliminary injunction.

We also believe that the entry of a preliminary injunction was improper in the instant case because the plaintiffs have an adequate remedy at law. Illinois courts have consistently held that money damages are the appropriate remedy for breach of contract. *Northrop Corp. v. AIL Systems, Inc., 218 Ill. App. 3d 951, 954-55, 161 Ill. Dec. 562, 578 N.E.2d 1208 (1991)*. In cases involving breach of contract, a monetary damage award is more complete, practical, and efficient than injunctive relief. *Northrop Corp., 218 Ill. App. 3d at 955.*

In the instant case, if an improper termination of the operating agreement occurred, the plaintiffs' damages would be their lost profits for the duration of the agreement. See *Rivenbark v. Finis P. Ernest, Inc., 37 Ill. App. 3d 536, 538-39, 346 N.E.2d 494 (1976)*. At the hearing, Seedorf testified that such profits are driven by the relatively "constant" monthly revenues received by the Av Group. Such revenues are generated from monthly hangar and tie-down lease payments and consistently total $ 17,100. Additionally, Seedorf acknowledged that the Av Group's financial records specifically detail the monthly income received since the onset of the operating agreement. We therefore believe that it would be a relatively simple task for the trial court to determine the plaintiffs' damages in the event that an improper termination of the operating agreement should occur.

The plaintiffs argue that a monetary remedy would be speculative because of the difficulty in calculating future lost profits. However, the plaintiffs fail to provide any convincing reason why its future profits may suddenly increase or decrease. Although there certainly is the possibility of an increased demand for hangar space and use of the airport's other facilities, such factors may be taken into account by the trial court in making a determination as to future lost profits. See *Kessler v. Continental Casualty Co., 132 Ill. App. 3d 540, 546, 87 Ill. Dec. 759, 477 N.E.2d 1287 (1985)* (lost profits can be measured on the basis of past performance and present predictions of future performance).

The plaintiffs also argue that a monetary remedy is inadequate because they will lose possession and use of the airport. They argue the airport is a unique piece of real estate and that they will have difficulty finding another location where they could conduct their business. However, the plaintiffs have failed to cite any authority for the proposition that the Av Group's removal from the airport, in and of itself, would be a compensable loss. Rather, as noted above, the plaintiffs' sole basis for recovery would be its lost future profits. See *Northrop, 218 Ill. App. 3d at 954-55.*

Additionally, although it is possible that the Av Group may ultimately be required to cease operations at the airport, there is no question that Meisner Aircraft, Finefield Aviation, and Northern Illinois Flight Center will be able to continue their individual business operations. These businesses have leases with the airport, and the Village has indicated that it has no intention of attempting to remove them from the premises. We therefore believe it disingenuous for plaintiffs to argue that they will not be permitted to use the airport or operate their businesses there.

Finally, the plaintiffs assert that the operating agreement conveys a possessory interest in the airport premises and that they cannot be removed absent an action by the Village pursuant to the Forcible Entry and Detainer Act (the Act) (*735 ILCS 5/9--101 et seq.* (West 1996)). See generally *City of Chicago v. Airline Canteen Service, Inc., 64 Ill. App. 3d 417, 435, 20 Ill. Dec. 897, 380 N.E.2d 1106 (1978).* We decline to consider the merits of this contention because it is not ripe for our determination. The plaintiffs filed the instant declaratory judgment action before the date that the operating agreement was to be terminated and before the Village made any attempt to reenter the property. As there has been no attempt to remove the Av Group from the premises, we decline the parties' invitation to determine the nature of Av Group's possessory interests under the operating agreement or the necessity to initiate proceedings under the Act.

In closing, we note that our discussion herein is offered solely for the purposes of explaining our determination to reverse the preliminary injunction. The discussion should not be taken as a resolution on the ultimate merits of the case. Rather, that determination is to be made by the trial court on the basis of the evidence presented at trial.

For the foregoing reasons, the judgment of the circuit court of McHenry County is reversed and the cause remanded.

Reversed and remanded.

AERONAUTICAL REPAIR STATION ASSOCIATION, INC. ET AL
v. FEDERAL AVIATION ADMINISTRATION

UNITED STATES COURT OF APPEALS FOR THE DISTRICT OF
COLUMBIA CIRCUIT

494 F.3d 161

July, 2007

OPINION

KAREN LECRAFT HENDERSON, *Circuit Judge*: The petitioners challenge a final rule (2006 Final Rule or Rule) of the Federal Aviation Administration (FAA) which amends its drug and alcohol testing regulations, promulgated pursuant to *49 U.S.C. § 45102(a)(1)*, to expressly mandate that air carriers require drug and alcohol tests of all employees of its contractors -- including employees of subcontractors at any tier -- who perform safety-related functions such as aircraft maintenance. *Antidrug and Alcohol Misuse Prevention Programs for Personnel Engaged in Specified Aviation Activities, 71 Fed. Reg. 1666 (Jan. 10, 2006).* The petitioners challenge the Rule on [various] grounds and [under] the *Fourth* and *Fifth Amendments to the United States Constitution.*

I.

The FAA first promulgated drug testing regulations in 1988 pursuant to the Congress's general directive in 49 U.S.C. app. § 1421(a)(6) (1988) that the Secretary of Transportation "promote safety of flight of civil aircraft in air commerce" by prescribing "reasonable rules and regulations, or minimum standards." *See Anti-Drug Program for Personnel Engaged in Specified Aviation Activities, 53 Fed. Reg. 47,024 (Nov. 21, 1988)* (1988 Rule). The 1988 Rule required that each employer test "each of its employees who performs" one of eight enumerated "sensitive safety -- or security -- related" functions, *14 C.F.R. § 121.457 (1992)*, and defined "employee" as "a person who performs, either directly or by contract" any of the enumerated functions, 14 C.F.R. pt. 121, app. I § II (1992).

[some legislative history omitted]

Pursuant to the Omnibus Act, in 1994 the FAA revised its drug testing regulations, *Antidrug Program for Personnel Engaged in Specified Aviation Activities, 59 Fed. Reg. 42,922 (Aug. 19, 1994)* (1994 Drug Rule), and promulgated regulations for the first time for alcohol testing, *Alcohol Misuse Prevention Program for Personnel Engaged in Specified Aviation, 59 Fed. Reg. 7380 (Feb. 15, 1994)* (1994 Alcohol Rule). Both the 1994 Drug Rule and the 1994 Alcohol Rule required that an "employer" test each covered "employee," again defined as "a person who performs, either directly or by contract" any of eight listed "safety-sensitive" functions, *59 Fed. Reg. at 7390* (alcohol), at 42,928 (drugs). Both rules also listed the same eight functions, which were substantially the same as those in the 1988 Rule:

1. Flight crewmember duties.

2. Flight attendant duties.

3. Flight instruction duties.

4. Aircraft dispatcher duties.

5. Aircraft maintenance or preventive maintenance duties.

6. Ground security coordinator duties.

7. Aviation screening duties.

8. Air traffic control duties.

59 Fed. Reg. at 7391, 42,928.

On February 28, 2002, the FAA issued a notice of proposed rulemaking seeking to revise its drug and its alcohol testing regulations. *Antidrug and Alcohol Misuse Prevention Programs for Personnel Engaged in Specified Aviation Activities, 67 Fed. Reg. 9366 (Feb. 28, 2002)* (NPRM). Significantly, the NPRM proposed to amend the definition of a covered "employee" subject to testing as "[e]ach employee who performs a function listed in this section directly or by contract (*including by subcontract at any tier* for an employer." *67 Fed. Reg. at 9377* (drugs) (proposed to be codified at 14 C.F.R. pt. 121, app. I § III), 9380 (alcohol) (proposed to be codified at 14 C.F.R. pt. 121, app. J § II) (emphasis added). The FAA explained that it proposed including the italicized language "to clarify that each person who performs a safety-sensitive function directly or by *any tier of* a contract for an employer is subject to testing." *67 Fed. Reg. at 9368* (emphasis added).

[some legislative history omitted].

The 2006 Final Rule, issued January 10, 2006, amended the testing regulations [ ] to require testing employees who perform the listed functions "directly or by contract (including by subcontract at any tier)." *Antidrug and Alcohol Misuse Prevention Programs for Personnel Engaged in Specified Aviation Activities, 71 Fed. Reg. 1666, 1676, 1677 (Jan. 10, 2006).* In addition, the FAA certified that the 2006 Final Rule "will not have a significant economic impact on a substantial number of small entities" and that it was therefore "not required to conduct an RFA analysis." *71 Fed. Reg. at 1674.*

The petitioners filed petitions for review on March 10 and March 13, 2006.

II.

The petitioners challenge the 2006 Final Rule [under several theories. All by the constitutional challenges are omitted].

C. Constitutional Challenges

The petitioners raise two constitutional challenges to the 2006 Final Rule, alleging the FAA violated the *Due Process Clause of the Fifth Amendment* and the *Fourth Amendment's* guarantee against unreasonable search and seizure. We reject each challenge in turn.

The petitioners first claim the 2006 Final Rule, insofar as it extends the testing to employees of noncertificated subcontractors, is so vague as to violate due process because it is unclear what constitutes "maintenance" for which testing is required -- and, in particular, where the FAA draws the line between "maintenance" and "preventive maintenance," for which testing is not required. *See 14 C.F.R. § 1.1* (defining "maintenance" as "inspection, overhaul, repair, preservation, and the replacement of parts, but exclud[ing] preventive maintenance"). Whatever uncertainty exists regarding the meaning of "maintenance," however, existed before -- and, according to the petitioners, was enhanced by guidance disseminated after -- the 2006 Final Rule issued and is therefore not attributable to it. In any event, the court "allow[s] greater leeway for regulations and statutes governing business activities than those implicating the *first amendment*" -- "no more than a reasonable degree of certainty can be demanded." *Throckmorton v. NTSB, 295 U.S. App. D.C. 338, 963 F.2d 441, 445 (D.C. Cir. 1992)* (internal quotations & citations omitted). In this case, employers can clarify the term's meaning as they always have -- by recourse to the written guidance which the FAA routinely provides on testing issues raised by interested parties. *See, e.g.,* JA 175, 180; Pet'rs Br. at 27-28 (noting guidance on meaning of "maintenance" issued since 2006 Final Rule). Thus, "the regulated enterprise" has "the ability to clarify the meaning of the regulation by its own inquiry, or by resort to the administrative process." *Vill. of Hoffman Estates v. Flipside, Hoffman Estates, Inc., 455 U.S. 489, 498, 102 S. Ct. 1186, 71 L. Ed. 2d 362 (1982).*

The petitioners next contend the 2006 Final Rule's drug testing requirement subjects employees of noncertificated subcontractors to unreasonable searches in violation of the *Fourth Amendment*. Again we disagree.

In *National Federation of Federal Employees v. Cheney, 280 U.S. App. D.C. 164, 884 F.2d 603 (D.C. Cir. 1989),* the court upheld against a *Fourth Amendment* challenge the U.S. Army's practice of subjecting civilian aviation maintenance personnel to compulsory, random toxicological urine testing because the Army had a compelling interest in ensuring air safety given "the quintessential risk of destruction to life and property posed by aviation." *884 F.2d at 610.* The same justification exists here. Nonetheless, the petitioners offer three grounds for finding the testing program unconstitutional.

First, the petitioners assert that the employees subject to testing are "ordinary citizens." The same is true, however, of the employees of certificated air carrier contractors and subcontractors and was true of the civilian employees in *National Federation*. Yet the petitioners do not suggest these groups may not constitutionally be tested.

Second, the petitioners object to the expansive scope of the testing insofar as it applies to all maintenance work, all employees who "participate" in the work and, especially, to current employees of noncertificated subcontractors. These objections applied as well to employees of a certificated contractor or subcontractor when they first became subject to testing in the late 1980s. Further, as to the first objection specifically, as indicated previously, the FAA can work out through guidance and consultation with subcontractors (as it has with certificated contractors and subcontractors) what is and is not test-triggering "maintenance" work. Further, as to the third objection, while testing of incumbents may as a general matter require a closer relationship between the employee's job and the government interest served than does testing of new applicants, *see Stigile v. Clinton, 324 U.S. App. D.C. 57, 110 F.3d 801, 805-06 (D.C. Cir. 1997); Willner v. Thornburgh, 289 U.S. App. D.C. 93, 928 F.2d 1185, 1188 (D.C. Cir. 1991)*, the nexus between aircraft mechanical work and aviation safety is sufficient, as our decision in *National Federation* made clear. Third, the petitioners argue, as earlier, that the additional testing "simply 'is not needed'" in light of the airworthiness testing all aviation components undergo before being placed in service. Pet'rs Br. at 46 (quoting *Chandler v. Miller, 520 U.S. 305, 320, 117 S. Ct. 1295, 137 L. Ed. 2d 513 (1997))*. We reject this argument here for the same reasons given earlier. *See supra* Part II.B.2. Because of "the quintessential risk of destruction to life and property" posed by substance impaired lapses by maintenance workers at any tier, the testing is justified under *National Federation*.

For the foregoing reasons, we uphold the substance of the FAA's 2006 Final Rule and remand for the limited purpose of conducting the analysis required under the Regulatory Flexibility Act, treating the contractors and subcontractors as regulated entities.

[non-constitutional analysis omitted]

So ordered.

[dissent omitted]

CRAIG BUCK ET AL v. AMERICAN AIRLINES, INC., ET AL.

UNITED STATES COURT OF APPEALS FOR THE FIRST
CIRCUIT

476 F.3d 29

February, 2007

OPINION

When the plaintiffs in this case purchased nonrefundable airline tickets that they ultimately were unable to use, they received no payback of any kind. In the lawsuit that followed, they conceded that they were correctly denied any refund of their base fares but accused the airlines of unlawfully failing to refund various fees and taxes that had been collected as part of the original ticket prices. The plaintiffs' core theory was that the word "nonrefundable" pertained only to their base fares, not to the various other charges (none of which became due without travel).

The district court found the plaintiffs' claims preempted and dismissed the suit for failure to state a viable cause of action. We too conclude that the plaintiffs are fruitlessly endeavoring to fly in unfriendly skies. Consequently, we affirm the order of dismissal.

I. BACKGROUND

On November 4, 2004, fifteen individuals filed suit against a number of airlines and related entities in a Massachusetts state court. The plaintiffs alleged that the defendants had wrongfully retained fees and taxes collected at the time of their purchase of nonrefundable tickets. This retention of funds was wrongful, the plaintiffs maintained, because they never used the tickets and, thus, the fees and taxes, which did not become due until the commencement of air travel, should have been returned.

The defendants removed the case to the federal district court. The plaintiffs, now reduced to nine in number, served an amended complaint (the operative pleading for our purposes) that named six domestic and seven international airlines as the culprits. The fees and taxes said to have been wrongly withheld include passenger facility charges, *see 14 C.F.R. § 158.5*; customs fees, *see 19 C.F.R. § 24.22(g)(1)*; immigration fees, *see 8 C.F.R. § 286.2*; agricultural quarantine fees, *see 7 C.F.R. § 354.3(f)*; security fees, *see 49 C.F.R. § 1510.5*; and charges on behalf of foreign sovereigns (collectively, the fees). The amended complaint named as additional defendants two trade associations (Airlines Reporting Corp. and Air Transport Association of America, Inc.), alleging that they had been complicit in allowing the airlines wrongfully to retain the fees.

The plaintiffs averred that, in keeping the fees, the defendants violated a host of federal regulations, most notably a regulation that provides:

> A passenger shall not be bound by any terms restricting refunds of the ticket price, imposing monetary penalties on passengers, or permitting the

157

carrier to raise the price, unless the passenger receives conspicuous written notice of the salient features of those terms on or with the ticket.

14 C.F.R. § 253.7. The plaintiffs claim that the retained fees constitute a forbidden monetary penalty, imposed without due notice. In this connection, they admit having had adequate notice that their tickets were nonrefundable; in their view, however, this only alerted them to the fact that they could not recover the base ticket price. They had no notice that the fees would be forfeit as well.

The plaintiffs cloaked this theory in pleochroic raiment; their multitudinous statements of claim included counts for declaratory judgment, rescission, breach of contract, unjust enrichment, breach of a covenant of good faith and fair dealing, breach of fiduciary duty, and civil conspiracy. In addition, the plaintiffs purposed to sue pursuant to an implied right of action arising under a federal regulation. Their prayer for relief requested certification of a class; a declaration that (i) the airlines had failed to provide adequate notice of an intention to withhold the fees and (ii) the airlines' retention of the fees was wrongful; treble damages; injunctive and other equitable remediation; and attorneys' fees.

A majority of the defendants moved to dismiss on the ground, inter alia, that all the claims were preempted by *section 105(a)* of the Airline Deregulation Act (ADA), *49 U.S.C. § 41713(b)(1)*. The district court granted the motion to dismiss. *Harrington v. Delta Air Lines, Inc., No. Civ. A. 04-12558, 2006 U.S. Dist. LEXIS 8144, 2006 WL 1581752, at 7-8 (D. Mass. Feb. 21, 2006)*. The court, acting sua sponte, extended its ruling to cover those defendants that had not joined in the original motion. *See id.* This timely appeal followed.

II. STANDARD OF REVIEW

This case arrives on our doorstep following the entry of a judgment of dismissal pursuant to *Rule 12(b)(6)*. Consequently, "we review the lower court's dismissal order de novo, accepting the plaintiffs' well-pleaded facts as true and indulging all reasonable inferences to their behoof." *McCloskey v. Mueller, 446 F.3d 262, 266 (1st Cir. 2006)*. In conducting that tamisage, however, "bald assertions, unsupportable conclusions, periphrastic circumlocutions, and the like need not be credited." *Aulson v. Blanchard, 83 F.3d 1, 3 (1st Cir. 1996)*.

III. DISCUSSION

We begin our analysis with the plaintiffs' lone federal-law claim: their claim of an implied right of action under *14 C.F.R. § 253.4* and *§ 253.7*. These provisions govern the disclosure of terms in contracts for air travel. Among other things, they prevent airlines from claiming the benefit of contract terms not incorporated by reference in a specified manner. *See 14 C.F.R. § 253.4(a)*. They go on to restrict the authority of airlines to impose monetary penalties on passengers without clear notice. *See id. § 253.7*. In this instance, the plaintiffs argue that they were denied notice that they would forfeit the fees (in addition to the base fares) in the event that they did not use their nonrefundable tickets.

In support of this argument, the plaintiffs invoke the test formulated in *Cort v. Ash, 422 U.S. 66, 95 S. Ct. 2080, 45 L. Ed. 2d 26*

(1975), which they insist controls whether a private right of action is to be implied in connection with a federal statute. Under that test, courts are to ask four questions:

> [I]s the plaintiff a member of the class for whose "especial benefit" the statute was passed? Is there any cogent indication of legislative intent to create or deny the remedy sought? Would recognition of the remedy be "consistent with the underlying purposes" of the statutory scheme? Would it be inappropriate to infer a federal remedy because "the cause of action [is] one traditionally relegated to state law . . ."?

Royal Business Grp., Inc. v. Realist, Inc., 933 F.2d 1056, 1060 (1st Cir. 1991) (quoting and paraphrasing *Cort*, 422 U.S. at 78) (alternations in original). The plaintiffs maintain that the regulations' goal is to protect consumers and, thus, that it is appropriate to imply a private right of action.

This argument cannot withstand scrutiny. In the first place, the plaintiffs misapprehend the relevant unit of analysis. Regulations alone cannot create private rights of action; the source of the right must be a statute. *See Alexander v. Sandoval, 532 U.S. 275, 291, 121 S. Ct. 1511, 149 L. Ed. 2d 517 (2001)*; *Iverson v. City of Boston, 452 F.3d 94, 100 (1st Cir. 2006)*. The regulations upon which the plaintiffs rely were promulgated pursuant to *49 U.S.C. § 41707* -- a statute that has its roots in the CAB Sunset Act, Pub. L. No. 98-443, § 7, 98 Stat. 1703, 1706 (1984). The CAB Sunset Act embodies a series of amendments to the ADA, which six years earlier had significantly revamped the Federal Aviation Act. We recently rejected an entreaty to imply a private cause of action pursuant to other regulations implementing the ADA. *See Bonano v. E. Carib. Airline Corp., 365 F.3d 81, 84-85 (1st Cir. 2004)*. In the process, we made clear that, for the purpose of implying private rights of action, the Federal Aviation Act (and, hence, the ADA, *see supra* note 5) is barren soil. *See id.* There is nothing about the case at bar that shakes our confidence in that assessment.

To cinch matters, "[e]very court faced with the question of whether a consumer protection provision of the ADA allows the implication of a private right of action against an airline has answered the question in the negative." *Casas v. Am. Airlines, Inc., 304 F.3d 517, 522 n.7 (5th Cir. 2002)* (quoting *Musson Theatrical, Inc. v. Fed. Express Corp., 89 F.3d 1244, 1252 (6th Cir. 1996)*); *see Statland v. Am. Airlines, Inc., 998 F.2d 539, 540-41 (7th Cir. 1993)* (declining to imply a private right of action under the statutory provision at issue in this case). We see no justification for creating a circuit split. Thus, we hold that the consumer protection provisions of the ADA do not permit the imputation of a private right of action against an airline and that, therefore, the plaintiffs do not have an implied right of action under *14 C.F.R. § 253.4 or § 253.7*.

Lacking a federal-law cause of action, the plaintiffs are relegated to their array of state-law claims. *See supra* note 3. Yet, even though Massachusetts law offers them a cornucopia of vehicles for their theory that the fees should have been refunded, this bounty avails them naught; state-law claims premised on that theory cannot survive the ADA's broad preemptive sweep. We explain briefly.

Pertinently, the ADA declares that no state may "enact or enforce a law, regulation, or other provision having the force and effect of law related to a price, route, or service of an air carrier." *49 U.S.C. § 41713(b)(1)*. The Supreme Court has offered considerable guidance as to how this preemption provision should be construed. In *Morales v. Trans World Airlines, Inc., 504 U.S. 374, 112 S. Ct. 2031, 119 L. Ed. 2d 157 (1992)*, the Court referred to the "sweeping nature" of the preemption provision, emphasizing the reach of the provision's "relationship" language. *Id. at 384*. The *Morales* Court held that the provision should be construed broadly. *Id. at 384-85*. This court has explained that, under *Morales*, the ADA preempts both laws that explicitly refer to an airline's prices and those that have a significant effect upon prices. *See United Parcel Serv., Inc. v. Flores-Galarza, 318 F.3d 323, 335 (1st Cir. 2003)*.

Three years after *Morales*, the Supreme Court reaffirmed the breadth of the ADA's preemption provision. *See Am. Airlines, Inc. v. Wolens, 513 U.S. 219, 223, 115 S. Ct. 817, 130 L. Ed. 2d 715 (1995)*. However, the Court carved out an exception for "suits alleging no violation of state-imposed obligations, but seeking recovery solely for the airline's alleged breach of its own, self-imposed undertakings." *Id. at 228*. It follows that, in order to avoid preemption, the plaintiffs in this case must demonstrate either that their state-law claims do not constitute state enforcement related to airline prices or services, or that they can navigate the straits of the *Wolens* exception.

The plaintiffs' doctrinal starting point is the assertion that their claims are outside the ambit of ADA preemption because they seek to enforce federal, not state, regulatory requirements. At the heart of this assertion lies the dubious premise that since federal rules govern the airlines' collection of the fees and provide certain forms of passenger protection in the contracting process, only federal policies are being advanced by this litigation. On this telling, "[s]tate court enforcement of Federal law is *not* the same as enforcement of a State-imposed requirement," and the fact that the causes of action themselves spring from state law is less important than the source of the underlying policies. Appellants' Br. at 29. This is so, the plaintiffs asseverate, because federal preemption should not disrupt federal policies; after all, nationwide uniformity is the driver for preemption, *see Morales, 504 U.S. at 378*, and that uniformity is not offended by enforcement of federal policies.

This sleight of hand will not work. While the plaintiffs strive to characterize their suit as one that invokes state remedies to right a federal wrong, that characterization does not ring true. More accurately, they are attempting to invoke state remedies to further a state policy: that those who are wronged should have individualized access to the courts in order to remediate that wrong. *Cf. Santagate v. Tower, 64 Mass. App. Ct. 324, 833 N.E.2d 171, 176 (Mass. App. Ct. 2005)* (discussing how Massachusetts provides an "equitable remedy" for those without "an adequate remedy at law"). It is the imposition of this state policy that would constitute forbidden state enforcement, in violation of the ADA's preemption provision, because the ADA itself provides no private right of action.

160

As an alternative, the plaintiffs posit that allowing their suit to proceed "does not -- and in fact cannot -- affect the prices (or rates), routes, or services [of airlines], since the redress occurs only *after* the prices (or rates), routes, and services have been determined by the Air Industry." Appellants' Br. at 19-20. In their view, "[a]irline ticket prices (or rates) are composed of two separate components: (1) the *fare prices* (or rates) set by the airlines, which comprise the base cost of a ticket, and (2) the *taxes, fees, and, charges* imposed by the Government or other fee-levying authorities." *Id. at 21.*

This dichotomy blurs when contextualized within the contours of the "significant effect" doctrine. Although the fees are in one sense separate from the base fare, the two are inextricably intertwined. In all events, an air traveler's concern is with the overall cost of his or her ticket. Thus, when an airline establishes the base fare, it must take cognizance of any surcharges that will be imposed by operation of law.

It is freshman-year economics that higher prices mean lower demand, and that consumers are sensitive to the full price that they must pay, not just the portion of the price that will stay in the seller's coffers. For that reason, an airline must account for the fees when setting its own rates. It follows that a finding for the plaintiffs in this case would impact base fares -- and since past judgments affect future behavior, this is as true of the retrospective relief requested by the plaintiffs as it is of the prospective relief that they request.

In view of these practical realities, it is not surprising that most of the courts to have considered suits for refunds of government fees associated with air travel have found those suits preempted. [Citations omitted]. We say "most" because at least one court has found to the contrary. *See In re Air Transp. Excise Tax. Litig., 37 F. Supp. 2d 1133, 1140 (D. Minn. 1999).* We regard that decision as mistaken.

The plaintiffs next argue that their suit was improvidently dismissed because their contract-based claims fit within the *Wolens* exception. But the plaintiffs' amended complaint identifies only a single word -- "nonrefundable" -- as common to their contracts of carriage with a multitude of airlines. It seems fanciful to suggest, in the circumstances of this case, that the word "nonrefundable" alone can anchor a breach of contract claim.

The same result would follow even if, as the plaintiffs insist, the word "nonrefundable" is ambiguous. At best, an ambiguity would furnish a rejoinder to a claim that the airlines gave clear notice about fees being forfeit. It could not, without more, support a claim that the defendants have breached their duty to treat the tickets as "nonrefundable" by withholding both the fare and the fees.

The plaintiffs attempt to circumvent this conspicuous obstacle by latching onto the federal regulatory guidelines relating to the disclosure of terms in airline contracts. These guidelines, they suggest, are "*federally* mandated terms of their air travel contracts." Appellants' Br. at 20. In making this point, the plaintiffs again emphasize *14 C.F.R. § 253.7,* the provision prohibiting the imposition of monetary penalties without clear notice. The plaintiffs allege that this regulation is written implicitly into every airline contract of carriage and thus, by retaining the fees, the airlines have breached their contractual duty not to levy an unwarned monetary penalty.

The plaintiffs have not directed us to a single case holding that a federal regulation incapable of spawning an implied private right of action may be enforced between private parties as an implicit contract term. The precedent that they most loudly trumpet -- the Texas Supreme Court's decision in *Delta Air Lines, Inc. v. Black, 116 S.W.3d 745, 46 Tex. Sup. Ct. J. 1147 (Tex. 2003)* -- is inapposite. The contract at issue there *explicitly* incorporated federal regulations. *See id. at 755.*

We conclude, without serious question, that the proposition asserted by the plaintiffs is untenable. As they conceded at oral argument, construing all federal regulations touching upon air travel as automatically incorporated into every airline's contracts of carriage would allow litigants freely to skirt the implied right of action doctrine. There is nothing to distinguish the regulation at issue here from the mine-run of federal regulations touching upon air travel, and we will not countenance the flagrant undermining of Supreme Court doctrine that the plaintiffs invite.

Our reluctance is evidently shared by the Fifth Circuit, which confronted a similar problem in *Casas*. There, the plaintiff argued for a remedy under federal common law with respect to violations of regulations prescribed by the federal Department of Transportation. The court rejected this argument, observing that a contrary holding "would be, in substance, to craft a private right of action for violations of [the regulation] -- and thus to circumvent the conclusion that the ADA, and therefore the regulations enacted pursuant to it, creates no private right of action." *Casas, 304 F.3d at 525.* Like the Fifth Circuit, we refuse to abet a blatant evasion of the implied right of action doctrine.

To say more on this point would be supererogatory. At bottom, the plaintiffs would have us believe that the implied right of action doctrine contains a gaping aperture that allows federal regulations, promulgated pursuant to a statute that creates no right of private enforcement, to be privately enforced through state-law mechanisms. We cannot imagine that the Supreme Court, which has devoted nearly three decades to cabining the implied right of action doctrine, *see* Richard H. Fallon et al., Hart & Wechsler's The Federal Courts and the Federal System 781-82 (5th ed. 2003), would approve so vagarious a course. We hold instead that, because no implied right of action exists under the ADA and the regulation at issue here, the regulation cannot be read as an implied contract provision.

Next, the plaintiffs launch a naked appeal to public policy. They tell us that if state-law causes of action are denied them, there will be a wrong (the airlines' withholding of the fees) without a remedy. Put in more hyperbolic terms, a rejection of the plaintiffs' claims would render "almost all airline contracts and certain provisions of Federal law" meaningless. Appellants' Br. at 34.

The first half of this lament -- that a finding for the defendants will jeopardize the enforceability of all airline contracts of carriage -- is empty rhetoric. A finding for the defendants merely retains the configuration of the *Wolens* exception crafted by the Supreme Court, which limited that exception to "self-imposed undertakings." *Wolens, 513 U.S. at 228.* The second half of this lament -- that a finding for the defendants will undercut the federal regulatory scheme -- is equally baseless. Refusing to treat federal regulations as implied contract terms does not in any way diminish the efficacy of the regulatory scheme itself. Contrary to the plaintiffs' importunings, we do not think it "inexplicabl[e]" that Congress might view certain regulations as sufficiently important to warrant their promulgation, yet "not sufficiently important to permit [private] enforcement in any court." Appellants' Br. at 35.

What the plaintiffs fail to grasp is that the unavailability of private enforcement is not the same as the unavailability of any enforcement at all. We made that point in *Bonano, 365 F.3d at 85*, where we remarked upon the power of the Secretary of Transportation to conduct investigations and issue orders with respect to the airline industry. This led us to the conclusion that Congress's preference in this area is for public, rather than private, enforcement. *See id.; see also 49 U.S.C. § 46106*. In other words, Congress reasonably expected the regulations to be enforced by the Secretary. *See Statland, 998 F.2d at 542*.

[two procedural arguments omitted].

IV. CONCLUSION

We need go no further. For the reasons elucidated above, we uphold the district court's order of dismissal.

Affirmed.

COALITION OF AIRLINE PILOTS ASSOCIATIONS, ET AL v.
FEDERAL AVIATION ADMINISTRATION AND
TRANSPORTATION SECURITY ADMINISTRATION.

UNITED STATES COURT OF APPEALS FOR THE DISTRICT OF
COLUMBIA CIRCUIT

370 F.3d 1184

June, 2004

TATEL, *Circuit Judge*: Several unions representing aviation
workers challenge regulations promulgated by the Transportation
Security Administration and the Federal Aviation Administration to
prevent individuals who pose security threats from flying, repairing, or
navigating airplanes in the United States. After the TSA and FAA
promulgated these rules, Congress enacted a new law directing the
agencies to accomplish this mission in a different way, prompting them
to pledge formally that they would no longer enforce the regulations as
written. Because these intervening events have mooted the unions'
claims, we dismiss the petitions for review.

I.

Recognizing that "the terrorist hijacking and crashes of passenger
aircraft on September 11, 2001, which converted civil aircraft into
guided bombs for strikes against the United States, required a
fundamental change in the way [the government] approaches the task
of ensuring the safety and security of the civil air transportation
system," Congress enacted the Aviation and Transportation Security
Act, Pub. L. No. 107-71, 115 Stat. 597 (2001), to improve security in
the nation's transportation system. H.R. CONF. REP. NO. 107-296, at
53 (2001), *reprinted in* 2001 U.S.C.C.A.N. 589, 590. In order to
achieve this goal, Congress created the Transportation Security
Administration within the Department of Transportation and charged it
with assuring "security in all modes of transportation." *49 U.S.C. §
114(d) (Supp. III 2003)*. Under the Act, the TSA assumed responsibility
not only for day-to-day security screening at the nation's airports, *id. §
114(e)*, but also for receiving, assessing, and distributing intelligence
information concerning transportation security, *id. § 114(f)(1)*.

To address the possibility that pilots, aircraft mechanics, or others
working in civil aviation might engage in terrorist activities, the Act
requires the nascent agency to "establish procedures for notifying the
Administrator of the Federal Aviation Administration ... of the identity
of individuals known to pose, or suspected of posing, a risk of air
piracy or terrorism or a threat to airline or passenger safety." *Id. §
114(h)(2)*. The statute also directs the FAA to modify its system for
issuing airman certificates in order to make it more effective at
combating terrorism. *Id. § 44703(g) (2000 & Supp. III 2003)*. Such
certificates are required for individuals who wish to work as pilots,
flight instructors, aircraft mechanics, or other civil aviation employees.
One year after creating the TSA, Congress transferred the agency to the
Department of Homeland Security, placing it under that Department's
Under Secretary for Border and Transportation Security. *See* Homeland

Security Act of 2002, Pub. L. No. 107-296, § 424, 116 Stat. 2135, 2185 (codified at *6 U.S.C. § 234 (Supp. IV 2004)*).

In January 2003, the TSA and FAA issued three new rules designed to coordinate their efforts to keep dangerous individuals from infiltrating the commercial aviation system. *See Threat Assessments Regarding Citizens of the United States Who Hold or Apply for FAA Certificates, 68 Fed. Reg. 3756 (Jan. 24, 2003)* (codified at *49 C.F.R. § 1540.115*); *Threat Assessments Regarding Alien Holders of, and Applicants for, FAA Certificates, 68 Fed. Reg. 3762 (Jan. 24, 2003)* (codified at *49 C.F.R. § 1540.117*); *Ineligibility for an Airman Certificate Based on Security Grounds, 68 Fed. Reg. 3772 (Jan. 24, 2003)* (codified at *14 C.F.R. §§ 61.18, 63.14, 65.14*). Together, these three rules--a TSA rule applicable to citizens, a TSA rule applicable to non-citizens, and an FAA rule applicable to both citizens and non-citizens--establish a system by which the TSA determines whether any airman certificate holder (or applicant for such certificate) poses a security threat. If the TSA makes such a determination, it informs the FAA of the threat, and the FAA in turn revokes or denies the certificate. Specifically, TSA's rules, codified at *49 C.F.R. § 1540.115* for citizens and *section 1540.117* for non-citizens, provide that when TSA's Assistant Administrator for Intelligence finds that any individual is "suspected of posing, or is known to pose" a security threat, *49 C.F.R. §§ 1540.115(c), 1540.117(c)*, the agency will serve that person, as well as the FAA, with an Initial Notification of Threat Assessment, *id. §§ 1540.115(e)(1), 1540.117(e)(1)*. The individual then has fifteen days in which to request any "releasable materials" on which the Initial Notification was based, meaning information that is not classified or otherwise sensitive for security reasons. *Id. §§ 1540.115(e)(2), 1540.117(e)(2)*. The individual may also file a written reply responding to the notification. *Id. §§ 1540.115(e)(4), 1540.117(e)(4)*. For citizens and aliens (both resident and non-resident), TSA's Deputy Administrator then reviews the Initial Notification, any information collected by the agency, and the individual's reply to determine whether the individual poses a security threat. *Id. §§ 1540.115(f)(1), 1540.117(f)(1)*. In the case of alien certificate holders, the Deputy Administrator then decides whether to issue a Final Notification of Threat Assessment or to withdraw the Initial Notification. *Id. § 1540.117(f)*. In the case of citizen certificate holders, if the Deputy Administrator determines that the individual poses a security threat, TSA's Administrator will conduct a separate, independent review of the Initial Notification before issuing a Final Notification. *Id. § 1540.115(f)(2)*. Under the rules, the TSA must serve on the FAA any Final Notification issued to either a citizen or alien certificate holder. *Id.*; *id. § 1540.117(f)(2)*. Although acknowledging that in most cases the TSA will rely on classified or otherwise sensitive information in determining whether an individual poses a security threat, *68 Fed. Reg. at 3758, 3765*, the rules provide that the TSA need not disclose such information to the certificate holder, *49 C.F.R. §§ 1540.115(g), 1540.117(g)*.

Under the FAA's rule, any person deemed a security threat by the TSA automatically becomes ineligible to hold an airman certificate. *14 C.F.R. §§ 61.18(a)* (pilots, flight instructors, and ground instructors), *63.14(a)* (flight crewmembers other than pilots), *65.14(a)* (airmen other than flight crewmembers). Thus, under this regulatory scheme, the FAA will suspend the airman certificate of any person to whom the

TSA issues an Initial Notification of Threat Assessment and then revoke the certificate upon the TSA's issuance of a Final Notification. *See, e.g.,* 14 *C.F.R.* §§ *61.18(b)(2)* (suspension), *61.18(c)(2)* (revocation).

Declaring that prior notice and comment would delay their ability to keep dangerous persons from holding airman certificates, the TSA and FAA both found that *section 553(b) of the Administrative Procedure Act*, which permits agencies to issue rules without notice and comment when they find "good cause" that "notice and public procedure ... are impracticable, unnecessary, or contrary to the public interest," *5 U.S.C. § 553(b) (2000)*, excused advance public participation here. *See 68 Fed. Reg. at 3759* (TSA rule governing citizens), *68 Fed. Reg. 3762, 3766* (TSA rule governing aliens), *68 Fed. Reg. 3772, 3773* (FAA rule). Accordingly, the agencies promulgated all three rules without notice and comment and made each immediately effective upon adoption.

In March 2003, the Coalition of Airline Pilots Associations, along with several labor organizations (collectively, "the Coalition"), filed petitions for review that asserted facial challenges to all three rules insofar as they affect citizen and resident alien airmen. (Challenges to these regulations insofar as they apply to non-resident alien airmen are resolved in *Jifry v. FAA, 361 U.S. App. D.C. 450, 370 F.3d 1174, 2004 U.S. App. LEXIS 11570, (D.C. Cir. 2004)*, issued simultaneously with this opinion.) The Coalition claims that the regulations violate the *Fifth Amendment's Due Process Clause* by failing to give affected airmen a meaningful opportunity to be heard at a meaningful time, that the rules are unconstitutionally vague and overbroad, that the TSA and FAA lacked statutory authority to promulgate the rules, and that the agencies violated the APA by promulgating the rules without prior notice and comment.

Nine months after the Coalition filed its petitions, Congress enacted the Vision 100-Century of Aviation Reauthorization Act, Pub. L. No. 108-176, 117 Stat. 2490 (2003). Significantly changing the legal landscape for threat assessments and certificate revocations, this new Act, in a section now codified as *49 U.S.C. § 46111 (Supp. IV 2004)*, expressly requires the FAA to amend, suspend, or revoke certificates in response to TSA threat assessments:

The Administrator of the [FAA] shall issue an order amending, modifying, suspending, or revoking any part of a certificate issued under this title if the Administrator is notified by the Under Secretary for Border and Transportation Security of the Department of Homeland Security that the holder of the certificate poses, or is suspected of posing, a risk of air piracy or terrorism or a threat to airline or passenger safety. If requested by the Under Secretary, the order shall be effective immediately.

Section 46111 also gives citizen airmen facing adverse certificate actions administrative appeal rights. *Id. § 46111(b)-(g)*. Specifically, affected citizen certificate holders are entitled to a hearing on the record before an administrative law judge, *id. § 46111(b)*, an appeal to the Transportation Security Oversight Board, *id. § 46111(d)*, and the opportunity for judicial review, *id. § 46111(e)*. *Section 46111* also ensures that citizen airmen receive a written explanation for the agency action and all relevant documents supporting adverse certificate actions

"to the maximum extent" permitted by national security interests, *id. §
46111(f)*, as well as an unclassified summary of any classified
information on which the FAA Administrator's order rests, *id. §
46111(g)(3)*.

Days after the President signed *section 46111* into law, the
government moved to dismiss as moot the Coalition's challenge to the
TSA and FAA rules. According to the government, this newly enacted
legislation, by requiring the two agencies to provide more robust
procedural protections for citizen airmen, superseded *section 1540.115*
and rendered it legally ineffective. The government also represented
that even though nothing in *section 46111* requires the agencies to
adopt new procedures for non-citizens, the TSA and FAA would
nonetheless not only craft new regulations to provide resident aliens
with administrative and judicial review procedures, but also cease
applying the rules against resident aliens in the interim. In view of these
developments, the government urged us to dismiss the Coalition's
petitions as non-justiciable. The Coalition objected, and we deferred
consideration of the mootness issue until oral argument. *Coalition of
Airline Pilots Ass'ns v. FAA*, No. 03-1074 (D.C. Cir. Jan. 15, 2004).

Two weeks before oral argument, on March 16, 2004, the
government informed us that the TSA had published its previous
representations to this court in its rulemaking dockets. Its
"Memorandum to the Dockets" provides:

> Although new implementing regulations have not been
> promulgated, the existing regulation governing
> certificate suspension and revocation procedures for
> citizens [*49 C.F.R. § 1540.115*] is no longer effective as
> to citizens. This regulation has not been applied by TSA,
> nor will it be applied by TSA, to citizens because it does
> not comport with Congress's new statutory directive.

> Although the new statute requires the FAA to take immediate
> certificate action when requested to do so by the Under Secretary [for
> Border and Transportation Security], it does not specify what appellate
> procedures apply when TSA determines that a resident alien who holds
> an FAA airman certificate poses a security threat. Nevertheless, the
> FAA and TSA will develop new procedures that govern resident aliens.
> The new procedures will contain an agency review process, followed
> by judicial review based on the entire record. In the meantime, TSA
> will not apply *49 CFR 1540.117* to resident aliens.

Memorandum to the Dockets, TSA Rulemaking Dockets Nos.
TSA-2002-13732 and TSA-2002-13733, Transportation Security
Administration, U.S. Department of Homeland Security (Mar. 16,
2004), *available at* http://dmses.dot.gov/docimages/p78/273780.pdf.

Then, just six days before oral argument, the government filed a
second post-briefing submission stating that the "FAA and TSA intend
to issue the permanent procedures pursuant to notice and comment
rulemaking." Letter from E. Roy Hawkens, Attorney, U.S. Department
of Justice, to Mark J. Langer, Clerk, U.S. Court of Appeals for the
District of Columbia Circuit (Mar. 24, 2004).

With a new statute on the books, a memorandum in the rulemaking dockets, and new agency representations to the court, we turn to the question of whether this case remains justiciable.

II.

Article III, section 2 of the Constitution limits federal court jurisdiction to cases or controversies, meaning that "a live controversy must exist at all stages of review." *Nat'l Black Police Ass'n v. District of Columbia, 323 U.S. App. D.C. 292, 108 F.3d 346, 349 (D.C. Cir. 1997).* We will thus "refrain from deciding [a case] if events have so transpired that the decision will neither presently affect the parties' rights nor have a more-than-speculative chance of affecting them in the future." *Id.* (internal quotation marks omitted). Of significance to this case, however, defendants cannot usually shelter their actions from judicial scrutiny simply by claiming that they will stop the challenged conduct. As the Supreme Court has explained, "voluntary cessation of allegedly illegal conduct does not deprive the tribunal of power to hear and determine the case, *i.e.*, does not make the case moot" unless "(1) it can be said with assurance that there is no reasonable expectation ... that the alleged violation will recur, and (2) interim relief or events have completely and irrevocably eradicated the effects of the alleged violation." *County of Los Angeles v. Davis, 440 U.S. 625, 631, 59 L. Ed. 2d 642, 99 S. Ct. 1379 (U.S. 1979)* (citations and internal quotation marks omitted) (omission in original). Moreover, the "burden of demonstrating mootness is a heavy one." *Id.* (internal quotation marks omitted).

Arguing that the two agencies' commitment to refrain from applying the challenged rules and *49 U.S.C. § 46111*'s enactment moot this case, the government urges us to dismiss the Coalition's petitions as non-justiciable. To assess this threshold jurisdictional issue, we apply the mootness standard to each of the Coalition's claims. *See Daingerfield Island Protective Soc'y v. Lujan, 287 U.S. App. D.C. 101, 920 F.2d 32, 37 (D.C. Cir. 1990)* ("Claim specific analysis [is] required before we [can] say that appellees have met the 'heavy' burden of demonstrating mootness." (citing *Davis, 440 U.S. at 631*)).

For its primary ground of attack, the Coalition contends that by denying airman certificates without adequate notice and opportunity to be heard, the rules violate the *Fifth Amendment's* procedural due process guarantee. For citizen airmen, however, not only has the TSA formally pledged to cease enforcing *section 1540.115*, but applying that regulation would now be unlawful under *49 U.S.C. § 46111*, which requires far more robust procedural protections than are available under the rule. *See Schering Corp. v. Shalala, 302 U.S. App. D.C. 35, 995 F.2d 1103, 1105 (D.C. Cir. 1993)* (finding moot a challenge to an FDA interpretation letter giving the agency discretion to define "bioequivalence" once the agency issued binding regulations defining that term). With respect to resident aliens, the agencies' commitment to draft new regulations that will provide additional administrative review procedures--a commitment made both to this court and in the formal entry in the TSA rulemaking dockets--provides sufficient assurance that the agencies will never return to *section 1540.117*'s allegedly unlawful procedures. *See Ariz. Pub. Serv. Co. v. EPA, 341 U.S. App. D.C. 222, 211 F.3d 1280, 1296 (D.C. Cir. 2000)* (finding a challenge moot when "there is no indication that the [agency] will revert to its past proposal"). Given the agencies' past practices, moreover, it seems highly unlikely that they would even consider using the existing regulations. Indeed, the TSA has never used *section 1540.115* against a citizen. Because there is thus no reasonable expectation that the alleged due process violations will recur, the first element of mootness is satisfied.

We also think that interim events have completely eradicated the effects of the alleged due process violations--the mootness test's second element. Not only has Congress wholly displaced *section 1540.115* procedures, but TSA has abandoned *section 1540.117* with respect to resident aliens, committing instead to provide them with greater procedural rights. Given these events, "any opinion regarding [the] rules would be merely advisory." *Nat'l Mining Ass'n v. U.S. Dep't of the Interior, 346 U.S. App. D.C. 192, 251 F.3d 1007, 1011 (D.C. Cir. 2001)* (finding moot a facial due process challenge to regulations after the agency promulgated new ones because the old rules "cannot be evaluated as if nothing has changed").

For its second claim, the Coalition argues that the rules are unconstitutionally vague and overbroad. As the Coalition sees it, the rules fail to give fair warning of the conduct they prohibit, delegate unfettered discretion to TSA officials, and chill constitutionally protected expression. Insisting this claim remains justiciable, the Coalition argues that *49 U.S.C. § 46111*'s enactment not only fails to prevent likely recurrence of the asserted constitutional violations, but also, by mandating certificate suspensions and revocations when the government merely "suspects" a certificate holder of posing a security threat, guarantees that the new rules will be unconstitutionally vague and overbroad. We disagree.

To begin with, the alleged constitutional violations are unlikely to recur. Because the agencies have promised to issue their new rules through notice-and-comment procedures, the Coalition will have every opportunity to push TSA to clarify the kinds of conduct or risks the agency would consider threats to air security. Indeed, Coalition counsel acknowledged at oral argument that whether the statute perpetuates an unconstitutionally vague regulatory regime "will depend on how the agency interprets the statute." Tr. of Oral Argument at 13. Moreover, intervening events-*section 46111*'s enactment and the agencies' representations that they will refrain from enforcing the rules--have eliminated the effects of the allegedly vague and overbroad rules. Emptied of legal effect, the challenged rules can neither chill protected speech nor punish certificate holders based on unclear standards of suspicion. Finally, to the extent the Coalition is attacking *section 46111*, and not the rules themselves, we lack jurisdiction to consider such a claim. If the Coalition wishes to challenge the new statute, it must do so in the district court. *Compare 28 U.S.C. § 1331 (2000)* (district courts' original jurisdiction), *with id. § 1291 (2000)* (courts of appeals' appellate jurisdiction).

Next, the Coalition claims that the agencies exceeded their statutory authority by effectively transferring FAA's power to suspend and revoke airman certificates to the TSA. We are confident, however, that the agencies cannot repeat this asserted violation, for as Coalition counsel acknowledged at oral argument, Congress has now clearly authorized--indeed required--the FAA to take immediate action when informed by the TSA of a security threat. *See 49 U.S.C. § 46111(a)*. In other words, even if, as the Coalition alleges, the agencies acted unlawfully in promulgating their rules, Congress has wholly cured the problem. Combined with the agencies' promise never to enforce the rules, Congress's action moots this claim as well.

We turn finally to the Coalition's claim that issuing the rules without advance public participation violated the APA's notice-and-comment requirement. *See 5 U.S.C. § 553(b), (c)*. Because the government has advised us that both agencies intend to issue the permanent procedures pursuant to notice-and-comment rulemaking, we have little trouble finding "no reasonable expectation ... that the alleged violation will recur." *Davis, 440 U.S. at 631* (internal quotation marks omitted) (omission in original). In addition, because the challenged rules are now devoid of any legal effect and because the agencies will use notice-and-comment procedures to promulgate the revised rules, the TSA and FAA have "eradicated the effects of the alleged violation." *Id.* Accordingly, "nothing [would] turn[] on the outcome" of our review of the Coalition's notice-and-comment claim. *Schering Corp., 995 F.2d at 1105*; *cf. Natural Res. Def. Council, Inc. v. U.S. Nuclear Regulatory Comm'n, 220 U.S. App. D.C. 261, 680 F.2d 810, 814 n.8 (D.C. Cir. 1982)* (finding that an agency's repromulgation of a challenged rule pursuant to notice-and-comment procedures mooted a notice-and-comment challenge to that rule).

For the foregoing reasons, we conclude that the petitions are no longer justiciable. At oral argument, Coalition counsel, still concerned about ongoing effects of the regulations, urged that we vacate the challenged rules with respect to citizens and resident aliens even if we determine that a live controversy no longer exists. Given the government's repeated and unequivocal assurances that the regulations are already effectively dead, however, we see no need to take this additional step. Indeed, at oral argument, government counsel not only reiterated that "there clearly is no operative regulation," Tr. of Oral Argument at 18, but also represented that "the agencies have already vacated" the rules, Tr. of Oral Argument at 24, *Jifry v. FAA* (No. 03-1085). Based on these assurances that the agencies have effectively erased the regulations as to both citizens and resident aliens, we dismiss the petitions.

So ordered.

TITLE 49. TRANSPORTATION
SUBTITLE VII. AVIATION PROGRAMS
PART A. AIR COMMERCE AND SAFETY
SUBPART IV. ENFORCEMENT AND PENALTIES
CHAPTER 461. INVESTIGATIONS AND PROCEEDINGS

49 USC § 46111

§ 46111. Certificate actions in response to a security threat

(a) Orders. The Administrator of Federal Aviation Administration shall issue an order amending, modifying, suspending, or revoking any part of a certificate issued under this title if the Administrator is notified by the Under Secretary for Border and Transportation Security of the Department of Homeland Security that the holder of the certificate poses, or is suspected of posing, a risk of air piracy or terrorism or a threat to airline or passenger safety. If requested by the Under Secretary, the order shall be effective immediately.

(b) Hearings for citizens. An individual who is a citizen of the United States who is adversely affected by an order of the Administrator under subsection (a) is entitled to a hearing on the record.

(c) Hearings. When conducting a hearing under this section, the administrative law judge shall not be bound by findings of fact or interpretations of laws and regulations of the Administrator or the Under Secretary.

(d) Appeals. An appeal from a decision of an administrative law judge as the result of a hearing under subsection (b) shall be made to the Transportation Security Oversight Board established by section 115 [*49 USCS § 115*]. The Board shall establish a panel to review the decision. The members of this panel (1) shall not be employees of the Transportation Security Administration, (2) shall have the level of security clearance needed to review the determination made under this section, and (3) shall be given access to all relevant documents that support that determination. The panel may affirm, modify, or reverse the decision.

(e) Review. A person substantially affected by an action of a panel under subsection (d), or the Under Secretary when the Under Secretary decides that the action of the panel under this section will have a significant adverse impact on carrying out this part, may obtain review of the order under section 46110 [*49 USCS § 46110*]. The Under Secretary and the Administrator shall be made a party to the review proceedings. Findings of fact of the panel are conclusive if supported by substantial evidence.

(f) Explanation of decisions. An individual who commences an appeal under this section shall receive a written explanation of the basis for the determination or decision and all relevant documents that support that determination to the maximum extent that the national security interests of the United States and other applicable laws permit.

(g) Classified evidence.

(1) In general. The Under Secretary, in consultation with the Administrator and the Director of Central Intelligence, shall issue regulations to establish procedures by which the Under Secretary, as part of a hearing conducted under this section, may provide an unclassified summary of classified evidence upon which the order of the Administrator was based to the individual adversely affected by the order.

(2) Review of classified evidence by administrative law judge.

(A) Review. As part of a hearing conducted under this section, if the order of the Administrator issued under subsection (a) is based on classified information (as defined in section 1(a) of the Classified Information Procedures Act (18 U.S.C. App.), such information may be submitted by the Under Secretary to the reviewing administrative law judge, pursuant to appropriate security procedures, and shall be reviewed by the administrative law judge ex parte and in camera.

(B) Security clearances. Pursuant to existing procedures and requirements, the Under Secretary shall, in coordination, as necessary, with the heads of other affected departments or agencies, ensure that administrative law judges reviewing orders of the Administrator under this section possess security clearances appropriate for their work under this section.

(3) Unclassified summaries of classified evidence. As part of a hearing conducted under this section and upon the request of the individual adversely affected by an order of the Administrator under subsection (a), the Under Secretary shall provide to the individual and reviewing administrative law judge, consistent with the procedures established under paragraph (1), an unclassified summary of any classified information upon which the order of the Administrator is based.

TAREK H. JIFRY AND MAAN H. ZARIE v. FEDERAL AVIATION
ADMINISTRATION, ET AL.

UNITED STATES COURT OF APPEALS FOR THE DISTRICT OF
COLUMBIA CIRCUIT

370 F.3d 1174

June, 2004

ROGERS, *Circuit Judge*: Petitions filed by two non-resident alien pilots challenge certain aviation regulations adopted in the wake of the September 11, 2001 terrorist attacks. From the establishment of the Transportation Security Administration ("TSA") in November 2001 to the promulgation of the challenged regulations in January 2003, aviation security has undergone a fundamental transformation. The pilots contend that the new procedures resulting in the revocation of their airman certificates issued by the Federal Aviation Administration ("FAA") violated the *Administrative Procedure Act* ("APA") and the *due process clause of the Fifth Amendment to the United States Constitution.* Specifically, they contend that the January 2003 regulations were unlawfully promulgated without notice and comment, that the revocations were not supported by substantial evidence in the record, and that they were denied meaningful notice of the evidence against them and a meaningful opportunity to be heard.

I.

Congress has delegated broad discretion to the Federal Aviation Administration ("FAA") to prescribe regulations and standards for safety in air commerce and national security. *See 49 U.S.C. § 44701(a)(5)*. The FAA may "at any time" reexamine the issuance of an airman certificate and issue an order "modifying, suspending, or revoking" a certificate if the Administrator determines that such action is required for "safety in air commerce" and "the public interest." *49 U.S.C. §§ 44709(a), (b)*. With regard to issuing airman certificates to qualified individuals, Congress distinguished between citizens and aliens, conferring broad discretion to the FAA regarding alien pilots. *See id. § 44703(e)*. After the September 11, 2001 terrorist attacks, Congress established the Transportation Security Administration ("TSA") on November 19, 2001, and transferred much of the responsibility for civil aviation security from the FAA to the TSA. *See id. §§ 114(d), (f)*.

This case concerns alien pilots only; citizens and resident alien pilots have challenged the applicable regulations in *Coalition of Air Line Pilots Ass'ns v. FAA, 361 U.S. App. D.C. 460, 370 F.3d 1184, 2004 U.S. App. LEXIS 11560, Nos. 03-1074 and 03-1076 (D.C. Cir. June 11, 2004)*. The two pilots, Jifry and Zarie, are citizens of Saudi Arabia who have used their FAA certificates to pilot flights abroad, but have not operated Saudi Arabian Airlines flights to the United States in the past nine and four years, respectively. On August 14, 2002, the TSA sent letters to the FAA requesting that Captain Jifry and Captain Zarie have their airman certificates revoked, stating that "based upon information available to us," they presented "a security risk to civil aviation or national security." The FAA notified Jifry and Zarie by letters of August 20, 2002, that their airman certificates would be revoked because the Acting Under Secretary of Transportation for Security, pursuant *49 U.S.C. §§ 44709(b)(1)(A)* and *46105(c)*, had determined that they presented risks to aviation or national security. The FAA revoked the pilots' certificates, *see 49 U.S.C. § 44709(b)*, and the pilots appealed the revocations to the National Transportation Safety Board ("NTSB"). *Id. § 44709(d)*. An administrative law judge ("ALJ") held a telephonic pre-hearing conference on January 17, 2003, and ordered that the FAA and the TSA provide a privilege log and that depositions of key witnesses take place by mid-February.

A week later, on January 24, 2003, the FAA dismissed the revocation actions against Jifry and Zarie, and in conjunction with the TSA, published, without notice and comment, new regulations governing the suspension and revocation of airman certificates for security reasons. *See 14 C.F.R. § 61.18, 49 C.F.R. § 1540.117*. The new FAA regulation, *14 C.F.R. § 61.18*, provides for automatic suspension by the FAA of airman certificates upon written notification from the TSA that the pilot poses a security threat and, therefore, is not eligible to hold an airman certificate. The TSA simultaneously promulgated *49 C.F.R. § 1540.117*, which establishes the procedure by which the TSA initially and finally notifies nonresident aliens who hold or apply for FAA certificates that they pose a security threat, and requires the TSA to notify the FAA once the TSA has determined that a pilot is a security threat. Upon finding that a pilot poses a "security threat," *see 49 C.F.R. § 1540.117(c)*, the TSA Assistant Administrator for Intelligence issues an Initial Notification of Threat Assessment ("Initial Notice") to the individual and serves that determination upon the FAA. *See id. § 1540.117(e)*. The FAA then suspends the pilot's certificate. *See 14 C.F.R. § 61.18(b)(2)*. No later than 15 days after service, the pilot may make a written request for copies of releasable materials upon which the Initial Notice was based. *See 49 C.F.R. § 1540.117(e)(1) & (2)*. The TSA must respond not later than 30 days after receiving the request, and the pilot may submit a written reply within 15 days of receiving the TSA's response. *See id. § 1540.117(e)(3) & (4)*. At that point, the TSA Deputy Administrator must review the entire record *de novo* to determine if the pilot poses a security risk. *Id. § 1540.117(f)(1)*. If the Deputy so determines, the TSA serves a Final Notification of Threat Assessment ("Final Notice"), *id. § 1540.117(f)(2)*, and the FAA revokes the certificate. *See 14 C.F.R. § 61.18(c)(2)*. The pilot may appeal the certificate revocation to the NTSB. *See 49 U.S.C. § 44709(d)*. Upon exhaustion of these administrative remedies, the pilot may seek review in the court of appeals, which may review the case on the merits. *See id. §§ 44709(f), 46110*.

On January 24, 2003, the TSA also served an Initial Notice of Threat Assessment designating Jifry and Zarie as security threats, and the FAA suspended their certificates. The pilots appealed the Initial Notice, and requested the materials upon which the Initial Notice had been issued. The TSA provided the releasable materials, but did not include the factual basis for TSA's determination, which was based on classified information. The pilots then appealed the suspension of their certificates to the NTSB. The ALJ granted the TSA's motion for summary judgment, ruling that the only question was procedural - whether the pilots had been duly advised by the TSA, in writing, that they posed a security threat, and finding that they had. Upon the pilots' appeals, the NTSB affirmed the ALJ's order in favor of the TSA. Jifry and Zarie then filed replies to the TSA's Initial Notice, stating that the "lack of evidence and information about the basis for the determination contained in the TSA's response" made it impossible for them to specifically rebut the TSA's allegations, and denying that they were security threats. On May 8, 2003, the TSA Deputy Administrator, upon *de novo* review of the administrative record, denied the pilots' challenge to the Initial Notice and issued a Final Notice based on finding that Jifry and Zarie posed security threats. *See 49 C.F.R. § 1540.117(c)*. The FAA then revoked the pilots' airman certificates. On August 13, 2003, the NTSB denied the pilots' appeal of the revocation of their certificates for the same reasons it had denied their challenges to the suspensions, and affirmed the ALJ's grant of summary judgment to the TSA and the emergency orders of revocation.

II.

The pilots make three challenges to the revocations of their FAA airman certificates: first, that the January 2003 regulations were unlawfully promulgated without notice and comment; second, that the revocations were not supported by substantial evidence in the record; and third, that the procedures provided by the January 2003 regulations violated their due process rights under the *Fifth Amendment to the Constitution*. We address each in turn.

Section 553 of the Administrative Procedure Act ("APA") requires an agency to publish a general notice of proposed rulemaking and to afford an opportunity for interested persons to participate in the rulemaking. *See 5 U.S.C. § 553(b), (c)*. The "good cause" exception, however, provides that "when the agency for good cause finds ... that notice and public procedure thereon are impracticable, unnecessary, or contrary to the public interest," the agency need not engage in notice and comment. *Id. § 553(b)(3)(B)*. The pilots contend that the regulations of January 2003 are invalid because they were unlawfully promulgated without notice and comment, and there was no rational basis for eliminating the right to a meaningful appeal before the NTSB. They maintain that the "good cause" exception does not apply because notice and comment had not been "impracticable, unnecessary or contrary to the public interest" inasmuch as the FAA already had the authority to immediately suspend or revoke a certificate upon finding that "safety in air commerce or air transportation and the public interest" required such an action. *See 49 U.S.C. § 44709, amended by* Pub. L. No. 108-176, 117 Stat. 2490 (2003).

Contrary to the position of respondents TSA, FAA, and the NTSB, the pilots' APA challenges to the FAA regulation, *14 C.F.R. § 61.18*, are not mooted by the enactment of the Vision 100 - Century of Aviation Reauthorization Act ("Act"), *49 U.S.C. § 46111*, on December 12, 2003. The Act provides that the FAA Administrator "shall issue an order ... suspending, or revoking any part of a certificate ... if the Administrator is notified by the Under Secretary for Border Transportation Security of the Department of Homeland Security that the holder of the certificate poses, or is suspected of posing, a risk of air piracy or terrorism or a threat to airline or passenger safety." *49 U.S.C. § 46111(a)*. The respondents maintain that through *§ 46111*, Congress approved the certificate-revocation process embodied in the FAA regulation by expressly commanding the FAA to suspend or revoke certificates if requested by the TSA. The respondents have not shown a

lack of a live controversy, however, because the effects of *14 C.F.R. §
61.18* remain very real for non-resident alien pilots like Jifry and Zarie.
The FAA has applied this regulation against the two pilots, and it
remains in effect notwithstanding the Act. The pilots therefore retain "a
legally cognizable interest in the outcome," *Powell v. McCormack, 395
U.S. 486, 496, 23 L. Ed. 2d 491, 89 S. Ct. 1944 (1969)*, of their APA
claims.

Generally, the "good cause" exception to notice and comment
rulemaking, *see 5 U.S.C. § 553(b)(3)(B)*, is to be "narrowly construed
and only reluctantly countenanced." *Tennessee Gas Pipeline Co. v.
FERC, 297 U.S. App. D.C. 141, 969 F.2d 1141, 1144 (D.C. Cir. 1992)*
(quoting *New Jersey v. EPA, 200 U.S. App. D.C. 174, 626 F.2d 1038,
1045 (D.C. Cir. 1980))*. The exception excuses notice and comment in
emergency situations, *Am. Fed'n of Gov't Employees v. Block, 210 U.S.
App. D.C. 336, 655 F.2d 1153, 1156 (D.C. Cir. 1981)*, or where delay
could result in serious harm. *See Hawaii Helicopter Operators Ass'n v.
FAA, 51 F.3d 212, 214 (9th Cir. 1995)*. The latter circumstance is
applicable here in examining the TSA's determination that "the use of
notice and comment prior to issuance of the [January 2003 regulations]
could delay the ability of TSA and the FAA to take effective action to
keep persons found by TSA to pose a security threat from holding an
airman certificate," and was "necessary to prevent a possible imminent
hazard to aircraft, persons, and property within the United States."

The pilots contend that the "good cause" exception does not apply
because the FAA already had unlimited power to revoke a certificate
immediately if it believed an airman to be a security risk, *see 49 U.S.C.
§ 44709*, and the TSA was already authorized to make security
assessments under *49 U.S.C. § 114(f)*. While true, the pilots fail to
acknowledge that at the time the challenged regulations were adopted,
the FAA's power to suspend or revoke certificates was permissive only.
See 49 U.S.C. § 44709. Congress had not yet enacted *49 U.S.C. §
46111*, which formalized the requirement that the FAA shall suspend,
modify, or revoke a certificate if notified by the TSA that an individual
posed a security risk. As the respondents explain, the January 2003
regulations mandated a "streamlined process" by which an individual's
pilot certificate would be automatically suspended or revoked by the
FAA upon notification by the TSA that a pilot posed a security threat.
The TSA and FAA deemed such regulations necessary "in order to
minimize security threats and potential security vulnerabilities to the
fullest extent possible." Given the respondents' legitimate concern over
the threat of further terrorist acts involving aircraft in the aftermath of
September 11, 2001, *see* Declaration of TSA Deputy Administrator
Stephen McHale (hereinafter McHale Decl.) at 4, the agencies had
"good cause" for not offering advance public participation. *See Utility
Solid Waste Activities Group v. EPA, 344 U.S. App. D.C. 382, 236 F.3d
749, 754-55 (D.C. Cir. 2001)*.

On the merits, the pilots' APA challenge fails. The court's review
of agency rulemaking is highly deferential, limited to determining
"whether the agency has considered the relevant factors and articulated
a 'rational connection between the facts found and the choice made.' "
*United States Air Tour Ass'n v. FAA, 353 U.S. App. D.C. 213, 298 F.3d
997, 1005 (D.C. Cir. 2002)* (quoting *Motor Veh. Mfrs. Ass'n v. State
Farm Mut. Auto. Ins. Co., 463 U.S. 29, 43, 77 L. Ed. 2d 443, 103 S. Ct.
2856 (1983))*. In *BellSouth Corp. v. FCC, 333 U.S. App. D.C. 308, 162*

F.3d 1215, 1221 (D.C. Cir. 1999), the court observed that "when ... an agency is obliged to make policy judgments where no factual certainties exist or where facts alone do not provide the answer, [the reviewing court's] role is more limited; we require only that the agency so state and go on to identify the considerations it found persuasive."

Contrary to the pilots' position, the regulations are not arbitrary and capricious for bearing no rational connection to the problem identified by the FAA. It is self-evident that the regulations are related to the TSA's and FAA's goals of improving the safety of air travel. Nor is the court in a position to second-guess the respondents' judgment that imposing stricter procedures for coordinating security risks and restricting individuals who pose security threats from holding airman certificates was necessary to further that goal. *See BellSouth Corp. v. FCC, 162 F.3d at 1221-22.* Moreover, the pilots' contention that the risk posed by the certificate holders alleged to be security threats was not remedied by providing fewer procedural protections to the certification holders and narrowing their right to NTSB review is to no avail because *49 U.S.C. § 46111* produces the same result. *Section 46111* makes no provision for NTSB review even for citizens, and the Conference Report states that non-resident aliens "have the right to the appeal procedures that [TSA] has already provided for them." H.R. Conf. Rpt. 108-334 at 152 (2003). In addition, *§ 46111(a)* requires the FAA to respond automatically to TSA threat assessments, providing that the FAA "shall issue an order amending, modifying, suspending, or revoking any part of a certificate issued under this title if the Administrator is notified by ... the Department of Homeland Security that the holder of the certificate poses, or is suspected of posing, a risk of air piracy or terrorism or a threat to airline or passenger safety." *49 U.S.C. § 46111(a).* Accordingly, if these pilots retain any right to NTSB review at all, it is no broader than the review for procedural regularity that they have received, and they would therefore garner no benefit from a remand. Indeed, an additional ground for rejecting the pilots' challenge to the promulgation of the FAA regulation without notice and comment exists precisely because *§ 46111* now provides an express statutory authorization for the automatic revocation that was previously predicated on the regulations alone; even were the court to invalidate the regulations for lack of notice and comment, the statute would compel the FAA to honor the TSA's notification and take immediate action against the pilots' certificates.

III.

The scope of the court's review of the pilots' challenges to the TSA's actions is limited to determining whether the actions were "arbitrary, capricious, an abuse of discretion, or otherwise not in accordance with law." *5 U.S.C. § 706(2)(A).* Under this standard, the court must consider whether those actions were "based on a consideration of the relevant factors and whether there has been a clear error of judgment." *Citizens to Preserve Overton Park v. Volpe, 401 U.S. 402, 416, 28 L. Ed. 2d 136, 91 S. Ct. 814 (1971) (overruled on other grounds). See Motor Veh. Mfrs. Ass'n v. State Farm Mut. Auto. Ins. Co., 463 U.S. 29, 43, 77 L. Ed. 2d 443, 103 S. Ct. 2856 (1983).* The court must affirm the agency's findings of fact if they are supported by "substantial evidence" and there is a "rational connection between the facts found and the choice made." *Burlington Truck Lines, Inc. v. United States, 371 U.S. 156, 168, 9 L. Ed. 2d 207, 83 S. Ct. 239 (1962).*

"Substantial evidence" is simply such relevant evidence as a reasonable person might accept as proof of a conclusion. *See Universal Camera Corp. v. NLRB, 340 U.S. 474, 477, 95 L. Ed. 456, 71 S. Ct. 456 (1981)* (quoting *Consol. Edison Co. v. NLRB, 305 U.S. 197, 229, 83 L. Ed. 126, 59 S. Ct. 206 (1938))*.

In contending that the revocations of their airman certificates are unsupported by substantial evidence in the record, the pilots do not challenge the definition of "security threat" under the TSA regulations. An individual poses a "security threat" if the individual "is suspected of posing, or is known to pose (1) A threat to transportation or national security; (2) A threat to air piracy or terrorism; (3) A threat to airline or passenger security; or (4) A threat to civil aviation security." *49 C.F.R. § 1540.117(c)*. Consistent with *Camp v. Pitts, 411 U.S. 138, 143, 36 L. Ed. 2d 106, 93 S. Ct. 1241 (1973)*, where the Supreme Court stated that when an agency official fails to adequately explain its decision, the agency should submit "either through affidavits or testimony, such additional explanation of the reasons for the agency decision as may prove necessary," the affidavit of TSA Deputy Administrator Stephen McHale provides an adequate basis for the TSA's determination that Jifry and Zarie each posed a "security threat" within the meaning of *§ 1540.117(c)*. The unsealed affidavit recounts that the Deputy Administrator affirmed the TSA's determination on the basis of classified intelligence reports, combined with reports from the intelligence community that aircraft would continue to be used as weapons of terrorism, and consideration of "the ease with which an individual may obtain access to aircraft in the United States once he or she has a pilot license." McHale Decl. at 4. The Deputy Administrator attested that "because it would be very difficult to avert harm once a terrorist had control of an aircraft, I concluded that it was important to err on the side of caution in determining whether [the two pilots] ... pose a security threat...." *Id.* at 4-5.

Viewing as a whole the record evidence before the TSA, including *ex parte in camera* review of the classified intelligence reports, we hold that there was substantial evidence to support the TSA's determination that the pilots were security risks. While we reject the pilots' contention that the court apply a *de novo* standard of review, we have carefully reviewed the classified intelligence reports on which TSA relied. The record is not lengthy and the basis for the TSA's conclusion is obvious. The court's review is limited, moreover, to the administrative record that was before the TSA when it determined that the pilots were security risks. *See 5 U.S.C. § 706; cf. United States v. Carlo Bianchi & Co., 373 U.S. 709, 715, 10 L. Ed. 2d 652, 83 S. Ct. 1409 (1963)*. Hence, the pilots' post-argument submission of May 3, 2004 is not properly before the court, although we note that the information it contains was known to the pilots in 2001 and could have, and still can be, submitted to the TSA.

The pilots' motion to bar the respondents' reliance on classified information in this court is not well-taken. Even assuming the respondents' failure to provide notice of its intention to rely on classified information on appeal until one month after the pilots filed their opening brief prevented the pilots from timely addressing the "classified information" question in their opening brief, the pilots' motion fails on its merits for several reasons. First, because the court reviewed the information designated by the respondents as "classified," the court is in a position to determine whether it was properly classified without the *Vaughn* Index, *see Vaughn v. Rosen, 157 U.S. App. D.C. 340, 484 F.2d 820, 826-28 (D.C. Cir. 1973)*, that the pilots urge be obtained. Reliance on *Vaughn* is misplaced, in any event, because that case involved the *Freedom of Information Act* and presented a very different situation than that presented here. Second, the court has inherent authority to review classified material *ex parte, in camera* as part of its judicial review function. *See Molerio v. FBI, 242 U.S. App. D.C. 137, 749 F.2d 815, 822 & n.2 (D.C. Cir. 1984). See also Holy Land Found. for Relief & Dev. v. Ashcroft, 357 U.S. App. D.C. 35, 333 F.3d 156, 164 (D.C. Cir. 2003); Nat'l Council of Resistance of Iran v. Dep't of State, 346 U.S. App. D.C. 131, 251 F.3d 192, 208-09 (D.C. Cir. 2001)*. The pilots' focus on the TSA Deputy Administrator's reliance on "sensitive security information," as defined by *49 U.S.C. §§ 114(s), 40119(b)(1)*, and 49 C.F.R. Part 1520, and "law enforcement sensitive" information, *see McHale Decl. at 5*, fares no better. Although *49 C.F.R. § 1520.5(b)* provides that a person has a "need to know sensitive security information" when the information is necessary to represent an individual in a judicial or administrative proceeding, *§ 1520.5(b)(5)* applies only to individuals representing persons listed in *§ 1520.5(a)*, and the pilots are not among the persons listed in subsection (a) who are required to restrict disclosure of and access to sensitive security information to those with a "need to know." *See 49 C.F.R. § 1520.5(a)*.

IV.

The court reviews *de novo* the pilots' challenge to the constitutionality of the procedures under the January 2003 regulations. *See Vt. Yankee Nuclear Power Corp. v. NRDC, 435 U.S. 519, 543, 55 L. Ed. 2d 460, 98 S. Ct. 1197 (1978); Ramirez-Alejandre v. Ashcroft, 319 F.3d 365, 377 (9th Cir. 2003); Grace Towers Tenants Ass'n v. Grace Housing Dev. Fund Co., 538 F.2d 491, 496 (2d Cir. 1976)*. They contend that the TSA and FAA procedures violate the *Fifth Amendment of the Constitution* by depriving the pilots of their property interest in their airman certificates without due process of law.

The Supreme Court has long held that non-resident aliens who have insufficient contacts with the United States are not entitled to *Fifth Amendment* protections. *See Johnson v. Eisentrager, 339 U.S. 763, 771, 94 L. Ed. 1255, 70 S. Ct. 936 (1950); Yamataya v. Fisher (Japanese Immigrant Case), 189 U.S. 86, 101, 47 L. Ed. 721, 23 S. Ct. 611 (1903); Yick Wo v. Hopkins, 118 U.S. 356, 369, 30 L. Ed. 220, 6 S. Ct. 1064 (1886). See also United States v. Curtiss-Wright Export Corp., 299 U.S. 304, 318, 81 L. Ed. 255, 57 S. Ct. 216 (1936); Pauling v. McElroy, 107 U.S. App. D.C. 372, 278 F.2d 252, 253 n.3 (D.C. Cir. 1960). Cf. United States v. Verdugo-Urquidez, 494 U.S. 259, 261, 108 L. Ed. 2d 222, 110 S. Ct. 1056 (1990)*. Exceptions may arise where aliens have come within the territory of the United States and established "substantial connections" with this country, *Verdugo-Urquidez, 494 U.S. at 271*, or "accepted some societal obligations." *Id. at 273*. In such situations, the Court has recognized that aliens may be accorded protections under the Constitution. *See Plyler v. Doe, 457 U.S. 202, 211-12, 72 L. Ed. 2d 786, 102 S. Ct. 2382 (1982); Kwong Hai Chew v. Colding, 344 U.S. 590, 596, 97 L. Ed. 576, 73 S. Ct. 472 (1953); Russian Volunteer Fleet v. United States, 282 U.S. 481, 489, 75 L. Ed. 473, 51 S. Ct. 229, 71 Ct. Cl. 785 (1931)*. This court has applied these principles in a series of cases concerning the designation of certain dissident organizations as "foreign terrorist organizations." *See People's Mojahedin Org. of Iran v. Dep't of State, 356 U.S. App. D.C. 101, 327 F.3d 1238, 1241 (D.C. Cir. 2003) ("People's Mojahedin II"); Nat'l Council, 251 F.3d at 201; People's Mojahedin Org. of Iran v. Dep't of State, 337 U.S. App. D.C. 106, 182 F.3d 17, 22 (D.C. Cir. 1999) ("People's Mojahedin I"). See also 32 County Sovereignty Comm. v. Dep't of State, 352 U.S. App. D.C. 93, 292 F.3d 797, 799 (D.C. Cir. 2002).* In *People's Mojahedin I, 182 F.3d at 22,* the court explained that "[a] foreign entity without property or presence in this country has no constitutional rights, under the due process clause or otherwise." We need not decide whether or not Jifry and Zarie are entitled to constitutional protections because, even assuming that they are, they have received all the process that they are due under our precedent.

"The fundamental requirement of due process is the opportunity to be heard 'at a meaningful time and in a meaningful manner.' " *Mathews v. Eldridge, 424 U.S. 319, 333, 47 L. Ed. 2d 18, 96 S. Ct. 893 (1976)* (quoting *Armstrong v. Manzo, 380 U.S. 545, 552, 14 L. Ed. 2d 62, 85 S. Ct. 1187 (1965))*. Generally, in determining whether administrative procedures are constitutionally adequate, courts weigh three factors:

> First, the private interest that will be affected by the official action; second, the risk of an erroneous deprivation of such interest through the procedures used, and the probable value, if any, of additional or substitute procedural safeguards; and finally, the Government's interest, including the function involved and the fiscal and administrative burdens that the additional or substitute procedural requirement would entail.

Mathews, 424 U.S. at 335. The pilots' interests at stake here - their interest in possessing FAA airman certificates to fly foreign aircraft outside of the United States - pales in significance to the government's security interests in preventing pilots from using civil aircraft as instruments of terror. As the Supreme Court has noted, "It is 'obvious and unarguable' that no governmental interest is more compelling than the security of the Nation." *Haig v. Agee, 453 U.S. 280, 307, 69 L. Ed. 2d 640, 101 S. Ct. 2766 (1981)* (quoting *Aptheker v. Secretary of State, 378 U.S. 500, 509, 12 L. Ed. 2d 992, 84 S. Ct. 1659 (1964))*. Whatever the risk of erroneous deprivation, the pilots had the opportunity to file a written reply to the TSA's initial determination and were afforded independent *de novo* review of the entire administrative record by the Deputy Administrator of the FAA, *see 49 C.F.R. § 1540.117(e)(4), (f),* and *ex parte, in camera* judicial review of the record. In light of the governmental interests at stake and the sensitive security information, substitute procedural safeguards may be impracticable, and in any event, are unnecessary under our precedent.

In *Nat'l Council of Resistance of Iran, 251 F.3d at 208,* the court concluded that in designating organizations as foreign terrorist organizations under the Anti-Terrorism and Effective Death Penalty Act, the Secretary of State had to "afford to the entities under consideration notice that the designation is impending," *id.,* and "the opportunity to present, at least in written form, such evidence as those entities may be able to produce to rebut the administrative record or otherwise negate the proposition that they are foreign terrorist organizations." *Id. at 209.* In light of the Supreme Court's instruction that "due process is flexible and calls for such procedural protections as the particular situation demands," *Morrissey v. Brewer, 408 U.S. 471, 481, 33 L. Ed. 2d 484, 92 S. Ct. 2593 (1972),* the court held that because of the extent to which security concerns were implicated in that case, the Secretary could upon "adequate showing to the court," provide the requisite notice after the designation of the organization as a terrorist organization, and needed only to disclose the unclassified portions of the record. *Nat'l Council of Resistance of Iran, 251 F.3d at 208.* In *People's Mojahedin II, 327 F.3d at 1242-43,* another case involving the designation of terrorist organizations, the court underscored that it "had established in [*National Council*] the process which is due under the circumstances of this sensitive matter of classified intelligence in the effort to combat foreign terrorism," and that "nothing further is due." *Id. See also Holy Land, 333 F.3d at 163-64.*

The TSA Assistant Administrator's Initial Notices informed the pilots that "based upon materials available to the [TSA], which I have personally reviewed, I have determined that you pose a security threat." The pilots were afforded an opportunity to respond to the designation and both filed written challenges to the TSA's Initial Notice, along with affidavits that they did not pose a threat to aviation or national security. *See 49 C.F.R. § 1540.117(e)(4).* These materials were considered by the TSA Deputy Administrator when he conducted a *de novo* review of the administrative record before issuing the Final Notice. While the pilots protest that without knowledge of the specific evidence on which TSA relied, they are unable to defend against the charge that they are security risks, the court has rejected the same argument in the terrorism listing cases. The due process protections afforded to them parallel those provided under similar circumstances in *National Council* and *People's Mojahedin II,* and are sufficient to satisfy our case law.

Accordingly, we affirm the NTSB revocation order of August 13, 2003, and deny the petitions for review and the pilots' motion to bar the respondents' reliance on classified information.

IV.   FAA ENFORCEMENT

A. *Falsification and Cheating*

ADMINISTRATOR, FEDERAL AVIATION ADMINISTRATION,

v.

STEVEN RICHARD COWELL

Order EA-1285;
Docket SE-4183

National Transportation Safety Board

May, 1975

Respondent has appealed from the initial decision of Administrative Law Judge William E. Fowler, Jr., issued orally at the conclusion of the hearing held in this matter on April 11, 1979. The law judge therein made the following findings:

1. Respondent is the holder of commercial pilot certificate No. 522766218, with airplane single and multi-engine land and instrument ratings; flight instructor certificate No. 522766218; and first class airman medical certificates issued to respondent on September 21, 1977, and on September 20, 1978.

2. In 1977 respondent appeared at the Air Carrier District Office, Aurora, Colorado, to apply for an airline transport pilot certificate.

3. Incident to said application, respondent presented his logbook for inspection.

4. In respondent's logbook entries, respondent alleged that he had logged a number of hours as pilot-in-command of the Grumman American Model AA-5 N5434L; that he had logged 111.6 hours as pilot in command of Mitsubishi MU-2 N304L; and that he had logged 8.1 hours as pilot in command of Piper PA-31 N432L.

5. Subsequent investigation revealed that at the times respondent logged flying time in Grumman American Model AA-5 N5434L, that airplane either had not yet been registered or had been totally destroyed in an accident.

6. Further investigation revealed that at the time respondent presented his logbook for inspection, while respondent had in fact logged some time as pilot-in-command of Mitsubishi MU-2F and Piper PA-31 airplanes, he had not in fact logged the time that he had originally claimed.

7. Respondent made intentionally false entries in his logbook in order to show compliance with the requirements for the issuance of an airline transport pilot certificate.

8. On September 21, 1977, respondent applied to Ronald E. Costin, M.D., designated aviation medical examiner, for first class airman medical certificate.

9. At the conclusion of his examination, Dr. Costin issued a first class airman medical certificate to respondent.

10. On September 20, 1978, respondent applied to M. A. Amundsen, M.D., a designated aviation medical examiner, for a first class airman medical certificate.

11. At the conclusion of his examination, Dr. Amundsen issued a first class airman medical certificate to respondent.

12. On the application for the medical certificate described in paragraph 8 hereinabove, respondent claimed in item 16 to have 3155 hours of pilot time.

13. The answer to No. 16 on the application described in paragraph 8 hereinabove is false in that respondent did not have 3155 hours pilot time.

14. On respondent's application for said medical certificates set forth in paragraphs 8 and 10 hereinabove, respondent stated on item 21 V. that he had no record of traffic convictions.

15. Respondent's answer to item 21 V. in the above-described applications was false in that he had a record of five traffic convictions in Colorado from 1972 through 1977.

16. By respondent's actions in making intentionally false statements in his logbook to show compliance with the requirements for an issuance of an airline transport pilot certificate, respondent has demonstrated that he lacks the qualifications to be the holder of any airman certificate.

17. By respondent's actions, knowingly making an intentionally false statement on his application for a medical certificate issued under part 67 of the Federal Aviation regulations, respondent has demonstrated that he lacks the qualifications to be the holder of any airman medical certificate.

18. By reason of the foregoing circumstances, it is found that respondent violated Section 61.59 (a) (2) of the Federal Aviation Regulations (FAR) in that he made intentionally false statements in his logbook to show compliance with the requirements for the issuance of an airline transport certificate; and it is also found that respondent violated Section 67.20 (a) (1) of the FAR n3 in that he made intentionally false statements on an application for a medical certificate issued under part 67 of the FAR.

The law judge thereupon affirmed the Administrator's emergency order revoking respondent's airman and airman medical certificates.

In support of his appeal, respondent has filed an appeal brief in which he alleges that the law judge erred in the following respects: (1) By refusing to grant respondent's motions to (a) strike from the complaint contentions of lack of qualifications, and (b) dismiss as stale that portion of the complaint pertaining to respondent's pilot certificate; (2) By receiving into the record testimony and documentary evidence which is irrelevant, immaterial and inflammatory; (3) By making findings Nos. 4, 6, and 7, which are unsupported by the evidence; and

(4) By concluding that respondent lacks the qualifications to hold either an airman or an airman medical certificate.

The Administrator has filed a reply brief opposing the appeal and urging the Board to affirm the initial decision.

Upon consideration of the briefs of the parties, and the entire record, the Board has determined that safety in air commerce or air transportation and the public interest require affirmation of the order of revocation. We adopt as our own the findings of the law judge.

Respondent first argues that the law judge erred by refusing to grant respondent's motion to dismiss those paragraphs of the complaint which assert that respondent lacks the qualifications to hold either an airman or an airman medical certificate. Respondent contends that these paragraphs fail to comply with section 821.31 (b) of the Board's Rules of Practice (49 C.F.R. 821.31 (b)), which provides that "If the Administrator claims that Respondent lacks qualifications as an airman, the order filed as the complaint, or an accompanying statement, shall recite on which of the facts pleaded this contention is based." The two paragraphs in question state that respondent's lack of qualifications is predicated on his "actions in knowingly and intentionally making fraudulent or intentionally false statements" both in his logbook and in his application for medical certificate. In our judgment, such a statement fully complies with the Board's Rules. Furthermore, since the paragraphs preceding the two in question recite in detail the manner in which respondent allegedly falsified the logbook and medical application, it is apparent that the charges of lack of qualifications are based on the entire complaint.

Respondent next maintains that the law judge erred in refusing to dismiss the complaint as stale. In support of this argument, respondent points out that the Administrator first suspected the logbook falsification violations in early 1977, and completed the investigation in May 1978, yet gave no notice of any action until the emergency order was issued in March 1979.

The Board's Rules contain a provision which subjects to a motion to dismiss allegations of offenses which occurred more than 6 months prior to the Administrator's advising respondent as to the reasons for the proposed certificate action. A motion to dismiss a complaint as stale does not apply, however, where an issue of qualifications would be presented if the allegations are assumed to be true. In this instance, the Administrator, as noted above, clearly alleged lack of qualifications. It is equally clear that these allegations, if assumed to be true, present a legitimate issue regarding qualifications in view of the fact that the Board has held that falsification of logbooks or medical certificate applications warrant revocation, a sanction which is associated with lack of qualifications. The fact that the Board, in other cases involving falsification of applications or logbooks, has not imposed revocation does not mean that an *issue* of qualifications is not presented by a complaint such as that filed herein.

As part of the stale complaint argument, respondent claims that the Administrator failed to comply both with section 609 of the Federal Aviation Act *(49 U.S.C. 1449)*, and with 14 CFR 13.19 of the Administrator's enforcement procedures, in that the Administrator failed to give prior notice of the proposed charges before issuing the emergency order. A similar argument was presented to the Safety

Board in *Administrator v. Stern, 2 N.T.S.B. 1240 (1974)*, whereupon the Board held as follows *(2 N.T.S.B. at p. 1241):*

"In our opinion, the legislative history of Section 609 of the Act supports the conclusion that the provisions of Section 609 and Section 1005(a) of the act must be considered together and the latter clearly provides that in cases of an emergency, the Administrator is not required either to give notice or to afford an opportunity to answer and be heard prior to the issuance of an emergency order. We find that the emergency revocations come within the intendment of section 1005(a) in its explicit and specific authorization to issue such orders as are deemed necessary with or without notice in emergency situations involving safety in air commerce."

The above holding, which was explicitly affirmed in *Stern v. Butterfield, 529 F.2d 407* (C.A.5, 1976), is dispositive of respondent's argument.

Respondent also contends that the law judge further erred by allowing into the record evidence which was both inflammatory and immaterial to the charges in the complaint in form of (a) medical certificate applications for the years 1975 and 1976 and (b) testimony regarding respondent's alleged false statements to prospective employers or pertaining to aircraft other than those listed in the complaint. We agree that there was both testimonial and documentary evidence entered into the record which went beyond the allegations listed in the complaint. We do not agree, however, that this evidence was irrrelevant or immaterial to those allegations. Rather, this evidence tended to show that the falsifications charged in the complaint were not isolated, inadvertent acts, but were part of a consistent pattern of misrepresentation. Such a pattern bears directly on the critical issue of the intentional falsity of the entries cited in the complaint and thus is clearly relevant. We therefore conclude that the law judge did not abuse his broad discretion by admitting this type of evidence into the record.

Turning to the specific charges regarding logbook entries, the record establishes that Grumman American AA-5, N5434L, was picked up from the factory on February 16, 1974, and was destroyed in a crash on October 12, 1975. Respondent's logbook indicates that he flew said aircraft on a number of flights in 1973 and 1976. Such entries are patently false. Respondent's logbook also reflects 111.6 hours in the Mitsubishi MU-2, N304L, during the months February-March 1975, and March 1976. This aircraft was owned and operated by Rapidair, Inc. (an air taxi operator) whose president testified that respondent has never been employed by Rapidair, either as a pilot or in any other capacity.

Respondent's attempts to explain the above logbook discrepancies were not persuasive to the law judge, nor are they convincing to this Board. Respondent testified that his listing of N5434L as the AA-5 he flew in 1973 and 1976 was the result of careless habits in maintaining the logbook. Such an explanation might have some plausibility if this discrepancy were an isolated occurrence. The record reflects, however, that respondent consistently overstated and fabricated his aviation experience on applications and during interviews, which indicates that the falsifications were part of a continuing campaign to further his ambitions as a pilot. He also testified that his flights in 1973 in N5434L were made with a flight instructor, and thus respondent did not serve as pilot-in-command. This testimony is made questionable by the fact that there are no entries by the flight instructor under the logbook section entitled "Remarks, Procedures, Maneuvers, Endorsements."

With respect to the MU-2, respondent testified that he had an informal arrangement with Rapidair which allowed him to go on flights and to manipulate the controls of the aircraft in order to gain experience. This testimony is difficult to accept in view of the fact that respondent was not employed by Rapidair and in the absence of any corroborative evidence that the president of Rapidair gave permission to his pilots to allow respondent to fly their aircraft. Respondent's ostensible operation of MU-2, N304L, in February-March 1975, is also belied by (a) respondent's own testimony that he commenced riding on Rapidair aircraft in June 1975, and (b) the fact that Rapidair did not operate this aircraft until October 1975.

In view of the above, the Board concludes that the logbook falsification charges pertaining to aircraft N5434L and N304L have been established by a preponderance of the evidence. As respondent points out in his brief, the logbook pages in the record are not sufficiently complete to disclose whether respondent listed himself on the subject flights as pilot-in-command, as charged in the complaint. As discussed hereinabove, the evidence indicates that respondent was the pilot-in-command on at least some of the flights. In any event, we do not regard the failure to prove that he listed himself as pilot-in-command in the logbook on all flights to be fatal to the ultimate charges. Regardless of his pilot station, the falsification charges stand proven. Furthermore, the evaluation of a pilot's qualification for an airline transport pilot (ATP) certificate are based on more than pilot-in-command time. A pilot's logbook is critical to the FAA's overall determination of whether an applicant for an ATP certificate has the requisite aeronautical experience. By presenting a logbook with false entries, respondent frustrated this determination. Viewed in this light, we believe the falsifications were sufficiently material to come within the required elements of intentional falsification prescribed in *Hart v. McLucas, 535 F.2d 516 (1976).*

Turning finally to the matter of sanction, the record reveals an airman who has falsified both his pilot logbook, as discussed in detail hereinabove, and his application for first class medical certificate. In our judgment, this pattern of falsification shows lacks the qualifications to hold any airman or airman medical certificate, not just in the sense that the Administrator has not received the necessary information to properly evaluate respondent, but in the sense that respondent has demonstrated that he lacks the degree of care, judgment and responsibility required of the holder of a certificate. Revocation is therefore the appropriate sanction. (The charge that respondent's listing his pilot time as 3155 hours on the medical application was false also appears to have been established. When questioned by the law judge about the validity of this figure at the hearing, respondent replied that he included (as pilot time) the time he served as "a safety pilot and an observer pilot" -- i.e., "time that I had flown in another aircraft with friends, that I rode in the forward seats, near the cockpit." (Tr. 214)).

ACCORDINGLY, IT IS ORDERED THAT:

1. Respondent's appeal be and it hereby is denied;

2. The Administrator's order and the initial decision, except as each is modified regarding the charge and finding pertaining to aircraft N432L, be and they hereby are affirmed; and

3. The revocation of respondent's airman and airman medical certificates is deemed effective March 6, 1979, the date of issuance of the Administrator's emergency order.

KING, Chairman, DRIVER, Vice Chairman, McADAMS and HOGUE, Members of the Board, concurred in the above opinion and order.

ELDON C. HART V. JOHN L. MCLUCAS, ADMINISTRATOR, FEDERAL AVIATION ADMINISTRATION

UNITED STATES COURT OF APPEALS FOR THE NINTH CIRCUIT

535 F.2d 516

May, 1976

SMITH, Circuit Judge:

Eldon C. Hart is an aviation enthusiast of long standing. He now appeals from a decision of the National Transportation Safety Board (hereinafter the NTSB) finding that Hart had violated *14 C.F.R. § 61.59(a)(2)* and ordering that Hart's flight instructor certificate be suspended for nine months.

For the reasons stated below, we remand this case for further proceedings before the NTSB. Further proceedings are required because the NTSB applied an incorrect interpretation of *§ 61.59 (a)(2)* below and because additional factual findings must be made before *§ 61.59(a)(2)* can be applied properly in this case.

Hart has been a leading promoter of aviation in eastern Idaho since the end of the Second World War. From 1964 until the spring of 1973, he was acting director of the aviation program of Ricks College in Rexburg, Idaho. When the college announced in May of 1972 that it was abandoning its program of aviation instruction, Hart formed a nonprofit corporation to continue the program as a separate school. All parties agree that Hart's frenetic exertions to save the aviation program put him under considerable emotional and physical strain.

Following a formal charge by the Federal Aviation Administration (FAA) and a hearing before an administrative law judge, the NTSB found that Hart had certified in the logbooks of three of his students that he had provided in-flight instruction when, in fact, Hart had not given such instruction. On these facts, the NTSB held that Hart had violated *14 C.F.R. § 61.59(a)(2)* which prohibits the making of a "fraudulent or intentionally false entry" in specified aviation records.

The incorrect entries were made several months after the alleged instruction would have been given. Hart, physically sick and admittedly overworked, certified the incorrect entries without first checking his own records. Hart freely admits that the statements in question were false.

On September 14, 1973, Administrative Law Judge Harley G. Moorhead found that Hart's actions were "more consistent with inattention than with an outright attempt to defraud anyone." Indeed, Judge Moorhead specifically found that Hart "was not engaged in a scheme to defraud."

However, while Judge Moorhead ruled that Hart had not acted fraudulently, he did rule that Hart had made "intentionally false" statements within the meaning of *14 C.F.R. § 61.59(a)(2)*.

Consequently, the administrative law judge ordered that Hart's flight instructor certificate be revoked.

On appeal, the NTSB adopted the position that an entry is "intentionally false" within the meaning of *§ 61.59(a)(2)* if the entry is factually incorrect (which is concededly the case here) and if the maker of the incorrect statement intends to make that statement. In short, it was the position of the NTSB that a person can make an "intentionally false" statement within the meaning of *§ 61.59(a)(2)* without knowing that the statement he is making is false.

The NTSB agreed with Judge Moorhead that Hart did not have an intention to deceive when he signed the incorrect entries in his students' logbooks. The NTSB also agreed that Hart's statements were nevertheless "intentionally false" within the meaning of *§ 61.59(a)(2)*.

However, the NTSB decided that a nine-month suspension of Hart's instructor certificate was sufficient penalty. From this decision, Hart now appeals.

I. FRAUD AND INTENT: ELEMENTS OF THE OFFENSE UNDER *§ 61.59(a)(2)*

There has been disagreement throughout this case as to the proper construction of *14 C.F.R. § 61.59(a)(2)*. It has been Hart's position that the terms "fraudulent" and "intentionally false" in *§ 61.59 (a)(2)* are synonymous and that, therefore, the finding of the NTSB that Hart did not act "fraudulently" necessarily implies that his statements were not "intentionally false" since the two terms, Hart asserts, mean the same thing.

This contention was rejected by the administrative law judge and by the NTSB, and properly so. On its face, *§ 61.59(a)(2)* prohibits statements which are "fraudulent *or* intentionally false," thereby indicating that there are two different offenses which the regulation proscribes (emphasis added). See, *e.g., Merchants Fire Assurance Corp. v. Lattimore, 263 F.2d 232, 240-41 (9th Cir. 1959); Adolfson v. United States, 159 F.2d 883, 885-86 (9th Cir.), cert. denied, 331 U.S. 818, 91 L. Ed. 1836, 67 S. Ct. 1307 (1947); Barkdoll v. United States, 147 F.2d 617, 618 (9th Cir. 1945).*

If the term "fraudulent" is synonymous with the expression "intentionally false," the regulation is hopelessly redundant and one or the other phrase is surplusage. Of course, in the construction of administrative regulations, as well as statutes, it is presumed that every phrase serves a legitimate purpose and, therefore, constructions which render regulatory provisions superfluous are to be avoided. *Jay v. Boyd, 351 U.S. 345, 360-61, 100 L. Ed. 1242, 76 S. Ct. 919 (1956); Klein v. Republic Steel Corp., 435 F.2d 762, 766 (3rd Cir. Pa. 1970); Rucker v. Wabash R.R., 418 F.2d 146, 149 (7th Cir. 1969)* ("Administrative regulations, like statutes, must be construed by courts, and the same rules of interpretation are applicable in both cases"); *Consolidated Flower Shipments, Inc. v. Civil Aeronautics Board, 205 F.2d 449, 450 (9th Cir. 1953).*

In short, it makes more sense to view *§ 61.59(a)(2)* as proscribing two overlapping, but nevertheless separate offenses, one involving fraud, the other involving "intentional" falsity.

Having decided that *§ 61.59(a)(2)* establishes two offenses, it is necessary to define and distinguish the elements of both.

The concept of "fraud" is one which arises frequently in the law and which is therefore well-defined. The Supreme Court has identified the elements of fraud as consisting of

> (1) a false representation (2) in reference to a material fact (3) made with knowledge of its falsity (4) and with the intent to deceive (5) with action taken in reliance upon the representation.

Pence v. United States, 316 U.S. 332, 338, 86 L. Ed. 1510, 62 S. Ct. 1080 (1942); *United States v. Kiefer, 97 U.S. App. D.C. 101, 228 F.2d 448 (D.C. Cir. 1955), cert. denied, 350 U.S. 933, 100 L. Ed. 815, 76 S. Ct. 305 (1956)*. Since this traditional definition of fraud is well-established, it is unlikely that the draftsman of § 61.59(a)(2) would have intended to use the word otherwise without saying so.

We further conclude that the elements of intentional false statement for the purpose of § 61.59(a)(2) are the first three elements of fraud: falsity, materiality and knowledge. Thus, intentional false statement is a lesser included offense within fraud. Thus, for both offenses, the person making the false entry must know of such falsity. However, fraud requires at least one additional element, *i.e.*, an intent to deceive.

The FAA argues that knowledge of falsity is not a required element for intentional false statement under § 61.59(a)(2). While the NTSB agreed with that construction of § 61.59(a)(2), we do not. And, indeed, at oral argument, attorneys for the government disavowed the NTSB's interpretation of § 61.59 (a)(2).

In effect, the FAA and NTSB would interpret § 61.59(a)(2) as establishing strict liability: the making of a false statement would be punishable, under their interpretation of § 61.59(a)(2), even if the person who made the statement did not know the statement to be false.

The obvious problem with this interpretation is that it effectively construes the term "intentionally" out of the regulation. The use of the word "intentionally," however, must be assumed to impart a *mens rea* requirement to the regulation. Were this not so, the draftsman of § 61.59(a)(2) could have defined the offense as the making of a false statement without any reference to the mental state of the person who makes the entry. Since, however, § 61.59(a)(2) explicitly includes an intent requirement, it is inconsistent to read the regulation as establishing strict liability.

Indeed, the Supreme Court has clearly indicated that *scienter* requirements, such as that established by § 61.59(a)(2), are not to be read out of administrative regulations when the express language of those regulations uses "the commonly understood terminology of intentional wrongdoing." *Ernst & Ernst v. Hochfelder, 425 U.S. 185, 214, 96 S. Ct. 1375, 47 L. Ed. 2d 668 (1976)*.

We conclude that § 61.59(a)(2) must be construed to require actual knowledge of falsity. It is readily conceded that fraud requires such knowledge. *Pence, supra; Kiefer, supra.* Since "a word is known by the company it keeps," (*noscitur a sociis*) it is unlikely that the draftsman of § 61.59 was establishing both strict and *scienter* liability with the simple phrase "fraudulent or intentionally false." *Jarecki v.*

G.D. Searle & Co., 367 U.S. 303, 307, 6 L. Ed. 2d 859, 81 S. Ct. 1579 (1961).

It may, indeed, be a sound policy, as the FAA suggests, for strict liability to apply in this or similar situations. The problem is that § 61.59(a)(2) does not establish it.

It is true, as the FAA asserts, that an administrative interpretation of a statute or regulation is to be accorded deference in judicial deliberations. However, when, as here, the administrative construction is clearly contrary to the plain and sensible meaning of the regulation, the courts need not defer to it. *White v. Bloomberg*, 345 F. Supp. 133, 147 (D. Md. 1972); *Francis v. Davidson*, 340 F. Supp. 351, 368 (D. Md.), *aff'd*, 409 U.S. 904, 34 L. Ed. 2d 168, 93 S. Ct. 223 (1972).

Finally, it should be noted that the concept of fraud in § 61.59(a)(2) is not rendered superfluous by the interpretation of "intentionally false" advanced here. It is true that one who makes a fraudulent statement must, under our construction of § 61.59(a)(2), also make a statement which is intentionally false since intentional falsity is a lesser included offense under fraud. However, the specification of fraud serves to indicate that there are varying degrees of culpability under § 61.59(a)(2) and that such degrees of culpability are to be considered in the choice of punishment.

In short, the administrative interpretation of § 61.59(a)(2) advanced below, which essentially establishes a strict liability offense, is incorrect since it violates the common and normal meaning of the phrase "intentionally false." A fair reading of § 61.59(a)(2) indicates a desire to require *scienter, i.e.,* knowledge of falsity, for liability. If the FAA thinks it would be better to establish strict liability, it is free to seek amendment of the regulation.

II. THE FACTUAL FINDINGS BELOW: THE NEED FOR REMAND

Judge Moorhead and the NTSB found that Hart had no intention to deceive when he entered incorrect entries into his students' logbooks. That finding is supported by substantial evidence and should not be overturned on appeal. 49 U.S.C. § 1486(e). Hart's character, his unblemished record, his cooperation with the FAA investigation of this incident, his failure to alter his other logbooks to conform to the entries in those of his students, his physical condition at the time of the entries, the time pressure which Hart was under, Hart's demeanor -- all these circumstances provide substantial evidence for the finding that Hart lacked an intent to defraud.

Thus, if Hart did violate § 61.59(a)(2), it must be that he made an "intentionally false" statement, *i.e.,* that he knew the entries were false when he made them, even though he did not act with an intent to deceive.

The problem this court confronts is that neither Judge Moorhead nor the NTSB squarely addressed the issue of Hart's knowledge of falsity. Apparently, neither felt it necessary since both viewed § 61.59(a)(2) as establishing strict liability for false statements. Since Hart admitted that the entries were false, the issue of Hart's *scienter* at the time the entries were made was not explicitly addressed.

Possibly the judge and the NTSB sought to spare Hart the obloquy of the direct finding, although there are indications that the administrative law judge and the NTSB believed that Hart was unaware of the falsity of the entries he made. Certainly, that is one possible interpretation of the finding that the false entries were the result of "inattention."

However, there are other comments by the NTSB which may be interpreted to the contrary. In particular, the NTSB said (somewhat obliquely) that Hart knew "the nature of the data he was signing." Does this mean that Hart knew the entries were false? We do not know.

In short, the finding of the NTSB on the issue of knowledge is understandably ambiguous because the NTSB incorrectly thought that knowledge was not a requisite element for a violation of § 61.59(a)(2).

Accordingly, we remand the case to the NTSB, in light of the correct legal standards, to rule on the factual issue of Hart's *scienter* at the time he entered the false statements into his students' logbooks. Remanded.

THOMAS F. TWOMEY, V. NATIONAL TRANSPORTATION
SAFETY BOARD, DONALD D. ENGEN, ADMINISTRATOR,
FEDERAL AVIATION ADMINISTRATION

UNITED STATES COURT OF APPEALS FOR THE FIRST
CIRCUIT

821 F.2d 63

June, 1987

Campbell, Chief Judge.

Thomas F. Twomey brings this petition for review of an order issued by the National Transportation Safety Board ("NTSB") affirming the initial decision and order of the Federal Aviation Administration ("FAA") revoking his airline transport pilot and other licenses. We uphold the NTSB's order.

On May 6, 1984, an FAA inspector monitoring a Delta Air Lines flight aboard which Twomey, a senior Delta captain, was to serve as pilot-in-command requested to inspect Twomey's pilot and medical certificates. Upon inspection, the FAA representative noted that Twomey's first-class airman medical certificate had expired on April 30, 1984. Twomey did not undertake the flight as a required flight crewmember.

On or about May 7, 1984, Twomey applied in Boston, Massachusetts, to Dr. David E. Rosengard for a first-class medical certificate. On his application, Twomey made an entry reflecting that the application was made on April 30, 1984, and asked Dr. Rosengard to backdate the medical certificate. Dr. Rosengard agreed and issued the certificate with the April 30, 1984 date.

Twomey thereafter presented the certificate to his employer, Delta Air Lines, to demonstrate that he had had a valid and current medical certificate on flights he had made subsequent to April 30, 1984. Twomey had participated as a required crewmember on a number of Delta flights between May 1, 1984 and May 6, 1984.

After learning of the falsification, the administrator of the FAA concluded that any flights conducted between May 1, 1984 and May 6, 1984, were in violation of *section 61.3* of the Federal Aviation Regulations ("FAR"). Moreover, the administrator determined that Twomey had made an intentionally false statement in his application for a medical certificate in violation of section 67.20(a)(1) of the FAR. The administrator then proceeded to revoke Twomey's medical, pilot, flight engineer and ground instructor certificates pursuant to his authority under 49 U.S.C. §§ 1429(a) and 1485(a) (1982) to issue emergency orders whenever, in the administrator's opinion, "an emergency requiring immediate action exists in respect of safety in air commerce."

Twomey administratively appealed pursuant to 49 U.S.C. § 1429. After an evidentiary hearing, an administrative law judge sustained the emergency order of revocation. Twomey appealed further to the National Transportation Safety Board which affirmed the FAA's order.

In this petition for review, Twomey raises three issues which we discuss below.

I.

Twomey argues that the backdating of his application for renewal of a pilot's first-class medical certificate did not constitute an intentionally false statement of a *material* fact. While section 67.20(a)(1) does not in so many words require the falsehood to relate to a "material fact," it is undisputed that such is required. *See, e.g., Cassis v. Helms, 737 F.2d 545, 546 (6th Cir. 1984).* In denying the materiality of the false date, Twomey asserts that it did not relate to his physical or psychological condition and hence lacked medical significance. Twomey says that in every case where the NTSB has previously found that the misstated or concealed fact was material, the fact carried some medical significance. He asserts that the FAA has never questioned his physical or mental health and, therefore, the false date on the application had no adverse effect on public safety.

The NTSB's conclusion of materiality was as follows:

> In the instant case, respondent's conspiracy with Dr. Rosengard to backdate the airman medical certificate that was issued May 7, 1984, was for the purpose of using the certificate, backdated to April 30, to deceive both his employer, Delta, and the FAA by falsely claiming that, during the flights that were conducted for Delta between May 1, 1984 and May 6, 1984, respondent was properly certificated when, in actuality, his certificate had expired. The Board therefore concludes that the false representation was in reference to a material fact.

We think the NTSB was well within its authority to reach this conclusion. For a statement to be material in situations like the one before us, it need only have a natural tendency to influence, or be capable of influencing, a decision of the agency in making a required determination. *Cassis v. Helms, 737 F.2d at 547; Poulos v. United States, 387 F.2d 4, 6 (10th Cir. 1968).* Regardless whether Twomey's health was or was not perfect from April 30 on, the false backdate could influence the FAA's determination whether he was qualified under its rules and regulations to fly as pilot-in-command during the period May 1-6.

In *Cassis* the court found that a pilot's false entries about 150 hours of flight time in his logbook were material where the logbook was required as part of an application for an airline transport pilot certificate, even when the pilot had enough hours to fulfill the 1,500 requirement without the false 150 hours. *737 F.2d at 547.* The court found that since the pilot did not inform the FAA which entries were accurate and which were false, "the false entries were capable of influencing the ultimate decision about whether [the pilot] had 1500 hours of flight experience." *Id.* Moreover, the court found that the false entries could be used by the pilot to show compliance with other FAA flight experience requirements.

The situation here is analogous to that in *Cassis.* The NTSB was entitled to conclude that the date of the application formed a critical element of the medical certificate's validity and, thus, of the applicant's qualifications for flight at a particular time. The date of the application here was material to the date the doctor wrote on the medical certificate and this, in turn, was material to the FAA's decisions concerning Twomey's qualifications for flight.

Had Twomey placed the true date of May 7 on the application, thus receiving a medical certificate of like date, it would have been apparent to the FAA that the flights Twomey conducted between May 1 and May 6 were in violation of FAA regulations requiring a pilot-in-command to have a current medical certificate. *14 C.F.R. § 67.3(c) (1987)*. Thus, the backdating of the application had the capability of making the FAA believe that Twomey had always held a current medical certificate and therefore of preventing the agency, as well as his employer, from taking action against him. We have no question, therefore, that the false date on the application was a material misstatement.

II.

The FAA also found Twomey in violation of *section 61.3* of FAR by acting as a required crewmember on a number of Delta Air Lines flights when he did not have an appropriate medical certificate.

At the hearing before the administrative law judge, evidence was introduced, and there was a stipulation, showing that Twomey had taken part in a number of Delta Air Lines flights as a regularly assigned crewmember between May 1, 1984 and May 6, 1984. There was evidence that as a very senior Delta captain, possessing some 28 years of experience, he had been allowed to "bid" on these routes as part of Delta's regular assignment process and, thereafter, flew as assigned crew. Twomey argues, however, that the FAA never established that he flew specifically as pilot-in-command rather than in some lesser position. If Twomey had served as pilot-in-command, *section 61.3(c)* required his medical certificate to be first class and current. If, however, he had served as first or second officer, his existing certificate which had "expired" as a first-class medical certificate on April 30, would still have had validity as a second-class medical certificate, making him "legal."

Twomey's attorney made this argument, along with a good many others, to the agency, but presented no evidence that Twomey, in fact, had flown in a subordinate role. The NTSB made no specific finding as to Twomey's capacity on these flights. However, it found that flights made between May 1 and May 6 were in violation of FAR 61.3 because Twomey's certificate had expired. Since the certificate could only have expired if he flew as pilot-in-command, this was tantamount to a finding that he flew in that capacity. The only question, therefore, is whether there is substantial evidence in the record to support a finding that he had flown as pilot-in-command rather than in a more junior capacity.

The record makes clear that Twomey was a *captain* for Delta. Delta's Chief Pilot in Boston also described him as one of the senior pilots with the airline, who had been with Delta and a predecessor airline about 28 years. The FAA argues that captains generally perform as pilots-in-command, an assertion which fits the dictionary definition of "captain" (derived from the Latin, "capitaneus" meaning "foremost, chief") as "a person having authority over and responsibility for a group or unit." Webster's New International Dictionary (3d ed. 1971). Twomey's likely command status was confirmed by the fact that on the date of the enroute inspection, May 6, 1984, which revealed his lack of a current medical certificate, Twomey was scheduled to fly as the captain and pilot-in-command of Delta Flight 164 from Memphis to Atlanta. We think the foregoing facts were sufficient to establish, prima facie, that Twomey flew as pilot-in-command on the flights between May 1 and May 6. In the unlikely event this senior captain had been flying in a junior role, his attorney could easily have brought this out by subpoenaing the relevant records or by seeking the information when examining Delta's Chief Pilot and other supervisory personnel. Twomey was represented by counsel at the administrative hearings, and the record suggests that he was present personally at at least one of them. He was in a position easily to correct any misimpression as to his true status should there have been one.

Given Twomey's command status on the flight where he was first questioned, the fact that he was both a captain and a very senior one, and the availability of an opportunity to present evidence that he flew in other than a command position had that been the fact, we believe the agency could properly have inferred that Twomey had acted as pilot-in-command in the mentioned flights in violation of *section 61.3* of the regulations.

III.

Twomey contends the revocation of his license constitutes action arbitrary, capricious, and abusive of discretion within the meaning of the Administrative Procedure Act, *5 U.S.C. § 706(2)(A) (1982)*, as incorporated by the Independent Safety Board Act of 1974, 49 U.S.C. § 1903(d) (1982). He argues that the use of the FAA's power to issue emergency orders was arbitrary in his case because there was no threat to public safety. His position is that since there was medically nothing wrong with him, the possibility that he might pilot airplanes without a proper medical certification was no real emergency as defined in the regulations.

In considering this argument, the NTSB said that its "review authority does not extend to consideration of the reasonableness of the Administrator's decision to invoke his emergency power." Without expressing ourselves as to the correctness of this statement, we hold that in order for someone to succeed before us in challenging an FAA's emergency determination, it must be shown "that the determination was 'a clear error of judgment' lacking any rational basis in fact." *Nevada Airlines, Inc. v. Bond, 622 F.2d 1017, 1021 (9th Cir. 1980), citing Bowman Transportation, Inc. v. Arkansas-Best Freight System, Inc., 419 U.S. 281, 285, 42 L. Ed. 2d 447, 95 S. Ct. 438 (1974)*.

We do not find the determination of an emergency to have been a clear error of judgment; there was basis in the record and in law for it. The ALJ stated,

> I have to concur with the National Transportation Safety Board's holdings in many previous cases of this type where they have held -- where there is an intentional falsification of a material fact as we have in

this case that this shows a lack of qualification on the part of the individual involved to hold any type of airman certificate issued by the Federal Aviation Administration that such a material false statement indicates, the board has said, indicates the lack of the necessary degree of care, judgment, and responsibility that the holder of any type of airman certificate could have or should have to be certified accordingly as a pilot by the Federal Aviation Administration.

Counsel for the FAA pointed out that the agency, and ultimately the flying public, depend heavily on the integrity of the system of self-reports that now exists. Deliberate falsification, even in relatively small matters, can undermine the effectiveness of the system, with adverse effects on airline safety. In arguing that the result here goes more to the morality of the pilot than to his danger to public safety, Twomey fails to recognize that the administrator could have found an important connection between the two.

Finally, Twomey argues that there could not have been any real emergency because seven months elapsed between the May 6, 1984, inspection (which revealed a problem concerning his medical certificate) and the issuance of the emergency order of revocation (on December 3, 1984). He adds that as late as October 10, 1984, he received a letter from an FAA inspector saying that "at this time the facts do not warrant legal enforcement action." However, it appears that the reason the FAA had taken no action against Twomey as of October 10, 1984, is that the agency was not convinced of the *backdating* of the application until sometime after that date. The record suggests that a far less serious view of the situation would have been taken had it been concluded that Twomey was merely negligent, for a period of several days, in renewing his medical certificate. The need for revocation was perceived when the FAA became satisfied of the deliberate falsification.

The petition for review is denied and the order of the Board is affirmed. Costs for respondent.

JOSEPH M. DEL BALZO, Acting
Administrator, Federal Aviation
Administration, v. LESLIE E.
THOMPSON.

EA-3854;
Docket SE-11495

National Transportation Safety Board

April, 1993

Respondent has appealed from an initial decision of Administrative
Law Judge Patrick G. Geraghty, issued orally at the conclusion of an
evidentiary hearing held on April 11, 1991. By that decision, the law
judge affirmed the Administrator's determination that respondent had
violated section 61.37(a)(5) of the Federal Aviation Regulations
("FAR," 14 C.F.R.) by using unauthorized material during a pilot's
written instrument rating examination that was conducted on February
12, 1990. In addition, the law judge sustained the revocation of
respondent's private pilot certificate, which had been ordered by the
Administrator as a sanction for that alleged FAR violation.

In connection with his appeal, respondent concedes that he brought
"a small cheat sheet with some answers on it" (a two-sided handwritten
document measuring approximately four and one-half inches by one
and one-half inches, which contains numbers corresponding to
questions found in the FAA examination question book and another set
of numbers indicating the correct multiple choice answer for each such
question) to the examination room, but maintains that he did not violate
FAR section 61.37(a)(5) because he did not "use" it before his
examination was confiscated by an FAA test examiner. Respondent
also contends that the revocation of his airman certificate is too harsh a
sanction for the FAR violation alleged in this case.

The Administrator has submitted a reply brief, in which he urges
the Board to affirm the law judge's initial decision.

Upon consideration of the briefs of the parties and the entire
record, the Board has determined that safety in air commerce or air
transportation and the public interest require affirmation of the
Administrator's order and the initial decision. We will therefore deny
respondent's appeal.

As has been noted above, respondent readily admits that he
brought a "cheat sheet" into the examination room. He has also
acknowledged that he placed the "cheat sheet" on one of his legs after
the examination began and that he intended to use it as an aid in
answering the examination questions. Although he has related that he
was unable to read the "cheat sheet" from that position and did not
obtain any answers from it before the test examiner confiscated his
examination, n6 respondent clearly attempted to answer questions by
referring to the "cheat sheet" while the examination was in progress.

198

The Board, therefore, believes that respondent's contention that he did not "use" an unauthorized test aid is without merit.

In this regard, we note that the facts of this case are analogous to those of *Administrator v. Slattery, 3 NTSB 1935 (1979),* in which we rejected a similar argument in finding a violation of section 61.37(a)(5). In Slattery, the respondent, under the pretext of needing to get change to purchase a candy bar, left the examination room and went to his car to retrieve an examination course book, which he referred to prior to returning to the room. This was detected by FAA monitors, who did not permit the respondent to continue taking the examination. While, as a consequence, he did not in fact utilize the information he obtained from the course book to answer any examination questions, the Board nevertheless held that the respondent had "used" an unauthorized test aid in contravention of section 61.37(a)(5). We see no significant distinction between the operative facts in Slattery and those presented in this case. The fact that respondent in the case now before us may have failed to obtain any answers from his "cheat sheet" for want of sharper vision or for having placed it in a poor location for viewing does not negate a finding that he "used" an unauthorized test aid. The purpose of the regulation in question is to prevent cheating, and we do not believe that there is a need to show that an attempt to cheat was successful in order for a violation of that regulation to be found. Thus, when respondent took the "cheat sheet" out and looked at it, he had "used" it within the meaning of FAR § 61.37(a)(5), even though he was unable to apply the information appearing on it to any of his answers.

In view of the above, the Board finds no error in the law judge's affirmation of the Administrator's determination that respondent violated FAR section 61.37(a)(5).

Turning to the matter of sanction, we note that we have previously held that "the integrity of the written examination process is a fundamental part of the system which ensures that only qualified applicants are granted ratings and certificates," and that an individual who compromises the integrity of that process by violating FAR section 61.37(a)(5) "has demonstrated that he lacks qualifications in the form of the degree of care, judgment, and responsibility required of the holder of an airman certificate." Consequently, we believe that the Administrator was justified in ordering the revocation of respondent's airman certificate and that the law judge did not err in sustaining that sanction.

ACCORDINGLY, IT IS ORDERED THAT:

1. Respondent's appeal is denied;

2. The Administrator's order and the initial decision are both affirmed; and

3. The revocation of respondent's private pilot certificate shall commence 30 days after the service of this opinion and order.

LOWELL G. FERGUSON v. NATIONAL TRANSPORTATION
SAFETY BOARD and LONGHORNE M. BOND, Administrator,
FEDERAL AVIATION ADMINISTRATION.

UNITED STATES COURT OF APPEALS, NINTH CIRCUIT

678 F.2d 821

June, 1982

OPINION

Lowell G. Ferguson appeals the decision of the National
Transportation Safety Board (NTSB) to suspend his Airline Transport
Pilot Certificate for 60 days for violations of the Federal Aviation
Regulations. Ferguson, the pilot-in-command of Western Airlines
Flight 44, landed his aircraft without clearance at Buffalo, Wyoming,
rather than at the scheduled stop at Sheridan, Wyoming. The NTSB
adopted as its own the decision of the Administrative Law Judge (ALJ)
affirming the order of suspension issued by the Administrator of the
Federal Aviation Administration (FAA).

Ferguson now requests this court to vacate and set aside the order
of the ALJ and the NTSB, or, in the alternative, to remand for further
proceedings.   Ferguson asserts an affirmative defense under the
FAA/NASA Aviation Safety Reporting Program (ASRP Advisory
Circular 00-46B), contending (1) he was entitled to a waiver of
punishment because his actions were "inadvertent and not deliberate;"
(2) his conduct was not reckless within the meaning of Federal
Aviation Regulation *§ 91.9 (14 C.F.R. § 91.9).* Jurisdiction in the
United States Court of Appeals for the Ninth Circuit is predicated upon
49 U.S.C. § 1486 (Federal Aviation Act of 1958), 49 U.S.C. § 1903
(Independent Safety Board Act of 1974), and *5 U.S.C. § 701*
(Administrative Procedure Act).

In our view, this appeal presents two issues: first, whether the
NTSB properly interpreted the phrase "inadvertent and not deliberate"
in Advisory Circular 00-46B of the FAA Aviation Safety Reporting
Program; and second, whether the NTSB was correct in affirming the
ALJ's conclusion from the findings of fact that Ferguson's operation of
Western Airlines Flight 44 was reckless within the meaning of Federal
Aviation Regulation *§ 91.9.*

We hold that the NTSB did not abuse its discretion in interpreting
the Advisory Circular 00-46B. Neither the historical background nor
the language of the circular indicates that reckless conduct can be
considered "inadvertent and not deliberate" and thus, qualify for a
waiver of punishment. We also conclude that the NTSB did not abuse
its discretion in affirming the ALJ's conclusion that Ferguson's conduct
was reckless. Although Ferguson did not knowingly land his aircraft at
the wrong airport, he should have known that his conduct demonstrated
a gross disregard for safety and created an actual danger to life and
property. Accordingly, we affirm the decision of the NTSB.

I. FACTUAL BACKGROUND

Ferguson was pilot-in-command of Western Airlines Flight 44 from Los Angeles, California to seven locations, including Las Vegas, Nevada, Denver, Colorado, and Sheridan, Wyoming. Ferguson, with over 12,000 hours of flying experience, had never been found in violation of any Federal Aviation Regulations.

Flight 44 left Los Angeles on July 31, 1979. By the time the flight departed on the leg from Denver to Sheridan, it was 35 minutes behind schedule. The original flight plan would have taken the aircraft from the Denver Air Route Traffic Control Center to the Crazy Woman navigational facility for an instrument landing in Sheridan. Shortly before reaching Crazy Woman, however, control of flight 44 was transferred to Salt Lake Air Route Traffic Control Center (Salt Lake Center). Visibility was unrestricted, and Salt Lake Center offered flight 44 a direct clearance to Sheridan along airway victor 19, which passed directly over an airport in Buffalo, Wyoming. Flight 44 accepted the new plan in order to save time and fuel.

Ferguson handled radio communications as the flight approached Sheridan, and the first officer, James Bastiani, flew the aircraft. Neither Ferguson nor Bastiani had flown into Sheridan before, but each believed the other had. Ferguson reviewed the navigational chart, but failed to note that the Buffalo airport was directly under the aircraft's flight path.

At approximately 10:00 p.m. both Ferguson and Bastiani saw runway lights and commenced a visual approach to what they assumed was the Sheridan Airport. Ferguson did not use available radio navigation aids to make positive identification of the airport. During the approach, flight 44 maintained radio contact with the Sheridan Flight Service Station. Although the Air Traffic Controller in Sheridan informed flight 44 that another aircraft was on final approach, neither Ferguson nor Bastiani inquired further when they were unable to see the other aircraft. Although the airport at Sheridan was equipped with visual approach slope indicator (VASI) lights, Ferguson did not ask the Sheridan Flight Service Station why the runway before him was not so lighted. In spite of the fact that Ferguson was under an obligation to land the aircraft himself (Western Airlines Flight Operational Manual, P 5.1.2 B), First Officer Bastiani landed the Boeing 737. It was not until the aircraft's landing gear nose wheel sank in the turnoff pad beyond the runway that Ferguson realized that flight 44 had landed in Buffalo instead of Sheridan. The error was confirmed when the jeep that drove up to meet them bore "Piper" insignia rather than the expected Western Airlines logo.

On November 28, 1979 the Administrator of the FAA issued an order of suspension of Ferguson's Airline Transport Pilot certificate for 60 days. The order was subsequently filed as the Administrator's complaint, and charged Ferguson with violation of four sections of the Federal Aviation Regulations: (1) § 91.75(a) (14 C.F.R. § 91.75, deviating from an air traffic control clearance; (2) *§ 121.590(a) (14 C.F.R. § 121.590)*, landing at an airport not certificated under part 139 of the Federal Aviation Regulations; (3) *§ 121.555(b) (14 C.F.R. § 121.555)*, landing at an airport not listed in the Western Airlines Operations Specifications; and (4) *§ 91.9 (14 C.F.R. § 91.9)*, operating an aircraft in a careless or reckless manner so as to endanger the life or property of another.

An evidentiary hearing was held before an ALJ on June 4, 1980. The ALJ concluded that the evidence in the record supported a finding that Ferguson had violated the sections of the Federal Aviation Regulations as charged. The Administrator's 60-day suspension of Ferguson's Airline Transport Pilot Certificate was affirmed by the ALJ.

Ferguson filed a timely notice of appeal, and on December 9, 1980 the NTSB affirmed the 60-day suspension. On January 7, 1981, Ferguson filed a motion to stay the order with the NTSB. The motion was granted on January 8, 1981, and the order of submission was stayed pending the disposition of the case by this court.

II. STANDARD OF REVIEW

Our review of the NTSB decision is limited by the standards set forth in the Administrative Procedure Act, *5 U.S.C. § 706(2)*. Unless the decision was "arbitrary, capricious, an abuse of discretion, or otherwise not in accordance with the law," *5 U.S.C. § 706(2)(A)*, or "unsupported by substantial evidence," *5 U.S.C. § 706(2)(E)*, we must affirm. Furthermore, we must give deference to an administrative agency's interpretation of its own regulations. *Udall v. Tallman, 380 U.S. 1, 16, 85 S. Ct. 792, 801, 13 L. Ed. 2d 616 (1965)*; *Sierra Pacific Power Co. v. EPA, 647 F.2d 60, 65 (9th Cir. 1981)*; see also, *Bellwood General Hospital v. Schweiker, 673 F.2d 1043 at 1044 (1982)* (administrative interpretation of regulation by agency responsible for promulgating and administering it is controlling unless it is plainly erroneous or inconsistent with regulation.)

It is important to note that in this case Ferguson's conduct is not in dispute. Rather, it is the agency's conclusions drawn from the conduct that are at issue. Ferguson failed to: (1) familiarize himself with the navigational chart depicting the Buffalo airport; (2) land the aircraft himself, as required by Western Airlines Flight Operational Manual (P 5.1.2 B); (3) use navigational aids such as the VOR/DME, the Instrument Landing System (ILS, and the Monarch low frequency beacon associated with the ILS to identify the airport; and (4) note visual indications that he was landing at the wrong airport.

The NTSB, affirming the FAA's interpretation of the scope of Advisory Circular 00-46B, determined that Ferguson was not entitled to a waiver of punishment under the "inadvertent and not deliberate" provision of the circular. The NTSB also concluded from the findings of fact that Ferguson's conduct was reckless within the meaning of Federal Aviation Regulation *§ 91.9 (14 C.F.R. § 91.9)*. Because both issues in this case center on agency interpretations of regulations and conclusions drawn from findings of fact, this court will review the decision of the NTSB under the abuse of discretion standard, giving deference to the agency's interpretation of its own regulations. *Udall, 380 U.S. at 16, 85 S. Ct. at 801*; *Sierra Pacific Power Co., 647 F.2d at 65.*

III. THE SCOPE OF ADVISORY CIRCULAR 00-46B

We first consider Ferguson's claim that he is entitled to a waiver of punishment under the terms of Advisory Circular 00-46B, which was issued on June 15, 1979, and was in effect at the time flight 44 landed at the Buffalo Airport. Unlike the two preceding Advisory Circulars (issued in 1975 and 1976), 00-46B does not include an express exclusion of reckless conduct from the scope of immunity. It does, however, provide for a waiver of punishment if the violation was "inadvertent and not deliberate. "

Ferguson contends that the removal of the express exclusion of reckless conduct from the scope of immunity evidences the intent of the FAA to waive disciplinary action in cases where conduct was reckless- as long as the conduct was also "inadvertent and not deliberate." He also suggests that this court should adopt what he terms a "lay interpretation" of "inadvertent." Under Ferguson's definition, "inadvertent" is synonymous with "not deliberate." Thus, violations that are not deliberate are also inadvertent.

The NTSB responds that the history of the FAA Aviation Safety Reporting Program (ASRP) indicates that the intent of the FAA was to limit rather than increase the number of instances in which a waiver of punishment would be afforded. Because reckless conduct had been expressly excluded in the past, the NTSB asserts that it would not be consistent with the FAA's intent to establish a new waiver for reckless conduct. Furthermore, the NTSB maintains that the phrase "inadvertent and not deliberate" inherently excludes reckless conduct.

A. The Administrative Interpretation

In 1979 the FAA Administrator promulgated Advisory Circular 00-46B, which modified the ASRP to provide for disciplinary action against violators whenever information about the violation is obtained from an independent source. 44 Fed.Reg. 18129. Waiver of punishment is granted if:

> (1) The violation was inadvertent and not deliberate;

> (2) The violation did not involve a criminal offense, or accident, or action under section 609 of the Act which discloses a lack of qualification or competency, which are wholly excluded from this policy;

> (3) The person has not been found in any prior FAA enforcement action to have committed a violation since the initiation of the ASRP of the Federal Aviation Act or of any regulation promulgated under that Act; and

> (4) The person proves that within 10 days after the violation, he or she completed and delivered or mailed a written report of the incident or occurrence to NASA under ASRS. Advisory Circular 00-46B, P 9c(1)-9c(4).

Although the language of the Advisory Circular 00-46B does not expressly exclude reckless conduct from the scope of immunity, the FAA Administrator's notice explains:

> In addition, where a timely report is filed, if the FAA
> has not initiated its investigation within 90 days after the
> incident, the Administrator will waive the taking of
> disciplinary action against the person filing the report;
> provided the incident does not involve reckless
> operations, gross negligence, willful misconduct, a
> criminal offense, or an accident. 44 Fed.Reg. 18128-
> 18129 (emphasis added).

Thus, the Administrator has determined that the circular, as presently formulated, excludes reckless conduct from the scope of immunity.

"The administrative interpretation of a regulation by the agency responsible for promulgating and administering it is "controlling ... unless it is plainly erroneous or inconsistent with the regulation.' *Immigration and Naturalization Service v. Stanisic, 395 U.S. 62, 72, 89 S. Ct. 1519, 1526, 23 L. Ed. 2d 101 (1969)*, quoting *Bowles v. Seminole Rock Co., 325 U.S. 410, 414, 65 S. Ct. 1215, 1217, 89 L. Ed. 1700 (1945).*" *Bellwood General Hospital at 1044.* We first examine whether this interpretation is clearly erroneous. An examination of the history of the ASRP reveals that the Administrator's interpretation of the scope of the circular is correct.

The FAA Administrator, in a notice at 44 Fed.Reg. 18128-18129 (1979), indicated that the FAA established the ASRP in 1975 in order to obtain information that would aid in discovering and preventing unsafe conditions in the National Aviation System. Much of this information had remained unreported because pilots and other involved individuals feared disciplinary action. Id. Therefore, the first Advisory Circular 00-46, promulgated in 1975, included a waiver of certain disciplinary actions in return for a timely written report. The 1975 circular, however, expressly stated that the waiver applied "except with respect to reckless operations, criminal offenses, gross negligence, willful misconduct and accidents." Id. P 3c (emphasis added).

In 1976, the FAA Administrator modified the ASRP to provide for submission of reports directly to the National Aeronautics and Space Administration (NASA). Advisory Circular 00-46A (1976). The NASA system was designed to guarantee absolute confidentiality and thus, to encourage reporting. 44 Fed.Reg. 18128 (1979). An important provision of the 1976 circular stated that disciplinary action could not be taken against a violator unless the FAA approached NASA to inquire about a particular incident within 45 days of its occurrence. Advisory Circular 00-46A, P 6a(1). Reckless conduct was expressly excepted from the provision: "Disciplinary action may be taken in such cases, however, on the basis of information obtained independently of the Aviation Safety Report." Id. P 6a(3). It appears, therefore, that reckless conduct was expressly excluded from the scope of immunity if the incident involving reckless conduct was independently reported. In keeping with the FAA's Administrator's intent to encourage reporting, an incident involving reckless conduct could not be used for disciplinary purposes unless an independent report was received.

In our view the FAA, by promulgating Advisory Circular 00-46B, did not intend to increase the number of circumstances in which waivers of punishment would apply. Rather, the 1979 circular decreases the availability of waivers by allowing disciplinary action when incidents are independently reported. Reckless conduct was not immune from disciplinary action under the 1975 and 1976 circulars, and we agree with the NTSB that the FAA did not intend to allow a waiver of punishment for reckless conduct under the 1979 circular. Thus, we conclude that the Administrator's interpretation of the circular is not clearly erroneous.

We next examine the language used in the 1979 circular to determine whether the phrase "inadvertent and not deliberate" excludes reckless conduct, and is therefore consistent with the interpretation of the Administrator. *Udall v. Tallman, 380 U.S. at 16-18, 85 S. Ct. at 801-802.*

B. The Meaning of "Inadvertent and Not Deliberate"

Ferguson urges this court to conclude that the term "inadvertent" is synonymous with "not deliberate." In affirming the order of the ALJ, the NTSB defined the terms "inadvertent and not deliberate" to mean not reckless. The NTSB stated:

> The terms "inadvertent' and "not deliberate' are used in the conjunctive (rather than disjunctive) in the Advisory Circular. Therefore, for immunity to apply, not only must a violation be not deliberate, it must also be inadvertent. While it is undisputed that the violations were not deliberate, it is also clear that, under any reasonable definition, they were not inadvertent. "Reckless" connotes a substantially greater degree of lack of care than "inadvertence", as exemplified by the difference between simple negligence and gross negligence, and approaches deliberate or intentional conduct in the sense of reflecting a wanton disregard for the safety of others. Exclusion of reckless conduct from the immunity protection of the circular is also consistent with the history and intent of the ASRP.

Thus, in the view of the NTSB the meaning of the phrase inadvertant and not deliberate is consistent with the FAA Administrator's interpretation of the circular. We agree.

The parties do not dispute that Ferguson's conduct was not deliberate. Therefore, we must determine whether his conduct was inadvertent. Ferguson, as pilot-in-command of Western Airlines Flight 44, was required by Federal Aviation Regulations and company policy to perform certain duties: (1) to familiarize himself with all flight information. FAR § 91.5 (*14 C.F.R. § 91.5*); (2) to utilize available radio navigation aids to identify the airport before landing. Western Airlines Flight Operation Manual, P 5.3.3.C; and (3) to land the aircraft himself until he accumulated 100 hours as pilot-in-command of a type aircraft. Western Airlines Flight Operation Manual P 5.1.2.B. It is undisputed that he failed to comply with these regulations.

In each instance, Ferguson's failure to comply with the regulation was the result of a purposeful choice. If he had thoroughly examined the navigational chart before the flight, his hasty in-flight examination of the new route (depicted on the same chart) might have revealed the presence of the Buffalo Airport in the same path as the Sheridan

Airport. He chose, however, not to familiarize himself with all flight information. If he had utilized his radio navigation aids, he could have positively identified the airport. He chose, however, not to persevere in his use of navigational aids. If he had flown the aircraft himself, he might have been more alert to the visual indications that he was landing at the wrong airport. He chose, however, to allow First Officer Bastiani to land the aircraft.

Ballentine's Law Dictionary defines "inadvertence" in the following manner: "The word includes the effect of inattention, the result of carelessness, oversight, mistake, or fault of negligence and the condition or character of being inadvertent, inattentive or heedless. Gross negligence is not inadvertence in any degree." It is evident that an inadvertent act is one that is not the result of a purposeful choice. Thus, a person who turns suddenly and spills a cup of coffee has acted inadvertently. On the other hand, a person who places a coffee cup precariously on the edge of a table has engaged in purposeful behavior. Even though the person may not deliberately intend the coffee to spill, the conduct is not inadvertent because it involves a purposeful choice between two acts-placing the cup on the edge of the table or balancing it so that it will not spill. Likewise, a pilot acts inadvertently when he flies at an incorrect altitude because he misreads his instruments. But his actions are not inadvertent if he engages in the same conduct because he chooses not to consult his instruments to verify his altitude.

In spite of the fact that Ferguson may not have consciously intended any particular consequences to occur as a result of his choice, he nevertheless made an election to act as he did. We agree with the NTSB's decision: "While it is undisputed that (Ferguson's) ... violations were not deliberate, it is also clear that, under any reasonable definition, they were not inadvertent."

Ferguson suggests that we should adopt a lay interpretation of inadvertent. In our view a lay interpretation of the phrase is consistent with a legal interpretation. Webster's Dictionary defines "inadvertent" as: "Not paying strict attention; failing to notice or observe; heedless; unwary." Clearly, Ferguson's conduct cannot fall within the ambit of this definition. Although his actions did not reflect the degree of deliberateness found in intentional misconduct, neither can they be found to be inadvertent. We hold that the NTSB did not abuse its discretion by determining that the scope of the 1979 circular does not allow a waiver of punishment for reckless conduct, and that the phrase "inadvertent and not deliberate" cannot encompass reckless conduct.

IV. RECKLESS CONDUCT WITHIN § 91.9

Federal Aviation Regulation § 91.9 (14 C.F.R. § 91.9) states: "No person may operate an aircraft in a careless or reckless manner so as to endanger the life or property of another." The term "reckless," as used on § 91.9 has been interpreted to mean "conduct that demonstrates a gross disregard for safety when coupled with the creation of actual danger to life and property ...." Administrator v. Understein, NTSB Order EA-1644 (1981). Thus, in order to find that the NTSB abused its discretion, this court would need to decide that the findings of fact do not lead to the conclusion that Ferguson's conduct demonstrated: (1) a gross disregard for safety; and (2) a danger to life and property.

A gross disregard for safety occurs when a person engages in conduct that show a disregard for foreseeable consequences. Administrator v. Understein, NTSB Order EA-1644 (1981). Ferguson should have known that his conduct could result in harm to the safety of his passengers. The ALJ commented that Ferguson's failure to use navigational aids was "unjustified. " Sound judgment should have dictated a verification of the airport. The NTSB indicated that Ferguson should have known that he was landing at the wrong airport because of the visual indications. VASI lights, which Ferguson knew were part of the Sheridan airport, were not visible. The Sheridan Flight Service Station relayed the information that another aircraft was in the traffic pattern, but Ferguson did not realize what he should have known-that he was landing at the wrong airport. Because the consequences of Ferguson's conduct were clearly foreseeable, the conclusion of the NTSB that Ferguson demonstrated a gross disregard for safety is not an abuse of discretion.

There is no question that Ferguson's conduct created an actual danger to life and property. The NTSB suggests several events that could have occurred as a result of Ferguson's conduct: (1) the hard landing and subsequent hard brake application could have caused the aircraft to swerve off the runway; (2) the landing gear could have collapsed if it had sunk into the ground near the runway; (3) a fire could have resulted if any of the fuel tanks had ruptured; and (4) the aircraft could have struck mountainous terrain because the flight was using the published elevation for Sheridan rather than Buffalo. Even though no actual injury resulted, the potential endangerment is sufficient to find reckless operation. Administrator v. Stretar, NTSB Order EA-1535 (1980).

Ferguson argues that emphasis should be placed on the fact that no accident, injury, or property damage occurred. He contends that "any act of inadvertence in light of its potential catastrophic consequences would constitute gross negligence or reckless conduct under the Administrator's theory." His contention is not accurate because an act of inadvertence, even one of potential catastrophic consequences, would not be reckless unless it was coupled with the requisite gross disregard for safety.

We hold that the NTSB did not abuse its discretion in drawing the conclusion that Ferguson should have known that he was landing at the wrong airport. Because Ferguson's conduct had clearly foreseeable consequences, it demonstrated a gross disregard for safety and created an actual danger to life and property. Thus, the conduct was reckless within the meaning of § 91.9.

V. CONCLUSION

In summary, we hold that the NTSB did not abuse its discretion by determining that the scope of Advisory Circular 00-46B does not allow a waiver of punishment for reckless conduct, and that the phrase "inadvertent and not deliberate" cannot encompass reckless conduct. Furthermore, we hold that the NTSB did not abuse its discretion in drawing a conclusion from the findings of fact that Ferguson's conduct was reckless within the meaning of Federal Aviation Regulations § 91.9 (14 C.F.R. § 91.9).

The decision of the NTSB is AFFIRMED.

J. LYNN HELMS, Administrator, Federal Aviation Administration, v.
THOMAS S. HOWARD

Order EA-1923;
Docket SE-5824

National Transportation Safety Board

July, 1983

This proceeding involves an emergency order of revocation, issued by the Administrator, which reads as follows:

"1. You [respondent] are now, and at all times mentioned herein were, the holder of Airline Pilot Certificate No. 575627487;

2. On or about February 1, 1983, you, as pilot-in-command, operated Civil Aircraft N5262J, a Cessna 414 owned by Jenkins Leasing, in the vicinity of Concord, California.

3. While you were acting as pilot-in-command during said flight, you were observed by another aboard to be in possession of and smoking marihuana, a drug that affects human faculties in a way contrary to safety.

4. On or about February 22, 1983, you, as pilot-in-command, operated Civil Aircraft N27309, a Piper PA-31-350 owned by Jenkins Leasing, in the vicinity of Concord, California.

5. While you were acting as pilot-in-command during said flight, you were observed by another aboard to be in possession of and smoking marihuana.

6. Your operations as described above were careless or reckless so as to endanger the lives and property of others.

By reason of the foregoing circumstances, you:

a. violated Section 91.11(a)(3) of the Federal Aviation Regulations, in that you acted as a crewmember of a civil aircraft while using a drug that affects your faculties in a way contrary to safety;

b. violated Section 91.12(a) of the Federal Aviation Regulations, in that you operated a civil aircraft within the United States with knowledge that marihuana was carried on the aircraft.

c. violated Section 91.9 of the Federal Aviation Regulations, in that you operated an aircraft in a careless or reckless manner so as to endanger the life or property of another.

d. failed to exercise the degree of care, judgment and responsibility required of the holder of an airline transport pilot certificate.

e. have demonstrated that you presently lack the qualifications required of the holder of an airline transport pilot certificate."

At the conclusion of the evidentiary hearing held on June 17, 1983, Administrative Law Judge Jerrell R. Davis issued an oral initial decision affirming the Administrator's order.

The Administrator has filed a reply brief opposing the appeal and urging that the initial decision be affirmed.

Upon consideration of the briefs of the parties, and the entire record, the Board has determined that safety in air commerce or air transportation and the public interest require affirmation of the Administrator's order of revocation. We adopt as our own the findings of the law judge.

At the beginning of his appeal brief, respondent cites several procedural errors allegedly committed by the law judge concerning rulings on pretrial motions, on admission of evidence and allowance of testimony at the hearing, and on respondent's motion to dismiss at the conclusion of the Administrator's case-in-chief. We have carefully examined these rulings, in the context of the record, and find that, in each instance, the law judge did not abuse his discretion.

The Administrator's case-in-chief, with respect to the circumstances of the 2 flights in question, was presented through the testimony of 2 witnesses who, like respondent, were employed by Cal-West Aviation, a repair station and Part 135 operator. The first witness, Nicholas Paganello, the Chief Inspector and temporary Director of Maintenance for Cal-West, testified that he was in the aircraft on both flights, which were conducted for the purpose of testing a plane following maintenance; and that he observed respondent, over a 4-5 minute period on each flight, take several puffs from a hand-rolled cigarette containing a green, plant material, that he understood to be marihuana, based on its appearance and unique smell as well as his passing conversation with respondent.

The Administrator's second witness, Clint La Fontaine, a mechanic for Cal-West, testified that he was in the right seat during the February 22nd flight; that respondent hand-rolled a cigarette, from a green, leafy substance, during the taxi-out; that respondent smoked about one-quarter to one-half of the cigarette over a 4-5 minute period during the flight; that respondent offered the cigarette to him; and that based on his experience of being "around the smoking of marihuana for quite a while" (Tr. 84), there was "no doubt" (Tr. 97) in his mind that, from the appearance and smell of the cigarette, it was marihuana.

The Administrator's third and final witness was an FAA aviation safety inspector whose testimony was based on (1) a 2 week course he had taken at the Transportation Safety Institute, part of which was devoted to human or physiological factors including drugs such as marihuana, (2) his comprehensive review of a document entitled "The Aeromedical Aspects of Marihuana" that was prepared by the FAA's Office of Aviation Medicine (Exhibit C-1); and (3) his own personal experience, which included at least one instance when he observed a pilot who had been smoking marihuana. The inspector testified that marihuana was a drug that adversely affects a pilot's faculties in that it impairs judgment, memory, vision and behavior.

Respondent, in his testimony, had no recollection of a flight on February 1st with Nick Paganello on board but denied that he flew a Cessna 414 on that date while he was in possession of and smoking marihuana. With respect to the February 22nd flight, he testified that he was pilot-in-command and that Messrs. Paganello and La Fontaine were on board the plane; that Nick Paganello told respondent before the flight that he had marihuana; and that during the flight Nick Paganello smoked part of a cigarette, represented to be marihuana, and that he offered it to respondent, who took several drags.

Respondent also presented as a witness a private investigator who interviewed Nick Paganello and Clint La Fontaine prior to the hearing. He testified that Mr. La Fontaine said he never observed respondent smoking marihuana and that Mr. Paganello stated he was under duress from his superiors to make a statement to the FAA.

We agree with the law judge that the violations of sections 91.12(a) and 91.11(a)(3) were established by a preponderance of the evidence. The law judge, "[h]aving carefully observed the demeanor of all witnesses who testified . . . found the witnesses testifying on behalf of [the Administrator], on balance, to be more believable and, in the final analysis, persuasive" (Tr. 221). In making this credibility determination, the law judge was well aware of the evidence in the record, stressed on appeal by respondent, of animosity between respondent and the owner of Cal West which apparently resulted in pressure being brought on Messrs. Paganello and La Fontaine (perhaps in the form of loss of employment) to make statements concerning the marihuana usage on the 2 flights. The law judge nevertheless made a clear and unequivocal credibility determination in favor of these witnesses and we have no reason to disturb that finding, which is within the exclusive province of the trier of fact who alone is in a position to gauge the demeanor of the witnesses. We therefore agree with the law judge that, notwithstanding the lack of a chemical analysis of the substance smoked by respondent, "the evidence, circumstantial or otherwise, is very persuasive that marihuana was, indeed, carried aboard the aircraft" (Tr. 221) in violation of section 91.12 of the FAR.

We are also satisfied that the record establishes that marihuana is a "drug that affects [a person's] faculties in any way contrary to safety". Again, while the best evidence on this issue would have been presented through a medical witness, the inspector's testimony, based on his training and personal experience, coupled with the document prepared by medical experts and detailing the effects of marihuana (Exhibit C-1), is sufficient to meet the Administrator's burden of proof that marihuana comes within the coverage of section 91.11(a)(3). It is our further view that, contrary to respondent's assertion, section 91.11(a)(3) sets forth a standard sufficiently specific to support the imposition of a sanction in this case.

Finally, with respect to sanction, the Board has consistently held that where the violation of section 91.12 (carriage of marihuana) or section 61.15 (conviction involving marihuana) involves the operation of an aircraft, revocation is the appropriate sanction. Although the previous cases have generally involved the carriage of a large amount of marihuana (i.e., as cargo), the instant matter, in addition to the section 91.12 violation, also involves the actual usage of marihuana by the pilot while operating an aircraft. By virtue of these circumstances, respondent has demonstrated a lack of qualifications and revocation is warranted.

ACCORDINGLY, IT IS ORDERED THAT:

1. Respondent's appeal is denied; and
2. The Administrator's order, and the initial decision, are affirmed.

DAVID R. HINSON, Administrator,
Federal Aviation Administration v.
DAVID R. KEARNEY

EA-4208;
Docket SE-13037

National Transportation Safety Board

July, 1994

Respondent has appealed from the oral initial decision of Administrative Law Judge William E. Fowler, Jr., rendered on July 22, 1993, at the conclusion of an evidentiary hearing. The law judge affirmed an order of the Administrator suspending respondent's airman certificate for 30 days for violating section 61.15(e) and (f) of the Federal Aviation Regulations ("FAR," 14 C.F.R. Part 61). We deny the appeal and affirm the law judge's decision.

Respondent was convicted of driving under the influence of alcohol (DUI) on March 30, 1992, in the State of California, but failed to report the incident to the FAA's Security Division within the next 60 days, as required by section 61.15. He maintains that he had decided in 1987 to "retire" from flying, did not have a current medical certificate at the time of his conviction and, as a consequence, could not legally have operated an aircraft. (Respondent had been a private pilot certificate holder since 1980).

In June 1992, respondent began exercising the privileges of his airman certificate again. He disclosed his DUI conviction on his medical certificate application on June 25, 1992, and learned from the aviation medical examiner that it was material to the FAA. In a letter dated January 27, 1993, from respondent to Joseph Standell, Assistant Chief Counsel, FAA Aeronautical Center, respondent states that he had "no way of knowing the FAA reporting requirement, because it was enacted when I was not involved with flying." He continues: "I did not become aware of the requirement until I became involved again with flying in June of 1992. In fact, it was not until my June 25 medical application that I understood my conviction to be an issue, when it was brought to my attention by Dr. Boris Schmiegel, the designated medical examiner. After examining the FAR that was enacted when I was retired from flying, I thought the information provided on the medical application was sufficient to meet the reporting requirement and that a separate statement was unnecessary."

From his statement, it appears that respondent, in fact, knew of the 61.15(e) reporting requirement before receiving the notification from the Security Division in November 1992. In any event, a certificate holder is charged with knowledge of the regulations that pertain to him.

He received a new medical certificate, issued on August 12, 1992. According to respondent, he believed he had fulfilled his obligation to report the conviction to the FAA. By letter dated November 20, 1992, the FAA's Security Division advised respondent that he had failed to submit notification of his DUI conviction as required by FAR section 61.15. The subject action ensued.

211

Although he admits that he failed to report his DUI conviction to the Security Division, respondent asserts that he was unaware of the requirements of section 61.15 because, when he retired from flying in 1987, he had no intention of returning to flying and as a result, he did not keep apprised of changes in the FARs. Since his medical certificate expired on March 31, 1988, respondent asserts, he did not and could not legally have operated an aircraft at the time of his conviction. Therefore, he claims that his failure to timely report the DUI conviction did not impact air safety. (We need not discuss respondent's argument that an inactive pilot should be treated no differently than a student pilot. Section 61.15 applies to present certificate holders, whether exercising the privileges of their certificates or not.)

The Administrator replies that since respondent remained a certificate holder, he had an obligation to be familiar with and comply with the FARs, irrespective of whether he was exercising the privileges of his airman certificate. This responsibility could only have been avoided had he voluntarily relinquished his certificate.

We agree that respondent's claim of ignorance is not a defense, as certificate holders are expected to be cognizant of the regulations that apply to them. Administrator v. Smith, NTSB Order No. EA-4088 at 8 (1994). In Smith, a case decided after the instant case was briefed, the respondent also asserted that he had been unaware of the 61.15(e) reporting requirements. However, it was not a claim of "mere ignorance," and though we found the respondent had committed a technical violation, no sanction was imposed, given the unique circumstances of the case. Specifically, Smith sought advice from a Flight Standards District Office about his obligation under the regulations to report a conviction for Driving While Intoxicated, but was given incomplete information.

By contrast, Respondent Kearney assumed that his decision to retire from flying (yet remain in possession of his airman certificate) released him from any obligation to keep informed of the regulations that pertained to him. Additionally, when he learned that his conviction had to be reported, as evidenced by his letter of January 27, 1993, he decided that the disclosure on the medical application rendered further notification to the FAA unnecessary.

Respondent's claim that he was unaware of the 61.15 reporting requirements or had misinterpreted the extent of his reporting obligation is not exculpatory, since intent is not an element of the violation. As for the Administrator's decision to prosecute this case, it is not a subject appropriate for Board review.

ACCORDINGLY, IT IS ORDERED THAT:

1. Respondent's appeal is denied;

2. The Administrator's order and the initial decision are affirmed; and

3. The 30-day suspension of respondent's airman certificate shall begin 30 days after service of this order.

PAUL LINDSAY v. NATIONAL TRANSPORTATION SAFETY
BOARD & FEDERAL AVIATION ADMINISTRATION

UNITED STATES COURT OF APPEALS FOR THE DISTRICT OF
COLUMBIA CIRCUIT

47 F.3d 1209

February, 1995

RANDOLPH, Circuit Judge: The most remarkable thing about this case is that petitioner thinks he is fit to hold a pilot's certificate. The Administrator of the Federal Aviation Administration revoked his certificate, a decision the National Transportation Safety Board sustained. To reconstruct the events precipitating this agency action, and to understand this petition for review of the Board's decision, we must go to central Florida and the pre-dawn hours of Sunday, October 17, 1993.

Two men and two women are at the Shamrock Lounge in Leesburg, drinking heavily. Their common interest is skydiving. Both men are also pilots. Neither woman is. One of the men, Phillip Smith, owns an aging Cessna Model 182, a single engine four-seater aircraft. He keeps his plane at the Leesburg Municipal Airport. Smith is with his girlfriend, Debra Hall, a bartender at the Shamrock. The other man, petitioner Paul Lindsay, holds an FAA airline transportation pilot certificate and has logged 4500 hours of flying time. Lindsay is with his girlfriend, Sandra Sprincis, a nurse who resides in a trailer in the nearby town of Umatilla. Lindsay lives with his mother some 10 miles away, but sometimes stays with Sprincis. They have driven to the bar together in Sprincis' car.

It is 1:30 a.m., and the Shamrock Lounge is about to close for the evening. "It's a nice night for a flight," the men observe. With that, their reckless, irresponsible plan is hatched. Lindsay wants to pilot Smith's plane. He has flown it before. Smith decides to fly it himself. That detail settled, the four men and women leave the bar and drive in Debra Hall's car to Leesburg Airport, 3 miles away. On the way, they stop to buy some beer.

Later, reports reach the Leesburg sheriff's office about a plane flying erratically over the town, a plane perhaps in trouble. Officers arriving at Leesburg Airport at 2:39 a.m. discover Hall's car and piles of clothing on the ground. No one is around. The runway is dark. While the officers wait, a Cessna 182 lands. Philip Smith is in the pilot's seat and very drunk. Hall is next to him. In the back are Lindsay and Sprincis, both naked.

The officers ask Smith to step out. He complies, promptly fails a sobriety test and is arrested for violating Florida law. A deputy sheriff escorts Smith to his cruiser and drives him to the county jail. Other officers stay behind interviewing Hall, Lindsay and Sprincis. Hall gets out of the plane. Lindsay refuses to budge. He is loud, obnoxious and, like Smith, very drunk. He brags about his flying skills. He refuses to tell the officers his address. His girlfriend Sprincis gives them her address in Umatilla and gives the same address for Lindsay.

Sprincis tries to persuade Lindsay to leave with her and Debra Hall. He refuses. He tells Sprincis to "go ahead with" Hall. Lindsay promises to "beat her home anyway." The officers radio the lieutenant to report Lindsay's recalcitrance. By this time, it is 4:00 a.m. The lieutenant radios back that Smith has given Lindsay permission to stay in his plane. Sprincis decides to remain with him. Hall departs in her car, apparently sufficiently recovered from the effects of alcohol. At 4:12 a.m., the officers drive out of the airport, leaving Lindsay and Sprincis there alone. Two of the officers park close by, hidden in the darkness, watching the airport entrance and runway, concerned that Lindsay might try to take off in Smith's plane. The officers maintain their lookout until 4:41 a.m. All is quiet, and they leave to respond to another call.

About 5:00 a.m., a lieutenant and his deputy, having left Smith in jail, return to the Leesburg Airport. It is not yet light. The Cessna is gone. So are Lindsay and Sprincis. Remembering the address Sprincis had given them, they drive 12 miles to Umatilla. There on the runway of the Umatilla Airport they find Smith's plane. Sprincis' trailer is a few hundred yards away, across the street. The door is locked, and when the lieutenant knocks, no one answers. Later that day the police impound the plane.

These largely undisputed facts were adduced during a two-day hearing before an administrative law judge on Lindsay's challenge to the FAA Administrator's emergency order revoking his pilot's certificate. FAA regulations prohibited Lindsay from recklessly operating an aircraft, *14 C.F.R. § 91.13*, and from acting as a crewmember of a civil aircraft "within 8 hours after the consumption of any alcoholic beverage," *14 C.F.R. § 91.17(a)(1)*. Attorneys for both sides stipulated that the only issue at the hearing would be whether Lindsay piloted Smith's plane on its October 17 flight from Leesburg to Umatilla. The ALJ, for reasons we will describe, found that the FAA Administrator had not proven his case. The National Transportation Safety Board reinstated the revocation on appeal.

We have three issues. The first is whether the Board erred in reversing the ALJ's decision. The second is whether the Board's decision upholding the order of revocation is supported by substantial evidence. The third is whether, by presenting an affirmative defense, Lindsay waived any objection to the ALJ's refusal to rule in his favor at the close of the Administrator's case-in-chief.

The Board overturned the ALJ's decision because the ALJ had failed to apply the preponderance of evidence standard in assessing the Administrator's proof. In order to put the Board's reversal in perspective, we need to recount some of the additional evidence produced during the hearing.

The FAA's investigation revealed that when Debra Hall left Leesburg Airport shortly after 4:00 a.m. on October 17 she took Smith's keys with her. Unknown to Hall, however, Smith's plane could be operated without those keys. The pilot-side door did not lock and any sort of key inserted into the ignition switch would turn on the engine. An FAA investigator called Hall on October 18, the day after the flights, and asked her whether she knew who flew the plane to Umatilla. Hall said Lindsay flew it. Asked about the source of her knowledge, Hall stated--in language the investigator recorded in his notes--that because she could not figure out how the plane could have been flown to Umatilla without the keys, "I confronted [Lindsay] at the jail when I bailed Phillip out [about noon on October 17] and he told me he flew it to Umatillo [sic]." At the hearing, Hall admitted having told the investigator that Lindsay piloted the plane to Umatilla. But she then denied having any knowledge to back up her assertion and said that when she had asked Lindsay at the jail, he told her he had not flown the plane. The investigator's contemporaneous notes show otherwise, of course, as does the investigator's testimony at the hearing. It is true, as Lindsay stresses, that at one point the transcript reports the investigator saying Hall told him Lindsay flew the plane to "Leesburg." But this appears to be either a slip of the tongue or a mistranscription. There is no other indication of any flight from Umatilla to Leesburg, and the ALJ understood the investigator to have been testifying about the flight from Leesburg to Umatilla.

When the Administrator rested, Lindsay moved for a judgment vacating the emergency revocation order on the ground that the FAA had failed to make out a prima facie case against him. The ALJ denied the motion, and Lindsay proceeded to put on his defense. There is no need to recite the defense in great detail. The ALJ found Lindsay's witnesses, including Lindsay himself, not credible. Lindsay testified that after the police left the airport, he and Sprincis got out of the plane, walked over to a phone booth and called Keith Jordan, a skydiver friend who lived in Leesburg. Jordan said he received the call about 4:00 a.m. With him in his apartment was Edward Carter, an aerial photographer who videotaped skydivers. Carter said he had travelled with Lindsay and Sprincis to Leesburg the evening before, and had been waiting for them to pick him up so that he could spend the night in Sprincis' trailer in Umatilla. After Lindsay's call awakened him, Jordan dressed, and he and Carter drove in Jordan's car to the Leesburg Airport, about 10 minutes away. When they arrived, Carter got out of the car, spoke with Lindsay, walked over to the plane with him, and together they unsuccessfully tried to secure the pilot-side door. Lindsay came back to the car and told Jordan and Sprincis that Carter was going to fly the plane to Umatilla. Jordan, Lindsay and Sprincis then drove out of the airport and back to Jordan's apartment, where they spent the night. Carter testified that he flew Smith's plane to Umatilla, about a 10-minute flight. He talked briefly with the security guard, Raymond Cruitt, and then walked over to Sprincis's trailer and fell asleep. He heard the officers knocking on the door of the trailer later in the morning, but decided not to answer.

The holes in this story are large, and the ALJ did not believe it. We will put aside the fact that if Jordan and Carter had arrived at the Leesburg Airport when they said, the officers maintaining surveillance would have seen them, but did not. The most glaring defect in Lindsay's defense is elsewhere--in the utter implausibility of Carter's having flown Smith's plane to Umatilla. Carter was a pilot, but he was not much of one. Since 1969 he had logged only 100 hours. When the FAA Administrator started inquiring about whether he still had a valid license to fly, Carter invoked his *Fifth Amendment* privilege against self-incrimination. Carter had never flown Smith's plane, and he did not have Smith's permission to fly it on October 17. He was unfamiliar with the Leesburg Airport. Yet according to him he decided to take off in the dead of night, without lights, on an unfamiliar runway that dropped off into a lake, in a plane he had never flown, without checking the oil level in the plane, and without even knowing how much, if any, fuel it had remaining. What was the urgency that caused Carter to decide to risk his life to get to Umatilla, a mere 15-minute drive away? When the FAA investigator asked him this rather obvious question before the hearing, Carter said he had no particular reason. At the hearing he changed his story. He explained that he had to get back to open up "Skyworld," a skydiving school at the Umatilla Airport, at 7:30 a.m., and when he met Lindsay and Sprincis at the Leesburg Airport he did not know where Sprincis had left her car. This is, to put it mildly, lame. Sprincis surely knew where she had left her car--at the Shamrock Lounge, only 3 miles from the Leesburg Airport. All Carter had to do was ask her. Besides, Jordan was supposedly there with his car. There is no reasonable explanation why, if he were telling the truth, Carter did not even ask Jordan to give him a lift to Umatilla. Carter still had hours to go before he supposedly had to open up at Skyworld. And yet he says he borrowed--that is, stole--Smith's plane to make the 12-mile trip.

What of Raymond Cruitt, the self-described person responsible for keeping "things clean and neat and security" at the Umatilla Airport, the person to whom Carter allegedly spoke as he was walking from Smith's plane to the trailer? In rambling and disjointed testimony, Cruitt said that Carter had committed "perjury," that Carter had not flown Smith's plane because the actual pilot was one "Lawrence Eugene Kavel," a member of a group dealing in "hypnosis, mind control, disguises," a person Cruitt met some twenty years ago in Washington, D.C., but still recognized through the darkness despite his older appearance, a person Cruitt thought might be a government agent. Cruitt "yelled out to him, I said, well who are you screwing over tonight?" and "he says, you better go back and get in bed because the police are on their way." And so Cruitt went back to bed. Needless to say, the ALJ found Cruitt to be "unreliable" and attached no weight to his "bizarre" testimony.

As to the Administrator's witnesses, the ALJ viewed them as "entirely credible." The ALJ also found that Debra Hall had made the statements the FAA investigator attributed to her; her contrary testimony at the hearing was not "credible." As to Jordan and Sprincis, they had an obvious "bias," and there was "considerable doubt" about their version of the events at the Leesburg Airport. Carter was simply not "a credible witness."

Despite these findings, the ALJ thought Lindsay had introduced "an element of doubt" sufficient to preclude a finding that the Administrator had satisfied his burden of proof. Nonetheless, the ALJ said that he was unconvinced Lindsay "did not commit the alleged violations."

We sustain the Board's ruling that the ALJ misapplied the preponderance of evidence standard. The ALJ had two versions of the events before him. For the Administrator to prevail, the ALJ had to find only that it was, in the familiar formulation, "more likely true than not true" that Lindsay flew the plane to Umatilla. 3 EDWARD J. DEVITT ET AL., FEDERAL JURY PRACTICE AND INSTRUCTIONS § 72.04 (4th ed. 1987); *see Concrete Pipe & Products of California, Inc. v. Construction Laborers Pension Trust, 124 L. Ed. 2d 539, 113 S. Ct. 2264, 2279 (1993).* This standard called for the ALJ to make a comparative judgment about the evidence, rather than a statement about what actually occurred. Certainty was not necessary, nor was the absence of any reasonable doubt. As the Board correctly put it, the ALJ's own findings reveal his belief that it was more probable than not that Lindsay made the flight.

As to the Board's ruling that Lindsay violated the regulations, there is substantial evidence to support it. Someone flew Smith's plane to Umatilla. All the credible evidence points to that someone being Lindsay. He had already demonstrated no hesitation about flying while intoxicated. At the bar he offered to fly the plane on its first outing of the night. Drunk or not, he was the only one among the cast of possible pilots who had the experience and ability to fly out of Leesburg in the dark and land safely in Umatilla. He had flown Smith's plane before. It is fair to assume that while he was sitting in the plane waiting for the police to leave, he knew that he could start the engine without Smith's keys. He was the one who defiantly remained in the plane. He is the one who bragged that without any means of transportation other than the plane, he would beat Sprincis back to Umatilla if she drove there with Hall. And he is the one Hall identified as having admitted to being the pilot on that flight. Substantial evidence is "such relevant evidence as a reasonable mind might accept as adequate to support a conclusion" (*Consolidated Edison Co. v. NLRB, 305 U.S. 197, 229, 83 L. Ed. 126, 59 S. Ct. 206 (1938))*, taking "into account whatever in the record fairly detracts from its weight" (*Universal Camera Corp. v. NLRB, 340 U.S. 474, 488, 95 L. Ed. 456, 71 S. Ct. 456 (1951))*. That standard has been satisfied.

All that remains is Lindsay's claim that the Board erred in making the following ruling:

> At the close of the Administrator's case the respondent moved to dismiss, arguing that the Administrator had not established a prima facie case. The law judge disagreed and denied that motion. On appeal here the respondent challenges that determination. However, since respondent put on evidence in defense of the charges after the rejection of his motion to dismiss, we think he effectively waived his right to object to the law judge's ruling, for once the case is appealed to us, the issue becomes not the correctness of the law judge's view that the burden of going forward with evidence had shifted to the respondent, but, rather, the sufficiency of the evidence in the record, viewed as a whole.

The Board's decision strikes us as entirely correct. The rule it embodies has long governed appeals in the federal courts. A defendant waives an appeal of the denial of a directed verdict motion by putting on evidence. The Supreme Court so held in *Bogk v. Gassert, 149 U.S. 17, 23, 37 L. Ed. 631, 13 S. Ct. 738 (1893)*: "A defendant has an undoubted right to stand upon his motion for a nonsuit, and have his writ of error if it be refused; but he has no right to insist upon his exception, after having subsequently put in his testimony and made his case upon the merits, since the court and jury have the right to consider the whole case as made by the testimony." *See, e.g., Alston v. Bowins, 236 U.S. App. D.C. 69, 733 F.2d 161, 163-64 (D.C. Cir. 1984)*. We have not considered whether all of the Board's previous decisions are consistent with this approach. Even if some are not, the Board's failure to follow or to explain those decisions is harmless. *5 U.S.C. § 706*. The Administrator's evidence in his case-in-chief surely was, for the reasons already given, enough to withstand Lindsay's motion.

The petition for review is denied.

Circuit Judge TATEL, concurring in part, and concurring in the judgment: I agree with the majority that substantial evidence supports the decision of the Board. I write separately to express a concern that the Board's reasoning regarding the burden of proof and certain related credibility determinations borders on the arbitrary and capricious.

The ALJ concluded that neither party had "proven" its version of events; neither established that Lindsay had, or had not, flown the plane. The Board considered this a misreading of the preponderance of the evidence standard. "This is not a complicated case," the Board wrote; Lindsay "either made the flight the Administrator believes he made or he did not. The law judge's task was to decide that issue one way or the other." The ALJ, however, had no duty to determine whether Lindsay did or did not fly the plane. His only duty was to determine whether the party with the burden of proof had established that its allegations were "more likely than not." The ALJ did just that, concluding that the Administrator had not proven, by a preponderance of the evidence, that Lindsay flew the plane.

The Board's confusion--and its insistence that the ALJ decide the matter "one way or the other"--is understandable: As a factual matter, Lindsay either was or was not in the pilot's seat that night. In a legal sense, however, the ALJ's findings were entirely plausible because neither party had provided him with the quantum of certainty that he needed to conclude that their version of events had occurred.

Lindsay, of course, was not responsible for proving he did not fly the plane; indeed, it was technically possible for Lindsay to have won without presenting any defense at all. But he did present a case, and his evidence was useful to the ALJ because it "created doubts" in his mind about the strength of the Administrator's case. This language of doubt is not, as the Board seems to think, evidence of an inappropriately applied burden of proof. Instead, it is merely one way of articulating the necessary weighing of evidence that goes on in circumstantial cases like this one. *See Administrator v. Williams,* No. Order EA-3588, Docket SE-10463, 1992 N.T.S.B. LEXIS 125, at 3 n.4 (May 26, 1992) (using language of "reasonable doubt" in a similar context); *Administrator v. Saunders,* No. Order EA-3672, Docket SE-10104, (Aug. 29, 1992) (using language of "sufficient doubt" in a similar context). Lindsay's failure to prove that he did not fly the plane--and the doubt that his witnesses cast on the Administrator's case--was thus entirely consistent with the ALJ's finding that the Administrator failed to prove his case. As Chairman Vogt recognized in dissenting from the Board's opinion, the Board's conclusion that the ALJ improperly applied the burden of proof was incorrect.

The Board compounded its error by failing to understand how Lindsay's witnesses could have "cast doubt" on the Administrator's case when the ALJ did not entirely believe their testimony. According to the Board, the ALJ's conclusion that Lindsay was "less than credible" "had to be equated" to a belief that Lindsay flew the plane--i.e. that the ALJ really must have believed the opposite of Lindsay's testimony. The Board also concluded that the ALJ had "unwittingly" given credence to the testimony of other witnesses that he considered biased or not fully credible. Although the ALJ *may* ignore the testimony of witnesses that appear "less than credible," and although the ALJ *may* even choose to believe the opposite of the testimony of a witness who appears particularly deceitful, *see* 2 Davis & Pierce, Administrative Law Treatise § 11.2, at 188-90 (3rd ed. 1994); *cf. United States v. Zeigler, 301 U.S. App. D.C. 298, 994 F.2d 845, 848-50 (D.C. Cir. 1994),* nothing requires, as the Board apparently concluded, that the factfinder *must* ignore the testimony of "less than credible" witnesses or must conclude the *opposite* of that testimony. Testimony by less than credible witnesses may be useful in several ways. For example, though the ALJ considers a portion of a witness' testimony to be deceptive, the rest of it may be credible. Such testimony might also cast doubt on the credibility or certainty of the Administrator's witnesses, or call into question the logical consistency of the Administrator's evidence or inferences that he seeks to draw from that evidence. As noted above, these considerations led the ALJ to conclude that the testimony of Lindsay's witnesses "cast doubt"--apparently significant doubt--on the Administrator's version of events. *See* Joint Appendix at 624, 626, 628, 630 (giving credence to less than credible witnesses).

I can understand the Board's frustration with trying to review seesawing credibility determinations like those made in this case. In such instances, the Board would be entirely justified in reviewing the evidence *de novo,* as it did here, or in directing its ALJs to provide less equivocal credibility determinations. The Board went further, however, resting much of its decision upon an apparent misconception of the burden of proof and a sweeping misunderstanding that testimony by less than credible witnesses can have no role in an adjudication. Since the Board's own finding that Lindsay violated flight regulations is supported by substantial evidence, I can nevertheless concur in its reversal of the ALJ. Should its misconceptions regarding the burden of proof and the role of less than credible testimony affect the results of future Board opinions, however, I will come to view them with even more skepticism.

ROBERT R. KRALEY, v. THE NATIONAL TRANSPORTATION
SAFETY BOARD & FEDERAL AVIATION ADMINISTRATION

UNITED STATES COURT OF APPEALS FOR THE SIXTH
CIRCUIT

165 F.3d 27

October, 1998

PER CURIAM. Petitioner Robert R. Kraley petitions for review of
a final order of the National Transportation Safety Board (NTSB or
Board) affirming an order of the Federal Aviation Administration
(FAA) suspending Kraley's commercial pilot certificate for violation of
14 C.F.R. § 61.15(d). We deny the petition.

I.

Section 61.15(d) of the Federal Aviation Regulations provides that
a motor vehicle action involving drugs or alcohol occurring within
three years of a previous motor vehicle action involving drugs or
alcohol is grounds for the suspension or revocation of any airman's
certificates or ratings. *14 C.F.R. § 61.15(d)*. On May 22, 1996, the
FAA Administrator found that Kraley had violated *§ 61.15(d)* because
he had been convicted of driving under the influence on January 16,
1992, in municipal court in Elyria, Ohio, and had his driver's license
suspended on June 9, 1994, for "refusal to submit to a chemical test
when arrested for Driving Under the influence of Alcohol." The
Administrator then suspended Kraley's commercial pilot certificate for
120 days.

Kraley filed a notice of appeal seeking review by the NTSB. After
a hearing, the Administrative Law Judge (ALJ) affirmed the FAA's
order and 120-day suspension. Kraley appealed that decision to the
Board. The Board denied Kraley's appeal and affirmed the 120-day
suspension. *Administrator v. Kraley*, NTSB Order No. EA-4581
(1997). This petition follows.

II.

As a general proposition, we will reverse a decision of the NTSB
only if we find the agency's action to be "arbitrary, capricious, an abuse
of discretion, or otherwise not in accordance with law." *5 U.S.C. §
706(2)(A)*; *McCarthney v. Busey, 954 F.2d 1147, 1153-54 (6th Cir.
1992)*.

A.

First, Kraley contends that the FAA's promulgation and
enforcement of *14 C.F.R. § 61.15(d)* was arbitrary and capricious
because there is no correlation between convictions for driving under
the influence of alcohol and alcohol-related flying fatalities or
accidents. In promulgating *§ 61.15(d)*, the FAA must have "examined
the relevant date and articulated a satisfactory explanation for its action
including a 'rational connection between the facts found and the choice
made.'" *Motor Vehicle Mfrs. Ass'n v. State Farm Auto Ins. Co., 463
U.S. 29, 43, 77 L. Ed. 2d 443, 103 S. Ct. 2856 (1983)*(quoting
Burlington Truck Lines, Inc. v. United States, 371 U.S. 156, 158, 9 L.

Ed. 2d 207, 83 S. Ct. 239 (1962)); *Simms v. NHTSA, 45 F.3d 999, 1004 (6th Cir. 1995)*. See also *BP Exploration & Oil, Inc. v. U.S. Environmental Protection Agency, 66 F.3d 784, 791-92 (6th Cir. 1995)*(articulating standards for evaluating informal rulemaking by administrative agency).

Based on an audit and resulting recommendations by the Office of Inspector General (OIG) for the United States Department of Transportation, the FAA issued a Notice of Proposed Rulemaking. Pilots Convicted of Alcohol- or Drug-Related Motor Vehicle Offenses or Subject to State Motor Vehicle Administrative Procedures, *54 Fed. Reg. 21,580, 21,580 (1989)*(to be codified at 14 C.F.R. pts. 61, 67)(hereinafter "Pilots Convicted"). The Notice of Proposed Rulemaking provides that the proposed rules were "intended to enhance aviation safety . . . by removing from navigable airspace pilots who have demonstrated an unwillingness or inability to comply with safety regulations." *Id.* The FAA reasoned that the proposed regulation was necessary because pilots with multiple substance abuse motor vehicle convictions have shown an inability or unwillingness to comply with regulations or laws and may not meet the medical standards of Part 67 of the Federal Aviation Regulations. Further, the FAA determined that information related to any conviction is needed to conduct effective investigations to ensure that such pilots are capable of safely exercising the privileges of a flight crewmember. *Id. at 21,581.*

Kraley attacks these justifications. First, he points to the FAA's admission in the Notice of Proposed Rulemaking that "statistics do not now indicate a significant positive correlation between convictions for driving under the influence of alcohol or drugs and flying fatalities or accidents." *Id.* However, in the Notice of Proposed Rulemaking, the FAA also noted that information collected by the FAA showed that 6.0% of general aviation pilots killed in aircraft accidents during the period from 1978 to 1987 had a blood alcohol level above .04% *Id.* It was therefore not unreasonable for the FAA to conclude that "some intoxicated or impaired pilots may operate aircraft in the United States." *Id.*

Kraley also attacks the FAA's reasoning that pilots with alcohol- and drug-related convictions may not meet medical standards of Part 67. Kraley relies on the FAA's "own research" that, between October 1987 and August 1990, the agency reviewed the medical files of approximately 24,000 airmen with DWI and DUI convictions, and that of those 24,000 airmen, only 2,400 were requested to submit additional information. Pilots Convicted of Alcohol- or Drug-Related Motor Vehicle Offenses or Subject to State Motor Vehicle Administrative Procedures, Final Rule, *55 Fed. Reg. 31,300, 31,301 (1990)*(to be codified at 14 C.F.R. pts. 61, 67). Further, "of this 2,400 airmen, an estimated 24 (1 percent) were denied medical certificates or had their medical certification suspended or revoked." *Id.* Kraley claims that "this extremely small positive correlation simply does not provide a rational basis for a regulation compelling the suspension or revocation of airman certificates due to alcohol-related motor vehicle offenses."

Yet, as the FAA points out, that 1% becomes significant when considered in view of the over 11,000 lives lost in general aviation accidents in a nine-year period. Pilots Convicted of Alcohol- or Drug-Related Motor Vehicle Offenses, *55 Fed. Reg. at 31,302.* In the Final Rule, the FAA reasoned that "if the rule were to result in the saving of a few lives, the potential benefits of the rule would exceed its potential cost." *Id.* We cannot say that this conclusion is irrational.

Kraley also criticizes the FAA's rationale that pilots with alcohol- and drug-related motor vehicle convictions display a disregard for compliance with safety regulations or laws. However, as the FAA explained in the Final Rule (in response to the 84 comments received in response to the Notice of Proposed Rulemaking) the number of pilots disclosing multiple alcohol- and drug-related convictions was consistent with the fact that "not all pilots show an appropriate concern for critical highway safety requirements. It is these pilots who are the focus of the detection mechanisms established by this rule." *Id.* The FAA reasoned that flying requires a higher degree of care than driving a vehicle. Furthermore, aviation-related errors of judgment pose a significantly higher risk of catastrophic damage than errors of judgment in driving. *Id.*

Again, we cannot say that the FAA's reasoning is arbitrary. We therefore conclude that the agency's consideration of such factors supports the reasonableness of its action and was within the scope of the statutory mandate. *See* 49 U.S.C.A. § 41003(a)(West 1997)(vesting Administrator with broad power to prescribe regulations, standards, and procedures regarding aviation safety).

B.

Next, Kraley argues that the FAA exceeded its statutory jurisdiction in promulgating *§ 61.15(d)* because the FAA has no authority to sanction airmen for violations of motor vehicle laws. In other words, Kraley complains that the regulation relates not to the operation of aircraft, but to the operation of motor vehicles.

This argument is without merit. The intent of *§ 61.15(d)* is clear--it is designed to enhance aviation safety by removing from navigable airspace pilots who have demonstrated, by being twice convicted in alcohol-related motor vehicle actions within a three-year period, an unwillingness to comply with safety regulations. Pilots Convicted of Alcohol- or Drug-Related Motor Vehicle Offenses, *54 Fed. Reg. at 21,580*. Congress vested the Administrator of the FAA with broad power to prescribe regulations, standards, and procedures relating to aviation safety. *See 49 U.S.C.A. §§ 40113(a)(West 1997)*(vesting Administrator with broad power to prescribe regulations, procedures relating to aviation safety); 44701(a)(5)(West 1997)(requiring Administrator to promote safe flight of civil aircraft in commerce by prescribing regulations and standards); 44703(a)(West 1997)(empowering Administrator to issue airman certificate); and 44709(West 1997)(authorizing Administrator to at any time reexamine, revoke, or suspend such certificates when safety and public interest requires). Because *§ 61.15(d)* is "reasonably related to the purposes of the enabling legislation," *Mourning v. Family Publications Serv., Inc., 411 U.S. 356, 369, 36 L. Ed. 2d 318, 93 S. Ct. 1652 (1973)*, it is a legitimate exercise of the FAA's statutory authority and therefore valid. *See United States v. Chesapeake and Ohio Railway Co., 426 U.S. 500, 514, 49 L. Ed. 2d 14, 96 S. Ct. 2318 (1976)*.

C.

Third, Kraley contends that the FAA violated substantive due process in promulgating § 61.15(d) because it lacks a rational relationship to a legitimate state goal or interest. *See Mansfield Apartment Owners v. City of Mansfield, 988 F.2d 1469, 1477 (6th Cir. 1993)*(regulation denies due process "if it fails to advance a legitimate governmental interest or if it is an unreasonable means of advancing a legitimate governmental interest"; (quotation omitted)). As noted above, the rule was promulgated pursuant to statutory authority and it serves legitimate governmental interest in safe skies. We cannot say that it is irrational to treat automobile-related drug or drunk driving incidents as a reliable proxy for their actual conditions in the air. Pilots Convicted of Alcohol- or Drug-Related Motor Vehicle Offenses, *54 Fed. Reg. at 21,580*. Kraley's claim is without merit.

D.

Kraley argues that the suspension of his driver's license in 1994 under Ohio's implied consent statute was not a "motor vehicle action" within the meaning of § 61.15 because he ultimately pleaded no contest to, and was found guilty of, the reduced charge of reckless operation of a motor vehicle. When he was stopped on June 9, 1994 for erratic driving, Kraley refused the police officers' request to take a breathalyzer test and was cited for refusal to take the test under the Ohio implied consent statute. His license was suspended from June 9, 1994, to June 9, 1995. On October 20, 1994, he was convicted of reckless operation of a vehicle, after pleading no contest. His driver's license was suspended from June 9, 1994 to June 9, 1995. Kraley therefore claims that reckless operation of a motor vehicle is not a "statute relating to the operation of a motor vehicle while intoxicated by alcohol or a drug . . . ."

This argument must also be rejected. Although arguably Kraley's conviction for reckless operation of a motor vehicle is not the same as operating a motor vehicle while under the influence of alcohol, Kraley's license was, by his own admission, suspended under Ohio's implied consent statute. The Ohio statute provides for the suspension of a driver's license for one year upon refusal to submit to a chemical test after properly being asked to do so by a police officer. Ohio Rev. Code § 4511.19.1(E)(1)(a)(Anderson Supp. 1997). Such a suspension constitutes "a cause related to the operation of a motor vehicle . . . while under the influence of alcohol" under the intent and wording of *14 C.F.R. § 61.15(c)*:

> (1) A conviction after November 29, 1990, for the violation of any Federal or State statute relating to the operation of a motor vehicle while intoxicated by alcohol or a drug, while impaired by alcohol or a drug, or while under the influence of alcohol or a drug;

> (2) The cancellation, *suspension*, or revocation of a license to operate a motor vehicle after November 29, 1990, for a cause related to the operation of a motor vehicle while intoxicated by alcohol or a drug, while impaired by alcohol or a drug, or while under the influence of alcohol or a drug . . . . (Emphasis added.)

The Notice of Proposed Rulemaking that sets forth the FAA's intent in promulgating *§ 61.15* provided that administrative suspensions would be included within the meaning of "motor vehicle action:"

> Under most state statutes, an individual's refusal to submit to a test to determine blood alcohol content, when requested by a law enforcement officer, automatically results in an "administrative" suspension or revocation of a driver's license by operation of state law. It is possible that an individual may "surrender" his or her driver's license, pursuant to a state's administrative suspension or revocation mechanism, to avoid a criminal conviction for an alcohol- or drug-related motor vehicle offense. The proposed amendment to *§ 61.15* is intended to address this situation by providing for certificate action in cases where there is no underlying criminal conviction for alcohol-or drug-related operation of a motor vehicle but a state has imposed an administrative sanction against a pilot's license to operate a motor vehicle on the basis of similar conduct or a related violation.

Pilots Convicted of Alcohol- or Drug-Related Motor Vehicle Offenses, *54 Fed. Reg. at 21,582. See also Administrator v. Wilson*, NTSB Order No. EA-4314, (Jan. 19, 1995)(holding that suspension for having a prohibited blood alcohol level but not one high enough to be convicted of operating a motor vehicle while intoxicated was nonetheless a "motor vehicle action" under *§ 61.15(d)* because regulation clearly intended to encompass causes "related to" operational offenses).

Kraley claims that "it is well settled under Ohio law" that when a person refuses to take a chemical test to determine the percentage of alcohol in his body, and subsequently enters a plea of guilty or no contest to the charges against him, any suspension of his license arises from the plea of guilty and not his refusal to take the test. The cases Kraley cites do not support his argument, however. Both *Appeal of Williamson, 18 Ohio Misc. 67, 246 N.E.2d 618 (Ohio Misc. 1969)*, and *Appeal of Dudley, 19 Ohio Misc. 165, 251 N.E.2d 527 (Ohio Misc. 1969)*, hold simply that under a prior version of the Ohio implied consent statute, failure to give consent for chemical testing could not result in an additional suspension of the driver's license if the driver's license was subsequently suspended as a result of the driver pleading guilty or no contest to the underlying driving under the influence charge. *See Williamson, 246 N.E.2d at 624-25; Dudley, 251 N.E.2d at 528.* This contention does not remove Kraley's violation of the Ohio implied consent statute from the scope of a "motor vehicle action" within the meaning of *§ 61.15.*

Moreover, under the current version of the Ohio implied consent statute (the one under which Kraley was convicted), "the registrar shall credit against any judicial suspension of a person's driver's . . . license . . . any time during which the person serves a related suspension imposed [under the implied consent statute]." Ohio Rev. Code Ann. § 4511.19.1(K)(Anderson Supp 1997). Thus, as the FAA argues, the suspension period, and not the underlying failure to comply with the implied consent statute for which the suspension was initially imposed, is all that is affected by a subsequent plea of guilty of no contest to driving while under the influence charges. In short, neither the applicable statute, nor *Williamson* or *Dudley*, supports Kraley's argument that his violation of the Ohio implied consent statute is a legal nullity in Ohio and, therefore, not a "motor vehicle action" within the meaning of *§ 61.15(c)(2)*. In any event, Kraley pled no contest and was convicted of "physical control" of a vehicle while under the influence of alcohol. In short, either the "physical control" conviction or his independent violation of Ohio's implied consent statute placed him in violation of *§ 61.15(d)*.

E.

Kraley contends that the FAA improperly relied upon an unpublished staff instruction in imposing a 120-day suspension. At the administrative hearing, FAA Special Agent Debra Bailey's testified that she relied on an unpublished staff manual in recommending Kraley's sanction. The Administrative Procedures Act requires each agency to make available to the public "administrative staff manuals and instructions to staff that affect a member of the public . . . ," and provides that in an enforcement action, an agency may not rely upon any manual or instruction that it has not made available to the public. *5 U.S.C.A. § 552(a)(2)(West 1996)*. The FAA concedes that it cannot rely on an unpublished sanction range in determining the suspension period for an airman certificate. *See Smith v. NTSB, 299 U.S. App. D.C. 124, 981 F.2d 1326, 1328-29 (D.C. Cir. 1993)*.

Nevertheless, the FAA points out that in recommending a 120-day suspension, Bailey testified that she made her evaluation based on the factors specified in the agency's written and publicly-available guidance related to sanctions contained in FAA Order 2150.3A, Ch. 2. That is, she considered Kraley's violation history, the type of penalties the State of Ohio imposed on Kraley for the motor vehicle violations, certain behavioral factors including evidence of a pattern of alcohol abuse, Kraley's compliance with the reporting requirements of *§ 61.15*, and any information Kraley submitted to the FAA for consideration. In so doing, Bailey followed the directive of FAA Order 2150.3A, which instructs FAA personnel to exercise discretion in weighing all factors to arrive at an appropriate sanction. The ALJ's extensive questioning of Kraley during the administrative hearing demonstrates that he independently concluded that the 120-day sanction was appropriate. The ALJ questioned Kraley about his drinking behavior, about the details of the 1994 stop, his traffic citation history, and future aspirations for flying.

We agree with the Board that the ALJ did not improperly rely on unpublished factors in determining Kraley's sanction. The Board did not improperly conclude that "in light of the severity of respondent's [Kraley's] conduct and its clear relevance to safety in the air, it is our view that a 120-day suspension is at the low end of the appropriate range of sanction."

F.

Kraley asserts that the ALJ erred in admitting testimony of "motor vehicle actions" not alleged in the FAA complaint. Agent Bailey testified on direct examination that in investigating Kraley's driving history, she learned of two previous convictions for driving under the influence--one in 1982 and one in 1987. In overruling Kraley's objection to admission of this evidence, the ALJ stated that the information had little to do with "the totality of the circumstances pertaining to [Kraley] . . . . That doesn't mean, of course . . . that it is necessarily pertinent and germane to the charges confronting [Kraley]."

We agree with the Board's assessment that Kraley's "other alcohol-related driving conviction may be irrelevant to the factual finding required by *§ 61.15(d)*, but it is not irrelevant to the issue of compliance disposition, which influences the sanction determination." The ALJ did not abuse his discretion.

Kraley also claims that the ALJ erred in admitting testimony regarding a 1996 suspension of his driver's license for driving under the influence. Kraley overlooks the fact that his own counsel opened the door for further discussion of the 1996 suspension by asking Bailey on cross-examination whether she had received court records pertaining to Kraley after she had closed her case file. This claim is therefore without merit. Upon these grounds, the ALJ had discretion to admit the evidence. *5 U.S.C.A. § 556(d)(West 1996)*.

G.

Kraley argues that the district court erred by excluding a doctor's report concluding that Kraley was not an alcoholic. At the FAA hearing, Bailey testified that the absence of a history of alcohol abuse is relevant in determining the sanction. Kraley subsequently proffered the report of a neurologist opining that Kraley was not an alcoholic. The ALJ excluded the doctor's report from evidence for lack of relevancy.

We find no abuse of discretion. Evidence of alcoholism would be relevant in a proceeding involving Kraley's qualifications to hold an airman medical certificate under Part 67 of the Federal Aviation Regulations, but is of limited evidentiary value to the issue of compliance disposition.

H.

Lastly, Kraley contends that the NTSB erred in finding that a 120-day suspension was at the low end of appropriate range of sanction. He cites *Administrator v. Gotisar*, NTSB Order No. EA-4544, (1997), where the Board found no error in the 90-day suspension imposed by the ALJ for a violation of *§ 61.15(d)*. *Gotisar* is inapposite because the length of the suspension was not at issue before the Board. In any event, this court has rejected the notion that sanctions for the violation of the same regulation must be the same in every case. *See Blackman v. Busey, 938 F.2d 659, 663 (6th Cir. 1991)*.

PETITION DENIED.

DAVID R. HINSON, Administrator,
Federal Aviation Administration, v.
CYNTHIA JANE WILSON.

No. EA-4314;
Docket SE-13582

National Transportation Safety Board

January, 1995

On June 14, 1994, Administrative Law Judge Patrick G. Geraghty granted the Administrator summary judgment on his allegation, in an order dated February 9, 1994, that the respondent's private pilot certificate should be suspended for her failure to file a report required by section 61.15(e) of the Federal Aviation Regulations ("FAR," 14 CFR Part 61). The respondent has appealed that ruling, arguing that she was not required to notify the Administrator that the State of California had suspended her motor vehicle operator's license for four months in 1993 because the reason for that suspension was not among those that trigger a duty to report under the regulation. Finding no error in the law judge's contrary determination, we affirm his decision and the Administrator's order of suspension.

FAR section 61.15(e) obligates Part 61 certificate holders to report, within 60 days, certain motor vehicle actions in which they have been involved to the FAA's Civil Aviation Security Division (AAC-700). The regulation defines "motor vehicle action" to mean, among other things, the "cancellation, suspension, or revocation of a license to operate a motor vehicle by a state . . . for a cause related to the operation of a motor vehicle while intoxicated by alcohol or a drug, while impaired by alcohol or a drug, or while under the influence of alcohol or a drug. . . ." (FAR section 61.15(c)(2)). Respondent takes the position that this regulation did not apply to the suspension she incurred because it was based only on the fact that she was found, following her arrest while operating a motor vehicle, to have a prohibited blood alcohol level (.08 per cent or above), not on the ground that she had operated a motor vehicle while intoxicated, impaired, or under the influence of alcohol. We have no difficulty concluding that the FAA reporting requirement applied to California's suspension of respondent's motor vehicle license for driving with an excessive blood alcohol level (BAL).

Respondent's argument that no report was required for the motor vehicle action in which she was involved is predicated on a reading of section 61.15(c)(2) that fails to take into account its plain intent to reach alcohol or drug related motor vehicle license actions that do not result in a conviction for operating a motor vehicle while intoxicated, impaired, or under the influence. That intent is manifest in the regulation's requirement that reports be made of license actions taken not just for those operational offenses, but also for causes "related to" those operational offenses. It is therefore irrelevant that the offense for which respondent's motor vehicle license was suspended under California law was not predicated on any finding that she was actually intoxicated, impaired or under the influence of alcohol. The issue

227

before us is not whether the evidentiary basis for the offense of driving with an excessive BAL is the same, under California law, as that for the offense of driving while intoxicated, impaired or under the influence of alcohol, but, rather, whether the two offenses involve associated conduct.

In our judgment, driving with an excessive blood alcohol level is unquestionably a cause related to operating a motor vehicle in a manner reflecting the adverse effects of too much alcohol consumption. Indeed, we think it fair to assume both that California would not outlaw driving with any specific BAL absent some concern over its potential impact on safe motor vehicle operation, and that a BAL of .08 would not be deemed or termed "excessive" unless it was believed to present an unnecessarily high risk that an individual having such a BAL may be intoxicated by alcohol, have alcohol-impaired judgment, or otherwise be under the influence of alcohol. In sum, we agree with the Administrator that a state motor vehicle license suspension based on excessive blood alcohol level is a cause related to the specifically enumerated offenses involving alcohol in the regulation. Even if we were not persuaded that a suspension for excessive blood alcohol level qualified as a cause related to operating a motor vehicle while impaired, intoxicated, or under the influence of alcohol, it would not necessarily follow that respondent had no duty to report under the regulation. Documents attached to the Administrator's motion for summary judgment reveal that while respondent's driver's record recites that her license was suspended for excessive blood alcohol level, that action was based on an order issued by a police officer, on January 12, 1993, which indicated that respondent's license, effective 45 days thereafter, would be suspended or revoked because she had been arrested *for driving under the influence of alcohol or drugs* and the officer believed that a blood test would show respondent's BAL to be .08 or greater. Given our view that the excessive BAL offense should have been reported, we need not decide whether the suspension ordered by the arresting officer, later temporarily stayed by a state court, created an additional or independent ground for reporting the incident to the FAA.

As noted, supra, the Administrator sought a 30-day suspension of respondent's private pilot certificate for the reporting failure, but did not appeal the law judge's reduction in sanction to a 25-day suspension, which was based on the, we think, questionable rationale that a reduction in an otherwise appropriate sanction was warranted because the respondent's decision not to file was attributable to the erroneous advice of counsel. On appeal, respondent in effect urges, in the event the violation finding is sustained, that no suspension period be imposed, in light of respondent's asserted good faith belief that no report was required. We do not believe that any further reduction of sanction can be justified. While, in our view, the reporting obligation was clear and unambiguous, there is no showing here that respondent or her counsel made any attempt to resolve, before the deadline for the report passed, any confusion they may have entertained over the applicability of the reporting requirement to the specific offense for which respondent's license was suspended in California.

ACCORDINGLY, IT IS ORDERED THAT:

1. The respondent's appeal is denied;

2. The June 14, 1994 "Decisional Order" of the law judge is affirmed; and

3. The 25-day suspension of respondent's private pilot certificate shall begin 30 days after service of this opinion and order.

JANE F. GARVEY, ADMINISTRATOR, FEDERAL AVIATION ADMINISTRATION v. NATIONAL TRANSPORTATION SAFETY BOARD AND RICHARD LEE MERRELL

UNITED STATES COURT OF APPEALS FOR THE DISTRICT OF COLUMBIA CIRCUIT

190 F.3d 571

September, 1999

GARLAND, Circuit Judge: The Federal Aviation Administration (FAA) issued an enforcement order to Captain Richard Merrell, a Northwest Airlines pilot whom the FAA determined had violated airline safety regulations. Merrell appealed to the National Transportation Safety Board (NTSB), which ruled in his favor and dismissed the FAA's order. The FAA petitions for review of that decision, arguing that the NTSB erroneously failed to defer to the FAA's reasonable interpretation of its own regulations. We grant the petition, reverse the NTSB, and remand for further proceedings consistent with this opinion.

I

The Federal Aviation Act, *49 U.S.C. §§ 40101 et seq.*, establishes a "split-enforcement" regime in which the FAA has regulatory and enforcement authority, while the NTSB acts as an impartial adjudicator. *See Hinson v. NTSB, 313 U.S. App. D.C. 59, 57 F.3d 1144, 1147 n.1 (D.C. Cir. 1995).* We begin by setting forth the facts and procedural history of Captain Merrell's case, and then describe the nature of the split-enforcement regime in more detail.

A

The facts of the case are undisputed. On June 19, 1994, Merrell was the pilot-in-command of a commercial passenger plane, Northwest Flight 1024. After Flight 1024 took off in the heavily trafficked Los Angeles area, air traffic control (ATC) instructed it to climb to and maintain an altitude of 17,000 feet. Merrell correctly repeated, or "read back," this instruction to ATC. About a minute later, ATC transmitted an altitude clearance to another aircraft, American Airlines Flight 94, directing it to climb to and maintain an altitude of 23,000 feet. The American flight promptly and correctly acknowledged this clearance with its own "readback. "

Merrell, however, mistakenly thought that the instruction to American was intended for his aircraft, so he also read the instruction back to ATC. Unfortunately, because Merrell made his readback at the same time as the American pilot, his transmission was blocked, or "stepped on." The ATC radio system can handle only one transmission at a time on any given frequency; when two transmissions overlap, both may become blocked or garbled, or the stronger signal alone may be heard (i.e., it may "step on" the weaker signal). ATC can often detect that a transmission has been stepped on because, unless the signals overlap completely, ATC will receive a portion of the stepped-on message, and because a loud buzzing noise usually accompanies the period of overlap. On rare occasions, however, two transmissions will overlap completely without creating an identifiable buzz. This appears to have happened in Merrell's case. His readback apparently coincided precisely with that of American Flight 94, and as a result his transmission was entirely blocked. ATC heard neither Merrell's readback nor any indication that it had occurred. And because ATC did not hear the erroneous readback, it could not correct Merrell's mistake.

Meanwhile Merrell, unaware that ATC had not received his transmission, proceeded to ascend toward 23,000 feet. As the Northwest flight rose from its assigned altitude, the ATC controller noticed the deviation and directed the aircraft to return to 17,000 feet. Before Merrell could comply, he had ascended to 18,200 feet and lost the standard safety separation required between commercial flights.

On November 3, 1995, the FAA issued an enforcement order against Merrell. The order alleged that Merrell had violated FAA safety regulations by, inter alia, (1) "operating an aircraft contrary to an ATC instruction in an area in which air traffic control is exercised," in violation of *14 C.F.R. § 91.123(b)*; and (2) "operating an aircraft according to a clearance or instruction that had been issued to the pilot of another aircraft for radar air traffic control purposes," in violation of *14 C.F.R. § 91.123(e)*. Joint Appendix (J.A.) at 7.

Merrell appealed the FAA's order to the NTSB. At the outset of the proceedings, the FAA agreed that because Merrell had filed a timely incident report pursuant to the FAA Aviation Safety Reporting Program, it would waive any sanction for the alleged violations. *See* J.A. at 11. It sought affirmance of its enforcement order, however, arguing that Merrell had deviated from clearly transmitted ATC instructions, that this mistake was due to his own carelessness rather than to ATC error, and that the deviation therefore constituted a regulatory violation. The Administrative Law Judge (ALJ) agreed and affirmed the order. The ALJ found, based on both the recording and the transcript of the radio communications, that the ATC transmission to American Flight 94 had been clear and that the instruction to climb to 23,000 feet had plainly not been intended for Merrell's aircraft. *Id.* at 14-15. Indeed, after Merrell listened to the tape, he conceded that he had simply "misheard" the instruction. *See id.* at 18-19; NTSB Record (R.) at 145. The ALJ concluded that the fact that Merrell's readback was stepped on did not absolve "Captain Merrell of his responsibility to hear that [the] initial clearance" was for another flight. J.A. at 26. He explained that: "Aviation is ... particularly unforgiving of carelessness or neglect. And in this particular case, the initial mistake was made by Captain Merrell, and he's going to have to be responsible for it." *Id.* at 27. Accordingly, the ALJ held that Merrell "was in regulatory violation as alleged." *Id.*

Merrell appealed the ALJ's decision to the Board. He argued that under NTSB precedent, a pilot cannot be held responsible for an inadvertent deviation caused by ATC error. His had been such a deviation, he contended, because he had taken actions which, but for ATC, would have kept him from leaving his assigned altitude. He reasoned that because ATC controllers are required to correct erroneous readbacks, his construction of ATC's silence as tacit confirmation had been reasonable and justified. In response, the FAA again argued that because the primary cause of the deviation had been Merrell's misperception of a clear instruction, his actions had violated the safety regulations. The FAA maintained that this outcome was consistent with Board precedent which, it contended, absolves pilots only when "ATC error is the initiating or primary cause of the deviation." R. at 321.

The NTSB accepted Merrell's arguments and dismissed the enforcement order. It found that Merrell had made only "an error of perception," and that there was "no evidence in the record ... that [he] ... was performing his duties in a careless or otherwise unprofessional manner." J.A. at 34. A "perception mistake," the Board said, does not always result from "a failure of attention," and therefore "careless inattention ... will not be automatically assumed in every case" in which a pilot mishears ATC instructions. *Id.* Moreover, there was no "failure of procedure" on Merrell's part, as he had "made a full readback so that the opportunity was there, absent the squelched transmission, for ATC to correct his error." *Id.* at 35.

The FAA then petitioned the Board for reconsideration of its decision. R. at 360-81. The agency argued that the Federal Aviation Act requires the Board to defer to the FAA's reasonable interpretation of its own safety regulations. In the FAA's view, *14 C.F.R. § 91.123* obligates pilots "to listen, hear, and comply with all ATC instructions except in an emergency." *Id.* at 366; *see id.* at 362. "Inattention, carelessness, or an unexplained misunderstanding," it said, "do not excuse a deviation from a clearly transmitted clearance or instruction." *Id.* at 367. "When there is an 'error of perception' resulting in a deviation, inattentiveness or carelessness are imputed in the absence of some reasonable explanation for the failure to comply with the ATC clearance." *Id.* According to the FAA, reasonable explanations include events such as "radio malfunction" or a controller error that precipitates a misunderstanding, but "to excuse [Merrell's] deviation in these circumstances as an acceptable, though unexplained, 'error of perception' " would be inconsistent with the agency's construction of *§ 91.123*. *Id.* at 368-69; *see id.* at 369, 371. Moreover, the FAA argued that the Board's decision would have a "profound" negative effect on air safety: "Under the decision, airmen can claim, without further proof, that they did not hear or that they misperceived safety crucial instructions as a means to avoid responsibility for noncompliance or erroneous compliance with ATC clearances and instructions." *Id.* at 374.

The Board denied the petition for reconsideration. Although it acknowledged its "general obligation to defer to the FAA's validly adopted interpretation of its regulations," the Board considered itself under no such obligation in this case because "the FAA cites no rule *it* has adopted that stands for the proposition the FAA urges here." J.A. at 38. The Board further noted that the FAA offered "no evidence of *any* policy guidance written by the FAA, validly adopted or otherwise," to support its interpretation, and instead offered only "counsel's litigation statements." *Id.*

Because the Board determined that it was not required to defer to the FAA's interpretation, it followed its own view of appropriate aviation policy. It stated:

> We ... disagree with the FAA's underlying belief that our policy threatens aviation safety. The premise of our

approach is this--human beings make mistakes, and there is no regulatory action, remedial or otherwise, that can eliminate all mistakes.... Where an inevitable error of perception does occur, the pilot should not face sanction if he has acted responsibly and prudently thereafter....

Id. Adhering to this principle, the NTSB announced the following rule:

If a pilot makes a mistake and mishears a clearance or ATC direction, follows all prudent procedures that would expose the mistake (e.g., reads back the clearance), and then acts on that mistaken understanding having heard no correction from ATC, the regulatory violation will be excused if that mistake is not shown to be a result of carelessness or purposeful failure of some sort.

Id. at 37. The FAA then petitioned for review in this court.

B

Under the Federal Aviation Act's split-enforcement regime, Congress has delegated rulemaking authority to the FAA: "The Administrator of the Federal Aviation Administration shall promote safe flight of civil aircraft in air commerce" by prescribing, among other things, "regulations and minimum standards for ... practices, methods, and procedure the [FAA] finds necessary for safety in air commerce and national security." *49 U.S.C. § 44701(a)*. Pursuant to that authority, the FAA promulgated the safety regulations at issue here, 49 C.F.R. §§ 91.123(b), (e). Congress has also given the FAA authority to enforce its regulations through a number of methods, including the issuance of "an order amending, modifying, suspending, or revoking" a pilot's certificate if the public interest so requires. *49 U.S.C. § 44709(b)*. The FAA exercised that authority in issuing its enforcement order to Captain Merrell. *See* J.A. at 7.

Congress has assigned adjudicatory authority under this regime to the NTSB. *See generally 49 U.S.C. § 1133*. A pilot whose certificate is adversely affected by an FAA enforcement order may appeal the order to the NTSB. *See id. § 44709(d)(1)*. Such an appeal is initially heard by an ALJ, *see 49 C.F.R. § 821.35(a)*, whose final decision may be appealed to the full Board, *see id. § 821.47(a)*. The Board's decision, in turn, may be reconsidered upon the petition of either party. *See id. § 821.50*. In reviewing an FAA order, "the Board is not bound by findings of fact of the [FAA] Administrator." *49 U.S.C. § 44709(d)(3)*. It is, however, "bound by all validly adopted interpretations of laws and regulations the Administrator carries out ... unless the Board finds an interpretation is arbitrary, capricious, or otherwise not according to law." *Id.*

If dissatisfied with a final order of the Board, either the FAA Administrator or any "person substantially affected" may petition for review in this court. *Id. §§ 1153(c), 44709(f), 46110.* [3] On judicial review, the "findings of fact of the Board are conclusive if supported by substantial evidence." *49 U.S.C. § 44709(f)*; *id. § 1153(c)*; *see also id. § 46110(c)*. We must, however, set aside Board decisions if they are "arbitrary, capricious, an abuse of discretion, or otherwise not in accordance with law." *5 U.S.C. § 706(2)(A)*. And, like the NTSB, we must defer to the FAA's interpretations of its own aviation regulations. *Cf. Martin v. Occupational Safety & Health Review Comm'n, 499 U.S. 144, 147, 150-57, 111 S. Ct. 1171, 113 L. Ed. 2d 117 (1991)* (holding that courts must defer to interpretations of Secretary of Labor rather than to those of OSHRC in split enforcement regime under Occupational Safety & Health Act).

II

As we have just described, Congress has "unambiguously directed the NTSB to defer to the FAA's interpretations of its own regulations." *Hinson, 57 F.3d at 1148 n.2* (citing *49 U.S.C. § 44709(d)(3)*); *see also id. at 1151*. Here, however, the NTSB explicitly declined to defer to the agency's interpretation of *14 C.F.R. § 91.123*. In this Part, we consider the argument that deference to the FAA was not required, either because its interpretation was not validly adopted or because that interpretation was really a factual finding in disguise.

A

The NTSB declined to defer to the FAA primarily because the agency had offered "no evidence of *any* policy guidance written by the FAA, validly adopted or otherwise," to support its interpretation. J.A. at 38. Instead, the agency had merely offered the "litigation statements" of FAA counsel, as well as citations to the Board's own case law. *See id.* The NTSB believed the former insufficient to qualify for Board deference under *section 44709(d)(3)*. Accordingly, it rejected the FAA's interpretation and expressly adopted its own policy to govern cases like that of Captain Merrell.

The NTSB's refusal to defer to the FAA on this question of regulatory interpretation and air safety policy was error. The FAA is not required to promulgate interpretations through rulemaking or the issuance of policy guidances, but may instead do so through litigation before the NTSB. We have said as much before, and the Supreme Court so held in *Martin v. Occupational Safety & Health Review Comm'n* with respect to the similar split-enforcement regime of the Occupational Safety & Health Act. Indeed, the NTSB itself has repeatedly made the same point. The fact that this mode of regulatory interpretation necessarily is advanced through the "litigation statements" of counsel does not relieve the NTSB of its statutory obligation to accord it due deference.

Nor was Merrell's the first case in which the FAA interpreted its regulations as it does here. The position the agency took in its petition for reconsideration can be summarized as follows: Failure to understand an ATC instruction is a valid defense to a *section 91.123* charge only if the pilot provides some exculpatory explanation, such as radio malfunction or precipitating controller error. *See* R. at 371. That is precisely the position the FAA took before this court in *Hinson*-- although there we refused to consider it because the agency had failed to raise it below. *See Hinson, 57 F.3d at 1150-51*. It is also the position the FAA has consistently taken in litigation before the Board. *See Administrator v. Gentile, 6 N.T.S.B. 60, 64 (1988); Administrator v.*

234

Wells, 1 N.T.S.B. 1472, 1474 (1971). As discussed in Part IV, while the NTSB's own position has wavered over the years, the FAA's has not.

In sum, the NTSB's rationale for denying deference to the FAA's interpretation of *14 C.F.R. § 91.123* was unjustified.

B

Merrell offers another potential justification for the NTSB's failure to defer to the FAA. The FAA's position below was not truly an "interpretation," he argues, but rather a determination of fact with which the Board was free to disagree. As Merrell observes, the FAA's petition for reconsideration states: "When there is an 'error of perception' resulting in a deviation, inattentiveness or carelessness are imputed in the absence of some reasonable explanation...." R. at 367. In addition, the FAA's appellate briefs consistently describe its interpretation as a presumption or inference. *See, e.g.,* FAA Br. at 23 ("FAA employs the following presumption: where evidence shows that a pilot mistakenly fails to understand and comply with a clear and distinct ATC transmission, and where the pilot fails to provide an exculpatory explanation for his mistake, FAA presumes that the pilot's mistake was due to inattention...."); *see also id.* ("It is fair and reasonable to infer that [Merrell's] mistake was attributable to inattention...."). The FAA's decision to "impute," "presume," or "infer" carelessness in a particular situation, Merrell argues, "is nothing more than a finding of fact, which can be reversed by the NTSB." Merrell Br. at 14.

We note first that Merrell did not make this argument below, *see* Opp'n to Pet. for Recons., and that the NTSB did not itself refuse to defer on the ground that the FAA's interpretation was really a finding of fact. Even if we could nonetheless consider the argument here, it is plain that the FAA's decision to infer carelessness from unexplained error does not represent a finding of fact in this, or any other, particular case. To the contrary, the FAA's inference is simply a justification for the regulatory interpretation the agency applies in all cases--a rationale for why it is reasonable to declare a violation when a pilot errs and has no explanation for his error. Although the agency's rule does act like a presumption, a presumption is a rule of law and not a finding of fact. *See* W. PAGE KEETON ET AL., PROSSER & KEETON ON THE LAW OF TORTS 240 (5th ed. 1984) ("There is ... general agreement that presumptions are rules of law....").

A presumption is valid if it is rational. *See Usery v. Turner Elkhorn Mining Co., 428 U.S. 1, 28, 49 L. Ed. 2d 752, 96 S. Ct. 2882 (1976)* (noting that a presumption will be upheld if there is "some rational connection between the fact proved and the ultimate fact presumed, and [if] the inference of one fact from proof of another shall not be so unreasonable as to be a purely arbitrary mandate"); *see also NLRB v. Baptist Hosp., 442 U.S. 773, 787, 61 L. Ed. 2d 251, 99 S. Ct. 2598 (1979); Chemical Mfrs. Ass'n v. Department of Transp., 323 U.S. App. D.C. 88, 105 F.3d 702, 705-06 (D.C. Cir. 1997).* And surely it is rational to infer that a pilot was careless or inattentive if he deviated from a clearance order without any explanation at all. In this case, everyone who listened to the recording of the ATC clearance instructions--including Captain Merrell-confirmed that those instructions were clear and understandable. *See* J.A. at 14-15, 18-19; R. at 145. Merrell's statement that he "misheard" the transmission is not an explanation for his deviation, but rather a concession that he has no explanation. Under such circumstances, it is not unreasonable to presume that he simply was not listening closely enough. Such a presumption is as common-sense as that employed in tort cases that hold that the running of a red light creates a presumption of negligence, rebuttable only by an exculpatory justification (such as brake failure).

There is also no merit to Merrell's contention that the FAA's presumption impermissibly reverses the burden of proof in NTSB proceedings--a point upon which, again, the Board did not rely. FAA regulations mandate that "in proceedings under [*49 U.S.C. § 44709*], the burden of proof shall be upon the Administrator." *49 C.F.R. § 821.32*. Merrell contends that the FAA's interpretation of *section 91.123* is in reality an attempt to circumvent this evidentiary requirement. He asserts that "having failed to carry its burden of proof," the FAA "sought to eliminate that burden by inventing a legal 'interpretation.' " Merrell Br. at 15. The Supreme Court considered a similar contention in *Director v. Greenwich Collieries, 512 U.S. 267, 129 L. Ed. 2d 221, 114 S. Ct. 2251 (1994)*. There, the Court construed § 7(c) of the Administrative Procedure Act (APA), *5 U.S.C. § 556(d)*, which imposes the "burden of proof" on the proponent of an order. The Court held that the phrase should be understood as having its "ordinary or natural meaning," which, it said, was the burden of persuasion. *512 U.S. at 272, 276*. Because the Labor Department rule at issue in *Greenwich* (the so-called "true doubt" rule) reversed the persuasion burden, the Court struck it down. *See id. at 280-81*. It indicated, however, that a presumption that did not shift the burden of persuasion would be acceptable under the APA because it would not affect the "burden of proof." *Id. at 280*. In accordance with this reasoning, every Circuit that has considered the issue since has concluded that a presumption that shifts only the burden of production does not shift the "burden of proof" as that phrase is used in the APA. *See Gulf & W. Indus. v. Ling, 176 F.3d 226, 232-34 (4th Cir. 1999)*; *Glen Coal Co. v. Seals, 147 F.3d 502, 510-13 (6th Cir. 1998)*; *Lovilia Coal Co. v. Harvey, 109 F.3d 445, 452 (8th Cir. 1997)*. Merrell offers no reason to read the same phrase in *section 821.32* any differently.

On this analysis, the FAA presumption at issue here is permissible if it shifts only the burden of production--and it does. That is the typical role of presumptions in modern evidence law, and the FAA's description of its presumption indicates that it functions in the same manner. That is, once the FAA shows that a pilot failed to follow a clear ATC instruction, the burden of production shifts to the pilot to offer an exculpatory explanation. Accordingly, we find no warrant for regarding the FAA's interpretation as the equivalent of a finding of fact or for concluding that it reverses the FAA's burden of proof, and hence no warrant for the NTSB's refusal to pay it appropriate deference.

III

Deference, of course, does not mean blind obedience. The agency's interpretation still must not be "plainly erroneous or inconsistent with the regulation" it is interpreting. *Cassell v. FCC, 332 U.S. App. D.C. 156, 154 F.3d 478, 484 (D.C. Cir. 1998)* (quoting *Auer v. Robbins, 519 U.S. 452, 461, 137 L. Ed. 2d 79, 117 S. Ct. 905 (1997)*). And even if the interpretation meets this standard, the NTSB need not follow it if it "is arbitrary, capricious, or otherwise not according to law." *49 U.S.C. § 44709(d)(3)*. We consider these two standards below.

First, we examine whether the FAA's interpretation was a reasonable construction of its regulation. The two subsections of *section 91.123* that Merrell was charged with violating state:

> (b) Except in an emergency, no person may operate an aircraft contrary to an ATC instruction in an area in which air traffic control is exercised.
>
> ....
>
> (e) Unless otherwise authorized by ATC, no person operating an aircraft may operate that aircraft according to any clearance or instruction that has been issued to the pilot of another aircraft for radar air traffic control purposes.

14 C.F.R. § 91.123.

Under the FAA's interpretation, a pilot who flies contrary to either of these commands is in violation unless he has an exculpatory explanation, such as "radio malfunction" or "ATC error resulting in a faulty transmission that precipitates a misunderstanding." FAA Br. at 15. This interpretation is consistent with the regulation. Indeed, the one respect in which it varies actually favors the pilot: it adds two exceptions (radio malfunction and precipitating ATC error) to the only two expressly listed in the rule itself (emergency and ATC authorization)--apparently because the FAA believes they are fairly implied. None of these exceptions assists Merrell, however, who has offered no explanation whatsoever for his failure to understand the clear and distinct ATC transmission. The FAA has also indicated, as a matter of its enforcement discretion, that in cases where ATC could have corrected a pilot's misunderstanding but did not, the agency will waive or reduce the sanctions for the violation (although it will still declare that the violation occurred). *See id. at 18*. Again, this offers Merrell no assistance, as it is undisputed that ATC could not have corrected Merrell's error, and in any event, the FAA has in fact waived any possible sanctions against him. We therefore find that the FAA's construction is a reasonable interpretation of its regulation, and that Merrell's case fits comfortably within that interpretation.

Second, we must determine whether the FAA's policy, as expressed in its interpretation, is arbitrary, capricious, or otherwise not in accordance with law. There is no question that the FAA's policy is harsh, but that does not make it unreasonable. The FAA contends that the rule's strictness is required by the potentially catastrophic consequences of noncompliance with ATC transmissions. In the agency's view, the only way to prevent air disasters is to ensure "that pilots exercise unflagging diligence in monitoring, understanding, and obeying clearly transmitted ATC instructions." *Id. at 16-17*. And the best way to ensure such diligence, the FAA has concluded, is to hold pilots to "an exacting standard of accountability." *Id. at 17*.

To continue our earlier analogy, the FAA's approach is somewhat akin to that of the motor vehicle safety laws. Although a driver may be able to defend the running of a red light on the ground of brake failure, the excuse that he simply "did not see it" does not avoid a ticket. Following the same logic, the FAA has concluded that while a radio malfunction can excuse a pilot's deviation from an ATC instruction, the claim that he simply "misheard it" does not. This approach is both rational and consistent with the Federal Aviation Act, which instructs the FAA to prescribe rules that, in its judgment, "best tend[] to reduce or eliminate the possibility or recurrence of accidents in air transportation." *49 U.S.C. § 44701(c)*.

We recognize that the NTSB prefers a different approach, one which might best be expressed, in the words of Alexander Pope, as, "To err is human...." ALEXANDER POPE, *An Essay on Criticism, in* COLLECTED POEMS 58, 71 (Bonamy Dobree ed., Everyman's Library 1983) (1711). The "premise" of its approach, the Board states, is that "human beings make mistakes, and there is no regulatory action, remedial or otherwise, that can eliminate all mistakes." Order on Recons., J.A. at 38. Hence, the Board maintains that "where an inevitable error of perception does occur, the pilot should not face sanction if he has acted responsibly and prudently thereafter...." *Id.* Although we cannot say that this view is unreasonable, that is not the issue. The NTSB is bound to follow the FAA's interpretation of a regulation unless the Board finds it arbitrary, capricious, or otherwise unlawful. *See 49 U.S.C. § 44709(d)(3)*. It was not arbitrary or capricious for the FAA to conclude that in the unforgiving environment of aviation, in which even good-faith error can lead to tragedy, the best way to encourage pilot attentiveness is through its harsh approach rather than the NTSB's more lenient one. This conclusion is consistent with the governing law, which makes clear that the FAA's principal responsibility is not to protect the interests of pilots, but rather to ensure that air carriers "provide service with the highest possible degree of safety in the public interest." *Id. § 44701*.

Finally, we consider Merrell's argument that the FAA's interpretation of subsections (b) and (e) of *section 91.123* is arbitrary because it conflicts with readback procedures assertedly contained in subsection (a) of the same section. The FAA's position, Merrell stresses, means that "a pilot who inadvertently mishears a clearance, reads it back to the controller to check his understanding, and receives no correction from the controller, would nevertheless be liable for a violation of *§ 91.123*" barring an exculpatory explanation for the initial misunderstanding. Merrell Br. at 19. Yet, he continues, subsection 91.123(a) states that a pilot who is "uncertain" about a clearance must "immediately request clarification from ATC." *Id. at 20* (quoting *14 C.F.R. § 91.123(a)*). That request, according to Merrell, "is made through a readback, and the written procedures governing air traffic controllers obligate controllers to correct any errors in the readback." Merrell Br. at 20; *see supra* note 2. Because of that obligation, Merrell argues, pilots are entitled to take ATC silence as acknowledgment that their readback was correct. Moreover, he contends that if the FAA's position were accepted, " *§ 91.123(a)* would be superfluous" because a pilot uncertain about a clearance "could follow the instruction of *§ 91.123(a)* precisely, but nevertheless be liable for violating *§ 91.123(b)* if ATC improperly failed, either because of human or system error, to respond to the pilot's recitation of an incorrect clearance." Merrell Br. at 20.

There is no conflict between the FAA's interpretation of subsections 91.123(b) and (e) and the language of *section 91.123(a)*. The latter provision refers to "clarifications," not readbacks, and the two are not the same. A request for clarification--which is mandatory when a pilot is "uncertain" about his clearance--requires ATC to transmit an affirmative clarifying response. If ATC fails to provide one, the pilot must renew his request until one is forthcoming. *See 14 C.F.R. § 91.123(a)*; FAA Reply Br. at 7-8. A readback, by contrast, is a non-mandatory acknowledgment by the pilot which, if correct, does not require an affirmative response from the controller. *See* ATC PROCEDURES P 2-72; *64 Fed. Reg. 15,912, 15,913 (1999)*. The clarification procedure is not implicated in the current case, as Merrell does not contend he was uncertain about the ATC instruction.

Nor is the FAA's interpretation either inconsistent with, or rendered irrational by, what Merrell contends is the routine pilot practice of reading back clearances and taking ATC silence as acknowledgment of accuracy. "Readbacks," the FAA points out, "add a layer of safety redundancy." FAA Reply Br. at 8. If a pilot transmits a readback, ATC will usually be able to correct a misunderstanding even if the pilot himself did not realize there was one. But as this case shows, the readback procedure is not failsafe; there is no guarantee that ATC's silence means it has received and confirmed the pilot's transmission. This underscores the reasonableness of the FAA's policy, which requires pilots to perceive ATC instructions correctly and not to depend upon the potentially unreliable readback mechanism. *See id. at 8, 17*.

IV

In support of the decision below, Merrell argues that the NTSB's holding is "thoroughly consistent with a wellestablished line of Board precedent." Merrell Br. at 17. The FAA contends that the opposite is true. As we discuss in this Part, the situation is far less clear than either party is willing to concede. But even if Merrell were correct, the fact that the Board followed its own precedent would not be a sufficient basis on which to uphold its decision. Because the FAA is entitled to launch new policies through administrative adjudication, it may sometimes be necessary for the NTSB to accommodate such policies by changing its jurisprudential course.

We begin by noting that there are actually two divergent lines of NTSB precedent in this area. One line contradicts Merrell's position, holding that if a pilot deviates from an ATC instruction in the absence of an emergency, the pilot is in violation unless an external factor precipitated the error. Under this line of cases, when the pilot cannot point to such a precipitating factor, the NTSB attributes the error to the pilot's own lack of care. And under this line, a violation is not excused even if the pilot reads back the misunderstood instruction and ATC fails to correct it, notwithstanding its ability to do so.

The second line of NTSB precedent, that cited by Merrell, is more supportive of his position although not wholly supportive. Under this line, the Board will excuse a pilot's deviation if ATC error was a contributing cause. In the typical case, a pilot misunderstands a clear ATC instruction, the pilot gives a readback that reflects this misunderstanding, and ATC receives the erroneous readback but fails to correct the error despite its ability to do so. The cases Merrell cites

239

indicate the NTSB will exonerate pilots who deviate from ATC instructions under such circumstances. The underlying rationale of these cases, however, appears to be that ATC could have corrected the pilot's misunderstanding before a violation occurred. *See* cases cited *supra* note 16. Indeed, the only precedent the NTSB itself cited in rejecting the FAA's petition for reconsideration, *Administrator v. Frohmuth & Dworak*, was a case in which the Board excused a violation because ATC, and not the pilot, was responsible for the initial misunderstanding. Here, ATC was neither responsible for the initial misunderstanding nor capable of correcting it since it never received Merrell's readback.

More important, even if the NTSB had followed an unvarying line contrary to the regulatory interpretation the FAA advances here, that would not be sufficient to uphold the Board's decision in this case. As we noted at the outset, the interpretation of air safety regulations is an area in which the Board owes deference to the FAA. For that reason, consistency with the FAA's position is more important than consistency with the Board's own. As both the NTSB and Merrell concede, the FAA is authorized to initiate new regulatory interpretations through adjudication. And because the Board is bound to follow such interpretations, it may at times be both necessary and proper for the Board to depart from its prior case law.

As discussed in Part II.A, the position the FAA takes here is neither new nor inconsistent with its previous view of a pilot's obligations. Nonetheless, there are still some constraints on the FAA's ability to bend the NTSB to its will in this case. For one, if a rule is to be applied to a regulated party, that party must have received fair notice. *See United States v. Chrysler Corp., 332 U.S. App. D.C. 444, 158 F.3d 1350, 1354 (D.C. Cir. 1998)*; *General Elec. Co. v. EPA, 311 U.S. App. D.C. 360, 53 F.3d 1324, 1328-29 (D.C. Cir. 1995)*; *see also Martin, 499 U.S. at 158* (noting that decision to use adjudication "as the initial means for announcing a particular interpretation may bear on the adequacy of notice to regulated parties"). In this case, however, there was fair notice. The plain language of *section 91.123* states that a pilot must follow ATC directions unless there is an emergency, and does not suggest that he may rely on readback procedures to absolve himself of responsibility.

An agency is also barred from applying a new rule in the adjudication in which it is announced if doing so would work a "manifest injustice." *Cassell, 154 F.3d at 486-87* (quoting *Clark-Cowlitz Joint Operating Agency v. FERC, 264 U.S. App. D.C. 58, 826 F.2d 1074, 1081 (D.C. Cir. 1987)*). In cases like this one, the issue boils down to the question of whether the regulated party reasonably and detrimentally relied on a previously established rule. *See 154 F.3d at 486*. For the reasons discussed above, however, there was no established, contrary rule upon which Merrell could have relied. Again, the FAA's position on this matter has been unwavering, while the NTSB's position has been at most internally inconsistent. Nor does Merrell suggest that there is anything he would have done differently as a pilot had he known how the FAA would interpret its rule. Accordingly, the NTSB's precedent in this area is insufficient to render the application of the FAA's interpretation to Merrell a "manifest injustice."

V

Finally, Merrell complains that the FAA did not begin to characterize its position as a regulatory interpretation until its petition for reconsideration. Both before the ALJ and initially before the Board, Merrell contends, FAA counsel presented the case as a straightforward charge of factual carelessness. But the NTSB did not refuse to consider the FAA's interpretation argument on the ground of tardy presentation, and Merrell himself stops short of contending that the agency's tardiness should have barred it from making the argument, saying only that the point is "worth noting." Merrell Br. at 14. He does, however, strongly suggest that the FAA pursued an unfair strategy by shifting to a second theory after losing on the first. Three considerations lead us to conclude that the FAA's delay should not affect our disposition of this case.

First, it is true that the FAA did not initially argue that it interpreted its regulation to presume inattentiveness or carelessness in the absence of explanation; nor did it initially argue that the NTSB was required to defer to such an interpretation. On the other hand, the FAA also did not appear to limit itself solely to a claim of factual carelessness. For example, during the initial hearing before the ALJ, the FAA's counsel argued: "The Board has stated that an altitude deviation in positive control airspace ... is carelessness in the absence of an emergency." R. at 201. Counsel also argued that pilots should be found in violation of *section 91.123* whenever their errors were not initiated by external factors. *See id. at 200, 213-14*. These arguments are consistent with the position the FAA took on reconsideration. They suggest that the FAA's litigating posture was not so much strategic as simply muddled.

Second, we are not precluded from considering a regulatory interpretation simply because the FAA raised it for the first time in a petition for reconsideration below--at least not where, as here, the Board went on to consider and resolve the petition on the merits. The pertinent statute states that "the court may consider an objection to an order of the Board only if the objection was made in the proceeding conducted by the Board or if there was a reasonable ground for not making the objection in the proceeding." *49 U.S.C. § 1153(b)(4)*; *see also id. § 46110(d)*. The reconsideration process qualifies as a proceeding conducted by the Board. *See 49 C.F.R. § 821.50*. Indeed, although in *Hinson* we rejected the FAA's effort to advance its regulatory interpretation because the agency had not raised it at all in the NTSB proceedings, we indicated we would have considered it had the FAA raised it at the reconsideration stage. *See Hinson, 57 F.3d at 1148-49, 1150-51*.

Third, and most important, Merrell does not suggest any way in which the late emergence of the FAA's interpretation argument prejudiced him. He does not contend, for instance, that if he had known of the argument earlier he would have litigated the factual issues differently. To the contrary, since Merrell construed the charge against him as one of pure factual carelessness, he had every reason to offer an explanation for his misperception of the ATC instructions at the initial hearing. And as he concedes he had no explanation, there was no further evidence he could have produced, regardless of how he understood the charge. Nor was Merrell disadvantaged in arguing the legal issues. After the FAA articulated its position in its petition for

241

reconsideration, Merrell had a full opportunity to respond in opposition to the petition, and he did so. *See* R. at 382-92.

None of this excuses the FAA's failure to be clear about its position from the start. Given that the agency lost *Hinson* in part because it failed to raise its interpretation argument in a timely manner, one would think it would have taken care not to wait until the last possible moment to raise the argument this time around. Employing the same presumption the FAA applies to pilots, we would have to conclude that only the agency's "inattentiveness" explains its tardiness. But unlike a pilot, the agency--and, derivatively, the flying public--cannot be sanctioned for its inattentiveness through dismissal of the enforcement order issued in this case.

VI

Because the NTSB failed to defer to the FAA's reasonable interpretation of its own regulations, we conclude that the Board's ruling was not in accordance with law. We therefore grant the petition for review, reverse the Board's decision, and remand the case for further proceedings consistent with this opinion.

RICHARD MERRITT and MARY-JO MERRITT, v. SHUTTLE, INC.

UNITED STATES COURT OF APPEALS FOR THE SECOND
CIRCUIT

187 F.3d 263

July, 1999

MESKILL, Circuit Judge:

Defendants-appellants, employees of the Federal Aviation
Administration, appeal from an order entered in the United States
District Court for the Eastern District of New York, Platt, J., denying
their motion to dismiss plaintiffs' Bivens claims on the basis of
qualified immunity. We remand with instructions to dismiss the Bivens
claims for lack of subject matter jurisdiction.

BACKGROUND

When we review the denial of a motion to dismiss we must accept
as true all material facts alleged in the complaint and draw all
reasonable inferences in the plaintiff's favor. See *Kaluczky v. City of
White Plains, 57 F.3d 202, 206 (2d Cir. 1995)*. According to his
complaint, plaintiff-appellee Richard Merritt is a commercial airline
pilot who was formerly employed by defendant Shuttle, Inc., d/b/a
USAir Shuttle (Shuttle). Defendant U.S. Airways owns a stake in
Shuttle and manages its operations, which consist mainly of running
commercial flights between airports in Washington, D.C., New York
and Boston. Defendants-appellants Joseph McNeil, John Blankenship
and Kevin O'Donnell are officials of defendant Federal Aviation
Administration (FAA). This lawsuit arises out of an incident that
occurred while Merritt was piloting a Shuttle aircraft on June 24, 1996.

I. The June 24, 1996 Incident

On the afternoon of June 24, 1996, Merritt was employed by
Shuttle as captain of a Boeing 727 assigned to fly from Washington
National Airport in Washington, D.C. to LaGuardia Airport in New
York City. Between 4:30 p.m. and 5:00 p.m., as Merritt prepared the
aircraft for takeoff, a band of severe weather, including a tornado,
rapidly approached the airport. Although other employees of Shuttle
and the FAA received repeated warnings about the approaching
weather system, they failed to communicate that information to
Merritt's crew. At 5:11 p.m., FAA officials prepared to evacuate their
control tower to avoid the impending tornado but nevertheless cleared
Merritt's plane for takeoff.

Unaware of the severity of the approaching storm, Merritt
proceeded to take off. As the plane was lifting off the runway, however,
the severe weather crossed its flight path. The plane experienced a
severe weather phenomenon known as "windshear," which buffeted the
plane violently and caused the left wingtip to strike the runway as the
plane became airborne. Although officials from Shuttle and the FAA
were aware that the plane's wingtip had been damaged on takeoff, they
failed to so inform the flight crew, who proceeded on route and landed
safely in New York.

Once the plane landed, Shuttle officials detained Merritt for six hours, a period during which Shuttle employees allegedly altered the aircraft's logbooks in an attempt to blame the takeoff incident on Merritt. The next day, Merritt refused Shuttle's demand that he submit to FAA interrogation, as he believed that the order violated federal air regulations. Shuttle fired Merritt on July 3, 1996, citing his general failure to follow Shuttle's instructions, and in particular his refusal to cooperate with federal investigators despite repeated requests from Shuttle and FAA officials that he do so. The FAA thereafter revoked Merritt's pilot certificate in an emergency order dated November 1, 1996.

II. Administrative Proceedings

Merritt challenged the emergency revocation order in a hearing before an administrative law judge (ALJ) of the National Transportation Safety Board (NTSB). The FAA defended its actions on the ground that Merritt had been careless and had exercised poor judgment in deciding to take off in the violent weather. The FAA presented evidence that the severity of the approaching storm was apparent and that Merritt's decision to take off was irresponsible.

Merritt, in contrast, blamed the incident on officials of Shuttle, U.S. Airways and the FAA, asserting their negligence in failing to provide him with adequate information about the danger of the approaching storm. Merritt also argued that Shuttle, U.S. Airways and the FAA immediately and without investigation, agreed to hold Merritt responsible for the incident, in an attempt to "cover up" their own culpability.

At the end of the four day hearing, the ALJ found enough blame to go around. For one, he noted that Merritt, as captain of the flight, bore ultimate responsibility for the decision to take off, and had exercised poor judgment and acted carelessly in making that decision. The ALJ concluded that Merritt had violated federal air safety regulations and that administrative action was warranted.

The ALJ also found, however, that employees of the FAA, U.S. Airways and Shuttle failed to communicate the latest weather information to Merritt, and that their failure constituted a "mitigating circumstance" that lessened Merritt's culpability. Indeed, the ALJ noted his belief that had the crew "been apprised of all the latest weather information, I would find virtually certain that the flight . . . wouldn't have come about."

In light of Merritt's prior, unblemished record, the ALJ modified the FAA emergency order by vacating the "supreme sanction" of revocation and imposing a nine month suspension in its place.

III. Merritt's Federal Suit

Merritt initially appealed the ALJ's order to the NTSB, which has authority to "amend, modify, or reverse" orders of the Administrator. See *49 U.S.C. § 44709(d)*. Merritt quickly abandoned that appeal, however, and filed this lawsuit in the district court, naming Shuttle, U.S. Airways, the FAA, and the three FAA officials who investigated the June 24 incident. In essence, the complaint laid blame for the incident at the defendants' door. It also alleged that the defendants failed to conduct a meaningful investigation and instead conspired to conceal their own negligence by blaming the incident on Merritt. Merritt advanced a host of common law, statutory and constitutional claims based on these allegations.

The defendants moved to dismiss on various grounds. In a lengthy written opinion, the district court granted a number of these motions and denied the balance. See *Merritt v. Shuttle, 13 F. Supp. 2d 371 (E.D.N.Y. 1998)*. The only ruling now on appeal concerns Merritt's claim, under *Bivens v. Six Unknown Named Agents of Federal Bureau of Narcotics, 403 U.S. 388, 29 L. Ed. 2d 619, 91 S. Ct. 1999 (1971)*, that the individual federal defendants' conduct in investigating the incident deprived Merritt of his *Fifth Amendment* due process rights. The defendants-appellants moved to dismiss the Bivens claim on qualified immunity grounds, but the district court denied their motion as a matter of law. As explained more fully below, we may review this interlocutory order now because it qualifies as a reviewable "collateral order" under the doctrine of *Cohen v. Beneficial Indus. Loan Corp., 337 U.S. 541, 93 L. Ed. 1528, 69 S. Ct. 1221 (1949)*. See *Mitchell v. Forsyth, 472 U.S. 511, 530, 86 L. Ed. 2d 411, 105 S. Ct. 2806 (1985)*.

In denying that motion, the district court noted that to establish immunity from suit, the FAA officials must demonstrate that the right that plaintiff claims was violated was not "clearly established" at the time of the investigation, or, if the right was clearly established, that it was "objectively reasonable" for the defendants to believe that their actions did not violate that right. *13 F. Supp. 2d at 382*. Without conclusively determining what right Merritt claimed was violated, the district court noted that "plaintiff appears to allege that he was terminated from employment because he refused to comply with an investigation that was contrary to federal air regulations." Id. The district court did not specify what constitutional right Merritt had in continued employment with Shuttle or in the FAA's compliance with federal regulations. Neither did it examine whether any such rights were clearly established at the time of the investigation. The district court did conclude, however, that the individual federal defendants were not entitled to qualified immunity because "if the investigation indeed was contrary to federal air regulations then it was not reasonable for the individual federal defendants to agree to participate in it." Id.

The individual federal defendants now appeal, arguing that they are entitled to qualified immunity on two alternative bases. First, they argue that (1) because the district court lacked subject matter jurisdiction over Merritt's Bivens claims it follows that (2) he has no federal cause of action and therefore (3) they may not be said to have violated any of Merritt's "clearly established rights." They also argue, in the alternative, that even if the court had jurisdiction, Merritt at most alleged a violation of agency regulations, and failed to allege that they violated any of his constitutional rights. As explained more fully below, we may review this interlocutory order now because it qualifies as a reviewable "collateral order" under the doctrine of *Cohen v. Beneficial Indus, Loan Corp., 337 U.S. 541, 69 S. Ct. 1221, 93 L. Ed. 1528 (1949)*. See *Mitchell v. Forsyth,. 472 U.S. 511, 105 S. Ct. 2806, 86 L. Ed. 2d 411 (1985)*. Also relevant here, the federal defendants and Shuttle challenged the district court's subject matter jurisdiction under *Fed. R. Civ. P. 12(b)(1)*. They characterized Merritt's action as a challenge to the FAA suspension order and noted that the Federal Aviation Act, *49 U.S.C. § 46110* (the "Aviation Act" or "Act"), locates judicial review of such orders exclusively in the courts of appeals. See *Merritt, 13 F. Supp. 2d at 379* & nn.4-5. The district court denied the motion, holding that even if judicial review of FAA orders was limited to the courts of appeals, Merritt's complaint sought more than mere review of the FAA order and in fact alleged separate constitutional violations sufficient to support a stand-alone suit. See id. As to the Bivens claims based on investigative improprieties, the district court reasoned that jurisdiction in the district court was proper because "plaintiff was not allowed" during the administrative review of his revocation, "to demonstrate that the investigation of the near-crash was tainted." *Id. at 382*. No one has appealed from the subject matter jurisdiction portion of the district court's order. The individual defendants' appeal from the order denying their claim of qualified immunity with respect to Merritt's *Fifth Amendment* Bivens claims is the sole issue on appeal. No other parties are before us and no other issues have been raised.

DISCUSSION

I. The Scope of This Appeal

As a general rule, we only hear appeals from "final decisions of the district courts." *28 U.S.C. § 1291*. An exception to this rule is the "collateral order" doctrine enunciated in *Cohen, 337 U.S. 541, 93 L. Ed. 1528, 69 S. Ct. 1221*. Cohen explained that interlocutory appeals may be taken from "claims of right separable from, and collateral to, rights asserted in the action, too important to be denied review and too independent of the cause itself to require that appellate consideration be deferred until the whole case is adjudicated." *Id. at 546*. Cohen permits immediate appeal from interlocutory orders that "[1] conclusively determine the disputed question, [2] resolve an important issue completely separate from the merits of the action, and [3] [are] effectively unreviewable on appeal from a final judgment." *Coopers & Lybrand v. Livesay, 437 U.S. 463, 468, 57 L. Ed. 2d 351, 98 S. Ct. 2454 (1978)*.

Here, the defendants-appellants seek review of the district court's order denying their motion to dismiss the complaint as to them on qualified immunity grounds. Generally speaking, an order denying a motion to dismiss is interlocutory and hence nonappealable. See *Hathaway v. Coughlin, 37 F.3d 63, 67 (2d Cir. 1994)*. Immediate appeal will lie, however, where such an order denies a claim of qualified immunity as a matter of law. Id. (citing *Mitchell, 472 U.S. at 530*). This is so because qualified immunity, if it applies, is a shield from litigation in the first instance, not merely a defense to liability. See *Kaminsky v. Rosenblum, 929 F.2d 922, 926 (2d Cir. 1991)*. Because that shield is effectively destroyed if a case is erroneously ordered to trial, Cohen permits immediate appeal when a district court denies an immunity defense as a matter of law. See *Mitchell, 472 U.S. at 530*; *Golino v. City of New Haven, 950 F.2d 864, 868 (2d Cir. 1991)*. We therefore have jurisdiction to review the district court's order denying qualified immunity because the issue here may be decided as a matter of law.

We may not reach the substance of that order, however, without first carrying out our "special obligation to satisfy [ourselves] not only of [our] own jurisdiction, but also that of the lower courts in [the] cause under review." *Steel Co. v. Citizens for a Better Environment, 523 U.S. 83, 95, 118 S. Ct. 1003, 140 L. Ed. 2d 210 (1998)* (citations and internal quotation marks omitted). This is because "'on every writ of error or appeal, the first and fundamental question is that of jurisdiction, first, of this court, and then of the court from which the record comes.'" *Steel Co., 523 U.S. at 94* (quoting *Great Southern Fire Proof Hotel Co. v. Jones, 177 U.S. 449, 453, 44 L. Ed. 842, 20 S. Ct. 690 (1900))*.

Appellate jurisdiction is proper because, as noted above, we have jurisdiction of the Cohen-based appeal from the denial of qualified immunity. Our review of the record, however, raises concerns about the district court's subject matter jurisdiction over the Bivens claim in the first instance. A defect in original jurisdiction would be dispositive here because, if the district court lacked jurisdiction, we would have "'jurisdiction on appeal, not of the merits but merely for the purpose of correcting the error of the lower court in entertaining the suit.'" *Bender v. Williamsport Area School Dist., 475 U.S. 534, 541, 89 L. Ed. 2d 501, 106 S. Ct. 1326 (1986)* (quoting *United States v. Corrick, 298 U.S. 435, 440, 80 L. Ed. 1263, 56 S. Ct. 829 (1936))*; see also *Fed. R. Civ. P. 12(h)(3)* ("Whenever it appears . . . that the court lacks jurisdiction of the subject matter, the court shall dismiss the action."). Accordingly, we must examine whether the district court had subject matter jurisdiction over the claim now on appeal. In making that examination, we heed the Supreme Court's admonition that we must "police" "subject-matter delineations . . . on [our] own initiative." *Ruhrgas A.G. v. Marathon Oil Co., 526 U.S. 574, 143 L. Ed. 2d 760, 119 S. Ct. 1563, 1570 (1999)*.

We pause only to explain that in examining this issue we do not run afoul of the boundaries of our appellate jurisdiction articulated in *Swint v. Chambers County Comm'n, 514 U.S. 35, 131 L. Ed. 2d 60, 115 S. Ct. 1203 (1995)*. Swint announced the general rule that when a federal appellate court reviews an order that is entitled to interlocutory review, the court may not at that time also review unrelated questions that are not themselves independently entitled to expedited consideration. see *id. at 51*. Because non-immunity based motions to dismiss for want of subject matter jurisdiction are not ordinarily entitled to interlocutory review, see *Catlin v. United States, 324 U.S. 229, 236, 89 L. Ed. 911, 65 S. Ct. 631 (1945)*, there is no independent basis for appellate jurisdiction over the district court's order denying the defendants' motion to dismiss for lack of subject matter jurisdiction. Indeed, perhaps aware of that limitation, none of the defendants appealed from that order. We nonetheless reach the subject matter jurisdiction issue of our own accord, however, and believe that in doing so we stay within the boundaries established in Swint.

In particular, we note that the Swint restrictions are not absolute. To the contrary, the Swint Court suggested and we have recognized that during the course of a properly grounded interlocutory appeal we may simultaneously consider another issue not itself entitled to interlocutory review if the otherwise unappealable issue is "'inextricably intertwined' with" the appealable one, or if review of the otherwise unappealable issue is "'necessary to ensure meaningful review of'" the appealable one. *Rein v. Socialist People's Libyan Arab Jamahiriya, 162 F.3d 748, 758 (2d Cir. 1998)* (quoting *Swint, 514 U.S.*

at 51), cert. denied, *144 L. Ed. 2d 235, 67 U.S.L.W. 3756, 119 S. Ct. 2337* (June 14, 1999).

We believe that our examination of the basis for the district court's subject matter jurisdiction over the Bivens claim is "necessary to ensure meaningful review of" the district court's order denying qualified immunity on that claim. The existence of subject matter jurisdiction goes to the very power of the district court to issue the rulings now under consideration. See *United States Catholic Conference v. Abortion Rights Mobilization, 487 U.S. 72, 77, 101 L. Ed. 2d 69, 108 S. Ct. 2268 (1988)* (noting that "the challenge in this case goes to the subject-matter jurisdiction of the court and hence its power to issue the order" under consideration). Indeed, as the Supreme Court recently reminded, "for a court to pronounce upon [the merits] when it has no jurisdiction to do so is, by very definition, for a court to act ultra vires." *Steel Co., 523 U.S. at 101-02*. Accordingly, our review of the district court's order on the Bivens claim would be meaningless if the district court was without jurisdiction over that claim in the first instance.

In reaching the subject matter jurisdiction issue in the context of a limited interlocutory appeal, we do not break new ground. In the past we have undertaken such review during appeals brought under *28 U.S.C. § 1292(a)*, which permits immediate appeal from the grant or denial of injunctive relief. See *San Filippo v. United Brotherhood of Carpenters and Joiners, 525 F.2d 508, 513 (2d Cir. 1975)* ("Where . . . there is an appeal otherwise properly before this Court, and the absence of subject matter jurisdiction is suggested, that issue may be reviewed."); see also *Volges v. Resolution Trust Corp., 32 F.3d 50, 51 (2d Cir. 1994)* (reviewing jurisdiction of lower court in context of appeal from grant of injunctive relief). The Supreme Court has sanctioned a similar practice. See *Deckert v. Independence Shares Corp., 311 U.S. 282, 287, 85 L. Ed. 189, 61 S. Ct. 229 (1940)* (noting, on properly grounded appeal from grant of preliminary injunction, that court of appeals' powers were "not limited to mere consideration of, and action upon, the order appealed from" because, "'if insuperable objection to maintaining the bill clearly appears, it may be dismissed and the litigation terminated'" (quoting *Meccano, Ltd. v. Wanamaker, 253 U.S. 136, 141, 64 L. Ed. 822, 40 S. Ct. 463 (1920)))* (cited with approval in *Swint, 514 U.S. at 50*).

The same practice should be followed in the collateral order context, and we believe that such a practice falls comfortably within the parameters contemplated by Swint. See Kanji, The Proper Scope of Pendent Appellate Jurisdiction in the Collateral Order Context, *100 Yale L.J. 511, 527 (1990)* (arguing that it "appears appropriate -- indeed, essential -- for collateral order courts, like their *section 1292(a)* counterparts, to consider all factors material to a determination of whether a collateral order was properly decided") (commentary cited with approval in *Swint, 514 U.S. at 51*).

We emphasize, however, that we examine only whether the district court possessed jurisdiction over the precise claims that are the basis for this appeal, i.e., Merritt's Bivens claims that the defendants-appellants' participation in a tainted investigation violated his *Fifth Amendment* due process rights. As we do not now have appellate jurisdiction over any other claims, we do not express an opinion on the merits of, or the district court's subject matter jurisdiction over, any other claims against these or any other defendants.

248

II. Did the District Court Have Subject Matter Jurisdiction Over Merritt's *Fifth Amendment* Bivens Claims?

Having explained how we reach the subject matter jurisdiction question, we now endeavor to answer it. We conclude that the district court lacked jurisdiction over the Bivens claims now on appeal.

The Aviation Act provides that the courts of appeals have "exclusive jurisdiction to affirm, amend, modify, or set aside" orders of the NTSB or the FAA. *49 U.S.C. § 46110(c)*. The appellants contended below, and we now conclude, that *section 46110* deprives the district court of jurisdiction over Merritt's Bivens claims against the defendants-appellants.

Other courts of appeals have addressed this precise question on very similar facts. See *Tur v. Federal Aviation Administration, 104 F.3d 290 (9th Cir. 1997)*; *Green v. Brantley, 981 F.2d 514 (11th Cir. 1993)*. In Green, when the FAA revoked Green's Designated Pilot Examiner certificate he eschewed administrative review entirely and instead filed a Bivens action in district court. See *981 F.2d at 517-18.* He charged that FAA officials had deprived him of constitutionally protected liberty and property interests. See *id. at 518.* The district court denied the defendants' motion for summary judgment on qualified immunity grounds and the defendants appealed. See id. The court of appeals sua sponte examined the district court's subject matter jurisdiction and remanded with instructions to dismiss the complaint. See *id. at 521.*

The court of appeals reasoned that Green's Bivens claim was an improper attempt to circumvent the Act's exclusive judicial review provisions. See id. It concluded that adjudication of the merits of Green's Bivens claim -- which challenged the procedures and reasons behind the agency action that aggrieved him -- would raise issues that were "inescapably intertwined" with a review of the procedures and merits surrounding the FAA's order. See id. As a result, the court concluded, the Act's exclusive judicial review procedures operated to deprive the district court of subject matter jurisdiction over the Bivens claim. See id.

A similar result obtained in *Tur, 104 F.3d 290.* There, the FAA revoked Tur's airman certificate on an emergency basis after Tur, a helicopter pilot, allegedly violated five separate FAA regulations. *Id. at 291.* An ALJ upheld the revocation order and both the NTSB and the Ninth Circuit affirmed. See id. When Tur later discovered that FAA officials had knowingly used false testimony in the course of the revocation proceedings, he sued those officials for money damages in federal district court, claiming that their knowing use of false testimony deprived him of his property interest in his airman's certificate without due process of law. See id.

The district court dismissed Tur's suit for want of subject matter jurisdiction and the Ninth Circuit affirmed. Applying the standard enunciated in *Green, supra*, the court of appeals concluded that Tur's claims were "inescapably intertwined with the merits of the previous revocation order." *Tur, 104 F.3d at 292.* In particular, the court reasoned that Tur's federal suit, which contested the manner in which FAA officials had conducted his investigation and revocation proceeding, would "result in new adjudication over the evidence and testimony adduced in the [prior revocation] hearing, the credibility determinations made by the ALJ, and, ultimately, the findings made by the ALJ." Id. Because the Act's judicial review provisions located jurisdiction over those issues exclusively in the court of appeals, the court concluded that the district court properly dismissed the suit for want of subject matter jurisdiction. See id.

We believe that the persuasive reasoning of these cases suggests an identical result in Merritt's case. As in both Green and Tur, the substance of Merritt's *Fifth Amendment* due process claim is "inescapably intertwined" with review of the revocation order. Although Merritt styles this claim in constitutional terms, he ultimately challenges the manner in which the officials conducted themselves during and after the June 24 incident, and disputes the ALJ's factual conclusion that he bore responsibility for an ill-considered decision to take off. As in Tur, advancing such a claim in district court would "result in new adjudication over the evidence and testimony adduced in the [prior revocation] hearing, the credibility determinations made by the ALJ, and, ultimately, the findings made by the ALJ" during the course of the proceedings under *section 46110*. See *Tur, 104 F.3d at 292*. The exclusive statutory scheme forbids such a result. See id.

We note that the district court distinguished Green on the ground that Green chose not to seek administrative review at all, while Merritt did have a hearing before the ALJ. Although Merritt did, in fact, seek review of his revocation order before the ALJ, and indeed had the revocation modified to a suspension, he nevertheless failed to complete the judicial review process by either perfecting an appeal to the NTSB or filing a petition for review in the appropriate court of appeals. Moreover, that an individual aggrieved by agency action avails himself of the specified administrative review procedures does not alter the exclusivity of those procedures. Indeed, in Tur the plaintiff had exhausted his administrative remedies, and the FAA revocation order was affirmed by an ALJ, the NTSB and the Ninth Circuit Court of Appeals. The fact remained, however, that *section 46110* rendered the district court Bivens action an improper collateral attack on the FAA order. See *Tur, 104 F.3d at 292*. The same may be said of Merritt's claim, whether or not he is deemed to have availed himself of the *section 46110* procedures.

We need not decide whether a broad-based, facial constitutional attack on an FAA policy or procedure -- in contrast to a complaint about the agency's particular actions in a specific case -- might constitute appropriate subject matter for a stand-alone federal suit. Cf. *Foster v. Skinner, 70 F.3d 1084, 1088 (9th Cir. 1995)* (holding that although courts of appeals have exclusive jurisdiction over claims that are "inescapably intertwined" with the FAA's actions on a particular final order, "a district court has subject matter jurisdiction over broad constitutional challenges to FAA practices"); *Mace v. Skinner, 34 F.3d 854, 859-60 (9th Cir. 1994)* (holding that district court had jurisdiction over suit waging a "broad challenge to allegedly unconstitutional FAA practices"). But see *Gaunce v. deVincentis, 708 F.2d 1290, 1293 (7th Cir. 1983)* (per curiam) (suggesting that Act bars any constitutional challenge not preceded by exhaustion of Act's judicial review procedures). See generally *Reno v. Catholic Social Servs., 509 U.S. 43, 56, 125 L. Ed. 2d 38, 113 S. Ct. 2485 (1993)* (holding that statutory provision governing review of single agency actions does not apply to challenge to "'a practice or procedure employed in making decisions'" generally) (quoting *McNary v. Haitian Refugee Center, 498 U.S. 479, 491-92 & n.12, 112 L. Ed. 2d 1005, 111 S. Ct. 888 (1991)* (holding that statutory review provisions of Immigration and Naturalization Act, which prescribed exhaustion of administrative remedies before judicial review in courts of appeals, precluded review of specific agency actions in individual cases, but did not preclude district court jurisdiction over "general collateral challenges to unconstitutional practices and policies")). Merritt's *Fifth Amendment* due process claim does not mount a broad-based attack on the FAA's practices or policies. He complains only of the circumstances that gave rise to his suspension and to the motivations and actions of those who allegedly engineered that suspension. In this regard, his *Fifth Amendment* due process claim is of the type that Mace specifically distinguished as properly preempted by *section 46110*, i.e., one in which it is "the conduct of FAA officials in adjudicating a specific individual claim that [is] under attack." *Mace, 34 F.3d at 858*. Because Merritt's *Fifth Amendment* due process claim against the individual federal defendants is "directed at the merits of a previous adjudication," see *Tur, 104 F.3d at 292*, rather than at any FAA policies or procedures generally, Merritt could not avail himself of the rule articulated in Mace even if it were the settled law of this Circuit.

CONCLUSION

The case is remanded with instructions to dismiss Merritt's *Fifth Amendment* due process claims against the defendants-appellants for lack of subject matter jurisdiction, and for other proceedings not inconsistent with this opinion.

RICHARD MERRITT & MARY-JO MERRITT, v. SHUTTLE, INC.,
U.S. AIRWAYS INC., TERRY V. HALLCOM, STEVEN K.
WILSON, & UNITED STATES OF AMERICA

UNITED STATES COURT OF APPEALS FOR THE SECOND
CIRCUIT

245 F.3d 182

April, 2001

SOTOMAYOR, Circuit Judge:

Plaintiffs-appellants Richard Merritt ("Merritt") and Mary-Jo Merritt (collectively, "plaintiffs") appeal from a May 2, 2000 judgment of the United States District Court for the Eastern District of New York (Thomas C. Platt, Jr., *Judge*) dismissing their action as against all defendants. More specifically, plaintiffs appeal the district court's *sua sponte* dismissal of their claim under the Federal Tort Claims Act (FTCA), *28 U.S.C. § 2671 et seq. (1994)*, against defendant United States of America (the "United States") for lack of subject matter jurisdiction.

The district court predicated its dismissal of plaintiffs' FTCA claim on *49 U.S.C. § 46110 (1994)*, which vests judicial review of certain administrative orders of the Federal Aviation Administration ("FAA"), the National Transportation Safety Board ("NTSB"), and the Department of Transportation ("DOT") exclusively in the courts of appeals. By order dated December 13, 1996, an administrative law judge ("ALJ") of the NTSB suspended Merritt's pilot's certificate for nine months. Instead of appealing that order to the full NTSB and then to this Court, Merritt filed this action in the United States district court for the Eastern District of New York. Finding that consideration of plaintiffs' FTCA claim was "inescapably intertwined" with review of the NTSB's nine-month suspension order, the district court *sua sponte* dismissed the claim for lack of subject matter jurisdiction.

For the reasons discussed, we conclude that *Section 46110* does not preclude the district court from hearing Merritt's FTCA claim, and we therefore reverse the district court's dismissal of the claim and remand for further proceedings consistent with this opinion.

BACKGROUND

Because we recited the allegations of Merritt's first amended complaint in some detail in our previous opinion, *Merritt v. Shuttle, Inc., 187 F.3d 263 (2d Cir. 1999) ("Merritt I")*, the following account is limited to those allegations that bear upon the issues that are the subject of the present appeal.

On June 24, 1996, Merritt was employed as a captain by defendant Shuttle, Inc. ("Shuttle") and assigned to captain flight number 6500 from Washington National Airport, Washington D.C. to LaGuardia Airport, New York City. At approximately 4:15 P.M., employees of the FAA ordered Merritt to proceed immediately to his aircraft for an early departure. Between 4:30 P.M. and 5:00 P.M., as Merritt prepared the aircraft for takeoff, a band of severe weather, including a tornado, rapidly approached the airport. Although FAA employees had been notified of the approaching storm, they failed to communicate that information to flight 6500. At approximately 5:11 p.m., as FAA officials prepared to evacuate their control tower to avoid the approaching tornado, they nevertheless cleared Merritt's plane for takeoff. Unaware of the severity of the approaching storm, Merritt proceeded to take off. As the plane was lifting off the runway, however, the severe weather crossed its flight path, causing a sudden loss of airspeed. The plane experienced a weather phenomenon known as "windshear," which violently buffeted the plane and caused the left wingtip to strike the runway as the plane became airborne. Although FAA employees were promptly informed of the damage to the plane, they failed to convey this information to flight 6500. Merritt continued the flight and landed the plane safely at LaGuardia Airport.

In the course of these events, Merritt claims that he suffered a near death experience, post traumatic stress syndrome, and other mental and physical ailments that rendered him disabled for an extended period of time. In his appellate brief, Merritt adds that "the FAA suspended [his] airman's medical certificate because of personal injuries he sustained on June 24, 1996." Similarly, at oral argument, Merritt alleged that "the FAA revoked [his] medical certificate for a two year period because of the medically documented damages that were involved with [the takeoff incident]."

The day after the takeoff incident, June 25, 1996, Merritt refused Shuttle's demand that he submit to FAA interrogation, as he believed that the demand violated federal aviation regulations. As a result of this refusal, Shuttle terminated Merritt's employment on July 3, 1996. The FAA thereafter revoked Merritt's airline transport pilot's certificate in an emergency order dated November 1, 1996. *See FAA v. Sachon*, No. SE-14698/SE-14700, 1996 WL 861978, at 1 (N.T.S.B. Dec. 13, 1996).

Merritt challenged the emergency revocation order in a hearing before an ALJ of the NTSB. *Id.* During the four day hearing in December 1996, the parties called a total of 31 witnesses and introduced 63 exhibits. *Id.* at 2. Merritt testified that, at the time he commenced takeoff, the visibility was very good, with just a few clouds in the sky. *Id.* at 2, 4. Some of the passengers testified, however, that they saw rain and lightning just prior to takeoff. *Id.* The ALJ found that Merritt, as captain of the flight, bore ultimate responsibility for the decision to take off, had exercised poor judgment and acted carelessly in making that decision, and had violated federal air safety regulations in the process. *Id.* at 2-3. The ALJ also found, however, that employees of the FAA failed to communicate the latest weather information to Merritt, and that this failure constituted a "mitigating circumstance" that lessened Merritt's culpability. *Id.* at 3. In light of this mitigating circumstance and Merritt's prior exemplary and unblemished record, the ALJ modified the FAA emergency order by vacating the "supreme sanction" of revocation of Merritt's pilot's certificate and imposing a nine-month suspension in its place. *Id.* at 4, 6.

Although Merritt initially appealed the ALJ's order to the NTSB, he soon thereafter abandoned that appeal and filed this action on May 27, 1997. Among numerous federal and state claims against several defendants, the amended complaint included a *Fifth Amendment* due process *Bivens* claim against three FAA officials, *Bivens v. Six Unknown Named Agents*, 403 U.S. 388, 29 L. Ed. 2d 619, 91 S. Ct.

1999 (1971), and an FTCA negligence claim against the United States based on the FAA's failure to warn him of the approaching storm. The defendants moved to dismiss on various grounds. The district court granted a number of these motions and denied the balance. *Merritt v. Shuttle, Inc., 13 F. Supp. 2d 371 (E.D.N.Y. 1998)*. Among the motions denied was the United States' motion to dismiss for lack of subject matter jurisdiction pursuant to *Section 46110* and the FAA officials' motion to dismiss the *Bivens* claim on qualified immunity grounds. *Id. at 379, 382*.

The FAA officials then brought an interlocutory appeal of the district court's rejection of their qualified immunity defense pursuant to the collateral order doctrine. *Merritt I, 187 F.3d 263, 266-67*. Instead of addressing this qualified immunity issue, we *sua sponte* reviewed the district court's denial of the United States' motion to dismiss for lack of subject matter jurisdiction under *Section 46110*. Finding that Merritt's *Bivens* claim was "inescapably intertwined" with review of the nine-month suspension order, and that permitting that claim to proceed to trial in the district court "would result in new adjudication over the evidence and testimony adduced in the prior [administrative] . . . hearing, the credibility determinations made by the ALJ, and, ultimately, the findings made by the ALJ during the course of the proceedings under *section 46110*," we concluded that *Section 46110* deprived the district court of jurisdiction over the *Bivens* claim. *Id. at 271*. (internal brackets and quotation marks omitted). We remanded the action "with instructions to dismiss Merritt's *Fifth Amendment* due process claims against the [FAA officials] for lack of subject matter jurisdiction, and for other proceedings not inconsistent with this opinion." *Id. at 272*.

On remand, the district court dismissed with prejudice the *Fifth Amendment* due process claims against the three FAA officials. Finding that Merritt's "common law torts [action] against the United States [was] 'inescapably intertwined' with the Administrative Law Judge's review of the revocation order," the district court also *sua sponte* dismissed with prejudice Merritt's FTCA claim against the United States. Merritt timely appealed.

DISCUSSION

We review the district court's *Fed R. Civ. P. 12(b)(1)* dismissal of the complaint against the United States *de novo*. *See Jaghory v. New York State Dept. of Educ., 131 F.3d 326, 329 (2d Cir. 1997)*. In reviewing the grant of a motion to dismiss we must accept as true all material facts alleged in the complaint and draw all reasonable inferences in the plaintiff's favor. *Id.*

In determining whether *Section 46110* deprives the district court of jurisdiction over Merritt's FTCA claim, we must begin with the text of the statute. *Section 46110(a)* provides in relevant part that "a person disclosing a substantial interest in an *order* issued by the . . . Administrator of the Federal Aviation Administration . . . under [United States Code, Title 49, Subtitle VII, Part A] may apply for review of the *order* by filing a petition for review in the United States Court of Appeals for the District of Columbia Circuit or in the court of appeals of the United States for the circuit in which the person resides or has its principle place of business." *49 U.S.C. § 46110(a)* (emphasis added).

Section 46110(c) provides in relevant part that the courts of appeals have "exclusive jurisdiction to affirm, amend, modify, or set aside any part of the [FAA's] *order.*" *49 U.S.C. § 46110(c)* (emphasis added). By its terms, *Section 46110(c)* precludes federal district courts from affirming, amending, modifying, or setting aside any part of such an order.

More broadly, statutes such as *Section 46110(c)* that vest judicial review of administrative orders exclusively in the courts of appeals also preclude district courts from hearing claims that are "inescapably intertwined" with review of such orders. *Merritt I, 187 F.3d at 271.* A claim is inescapably intertwined in this manner if it alleges that the plaintiff was injured by such an order and that the court of appeals has authority to hear the claim on direct review of the agency order. *City of Tacoma v. Taxpayers of Tacoma, 357 U.S. 320, 336, 339, 2 L. Ed. 2d 1345, 78 S. Ct. 1209 (1958).*

City of Tacoma is the seminal Supreme Court case discussing the scope of exclusive jurisdiction provisions such as 46110(c). *See Williams Natural Gas Co. v. City of Oklahoma City, 890 F.2d 255, 261 (10th Cir. 1989)* (stating that the "watershed case" interpreting such provisions is *City of Tacoma*). *City of Tacoma* concerned a license to construct a power project issued to the City of Tacoma by the Federal Power Commission (the "Commission") pursuant to Section 21 of the Federal Power Act, *16 U.S.C. § 791a et seq. City of Tacoma, 357 U.S. at 323.* The relevant exclusive jurisdiction statute, Section 313(b) of the Federal Power Act, *16 U.S.C. § 825l(b),* provided that the courts of appeals "shall have exclusive jurisdiction to affirm, modify, or set aside" orders of the Commission. *Id. at 335.* The State of Washington appealed to the Ninth Circuit the issuance of the license, arguing that the Commission lacked the authority to issue the license because, *inter alia,* "the City had not complied with applicable state laws nor obtained state permits and approvals required by state statutes." *Id. at 328.* The Ninth Circuit eventually affirmed the issuance of the license. *Id.* While the State's appeal was pending in the Ninth Circuit, however, the City brought a state court action against, *inter alia,* the State seeking a judgment declaring valid an issuance of bonds to finance the power project. *Id. at 329.* The State filed a cross-claim, "reasserting substantially the same objections [it] had made before the Commission, and that had been made in, and rejected by, the Court of Appeals." *Id.* After two rounds of direct review in the state courts, the Washington Supreme Court affirmed an order enjoining the City from proceeding to construct the project. *Id. at 329-32.*

The United States Supreme Court reversed. *Id. at 341.* The Court reasoned that because Section 313(b) of the Federal Power Act provides that "any party *aggrieved by the Commission's order* may have judicial review, upon all issues raised before the Commission . . . by the Court of Appeals which 'shall have exclusive jurisdiction to affirm, modify or set aside such order in whole or in part,'" the provision

> necessarily precludes *de novo* litigation between the parties of all issues inhering in the controversy, and all other modes of judicial review. Hence, upon judicial review of the Commission's *order,* all objections to *the order,* to the license [the order] directs to be issued, and to the legal competence of the licensee to execute [the

> order's] terms, must be made in the court of appeals or
> not at all.

Id. at 336 (footnote omitted and emphasis added) (quoting *16 U.S.C. §
825l(b)*). The Supreme Court added that the test for determining
whether Section 313(b) precludes a district court from hearing a
particular claim is not whether the claim was presented to and decided
by a court of appeals, but rather whether the claim "could and should
have been" presented to and decided by a court of appeals. *Id. at 339*.

In formulating *City of Tacoma*'s holding, it is important not to take
out of context the Court's statement that Section 313(b) "necessarily
precludes *de novo* litigation between the parties of all issues inhering in
the controversy, and all other modes of judicial review." Because the
notion of issues "inhering in a controversy" is inherently vague, this
statement could be taken to mean that district courts are precluded from
hearing *any* issue that was raised or decided in a prior administrative
proceeding. The "inhering in the controversy" statement, however,
must be read in relation to the Supreme Court's other statements that,
under Section 313(b), a party aggrieved by an administrative *order* may
seek judicial review of the order in the courts of appeals, that the courts
of appeals have exclusive jurisdiction to affirm, modify or set aside
such *orders*, and that all objections to such *orders* must be made in the
courts of appeals or not at all. We thus read *City of Tacoma* as holding
that Section 313(b) precludes (i) *de novo* litigation of issues inhering in
a controversy over an administrative *order*, where one party alleges that
it was *aggrieved by the order*, and (ii) all other modes of judicial
review *of the order*. Cf. *Thunder Basin Coal Co. v. Reich, 510 U.S.
200, 212-13, 127 L. Ed. 2d 29, 114 S. Ct. 771 (1994)* (stating that
exclusive jurisdiction provisions do not preclude district court
consideration of claims that are "'wholly collateral' to a statute's review
provisions and outside the agency's expertise, particularly where a
finding of preclusion could foreclose all meaningful judicial review")
(internal quotation marks and citations omitted); *FCC v. ITT World
Communications, Inc., 466 U.S. 463, 468, 80 L. Ed. 2d 480, 104 S. Ct.
1936 (1984)* (holding that "litigants may not evade [*28 U.S.C. §
2342(1)*] by requesting the District Court to enjoin action that is the
outcome of the agency's *order*") (emphasis added).

Similar caution must be taken with respect to our statement in
Merritt I that Section 46110 precludes a district court from hearing a
particular claim when "advancing [it] in district court would result in
new adjudication over the evidence and testimony adduced in . . . [the
prior administrative proceeding], the credibility determinations made
by the ALJ, and, ultimately, the findings made by the ALJ." *187 F.3d
at 271* (internal quotation marks omitted). Read in isolation, this
statement could suggest that *Section 46110* precludes a district court
from hearing virtually any issue that was raised and considered in a
prior administrative proceeding. This statement, however, must be read
in light of *City of Tacoma* and in connection with our other statement in
Merritt I that the test is whether the claim is "inescapably intertwined
with review of the [administrative] *order*." *Id.* (internal quotation marks
omitted) (emphasis added). This means that the mere overlap of
evidence and testimony adduced in the two proceedings, or the mere
overlap of findings made by an ALJ and by a district court judge are
insufficient to preclude the district court from hearing a given claim.

Such overlap is relevant only if the claim attacks the matters decided by the administrative order..

In *Merritt I*, we held that the district court lacked subject matter jurisdiction to hear Merritt's *Bivens* claim precisely because that claim challenged the ALJ's order suspending Merritt's pilot's certificate for nine months. We noted that Merritt complained of "the circumstances that gave rise to his suspension" and "the motivations and actions of those who allegedly engineered that suspension," and that his *Bivens* claim was "directed at the merits of a previous [administrative] adjudication." *Id. at 272* (internal quotation marks omitted).

In the present case, it is evident that Merritt's FTCA claim does not allege that he was injured or aggrieved by the ALJ's December 13, 1996 order suspending his pilot's certificate for nine months. Rather, Merritt claims that he was injured by the failure of FAA employees to provide him with accurate weather information prior to takeoff on June 24, 1996.

Nor could Merritt raise his FTCA claim in an appeal of the order suspending his pilot's certificate to this Court. Merritt asserted at oral argument -- and the Government agreed -- that there is "no subject matter jurisdiction in the NTSB court to hear negligence claims" against the FAA. This assertion is supported by review of the statute that vests the NTSB with the authority to review FAA orders, namely, *49 U.S.C. § 44709 (1994). Section 44709* vests the FAA with authority (i) to "reexamine an airman holding a [pilot's] certificate," *id. § 44709(a)*, and *(ii)* to "issue an order amending, modifying, suspending, or revoking-(1) any part of [such] a certificate . . . if-(A) [it] decides . . . that safety in air commerce or air transportation and the public interest require that action," *id. § 44709(b). Section 44709(d)* gives the NTSB authority, upon the appeal of such an order, to "amend, modify, or reverse the order." *49 U.S.C. § 44709(d)(1).* These provisions indicate that the entire focus of such review proceedings is whether the suspension or revocation of a pilot's certificate was warranted; no provision is made for claims by the pilot that the FAA was responsible for the incident that led to the suspension of his certificate. Indeed, reported decisions of the NTSB affirmatively state that the NTSB has no authority to hear such claims against the FAA in a *Section 44709* proceeding. *See FAA v. Smedley*, No. SE-15798, 2000 WL 576184, at 3 (N.T.S.B. Apr. 6, 2000) (stating that "unlike civil cases and juries and a lot of tort cases, [the NTSB in a *Section 44709* proceeding lacks authority to] . . . compare negligence. The FAA could be 70 percent negligent and the pilot could be 30 percent negligent, but if there's a regulatory allegation shown, the pilot is going to lose because [the NTSB] can't hold the FAA in any way responsible"); *FAA v. Tate*, No. SE-11734, 1991 WL 345903, at 2-3 (N.T.S.B. Sept. 13, 1991) (same); *cf. Beins v. United States, 224 U.S. App. D.C. 397, 695 F.2d 591, 598 (D.C. Cir. 1982)* (holding that Section 1486 did not preclude the district court from hearing pilot's FTCA claim against the FAA because, *inter alia*, "an administrative appeal determines whether the agency action was in excess of statutory jurisdiction and authority, without observance of procedure required by law, contrary to constitutional right and power, arbitrary and capricious, or otherwise not in accordance with law, *5 U.S.C. § 706*; these determinations are distinct conceptually from a finding of negligence, the linchpin of the FTCA"). Hence, because our review of an NTSB order is generally limited to the issues considered by the NTSB, *49 U.S.C. § 44110(b)*, Merritt could not raise his FTCA claim in an appeal of the order suspending his pilot's certificate to this Court.

Furthermore, as the Court of Appeals for the District of Columbia Circuit explained in *Beins*, consideration of the nature and purpose of the FTCA provides an independent basis for concluding that FTCA claims are not precluded by *Section 46110*:

> On its face the FTCA provides a remedy for negligent acts of government employees; none of the several explicit exceptions in the FTCA exempts negligent acts solely because the legal validity of the employee's actions is appealable on other grounds to other administrative bodies or eventually to the courts through the Administrative Procedure Act . . . . "The [FTCA] was the product of nearly thirty years of congressional consideration and was drawn with numerous substantive limitations and administrative safeguards." . . . .
>
> [Given the] considerable care [taken] by Congress in crafting when and how the FTCA would be available to a claimant . . . we are disinclined to add a jurisdictional exception . . . .

695 F.2d at 597-98 (quoting *Indian Towing Co. v. United States, 350 U.S. 61, 68, 100 L. Ed. 48, 76 S. Ct. 122 (1955))*.

A final consideration that weighs against the district court's interpretation of *Section 46110* as depriving it of jurisdiction to hear Merritt's FTCA claim is that it yields several unreasonable consequences -- the first two of which the government at oral argument acknowledged and urged us to accept. Whenever possible, however, we interpret statutes to avoid unreasonable results. *See Dougherty v. Carver Fed. Sav. Bank, 112 F.3d 613, 624 (2d Cir. 1997)* (citing *Am. Tobacco Co. v. Patterson, 456 U.S. 63, 71, 71 L. Ed. 2d 748, 102 S. Ct. 1534 (1982))*. First, under the district court's interpretation, although every passenger of flight 6500 could bring an FTCA claim for injuries allegedly suffered during the June 24, 1996 takeoff incident, Merritt could not -- even though his allegations of FAA negligence, like the allegations of FAA negligence that could be made by the passengers, are directed against FAA acts and omissions that occurred on June 24, 1996, not against the FAA's suspension of his pilot's certificate. *See Tinkler v. United States, 982 F.2d 1456 (10th Cir. 1992)* (presupposing that district court had jurisdiction to hear FTCA claim brought by wife of aircraft passenger killed as a result of alleged failure of FAA employee to furnish weather information to the pilot of the aircraft). Second, even if the ALJ had found that Merritt bore no responsibility whatsoever for the June 24, 1996 takeoff incident, the district court's interpretation of *Section 46110* would nonetheless unjustly bar him from bringing an FTCA claim in district court. Third, while the district court's interpretation precludes Merritt from bringing an FTCA claim for the injuries he suffered during the takeoff incident, it would have permitted Merritt's estate to bring an FTCA claim had Merritt died as a result of the takeoff incident. *See Budden v. United States, 15 F.3d 1444 (8th Cir. 1994)* (presupposing that district court had jurisdiction

258

to hear FTCA claim brought by estate of deceased pilot alleging that pilot had been killed as a result of failure of FAA employee to fully notify pilot of forecasted adverse weather conditions during a pre-flight briefing).

For the reasons discussed, we hold that *Section 46110* does not preclude the district court from hearing Merritt's FTCA claim.

Finally, we caution that our holding has no bearing on the question of whether the ALJ's determination of particular issues raised in the administrative hearing may be given issue preclusive effect by the district court upon remand. The jurisdictional preclusion effected by statutes such as *Section 46110* (as interpreted herein) is distinct from the doctrine of issue preclusion or collateral estoppel. Issue preclusion applies when "(1) the issues in both proceedings are identical, (2) the issue in the prior proceeding was actually litigated and actually decided, (3) there was full and fair opportunity to litigate in the prior proceeding, and (4) the issue previously litigated was necessary to support a valid and final judgment on the merits." *Liona Corp. v. PCH Assocs. (In re PCH Assocs.), 949 F.2d 585, 593 (2d Cir. 1991)*. Statutes such as *Section 46110*, in contrast, preclude district courts from deciding issues that "could and should have been" raised in an administrative proceeding or at least in a court of appeals, not merely those that were actually considered and necessarily decided in the administrative proceeding. *City of Tacoma, 357 U.S. at 339.*

CONCLUSION

For the reasons discussed, the district court's judgment dismissing Merritt's FTCA claim for lack of subject matter jurisdiction is reversed, and the case is remanded for further proceedings consistent with this opinion.

MARION C. BLAKEY, Administrator, Federal Aviation Administration v. CHARLES FRANCIS DRESS.

No. EA-5115;
Docket SE-16768

National Transportation Safety Board

October, 2004

Respondent and the Administrator have both appealed from the oral initial decision of Administrative Law Judge William E. Fowler, Jr., issued on June 4, 2003, following an evidentiary hearing. The law judge affirmed alleged violations of 14 C.F.R. 91.103 and 91.141, but dismissed the alleged violation of section 91.13(a), and modified the sanction from a 150-day suspension, as requested by the Administrator, to a 100-day suspension of respondent's pilot certificate. We grant respondent's appeal, deny the Administrator's appeal, and dismiss the complaint.

It is undisputed that on November 20, 2001, respondent was the pilot in command of a PA-28-161 on an instructional flight from Northeast Philadelphia Airport to Hagerstown, Maryland, and that the flight penetrated an area of prohibited airspace known as P-40. It is further undisputed that the radius of area P-40, which encircles the Presidential retreat of Camp David, had been temporarily expanded from 3 miles to 8 miles, after September 11, 2001. While the original prohibited area (which respondent's flight did not penetrate) was depicted on sectional aeronautical charts published by the Department of Transportation, no government publications were available prior to respondent's November 20 flight that depicted or referred to the expanded prohibited area. The temporary expansion was announced by way of a NOTAM, the contents of which were supposed to have been conveyed to affected pilots by Flight Service Station (FSS) briefers during pre-flight briefings.

Respondent and his student both stated they were aware of the existence of the P-40 prohibited airspace (as published on the sectional chart with a 3-mile radius), and that they discussed it as part of their pre-flight planning. However, respondent's student, who obtained the pre-flight briefing, testified that the FSS briefer did not mention the NOTAM pertaining to the expansion of P-40 during the briefing. No recording of the briefing or any other FAA record of its contents was available, because no preservation request was made within the 15-day window that such records are routinely maintained.

The Administrator argues that the evidence supports a finding that the NOTAM information was provided during the briefing, citing witness testimony describing the prescribed process by which FSS briefers were supposed to retrieve and disseminate relevant NOTAM information to pilots during the time period at issue, and asserting that there is a presumption of regularity in the official acts of public officials. The Administrator argues that it is more likely that the student made a mistake and missed the NOTAM information than it is that the FSS briefer made a mistake in failing to provide the information.

In affirming the violations of section 91.103 and 91.141, the law judge suggested that the respondent may have shown a lack of care, judgment, and responsibility in relying on his student to obtain the FSS briefing. However, in dismissing the section 91.13(a) charge and reducing the sanction, the law judge stated he had "a feeling that if NOTAMs had been mentioned to the student he would have conveyed that" to respondent. (Transcript (Tr.) 215.) Further, in finding that respondent's entry into prohibited airspace was inadvertent, the law judge stated that he was aware of other cases in which the FAA failed to disseminate NOTAM information to pilots. Accordingly, although the law judge did not make a direct finding as to the content of the briefing, the law judge appears to have implicitly concluded that the FSS briefer did not provide the NOTAM information.

Respondent contends that the law judge's implicit finding that the NOTAM information was not provided in this instance is supported by the weight of the evidence. Respondent argues that he should not be held responsible for violating an airspace restriction about which neither he nor his student had been given notice. He also argues that a negative inference as to the content of the briefing is appropriate in cases such as this when the Administrator does not preserve the briefing tapes.

We agree with respondent that the law judge's apparent finding that the briefer did not provide the NOTAM information is supported by the evidence in this case. While official acts may be entitled to a presumption of regularity, it was not unreasonable for the law judge to find that this presumption was overcome by the testimony that the NOTAM information was not provided on this occasion, especially in light of the other evidence in the record. Specifically, we note the dramatic increase in NOTAM information that briefers had to assimilate and summarize in the aftermath of September 11, and the FAA's acknowledgment that there have been other instances in which pilots have not been informed of temporary NOTAM restrictions. In light of these factors, and given the absence of any official record documenting the contents of the briefing, a conclusion that the information was not given in this instance is not unreasonable.

However, we do not agree with respondent that the Administrator's failure to preserve the briefing tape should automatically result in an adverse inference. Nonetheless, we note that in cases involving airspace violations potentially related to national security, such as this one, taking timely action to preserve briefing tapes would clearly aid the Administrator not only in litigating subsequent enforcement cases, but also in improving quality control regarding the transmittal of such information and, thereby, potentially improving safety and security. The heightened security concerns associated with violations of prohibited airspace following the events of September 11, 2001, and the seriousness with which FAA and law enforcement agencies address such violations would seem to dictate extra care in preserving evidence.

The Air Traffic Manager at the local FSS testified that briefing tapes are preserved only if there is a request or a formal complaint within 15 days of the briefing. According to the Administrator, it currently takes 20 days for information about a potential enforcement action to reach the Flight Standards District Office responsible for processing the case. But other arms of the Federal government, including the FAA's air traffic control service, knew immediately of

261

respondent's airspace violation and, presumably, that it would likely result in an eventual enforcement action.

In any event, if, as indicated in this case by the weight of the evidence, the briefer did not provide the NOTAM information, it is inappropriate to hold respondent responsible for violating its prohibition. See *Graves and Davis, 3 NTSB 3900, 3903 (1981)* (no violation when the respondent's inadvertent entry into restricted area resulted from reliance on erroneous information). Pilots are not held to a standard of strict liability. Administrator v. Rolund, Order Denying Reconsideration, NTSB Order No. EA-4123 at 5 (1994), citing Administrator v. Frohmuth and Dworak, NTSB Order No. EA-3816 (1993).

Further, if the briefing was deficient, then it is of little import whether respondent or his student called for the briefing. However, we do not endorse respondent's position that it was reasonable for him to rely on his student (who at that time had only 26 hours of flight time) to obtain the briefing. In light of the student's inexperience and the highly-charged nature of airspace security concerns that prevailed in the aftermath of September 11, we believe respondent would have been well-advised (even if he were not required) to independently verify the pre-flight planning information provided to him by the student.

In light of our granting of respondent's appeal, we need not address the issues raised by the Administrator's appeal.

ACCORDINGLY, IT IS ORDERED THAT:

1. Respondent's appeal is granted;

2. The Administrator's appeal is denied; and

3. The Administrator's complaint is dismissed.

MARION C. BLAKEY, Administrator, Federal Aviation Administration, v. LOWELL G. PATE and LEANNA J. YODER.

No. EA-5105;
Dockets SE-16583 and SE-16590
National Transportation Safety Board

July, 2004

Respondents appeal the written initial decision of Administrative Law Judge William R. Mullins, issued on October 29, 2002. By that decision, the law judge affirmed the Administrator's Orders of Suspension charging violations of sections 91.123(b) and 91.13(a) of the Federal Aviation Regulations (FARs) and imposing, respectively, a 15-day and 7-day suspension against respondent Pate's and respondent Yoder's Airline Transport Pilot certificates. We grant the appeal.

Prior to the hearing, respondents admitted all factual allegations in the Administrator's Orders of Suspension. Briefly, on May 19, 2000, respondent Pate was pilot-in-command and respondent Yoder was second-in-command of United Airlines Flight 1711, a Boeing 737-522. As Flight 1171 approached Cedar Rapids, Iowa, its destination, Flight 1171 was instructed to, and did, descend to and maintain 2,500 feet. Subsequently, Flight 1171 was instructed to turn to a heading of 50 degrees. However, Flight 1171 turned to a heading of 250 degrees and climbed to 3,000 feet. As a result, there was a loss of "standard separation" when respondents' aircraft came within 500 feet vertically and two and one-half miles laterally of another airliner, Trans World Airlines Flight 541.

The ATC transcript, verified by respondents as accurate, is a part of the record. At the relevant time period, according to the transcript, Flight 1171's last assigned altitude was 2,500 feet and the last assigned heading was 360 degrees. Thereafter, the following exchange occurred:

> CID Apch -- 1171, roger, plan runway 13, I'll tell you what, make the heading 050, I'll bring you up on a left downwind at 13.
>
> UALA 1171 -- OK, 050.
>
> CID Apch -- United 1171, they just said runway 9's available. I guess you probably want to stick with that? 2500 on the altitude.
>
> UALA 1171 -- Yeah, we'll do that.
>
> CID Apch -- 1171, roger. What heading are you on.
>
> UALA 1171 -- Just turned left here. We'll come, we'll, I'll tell you what. Let's go to Cindy [intersection], we'll do a right 270 and land that way, OK.

CID Apch -- That's fine with me, and just to verify, your traffic 2 o'clock and 3 miles, you're at 2500, right?

UALA 1171 -- Ah, we're going back down to it [sic] little bit.

CID Apch -- And you got that traffic in sight?

UALA 1171 -- I don't have him but we're going back down to 2500.

Upon a joint motion filed by the parties, the case proceeded without a hearing, and, after the parties submitted briefs, the law judge reviewed the Administrator's Orders of Suspension only as to respondents' "affirmative defense of entitlement to waiver of sanction.

Before the law judge, respondents argued that *Administrator v. Brasher, 5 NTSB 2116 (1987),* requires that no sanction be imposed for the FAR violations because Air Traffic Control ("ATC") personnel did not provide a timely "deviation" notice. Respondents cite to paragraph 2-1-26 ("Pilot Deviation Notification") of FAA Order No. 7110.65M ("Air Traffic Control") which states: "When it appears that the actions of a pilot constitute a pilot deviation, notify the pilot, workload permitting. Phraseology - (Identification) POSSIBLE PILOT DEVIATION ADVISE YOU CONTACT (facility) AT (telephone number)."

Respondents also argued that ATC's failure to provide a deviation notice precluded them from taking advantage of the sanction waiver benefits of filing a report pursuant to the Aviation Safety Reporting System ("ASRS"). Respondents' July 2, 2002 Amended Answer and Affirmative Defense to the Administrator's complaint admitted all numerated factual allegations, and premised their "affirmative defense" on the "Brasher doctrine." In doing so, respondents specifically complained that "as a direct consequence of the controller's failure to comply with the Administrator's notice requirement ... respondents failed to avail themselves of the immunity protections available under the [ASRS]." The purpose of the ASRS is not to grant immunity. Cf. Brasher at footnote 8 (1987) ("we take note of the assertion of the Administrator ... that the purpose of immediately notifying pilots of possible deviation is not to allow that pilot to file a timely report under [ASRS] and thus gain the immunity conferred by that program"). Were ASRS the only basis for respondents' appeal, it would fail. However, we accept, over the objections of the Administrator, respondents' counsel's assertion on appeal that respondents "elected to admit the facts alleged ... but relied on the Board's well-established Brasher doctrine as an affirmative defense because their ability to defend their actions had been prejudiced by the FAA's failure to timely notify them of any deviation." Respondents' Brief at 2.

The law judge rejected these arguments, and affirmed the Orders of Suspension.

On appeal, respondents essentially repeat the Brasher argument they raised before the law judge. The Administrator urges us to uphold the law judge's decision.

Our review of Brasher, and the other cases cited by the parties that resolved similar issues of ATC notice, establishes that a failure by ATC to provide a required notice of a deviation generally requires that sanction be waived for the associated FAR violation. See, e.g., Administrator v. McIntosh & Spriggs, NTSB Order No. EA-4174 at 12 (1994) ("the remedy for non-compliance with the [ATC] notice requirement is to impose no sanction for the violation, not dismissal of the charges") (internal citations omitted).

On April 30, 2004, the parties were asked to provide supplemental information about "whether, at the time of the incident in the subject appeal, there was any published guidance or requirement concerning Air Traffic Control ("ATC") notice to pilots observed to have deviated from a clearance or instruction." The parties were also instructed to provide information about "the current status of the notice of deviation policy discussed in [Brasher], any superceding provision or policy if that one is no longer extant, and any regulatory or administrative history applicable to the issue."

The supplemental information provided by the Administrator indicates that the ATC notification requirement (FAA Notice N7210.251) cited in Brasher is substantively the same as the ATC notification requirement set forth in the ATC manual that was in effect on May 19, 2000 (FAA Order 7110.65M).

The Administrator provides no cognizable basis to depart from the central holding of Brasher that the pilot deviation notice provisions "prescribe a duty, ... imposed on FAA employees and instituted, at least in part, for the benefit of pilots." Brasher at 2118. And, as we observed in Brasher, the Administrator specifically informed the pilot community that at least one of the purposes of the deviation notification procedures is to permit pilots to prepare a response to allegations of an ATC clearance deviation. The Administrator has not shown that this guidance has been rescinded (particularly in light of the consistently-similar phraseology specified within the FAA publications).

In view of the foregoing, we hold that respondents were entitled to a waiver of sanction under the rationale of Brasher because they were not notified of an ATC deviation in accordance with the provisions of paragraph 2-1-26 of the ATC manual. We disagree with the Administrator's contention that the controller complied with the deviation notice provision when he queried respondents about their heading and altitude. Such inquiries do not provide the information required by the notice. To the extent that our opinion and order in *Administrator v. Palmquist, 6 NTSB 476 (1988),* suggests otherwise, it is overruled.

ACCORDINGLY, IT IS ORDERED THAT:

1. Respondents' appeal is granted;

2. The law judge's decision as to sanction is vacated; and

3. The Administrator's Orders of Suspension are affirmed, but sanction is waived.

MARION C. BLAKEY, Administrator, Federal Aviation
Administration, v. GREGORY ALAN SIMMONS

No.EA-5275;
Docket No. SE-17468

National Transportation Safety Board

March 26, 2007

Respondent appeals the oral initial decision of Administrative Law
Judge Patrick G. Geraghty, issued February 1, 2006, following a
hearing limited to the issue of sanction. By that decision, the law judge
affirmed the 240-day suspension of respondent's private pilot certificate
for respondent's violation of sections 91.13(a), 91.111(a), and 91.155(a)
of the Federal Aviation Regulations (FAR). Respondent has appealed
the law judge's order with regard to sanction. We deny respondent's
appeal.

The Administrator's order alleged the following facts and
circumstances:

> 1. You are now, and at all times mentioned herein were,
> the holder of Private Pilot Certificate No. 483942326.

> 2. On or about December 31, 2002, you acted as pilot in
> command of a Beech Baron aircraft, N82LB, that
> departed from the Telluride Regional Airport, Colorado
> under visual flight rules (VFR).

> 3. After your departure you headed towards the Cones
> VOR and, while in Class E airspace, you failed to
> maintain the required VFR cloud clearance.

> 4. You entered instrument meteorological conditions
> without activating your IFR flight plan and obtaining the
> appropriate ATC clearance.

> 5. You passed within 400 - 700 feet of a passenger
> carrying commercial aircraft creating a collision hazard.

> 6. Your operation of N82LB as described above was
> careless or reckless, endangering the lives and property
> of others.

Based on these alleged violations, the Administrator ordered
respondent's private pilot certificate suspended for 240 days. After the
Administrator issued this order, respondent failed to file a timely
answer. The Administrator subsequently filed a motion for summary
judgment, and Chief Administrative Law Judge William E. Fowler, Jr.
partially granted the motion and deemed the factual allegations of the
complaint to be admitted. The chief law judge's order also partially
denied the motion with regard to the issue of sanction, and ordered a
hearing, at which parties could, "present evidence both in support and

in mitigation of [the 240-day] sanction." Order Granting in Part Administrator's Mot. for J. on the Pleadings and Limiting Hr'g to the Issue of Sanction (Oct. 21, 2005) at 7. Subsequently, the Safety Board's Office of Administrative Law Judges assigned this case to Administrative Law Judge Patrick G. Geraghty to resolve the issue of appropriate sanction. Judge Geraghty conducted a hearing on February 1, 2006, and upheld the imposition of the 240-day suspension.

At the hearing, the Administrator called Captain Matthew Ian Rapp, who acted as captain of the Great Lakes Airlines flight on December 31, 2002, that respondent closely passed. Captain Rapp verified that respondent closely passed over the Great Lakes flight on Captain Rapp's approach into Telluride. Captain Rapp also testified that he notified Great Lakes Airlines, which in turn informed the appropriate Flight Standards District Office of the close proximity within which respondent's aircraft passed him. Transcript (Tr.) 19; Exhibit (Exh.) R-6. The Administrator also called FAA Inspector Carl Miller, who testified that respondent had filed an IFR flight plan, but, when attempting to activate the plan, learned that, "there would be a significant delay and he was like number four for departure." Tr. 31. Respondent never activated the IFR flight plan. Id. Inspector Miller also testified that he referred to the Administrator's Sanction Guidance Table, and stated that he relied on the Table when proposing the 240-day suspension, as well as FAA Advisory Circular 00-46D, which sets forth the requirements for the Aviation Safety Reporting Program (ASRP), because respondent had timely filed a report under the ASRP. See Tr. 32, 44. Inspector Miller stated that, after concluding his investigation into the events described herein, he determined that respondent did not qualify for a sanction waiver under the ASRP. Tr. 45. Inspector Miller stated that he reached this conclusion because he "felt that this violation ... was deliberate and it was intentional." Id. Finally, on rebuttal, the Administrator called Mr. Mike Aronovich, who, as a pilot for Great Lakes Airlines on December 31, 2002, observed respondent's flight from the ground. Mr. Aronovich testified that the weather conditions in and around Telluride "[were] not suitable for VFR flight" in his judgment. Tr. 80. Mr. Aronovich also described the conditions in and around Telluride as "dynamic," and stated that, "the weather was very, very marginal out to the west, because it is a boxed canyon," and that, "just a mile or two miles away to the west the clouds could be obscuring the area completely." Tr. 82. Mr. Aronovich concluded that, in his opinion, "[t]he weather was very marginal." Id.

Respondent testified that he departed under VFR, and never intended to fly in IFR conditions. We note that this claim is at odds with respondent's decision to file an IFR flight plan. Respondent stated that he was surprised by his entry into IMC conditions. Tr. 56. We note that the record indicates that the flight at issue occurred in daylight conditions. See Exh. R-10 (NASA Aviation Safety Reporting System Identification Strip, listing the time of occurrence as 10:30 am).

Respondent also stated that he had instrument charts in his aircraft, but that they were on the floor of the aircraft and he did not use them for the flight. Tr. 59. Respondent then called Mr. Adam Peck, who was the sole passenger who accompanied respondent during the flight that is the subject of this appeal. Mr. Peck testified that, within 2 to 3 minutes after taking off, respondent was "in the clouds." Tr. 67.

Finally, respondent called Mr. Paul Mackey to provide expert testimony, as an independent aviation consultant, with regard to whether respondent's report pursuant to the ASRP should qualify as an affirmative defense, and other potentially mitigating factors. Mr. Mackey opined that the respondent's reporting of the incident to the National Aeronautics and Space Administration (NASA) met the requirements of the ASRP, and that such reporting should obviate the imposition of any sanction against respondent. Tr. 74. Mr. Mackey also stated that he had reviewed the evidence in the record for this case, and that he believed that respondent's actions were, "unintentional and inadvertent." Id.

The law judge, in evaluating whether respondent's report to NASA of the incident obviated the need for a sanction under the ASRP, concluded that respondent's actions were reckless; therefore, the law judge held that a 240-day suspension of respondent's private pilot certificate was appropriate. In his decision, the law judge summarized the evidence in the record, stating that respondent's close encounter with Captain Rapp's aircraft was foreseeable and not inadvertent, because the VMC conditions were marginal and IMC conditions were present to the west. The law judge stated, "[p]roceeding directly out on the reciprocal of the inbound localizer in IMC conditions not knowing whether or not another aircraft is making the approach is a foreseeable hazard. You're taking the chance that nobody's coming in." Tr. 102. In rejecting respondent's claim that he inadvertently entered IMC conditions, the law judge emphasized that respondent's unapproved entry into IMC conditions caused a significant, foreseeable risk under the circumstances:

> In my view, it was foreseeable on the conditions as they have been established on what I believe the credible and reliable evidence as to the marginality of the VMC conditions at the airport and the fact that it's not disputed that IMC conditions were to the west ... In my view, therefore, that the departure by the Respondent and climbing out into IMC conditions, not contacting anybody to alert them to the fact, and continuing on the reciprocal when it was reasonable to also assume that other aircraft could be coming in, and whether or not they were he didn't know ... [was] not an inadvertent encounter with IMC.

The law judge concluded, therefore, that respondent operated the aircraft in a reckless manner. Id. The law judge upheld the Administrator's choice of sanction, noting that the Board typically shows deference to the choice of sanction, and that the gravity of respondent's near-miss with another aircraft warranted upholding the Administrator's choice of sanction. The law judge also noted that such a sanction was consistent with the public interest in aviation safety, as it would hopefully act as a deterrent to other operators. Tr. 102-103. Respondent demonstrates no error, nor do we discern one, in the law judge's analysis and conclusion. Accordingly, the record affords no basis to disturb the law judge's decision regarding sanction.

On appeal, respondent presents three issues. Respondent argues that the law judge's failure to allow respondent to cross-examine the Administrator's witnesses and place ATC tape recordings in the record denied respondent due process. Respondent also argues that the law judge's affirmation of the sanction was contrary to the weight of the evidence. Finally, respondent argues that the law judge misinterpreted the applicable Safety Board case law, precedent, and policy with regard to the imposition of sanction after respondent reported the incident in accordance with the ASRP. The Administrator opposes each of respondent's arguments, and urges the Board to affirm the law judge's decision concerning sanction.

The Board allows law judges significant discretion in overseeing administrative hearings. See 49 C.F.R. § 821.35(b); Administrator v. Kachalsky, NTSB Order No. EA-4847 at n.4 (2000); see also Administrator v. Reese, NTSB Order No. EA-4896 at n.4 (2001). A careful review of the transcript of the administrative hearing indicates that the law judge did allow respondent's counsel to cross-examine witnesses, and that he appropriately considered allowing respondent's counsel to place the relevant ATC tape recordings into evidence. The law judge concluded that respondent's counsel did not articulate how the ATC tape recordings would be relevant to sanction, and we find no error in the law judge's conclusion.

Respondent further contends that the law judge erred in not allowing respondent's counsel to cross-examine Inspector Miller with regard to how the inspector conducted his investigation into the allegations, and that the law judge should not have allowed Inspector Miller to mention the ATC recordings. These arguments are irrelevant to the issue of sanction and are meritless. Overall, after a careful review of the transcript of this hearing, we find that the law judge's conclusions with regard to the scope of the testimony and the cross-examination were not erroneous.

In addition, respondent argues that the weight of the evidence does not support some of the factual conclusions on which the law judge based his analysis. However, the chief law judge's previous order that partially granted summary judgment in favor of the Administrator already established the facts of the case. Overall, we find that respondent's assortment of arguments regarding the law judge's conclusions concerning the weight of the evidence, and evidentiary rulings at the hearing, are not persuasive.

Finally, respondent argues that the law judge was obligated to waive the sanction for respondent's violations under the ASRP, and that this failure to waive the sanction is contrary to law, precedent, and policy. The law judge carefully considered the application of the ASRP to the facts of the instant case, and concluded that, although respondent had filed a timely report with NASA, his operation of the aircraft in the IMC environment was not inadvertent. The law judge stated that, when one places oneself at a significantly increased risk of committing a violation, then the violation is foreseeable and therefore not inadvertent. Tr. 99-100. We find that the relevant case law supports this conclusion. We have long held that the ASRP will not obviate the imposition of a sanction when an operator's conduct is deliberate or

269

intentional such that it reflects a "wanton disregard of the safety of others" or a "gross disregard for safety." *Administrator v. Fay, 7 NTSB 951, 956 (1991);* see also *Ferguson v. NTSB, 678 F.2d 821 (9th Cir. 1982); Administrator v. Understein, 3 NTSB 3552, 3558,* order den. recon., *3 NTSB 3564 (1981).* We have also stated that, in general, the ASRP was never designed to protect those who exhibit a reckless disregard for safety. Administrator v. Halbert, NTSB Order No. EA-3628 at 3 (1992). The law judge elaborated on the characterization of intentional, reckless, and deliberate behavior, and then applied the Board's precedent regarding such behavior to the facts of this case. Tr. 99-102. In addition, Mr. Mackey's expert testimony was cursory and did not provide persuasive justification for a waiver of sanction under the ASRP. Therefore, we do not agree with respondent's argument that the law judge's conclusions were contrary to law, precedent, or policy.

Respondent's close proximity to Captain Rapp's aircraft at the time of the relevant events presents a significant safety issue. Moreover, respondent entered the IMC area very soon after taking off, and the approach plate shows that respondent proceeded over 2,000 vertical feet while in IMC conditions without the requisite ATC clearance. Even though respondent had filed for an IFR flight plan, he never activated it, and then encountered IMC conditions that were foreseeable. Overall, the facts on this record indicate that respondent's encounter with the IMC area was reckless. We find that waiving the sanction in this case would be inconsistent with our precedent regarding sanction waivers in response to ASRP reports. Specifically, *Understein, 3 NTSB at 3558,* contains facts that are closely similar to the factual background of the case at issue here, and in that case, we concluded that the respondent's takeoff into clouds without proper IFR clearance was reckless, and that, as a result, he was not within the grant of immunity that the ASRP provides. *Id. at 3555.* In Understein, we also cited previous case law for the rule that, when an airman files a report pursuant to the ASRP, "a pilot can only be exonerated from full responsibility for unintentional flight into IFR weather when the IFR weather conditions are unforeseeable and not avoidable by the exercise of sound [judgment] both before and during the flight." *Id. at 3558* (citing *Administrator v. Hollis, 2 NTSB 43 (1973)).*

On the record of the case at hand, the facts indicate that IFR conditions were foreseeable to many witnesses and airmen in the area, and that respondent's entry into IFR weather conditions was avoidable, because respondent could have activated his IFR flight plan or otherwise arranged to avoid the area. Therefore, in spite of respondent's reporting of the incident in accordance with the ASRP, we find that, on this record and based on our precedent, respondent's unapproved entry into IMC and close proximity to another aircraft was foreseeable, and waiver of sanction under the ASRP would be inappropriate. The Board finds that safety in air commerce or air transportation and the public interest requires the affirmation of the law judge's decision.

ACCORDINGLY, IT IS ORDERED THAT:

1. Respondent's appeal is denied; and

2. The 240-day suspension of respondent's private pilot certificate shall begin 30 days after the service date indicated on this opinion and order.

ROBERT A. STURGELL, Acting Administrator, Federal Aviation Administration v. SPENCER A. MURPHY and DENNIS S. VERNICK

No. EA-5355;

National Transportation Safety Board

January 16, 2008,

The Administrator has appealed from the written initial decision and order of Administrative Law Judge William A. Pope, II, issued on November 22, 2006, following an evidentiary hearing held on November 14-15, 2006. The law judge granted respondents' appeals and, although he found that the respondents committed most violations as alleged, reversed the Administrator's orders of suspension, and dismissed the complaints. The Administrator had alleged that Respondent Murphy violated 14 C.F.R. §§ 91.13(a), 91.123(b), and 91.111(a); and that Respondent Vernick violated those sections in addition to §§ 91.123(a) and 91.183(c). Section 91.13(a) states that no person may operate an aircraft in a careless or reckless manner so as to endanger the life or property of another. Section 91.111(a) states that no person may operate an aircraft so close to another aircraft as to create a collision hazard. Section 91.123(a) states that when a pilot obtains an ATC clearance, he may not deviate from that clearance, except in an emergency, unless an amended clearance is obtained or the deviation is in response to a traffic alert and collision avoidance system resolution advisory. Section 91.123(b) states that, except in an emergency, no person may operate an aircraft contrary to an ATC instruction in an area in which air traffic control is exercised. Section 91.183(c) requires a pilot-in-command of an aircraft operated under IFR [instrument flight rules] in controlled airspace to maintain a continuous watch on the appropriate frequency and to report by radio as soon as possible any information relating to the safety of flight.

The Administrator proposed 60-day suspensions of Respondent Murphy's commercial pilot certificate and of Respondent Vernick's airline transport pilot certificate. We grant the Administrator's appeal.

Facts

We adopt the law judge's summary of evidence and factual findings of fact as our own. A recounting of pertinent facts, however, is in order. On April 17, 2005, Respondent Vernick was pilot-in-command and Respondent Murphy was second-in-command of a Lear 35 aircraft, number N89TC. After receiving an air traffic control (ATC) clearance to climb to 26,000 feet (Exh. A-2 (ATC transcript) at 4), they leveled off at 26,000 feet, and Respondent Murphy, who was at the controls, testified that he engaged the autopilot. When he checked the altitude indicator, they were 120 feet above the assigned altitude. Respondent Vernick, performing pilot-not-flying duties, noticed the altitude-hold function was not on. N89TC had already arrested the ascent and started back down to 26,000 feet. Tr. at 341-42; see Exh. A-2 at 5-6.

In the meantime, a conflict alert activated on the air traffic controller's radar screen as to N89TC and a Canadair Bombardier

CRJ2, FLG5700, meaning that data blocks on his radar screen started to flash in unison. The data blocks showed N89TC was at 26,300 feet, and FLG5700 was at its assigned altitude of 27,000 feet. The controller contacted respondents and asked them to verify they were at 26,000 feet. Respondent Vernick advised they were back at 26,000 feet. Exh. A-2 at 5-6. The controller testified that, because N89TC had already descended back to the assigned altitude, he took no other control actions. Tr. at 107. The parties stipulated this was a computer-detected altitude deviation. The separation criteria in the en route environment are 5 miles of lateral separation or 1,000 feet of vertical separation. At the time of the activation, the separation between the aircraft was 3.4 miles laterally and 700 feet vertically. A radar track analysis showed the aircraft were both generally proceeding to the southeast on converging courses.

FAA Order 2150.3A, Compliance and Enforcement Program, Compliance/Enforcement Bulletin No. 86-1 (86-1) (Exh. R-1), discusses computer-detected altitude deviations of 500 feet or less. It states that:

> . . . a computer detected altitude deviation of 500 feet or less, where no near midair collision resulted, should normally be addressed by means of administrative action, unless a prior altitude deviation occurred within 2 years of the date of the subject altitude deviation or other aggravating circumstances require initiation of legal enforcement action. In determining whether a violation is "aggravated," all circumstances surrounding the incident (e.g., whether the deviation was deliberate or inadvertent, the hazard to safety, etc.) shall be considered.

Hearing and Written Initial Decision

At the hearing, the Administrator presented the testimony of the controller, David Gish; the aviation safety inspector who investigated the incident, Robert Rogers; the quality assurance specialist who prepared the track analysis, Paula Peters; the operations manager, John Reider; and the controller's supervisor, Todd Moore. Mr. Rogers testified that the loss of standard separation between aircraft is an aggravating circumstance under 86-1 if the loss is 100 feet or more, and that the loss of separation here created a safety hazard because N89TC penetrated the separation bubble around FLG5700. He pointed out that the aircraft were on converging courses. Mr. Moore defined "collision hazard" as "aircraft operating . . . with less-than-standard separation," but admitted that the term is not defined in FAA regulations. Tr. at 348-49.

Respondents presented the testimony of Jack Overman, a former FAA air traffic controller; Francis DeJoseth, a former FAA flight standards inspector; and the respondents, themselves. Respondents offered into evidence Advisory Circular 00-46C, Aviation Safety Reporting Program (ASRP), and verifications that timely ASRP reports were filed. Mr. Overman gave his opinion that the criteria in 86-1 were met, that the altitude deviation did not create a collision hazard, and that the Administrator should have issued a warning letter. Mr. DeJoseth testified that he would have resolved the case with a warning letter because he did not think there were any aggravating circumstances. He reached that conclusion because there was no urgency in the voice of the controller, who did not issue a turn to either aircraft. Tr. at 305.

The law judge found that Respondent Murphy violated the alleged FAR provisions, and that Respondent Vernick violated all but § 91.183(c). The law judge further found that there were no aggravating circumstances that would "make the Respondents ineligible under [86-1] for administrative action, rather than enforcement action." Written Initial Decision at 8. He also found "that the Respondents meet all of the criteria for application of the Administrator's policy of handling altitude deviations administratively," and that, "[b]y bringing this matter as an enforcement action, and not handling it administratively, the Administrator violated her policy set out in [86-1], and deprived the Respondents of the benefits they were entitled to under that FAA policy," and he therefore dismissed the complaints. Id. at 9-10.

Appeal

Because of our disposition of the appeal, we address only one of the Administrator's arguments. The Administrator argues that his exercise of prosecutorial discretion is not subject to Board review. Administrator's Appeal Br. at 18-22. He contends that the law judge substituted his judgment for that of the Administrator to elect one remedy over another; that it is the Administrator's prerogative to issue an order of suspension when the facts support one; and that the Board has no direct authority over his exercise of prosecutorial discretion. Id. at 18-19.

Respondents contest the arguments in the Administrator's appeal and urge the Board to affirm the law judge's decision. They argue that due process of law binds the Administrator to follow the policy adopted in 86-1. Respondents' Reply at 25-36. Respondents contest the Administrator's argument that 86-1 applies only to computer-detected altitude violations discovered through the Air Traffic Quality Assurance Program. Id. at 36-38. Finally, respondents dispute the Administrator's argument that their altitude deviation involved aggravating circumstances. Id. at 39-40.

Discussion and Analysis

The Board will not review the Administrator's determination to pursue a matter through legal enforcement action. This is a matter of jurisdiction. Jurisdiction "commences with the filing of a petition for review of an order of the Administrator and does not extend to an evaluation of the procedural steps leading to the issuance of that order." The Board's charter prevents that. The discretion to pursue one remedy over another or to pursue enforcement action at all is within the Administrator's purview.

The law judge states that it is "well established that the Administrator is bound to follow her own regulations and policies." Written Initial Decision at 10, citing *Steenholdt v. FAA, 314 F.3d 633*

(D.C. Cir. 2003), and *Lopez v. FAA, 318 F.3d 242, 249 (D.C. Cir. 2003).* Respondents also cite those cases. We have reviewed those cases and have determined that reliance on them, for analyzing the instant case, is misplaced. Although noting that agencies are required to follow their own rules, the D.C. Circuit, in Steenholdt, denied a petition for review of a decision of the FAA not to renew the authority to examine aircraft repairs for compliance with airworthiness regulations (not related to a certificate action appealable to this Board). The court held that the decision "is committed to agency discretion by law," and that the court *did not have jurisdiction* to review the substance of the FAA's decision. *Steenholdt, 314 F.3d at 634, 640.* The Lopez court also denied such a petition for review upon finding that it did not have jurisdiction.

Respondents and the law judge also cite two *Board cases. In Administrator v. Randall, 3 NTSB 3624 (1981),* the only evidence that supported the Administrator's alleged violations came from flight data recorder (FDR) tapes, which inspectors specifically reviewed for the sole purpose of pursuing enforcement action. The respondent objected to use of the tapes based on FAA policy, set forth in the Compliance and Enforcement Program manual (Order 2150.3). That policy stated, among other things, that, ". . . flight recorder tapes will not be utilized as a means to discover violations when the FAA has no other evidence of possible violations; and flight recorder tapes will not be used as evidence in an FAA enforcement action except for the purpose of corroborating other available evidence or to resolve conflicting evidence." *Randall, supra at 3625.* The Board would not allow the Administrator to rely on the tapes as evidence in its enforcement action. *Administrator v. Brasher, 5 NTSB 2116 (1987),* as in the instant case, involved an altitude deviation, and resulted in what is now known as the "Brasher warning." The Board noted that FAA Notice N7210.251, "System Evaluation of Pilot Deviations as a Result of Operational Error Detection Alerts," instructed ATC to notify the pilot, with specific phraseology, when a possible deviation had occurred. Brasher, supra at 2116-17. The law judge there found that the Administrator proved FAR violations, but concluded no sanction should be imposed "because the FAA failed to comply with its own policy of notifying the pilot immediately when a deviation has occurred." Id. at 2116. The Board denied the Administrator's appeal, finding that, "the law judge's application of *Notice 7210.251* was consistent both with the circumstances of this case and with Board precedent . . . ." Id. at 2119.

Randall and Brasher did not involve prosecutorial discretion at the point of the initiation of enforcement action. As the Board noted in Randall, "the conclusion that the FAA was not free to use a specific item of evidence has absolutely no bearing on the agency's right to prosecute the respondent for the alleged violations." Randall, supra at n.6. A similar rationale applies to the waiver of imposition of sanction in Brasher. Our review of Brasher and like cases establishes that a failure by ATC to provide a required notice of a deviation requires that sanction be waived for that violation, not that enforcement action for the violation be waived or dismissed. The Board, in Randall and Brasher, did not address the Administrator's prosecutorial discretion to pursue an enforcement action. The Board addressed only the evidence that could be used to support the action and the sanction that could be imposed, respectively--the Board did not address the decision to bring the action.

We apply a similar principle today. The Board does not have jurisdiction to review the Administrator's discretion in choosing to bring an enforcement action against a respondent. We reject respondents' arguments that 86-1 precluded the Administrator from pursuing enforcement actions against respondents. In sum, the Board finds that the law judge's application of Bulletin No. 86-1 was not consistent with the Board's statutory charter or with Board precedent, and his decision in that regard is reversed.

Sanction

As to sanction, the Board finds that safety in air commerce or air transportation and the public interest do not require affirmation of the Administrator's sanction, and we will apply a waiver of sanction, for the following reasons. The Administrator did not introduce the Sanction Guidance Table, FAA Order 2150.3A, Compliance and Enforcement Program, Appendix, into evidence at the hearing. It is the Administrator's burden under the FAA Civil Penalty Administrative Assessment Act n13 to articulate the sanction sought, and to ask that the Board defer to that determination, supporting the request with evidence showing that the sanction has not been selected arbitrarily, capriciously, or contrary to law. It is "the Administrator's obligation explicitly and timely to raise the deference argument." Next, we concur with the law judge's comments as to the circumstances surrounding respondents' violations that tend to make the offenses seem less serious: "In the instant case, while it is clear that while there was a loss of separation, there was no near mid-air collision, as defined in the Aeronautical Information Manual, Exhibit R-2, at 7-6-3(b)." Written Initial Decision at 9. That definition is, "an incident associated with the operation of an aircraft in which a possibility of collision occurs as a result of proximity less than 500 feet to another aircraft. . . ." Id.; see Exh. R-2. The law judge noted that the controller "did not feel it was necessary to divert either aircraft." Id. The law judge also noted that Mr. Rogers, "although characterizing the loss of separation as an aggravating circumstance, acknowledged that the collision hazard was slight, and there was a timely correction of the altitude deviation by [respondents]." Id.; see also Tr. at 204 (Mr. Rogers defined "slight" as "[o]ne in 100,000, one in a larger number, slight."). The law judge also noted that the altitude deviation resulted in a "fairly minor loss of separation," and that the risk to safety was "minimal." Id. Finally, filing a report under the ASRP concerning a FAR violation may preclude the imposition of a sanction when: (1) the violation was inadvertent and not deliberate; (2) it did not involve a criminal offense, accident, or action at *49 U.S.C. § 44709;* (3) the person has not been found in an enforcement action to have committed a violation in the past 5 years; and (4) the person files a report within 10 days of the violation. Advisory Circular 00-46C at P 9c. The parties stipulated that respondents filed timely reports under the ASRP. Tr. at 321. The Administrator does not dispute that the ASRP waiver of sanction applies here. Based on the particular circumstances of this case and these respondents, we will apply waiver of sanction.

Conclusion

The law judge found, with the exception of one regulatory violation, that the Administrator established all of the other allegations by a preponderance of the reliable, probative, and substantial evidence. The Board concludes that safety in air commerce or air transportation and the public interest require affirmation of the law judge's findings as to the regulatory violations, and we therefore affirm his findings.

ACCORDINGLY, IT IS ORDERED THAT:

1. The Administrator's appeal is granted;

2. The law judge's decision, finding violations of all but one of the Administrator's allegations, as noted in this opinion and order and in the law judge's decision and order, is affirmed;

3. The law judge's order, as to granting respondents' appeal, reversing the Administrator's orders of suspension, and dismissing the complaints, is reversed; and

4. The Administrator's orders of suspension are affirmed, but sanction is waived.

IN RE: AIR CRASH AT LEXINGTON, KENTUCKY, AUGUST 27, 2006 RELATING TO: ALL CASES

CIVIL ACTION (MASTER FILE) NO. 5:06-CV-316 - KSF

UNITED STATES DISTRICT COURT FOR THE EASTERN DISTRICT OF KENTUCKY, CENTRAL DIVISION

January, 2008

This matter is before the Magistrate Judge on the motion of Comair, Inc. ("Comair") for a protective order against disclosure of its Aviation Safety Action Program reports and motion to quash Rule 30(b)(6) deposition notice [DE # 1200]. A telephone conference between the parties was conducted December 17, 2007 and a briefing schedule established for the motion. The deposition was continued pending a ruling on the motion for protective order. Motions by the Air Line Pilots Association ("ALPA") and the Regional Airlines Association ("RAA") to file amicus briefs were also granted. All briefs having been filed, the motion is ripe for review.

I. FACTUAL BACKGROUND AND PROCEDURAL HISTORY

On November 21, 2007, Plaintiffs noticed the deposition on December 20 of a corporate representative most knowledgeable regarding Comair's Aviation Safety Action Program ("ASAP") reports. Comair was also asked to produce:

All ASAP reports involving or in any way connected to any runway incursion; attempted take-off from a runway other than the runway for which the subject aircraft was cleared for take-off; any report relating to an aircraft lining up on an incorrect runway prior to commencing the take-off roll; any attempted take-off from a taxiway; any confusion at Blue Grass Airport regarding runway and/or taxiway configuration; and/or any report wherein a flight crew violated air traffic control instructions during ground operations.

[DE # 1105].

By way of background, ASAP reports arise from voluntary programs initiated in 1996 by the FAA whereby airline employees may report safety-related incidents to an Event Review Committee, typically consisting of a representative of the airline, the airline pilots' union and the FAA. 70 J. Air L. & Com. 83, 104 (Winter 2005). The FAA takes "no action" if the report is the only source of information. The FAA is limited to administrative action, a letter of correction or a warning notice, if the report is not the only source. In any event, the report cannot be used by the company for disciplinary action, although corrective action may be required. Id. In summary:

An ASAP provides a vehicle whereby employees or participating air carriers and repair station certificate holders can identify and report safety issues to management and to the FAA for resolution, without fear that the FAA will use reports accepted under the program to take legal enforcement action against them, or that companies will use such information to take disciplinary action.

FAA Advisory Circular No: 120-66B issued November 15, 2002. On September 3, 2003, the FAA issued Order 8000.82 providing that the FAA will not release ASAP information unless agreed to by the submitting party or unless ordered by a court of competent jurisdiction. Id. at 105. See also 49 U.S.C. § 40123.

In the present case, Comair moved on December 13, 2007, for a protective order against disclosure of any ASAP reports and to quash the 30(b)(6) deposition notice claiming that disclosure of any ASAP reports would contradict the intent of Congress and the FAA and, further, that the reports were privileged under the self-critical analysis privilege [DE # 1199]. A memorandum in support of the motion followed on December 14 in which Comair claimed that disclosure of safety information submitted to the FAA was prohibited by statute [DE # 1204, p. 4] and that there was significant public interest in protecting the reports [id., p. 6]. Comair further relied on the common law privilege recognized under FRE 501 in In re Air Crash Near Cali, Colombia on December 20, 1995, 959 F. Supp. 1529 (S.D. Fla. 1997) and Tice v. American Airlines, Inc., 192 F.R.D. 270 (N.D. Ill. 2000), as well as the self-critical analysis privilege recognized in ASARCO, Inc. v. N.L.R.B., 805 F.2d 194, 199-200 (6th Cir. 1986) where a labor union was denied an internal investigative report to use for collective bargaining. To the extent that state law governs, Comair claimed that Kentucky courts would adopt such a privilege under the facts of this case [id., p. 13]. Lastly, Comair claimed that Plaintiffs cannot show a substantial need for the ASAP reports.

The ALPA, a labor organization representing pilots employed by numerous commercial airlines, filed an amicus brief in support of Comair's motion to preclude disclosure of the ASAP reports [DE # 1253]. It noted that the United States is a party to the 1947 Convention on International Civil Aviation (also known as the Chicago Convention), which offered in 2001 "Legal Guidance for the Protection of Information From Safety Data Collection and Processing Systems" that included the use of safety information for civil proceedings against operational personnel as an "inappropriate use." [DE # 1253, Ex. 1; ANNEX 13]. The ALPA urges that use of self-reporting information for purposes other than safety "will inhibit pilots from making reports" [DE # 1253, p. 5]. It argues that pilots make reports "with the understanding that they are confidential and will be used solely for purposes of flight safety and will not be used to support litigation against themselves or their company." As authority for this understanding, it cites 49 U.S.C. § 40123 and 14 C.F.R. Part 193. Id., p. 6. The amicus brief further relies on the Declaration of Donald H. McClure, ALPA's Air Safety Coordinator, who has extensive experience with the ASAP program. Mr. McClure offers several examples of safety improvements resulting from pilots reports and opines that "the release of ASAP reports for use in litigation will have a chilling effect on this highly successful safety program and the willingness of pilots to voluntarily provide this critical safety information. . . ." Id., Ex. 2, p. 2]. The amicus brief expands on this opinion to suggest that pilots would refrain from self-reporting if it might lead to "the hostility of cross-examination, the threat of acting as [a] witness against their employer, or to the danger of their own possible civil liability." [DE # 1253, p. 7]. It further suggests that airlines would not participate "if the data has the potential to be used by litigants to support a case against the company." Id., p. 8. The ALPA also agrees with Comair that ASAP information should be protected under the self-critical analysis privilege.

The RAA, a trade association representing regional airlines, filed an amicus brief in support of Comair [DE # 1261]. It argued that the program was designed to encourage disclosure of safety information "without fear of punitive legal enforcement sanctions." [Id., p. 3]. It expressed concern the information would not be provided "if employees and carriers feared the consequences of public disclosure." Id., p. 5. It urged that disclosure of the information to civil litigants would deprive the public of the safety benefits and "contradict well-established Congressional intent." Id., p. 6. Finally, it argued that ASAP information is protected under a common law privilege and the self-critical analysis privilege. Id.

The FAA's brief in support of Comair noted that the voluntary ASAP program encourages employees to self-report their own mistakes "without fear of discipline or punishment from either the airline or FAA." [DE # 1263, pp. 1-2]. It mentioned that the reports are not subject to Freedom of Information Act ("FOIA") requests, but acknowledged that it will produce the reports where "ordered to do so by a court of competent jurisdiction" pursuant to 14 C.F.R. § 193.7(f). It suggested that airlines and employees would be less likely to report ASAP information if the reports "were not kept from public disclosure" of if they could be used for "other than safety enhancement purposes." [Id., pp. 2-3].

In response to the ALPA and RAA, Plaintiffs note that Congress has not found it necessary to make ASAP reports privileged [DE # 1286, p. 2]. The protection offered was that air crews could report safety incidents "without fear of reprisal by their employers"; it was "not to allow airlines to keep reports of safety concerns secret." Id. Plaintiffs argue that the "Amici ask this Court to do what Congress did not do: create a privilege for ASAP reports." Id. Plaintiffs note that little more than speculation supports the claims that pilots and carriers would cease participation in the program if reports were disclosed in this litigation under a protective order. Plaintiffs characterize ALPA's argument as follows: "ALPA believes that its pilots will intentionally ignore or suppress safety issues that they witness, issues which could lead to the death of hundreds of passengers, and of the pilots themselves, in order to avoid having to be deposed." Id., p. 3. Plaintiffs cite a recent article in Air Line Pilot published by ALPA stating that initially "pilots tend to send in [ASAP] reports primarily because of the reporting incentives" of no company discipline or FAA enforcement action. As they get feedback and see changes made to fix problems, they "begin to submit the sole-source reports that are the real nuggets of an ASAP program." Id., p. 4.

Plaintiffs also argue that the "goals" reflected in the federal statutes, regulations and FAA advisory circulars are to protect the reports from disclosure to the general public in response to FOIA requests and not to prohibit discovery of relevant evidence by litigants. Id. Plaintiffs say they seek the reports solely for purposes of this litigation, and that the reports would be subject to the Court's protective order for confidential documents. Id., p. 5. They claim that air safety would be undermined if carriers could refuse to take corrective action after repeated warnings of a safety issue, but then hide that information from victims harmed by the safety problem by refusing to disclose the relevant ASAP reports. Finally, Plaintiffs argue that the possibility of future reluctance to report does not warrant the extraordinary step of judicially creating a privilege where Congress felt none was necessary. Id., pp. 5-6.

Regarding the FAA's submission, Plaintiffs claim it should be disregarded because the FAA did not request permission to file a brief during the December 17 conference call. 2 They also note that the FAA confirms there is no statutory privilege and that it can be compelled by a court to produce ASAP reports. They attach significance to the absence of any FAA argument regarding a common law privilege and characterize the submission, generally, as focusing on an objection to broad, public disclosure. Id., pp. 6-7. Plaintiffs also state that the FAA has already produced ASAP post-accident reports in this litigation without objection by Comair.

In response to Comair's motion, Plaintiffs note Comair's acknowledgment that no statute or regulation creates a privilege for ASAP reports and that Kentucky does not recognize a self-critical analysis privilege [DE # 1259, p. 3]. Plaintiffs rely on FAA Advisory Circular ("AC") 120-66B which focuses on voluntary reporting "without fear that the FAA will use reports accepted under the program to take legal enforcement action against them, or that companies will use such information to take disciplinary action." Id., p. 4. The focus of FAA Order 8000.82 is to protect the reports from "public" disclosure by the FAA, but Plaintiffs say they are seeking only disclosure for purposes of this litigation and subject to the general protective order in place. Id., p. 10. Plaintiffs note that even the FAA will publically disclose ASAP reports "to correct a condition that compromises safety or security, if that condition continues uncorrected." 14 C.F.R. § 193.9.

Plaintiffs disagree that disclosure under the limited circumstances they propose would have the chilling effect urged by Comair. They argue it is in every pilot's interest to report safety issues voluntarily so that corrective action can be taken and safety for everyone, including the crew, can be further enhanced. Plaintiffs alleged in their complaints that the captain and first officer of Comair Flight 5191 committed numerous specific violations involving basic pilot practices. They claim if Comair's ASAP reports relate to those issues or to the practices of these pilots but Comair did not address those concerns, it must be held accountable for its failure. Id., p. 6.

Plaintiffs contend that state law controls the availability of privileges in this case and that Kentucky specifically declined to judicially adopt a self-critical analysis privilege. It distinguishes Comair's authorities as all arising under federal law and as not encompassing facts such as these. Id., pp. 6-8, 11-13. Even if federal law were applicable, Plaintiffs note that Comair concedes there is no statutory privilege per se for the reports. Plaintiffs claim that Congress spoke loudly with that silence. Id., p. 9.

Finally, Plaintiffs argue that, even if a self-critical analysis were to be recognized, their need for the reports outweighs any privilege [DE # 1259, pp. 13-19]. They assert that it is not fair for Comair and its witnesses to provide "selective glimpses" into the ASAP program based upon vague recollections. They note that different Comair witnesses testified inconsistently regarding the ASAP reports of incidents such as runway incursions. Id., p. 14. They cite testimony reflecting that ASAP

Coordinator Paul Vislosky had only his memory to rely upon regarding whether reports of certain types of incidents were made or might even exist. They also note that no objections regarding confidentiality were raised during questioning of Mr. Vislosky about the ASAP reports.

Comair replies relying on the Amici briefs' suggestion that "disclosure of the reports would have a crippling effect on the ASAP." [DE # 1289, p. 2]. Comair urges that the program "was built on and recognized the value of confidentiality." Id., p. 3. Comair urges the court to create a privilege for ASAP reports to protect confidentiality. Comair claims it, the ALPA, the RAA, and the FAA cannot rely on "Plaintiffs' promise that the reports will remain confidential." Id., p. 4. Comair disputes that state law provides the rule of decision in these cases and notes that some cases are brought under federal law. Id., p. 5. It further argues that a uniform, federal law should apply to any issue of privilege and urges that a common law or self-critical analysis privilege be applied. Id., pp. 6-7. Comair claims that Plaintiffs have not shown a compelling need for the reports. Id., p. 10. Finally, they reply that the prior deposition of Mr. Vislosky satisfied Plaintiffs' needs and the deposition notice should be quashed. Id., p. 11.

II. ANALYSIS

When addressing similar arguments regarding the need for confidentiality and the creation of a privilege, the United States Supreme Court said that privileges "are not lightly created nor expansively construed, for they are in derogation of the search for truth." United States v. Nixon, 418 U.S. 683, 710, 94 S. Ct. 3090, 41 L. Ed. 2d 1039 (1974). "The allowance of the privilege to withhold evidence that is demonstrably relevant in a . . . trial would cut deeply into the guarantee of due process of law and gravely impair the basic function of the courts." Id. at 712.

A. Congressional Intent to Protect ASAP Reports from Discovery by Litigants

Comair argues that "disclosure of any ASAP reports will contradict the intent of Congress as expressed in 49 U.S.C. § 40123." [DE # 1204, p. 3]. It later admits, however, that "Congress did not create a statutory privilege specifically for ASAP reports." [DE # 1289, p. 4]. Congress is well aware of how to protect sensitive aviation information from litigation discovery. It expressly prohibited discovery of cockpit voice recorder transcripts as follows:

Discovery and use of cockpit and surface vehicle recordings and transcripts

(a) Transcripts and recordings -
(1) Except as provided by this subsection, a party in a judicial proceeding may not use discovery to obtain -
(A) any part of a cockpit or surface vehicle recorder transcript that the National Transportation Safety Board has not made available to the public under section 1114(c) or 1114(d) of this title; and

(B) a cockpit or surface vehicle recorder recording.

(2) (A) Except as provided in paragraph (4)(A) of this subsection, a court may allow discovery by a party of a cockpit or surface vehicle recorder transcript if, after an in camera review of the transcript, the court decides that -
(i) the part of the transcript made available to the public under section 1114(c) or 1114(d) of this title does not provide the party with sufficient information for the party to receive a fair trial; and

(ii) discovery of additional parts of the transcript is necessary to provide the party with sufficient information for the party to receive a fair trial.
49 U.S.C. § 1154 (emphasis added). The parties are familiar with this statute, as they relied on it when Plaintiffs recently moved to compel production of the cockpit voice recorder recording [DE # 861]. As this statute reflects, when Congress believes protection from discovery is important, it says so and spells out requirements for prior in camera review and findings by a court.

By contrast, 49 U.S.C. § 40123 simply provides that the FAA, or any agency receiving information from the FAA, shall not disclose voluntarily-provided safety related information. The regulation implementing this statute, 14 C.F.R. Part 193 discusses the expressed concerns that this information, "when in the hands of a government agency, may be required to be released to the public through FOIA or other means." It also cites the legislative history regarding "reluctance to share such information if it will be publicly released because it could easily be misinterpreted, misunderstood, or misapplied." The Background discussion says that 49 U.S.C. § 40123 was added to provide "relief from these concerns." FAR Part 193 Final Rule [DE # 1288, Ex. 3]. Public disclosure is expressly provided for when it is "to correct a condition that compromises safety or security, if that condition continues uncorrected" and "to carry out a criminal investigation or prosecution." 14 C.F.R. § 193.9. Additionally, 14 C.F.R. § 193.7(f) provides that information will be released when "ordered to do so by a court of competent jurisdiction." FAA Order No. 8000.82 states as its purpose: "This order designates information received by the agency from an Aviation Safety Action Program (ASAP) as protected from public disclosure in accordance with the provisions of Title 14 of the Code of Federal Regulations (14 C.F.R.) part 193."

The briefs filed by the RAA and FAA also focus on the concerns associated with "public" disclosure of the reports. The ALPA argues that reporting employees understand the reports "will not be used to support litigation against themselves or their company" and relies on the statute and regulation for support [DE # 1253, p. 6]. It does not explain how such an understanding could arise or survive, however, in light of FAA regulations expressly providing for disclosure for uncorrected safety conditions, criminal investigations or prosecutions, and court orders. 14 C.F.R. §§ 193.7(f), 193.9.

This Magistrate Judge is not persuaded by the Legal Guidance offered regarding the Chicago Convention. There is no indication that this document has any binding effect on any party to the treaty. Instead, it appears to be a suggestion to legislative bodies in signatory states because the members noted that "existing national laws and regulations in many States may not adequately address the manner in which safety information is protected from inappropriate use." [DE #!253, Ex. 1, p. 3]. This Court is bound by the existing law expressed by Congress, not some possible future law. Ellis ex rel. Pendergrass v. Cleveland Mun. School Dist., 455 F.3d 690, 697 (6th Cir. 2006) ("We cannot allow a propensity to speculate as to yet unarticulated law to allow us to indulge our own predisposition").

The plain language used by Congress and the FAA reveals that the protection given ASAP reports is limited, and simply precludes government agencies from publicly disclosing the information pursuant to FOIA requests. Disclosure in litigation was obviously contemplated, as the FAA agreed to produce the reports pursuant to a court order. There is no provision to protect carriers from discovery requests such as the present one where the information is unquestionably relevant and any documents produced could be subject to a protective order. Accordingly, it is the opinion of this Magistrate Judge that the ASAP reports are not protected from discovery by any statutory or regulatory privilege.

B. Common Law Privilege

Comair requests that this Court, nonetheless, grant a privilege to the ASAP reports in light of the value of the information provided and the possibility that there might be some chilling effect on voluntary reports. An initial consideration is whether state or federal law provides the rule of decision in the various cases, as that same law would determine whether or not there might be a privilege. Federal Rule of Evidence 501 Invesco Institutional (N.A.), Inc. v. Paas, 244 F.R.D. 374, 378 n. 7 (W.D. Ky. 2007). Although most Plaintiffs filed their claims under state law, Comair correctly notes that some Plaintiffs brought their claims under federal law pursuant to the Montreal Convention [DE # 1289, pp. 5-6]. Additionally, the Court has not been asked to determine what law provides the rule of decision in these cases. See DE # 406, pp. 8-9. Regardless of whether state or federal law applies, the outcome is the same for a common law or self-critical analysis privilege for ASAP reports.

The United States Supreme Court rejected an argument similar to Comair's regarding a privilege for university peer review reports as follows: "We are especially reluctant to recognize a privilege in an area where it appears that Congress has considered the relevant competing concerns but has not provided the privilege itself. The balancing of conflicting interests of this type is particularly a legislative function." University of Pennsylvania v. E.E.O.C., 493 U.S. 182, 198, 110 S. Ct. 577, 107 L. Ed. 2d 571 (1990) (citation omitted). This reluctance is in addition to the usual concerns that privileges are in derogation of the search for truth and that there due process implications in withholding demonstrably relevant evidence. See Nixon, 418 U.S. at 710, 712.

As discussed above, the focus of the legislative protection for ASAP reports is to prevent disclosure to the "public" through FOIA requests. FAR Part 193 Final Rule. Noting that use of the information for enforcement was of "prime interest" to reporting parties, the FAA designed "enforcement-related incentives" into the program." AC No: 120-66B. Those incentives are that FAA enforcement will be limited to administrative action, no action or corrective action, depending upon the circumstances. Id. § 11.b. Additionally, the contents of an ASAP report will not be used to initiate or support company disciplinary action. 70 J. Air. L. & Com. 83, at 104; AC No: 120-66B; Comair ASAP MOU, § 10.i. Employees have the additional strong incentive that their voluntary reports are making aviation safer for themselves and their passengers. See DE # 1253, p. 2. In Dowling v. American Hawaii Cruises, Inc., 971 F.2d 423 (9th Cir. 1992), the court considered whether allowing discovery of pre-accident safety reviews would stifle voluntary reporting and said: "[P]re-accident safety reviews are designed to preempt litigation; it is perverse to assume that the candid assessments necessary to prevent accidents will be inhibited by the fear that they could later be used as a weapon in hypothetical litigation they are supposed to prevent." Id. at 427.

Comair relies on the common-law qualified privilege created by In re Air Crash Near Cali, Colombia on December 20, 1995, 959 F. Supp. 1529 (S.D. Fla. 1997). It has been nearly eleven years since that decision, and no other court has relied upon it to create a similar common-law privilege. This Magistrate Judge, likewise, does not find the Cali analysis persuasive.

It is the opinion of this Magistrate Judge that the failure of Congress to create any privilege for ASAP reports weighs heavily against the creation of any privilege by this Court. The concerns regarding reluctance to report were considered by Congress and the FAA, and the incentives deemed sufficient to protect the program were provided.

C. Self-Critical Analysis Privilege

Comair also asks this Court to apply a self-critical analysis privilege to the ASAP reports. No such privilege is available under Kentucky law. University of Kentucky v. Courier-Journal & Louisville Times Co., 830 S.W.2d 373, 378, 39 4 Ky. L. Summary 51 (Ky. 1992) ("The University asks the Court to adopt a 'self-critical analysis' privilege which would exempt from disclosure self-evaluative documents. We refuse to judicially adopt such a privilege"). Comair argues that the Supreme Court of Kentucky would decide the issue differently if presented with the facts of this case. [DE # 1289, p. 8]. This Court is bound by existing law. "Until the [state] courts have spoken on the subject, we must follow the law as it is. We should not attempt to make new law for the state in conflict with its existing decisions." Goranson v. Kloeb, 308 F.2d 655, 656-657 (6th Cir. 1962). See also Angelotta v. American Broadcasting Co., 820 F.2d 806, 807 (6th Cir. 1987) (A district court "must apply state law in accordance with the then controlling decision of the state's highest court").

Comair's argument regarding a self-critical analysis privilege also fails under federal law. The Cali court was "unpersuaded that the self-critical analysis privilege" applied to ASAP reports. Cali, 959 F. Supp. at 1532-33. It particularly noted that the privilege was for "in house" reviews, but not reports send to others like the ASAP reports. Id. at 1532 ("unless the report is prepared for purely internal review purposes, no self-critical analysis privilege should attach"). That factual distinction also applies to the self-critical analysis privilege recognized for an internal post-accident report in ASARCO, Inc. v. National Labor Relations Board, 805 F.2d 194 (6th Cir. 1986). In United States v. Allison Engine Co., Inc., 196 F.R.D. 310 (S.D. Ohio 2000), the court considered a claim of self-critical analysis privilege regarding internal audits of quality control for products supplied to the United States Navy. It applied a four-part test from Bredice v. Doctors Hosp., Inc., 50 F.R.D. 249 (D.D.C. 1970):

(1) the information must result from self-critical analysis undertaken by the party seeking protection; (2) the public must have a strong interest in preserving the free flow of the type of information sought; (3) the information must be of the type whose flow would be curtailed if discovery were allowed; and (4) no documents should be accorded the privilege unless it was prepared with the expectation that it would be kept confidential.

Allison Engine, 196 F.R.D. at 312. The court rejected the privilege in that case, noting that the privilege had rarely been applied and that its very rationale had been called into doubt by University of Pennsylvania. Id. at 313. Particularly, the court held that the quality control audits failed to meet the third and fourth tests. In rejecting that the flow of information would be curtailed by discovery, it noted that abandoning safety reviews would be bad for business and that the documentation may form an affirmative defense to a claim. Id. at 314. The court also rejected the argument that the documents were created with the expectation that they would remain confidential since the company was required to maintain records of inspections and corrective action and make them available for inspection by the contracting party. Id. at 314-315.

Similarly, the Ninth Circuit reversed a decision that routine, internal self-critical safety reviews on a ship were privileged. Dowling, 971 F.2d at 426. The court concluded that "such reviews will rarely, if ever, be curtailed simply because they may be subject to discovery." Id. It noted that the "many incentives" to conduct safety reviews outweigh any harm from disclosure. Particularly, there "is surely the desire to avoid law suits arising from unsafe conditions." Id. The court found it noteworthy that automobile manufacturers continue to conduct safety tests despite discovery of a cost-feasibility memorandum that subjected Ford Motor Company to punitive damages. Id. The court also doubted the claim that the reviews were performed with the expectation that they would be kept confidential. Id.

Comair's claim of a self-critical analysis privilege likewise must fail. First, the ASAP reports are not prepared for purely internal review. Cali 959 F. Supp. at 1532-33. They are prepared to be shared with the FAA and the pilots' union. Second, there are many incentives for reporting to continue, not the least of which is the future personal safety of the crew and passengers. There is also the desire to prevent lawsuits from unsafe conditions and the possibility of documenting an affirmative defense in the event a lawsuit should arise. Congress and the FAA considered the need to encourage future reporting and determined that incentives regarding enforcement and company discipline were sufficient. Courts should be particularly reluctant to recognize a privilege when Congress has chosen not to do so. Pennsylvania, 493 U.S. at 198. Third, there is no reasonable basis for expecting confidentiality of the ASAP reports when the regulations expressly provide circumstances under which they will be publicly disclosed, and they further authorize disclosure pursuant to court order. 14 C.F.R. Part 193. This fact distinguishes the conclusion in Tice v. American Airlines, Inc., 192 F.R.D. 270, 273 (N.D. Ill. 2000) that the different reports at issue there "were prepared with the expectation that they would be kept confidential." Accordingly, is it the opinion of this Magistrate Judge that Comair's ASAP reports are not subject to a self-critical analysis privilege or any similar qualified privilege.

D. Substantial need for documents

Relying upon Cali, Comair argues that Plaintiffs failed to demonstrate a substantial or compelling need for the documents [DE # 1289, p. 8]. There is no heightened burden on Plaintiffs when there is no privilege. Moreover, Plaintiffs here are seeking information that the carrier had notice of safety hazards similar to the ones involved in the crash of Flight 5191. The Cali court recognized that "[e]vidence of this sort ... might be vital to its cause of action for willful misconduct." Plaintiffs in the present cases are seeking punitive damages on several grounds. Additionally, Plaintiffs have demonstrated that they were severely handicapped in questioning Mr. Vislosky about specific incidents in ASAP reports when they had no basis for assessing the accuracy of his testimony or his recollection.

E. Motion to Quash Deposition

Comair argues that no deposition of a corporate representative regarding the ASAP reports is necessary since Mr. Vislosky has already been deposed. Without the ASAP reports, Plaintiffs were blindfolded while deposing the witness. Additionally, they are entitled to the benefit of a 30(b)(6) deposition and the "information known or reasonably available to the organization," rather than being limited to Mr. Vislosky's personal knowledge.

III. CONCLUSION

IT IS ORDERED:
1. Comair's Motion for a Protective Order and Motion to Quash Deposition [DE # 1200] is DENIED;

2. Comair shall immediately produce to Plaintiffs the documents requested in Plaintiffs' November 21, 2007, Notice of Deposition and Request for Production of Documents [DE # 1105]; and

3. Comair shall promptly make a corporate representative available to Plaintiffs for a deposition in accordance with Plaintiffs' November 21 Notice.

V.   PROPERTY LAW – AIRCRAFT OWNERSHIP

A. *Bailment*

PURITAN INSURANCE COMPANY v. BUTLER AVIATION-PALM BEACH, INC.

UNITED STATES COURT OF APPEALS FOR THE ELEVENTH CIRCUIT

715 F.2d 502

September, 1983

Opinion

This appeal arises out of the theft of an airplane from the premises of Butler Aviation, a fixed based operator at Palm Beach International Airport. Upon landing at Palm Beach, the owner, Gullia, taxied his plane to Butler Aviation so that it could be parked and tied down. He locked the plane, retained his key and sent another key to a person who planned to use the plane for business purposes. No key is necessary, however, to operate this model aircraft. The keys Gullia retained opened the door locks and baggage compartments.

Gullia was a visitor to the area and did not store his plane at Butler Aviation on a regular basis. Pursuant to Butler's procedure, Gullia completed a registration card indicating that he was the owner of the aircraft and giving his local address and intended length of stay. The plane was then logged on Butler's daily arrival sheet. A Butler employee towed the plane to a parking area and tied it down.

The Palm Beach County Department of Airports maintains a fence around the airport perimeter. Other than the fence, each fixed based operator is responsible for providing security for its facilities. Butler controlled its area by stationing a security guard at its access gate and a dispatcher at a service counter at the other entrance. Another Butler employee checked nightly to see which aircraft were in the parking area.

The day after his arrival Gullia returned to Butler Aviation. He stowed his flight case in the wing locker and relocked the plane. He did not move the aircraft.

A little more than a week after Gullia's arrival in Palm Beach an unknown person entered Butler's lot, paid the parking and refueling charges, and absconded with the plane. Puritan Insurance Company paid Gullia for his loss and now seeks to recover from Butler, alleging that Butler's negligence caused the theft. The district judge determined as a matter of law that a bailment relationship existed between Gullia and Butler, and the jury then found for Puritan. We affirm.

On appeal Butler argues that the district court erred in holding that a bailment existed, and alternatively that the jury instructions were erroneous. Under Florida law a bailment requires complete delivery of possession, custody and control of the chattel. *Blum v. Merrill Stevens Dry Dock Co., 409 So.2d 192 (Fla.App.1982)*. Butler contends that in light of the circumstances surrounding the storage of the plane, specifically Gullia's retention of the key, there was not a complete delivery. We disagree. The facts that we have set out -- a fenced area, control of the access gate, a dispatcher on duty, registration procedures, placement and tying down of the plane by Butler, and a nightly check -- indicate that Butler had control over the aircraft and was properly considered a bailee. *See Palm Beach Aviation, Inc. v. Kibildis, 423 So.2d 1011 (Fla.App.1982)*; *Empire Tool Co. v. Wells, 227 So.2d 76 (Fla.App.1969)*. Although Gullia retained his key (and sent another to a third party) practical control remained with Butler. Other jurisdictions have held that no bailment exists where the owner retains the keys to the plane. *See Balcar v. Aircrafters, Inc., 360 A.2d 155 (Del.Super.1976)*; *Nelson v. Schroeder Aerosports, Inc., 280 N.W.2d 107 (S.D.1979)*. The Florida courts, however, have not indicated that they would consider retention of the key to be the dispositive factor. The district court did not err in finding a bailment existed.

Butler also objects to the following jury instruction:

> The burden is on the defendant to show that it exercised the requisite degree of care. A bailee is not an insurer for the property bailed and without fault on his part he is not liable for the loss of the property bailed. Thus where the plaintiff [sic] has delivered its property in a bailment relation with another, and that property is not redelivered upon the demand of the plaintiff, then unless the defendant can show it has exercised the degree of care required by the nature of the bailment, your verdict should be for the plaintiff.
>
> Thus the defendant must show that it was not negligent.

Relying on *Insurance Company of the State of Pennsylvania v. Estate of Guzman, 421 So.2d 597 (Fla.App.1982)*, Butler argues that this instruction is contrary to Florida law because it places upon the bailee the burden of proving freedom from negligence. Butler did not object specifically to this instruction or submit an alternate instruction. Absent plain error, we cannot consider an objection to a jury instruction not made at trial. *Johnson v. Bryant, 671 F.2d 1276 (11th Cir.1982)*. Given the confusion in the Florida courts on this issue, cf. *Guzman, 421 So.2d 597*, with *Clermont Marine Sales, Inc. v. Harmon, 347 So.2d 839 (Fla.App.1977)*, and the fact that the jury was also instructed that the burden is on the plaintiff to prove every element of his claim, we decline to find plain error. *See G.A. Thompson & Co. v. Partridge, 636 F.2d 945 (5th Cir.1981)*.

AFFIRMED.

Muriel STUBBS v. Ralph W. HOOK, Jr.

Court of Appeals of Indiana, First District

467 N.E.2d 29

August, 1984

Muriel Stubbs as administratrix of her husband's estate, Stubbs Aviation Service, Speedway Airport, and the Indianapolis Metropolitan Airport Authority appeal an adverse judgment rendered by the court which found them liable for damage to an airplane owned by Ralph Hook.

George Stubbs, deceased, did business at the Speedway Airport as Stubbs Aviation Service; Speedway Airport operates under the supervision of the Indianapolis Metropolitan Airport Authority. Hook owned a Piper Cherokee airplane and rented a tie-down space from Stubbs for $180.00 per year in 1979 and 1980. In July, 1979, the airplane was given an annual inspection and determined to be airworthy. Thereafter, Hook and a friend flew the airplane as late as September, 1979. On December 3, 1979, Hook went to Stubb's office to pay his fee for 1980 and was told his airplane had been damaged two or three weeks earlier.

The damage was located on the upper part of the right wing and on the engine cowling. In Hook's opinion and the opinion of an airplane dealer, who was called as a witness by the defendants, the damage was caused by a ground vehicle.

The airplane was parked in a space designated by Stubbs and located in the second strip of parking spaces at the end of a 2,500 foot grass runway. Stubbs furnished the tie-down equipment. It consisted of brackets set in the ground linked to chains with manual fasteners that could be opened by anyone. Stubbs possessed a set of keys for the airplane and moved it occasionally by using the key and manually. Hook and his friend retained keys to the airplane. It was not necessary for pilots to check in with the office on take off or landing.

The trial court made specific findings of fact and conclusions of law. The court concluded Stubbs and Hook had made a bailment contract. Relying on this conclusion and applying the doctrine of *res ipsa loquitur,* the trial court found the defendants liable for the unexplained damage to the airplane. Because of provisions in a lease agreement between Stubbs and the airport authority concerning the location of tie-down space and the apportionment of rental fees, the trial court held the airport authority liable.

On appeal, the defendants argue the judgment is contrary to law alleging: 1) that the doctrine of *res ipsa loquitur* is not applicable absent evidence that the defendants controlled the instrumentality causing the damage; 2) the contract between Stubbs and Hook was not a bailment contract because Stubbs did not have exclusive possession and control of the airplane; 3) the Indianapolis Metropolitan Airport Authority should not be liable to Hook because it did not participate in managing the tie-down facilities; and 4) that the trial court erred by allowing witnesses to speculate about the cause of the damage.

We reverse because Stubbs did not have exclusive possession and control of the airplane and therefore, a bailment was not created.

In cases tried by the court, we may not reverse the trial court's decision unless it is clearly erroneous and we give due regard to the trial court's opportunity to judge the credibility of witnesses. *Litzelswope v. Mitchell*, (1983) *Ind.App., 451 N.E.2d 366*. Ind. Rules of Trial Procedure, Trial Rule 52(A). When a judgment is attacked as being contrary to law, we neither consider credibility of witnesses nor weigh the evidence. Rather, we look solely to the evidence most favorable to the judgment, together with all reasonable inferences therefrom, and it is only when this evidence is without conflict and leads to but one conclusion and the trial court reached a contrary conclusion that we will reverse that decision as being contrary to law. *Dominguez v. Gallmeyer*, (1980) *Ind.App., 402 N.E.2d 1295*, trans. denied.

A bailment is an agreement, either express or implied, that one person will entrust personal property to another for a specific purpose and that when the purpose is accomplished the bailee will return the property or the bailor will reclaim it. 8 Am.Jur.2d (Rev.) § 2 (1980). In an action based upon breach of a bailment contract, proof that the property was received by the bailee in good condition and was damaged prior to being returned to the bailor raises an inference the bailee was negligent. *Spencer v. Glover*, (1980) *Ind.App., 412 N.E.2d 870*. This rule is a recognition of the bailee's duty to exercise reasonable care to protect the bailor's property. *Central Transport, Inc. v. Great Dane Trailers, Inc.*, (1981) *Ind.App. 423 N.E.2d 675*.

In order for a bailment to exist, the bailed property must be delivered into the bailee's exclusive possession and accepted by the bailee. This point was discussed in *Weddington v. Stolkin*, (1952) 122 *Ind.App. 670, 675, 106 N.E.2d 239, 241-242*.

> It is essential to the creation of the relation of bailor and bailee that there be a delivery of the property to the bailee. In order to constitute a sufficient delivery in any given case, it is the general rule that there must be such a full transfer, either actual or constructive, of the property to the bailee as to exclude the possession of the owner and all other persons and give to the bailee, for the time being, the sole custody and control thereof.

We have not found any Indiana cases that apply this rule to factual situations analogous to the case at bar. Hook cites several cases from other jurisdictions for the proposition that rental of a tie-down space creates a bailment. In some of these cases, the parties agreed a bailment existed, *Naxera v. Wathan*, (1968) *Iowa, 159 N.W.2d 513*, *Alamo Airways, Inc. v. Benum*, (1962) *78 Nev. 384, 374 P.2d 684*, and in others, the possession issue was not raised, *Meyer v. Moore*, (1958) *Okla.Supr., 329 P.2d 676*, therefore they are not applicable to the case at bar. However, a South Dakota case is exactly on point with the case before us.

In *Nelson v. Schroeder Aerosports, Inc.,* (1979) *S.D., 280 N.W.2d 107* the owner of an airplane sought to recover damages his plane sustained in a storm. He had rented a tie-down space from the defendant-airport operator. The plaintiff retained the keys to his airplane and allowed a third party access to it. Apparently, the plaintiff's case was predicated on the theory that the defendant negligently failed to properly anchor the aircraft prior to the storm, although the tie-downs were secure. The trial court directed a verdict for the defendant, which was affirmed on appeal, on the grounds that a bailment did not exist because the plaintiff had not relinquished exclusive control of the aircraft.

The only factual distinction between *Nelson* and Hook's case is that Stubbs had a set of keys for the airplane. Nevertheless, Hook retained keys to the aircraft and allowed a third party access to it. Therefore, the trial court erroneously concluded a bailment existed that put the burden of proof and ultimately the responsibility for the damage on the defendants. *See also, State ex rel. Mather v. Carnes,* (1977) *Mo.App., 551 S.W. 2d 272.*

Hook argues the judgment can be sustained on any of three theories: bailment, *res ipsa loquitur* or contract. However, the trial court did not base its decision on separate alternative theories. The duty to safely store the airplane and the burden of explaining the damage are interwoven with the finding that a bailment existed. Hook did not introduce evidence he had contracted for safe storage. He gave his opinion that he expected a safe place, but he did not show that Stubbs made representations about storage conditions.

Furthermore, the doctrine of *res ipsa loquitur* is a mechanism for proving breach of a duty, once the duty has been established. The trial court went from its conclusion that a bailment existed, with the object being safe storage, to the conclusion that the airport had a duty to control ground traffic to effectuate safe storage. The trial court equated control of the ground traffic and the airport as a whole with the control of an instrumentality necessary for the application of *res ipsa loquitur. Bituminous, Etc. v. Culligan Fyrprotexion, Inc.,* (1982) *Ind.App., 437 N.E.2d 1360* (the case contains a good explanation of control of an instrumentality.) Absent a bailment, Stubbs did not have a duty to provide safe storage.

Judgment reversed.

INTERNATIONAL ATLAS SERVICES, INC. v. TWENTIETH CENTURY AIRCRAFT COMPANY et al.

Court of Appeal of California, Second Appellate District, Division Two

251 Cal. App. 2d 434

May, 1967

Atlas, a corporation in the business of repairing and maintaining aircraft engines, sued for claim and delivery of three aircraft engines and one QEC (quick engine change) unit attached to a DC-6B aircraft, No. 90771. From a judgment in favor of Twentieth Century, which had repossessed the aircraft as legal owner and conditional seller, Atlas appeals.

The controversy developed out of the sale of a four-engine DC-6B in 1961 by Twentieth Century to President Airlines under conditional sales contract. President Airlines, an operator of aircraft and not a party to this suit, employed Atlas to service and maintain the aircraft, the maintenance service to include scheduled engine changes and engine overhauls. Both Atlas and Twentieth Century now claim ownership of engines installed in the aircraft by Atlas in the course of scheduled maintenance, engines which came into the possession of Twentieth Century when it repossessed the aircraft on President Airlines' default.

Under the 1961 conditional sale of the aircraft to President Airlines, monthly installments on the purchase price ran from $ 12,500 to $ 20,000, and legal title and ownership of the aircraft remained in Twentieth Century until full payment of the purchase price, $ 525,000 plus interest. Before delivery Twentieth Century affixed two plaques to the aircraft announcing its legal ownership of the airplane and the conditional nature of the interest of President Airlines. On June 6, 1961, President Airlines registered its ownership with the Federal Aviation Agency, and on the same day Twentieth Century recorded its conditional sales contract with the Aircraft Records Branch of the Federal Aviation Agency at Oklahoma City, Oklahoma. The contract of sale required President Airlines to keep the aircraft in good order and repair and to pay all expenses of maintenance and overhaul. With respect to replacement of equipment the contract provided: "Buyer [President] shall, at its own cost and expense, replace in or on said aircraft, any and all parts, equipment . . . or accessories which may be worn out . . . or otherwise rendered unfit for use . . . with other property which shall . . . be owned by Buyer free and clear of all liens and encumbrances. Buyer shall, at its own expense, perform all engine . . . overhaul and inspection and maintenance service on said aircraft . . . Buyer shall have the right to remove from said aircraft any engine . . . or other article of equipment . . which may have become unfit for use, but only if Buyer shall have substituted for the same another engine, . . . or other article of equipment which is owned by Buyer and is not at the time subject to any lien or other . . . claim, charge or encumbrance. . . ."

On taking possession of the aircraft President Airlines contracted for maintenance with Atlas, which agreed among other services to make all engine changes and engine overhauls needed to keep N-90771 airworthy. The customary method of servicing engines in large aircraft is by engine substitution, sometimes including a QEC to support the engine. An engine which needs overhauling or whose time has run out is replaced by a newly overhauled engine with zero time, and the old engine in turn is completely overhauled and rebuilt. It then becomes an engine with zero time and thereafter may be installed in the same or other aircraft as the need for engine replacement arises. Aircraft engines bear serial numbers for identification, and their ownership may be recorded with the Aircraft Records Branch of the Federal Aviation Agency in Oklahoma City.

When President Airlines defaulted in its payments, Twentieth Century repossessed the aircraft, as it was entitled to do under its conditional sales contract. At the time of repossession the aircraft was equipped with three engines and a QEC which Atlas had installed in the ordinary course of scheduled maintenance and to which Atlas retained legal title. Atlas claimed ownership and the right to possession of these three engines, relying on the terms of its maintenance agreement with President Airlines, "Title to all spare QEC's and engines shall at all times remain in IAS [Atlas] . . ." Issue was thus joined of priority of right between the legal owner of a component part and the legal owner of the principal property in which the component part had been installed.

Under California law in effect in 1961 this controversy would normally have been governed by the provisions of *Civil Code section 1025* dealing with accessions to personal property: "When things belonging to different owners have been united so as to form a single thing, and cannot be separated without injury, the whole belongs to the owner of the thing which forms the principal part; who must, however, reimburse the value of the residue to the other owner, or surrender the whole to him." Under this rule if the component part cannot be detached without severely diminishing the market value of the principal part, then the component part belongs to the owner of the principal part, who must, however, reimburse the owner of the component part for its value. Since aircraft cannot function without engines, the facts of the present case place it squarely within the provisions of this rule. (*Sasia & Wallace, Inc. v. Scarborough Implement Co., 154 Cal.App.2d 308 [316 P.2d 39]*; cf. *A. Meister & Sons v. Harrison, 56 Cal.App. 679 [206 P. 106]*.) Following this rule we would be required to determine the value of the engines at the time of repossession and then decide whether that value should be compared with the value of the engines on the aircraft at the time of its sale to President Airlines or with the value of the run-out engines removed from the aircraft at the time of their replacement.

Were we to consider the rights of the parties under current California law, we would find the position of the owner of a component part in relation to the owner of the principal property even stronger than it had been under prior law, and we would be required to give full recognition to the continued separate ownership of the component part installed in the aircraft. *Commercial Code, section 9314*, reads: "(1) A security interest in goods which attaches before they are installed in or affixed to other goods takes priority as to the goods installed or affixed (called in this section 'accessions') over the claims of all persons to the whole except as stated in subdivision (3) . . ." [Subdivision (3) has no application, since it relates to subsequent purchases and subsequent advances.] The official comment under *section 9314 of the Uniform Commercial Code* has this to say: "This Section changes prior law in that the secured party claiming an interest in a part (e.g., a new motor in an old car) is entitled to priority and has a right to remove even though under other rules of law the part now belongs to the whole."

It would appear, then, that under California law Atlas at a minimum should recover the value of its engines and at a maximum should recover the engines themselves. Nevertheless, we have concluded that California law does not apply to this case, that the controversy is governed by the laws of the United States, and that under federal law Twentieth Century must prevail. (1) As we see it, general California law on the subject of title and liens to personal property in relation to component parts has been superseded by specific federal law with respect to aircraft. Section 503 of the Federal Aviation Act of 1958, derived from the Civil Aeronautics Act of 1938, provides for centralized registration and recordation of interests in aircraft with the Federal Aviation Agency. The pertinent provisions of the statute are found in 49 United States Code, section 1403:

"(a) The Administrator shall establish and maintain a system for the recording of each and all of the following:

"(1) Any conveyance which affects the title to, or any interest in, any civil aircraft of the United States;

"(2) Any *lease*, and any mortgage, equipment trust, contract of conditional sale, or other instrument executed for security purposes, which lease or other instrument affects the title to, or any interest in, *any specifically identified aircraft engine* [over 750 horsepower] . . . or any specifically identified aircraft propeller [capacity over 750 horsepower] . . .

" (3) Any lease, and any mortgage, equipment trust, contract of conditional sale, or other instrument executed for security purposes, which lease or other instrument affects the title to, or any interest in, any aircraft engines, propellers, or appliances . . . which instrument need only describe generally by types the engines, propellers, appliances, and spare parts covered thereby and designate the location or locations thereof; . . .

"(c) *No* conveyance or *instrument the recording of which is provided for by subsection (a)* of this section *shall be valid in respect of such aircraft*, aircraft engine or *engines*, propellers, appliances, or spare parts against any person other than the person by whom the conveyance or other instrument is made or given, his heir or devisee, or any person having actual notice thereof, *until such conveyance or other instrument is filed for recordation* in the office of the Administrator: . . .

"(d) Each conveyance or other instrument recorded by means of or under the system provided for in subsection (a) or (b) of this section shall from the time of its filing for recordation be valid as to all persons without further or other recordation, except that an instrument recorded pursuant to subsection (a) (3) of this section shall be effective only with respect to those of such items which may from time to time be situated at the designated location or locations and only while so situated: *Provided*, That an instrument recorded under subsection (a) (2) of this section shall not be affected as to the engine or engines, or propeller or propellers, specifically identified therein, by an instrument theretofore or thereafter recorded pursuant to subsection (a) (3) of this section." (Italics added.)

It seems clear that Congress has recognized the extreme mobility of large aircraft for which neither state nor national boundaries can delineate or assure any fixed controls. Without some central system of recording ownership and other property interests in aircraft, security transactions involving aircraft engaged in continuous movement would amount to little more than attempts to control ownership of fish and game, which become objects of ownership only when taken. (*Civ. Code, § 656.*) To bring order into the field of aircraft ownership and finance, the federal government in a manner within its sphere set up a comprehensive scheme of centralized recordation, which, if properly used, provides adequate protection for all substantial property interests in large aircraft, both for the aircraft itself and for its principal component parts. Under section 1403(a) (1) a security interest in the aircraft as a whole can be recorded. Under section 1403(a) (2) an interest in its specific engines and propellers can be recorded. A conveyance, lease, or security instrument recorded under section 1403(a) is fully valid against all persons from the time of its filing without further or other recordation. Under section 1403(c) a conveyance or instrument which could have been recorded but was not, is, until so recorded, invalid against a person without actual notice of the conveyance or instrument. The section also provides for bulk registration of engines, propellers, and spare parts (§ 1403(a) (3)), but it is careful to subordinate this bulk registration to the specific registration of particular property under subsection (a) (2) (i.e., engines and propellers).

(2) Here we have a complete and comprehensive system of recordation which necessarily supersedes inconsistent state law. Constitutionally, the federal government may be said to have fully occupied the field of recordation of interests in aircraft and of rights derived from recordation, and to have established paramount law in this area. (3) Atlas could have fully protected its rights in these engines and preserved a good title throughout the world by taking advantage of this national system of recordation and recording its interest in specifically numbered aircraft engines with the Federal Aviation Agency. Its failure to record in Oklahoma City its ownership of the engines prior to repossession of the aircraft by Twentieth Century resulted in the subordination of its interest in the engines to the recorded interest of Twentieth Century in the aircraft as a whole. The latter, by recording with the Federal Aviation Authority, established a superior right to the aircraft, its engines, and its propellers, effective against all other interests in the aircraft except known or recorded adverse interests. This paramount interest under federal law effectively superseded any inconsistent interest derived from state law.

On federal preemption as overriding state law in this field, we find persuasive *United States v. United Aircraft Corp., 80 F.Supp. 52.* In that case the United States, as a mortgagee, had recorded under federal law a purchase money chattel mortgage on a particular aircraft. Later United Aircraft, to whom the engines from the aircraft had been delivered by the mortgagor for overhaul, asserted an artificer's lien against the engines under Connecticut law. The court declared that Congress had preempted the field of liens on aircraft and that federal law was controlling. In the particular case, however, the artificer's lien was upheld because of the insufficiency of the notice to third parties of the mortgagee's lien -- only the number of the aircraft itself having been recorded and not the serial numbers of its individual engines. Since the time of this decision the gap which then existed in the law has been closed, and federal law now authorizes the recording of specifically numbered engines. *Crescent City Aviation, Inc. v. Beverly Bank (1966) Ind.App.   [219 N.E.2d 446].*)

(4) To avoid the impact of the recordation statute, Atlas argues that the provisions of the law are limited to the recordation of security interests; that its installation of engines in N-90771 was only a loan of personal property which did not fall within the classification of a transaction executed for security purposes. We think this argument is sufficiently answered by the text of the statute itself, section 1403 (a)(2), which specifically applies to "Any lease" [and any mortgage or other security instrument] "which lease or other instrument affects the title to, or any interest in, any specifically identified aircraft engine . . ." The term lease is broad enough to include a bailment of personal property, and the statute clearly applies. (*Carstensen v. Gottesburen, 215 Cal.258 [9 P.2d 831].*)

Finally, Atlas argues that since there was no testimony to prove that section 1403(a) (2) had ever been used to record interests in aircraft engines we must assume it was a custom of the industry not to use the statute for that purpose. The assumption does not follow from the premises and is contradicted by the congressional committee report on the subject, 1959 U.S. Code Congressional News, pp. 1762, 1764. Nor does it follow from the proof in this very case, for the record reflects that Bank of America, a prior lienholder recognized as such by all parties, had recorded with the Federal Aviation Agency a security interest in the plane and in specified aircraft engines identified by number, a paramount interest which no one saw fit to challenge.

(5) We conclude that the failure of Atlas to record its interest in the airplane engines installed in an aircraft to which Twentieth Century held legal title, which title the latter had properly recorded under federal law, subordinated its interest in the engines at the time of repossession to the interest of Twentieth Century in the aircraft as a whole.

Judgment affirmed.

DONALD A. DOWELL v. BEECH ACCEPTANCE
CORPORATION, INC., et al.

Supreme Court of California

476 P.2d 401

November, 1970

We consider whether the system of recordation of title to aircraft under the Federal Aviation Act (49 U.S.C.A. § 1403) affects the priorities under state law between prior security holders and subsequent buyers in the ordinary course of business. (1) Specifically, we must decide whether the holder of a prior, recorded security interest in a new airplane prevails over a subsequent buyer in the ordinary course of business who neither recorded his own title nor searched the Federal Aviation Agency (F.A.A.) records to discover the security holder's prior claim. We conclude that the federal statute requires judgment in favor of the holder of the prior recorded security interest.

The facts are not in dispute: The airplane in question, a Beechcraft Bonanza aircraft, was sold by the manufacturer to Nevadair, one of its distributors. On October 26, 1965, Nevadair delivered the plane to Marion Tanger, a duly authorized Beechcraft dealer, pursuant to a conditional sales contract. The contract provided that Tanger was not to sell the plane without Nevadair's consent and that Nevadair retained a security interest in the plane to the extent of the unpaid balance of the purchase price. Nevadair assigned its security interest to defendant Beech Acceptance Corporation, a company in the business of aircraft financing. On October 27, 1965, Beech filed the conditional sales contract and the assignment with the Federal Aviation Agency, pursuant to 49 United States Code Annotated section 1403, and the instruments were recorded as of November 4, 1965.

In July of 1966, plaintiff purchased the plane from Tanger for $ 30,000, the sum being paid in full. He made no inquiry as to the state of the title ostensibly because the plane was new and Tanger was an authorized dealer. However, plaintiff was not inexperienced in the field of aviation. He was a member of the Aircraft Owners and Pilots Association, was familiar with F.A.A. rules and was aware that he could have checked the title with the F.A.A. for a $ 3.50 fee. Apparently Tanger promised plaintiff that he would file plaintiff's bill of sale with the F.A.A. Aircraft Registry but failed to do so. At the time of the sale to plaintiff, Tanger owed Beech $ 21,366.03 plus interest, but not until September 22, 1966, did he confess to Beech that he had sold the plane. The following day, Beech, Nevadair, and Larson (Nevadair's parent corporation), on the advice of counsel, removed the plane from plaintiff's possession without his knowledge or consent.

Plaintiff thereupon brought this action to establish his title to the plane and to recover compensatory and punitive damages against defendants. Through a claim and delivery proceeding at the outset of his action, plaintiff recovered possession of the airplane on October 22, 1966, pending trial. After trial, the court awarded the plane to plaintiff along with $ 175 compensatory damages, representing the value of the use of the plane between September 23 and October 22, 1966. Plaintiff was also awarded $ 1,000 punitive damages, on the theory that defendants' seizing possession of the airplane without plaintiff's consent on September 23 constituted oppressive conduct.

Section 503 of the 1958 Federal Aviation Act, 49 United States Code Annotated section 1403, provides in relevant part: "(a) The Administrator shall establish and maintain a system for the recording of each and all of the following: (1) Any conveyance which affects the title to, or any interest in, any civil aircraft of the United States; (2) Any lease, and any mortgage, equipment trust, contract of conditional sale, or other instrument executed for security purposes, which lease or other instrument affects the title to, or any interest in, any specifically identified aircraft engine . . . or any specifically identified aircraft propeller . . . and also any assignment or amendment thereof or supplement thereto . . . . (b) The Administrator shall also record under the system provided for in subsection (a) of this section any release, cancellation, discharge, or satisfaction relating to any conveyance or other instrument recorded under said system. (c) No conveyance or instrument the recording of which is provided for by subsection (a) of this section shall be valid in respect of such aircraft, aircraft engine or engines, [or] propellers . . . against any person other than the person by whom the conveyance or other instrument is made or given, his heir or devisee, or any person having actual notice thereof, until such conveyance or other instrument is filed for recordation in the office of the Administrator. . . . (d) Each conveyance or other instrument recorded by means of or under the system provided for in subsection (a) or (b) of this section shall from the time of its filing for recordation be valid as to all persons without further or other recordation . . . . (f) The Administrator shall keep a record of the time and date of the filing of conveyances and other instruments with him and of the time and date of recordation thereof. He shall record conveyances and other instruments filed with him in the order of their reception, in files to be kept for that purpose, and indexed according to . . . the identifying description of the aircraft, aircraft engine, or propeller . . . and . . . the names of the parties to the conveyance or other instrument."

Section 506 of the Act, 49 United States Code Annotated section 1406, was added in 1964 and provides: "The validity of any instrument the recording of which is provided for by section 1403 of this title shall be governed by the laws of the State . . . in which such instrument is delivered, irrespective of the location or the place of delivery of the property which is the subject of such instrument."

Our task is to determine whether the foregoing federal system of recording interests in aircraft affects priorities recognized by applicable state law. The issue is squarely before us because, absent the federal recording system and its possible impact on state law, there can be no doubt that Tanger had the power to defeat Beech's security interest by a sale to a buyer in the ordinary course of business and that plaintiff was such a buyer. *Section 9307 of the California Commercial Code* provides that, "A buyer in ordinary course of business (*subdivision (9) of Section 1201*) . . . takes free of a security interest created by his seller even though the security interest is perfected and even though the buyer knows of its existence." Hence, under California law, plaintiff would prevail over defendant Beech Acceptance Corporation regardless of whether defendant recorded its security interest and even if plaintiff knew of the existence of the security interest, so long as he was not aware of any terms of the security agreement that were violated by the sale to him. (See Uniform Commercial Code Comment 2, *Com. Code, § 9307.*)

Although this matter is of first impression in our court, we are cognizant of helpful authority in the Courts of Appeal on the question of the relationship between the federal recording system and state priorities. In *Pope v. National Aero Finance Co. (1965) 236 Cal.App.2d 722 [46 Cal.Rptr. 233]* (hg. den.), Justice Sullivan considered the assertion of plaintiffs that they held an interest in an aircraft superior to that of the prior record security interest of a mortgagee. Although there was doubt as to whether plaintiffs had any interest in the plane, the Court of Appeal assumed arguendo that they had acquired ownership. Plaintiffs had obtained their interest subsequent to the defendant-mortgagee's acquisition of its security interest, but two days before the latter's interest was recorded. Said the court, "The federal statute requiring recordation and providing for the effect to be given to instruments not recorded pursuant thereto, preempts any state laws which might otherwise apply. . . . Even if, as we here assume for the sake of argument, plaintiffs actually acquired some interest in the [aircraft] by virtue of their agreements, we are of the opinion that under the above-mentioned federal statute and the . . . cases interpreting it, it was incumbent upon them to record the documents under which they claimed ownership and having failed to do so at any time are not entitled to priority over NAFCO, the chattel mortgagee who in addition to acquiring its interest under a prior chattel mortgage filed the same for record in good faith and without any notice of plaintiffs' claims. . . . [It] would be violative of the purpose of the federal act to permit plaintiffs, who did nothing to comply with its registration and recordation provisions, to prevail over NAFCO which lent money on the strength of the record title in [the seller-mortgagor] and recorded its mortgage with the federal agency." (Fn. omitted.) (*Pope v. National Aero Finance Co., supra, 236 Cal.App.2d 722, 733, 734-735.*)

Although the facts are distinguishable from those in the case at bar, the reasoning of the *Pope* court has clear application here. In deciding the priorities between a mortgagee with a recorded interest and a subsequent purchaser who acquired his interest before the mortgagee's interest was recorded but who failed to record his own interest, the court looked to the federal law and determined that the policy underlying the recordation system precluded judgment for plaintiffs who had failed to comply with the recordation provisions. In the instant action, it was conceded that defendant Beech's interest was recorded months before plaintiff's purchase, and plaintiff was aware he could have checked title with the F.A.A. by telephone for a mere $ 3.50. As in *Pope*, defendant-mortgagee did all it could to protect its security interest by giving notice in the form of recordation to potential third-party purchasers. We would undermine any federal policy requiring recordation to protect previously acquired aircraft titles if we held that state law governed the rights of the parties irrespective of recordation.

Further persuasive precedent is provided by *International Atlas Services, Inc. v. Twentieth Century Aircraft Co. (1967) 251 Cal.App.2d 434 [59 Cal.Rptr. 495]* (hg. den.). In that case defendant sold an airplane to a retailer pursuant to a conditional sales contract by which defendant retained a security interest in the plane. The security interest was recorded with the F.A.A. Subsequently, the retailer hired plaintiff Atlas to repair the engines of the plane and became indebted to plaintiff for the repairs. The retailer eventually defaulted on all of his obligations, and defendant repossessed the airplane. Atlas claimed ownership of the engines by virtue of its mechanics' lien.

At the outset, the Court of Appeal reviewed the California law on priorities in both the Civil Code and the new Commercial Code and concluded "that under California law Atlas at a minimum should recover the value of its engines and at a maximum should recover the engines themselves. Nevertheless, we have concluded that California law does not apply to this case, that the controversy is governed by the laws of the United States, and that under federal law Twentieth Century must prevail. As we see it, general California law on the subject of title and liens to personal property in relation to component parts has been superseded by specific federal law with respect to aircraft." (*Id. at p. 438.*)

After quoting from the relevant subsections of section 1403, the Court of Appeal continued: "To bring order into the field of aircraft ownership and finance, the federal government in a manner within its sphere set up a comprehensive scheme of centralized recordation, which, if properly used, provides adequate protection for all substantial property interests in large aircraft . . . . A conveyance, lease, or security instrument recorded under section 1403(a) is fully valid against all persons from the time of its filing without further or other recordation. Under section 1403(c) a conveyance or instrument which could have been recorded but was not, is, until so recorded, invalid against a person without actual notice of the conveyance or instrument. . . .

"Here we have a complete and comprehensive system of recordation which necessarily supersedes inconsistent state law. Constitutionally, the federal government may be said to have fully occupied the field of recordation of interests in aircraft and of rights derived from recordation, and to have established paramount law in this area. Atlas could have fully protected its rights in these engines and preserved a good title throughout the world by . . . recording its interest in specifically numbered aircraft engines with the Federal Aviation Agency." (*Id. at p. 440.*)

Despite the factual distinctions between *Atlas* and the case at bar, the above-quoted passages would seem to be a compelling rationale for the proposition that the federal system of recordation affects the priorities under state law between prior security holders and subsequent lienholders and purchasers. (2) As construed by the Court of Appeal, section 1403 provides a comprehensive system of recordation the purpose of which is to bring order to the field of aircraft titles and to protect the holders of substantial property interests in aircraft. Neither of those purposes is served if we apply state law in a manner virtually ignoring the existence of the federal system. If prior recorded interests are not protected against subsequent buyers who fail to search title, the federal policy in favor of the recordation of aircraft titles will be frustrated and subsequent purchasers in California will cavalierly decline to investigate title so as to avoid "actual notice" under *Commercial Code section 9307.*

The California Courts of Appeal have not been alone in suggesting that prior recorded security interests under federal law should take precedence over subsequent purchasers. Although decisions in other jurisdictions have varied widely (see generally Annot. (1968) 22 A.L.R.3d 1270), most courts have taken a view consistent with that espoused in *Pope* and *Atlas*. (3) The case of *In re Veterans' Air Express Co. (D.N.J. 1948) 76 F.Supp. 684*, contains some particularly appropriate language: "It is clear that the Congress has prescribed the only way in which aircraft may be transferred and in which liens upon aircraft may be duly recorded. In this manner, all persons dealing with aircraft are upon full legal notice concerning possible liens *and are charged with the duty of inquiry at the central recording office of the Civil Aeronautics Administration* [predecessor to the Federal Aviation Agency] *with respect to any aircraft in which they might be concerned.*" (*Id. at p. 688.*) (Italics added.)

In *Dawson v. General Discount Corporation (1950) 82 Ga.App. 29 [60 S.E.2d 653]*, a Georgia appellate court considered facts almost identical to those before us. There, the plaintiff-mortgagee, who had acquired and recorded his security interest while the subject aircraft was in the possession of the conditional buyer, brought suit for possession of the plane against a subsequent purchaser who had failed to search title before his purchase. In affirming a judgment for the plaintiff-mortgagee, the court concluded: "[Constructive] notice was given by the recording of the instrument with the Civil Aeronautics Authority under the provisions of Title 49, U.S.C.A., which provides that every conveyance so recorded shall be valid as to all persons. No further act was required of the plaintiff to protect his rights. The defendant, before purchasing, had the opportunity to ascertain the paramount outstanding title by checking the records of the Civil Aeronautics Authority." (*Id. at p. 658.*)

Other cases adopting a view as to priorities based upon the federal recordation provisions include *Marsden v. Southern Flight Service, Inc. (M.D.N.C. 1964) 227 F.Supp. 411, 415, 418-419*; *United States v. United Aircraft Corporation (D.Conn. 1948) 80 F.Supp. 52*; *Smith v. Eastern Airmotive Corp. (1968) 99 N.J.Super. 340 [240 A.2d 17]*; *Crescent City Aviation, Inc. v. Beverly Bank (1966) 139 Ind.App. 669 [219 N.E.2d 446]*; *Continental Radio Co. v. Continental Bank & Trust Co. (Tex. 1963) 369 S.W.2d 359, 362*; and *James Talcott, Inc. v. Bank of Miami Beach (Fla. 1962) 143 So.2d 657, 659*.

In deciding that defendant's prior recorded security interest must prevail over a buyer in the ordinary course of business in order to further the policies expressed in section 503 of the Federal Aviation Act, we do not overlook those few cases reaching a contrary conclusion. Rather we do not find them persuasive and simply decline to follow them. In *Northern Illinois Corp. v. Bishop Distributing Co. (W.D.Mich. 1968) 284 F.Supp. 121* and *Texas National Bank of Houston v. Aufderheide (E.D.Ark. 1964) 235 F.Supp. 599*, the courts looked to state law and held that a buyer in the ordinary course of business should prevail over a prior mortgagee with a recorded security interest. Both courts concluded that state law governed priorities to aircraft and that persons buying new aircraft from authorized dealers without actual notice of prior claims (buyers in ordinary course of business) should not have to search title to protect their claims. While the view espoused in those cases has appeal from a policy perspective, it ignores the impact of the overriding federal policy in section 1403. The federal policy to foster recordation and to protect recorded interests is eviscerated by a rule which relies on state laws to protect the buyer in the ordinary course of business even though he fails to undertake a simple title search which would have readily revealed all encumbrances.

(4) For the foregoing reasons, we conclude that the judgment granting possession of the disputed airplane to plaintiff must be reversed. Because we have decided that the mortgagee holds a superior right to the aircraft, to the extent of his investment in it, the award of compensatory damages to plaintiff for his loss of use of the plane must be reversed; and it also follows that the award of punitive damages may not be sustained.

The judgment is reversed and remanded to the trial court with directions to amend its findings of fact and conclusions of law in accord with the views expressed herein and to enter judgment for Beech establishing the priority of Beech's security interest in the airplane.

PHILKO AVIATION, INC. *v.* SHACKET ET UX.

SUPREME COURT OF THE UNITED STATES

462 U.S. 406

June, 1983

JUSTICE WHITE delivered the opinion of the Court.

This case presents the question whether the Federal Aviation Act of 1958 (Act), 72 Stat. 737, as amended, 49 U.S.C. § 1301 *et seq.* (1976 ed. and Supp. V), prohibits all transfers of title to aircraft from having validity against innocent third parties unless the transfer has been evidenced by a written instrument, and the instrument has been recorded with the Federal Aviation Administration (FAA). We conclude that the Act does have such effect.

On April 19, 1978, at an airport in Illinois, a corporation operated by Roger Smith sold a new airplane to respondents. Respondents, the Shackets, paid the sale price in full and took possession of the aircraft, and they have been in possession ever since. Smith, however, did not give respondents the original bills of sale reflecting the chain of title to the plane. He instead gave them only photocopies and his assurance that he would "take care of the paperwork," which the Shackets understood to include the recordation of the original bills of sale with the FAA. Insofar as the present record reveals, the Shackets never attempted to record their title with the FAA.

Unfortunately for all, Smith did not keep his word but instead commenced a fraudulent scheme. Shortly after the sale to the Shackets, Smith purported to sell the same airplane to petitioner, Philko Aviation. According to Philko, Smith said that the plane was in Michigan having electronic equipment installed. Nevertheless, Philko and its financing bank were satisfied that all was in order, for they had examined the original bills of sale and had checked the aircraft's title against FAA records. At closing, Smith gave Philko the title documents, but, of course, he did not and could not have given Philko possession of the aircraft. Philko's bank subsequently recorded the title documents with the FAA.

After the fraud became apparent, the Shackets filed the present declaratory judgment action to determine title to the plane. Philko argued that it had title because the Shackets had never recorded their interest in the airplane with the FAA. Philko relied on § 503(c) of the Act, 72 Stat. 773, as amended, 49 U.S.C. § 1403(c), which provides that no conveyance or instrument affecting the title to any civil aircraft shall be valid against third parties not having actual notice of the sale, until such conveyance or other instrument is filed for recordation with the FAA. However, the District Court awarded summary judgment in favor of the Shackets, *Shacket v. Roger Smith Aircraft Sales, Inc., 497 F. Supp. 1262 (ND Ill. 1980)*, and the Court of Appeals affirmed, reasoning that § 503(c) did not pre-empt substantive state law regarding title transfers, and that, under the Illinois Uniform Commercial Code, Ill. Rev. Stat., ch. 26, P1-101 *et seq.* (1981), the Shackets had title but Philko did not. *681 F. 2d 506 (1982)*. We granted certiorari, *459 U.S. 1069 (1982)*, and we now reverse and remand for further proceedings.

Section 503(a)(1) of the Act, 49 U.S.C. § 1403(a)(1), directs the Secretary of Transportation to establish and maintain a system for the recording of any "conveyance which affects the title to, or any interest in, any civil aircraft of the United States." Section 503(c), 49 U.S.C. § 1403(c), states:

"No conveyance or instrument the recording of which is provided for by [§ 503(a)(1)] shall be valid in respect of such aircraft . . . against any person other than the person by whom the conveyance or other instrument is made or given, his heir or devisee, or any person having actual notice thereof, until such conveyance or other instrument is filed for recordation in the office of the Secretary of Transportation."

The statutory definition of "conveyance" defines the term as "a bill of sale, contract of conditional sale, mortgage, assignment of mortgage, or other instrument affecting title to, or interest in, property." 49 U.S.C. § 1301(20) (1976 ed., Supp. V). If § 503(c) were to be interpreted literally in accordance with the statutory definition, that section would not require every transfer to be documented and recorded; it would only invalidate unrecorded title *instruments,* rather than unrecorded title *transfers*. Under this interpretation, a claimant might be able to prevail against an innocent third party by establishing his title without relying on an instrument. In the present case, for example, the Shackets could not prove their title on the basis of an unrecorded bill of sale or other writing purporting to evidence a transfer of title to them, even if state law did not require recordation of such instruments, but they might still prevail, since Illinois law does not require written evidence of a sale "with respect to goods for which payment has been made and accepted or which have been received and accepted." Ill. Rev. Stat., ch. 26, P2-201(3)(c) (1981).

We are convinced, however, that Congress did not intend § 503(c) to be interpreted in this manner. Rather, § 503(c) means that every aircraft transfer must be evidenced by an instrument, and every such instrument must be recorded, before the rights of innocent third parties can be affected. Furthermore, because of these federal requirements, state laws permitting undocumented or unrecorded transfers are pre-empted, for there is a direct conflict between § 503(c) and such state laws, and the federal law must prevail.

These conclusions are dictated by the legislative history. The House and House Conference Committee Reports, and the section-by-section analysis of one of the bill's drafters, all expressly declare that the federal statute "requires" the recordation of "every transfer . . . of any interest in a civil aircraft." The House Conference Report explains: "This section requires the recordation with the Authority of every transfer made after the effective date of the section, of any interest in a civil aircraft of the United States. The conveyance evidencing *each such transfer* is to be recorded with an index in a recording system to be established by the Authority." Thus, since Congress intended to require the recordation of a conveyance evidencing *each transfer* of an interest in aircraft, Congress must have intended to pre-empt any state law under which a transfer without a recordable conveyance would be valid against innocent transferees or lienholders who have recorded.

Any other construction would defeat the primary congressional purpose for the enactment of § 503(c), which was to create "a central clearing house for recordation of titles so that a person, wherever he may be, will know where he can find ready access to the claims against, or liens, or other legal interests in an aircraft." Hearings on H.R. 9738 before the House Committee on Interstate and Foreign Commerce, 75th Cong., 3d Sess., 407 (1938) (testimony of F. Fagg, Director of Air Commerce, Dept. of Commerce). Here, state law does not require any documentation whatsoever for a valid transfer of an aircraft to be effected. An oral sale is fully valid against third parties once the buyer takes possession of the plane. If the state law allowing this result were not pre-empted by § 503(c), then any buyer in possession would have absolutely no need or incentive to record his title with the FAA, and he could refuse to do so with impunity, and thereby prevent the "central clearing house" from providing "ready access" to information about his claim. This is not what Congress intended.

In the absence of the statutory definition of conveyance, our reading of § 503(c) would be by far the most natural one, because the term "conveyance" is first defined in the dictionary as "the action of conveying," *i.e.,* "the act by which title to property . . . is transferred." Webster's Third New International Dictionary 499 (P. Gove ed. 1976). Had Congress defined "conveyance" in accordance with this definition, then § 503(c) plainly would have required the recordation of every transfer. Congress' failure to adopt this definition is not dispositive, however, since the statutory definition is expressly not applicable if "the context otherwise requires." 49 U.S.C. § 1301 (1976 ed. and Supp. V). Even in the absence of such a caveat, we need not read the statutory definition mechanically into § 503(c), since to do so would render the recording system ineffective and thus would defeat the purpose of the legislation. A statutory definition should not be applied in such a manner. *Lawson v. Suwannee Fruit & S.S. Co., 336 U.S. 198, 201 (1949).* Accordingly, we hold that state laws allowing undocumented or unrecorded transfers of interests in aircraft to affect innocent third parties are pre-empted by the federal Act.

In support of the judgment below, respondents rely on *In re Gary Aircraft Corp., 681 F. 2d 365 (CA5 1982),* which rejected the contention that § 503 pre-empted all state laws dealing with priority of interests in aircraft. The Court of Appeals held that the first person to record his interest with the FAA is not assured of priority, which is determined by reference to state law. We are inclined to agree with this rationale, but it does not help the Shackets. Although state law determines priorities, all interests must be federally recorded before they can obtain whatever priority to which they are entitled under state law. As one commentator has explained: "The only situation in which priority appears to be determined by operation of the [federal] statute is where the security holder has failed to record his interest. Such failure invalidates the conveyance as to innocent third persons. But recordation itself merely validates; it does not grant priority." Scott, Liens in Aircraft: Priorities, 25 J. Air L. & Commerce 193, 203 (1958) (footnote omitted). Accord, Sigman, The Wild Blue Yonder: Interests in Aircraft under Our Federal System, 46 So. Cal. L. Rev. 316, 324-325 (1973) (although recordation does not establish priority, "failure to record . . . serves to subordinate"); Note, 36 Wash. & Lee L. Rev. 205, 212-213 (1979).

In view of the foregoing, we find that the courts below erred by granting the Shackets summary judgment on the basis that if an unrecorded transfer of an aircraft is valid under state law, it has validity as against innocent third parties. Of course, it is undisputed that the sale to the Shackets was valid and binding as between the parties. Hence, if Philko had actual notice of the transfer to the Shackets or if, under state law, Philko failed to acquire or perfect the interest that it purports to assert for reasons wholly unrelated to the sale to the Shackets, Philko would not have an enforceable interest, and the Shackets would retain possession of the aircraft. Furthermore, we do not think that the federal law imposes a standard with which it is impossible to comply. There may be situations in which the transferee has used reasonable diligence to file and cannot be faulted for the failure of the crucial documents to be of record. But because of the manner in which this case was disposed of on summary judgment, matters such as these were not considered, and these issues remain open on remand. The judgment of the Court of Appeals is reversed, and the case is remanded for further proceedings consistent with this opinion.

So ordered.

JUSTICE O'CONNOR, concurring in part and concurring in the judgment.

I join the opinion of the Court except to the extent that it might be read to suggest this Court's endorsement of the view that one who makes a reasonably diligent effort to record will obtain the protections ordinarily reserved for recorded interests. I would express no opinion on that question, for it is not before us and has not been addressed in brief or in argument or, indeed, in the statute.

GARY AIRCRAFT CORPORATION v. GENERAL DYNAMICS CORPORATION.

UNITED STATES COURT OF APPEALS FOR THE FIFTH CIRCUIT

681 F.2d 365

July, 1982

WISDOM, Circuit Judge:

I.

This dispute over the ownership of one airplane and of the proceeds of the sale of another requires us to determine the reach of the Federal Aviation Act and its impact on state law. We also explore the protection accorded buyers against secured creditors by state law.

In December 1971, Gary Aircraft Corporation ("Gary"), the plaintiff-appellee, entered into a letter of understanding stating its intention to purchase four airplanes from Frederick B. Ayer & Associates, Inc. ("Ayer"), a dealer in aircraft. Two of these airplanes are the subject of the controversy here. Gary did not complete the purchase, but Arthur Stewart, its president, carried out the transaction in his individual capacity, purchasing the first plane in controversy here, N8222H, on December 22, 1971 for $ 5,000, and the second, N8221H, on January 4, 1972, also for $ 5,000. On the date of each sale, the airplane purchased was subject to a security interest held by General Dynamics Corporation ("General Dynamics"), the defendant-appellant. General Dynamics held its interest under a security agreement executed by Ayer on February 20, 1969. Under that agreement, Ayer was authorized to sell the collateral, unless it was in default on its obligations to General Dynamics. In case of default, Ayer could not sell without the written consent of General Dynamics. General Dynamics recorded its security agreement with the Federal Aviation Administration on March 3, 1969. On the dates of the sales to Stewart, Ayer was in default.

Crawford, the vice-president of Gary, requested a title search from the Aircraft Owners and Pilots Association on January 4, 1972. The AOPA reported the results on January 5, 1972. On August 3, 1972, approximately seven months after the sale, Stewart recorded his bill of sale with the FAA. Over the next four years, Crawford communicated periodically with Ayer, requesting that Ayer take action to secure the release of General Dynamics's security interest.

In March 1974, Stewart sold one of the group of four planes to Gary for $ 13,275. He transferred the two planes at issue here to Gary on November 7, 1975, apparently without consideration. Gary executed a mortgage on the aircraft in favor of the Victoria Bank and Trust Company, the third party defendant. The Victoria Bank recorded its interest with the FAA. On May 28, 1976, General Dynamics informed Gary that it had learned that the aircraft were registered in Gary's name and that General Dynamics was asserting a security interest in the property.

On October 28, 1976, Gary initiated Chapter XI proceedings under the Bankruptcy Act. It brought this action in the bankruptcy court, seeking to sell Airplane N8222H free and clear of liens. Upon the agreement of all interested parties, the court permitted the sale of the airplane, and the proceeds were deposited with the court. The second airplane remains in the possession of Gary.

The bankruptcy court, affirmed by the district court, held that Gary was entitled to the proceeds of the sale of Airplane N8222H and to the possession of Airplane N8222H, free of any interest asserted by General Dynamics. General Dynamics appeals, presenting three theories. First, it contends that the Federal Aviation Act grants it priority because it recorded its security interest with the Federal Aviation Administration before Stewart purchased the aircraft. Second, even if the FAA does not govern the priority question but instead remits it to Texas law, which protects a buyer in the ordinary course of business against the perfected security interest of his seller's creditor, General Dynamics argues that Stewart could not take free of its interest because, according to General Dynamics, Stewart could not qualify as a buyer in the ordinary course of business. Finally, General Dynamics contends that, even if Stewart did qualify as a buyer in the ordinary course, he could not transfer his status to Gary, and Gary did not qualify in its own right so, in Gary's hands, the aircraft are subject to the interest of General Dynamics. Concluding that the FAA does not govern priorities in interests in aircraft, that Stewart, as a buyer in the ordinary course of business, took free of General Dynamics's interest, and that Gary takes the title of its transferor, we affirm.

II.

General Dynamics's first theory presents this court, for the first time, with the question to what extent the provisions of the Federal Aviation Act, 49 U.S.C. §§ 1301-1542, preempt state regulation of interests in aircraft. The Civil Aeronautics Act of 1938, and its successor, the Federal Aviation Act of 1958, both create a single national recording system for interests in aircraft. Section 503 of the FAA, 49 U.S.C. § 1403, establishes the recording system and provides,

> (c) No conveyance or instrument the recording of which is provided for by subsection (a) of this section shall be valid in respect of such aircraft . . . against any person other than the person by whom the conveyance or other instrument is made or given, his heir or devisee, or any person having actual notice thereof, until such conveyance or other instrument is filed for recordation. . . .

> (d) Each conveyance or other instrument recorded by means of or under the system provided for in subsection (a) or (b) of this section shall from the time of its filing for recordation be valid as to all persons without further or other recordation.

In 1964, Congress added section 506, 49 U.S.C. § 1406, providing,

> The validity of any instrument the recording of which is provided for by section 1403 of this title shall be governed by the laws of the State, District of Columbia, or territory or possession of the United States in which such instrument is delivered. . . .

Without question, section 506 reserves some areas of regulation for the states by assigning questions of "validity" to state law. At the same time, Congress has provided the exclusive means of recordation and has preempted state laws providing filing systems for interests in aircraft. *See, e.g., Bank of Lexington v. Jack Adams Aircraft Sales, Inc., 570 F.2d 1220,* 5 Cir. 1978 (dictum); Scott, *Liens in Aircraft: Priorities,* 25 J. Air L. & Com. 193, 200 (1958).

Whether Congress intended to preempt a broader field of state law by federalizing also the assignment of priorities to various interests in aircraft is not as clear. The courts have split on that question. [citations omitted].

After considering the language of the FAA and the CAA as well as their legislative history, we conclude that the FAA does not displace state law assignment of priorities to interests in aircraft. That conclusion is in accord with the weight of recent authority, [citations omitted]. A majority of the commentators agree. [citations omitted].

Although Congress has acted in the general field of aircraft interests, the supremacy clause, U.S.Const. art. VI, requires us to invalidate state law only if it conflicts with a federal statute, if it would frustrate a federal scheme, or if the totality of the circumstances shows that Congress sought to occupy the field. The intent of Congress is determinative. *Malone v. White Motor Corp., 1978, 435 U.S. 497, 504, 98 S. Ct. 1185, 1189, 55 L. Ed. 2d 443, 450.* The courts do not favor the preemption of state law, however, and, in the absence of strong reasons to believe that Congress intended to displace it, state law governs. *Chicago and Northwestern Transportation Co. v. Kalo Brick & Tile Co., 1981, 450 U.S. 311, 315-316, 101 S. Ct. 1124, 1129, 67 L. Ed. 2d 258, 264-65.*

Before examining the statute itself, we reject General Dynamics's contention that it would be meaningless to create a central recording system without according priority to earlier recorded interests. Refusing to grant priority to recorded interests over all others would make sense if Congress were attempting to deal with the problems created by the mobility of aircraft. Before the enactment of the CAA, to be certain of protecting his interest insofar as an interest in an airplane was protectible by recordation, the holder had to record in all states in which the aircraft might be located. Similarly, a subsequent creditor or purchaser had to undertake a title search in all states if he wished to be certain that no prior recorded interests existed. By creating a single federal recording system, Congress eliminated the need for multiple recordation and multiple title searches. If that was the only problem that Congress intended to resolve, it would not be necessary to address the question of priorities at all, for the establishment of a recording system does not compel any given set of priority rules. The Uniform Commercial Code is a case in point. Although it sets up a recording system for interests in personal property, *see U.C.C. §§ 9-401--9-403* (1962), it also creates a priority system under which a recorded interest does not take precedence over all unrecorded interests or all interests recorded later, *e.g., id. §§ 9-307(2), 9-310.* These special priority rules further goals other than encouraging recordation, such as promoting the free alienability of goods by protecting good faith buyers from the interests of the creditors of their retailer-sellers. In enacting the CAA and the FAA, Congress could have intended to eliminate the problems inherent in local recordation of mobile property but to leave to the states the task of striking the balance between competing interests that dictates the effect that recordation of an interest will have on its priority.

Looking to the statute itself, we find that the language is ambiguous. Subsections 503(c) and (d) provide that no instrument shall be "valid" (except against the parties to the instrument and parties with actual knowledge) until filed and that, once filed with the Federal Aviation Administration, all instruments shall be "valid" without further recordation. But "validity" need not establish priority. On the contrary, it may mean nothing more than that recordation with the FAA will assure the instrument such "validity" as state law grants a recorded instrument. As the district court noted, if the term "valid" refers to enforceability, a literal interpretation of the language would lead to irrational results--one could create an enforceable interest in an aircraft without giving any value simply by recording it with the FAA. Still, we could read the statute as giving "validity" in the sense of priority to recorded interests *otherwise* "valid" under state law--that is, "valid" in the sense of complying with formalities and requirements of consideration. Under that interpretation, the choice of law rule in section 506, which refers questions of "validity" to the law of the state where the instrument was delivered, would mean only that the law of that state governs these questions of formality and adequacy of consideration.

The statute does undertake to assign some substantive priorities. For instance, it recognizes and provides for recordation of the "basket lien"--a lien over stocks of spare parts maintained for installation in aircraft, 49 U.S.C. § 1403(a)(3)--and provides that a recorded interest in a specific engine shall have priority over both previously and subsequently recorded basket liens. § 1403(d). *See* 1 G. Gilmore, Security Interests in Personal Property § 13.5 (1965). But the treatment of this special lien, *see id.,* does not necessarily indicate that Congress was legislating a full set of priority rules to cover all interests. On the contrary, the use of specific language to cover this special case could just as readily suggest that Congress meant to leave other priority rules remain unchanged--that is, they are left to state law.

[a discussion about maritime liens is omitted].

III.

[further discussion omitted]

V.

We hold that the FAA does not preempt the provisions of the Texas Business and Commerce Code relating to the priority of interests in aircraft. Therefore, Stewart, as a buyer in the ordinary course of business, took the aircraft free and clear of the lien of General Dynamics. And Gary, as the transferee of Stewart, also took free and clear of the lien. Consequently, Gary is entitled to the possession of the remaining airplane and the proceeds of the airplane that was sold. The case is AFFIRMED.

CHAD M. KOPPIE v. UNITED STATES OF AMERICA and LIGON
"AIR", an Indiana partnership.

UNITED STATES COURT OF APPEALS FOR THE SEVENTH
CIRCUIT

1 F.3d 651

August, 1993

CUMMINGS, *Circuit Judge.*

Plaintiff Chad M. Koppie sued Ligon "Air", an Indiana partnership, and the Federal Aviation Administration ("FAA"), over the ownership of a plane. Koppie claims that Ligon "Air" is in control of the aircraft, a Convair 880, which he rightly owns, and that the FAA took the wrong side in the dispute by issuing a Certificate of Registration to Ligon "Air" rather than to him. Plaintiff claims that these misdeeds by Ligon "Air" and the federal government cost him $ 667,000, but the district judge was not convinced and neither are we. Koppie's case against Ligon "Air" is based on diversity jurisdiction and his claim against the government is a federal question stemming from the Federal Tort Claims Act, *28 U.S.C. §§ 2671-2680.*

Koppie purchased, or thought he purchased, the Convair from Hudson General Corporation in 1987 for a mere $ 5,000, a strikingly good deal for an aircraft that originally cost $ 10 million. Hudson had obtained title through satisfaction of a garnishment lien against Ligon "Air", which owed it money for storing and maintaining the plane. But unbeknownst to Koppie, the aircraft had made its way back into the hands of Ligon "Air" through a circuitous route. Koppie took ownership subject to the recorded interest of Cromwell State Bank, the original lienholder, and Cromwell assigned its interest to something called the "880 Partnership", which then resold the plane to Ligon "Air". Both the "880 Partnership" and Ligon "Air" are owned by the same two people, Susan and Cliff Pettit. Koppie knew something was amiss when in June or July of 1987 he went to the airport to look after his plane and discovered Michael Potter, whom he thought was an agent for Ligon "Air", working on the aircraft.

In the meantime, Koppie had applied for a Certificate of Aircraft Registration from the FAA. On June 23, 1987, he received a letter denying his request because of the conflicting claims over ownership. The letter said in part:

> Review of the aircraft file indicates it was repossessed May 23, 1987, premised upon a security agreement, which was recorded by the FAA on July 9, 1982, and subsequently sold to Ligon Air, 105 West 2nd St., Ligonier, IN 46767. In view of the repossession and subsequent sale, we are unable to issue a certificate of aircraft registration in your name at this time.

Having learned that his ownership of the plane was in serious dispute, Koppie signed two documents releasing whatever interests he might have had in the Convair in return for consideration of $ 36,000 from Michael Potter. Koppie eventually received and accepted the money, and the plane was flown to South Africa, where it remains.

The district court granted Ligon "Air"'s motion for summary judgment in December 1991, but judgment was not officially rendered until August of 1992 (plaintiff's app. at 29). At that time the district judge also handed down an order and judgment granting the FAA's motion for summary judgment. Koppie now claims that the release of his interests in the Convair was nullified by a subsequent document between him and Michael Potter and Western Continental Holdings, Ltd. But in that document Potter and Western Continental Holdings acknowledged that they have no interest of any kind in the plane. The document is thus meaningless. Clearly, it is impossible for a person who owns no interest in a piece of property to execute an agreement for consideration transferring ownership of the property to another. This is akin to the proverbial selling of the Brooklyn Bridge. Since the subsequent document has no validity, Koppie's earlier decision to accept $ 36,000 for the relinquishment of all claims to the Convair prevents him from now complaining that he, not Ligon "Air", owns the aircraft.

As for the FAA, Koppie alleged in his first amended complaint under the Federal Tort Claims Act that the agency wrongfully denied him a Certificate of Aircraft Registration and tortiously converted Koppie's property. The major flaw in this argument is that merely registering an aircraft with the FAA does not determine ownership and has no legal effect. Under 49 U.S.C. § 1401(f), the purpose of registering a plane is to define its nationality for international travel, and the statute states explicitly: "Such certificate shall be conclusive evidence of nationality for international purposes, but not in any proceeding under the laws of the United States. Registration shall not be evidence of ownership of aircraft in any proceeding [such as here] in which ownership by a particular person is, or may be an issue." See *Northwestern Flyers, Inc. v. Olson Bros. Mfg. Co., Inc., 679 F.2d 1264, 1270 n.13 (8th Cir. 1982)* (registration does not control questions of title). Since the registration does not even have effect in American courts, and the statute expressly forbids the kind of ownership claim made here based on certification, Koppie is clearly stretching credulity in arguing that the FAA harmed him with regard to ownership by failing to grant him, rather than Ligon "Air", a certificate. In essence, such a certificate is worthless as far as proving ownership, and thus Koppie could not by definition have lost anything by its denial.

The district court also held that Koppie's claims against the FAA were barred by the Federal Tort Claims Act's exception for government officials performing discretionary functions, *28 U.S.C. § 2680*, and by the doctrine of collateral estoppel because a summary judgment order had already been issued against Koppie in favor of Ligon "Air". Having decided that the federal government is simply not liable in these circumstances for rendering an opinion about ownership, we need not reach these two issues. The judgments for both defendants are affirmed, but Ligon "Air"'s motion for sanctions is denied because, although unsuccessful, plaintiff's appeal was not frivolous within the meaning of *Rule 38 of the Federal Rules of Appellate Procedure.*

FALL CREEK CONSTRUCTION COMPANY, INC. vs. DIRECTOR OF REVENUE.

SUPREME COURT OF MISSOURI

109 S.W.3d 165

July, 2003

I.

Fall Creek Construction Company seeks review of the decision of the Administrative Hearing Commission ("AHC") that Fall Creek is liable for $ 43,369.63 in use tax, plus accrued interest, on its fractional ownership interests in two aircraft enrolled in a fractional ownership program. The decision of the AHC is affirmed.

II.

The underlying facts are not in dispute. Fall Creek is a real estate development company with its principal place of business in Branson, Missouri. Fall Creek develops real estate in Missouri, Mississippi, Arizona, Virginia and Tennessee. Fall Creek's employees regularly travel to and from locations where it develops real estate.

On October 30, 1998, Fall Creek acquired fractional interests in two aircraft from Raytheon Travel Air Company, a Kansas Corporation. Fall Creek purchased a 1/16 (6.25%) undivided interest in a King Air B200 aircraft, tail number N713TA for $ 254,000 and a 1/8 (12.5%) undivided interest in a Beech Jet 400A aircraft, tail number N798TA for $ 772,500. Delivery of these interests occurred in Wichita, Kansas and neither Fall Creek nor Raytheon paid any sales or use tax to either Kansas or Missouri.

In order to purchase these interests, Fall Creek was required to enter into a series of four separate agreements for each aircraft -- an aircraft purchase agreement, a joint ownership agreement, a management agreement, and a master interchange agreement (these documents are collectively referred to as the "governing documents"). The purchase agreement indicates that Fall Creek "desires to purchase... an undivided property interest in the aircraft" and also provides: (1) the buyer must execute the governing documents and must perform such actions as are required by the closing date; (2) no buyer may place a lien on the aircraft; (3) transfers to third parties are conditioned upon meeting strict requirements of Raytheon; (4) Raytheon has a right of first refusal on the transfer of interest; and (5) after 60 months, Raytheon must purchase the interest back from the buyer. Each owner also must execute an irrevocable power of attorney allowing Raytheon to file the appropriate application with the Federal Aviation Administration ("FAA") on each occasion that a fractional interest in the aircraft is purchased.

While the purchase agreement places restrictions on the fractional owners, the bill of sale recites that Raytheon "does ... hereby sell, grant, transfer and deliver all rights, title, and interests in and to an undivided ... interest in such aircraft unto: Fall Creek Construction Company, Inc." The FAA recognizes Fall Creek and the other co-owners as legal owners of a partial interest in each particular aircraft. Additionally, Fall Creek depreciates the aircraft on its accounting ledgers.

The joint ownership agreement provides that co-owners place the aircraft into the master interchange program and agree that they are all tenants in common with respect to the aircraft. The co-owners waive any right to partition and agree to divest themselves solely in accordance with the governing documents.

Under the management agreement, co-owners hire Raytheon to manage the aircraft. Owners pay a separate monthly management fee and a variable hourly rate for flight hours. Raytheon manages aircraft scheduling and must make reasonable efforts to obtain the owner's actual aircraft before providing a similar aircraft under the interchange program. Raytheon must also: (1) have the aircraft inspected, maintained, serviced, repaired, overhauled and tested; (2) maintain all required aircraft records and logs; (3) provide pilots, pilot training, pilot medical examinations and pilot uniforms; (4) provide hangaring and tie-down space, in-flight catering, flight planning, weather services, and communications; (5) maintain insurance on the aircraft; and (6) provide consulting regarding FAA issues, warranty claims, and insurance matters.

The master interchange agreement requires each owner to participate in the master interchange program by sharing its aircraft with other participants in the program. If an owner's aircraft is unavailable, Raytheon may substitute another similar aircraft from among the 110 aircraft in the program. Under the program, a participant informs Raytheon of the date and destination of the trip. Raytheon arranges for a program aircraft to carry the participant. Raytheon or the pilot determines whether the aircraft will fly to a location due to adverse weather conditions or other restrictions. However, the owner is in "operational control" of the aircraft while in the air and may direct the pilot to an alternate destination.

During the tax period, October 30, 1998, through December 31, 1999, aircraft 713TA made a total of 840 flights. Twenty-six flights were arrivals to or departures from Missouri. The aircraft remained overnight in Missouri thirteen times and Fall Creek used the aircraft in Missouri eight times.

Aircraft 798TA completed 897 flights during the tax period. Sixteen flights were arrivals to or departures from Missouri. The aircraft remained overnight in Missouri eleven times and Fall Creek used the aircraft in Missouri three times.

Fall Creek made a total of sixty-seven flights from or to Missouri during the tax period. These flights were made while traveling on a combination of its own aircraft and others from the interchange program. Fourteen of these sixty-seven flights were intrastate flights within Missouri.

The Director of Revenue conducted a sales and use tax audit of Fall Creek. After her audit, the Director assessed unpaid use tax in the amount of $ 60,453.42 and accrued interest totaling $ 8,120.67. The parties stipulated that, after allowing trade-in credit for aircraft 600TA, the total disputed amount is $ 49,928.79.

[discussion of jurisdiction omitted]

IV.

Missouri's use tax, *section 144.610*, states:

1. A tax is imposed for the privilege of storing, using or consuming within this state any article of tangible personal property purchased on or after the effective date of *sections 144.600 to 144.745* in an amount equivalent to the percentage imposed on the sales price in the sales tax law in *section 144.020*. This tax does not apply with respect to the storage, use or consumption of any article of tangible personal property purchased, produced or manufactured outside this state until the transportation of the article has finally come to rest within this state or until the article has become commingled with the general mass of property of this state.

This tax is a levy on the privilege of using within this state property purchased outside Missouri, where the property would have been subject to the sales tax if purchased locally. *Dir. of Revenue v. Superior Aircraft Leasing Co., 734 S.W.2d 504, 505* (Mo. banc 1987). Its purpose is to "complement, supplement, and protect the sales tax." *Id. at 506* (quotation omitted). This tax "eliminates the incentive to purchase from out-of-state merchants in order to escape local sales taxes thereby keeping in-state merchants competitive with sellers in other states, and it also provides a means to augment state revenues." *Id.* (quotation omitted).

Fall Creek calls on this Court to determine whether its fractional ownership of two aircraft is taxable under Missouri's use tax and asserts four reasons why its interests are not taxable.

1.

Fall Creek first contends that it does not owe use tax because its fractional ownership interest in each aircraft does not constitute a purchase of tangible personal property, but merely represents the right to use any aircraft in the interchange program for a specified number of hours per year.

"Purchase" is defined as "the acquisition of the ownership of, or title to, tangible personal property, through a sale, as defined herein, for the purpose of storage, use or consumption in this state." *Section 144.605(5)*. "Sale" is:

any transfer, barter or exchange of the title or ownership of tangible personal property, or the right to use, store or consume the same, for a consideration to be paid, and any transaction whether called leases, rentals, bailments, loans, conditional sales or otherwise, and notwithstanding that the title or possession of the property is retained for security.

Section 144.605(7). "Tangible personal property" is defined as "all items subject to Missouri sales tax as provided in subdivisions (1) and (3) of *section 144.020*." *Section 144.605(11)*. The non-exclusive list of tangible personal property includes "motor vehicles, trailers, motorcycles, mopeds, motortricycles, boats and outboard motors...." *Section 144.020(1)*. An aircraft is an item subject to Missouri sales tax. *See Westwood Country Club v. Dir. of Revenue, 6 S.W.3d 885, 887* (Mo. banc 1999) (Where aircraft are sold to non-exempt entities a sales or use tax is to be collected on the sale of the final product.).

Fall Creek cites a New York advisory opinion and an "FYI" notice in *Tax Policy News* by the Texas Comptroller in support of its argument. While these sources do offer some support for Fall Creek's contention, they are not binding on this Court and, upon close review, appear to offer an incomplete analysis of fractional ownership taxation. The "FYI" is a half-page announcement applying to no specific case or controversy and with no citation to law, Carole Keeton Rylander, *FYI: Sales Tax*, TAX POLICY NEWS (Vol. X, Issue 8 Dec. 2000), while the New York advisory opinion concludes that there is never an actual sale at all in fractional aircraft ownership. *Gap, Inc.*, No. S990720A, *2000 N.Y. Tax LEXIS 37* (N.Y. Dept. of Taxation and Fin. Jan. 28, 2000). Neither source is persuasive in this case. Missouri law is well settled that where no ambiguity exists in the contract language, "the court need not resort to construction of the contract, but rather the intent of the parties is determined from the four corners of the contract." *Eisenberg v. Redd, 38 S.W.3d 409, 411* (Mo. banc 2001).

Here, the purchase agreement is unambiguous. It states that "Buyer desires to purchase from Seller, and Seller desires to sell to Buyer, the undivided property interest ... in the aircraft...." Were this Court to look beyond the four corners of the purchase agreement, other governing documents would also evidence Fall Creek's intention to purchase property interests in the aircraft. Raytheon executed a bill of sale indicating that it "does ... hereby sell, grant, transfer and deliver all rights, title, and interests in and to an undivided ... interest in such aircraft" to Fall Creek. Further, the separate master interchange agreement specifically states that it is "an arrangement whereby a person leases *his airplane* to another person in exchange for equal time, when needed, on the *other person's airplane*...." (emphasis added). The purchase agreement clearly and unambiguously demonstrates that Fall Creek intended and understood that it was purchasing an interest in tangible personal property -- the aircraft.

Despite this unambiguous contract language, Fall Creek argues that an "essence of the transaction" test should determine the nature of the transaction. Fall Creek claims that its ownership of the physical aircraft is merely incidental and that the true nature of the transaction is one for transportation services. Clearly this was a complex transaction between sophisticated parties designed to maximize regulatory and tax advantages. However, the mere fact that the purchase agreement was executed along with other agreements does not render the contract ambiguous nor does it change the nature of Fall Creek's interest. Extrinsic evidence of contractual intent, including a determination of the "essence of the transaction," is necessary only if the contract contains an ambiguity. There is no ambiguity as to Fall Creek's purchase of fractional interests in the aircraft; therefore, an "essence of the transaction" analysis is not necessary.

Fall Creek unambiguously purchased an undivided fractional ownership interest in two aircraft as evidenced by the purchase agreement. The mere fact that it entered into additional management agreements with Raytheon does not change the nature of Fall Creek's ownership interest. Point one is denied.

2.

Next, Fall Creek argues that imposition of Missouri's use tax on its fractional ownership interest in the aircraft impermissibly burdens interstate commerce.

Historically, states could not tax interstate commerce and could only impose a sales or use tax during a "taxable moment" -- that period of time "during which the property [had] reached the end of its interstate movement and [had] not yet begun to be consumed in interstate operations." *Superior Aircraft, 734 S.W.2d at 506*. However, the United States Supreme Court later declared that interstate commerce is not immune from state and local taxation and "may constitutionally be made to pay its way." *Id.* (quoting *Maryland v. Louisiana, 451 U.S. 725, 754, 68 L. Ed. 2d 576, 101 S. Ct. 2114 (1981))*.

While interstate commerce must "pay its way," a state's right to tax interstate commerce is limited. *Superior Aircraft, 734 S.W.2d at 507*. No state tax may be imposed unless the tax: "(1) has a substantial nexus with the State; (2) is fairly apportioned; (3) does not discriminate against interstate commerce; and (4) is fairly related to the services provided by the State." *Id.* (citing *Maryland v. Louisiana, 451 U.S. at 754*). Fall Creek challenges only the first element of this test -- that there is a substantial nexus with Missouri.

There exists the requisite nexus with Missouri, even though these aircraft were hangared and maintained primarily outside of this state. These aircraft departed from or arrived in Missouri forty-two times and remained overnight in Missouri twenty-four times during the tax period. "The use in Missouri, however brief, is a taxable incident" and was sufficient to create a substantial nexus. *R & M Enter., Inc. v. Dir. of Revenue, 748 S.W.2d 171, 173* (Mo. banc 1988) (citing *Superior Aircraft, 734 S.W.2d 504*) (other citation omitted), *overruled on other grounds by House of LLoyd, Inc. v. Dir. of Revenue, 884 S.W.2d 271* (Mo. banc 1994). Point two is denied.

3.

Fall Creek also claims that it had insufficient dominion and control over its aircraft to constitute "storage" or "use" under *section 144.610*. Fall Creek argues that Raytheon maintained control of the aircraft and that Fall Creek merely contacted Raytheon to request transportation to a particular location. Fall Creek cites to no other law supporting its contention.

"Storage" is defined as "any keeping or retention in this state of tangible personal property purchased from a vendor, except property for sale or property that is temporarily kept or retained in this state for subsequent use outside the state." *Section 144.605(10)*. "Use" is:

the exercise of *any right or power* over tangible personal property incident to the ownership or control of that property, except that it does not include the temporary storage of property in this state for subsequent use outside the state, or the sale of property in the regular course of business[.]

Section 144.605(13) (emphasis added).

Fall Creek is simply incorrect in its assertion that "operational control" is *de minimus* control of the aircraft. One of the regulatory advantages of fractional ownership is the ability to operate within Part 91 of the Federal Aviation Regulations. Philip E. Crowther, *Taxation of Fractional Programs: "Flying Over Uncharted Waters"*, 67 J. AIR L. & COM. 241, 249 (Spring 2002). "With certain exceptions, in order to operate under Part 91, the user must accept responsibility for 'operational control' of the aircraft." *Id.* Such responsibility is more than token. *Id.* The user-owner is held responsible by the FAA and civil courts if there is an incident. *Id.*

The Federal Aviation Regulations ensure that owners are fully aware of the consequences of having operational control. *Id.* An aircraft owner accepting "operational control" must acknowledge that he or she: "(i) has responsibility for compliance with all Federal Aviation Regulations applicable to the flight; (ii) may be exposed to enforcement actions for noncompliance; and (iii) may be exposed to significant liability risk in the event of a flight-related occurrence that causes personal injury or property damage." *Id.* (internal quotations omitted); *14 C.F.R. section 91.1013.*

Operational control of an aircraft is a significant assumption of control and responsibility and is clearly sufficient to constitute "the exercise of any right or power." *Section 144.605(13).* Fall Creek used its aircraft when it boarded the aircraft and assumed operational control. Point three is denied.

4.

Last, Fall Creek maintains that the aircraft did not "finally come to rest" within Missouri as required by *section 144.610.* The use tax does not apply "until the transportation of the article *has finally come to rest* within the state or until the article has become commingled with the general mass of property of this state. " *Section 144.610(1)* (emphasis added). Fall Creek insists that, because of the nature of the interchange program, the aircraft are purely transient and never come to rest in any location.

Fall Creek relies on *Nubo v. Director of Revenue*, No. RS-84-1778, 1987 Mo. Tax LEXIS 226 (Mo. Admin. Hearing Comm'n Dec. 30, 1987), in support of its argument. AHC decisions do not constitute precedent in this Court, *Ovid Bell Press, Inc. v. Dir. of Revenue, 45 S.W.3d 880, 886 (Mo. banc 2001),* and this Court is not bound by the AHC's interpretation of revenue law and exercises *de novo* review.

This issue is controlled by *Director of Revenue v. Superior Aircraft Leasing Co., 734 S.W.2d 504 (Mo. banc 1987).* There, a Missouri corporation purchased an aircraft in Kansas in order to lease it to an Ohio-based charter / aircraft retail company. *Id. at 505.* The aircraft was hangared and maintained in Ohio and was used infrequently in Missouri. *Id.* Although the language of *section 144.610(1)* was not expressly discussed in the majority opinion, this Court tacitly rejected the argument as evidenced by the dissenting opinion of Judge Welliver. *See id. at 508-09* (Welliver, J., dissenting) ("Under these circumstances, I think that the airplane did not 'finally come to rest within this state'...."). Judge Welliver's dissent received no other votes and this Court applied the use tax despite the fact that Missouri was not the aircraft's permanent base or home. *Id. at 508.*

This Court also addressed the language of *section 144.610(1)* in *R & M Enterprises, Inc. v. Director of Revenue, 748 S.W.2d 171* (Mo.

banc 1988), *overruled on other grounds by House of Lloyd, Inc. v. Dir. of Revenue, 884 S.W.2d 271* (Mo. banc 1994). *R & M Enterprises* applied the use tax to books that were bound outside of Missouri but stored briefly in the state before being shipped to retailers both inside and outside of Missouri. *Id. at 171.* This Court said:

> ... Appellant ... has complete dominion and control over [the books]. They come to rest in Missouri.... [Appellant] has the privilege of "using," in the sense of the statute. It makes no difference that it may assert this privilege only a very brief time. The privilege of using is the occasion for taxation.

Id. at 172. The aircraft here are no different than the books in *R & M Enterprises*. Once the aircraft were delivered to Missouri, Fall Creek obtained operational control and had the privilege of using the aircraft in Missouri. That privilege triggered imposition of the use tax and brought the aircraft within the statute, such that the aircraft finally came to rest in Missouri and became commingled with the general mass of property of the state. "It makes no difference that [Fall Creek asserted] this privilege only a very brief time." *Id.*

The phrase "finally comes to rest" must necessarily be considered in relation to the object to which it applies. Were this Court to adopt Fall Creek's strict construction of the statute, no aircraft, motor vehicle or other transitory object could ever finally come to rest in Missouri until it "finally" entered the junkyard or scrap heap, for until then such objects always have the capability of leaving the state. The term "finally" cannot have such an exclusive meaning in this context. Rather, "finally" merely indicates that the property is "finally" in Missouri ready for use. In this context, the term "finally" need not mean that the property must remain here forever or be "domiciled" here, especially transitory property like airplanes whose use may require that they fly in and out of the state. Just as "vegetables do not have to 'come to rot' in order to [finally] 'come to rest,'" aircraft need not be interred in an airplane graveyard to satisfy the statute.

Here, the aircraft finally came to rest in Missouri when they landed in this state and Fall Creek exercised control over them and used them in this state. Point four is denied.

V.

For the foregoing reasons, the decision of the Administrative Hearing Commission is affirmed.

WILLIAM RAY PRICE, JR., Judge

All concur.

VI.   CONTRACT LAW – INSURANCE

A. *Basic Insurance Law*

Mary Jo HAWKINS v. STATE LIFE INSURANCE COMPANY

UNITED STATES DISTRICT COURT FOR THE EASTERN
DISTRICT OF TENNESSEE, NORTHERN DIVISION

366 F. Supp. 1031

July, 1972

ROBERT L. TAYLOR, District Judge.

This is an action by the beneficiary of a life insurance policy to
recover the proceeds allegedly due and payable on the insured's death
which occurred June 11, 1968. Defendant seeks to defeat recovery on
the ground that the circumstances of death preclude recovery under the
aviation exclusion provision attached to the policy. Plaintiff contends
that the insured's death resulted from a war risk instead of an aviation
risk.

When he applied to defendant for insurance, the insured
represented that he would enter the United States Army as a pilot. In
making the application, he signed a "Supplement to Application"
concerning aviation wherein he agreed that the following would
constitute a part of the policy:

> "This policy is issued subject to the express condition
> and agreement that the following risks are specifically
> excluded from the coverage afforded by this policy,
> notwithstanding anything contained in the policy to the
> contrary:
>
>> "'Death of the Insured as a result of
>> travel or flight in, or descent from or with
>> any kind of aircraft, provided the Insured
>> is a pilot, officer, or member of the crew
>> of such aircraft, or is giving or receiving
>> any kind of training or instruction or has
>> any duties aboard such aircraft or
>> requiring descent therefrom.'"

The policy's "Premium Waiver Disability Provision" provides that
no premiums shall be waived if the disability of the insured results
from "an act of war, declared or undeclared." The policy does not
contain a war risk exclusion clause. This implies that war risks are
contemplated as covered by the policy. Defendant makes no claim that
war risks are excluded by this policy.

On the date of death the insured left his base in a light observation
aircraft and did not return. His plane was found later that day. The
Department of the Army's "Report of Casualty," which by its own
terms is an official certificate of death, states:

"DIED 11 June 1968 in Vietnam from burns received while pilot aboard military aircraft which was hit by hostile fire, crashed and burned."

Captain David Creasman of the United States Army, who knew the deceased both in flight school and in Vietnam, was a witness in the case. Both the deceased and Captain Creasman were reconnaissance pilots who flew single-engine, light observation planes in Vietnam. The plane is a two-man, high wing craft with stick control and air speed of 85 to 290 miles per hour. It is a very responsive, highly maneuverable aerobatic craft. It has gliding capability and can land as safely without power as with power. It has three radio systems including a UHF emergency channel that is monitored by all military aircraft at all times. In the event of trouble it takes only a half second to hit the emergency switch, and get out a "Mayday" signal stating the plane's location. This action does not interfere with operating the plane. All pilots in Vietnam received intensive training in getting off this signal.

Captain Creasman was the first person to locate the deceased's crash site. Because of well established military procedures he knew that the deceased was unconscious before he could get off a distress signal. None of several aircraft fire control towers or several subsectors within communication distance had received a distress signal from anyone that morning.

The crash site was a wooded area on the side of a mountain approximately 100 meters from Highway 19, which was an ideal landing site. There were other less suitable, but survivable, landing sites within gliding distance of the crash site. The plane was upright, intact and its cockpit was burned out. The tree tops had not been knocked off, indicating that there had been no normal glide as would occur in a landing attempt. No conscious pilot would have landed with his nose pointing downhill as was this plane.

The crash site was in Viet Cong controlled territory where observation planes frequently received small arms fire from the ground. The condition of the plane indicated that its fuel tanks on the wings had exploded, thereby burning out the cockpit.

In general, where an insurer seeks to avoid payment under an exclusion clause it has the burden of showing the facts necessary to defeat recovery. *American Indemnity Company v. Sears, Roebuck & Co., 195 F.2d 353* (C.A. 6, 1962). Because the insurer chooses the language in its policies, its policies are construed against it and in favor of the insured. *Sturgill v. Life Insurance Co. of Georgia, 62 Tenn. App. 550, 465 S.W.2d 742* (Tenn.App., 1970). An aviation exclusion clause is a valid provision in a life insurance policy. *Bennett v. Metropolitan Life Insurance Company, 206 Tenn. 652, 337 S.W.2d 9 (1960)*.

The question presented is whether the insured's death is within the scope of the aviation exclusion clause. The question is a difficult one to answer. Clearly the insured died while acting as a pilot aboard an aircraft which was in flight, descended and crashed at the time of his death. For this reason it might appear that recovery should be barred under a literal interpretation of the aviation exclusion clause. On the other hand, the insured died from burns which presumably resulted from a fire in his aircraft. The fire was caused either directly or indirectly by hostile action in a combat zone. Whether the hostile gunfire or the crash ignited the flames is immaterial. Either way the proximate cause of death was an act of war. These circumstances show the insured's death to have been within both a war risk covered by the policy and an aviation risk excluded by the policy. The problem is to which risk is his death to be attributed.

The relevant cases are in conflict. We are advised during oral argument and in briefs that this is a case of first impression in Tennessee. *Bennett v. Metropolitan Life Insurance Company, supra*, is not helpful as it involved a routine training flight outside combat zones.

Wilmington Trust Company v. Mutual Life Insurance Company, 177 F.2d 404 (C.A. 3, 1949), concerned a policy with a general aviation exclusion clause and a statement that there were no occupational or military restrictions in the policy. The insured, while in military service, was engaged in a test flight of a glider in California. He was forced to bail out and died because his parachute failed to open. The Court held there was no ambiguity in the policy and that the aviation exclusion clause was to be literally applied, thereby barring recovery. This case is not in point because there was no war risk coinciding with the aviation risk.

In *United Services Life Insurance Company v. Bischoff, 86 U.S.App.D.C. 328, 181 F.2d 627 (1950)*, the insured was killed as he banked away from a locomotive he was strafing and his right wing struck the locomotive causing the plane to crash and burn. The general aviation exclusion clause in that case did not except war risks and stated that its terms applied "any provision . . . to the contrary notwithstanding." The Court denied recovery on the ground that the exclusion was unqualified and applied equally to all risks.

Defendant argues that *Barringer v. Prudential Insurance Company of America, 62 F. Supp. 286 (E.D.Pa., 1945)* is on all fours with the instant case. The insured in *Barringer* was last seen boarding a military plane in Puerto Rico that was under orders to fly to Trinidad. The plane was never seen again after its take-off. In finding that death resulted from riding in an airplane thereby precluding recovery because of the policy's aviation exclusion clause, the Court observed that the possibility that the plane had been shot down by a German submarine was too remote to be accepted as the cause of death. The most probable inference was that the insured died as a result of an aviation risk. The court in *Boye v. United Services Insurance Co., 83 U.S.App.D.C. 306, 168 F.2d 270 (1948)*, stated that the *Barringer* opinion indicates that recovery would have been allowed if there were reason to believe an enemy submarine shot down the plane. We agree that the *Barringer* rationale supports this view.

Boye, supra, granted a recovery on the proposition that an insuror invoking an exclusion in the policy has the burden of demonstrating that the facts are within the exclusion. In that case the insured was a pilot who never returned from a bombing mission over enemy controlled territory. There was no proof of the cause of death. One of the two planes that did not return from this mission was seen going down. Whether this was the insured's plane was not known. The Court held that death resulting either directly or indirectly from an act of war results from a war risk instead of an aviation risk. It compares the case to the situation of a policy excluding coverage when "operating or riding in an automobile" where the insured was killed by gunfire while riding in a car. Death results from being shot, not from riding in the car.

In *Bull v. Sun Life Assurance Co., 141 F.2d 456* (C.A. 7, 1944), the insured was attempting to inflate a life raft on the wing of a seaplane downed by anti-aircraft fire when he was killed by the strafing of a Japanese fighter. The policy excluded coverage where death resulted from "service, travel or flight in . . . aircraft." In allowing recovery, the Court observed that the policy stated it shall not apply:

> ". . . if the death is *contributed to* directly or indirectly by the service, travel or flight in the aircraft. The policy deals with results and not causes or contributing causes. Aviation may have been a contributing cause, but that did not make the death an indirect result of aviation. No risk of aviation resulted in death. A risk of war resulted in death. That was a risk not excluded by the policy."
> *141 F.2d at 459.*

Although distinguishable on its facts from the instant case, this reasoning is applicable to our case in that aviation was merely a "contributing cause" of death rather than a "result" of aviation. Aviation was a condition of Captain Hawkins' death but not its proximate cause. The proximate cause was the enemy fire.

Mann v. Service Life Insurance Company, 284 F. Supp. 139 (E.D.Va., 1968), involved an insured serving as co-pilot in a military helicopter in a Vietnam war zone who was hit by hostile fire. The helicopter was not damaged and returned to its base. The insured died from his wounds the next day. The Court held an aviation exclusion clause to be inapplicable because death resulted from an "intervening cause totally unrelated to the operation of the aircraft." (*284 F. Supp. at 140*).

It is to be observed that no conflicts of law problem is presented despite the facts that the insurer is a resident of Indiana, the insured a resident of Tennessee, the policy was written in Georgia, and the death occurred in Vietnam. We have been advised by counsel that the question is one of first impression in each of these jurisdictions.

The insuror's primary obligation under the terms of the policy, is to pay "the Sum Insured to the Beneficiary immediately upon receipt at the Home Office of due proof of the death of the Insured" subject to the provisions of the policy. This language is to be construed liberally and any exclusory language is to be construed strictly.

The policy makes no attempt to limit this obligation in the event death results from an act of war. It is obvious that the insuror considered war risks when it chose the policy language. The Premium Waiver Disability Provisions declines to waive premiums "if the disability . . . should occur as a result of . . . an act of war, declared or undeclared." The failure to mention war risks anywhere else in the policy is an indication of the intention to cover death as a result of "an act of war."

The policy, however, excludes from coverage death "as a result of aviation where the insured is a pilot." Where an insured is engaged in aviation and, simultaneously, engaged in an act of war, the policy is ambiguous on the question of coverage. Under these circumstances the language of the policy taken as a whole both allows and denies coverage on the same set of facts. It is well settled that ambiguities in insurance policies are resolved in favor of the insured. See *Sturgill v. Life Insurance Company of Georgia, supra.*

Even if the policy taken as a whole is not ambiguous, a strict reading of the Aviation Provisions indicates that the insured's death was within an insured risk. The key phrase is "death. . . as a result of [aviation]." The facts of this case show that the insured did not die as a result of aviation. On the contrary his death was a result of an act of war. Had it not been for an act of war his plane would not have crashed. In all probability he died before his plane crashed. Either way death was not the result of an aviation risk. Aviation was merely an incidental condition (circumstance) at the time of death.

At the time the insuror entered into this contract with the insured, it knew that the insured was going to enter military service shortly thereafter as a pilot. It also knew that there was a military conflict in Southeast Asia where the insured might be assigned. Having accepted premium payments to the time of death, it should not now be permitted to deny liability for this combat death.

NEW ZEALAND INSURANCE COMPANY et al v. GRIFFITH
RUBBER MILLS.

SUPREME COURT OF OREGON

526 P.2d 567

September, 1974

This is an insurance subrogation action. The controlling facts are admitted in the pleadings.

Plaintiff Roy D. Wright in May 1971 leased a Piper Cherokee airplane to Sky Tech, Inc., an Oregon corporation, under a rental agreement, a copy of which is attached to the amended answer.

Sky Tech, Inc., rented the airplane to George W. Smith, a member of Sky Tech Flyers, a Sky Tech, Inc., organization. Plaintiff New Zealand issued a policy of aircraft hull and liability insurance to Sky Tech, Inc., and the plaintiff Roy D. Wright was an additional insured under said policy.

That George W. Smith was an employe of defendant Griffith Rubber Mills and that while Smith was piloting the plane within the scope of his employment it was damaged in a landing at an airfield. That the damage to the plane amounted to $ 21,024.35, of which New Zealand paid all but the policy deduction of $ 1,000.

The agreement between Sky Tech and Smith was contained in the document entitled "APPLICATION AND CONDITIONS OF SKY TECH FLYERS". A 14-paragraph portion of that document was captioned "SKY TECH, INC. OPERATING PROCEDURES", a portion of which we will quote below. The parties assume that Smith was a member of Sky Tech Flyers.

The trial court held that the right of subrogation had been waived by the rental contract between Sky Tech and Smith and entered judgment on the pleadings in favor of defendant. The plaintiffs appeal. The issue is whether the right of subrogation was waived by certain provisions of the contract between Sky Tech and Smith.

The portions of the "SKY TECH, INC. OPERATING PROCEDURES" which the parties regard as determinative of this case read as follows:

"SKY TECH, INC. OPERATING PROCEDURES

"The following applies to all members of SKY TECH FLYERS and also to all persons renting SKY TECH, INC.'s aircraft.

.....

"2. Each pilot shall agree to return the aircraft to SKY TECH, INC. at Aurora State Airport within the time and in the same condition as he received it. (Ordinary wear and tear excepted.)

.....

"5. Each pilot shall agree to indemnify SKY TECH, INC. and its insurance carrier for any and all

326

loss, damage, cost, and expense paid or incurred by SKY TECH, INC. or its insurance carrier because of injuries or damages sustained as a result of operation of the aircraft in violation of any of the terms and conditions of this agreement.

"6. Each pilot shall agree to pay SKY TECH, INC., on demand, a sum equal to the cost of all damages to the aircraft while in his possession or in his custody provided that they are *not* covered by insurance.

.....

"14. All pilots should understand that insurance carried by SKY TECH, INC. is to protect SKY TECH *only* and does not extend in any way to him for either hull damage or liability for bodily injury or property damage; such exposure on the part of a member or renter pilot is his own. Students taking instruction from an instructor employed by SKY TECH, INC. *are* covered.

"I certify that I have read the foregoing and agree to be bound by the terms thereof.

"Dated this   day of   197_ .

"SKY TECH FLYERS

MEMBER

CHIEF PILOT

SKY TECH, INC."

The trial court found that paragraph 6 quoted above "is not ambiguous and does not require or permit parol evidence in aid of construction" and, based on said finding, entered judgment for defendant on the pleadings.

We conclude that when paragraph 6, on which the defendant relies, is construed together with paragraph 2, paragraph 5, and paragraph 14, it must be given a different meaning or at least is so ambiguous as to permit the introduction of extrinsic evidence to aid the court in construing it.

We note at the outset that Sky Tech is not a party to this action and that neither the Wrights nor New Zealand is a party to the agreement between Sky Tech and Smith.

It is a fundamental rule in the construction of contracts that it is the duty of a court to construe a contract as a whole employing any reasonable method of interpretation so that no part of it is ignored and effect can be given to every word and phrase. *Automotive Equip. v. 3 Bees Logging*, 251 Or 105, 111, *444 P2d 1019 (1968)*; *Hardin v. Dimension Lbr. Co.*, 140 Or 385, 389, 13 P2d 602 (1932). As a necessary consequence, the court in performing this function must reconcile inconsistent provisions if it is at all possible. *Hardin supra at 388*; *Lachmund v. Lope Sing, 54 Or 106, 111, 102 P 598 (1909)*. See, also, 17A CJS 163, Contracts § 309.

Turning to paragraph number 2 we note that it imposed on the pilot the basic liability to return the aircraft to Sky Tech in the same condition as he received it. We need not decide the full scope of the pilot's liability under paragraph 2, but, if construed literally, it makes the pilot a virtual insurer of the safe return of the aircraft.

Paragraph 5, in turn, imposes a broad liability on the pilot "to indemnify SKY TECH, INC. and its insurance carrier for any and all loss, damage, cost, and expense paid or incurred by SKY TECH, INC. or its insurance carrier because of injuries or damages sustained as a result of operation of the aircraft in violation of any of the terms and conditions of this agreement." Again, we need not decide the full scope of the liability imposed on the pilot nor whether a failure to return the plane in the same condition as the pilot received it would constitute damages "sustained as a result of operation of the aircraft in violation of any of the terms and conditions of this agreement". Suffice it to say that the potential liability imposed on the pilot by paragraph 5 is very broad, both to Sky Tech and its insurer.

Any doubt about the intent of the agreement to impose liability on the pilot is removed by a reading of paragraph 14. It warns the pilot that insurance carried by Sky Tech does not protect the pilot against liability for either hull damage or for bodily injury or property damage and that the risk of all of said liability rests on the pilot. It is the apparent purpose of paragraphs 2, 5, and 14 to shift to the pilot the burden of all liability resulting from the operation of the aircraft for both hull damage and for injuries or damages to third parties and to hold Sky Tech and its insurer harmless from any of such loss or damage.

Against this background of paragraphs 2, 4, and 14, we turn to the construction of paragraph 6. We note that paragraph 6 concerns only Sky Tech and the pilot and the liability of each for damage to the aircraft. It is obvious that paragraph 6, as interpreted by the trial court, would relieve the pilot from all liability for damage to the aircraft except that portion thereof not covered by insurance. Under the facts in this case that would only be the portion excluded by the $ 1,000 deductible clause of the policy.

The construction adopted by the trial court renders paragraphs 2, 5, and 14 meaningless insofar as they impose liability on the pilot for damage to the aircraft. We think the parties more probably intended that the pilot should pay to Sky Tech that portion of the hull damage not covered by insurance in addition to his liability to Sky Tech and its insurance carrier under paragraphs 2, 5, and 14.

As we have pointed out, paragraph 6 concerns only Sky Tech and does not indicate any intention to bar Sky Tech's insurer from subrogating against the pilot. To construe paragraph 6 as a waiver by Sky Tech of its insurer's right of subrogation would make that paragraph inconsistent with Sky Tech's duty under its policy of insurance to preserve this right on behalf of its insurer. We think paragraph 6 must be construed to mean that the pilot would be liable for the amount of the deductible to Sky Tech and liable to Sky Tech's insurer for the balance of the loss. So construed paragraph 6 would be consistent with paragraphs 2, 5, and 14.

The antecedent for paragraph 6 is found in the Airplane Rental Agreement between the owner of this aircraft and Sky Tech as renter, a copy of which is attached to the amended answer. That agreement contained the following provision:

> "8. *Insurance*. Owner warrants that the airplane is insured for commercial operation and against physical loss and that such insurance cover[s] the airplane while rented to Renter. Renter agrees to pay an[y] deductible required by such insurance on any accident caused by its occurring during a rental period."

We think the uninsured damage clause of paragraph 6 operates to make the owner whole by receiving the amount of the deductible from the renter and the balance from the insurer. In view of the foregoing paragraph we think that if Sky Tech had intended to shield the pilot from a subrogation claim from Sky Tech's insurer it would have expressed that intention more clearly.

We note that a special endorsement was attached to New Zealand's policy which expressly waived the insurer's right of subrogation against two individuals. If Sky Tech had intended to waive its subrogation rights against members of Sky Tech Flyers by paragraph 6 of its Operating Procedures such a special endorsement would have been completely unnecessary.

Since the court below refused to consider any extrinsic evidence as an aid to construction of the agreement, we remand the case to the trial court to hear such extrinsic evidence as the parties may offer and with the aid of such evidence construe the meaning of the contract.

The cause is reversed and remanded for further proceedings not inconsistent herewith.

AVEMCO INSURANCE COMPANY v. N. R. ROLLINS et al.

UNITED STATES DISTRICT COURT FOR THE NORTHERN
DISTRICT OF GEORGIA, NEWNAN DIVISION

380 F. Supp. 869

March, 1974

Henderson, District Judge.

This is a diversity action for declaratory judgment and rescission of the insurance policy Avemco Insurance Company (hereinafter referred to as "Avemco" or "insurer") issued to N. R. Rollins and Larry R. Flowers. The plaintiff insurer seeks a determination of its obligation to indemnify and defend defendants Rollins and Flowers in suits now pending and which may arise from circumstances involving an aircraft crash on November 21, 1971. Presently pending are the summary judgment motions of Avemco and the defendants McGees and Nixons, each contending no genuine issue of material fact remains and that, as a matter of law, they are entitled to judgment.

Avemco contends that the defendants, Rollins and Flowers, in applying for a policy of aviation insurance, knowingly and willfully misrepresented certain material facts. These misrepresentations are claimed to be critical to the acceptance of the risk and the hazard assumed by the plaintiff. In response, the defendants deny Avemco is entitled to relief or that the policy should be rescinded. Michael Eugene McGee, Joyce McGee, Melvin McGee, Mildred Nixon and Jerrell Nixon, contend that the plaintiff waived and ratified the alleged misrepresentations by Rollins and Flowers and is estopped to deny coverage; that it had no right to rely upon the alleged misrepresentations of the defendants, Rollins and Flowers; that the plaintiff failed to use reasonable diligence to protect itself from the alleged misrepresentations, if they existed; and that the suit is barred by laches.

Avemco issued to Rollins and Flowers a policy of comprehensive aircraft insurance, effective January 21, 1971, for a term of one year in payment of a premium of $600.00. In applying for coverage, the insureds represented to Avemco that they held a private pilot's license, when in fact each held only a student pilot certificate rating. Had the truth of the matter been known, Rollins and Flowers would probably have been insured by Avemco, but at a higher premium rate and the policy would have contained a declaration for coverage extending only to Rollins and Flowers and "any private or commercial pilot who has not less than 100 hours experience as pilot in command, of which at least ten hours were in aircraft having 188 H.P. or over and one hour was in the same model as the insured aircraft." (Affidavit of Charles W. Hubbard, July 20, 1973).

On November 21, 1971, the defendant, Rollins, while transporting passengers in his aircraft, was involved in an accident which resulted in injury to Rollins and Michael Eugene McGee and the death of Terry Wayne Nixon. Upon being notified of the crash on November 23, 1971 Avemco discovered, in verifying the license status of Rollins through the Aircraft Owners & Pilots Association in Oklahoma City, Oklahoma, that the insured held only a student's license. (Deposition of

Don Kehaya of October 12, 1973 at 7, 9). Subsequently, on December 2, 1971, the plaintiff notified Rollins and Flowers that it would not provide coverage under the policy because of the alleged misrepresentations contained in the application. In February of 1972 the insurer paid the Fulton National Bank its mortgage interest on the destroyed aircraft as loss payee under the breach of warranty provisions of the insurance contract. Thereafter, on April 5, 1972, Avemco returned to the insured the unearned liability premium of $22.00 on the policy. Allegedly, the return of the premium was a routine function of the insurer's accounting department and made by persons unaware of the plaintiff's denial of coverage. (Shrout Deposition of November 2, 1973, at pp. 12-13, 16-17).

In diversity actions, the substantive legal issues must be resolved by the forum state's conflict of law rules. *[citations omitted]*. Under the Georgia choice of law rule, the validity, form and effect of insurance contracts are governed by the laws of the place where they are made under the principle of *lex loci contractus*. *[citations omitted]*. The law of this state provides that insurance contracts are considered made at the place where the contract was delivered. *[citations omitted]*. Because this policy was delivered to Rollins and Flowers in Carroll County, Georgia, it was made in Georgia and is controlled by Georgia law.

A false representation or misrepresentation avoids a contract of insurance when it is material, regardless of the intent with which it was made. Vance, The Law of Insurance (3rd ed. 1951) § 67 at 389.

> "Correlatively speaking, a misrepresentation in insurance is an oral or written statement, made by the insured or his authorized agent to the insurer or his authorized agent, of something as a fact which is untrue, is known to be untrue, and is stated with intent, or has a tendency, to mislead or deceive, or which is stated positively as true without its being known to be true, and which has a tendency to mislead, such statement relating in every case to material facts. A misrepresentation is a false representation of a material fact tending directly to induce the making of the contract. In other words a misrepresentation is a statement of something as a fact which is untrue and material to the risk, and which the insured states, knowing it to be untrue, in an attempt to deceive, or which he states positively is true, without knowing it to be true, and which has a tendency to mislead.
>
> The word "misrepresentation" in policies of insurance is taken in the same sense as that in which it is ordinarily used in common speech and is not a technical term, meaning merely a false statement touching a matter material to the risk. " (footnotes omitted).

Couch on Insurance 2d, § 35:4 at 11-12. Following the general rule, Ga. Code Ann. § 56-2409 provides:
> "All statements and descriptions in any application for an insurance policy or annuity contract, or in negotiations therefor,

by or in behalf of the insured or annuitant shall be deemed to be representations and not warranties. Misrepresentations, omissions, concealment of facts, and incorrect statements shall not prevent a recovery under the policy or contract unless:

(1) Fraudulent; or

(2) Material either to the acceptance of the risk, or to the hazard assumed by the insurer; or

(3) The insurer in good faith would either not have issued the policy or contract, or would not have issued a policy or contract in as large an amount, or at the premium rate as applied for, or would not have provided coverage with respect to the hazard resulting in the loss, if the true facts had been known to the insurer as required either by the application for the policy or contract or otherwise. "

The undisputed facts make it clear that the incorrect statements would ordinarily prevent recovery under the policy. Their statements relating to their flying status were material to the acceptance of the risk or the hazard insured by Avemco. 45 C.J.S. Insurance, § 473 (4)(d); *Lee v. Metropolitan Life Insurance Co., 158 Ga. 517, 520-21, 123 S.E. 737 (1924)*. Had the insurer possessed the correct information the policy would not have been issued at the lower rate and the coverage would have been more restrictive. Ga. Code Ann. § 56-2409(2) (3). In a recent and similar case, All *American Life & Casualty Co. v. Saunders, 125 Ga. App. 7, 10-11, 186 S.E.2d 328 (1971)*, the Court of Appeals of Georgia noted:

"In cases where the application for insurance is attached to and becomes a part of the policy, in order to avoid the policy for misrepresentation, the insurer need only show that the representation was false and that it was material in that it changed the nature, extent or character of the risk and this is true although the applicant may have made the representation in good faith, not knowing that it was untrue. *Preston v. Nat. Life & Accident Ins. Co., 196 Ga. 217, 229, 26 SE 2d 439, 148 A.L.R. 897; General Assurance Corp. v. Roberts, 92 Ga. App. 834, 837 (90 SE 2d 70)*." *Gilham v. National Life & Accident Ins. Co., 104 Ga. App. 459, 460, 122 SE 2d 164*. See *Mutual Benefit Health & Accident Assn. v. Bell, 49 Ga. App. 640 176 SE 124*. "An applicant is prima facie charged with knowledge of the contents of an application signed by him. . . ." *Jessup v. Franklin Life Insurance Company, 117 Ga. App. 389, 391, 160 S.E.2d 612 (1968)*.

Reserve Life Insurance Company v. Chalker, 127 Ga. App. 565, 194 S.E.2d 290 (1972); see *Reserve Life Insurance Co. v. Bearden, 96 Ga. App. 549, 550-51, 101 S.E.2d 120 (1957)* aff'd *213 Ga. 904, 102 S.E.2d 494*.

In opposing the plaintiff's motion for summary judgment, the defendants, McGee and Nixon, assert that Avemco "had no right to rely upon these representations and that it failed to use reasonable diligence to protect itself from the misrepresentation of the insureds." (Defendant's Brief in Opposition to Plaintiff's Motion for Summary Judgment, at p. 12).

The court is not aware of any legal requirement for an insurance company to determine the truth or falsity of representations made in an application for insurance. Indeed, it is a time honored rule that the highest degree of good faith is demanded of the parties to an insurance contract. Vance, supra, § 13 at p. 100. 45 C.J.S. Insurance, § 473(4)(d) at 170-79. In an analogous situation, the Supreme Court of Georgia held that failure of an insurer to confirm, by way of investigation, material representations made in the procurement of a policy does not deny the insurer a defense of fraud or misrepresentation, even though the examination would have revealed a false statement. *Lee v. Metropolitan Life Insurance Co., supra, 158 Ga. at 522-23 (1924)*. Because of the relationship between insurer and insured, the reliance by Avemco on the representation respecting the flying status was reasonable. This contention of the defendants is without merit.

It is further urged that this action for declaratory judgment is barred because of laches. The chronology of events, however, does not demonstrate delay or neglect on the part of the insurer sufficient to bar this suit. The policy was cancelled within seven days after the crash. Thereafter, the mortgagee's claim was settled under the breach of warranty provision of the contract and the unearned premium returned. The present action was brought within one month after the filing of death and personal injury claims in the Superior Court of Carroll County, Georgia. Until the state court suits were filed the defendant insurer had no reason to seek a declaration of its rights since it had disavowed any liability under the policy. Had Avemco sought a declaratory judgment immediately after it learned of the misrepresentation, as suggested by the defendants, it would not have been entertained by this court or a state court.

The federal case law respecting declaratory judgments is well settled. "The Declaratory Judgment Act was an authorization, not a command. It gave the federal courts competence to make a declaration of rights; it did not impose a duty to do so." *Public Affairs Associates v. Rickover, 369 U.S. 111, 112, 7 L. Ed. 2d 604, 82 S. Ct. 580 (1962)* (and cases cited therein.) The Declaratory Judgment Act, *28 U.S.C. § 2201*, provides that an "actual controversy" must exist before declaratory relief may be granted. The Supreme Court defines a case ripe for adjudication as one of "concrete legal issues, presented in actual cases, not abstractions." *Golden v. Zwickler, 394 U.S. 103, 108, 22 L. Ed. 2d 113, 89 S. Ct. 956 (1969)*, citing *United Public Workers of America v. Mitchell, 330 U.S. 75, 89, 91 L. Ed. 754, 67 S. Ct. 556 (1947)*. In *Maryland Casualty Co. v. Pacific Coal & Oil Co., 312 U.S. 270, 273, 85 L. Ed. 826, 61 S. Ct. 510 (1941)* the Court sought to fashion a test to determine a "controversy" contemplated by the Declaratory Judgment Act as opposed to an abstract question. It was there held that "the question in each case is whether the facts alleged, under all the circumstances, show that there is a substantial controversy, between parties having adverse legal interests, of sufficient immediacy and reality to warrant the issuance of a declaratory judgment."

The Georgia appellate courts have likewise decided that declaratory judgment is a proper remedy where there is a "substantial controversy between parties having adverse legal interests of sufficient immediacy and reality to warrant the issuance of a declaratory judgment." *LaSalle National Insurance Co. v. Popham, 125 Ga. App. 724, 728, 188 S.E.2d 870 (1972)*, citing *St. Paul Fire and Marine Insurance Co. v. Johnson, 216 Ga. 437, 438, 117 S.E.2d 459*, quoting *Maryland Casualty Co. v. Pacific Coal & Oil Co., supra at 312 U.S. 273*. In *Popham, 125 Ga. App. at page 728*, the court stated:

> "the rule as to when an insurer may properly proceed for declaratory judgment is clearly stated in *Nationwide Mut. Ins. Co. v. Peek, 112 Ga. App. 260, (145 SE 2d 50)*; "Where an insurer denies coverage under a particular policy and seeks to relieve itself of its obligation to defend a pending suit against an insured because of circumstances pleaded which cast doubt on the coverage of the policy as applied to those circumstances, *there is such an immediacy of choice imposed upon it as to justify an adjudication by declaratory judgment.*" "
> (italics added).

Consequently, this action is timely and the assertion that it is barred by laches is untenable.

The defendants also maintain that the insurer waived its right to contend the policy was void because it (a) cancelled the policy after the date of the crash and returned the unearned premiums or (b) made payment to a lienholder under the policy's breach of warranty provisions. As previously noted, liability may be *avoided where a material misrepresentation* is made concerning the risk or hazard or if the premium rate or coverage would have been different had the true facts been known. Ga. Code Ann. § 56-2409. Avoidance or rescission is not cancellation. Couch, *supra*, § 67:35 at 412. Rescission voids the policy *ab initio* and this is the remedy the plaintiff now seeks. The insurance company took immediate action to avoid the policy upon hearing of the false statements. Furthermore, the Georgia courts have held that avoidance of liability under a policy induced by fraud or misrepresentation may be asserted without return of premiums to the insured. *Columbian National Life Insurance Co. v. Mulkey, 146 Ga. 267, 268-72, 91 S.E. 106 (1916)*; *Golden v. National Life & Accident Insurance Co., 189 Ga. 79, 88, 5 S.E.2d 198 (1939)*; cf. *Curry v. Washington National Insurance Co., 56 Ga. App. 809, 810-11, 194 S.E. 825 (1937)*. Thus, the remittance of the unearned premiums and the later payment of the entire premium paid by the insured into the registry of the court, while necessary for cancellation, is not necessary in the case of rescission. Ga. Code Ann. §§ 56-2430, 2409. This act of Avemco does not constitute a waiver of its right of rescission.

The defendants go further and claim that the right of avoidance was waived by the insurer's payment to Fulton National Bank, the mortgagee. The payment to the bank for the physical loss of the aircraft was an act wholly unrelated to the obligation once owed to the named insured. The breach of warranty provision of the policy is an agreement with the mortgagee whereby the insurer shall pay the lienholder for its loss in the event of the destruction of the mortgaged property and thereby be subrogated to the mortgagee's rights. (Plaintiff's Exhibit A). Such agreements are standard requirements of financial institutions dealing with aviation financing and placed in policies for their protection since they have no control over an insured's representation to the insurer or the use of the aircraft. The breach of warranty provision is a contract separate from the agreement between the insurer and insured and as such, requires a separate premium charge which, in this case, was $29.00. (See Shrout Deposition, Nov. 2, 1973 at 21-23, 25-27; Kehaya Deposition, Oct. 12, 1973 at 9, 12-13, 23-25). The payment of the mortgage balance by Avemco to the bank was satisfaction of that contract between them and is irrelevant to any obligation the insurer had to Rollins and Flowers. Therefore, this conduct by Avemco does not amount to a waiver of its right to void the policy.

The plaintiff's motion for summary judgment is granted. The plaintiff is directed to submit a proposed judgment in accordance with the terms of the order, within ten (10) days of the filing of this order.

B. *Limits of Insurance Coverage*

DEAN S. EDMONDS, JR. *v.* UNITED STATES OF AMERICA, ET AL.

United States Court of Appeals For the First Circuit

642 F.2d 877

April, 1981

SKINNER, District Judge . This is an appeal from an order of the District Court granting summary judgment for defendant-appellee Avemco Insurance Company ("Avemco") against plaintiff-appellant Dean S. Edmonds, Jr. We affirm the District Court's judgment.

The following facts are essentially undisputed. Edmonds is a licensed pilot who resides in Massachusetts. Avemco is an aircraft insurance company incorporated under the laws of Maryland with its principal place of business in Bethesda, Maryland. On May 14, 1974, Edmonds purchased a Beech Baron Aircraft. Avemco subsequently issued an aircraft insurance policy to Edmonds effective May 15, 1974 for a period of one year ("1974-75 policy"). The 1974-75 policy insured Edmonds against personal injury and property damage while operating the aircraft. Item 7 of the "DECLARATIONS" section stated:

PILOTS: This policy applies when the aircraft is in flight, only while being operated by one of the following pilots, while such pilot is holding a valid and effective Pilot and Medical Certificate:

(a) Dean S. Edmonds....

The 1974-75 policy also contained a section entitled "EXCLUSIONS" and one entitled "CONDITIONS". Neither section set out a requirement that Edmonds undergo a periodic review of his piloting skills in order to qualify for coverage.

In 1974 the Federal Aviation Administration [FAA] amended Part 61 of the Federal Air Regulations by inserting therein *§ 61.57, 14 C.F.R. § 61.57 (1980)*, which provides, in part:

§ 61.57 Recent Flight experience:

Pilot in command.

(a) Flight Review . After November 1, 1974, no person may act as pilot in command of an aircraft unless, within the proceeding 24 months, he has --

(1) Accomplished a flight review given to him, in an aircraft for which he is rated, by an appropriately certified instructor or other person designated by the Administrator; and

(2) Had his log book endorsed by the person who gave him the review certifying that he has satisfactorily accomplished the flight review.

Edmonds successfully completed a biennial flight review under the supervision of an FAA-certified instructor on November 24, 1974.

Prior to the expiration date of the 1974-75 policy, Avemco sent Edmonds an "Aircraft Policy Renewal Information" form ("policy renewal form"). The form stated, in part:

Your present AVEMCO Aircraft Insurance Policy expires on the date indicated. So that we may serve you better and have current information on both your aircraft and flying experience, please take a moment to complete and return this postage paid card. As soon as we receive this completed form, we will immediately send you our renewal quotation for your consideration.

Note: If you do not return this completed card within 10 days, we will forward our renewal quotation based upon your estimates of flying time and aircraft value from information in our files.

DO ALL PILOTS HAVE:

Current Biennial Flight Review

Yes

No

Current Medical Certificate

Yes

No

Edmonds checked the box indicating that he had a current biennial flight review and mailed the form to Avenco, which issued Edmonds a renewal policy for the term May 15, 1975 to May 15, 1976 ("1975-76" policy"). Edmonds later received a new "DECLARATIONS" section. Item 7 of that section had been amended to read:

Item 7, PILOTS: This policy applies when the aircraft is in flight, only while being operated by one of the following pilots (indicated by [X] below) who, (1) holds a valid and effective Pilot and Medical Certificate, (2) has a current biennial flight review and (3) if carrying passengers, has completed at least three Take-Offs and Landings within the preceding 90 days in an aircraft of the same make and model as the insured aircraft.

In March of 1976, Avemco again sent Edmonds a policy renewal form. Edmonds replied that he had a current biennial flight review and mailed the form to Avemco, after which he received a renewal policy for the term May 15, 1976 to May 15, 1977 ("1976-77 policy").

This renewal procedure was repeated again the following year. Avemco sent Edmonds a policy renewal form in March of 1977. Edmonds indicated that he had a current biennial flight review and mailed the form back to Avemco. Avemco subsequently issued a renewal policy covering the period May 15, 1977 to May 15, 1978. ("1977-78 policy"). As with the previous two policies, Item 7 of the "DECLARATIONS" section provided that the 1977-78 policy "applies when the aircraft is in flight, only while being operated by one of the following pilots [Edmonds]... who... (2) has a current biennial flight review...." The 1977-78 policy also contained a new provision in the "EXCLUSIONS" section:

This policy does not apply:

(g) Under Coverages A, B and C, to any aircraft while in flight

(3) being operated by a pilot not meeting the requirements set forth in item 7 of the declarations

When Edmonds returned the policy renewal form to Avemco to obtain the 1977-78 policy, however, he did not have a current biennial flight review within the meaning of *14 C.F.R. § 61.57.* His previous flight review took place on November 24, 1974, more than two years earlier. In 1977, Edmonds twice piloted an airplane accompanied by Gary Brigham, a demonstrator pilot employed by the Beech Air Company. Brigham latter wrote to Avemco that Edmonds performed all of the maneuvers necessary to complete a biennial review during these flights. Brigham, however, was not an FAA-certified instructor, did not have authority to conduct biennial flight reviews, and did not enter his findings in Edmonds' log book.

On January 14, 1978, Edmonds had an accident at Hanscom Field in Bedford, Massachusetts. As he brought his plane down for a landing on Runway 23, it hit a mound of snow and crashed. The aircraft was extensively damaged. Edmonds promptly filed a claim under the 1977-78 policy. Avemco refused to honor his claim on the theory that by failing to maintain a current biennial flight review Edmonds breached a condition precedent to Avemco's contractual duty.

Edmonds then brought suit for damages against the United States, the Massachusetts Port Authority and Avemco. Count II, the only court before us on this appeal, alleged that Avemco breached its contract of insurance with Edmonds by refusing to cover the accident as required by the 1977-78 policy. Massachusetts law governs this claim since jurisdiction is based on diversity of citizenship.

In the proceedings below, the District Court granted Avemco's motion for summary judgment on Count II. The Court ruled that Edmonds was bound by Item 7 of the "DECLARATIONS", that Item 7 incorporated the federal regulatory standard for flight reviews, and that Edmonds did not comply with Item 7. The District Court then turned to what it perceived as the more difficult question: whether Edmonds' failure to comply with Item 7 voided Avemco's obligations under the policy. The Court noted that under Massachusetts law it was necessary to characterize Item 7 as either a condition precedent, in which case Avemco's obligation was terminated, or a warranty or representation, in which case coverage could be avoided only if the breach contributed to the accident or increased the insurer's risk of loss. *M.G.L. c.175, § 186.* In the District Court's view, the standard for determining whether Item 7 is a condition precedent is set out in *Charles, Henry & Crowley Co. Inc. v. The Home Insurance Co ., 349 Mass. 723, 726 (1965):*

[A] statement made in an application for a policy of insurance may become a condition of the policy rather than remain a warranty or representation if: (1) the statement made by the insured relates essentially to the insurer's intelligent decision to issue the policy; and (2) the statement is made a condition precedent to recovery under the policy, either by using the precise words "condition precedent" or their equivalent.

The Court found that both branches of the standard were met in the instant case and ruled that Item 7 was a condition precedent. It held, accordingly, that Edmonds' failure to comply with Item 7 prevented Avemco's duty of covering the accident from arising.

Edmonds' first contention on appeal is that the District Court incorrectly ruled that the term "current biennial flight review" in Item 7 of the "DECLARATIONS" incorporated by reference the federal regulatory requirements set out in *14 C.F.R. § 61.57*. He argues that it is impossible to determine from the face of the contract whether the parties intended that all of the technical requirements of *14 C.F.R. § 61.57* apply and, therefore, that a genuine issue of material fact exists as to the meaning of Item 7.

Under Massachusetts law, interpretation of a contract is ordinarily a question of law for the court. *Freelander v. G. & K. Realty Corp., 357 Mass. 512, 516 (1970).* The circumstances surrounding the making of the agreement must be examined to determine the objective intent of the parties. *Louis Stoico, Inc. v. Colonial Development Corp., 369 Mass. 898, 902 (1976),* where the wording of the contract is unambiguous, the contract must be enforced according to its terms. *Freelander v. C. & K. Realty Corp., 357 Mass. at 516.* It is only where the contract contains ambiguities that a question of fact for the jury is presented. *Trafton v. Custeau, 338 Mass. 305, 307-08 (1959); Gillentine v. McKeand, 426 F.2d 717, 721 (1st Cir. 1970).*

We hold that the District Court properly construed the term "current biennial flight review" as incorporating the federal regulatory standard. This term is unambiguous. It was added to Avemco's standard aircraft policy shortly after the FAA adopted the biennial flight review requirement and tracks the exact language used in *14 C.F.R. § 61.57.* Edmonds has offered no other plausible definition of "current biennial flight review". We thus have no doubt that the parties understood this term as requiring Edmonds to comply with *14 C.F.R. § 61.57.*

Edmonds' second contention on appeal is that the District Court erred in ruling that Item 7 of the "DECLARATIONS" operated as a condition precedent to Avemco's contractual liability. This argument has two alternative branches. The first is that the District Court's reliance upon *Charles Henry & Crowley Co. Inc. v. The Home Insurance Co., supra* [hereinafter, "Charles "], was misplaced. Rather, in Edmond's view, the Supreme Judicial Court's opinion in *Johnson Controls, Inc. v. Bowes, 1980 Mass. Adv. Sh. 1831, 409 N.E.2d 185 (1980),* decided after the District Court granted summary judgment, is controlling and establishes that breach of a condition in an insurance policy avoids coverage only where the insurer shows that such breach increased the risk of loss or contributed to the accident.

At issue in Charles was the construction of a provision in a policy of insurance against theft. The insured, a jewelry firm, represented in its application for insurance that the maximum value of jewelry to be displayed in its store windows would be $ 15,000. Provision 1B of the policy stated: "It is a condition for this insurance precedent to any recovery hereunder that the values of property displayed will not exceed the amount represented...." Subsequently, $ 13,620 worth of jewelry was stolen from the windows on a day in which over $ 19,000 worth of jewelry was on display. Arguing that the jeweler breached a condition precedent, the insurer refused to extend coverage. The Supreme Judicial Court noted that § 1B of the policy had to be characterized as either a condition precedent which would bar recovery if not complied with or a representation or warranty which, if not fulfilled, would bar recovery only if the proof required by *M.G.L. c.175*

339

§ 186, existed. Analyzing a long line of Massachusetts cases the Court enunciated a two-pronged standard for making this determination:

[A] statement made in an application for a policy of insurance may become a condition of the policy rather than remain a warranty or representation if: (1) the statement made by the insured relates essentially to the insurer's intelligent decision to issue the policy; and (2) the statement is made a condition precedent to recovery under the policy, either by using the precise words "condition precedent" or their equivalent.

On the facts before it the Court concluded that § 1B constituted a condition precedent.

Johnson Controls involved a notice provision in a malpractice insurance policy. The provision required the insured, an attorney, immediately to notify the insurer of any malpractice lawsuit brought against him. The issue before the Court was whether the insured's failure to comply with the notice provision barred recovery regardless of lack of prejudice to the insurer. Rejecting a strict contractual approach, the court held that in order to avoid its obligations an insurance company must prove "both that the notice provision was in fact breached and that the breach resulted in prejudice to its position." The Court then decided, however, to apply its rule only to claims arising after the date of the opinion because to do otherwise "would disturb retroactively the contractual arrangements of the insurer and the insured...." *1980 Mass. Adv. Sh. at 1835-36, 409 N.E.2d at 188.*

We hold that the District Court properly looked to Charles to determine whether Item 7 constituted a condition precedent. The insurance provision at issue in Charles and in this case are similar in one critical aspect: both relate to the insurer's initial decision to issue the policy and take the insurance risk. The notice provision in Johnson Controls, on the other hand, has no bearing on insurability; its purpose is to protect an insurance company's interests after a claim against the insured has arisen. While a standard based on prejudice to the insurer has merit in the latter situation, there is nothing in Johnson Controls to suggest that the Supreme Judicial Court meant to extend such a standard to provisions relating to the decision to insure. Moreover, Johnson Controls has prospective application only. Edmonds brought this case long before Johnson Controls was decided and would be foreclosed from relying on that decision even if it were on point.

Edmonds' alternative argument is that the District Court misapplied the Charles standard. In Edmonds' view, application of the two-pronged standard requires a court to make findings of fact. He contends that there is a genuine dispute of fact over the first part of the standard, i.e ., whether his representation in the policy renewal form that he had a current biennial flight review "relates essentially to the insurer's intelligent decision to issue the policy". Edmonds points out that the very same renewal form contained a notation stating that a quotation would be sent to Edmonds even if Avemco did not receive the form, which arguably supports an inference that the current biennial flight review requirement was not of central concern to Avemco. Edmonds argues, accordingly, that summary judgment on this issue was inappropriate. Edmonds further contends that the second prong of the Charles standard, whether there is language in the policy expressly making the statement a condition precedent, is not met because Avemco did not clearly indicate in Item 7 that failure to maintain a current biennial flight review would avoid Avemco's duties.

The determination whether contractual language operates as a condition precedent or merely as a warranty of representation is a question of law for the court. *Shaw v. Commercial Insurance Co., 359 Mass. 601, 605 (1971)*. The first branch of the Charles standard does not require the court to determine whether the insurer would in fact have issued the insurance regardless of the false statement, as a question of fact. None of the Massachusetts cases employing this standard have considered evidence of the insurer's subjective state of mind. Rather, the Court has considered whether the contract term is properly categorized as a condition precedent as a matter of law because it has a reasonable bearing on the extent of the risk assumed by the insurer. See *Lopardi v. John Hancock Mutual Life Insurance Co., 289 Mass. 492 (1935)*; *Kravit v. United States Casualty Co., 278 Mass. 178, 179-80 (1932)*; *Faris v. The Travelers Indemnity Co., 278 Mass. 204 (1932)*; *Penta v. Home Fire & Marine Insurance Co., 263 Mass. 262 (1928)*.

We hold that the District Court properly applied the Charles standard to the aircraft insurance policy in this case. By requiring a formal, FAA designated biennial flight review, Avemco accomplishes several things. It avoids having to design its own independent test of an insured pilot's competence; it is assured that the pilot who examines the insured is certified by the FAA as competent to instruct and to review; and it imposes on the pilot and itself the least administrative burden possible -- to be eligible for renewed coverage the insured pilot need only show that he has passed a flight review that he is required by FAA regulations to have passed anyway.

The first branch of the standard is satisfied because the biennial flight review requirement has a rational relationship to Avemco's decision to issue the policy. As to the second branch, Item 7 explicitly states that the policy applies only while the aircraft is being operated by a pilot who has a current biennial flight review. Section (g)(3) of the "EXCLUSIONS" adds that the policy does not apply unless the insured complies with Item 7. Though the term "condition precedent" does not appear, we hold that the language that was used is the equivalent and, therefore, that the second part of the standard is satisfied. See, e.g., *Krause v. Equitable Life Insurance Co., 333 Mass. 200 (1955)*; *Massachusetts Mutual Life Insurance Co., v. Sullivan, 5 Mass. App. 816 (1977)*.

Affirmed.

NORTHWESTERN FLYERS, INC., ET AL, V. OLSON BROS. MFG.
CO., INC., ET. AL.

UNITED STATES COURT OF APPEALS, EIGHTH CIRCUIT

679 F.2d 1264

June, 1982

These controversies arise from the crash and destruction of a new Cessna airplane. At the time of the crash, the buyer, Olson Brothers Manufacturing Company (Olson Brothers), had taken delivery of the airplane but had not fully paid for it. As a result, the seller, Northwestern Flyers, Inc. (Northwestern Flyers), and its financing agent, Cessna Finance Corporation (Cessna Finance), instituted this action against Olson Brothers and its financing agent, Commercial Credit Equipment Company (Commercial Credit) to recover the balance of the purchase price. In addition, Olson Brothers, Northwestern Flyers, and their respective financing agents, filed claims against the Aviation Office of America and the United States Fire Insurance Company (Insurance Company), which had issued two separate insurance policies on the hull of the airplane, one covering Northwestern Flyers and its financing agent, and the other covering Olson Brothers and its financing agent. The Insurance Company refused to pay on either policy. Both Northwestern Flyers and Olson Brothers have been adjudicated bankrupt since the date of the crash.

In consolidated actions, the jury returned verdicts for Northwestern Flyers and against Olson Brothers for the unpaid purchase price of the airplane, and for Cessna Finance on its claim under Northwestern Flyers' insurance policy. In addition, the jury returned a verdict for Olson Brothers on its claim based on its separate insurance policy. Following various post-trial motions, the trial court set aside the verdict for Olson Brothers and distributed the proceeds of the policy held by Northwestern Flyers in accordance with its views of the rights of the parties. All parties, with the exception of Commercial Credit, filed appeals or cross-appeals. We reverse and remand, and direct entry of judgments consistent with this opinion.

I. Background.

Northwestern Flyers, an Iowa corporation, sells and leases small aircraft in Sioux City, Iowa. It served as an authorized Cessna dealer when it sold the airplane to Olson Brothers.

On February 10, 1979, Northwestern Flyers entered into a sales agreement with Olson Brothers, a Nebraska corporation, for sale and delivery of a 1979 Cessna Turbo 210 airplane, FAA registration number N6995N, for the sale price of $ 97,616.49. According to the contract, Olson Brothers agreed to pay $ 4,600 down and deliver a used Piper airplane, valued at $ 50,221.49, as a trade-in. Olson Brothers made the downpayment and turned over the used airplane to Northwestern Flyers.

On February 16, 1979, Northwestern Flyers obtained the Cessna airplane (N6995N) from Cessna Aircraft Company. To finance its purchase, Northwestern Flyers borrowed $ 84,037.69 from Cessna

Finance Corporation, which retained and perfected a security interest in the airplane.

During this time, Northwestern Flyers carried insurance on all its aircraft through a policy with the Aviation Office of America and United States Fire Insurance Company. Northwestern Flyers filed monthly reports with the Insurance Company listing the specific airplanes for which it sought coverage and remitted the premiums for those airplanes. Northwestern Flyers listed the Cessna Turbo 210 (N6995N) on its February report form, and specified policy coverage from February 16, 1979 to February 19, 1979, in the amount of $ 85,000. The Insurance Company attached to this policy a lienholder's endorsement in favor of Cessna Finance, which entitled Cessna Finance to recover directly for any damage or loss to the airplane.

On February 28, 1979, the airplane crashed while on a flight over Montana. The pilot, Larry McAfee, an employee of Olson Brothers, perished in the accident.

Following this crash, Northwestern Flyers and Cessna Finance brought this action to recover the unpaid portion of the purchase price from Olson Brothers and the value of the airplane from the Insurance Company. Olson Brothers denied that it owed Northwestern Flyers any amount and asserted a cross-claim against the Insurance Company based on its separate insurance policy.

Following a seven-day trial, the court submitted the case to the jury, asking it to determine whether Cessna Finance could recover under Northwestern Flyers' insurance policy, whether Olson Brothers' separate policy entitled it to recovery, and whether Northwestern Flyers should recover from Olson Brothers the balance of the purchase price of the aircraft. The jury returned verdicts for both Cessna Finance and Olson Brothers on their claims under their separate insurance policies. In addition, the jury returned a verdict for Northwestern Flyers on its claim against Olson Brothers under the purchase agreement.

Following posttrial motions, the court entered judgment on the verdict for Cessna Finance and against the Insurance Company. The court, however, entered judgment n. o. v. for the Insurance Company on Olson Brothers' claim under its policy, on the theory that Olson Brothers did not have an insurable interest in the airplane at the time of the accident. Finally, while acknowledging Northwestern Flyers' rights against Olson Brothers under the purchase agreement, the court refused to enter judgment on the verdict in favor of Northwestern Flyers and against Olson Brothers for the unpaid purchase price of the Cessna airplane. Moreover, instead of entering judgment for Cessna Finance in the full amount of the insurance policy, the court directed the Insurance Company to deposit with the court $ 84,000, plus interest from the date of the crash.

The court then ordered the clerk of court to distribute this money as follows: $ 33,778.51, plus interest at the statutory rate from the date of the crash, to Cessna Finance; and $ 50,221.49, plus interest at the statutory rate from the date of the crash, to Olson Brothers.

In addition to the cash award, the court concluded that Cessna Finance should take title to the trade-in airplane. It also ordered Northwestern Flyers to pay Olson Brothers $ 1,079.51, plus interest from the date of the judgment. Finally, the court ordered the Insurance Company to pay $ 21,934.95 in attorneys' fees to Olson Brothers.

Cessna Finance, Northwestern Flyers, and Olson Brothers appealed the district court's rulings following entry of the judgments. The Insurance Company filed a cross-appeal, contending that neither insurance policy afforded any coverage for the Cessna airplane at the time of the crash.

II. Discussion.

A. Northwestern Flyers' Hull Policy.

Both Cessna Finance and the Insurance Company appeal from the district court's order awarding insurance proceeds to Cessna Finance, as lienholder, under Northwestern Flyers' hull policy. Cessna Finance maintains that the court should have entered judgment in the full amount to which it was entitled under the policy, rather than awarding it title to the trade-in aircraft and $ 33,778.51 in cash. The Insurance Company contends that Cessna Finance could not recover as a matter of law under Northwestern Flyers' policy because Northwestern Flyers did not have title to the aircraft at the time of the crash.

Northwestern Flyers' hull policy contains a lienholder's interest endorsement in favor of Cessna Finance, entitling the lienholder to recover the unpaid balance due on any liens on the aircraft. The "ownership" clause recites the named insured, Northwestern Flyers, as the sole owner of the airplane, and reads as follows:

> OWNERSHIP: Unless otherwise stated herein and except with respect to bailment, lease, conditional sale, purchase agreement, mortgage or other encumbrance, the Named Insured is the sole owner of the aircraft.

The Insurance Company argues that, under the terms of the policy, Northwestern Flyers' coverage ceased after it sold and delivered the aircraft to Olson Brothers. Because Cessna Finance's rights as a lienholder depend upon Northwestern Flyers' rights under the policy, the Insurance Company contends that Cessna Finance cannot prevail unless the lienholder endorsement affords it greater protection than that afforded Northwestern Flyers.

The lienholder's endorsement provides that the insurance

> shall not be invalidated as respects the interest of the Lienholder by any act or neglect of the Insured; except that any change in title of ownership of the aircraft ..... (is) not covered hereunder(.)

Cessna Finance, therefore, can recover only if the sale of the airplane to Olson Brothers did not effect a "change in title of ownership." The parties dispute the meaning of this phrase. Cessna Finance claims that the phrase "title of ownership" refers to the paper title to the aircraft. It contends that because Northwestern Flyers retained possession of the bill of sale and the FAA registration, "title" remained in Northwestern Flyers. The Insurance Company argues that the concept of title used in commercial transactions governs the interpretation of the policy. We agree with this latter approach.

The phrase "title of ownership" simply refers to lawful ownership of the airplane. Because the parties entered into a commercial relationship, the Iowa Uniform Commercial Code (UCC) governs the rights of the parties. Ordinarily, title to goods passes to the buyer upon delivery. *Iowa Code Ann. § 554.2401* (West 1967). Retention of title by the seller in goods delivered to the buyer is limited, in effect, to reservation of a security interest. Id. Thus, upon Northwestern Flyers' delivery of the airplane to Olson Brothers, title to the aircraft passed to Olson Brothers, although Northwestern Flyers may have retained a security interest. See *Herington Livestock Auction Co. v. Verschoor, 179 N.W.2d 491 (Iowa 1970)*; *Iowa Code Ann. § 554.2401* (West 1967). Because title to the airplane passed to Olson Brothers upon delivery, Cessna Finance cannot recover as a lienholder under the terms of Northwestern Flyers' policy.

B. Olson Brothers' Hull Policy.

The jury returned a verdict for Olson Brothers based on its claim under its separate insurance policy, which carried a stated value of $110,000. The district court, however, entered judgment n. o. v. for the Insurance Company on the ground that Olson Brothers did not hold an insurable interest in the airplane at the time of the crash.

The Insurance Company concedes that Olson Brothers had an insurable interest in the airplane, and, therefore, admits that the basis for the trial court's ruling was erroneous. It argues, however, that the court properly entered judgment n. o. v. because the pilot's flight pattern, which resulted in the crash, violated the terms of the policy's pilot clause, thereby cancelling Olson Brothers' insurance coverage.

Item 7 of the policy declarations provides:

> PILOT CLAUSE: Only the following pilot or pilots holding valid and effective pilot and medical certificates with ratings as required by the Federal Aviation Administration for the flight involved will operate the aircraft in flight(.) (Emphasis supplied.)

The policy specifically excludes from coverage any damage or loss "occurring while the aircraft is operated in flight by other than the pilot or pilots set forth under Item 7 of the Declarations(.)"

The parties do not dispute that the policy lists Larry McAfee as a pilot authorized to fly the aircraft, and that he was rated for flight only under Visual Flight Rules (VFR). The parties, however, disagree on whether the fatal flight should be characterized as a VFR flight, for which McAfee carried a proper rating.

Prior to takeoff, VFR weather conditions prevailed at Great Falls, Montana, the point of departure, and at McAfee's destination in O'Neill, Nebraska. Although some cloud cover existed in the flight path, Olson Brothers' expert testified that McAfee could have completed the entire flight under VFR conditions. However, seventeen minutes after takeoff, McAfee requested and received permission from the air traffic control center in Salt Lake City, Utah, to fly at altitudes of 21,000 and 23,000 feet. Shortly after climbing to 23,000 feet, McAfee apparently lost control of the airplane and it crashed.

Under FAA regulations, Instrument Flight Rules (IFR) govern flight into air space above 18,000 feet. The Insurance Company contends that the flight in question became an IFR flight and that insurance coverage ceased when McAfee flew above that altitude. According to the Insurance Company, the trial judge incorrectly permitted a determination that the flight in question was a VFR flight for which McAfee was properly rated, when he instructed the jury that "a flight (was) to be characterized or determined at the time of take-off." We disagree.

At the outset, we note that Nebraska law governs whether McAfee was properly rated for the flight within the terms of the Olson Brothers' policy. We have been unable to find controlling Nebraska precedent to guide our determination of whether the trial court properly instructed the jury that the flight was to be characterized as VFR or IFR at the time of takeoff.

The Insurance Company refers to *Arnold v. Globe Indemnity Co., 416 F.2d 119 (6th Cir. 1969)*, and *Jim Hawk Chevrolet-Buick, Inc. v. Insurance Co. of North America, 270 N.W.2d 466 (Iowa 1978)*, as authority for its argument that insurance coverage ceased when McAfee flew into a positive control area without holding an instrument rating. These cases, however, may be distinguished.

In Arnold and Jim Hawk, the pilots took off under IFR conditions, while holding only VFR ratings. In Arnold, IFR weather conditions prevailed at takeoff. *416 F.2d at 122.* In Jim Hawk, the evidence suggests that IFR conditions existed throughout the entire flight: "(A)t the time of operation and the crash ..... weather conditions were such that the sky was overcast, there was a 600 foot ceiling, it was dark at night, foggy and raining(.)" *270 N.W.2d at 467.* Thus, the facts of both Arnold and Jim Hawk differ materially from those in the present case. Here, the flight unmistakably began under VFR conditions.

National Insurance Underwriters v. King Craft Custom Products, Inc., 368 F. Supp. 476 (N.D.Ala.1973), aff'd, *488 F.2d 1393 (5th Cir. 1974)*, and *Glover v. National Insurance Underwriters, 545 S.W.2d 755 (Tex.1977)*, support the district court's instruction that the character of the flight should be determined at takeoff.

In King Craft, an insurance carrier denied coverage based on a policy exclusion similar to the one at issue in the instant case. The pilot in King Craft, while holding only a VFR rating, flew into IFR weather conditions and crashed when attempting to land. *368 F. Supp. at 477-78.* The insurer argued that the pilot was not properly rated for the flight under the policy's pilot clause. The court noted that, at the time of takeoff, VFR weather conditions prevailed at both the point of departure and destination. *Id. at 478*. The insurance carrier there, as here, urged the court to break the flight into segments, and to treat that portion of the flight when the crash occurred as an IFR flight for which the pilot did not hold an appropriate rating. The court declined, observing that such an interpretation of the policy "could result in coverage during a particular flight flickering on and off as particular weather conditions were encountered." *Id. at 479*.

The court in Glover similarly confronted the question whether a pilot holding a VFR rating was properly rated for the flight when he encountered IFR weather conditions and crashed. *545 S.W.2d at 758-59*. The pilot in Glover began his flight in VFR weather conditions and later encountered IFR weather conditions. The evidence in Glover, however, indicated that at the time of takeoff IFR weather conditions prevailed over the final one-third of the flight as well as the destination. *Id. at 759*. The court, nevertheless, declined to characterize the flight as an IFR flight. Instead, the court held that a flight must be characterized at its inception. *Id. at 762*. Because the pilot took off under VFR conditions and VFR conditions prevailed throughout the first one-third of the flight, the court determined the flight to be a VFR flight. *Id. at 763*.

The Insurance Company would distinguish King Craft and Glover from this case on the ground that the pilots in those cases encountered IFR weather conditions. The Insurance Company contends that McAfee did not encounter IFR weather conditions, but simply chose to fly into air space that required an instrument rating.

The Insurance Company's contention must be examined in light of the well-settled rule that "exceptions, limitations and exclusions to insuring agreements require a narrow construction on the theory that the insurer, having affirmatively expressed coverage through broad promises, assumes a duty to define any limitations upon that coverage in clear and explicit terms." *Roach v. Churchman, 431 F.2d 849, 851 (8th Cir. 1970)*; see also *City of Cedar Rapids v. Northwestern National Insurance Co., 304 N.W.2d 228, 230 (Iowa 1981)*; cf. *Neal v. St. Paul Fire & Marine Insurance Co., 197 Neb. 718, 250 N.W.2d 648, 650 (1977)* (insurance policy will be liberally construed in favor of the insured).

The Insurance Company here knew how to exclude coverage for a flight into air space requiring an instrument rating. It failed to do so in clear and explicit terms in Olson Brothers' policy. In such circumstances, the pilot clause should not be interpreted to exclude coverage as a matter of law. See *National Insurance Underwriters v. King Craft Custom Products, Inc., supra, 368 F. Supp. at 479*; *Glover v. National Insurance Underwriters, supra, 545 S.W.2d at 764*.

Accordingly, the district court correctly instructed the jury that the flight was to be characterized at the time of takeoff. Because the Insurance Company failed to establish a basis for exclusion of coverage as a matter of law, the jury verdict in favor of Olson Brothers on the hull policy must stand.

347

C. Northwestern Flyers' Claim Against Olson.

Although the jury returned a verdict for Northwestern Flyers on its claim for the purchase price of the airplane it had sold Olson Brothers, the district court declined to enter judgment for Northwestern Flyers. Instead, as we have already observed, the court ordered Northwestern Flyers to pay Olson Brothers $ 1,079.51, the difference between lost profits on the sale of the airplane and the amount Northwestern Flyers had received from Olson Brothers as a downpayment.

The jury determined that Northwestern Flyers should recover the unpaid portion of the purchase price from Olson Brothers. The evidence in this case establishes that amount to be $ 70,473.65: the balance due on the airplane sold, $ 37,160, plus credit for the $ 33,313.65 lien Commercial Credit holds on the trade-in airplane, which Olson Brothers represented to be free and clear of liens. Northwestern Flyers should also receive interest on this balance from date of the delivery of the aircraft.

D. Olson Brothers' Attorneys' Fees.

The district court awarded Olson Brothers attorneys' fees pursuant to *Neb.Rev.Stat. § 44-359*. Having concluded that Olson Brothers should recover on its claim under its own insurance policy, we affirm the district court's award of $ 21,934.95 in attorneys' fees. The amount of attorneys' fees awarded falls within the discretion of the district court, *Schmer v. Hawkeye-Security Insurance Co., 194 Neb. 94, 230 N.W.2d 216, 218 (1975)*, and the district court did not abuse that discretion.

In addition, because *Neb.Rev.Stat. § 44-359* authorizes attorneys' fees for appellate proceedings, Olson Brothers may petition this court for its attorneys' fees on appeal by complying with the rules of this court. See *8th Cir. R. 17*.

E. Insurance Company's Assertions of Trial Error.

The Insurance Company raises several allegations of error in the trial court's evidentiary rulings and jury instructions. We have reviewed those claims, and, in light of our prior rulings, conclude that any error committed must be deemed harmless.

III. Conclusion.

In sum, we hold that Cessna Finance may not recover under the provisions of Northwestern Flyers' insurance policy for the loss of the airplane. Olson Brothers is entitled to recover the stated value of the airplane under its separate insurance policy along with the amount of attorneys' fees awarded by the district court. Finally, Northwestern Flyers is entitled to recover on its contract claim against Olson Brothers in the amount of $ 70,473.65, plus interest at Iowa's statutory rate from the date of delivery of the airplane.

We affirm in part, reverse in part, and remand to the district court for such further proceedings as may be necessary and for entry of appropriate judgments consistent with this opinion. Olson Brothers shall have costs assessed against the Insurance Company. Northwestern Flyers shall have fifty percent of its costs assessed against Olson Brothers. Otherwise, the parties shall bear their own costs.

VII. TORT LAW – NEGLIGENCE & PRODUCTS LIABILITY

A. *Negligence*

BURTON QUAM V. NELSON-RYAN FLIGHT SERVICE

Supreme Court of Minnesota

144 N.W.2d 551

July, 1966

This is an appeal from a judgment entered in the municipal court of Minneapolis for damages caused to a light, 4-passenger plane while it was parked on defendant's premises. It is contended that the verdict is not supported by the evidence.

It appears that plaintiff, an airplane pilot, is the owner of a small, single-engine airplane which he uses to teach instrument flying. At the time of the occurrences hereinafter related that activity was a hobby of the plaintiff which he intended to develop into a business on retirement. He maintained the plane on premises owned by defendant, Nelson-Ryan Flight Service, where there was assigned to him a space to keep the plane for which he paid $ 7.50 a month. It was recognized that the plane would be exposed to the elements and, in order to safely keep it in place, defendant had installed three stakes to which ropes were attached. When the plane was parked the ropes would be tied to rings located on each wing of the plane and at the tail spring. In the late afternoon of July 22, 1962, while the plane was parked on defendant's premises, one of the ropes broke during a severe storm, causing the plane to be thrown about and resulting in damage which is the subject of this lawsuit.

The trial court indicated to the jury:

"In order to recover on his claim, the plaintiff must prove by the preponderance of the evidence that the rope furnished by the defendant was defective or insufficient for its intended use; that the plaintiff's property was damaged and that defendant's failure to furnish a rope sufficient for its intended use was a direct cause of the damage to plaintiff's property.

"The defendant must prove by a preponderance of the evidence its affirmative defenses, the contributory negligence of the plaintiff and the assumption of risk by the plaintiff and the Act of God."

It is not contended by defendant that the jury was not correctly instructed as to the law. The principle of law to be applied in this case is that a person who furnishes equipment for compensation for a business use by another, under circumstances where such person retains the exclusive right to maintain the equipment and it is foreseeable that damage might result from defects in it, owes a duty to use reasonable care to provide equipment that is safe for its intended use and free from defects of which such person has knowledge or which he could have discovered by the use of reasonable care.

On the basis of the record here there was a fact question as to whether or not the rope which broke in the storm was defective and unsafe for its intended use. The jury had an opportunity to examine the rope and from the evidence in the record could fairly find that there was in fact a breach of duty on the part of defendant in failing to provide equipment which was safe for its intended use. *Campbell v. Siever, 253 Minn. 257, 91 N.W. (2d) 474.*

Affirmed.

CHARLES LECKBEE V. CONTINENTAL AIRLINES, INC.

UNITED STATES COURT OF APPEALS FOR THE FIFTH
CIRCUIT

410 F.2d 1191

May, 1969

GEWIN, Circuit Judge:

The *SUDDEN JERK* which has plagued carriers engaged in surface transportation for years now forms the basis of a complaint against an air carrier. By an action in the United States District Court for the Western District of Texas, Charles Leckbee seeks to recover damages from Continental Airlines for personal injuries allegedly inflicted upon him by the abrupt and unexpected movement of Continental's commercial airliner on which he was a passenger. The case was heard by a jury, but the issues never reached the jurors. After both parties had presented their evidence and rested, the court directed a verdict in favor of Continental, expressing the view that there was no evidence from which the jury could find that Leckbee suffered an injury *PROXIMATELY CAUSED* by Continental's negligence. We disagree with this assessment of the evidence and reverse.

The suit arose from an incident which occurred on December 12, 1966, as Continental's four-engine, turbo-prop aircraft commenced its takeoff from the Greater Southwest Airport in Fort Worth, Texas. As the plane sped along the runway approaching the point of lift-off, the captain's adjustable seat unexpectedly slid backwards projecting him away from the instrument panel and controls. This malfunction of the seat prompted the captain to abort the takeoff by immediately retarding the throttles and executing a maneuver characterized as "ground fine," whereby movement of the aircraft was slowed and the plane eventually brought to a full stop. Appellant Leckbee alleges in his complaint that the deceleration was so abrupt that it threw him across his seat belt, causing injury to the bones, nerves, and soft tissue of his back. At the trial, his account of the incident was, in pertinent part as follows:

> I had my seat belt on and the acceleration pushed me back into the seat. Everything was apparently normal and the first thing I knew, why this thing -- bingo, she stopped, not necessarily like hitting a brick wall, but just reversed the thrust, and I found myself leaning over the seat belt and I tried to catch myself using my back muscles et cetera, and I guess I put my hand up in front of me and they slowed the plane down and it eventually turned off. I didn't know what had happened.
>
> Q. Did you have any kind of a warning whatsoever that the plane wasn't going to take off normally until this abortive take-off occurred?
>
> A. No warning whatsoever.
>
> Q. Did you feel any kind of sensation in any part of your body that was out of the ordinary when that occurred, when the airplane deaccelerated?

A. Well, I felt a little pull, a twing or twang, something or another back in the back. I didn't think too much about it at the time.

About two months prior to this incident, Leckbee had undergone a surgical operation for the removal of a herniated disc in the lower region of his back. The neurosurgeon who performed the operation, Dr. Meek, testified that his last examination of Leckbee *BEFORE* the aborted takeoff was on November 8, 1966, slightly over a month before this occurrence, and on that date Leckbee reported no back pain and complained of only slight pain in his left leg. Leckbee testified that at the time he boarded the plane on December 12, he had no pain in any part of his body, but that on the day following the aborted takeoff, he experienced discomfort in his left leg and hip which progressively worsened. On December 23, 1966, Leckbee returned to Dr. Meek complaining of severe leg and hip pain. When a period of bed rest failed to produce relief from this condition, a second surgical procedure was performed February 6, 1967, at which time more herniated disc was removed from Leckbee's back. Dr. Meek testified that an abrupt movement like the one described by Leckbee as having occurred at the time of the aborted takeoff could lead to the condition which required Leckbee's second surgical operation and that, assuming no other injury to Leckbee's back, he believed "there would be a relationship between such an incident and the subsequent development of his symptoms and physical condition."

The district court viewed the evidence as adequately presenting for jury consideration the question of whether Continental had acted negligently in permitting the captain's seat to malfunction, but concluded that the evidence was insufficient to establish proximate causation linking Leckbee's injury with the malfunction. On appeal the parties have not seriously challenged the district court's evaluation of the evidence relating to Continental's *NEGLIGENCE* and, after examining the record, we concur in this aspect of the court's analysis. In our opinion there was sufficient evidence of probative force to support a finding of negligence. However, we are unable to agree with the district court that the evidence was insufficient to raise a jury question on the matter of *PROXIMATE CAUSE*.

The concept of proximate cause as fashioned by Texas jurisprudence has two basic elements: cause in fact and foreseeability. *CAUSE IN FACT* requires evidence that the negligent act was a substantial factor in bringing about the injury and that but for the negligent act no harm would have been incurred. Viewing the evidence in a light most favorable to Leckbee, we are unable to say that reasonable and fair-minded men in the exercise of impartial judgment could not find these requirements fulfilled and conclude that the aborted takeoff of Continental's aircraft was the *CAUSE IN FACT* of Leckbee's subsequent decline in health. The evidence is clearly susceptible of such a finding once the jury gives credence to the following: (1) Leckbee's testimony that the unexpected deceleration threw him forward, instantly causing pain in his left leg and hip; (2) testimony describing the deceleration as sufficiently abrupt to cause a handbag or purse to slide up the aisle; (3) testimony contrasting Leckbee's physical condition before and after the aborted takeoff; and

(4) medical testimony relating the abrupt movement of the aircraft to Leckbee's injury.

Continental would avoid the result we reach by its contention that the *DECELERATION* of the plane was not an act of negligence. It is true that there was no evidence of the captain's having acted negligently in aborting the takeoff. Common sense suggests that under the circumstances he exercised good judgment. Nevertheless, the prudence of Continental's pilot in aborting the takeoff cannot be invoked to absolve the carrier from liability if the emergency necessitating the abortion was created by Continental's negligence, *i.e.*, permitting the captain's seat to malfunction. As stated by the Texas court,

> the issue as to responsibility is in . . . circumstances [of emergency] to be resolved by reference to the act or omission which brought the dangerous situation into existence.

FORESEEABILITY, the second element in the makeup of proximate cause, requires that

> as a person of ordinary intelligence and prudence, . . . [the actor] should have anticipated the danger to others created by his negligent act, and the rule does not require that he anticipate just how injuries will grow out of that dangerous situation.

We have no difficulty concluding that a jury might justifiably find from the evidence that Continental's employees should have reasonably foreseen the danger to passengers created by a failure adequately to adjust or properly to inspect the captain's seat, since a malfunction of the seat might deprive the pilot of access to the controls of the swift and mammoth machine he operates. [There was evidence indicating that the malfunction could have resulted from either the captain's failure properly to adjust his seat or a broken pen under the seat].

The judgment directed by the district court is reversed and the case is remanded for a new trial.

Reversed and remanded.

KANDIE NEWING, a Minor, etc., et al., v. STEVEN EUGENE CHEATHAM, as Administrator, etc.

Supreme Court of California

540 P.2d 33

October, 1975

In this action for damages for wrongful death arising out of the crash of a private airplane, defendant Steven Eugene Cheatham as administrator of the estate of Harold Cheatham (hereafter Cheatham) deceased appeals from a judgment entered upon a jury verdict in favor of plaintiffs and against decedent's estate in the sum of $ 125,000. Plaintiffs are the surviving wife and children of Richard Newing, an occupant of the plane who died in the crash. Defendant's decedent who also died in the crash was the owner and pilot of the plane.

[note: "wrongful death" is a type of negligence claim brought by a decedent's survivors. Obviously, a dead person cannot sue anyone, so the deceased's relatives usually sue in his or her place under the wrongful death theory.] –JJV, ed.

About 1 p.m. on Sunday, October 25, 1970, Richard Newing, Harold Cheatham, and Ronald Bird departed from Brown Field at Chula Vista, California, aboard a single-engine Cessna 172 aircraft owned and piloted by Cheatham. Neither Newing nor Bird was a licensed pilot. At the time of take-off the weather was clear and the visibility unrestricted. There was no evidence that the plane landed at any other field that afternoon, or that it sent any radio messages. When it failed to return, a search was commenced. On the following day the plane's wreckage was located by a search aircraft in mountainous terrain about 13 miles east of Tijuana, Mexico, and an equal distance southeast of Brown Field. A rescue party found all occupants of the airplane dead. The clock on the instrument panel was stopped at 5:18.

Plaintiffs brought this action for wrongful death alleging that the crash had been caused by Cheatham's negligence. At trial, three theories were advanced in support of plaintiffs' case. The first was that Cheatham had negligently permitted the airplane to run out of fuel while in flight. The second was that he had been negligent as a matter of law in that he had violated applicable federal air regulations. Finally, Cheatham's negligence was said to be established by the doctrine of res ipsa loquitur.

[note: res ipsa loquiter is Latin for "the thing speaks for itself." It is also an alternative way of establishing a negligence claim. The elements of a res ipsa loquiter claim are enumerated below.] –JJV, ed.

In support of the first of these theories, plaintiffs offered the testimony of Jorge Areizaga Rojo, then Commandante of the Tijuana Airport, and of Jesus Leon an airport mechanic. Rojo, who testified as an expert witness, had been a member of the rescue party that first reached the wreckage of the aircraft. Accompanied by Leon, he returned to the site on the second day after the crash in order to gather information for a report to the Mexican authorities. Rojo testified that he visually inspected the fuel tanks of the aircraft, which were carried on its wings, but saw no fuel. He also attempted, but without success, to drain fuel from the bottom of each tank by removing drain plugs.

Leon testified that he had inspected the aircraft's fuel system, although he had not dismantled it, but had found no trace of fuel. Both men visually inspected the ground beneath the aircraft, but saw no indication of fuel spillage. They also attempted to measure the fuel in one of the wing tanks; Leon estimated the level of the fuel to be three-sixteenths of an inch. Rojo indicated that whatever fuel remained in the tanks was probably "unusable," in the sense that it was not a sufficient quantity to reach the engine. Rojo also testified concerning the general structural condition of the aircraft, the appearance of the propeller and control surfaces, the upright position in which the plane had come to rest, and general description of the accident site. All of these factors, he said, indicated that the crash had been caused by fuel exhaustion.

On cross-examination, however, Rojo conceded that the appearance and condition of the plane would have been the same if the crash had been caused by engine failure or some similar mechanical malfunction resulting in loss of power. He also indicated that since the aircraft had not been brought to a level position before he had attempted to drain fuel from the tanks, a usable amount of fuel might have remained within. He admitted that there had been no very thorough investigation of other potential causes of the crash. Despite the foregoing, however, he remained of the opinion that the plane had crashed because it had run out of fuel.

Plaintiffs also called as an expert witness Michael Potter, an airline pilot who had logged some 1,200 hours of flight time in small aircraft, including 200 hours in a Cessna 172. Potter testified at length concerning the training received by student pilots with respect to fuel management and emergencies in flight. He stated that a prudent pilot maintains at the minimum a 45-minute reserve of fuel, and ordinarily flies high enough above surrounding terrain to permit his aircraft to glide to a safe landing in the event of a power failure. Potter also testified that, according to the operator's manual, a Cessna 172 has sufficient fuel capacity to fly to 4.3 hours when operated at the usual power settings and with a "lean" fuel mixture. Thus, he said, the Cheatham plane, if operated in the usual manner with respect to power settings, fuel mixture, and altitude, should have run out of fuel at just the time indicated on its damaged clock. However, he indicated on cross-examination that the endurance of a Cessna 172 can be greater or less than 4.3 hours depending upon the manner in which it is operated. Despite this, Potter said that the crash had probably been caused by fuel exhaustion and the pilot's failure to maintain proper terrain clearance. This opinion was based upon his examination of photographs of the wreckage, his observations made during overflights of the crash site, the testimony of Rojo and Leon, and an experiment in which he ran the engine of a stationary Cessna 172 until its fuel supply was exhausted. From such experiment Potter found that five-sixteenths of an inch of fuel remained in the tanks after the engine had stopped.

Defendant called as an expert witness Robert Rudich, an experienced air traffic controller who had written widely on the subject of air crash investigations and had participated in many such investigations, though chiefly as an analyst of cockpit recording devices and as an editor of final reports. Rudich expressed no opinion as to the cause of the crash, but testified instead about the procedures that must be employed in a sound air crash investigation. According to Rudich, such an inquiry must consist of a progressive "ruling out" of the whole gamut of potential causes ranging from human error to mechanical or structural failure. Where fuel exhaustion is suspected, the entire fuel system must be dismantled and painstakingly inspected from end to end in order to eliminate the possibility that one of its components has malfunctioned. In addition, the plane's other systems must be checked for signs of similar mechanical failure. The court did not permit Rudich to express an opinion as to the quality of the investigation conducted by Rojo and Leon, although the implication of his testimony was that their investigation had been rudimentary at best. However, Rudich was allowed to testify about an experiment he performed on a detached Cessna 172 wing arranged at an angle approximating that of the wing of the downed plane as shown in photographs of the wreckage. Rudich found that it required 7.5 gallons of gasoline to raise the fuel level in the wing tank to three-sixteenths of an inch. This was said to constitute a usable amount of fuel.

In addition to this expert testimony, defendant introduced evidence that the three dead men had been drinking beer together on the day of the crash. The owner of a National City tavern testified that Newing, a man named "Harold," and another man had drunk draft beer in his establishment for about an hour that morning, although he was unable to say how much beer they had consumed. A member of the rescue party testified that eight or nine empty beer cans had been found in the wreckage of the Cheatham plane. Evidence was also produced that the Mexican physicians who had performed autopsies on the bodies of the three men, had noted a strong odor of alcohol emanating from the remains of Cheatham and Bird, but not from Newing's.

After the close of the evidence, the trial judge advised counsel that he would not instruct the jury on the defenses of assumption of risk and contributory negligence. He then granted plaintiffs' motion for a directed verdict on the issue of liability, concluding that the elements of res ipsa loquitur had been established as a matter of law and that the inference of negligence arising from the doctrine had not been rebutted as required by *Evidence Code section 646*. The jury returned a verdict in favor of plaintiffs in the amount of $ 125,000. Judgment was entered accordingly. This appeal followed.

We address ourselves at once to defendant's main contention that the trial court committed prejudicial error by directing a verdict on the issue of liability. Our consideration of this issue requires us to resolve two subordinate questions: First, whether, as the trial court concluded, the doctrine of res ipsa loquitur established Cheatham's negligence as a matter of law; second, whether, as it also determined, the defenses of contributory negligence and assumption of risk as a matter of law were not applicable to the case.

We proceed to discuss these questions in the above order. We do so mindful of the familiar rules governing the granting of a motion for a directed verdict. Adverting to them in the context of a directed verdict in favor of the plaintiff, we had this to say in *Walters v. Bank of America (1937) 9 Cal.2d 46, 49:* "The trial court, in a proper case, may direct a verdict in favor of a party upon whom rests the burden of proof, in this case the plaintiff. Substantially the same rules apply to directed verdicts in favor of plaintiffs as apply to such verdicts in favor of defendants. [Citations omitted.] A directed verdict may be granted, when, disregarding conflicting evidence, and indulging every legitimate inference which may be drawn from the evidence in favor of the party against whom the verdict is directed, it can be said that there is no evidence of sufficient substantiality to support a verdict in favor of such party, if such a verdict has been rendered. [Citations omitted.] In passing on the propriety of the trial court's action in directing a verdict, the doctrine of scintilla of evidence has been rejected in this state. [Citation omitted.] A motion for a directed verdict may be granted upon the motion of the plaintiff, where, upon the whole evidence, the cause of action alleged in the complaint is supported, and no substantial support is given to the defense alleged by the defendant. [Citations omitted.]"

(1) It is settled law in this state that the "doctrine of res ipsa loquitur is applicable where the accident is of such a nature that it can be said, in the light of past experience, that it probably was the result of negligence by someone and that the defendant is probably the one responsible. [Citations omitted.]" According to the classic and oft-repeated statement, there are three conditions for the application of the doctrine: "'(1) the accident must be of a kind which ordinarily does not occur in the absence of someone's negligence; (2) it must be caused by an agency or instrumentality within the exclusive control of the defendant; (3) it must not have been due to any voluntary action or contribution on the part of the plaintiff.'" (*Ybarra v. Spangard (1944) 25 Cal.2d 486, 489 [154 P.2d 687, 162 A.L.R. 1258]*; see *Wolfsmith v. Marsh (1959) 51 Cal.2d 832, 835 [337 P.2d 70].*) The existence of one or more of these conditions is usually a question of fact for the jury. [Citations omitted.] In a proper case, however, they all may exist as a matter of law. [Citations omitted.] The question to be answered here is whether, as the trial judge determined, this is such a case.

(2) Turning to consider the foregoing three conditions for the application of the doctrine, we direct our attention to the first condition, namely that the accident must be of a kind which ordinarily does not occur in the absence of negligence. In determining whether this condition is satisfied, a court may consider common knowledge, the testimony of expert witnesses, and the circumstances relating to the particular accident at issue. (*Zentz v. Coca Cola Bottling Co. (1952) 39 Cal.2d 436, 446 [247 P.2d 344].*) It need not be concluded that negligence is the only explanation of the accident, but merely the most probable one. [Citations omitted.] We deal here in probabilities, not certainties.

Whether aircraft accidents are more often than not the result of negligence is a question that has vexed the courts of many jurisdictions for decades. (See cases collected in Annot., 6 A.L.R.2d 528 (1949), and Speiser, Res Ipsa Loquitur (1972) § 10:1 et seq.) According to Prosser, many early cases took the position that not enough was known about the hazards of flight to permit an inference of negligence to arise from the mere fact of a plane crash. (Prosser, Law of Torts (4th ed. 1971) p. 216.) Advances in the safety and frequency of air travel, however, have led to a trend in the opposite direction. Thus, while judicial opinion on the subject is by no means unanimous, res ipsa loquitur, over the years, has been applied to an increasing variety of aircraft mishaps. [Citations omitted.]

It is not fatal to the ruling here under review that the above cited cases dealt with the application of the doctrine of res ipsa loquitur as a question of fact to be determined by the jury whereas in the case at bench, it was applied by the trial judge to the air crash here involved as a matter of law. Essentially any differences in the manner of establishing the doctrine lies in the state of the evidence and the posture of the case. (*Zentz v. Coca Cola Bottling Co., supra, 39 Cal.2d 436, 440.*) Although whether any one of the conditions for the application of the doctrine has been met may be usually a question of fact (*Seneris v. Haas, supra, 45 Cal.2d 811, 827*), nevertheless under the particular circumstances of the case, any one of them may exist as a matter of law (*Roddiscraft, Inc. v. Skelton Logging Co., supra, 212 Cal.App.2d 784, 794*). Where no issue of fact has been raised as to any of the three conditions, the application of the doctrine is compelled as a matter of law. (*Di Mare v. Cresci, supra, 58 Cal.2d 292, 300*; *Roddiscraft, Inc. v. Skelton Logging Co., supra*; as to the first condition compare *Roddiscraft at pp. 795-797*, question of fact, conditional res ipsa instruction with *Di Mare at pp. 299-300*, question of law, unconditional res ipsa instruction.) In sum, the fact that usually the application of the doctrine involves the resolution of a question of fact as to one or more of the conditions does not foreclose the possibility that in the light of the circumstances surrounding the particular air crash, the application of the doctrine may be compelled as a matter of law.

As we previously noted, the first condition for invocation of the res ipsa doctrine is satisfied if under the facts of the case, common experience indicates that the accident would not have occurred unless there had been negligence on the part of someone. In the instant case, it seems reasonably clear in light of the circumstances surrounding the crash that the accident ordinarily would not have taken place in the absence of negligence. The evidence is uncontradicted that the airplane took off from Chula Vista in clear weather with no restrictions on visibility. There is no evidence that weather conditions contributed in any way to the crash of the plane. Nor was there any evidence that the plane had collided with other aircraft while in flight. Indeed the condition of the plane after the crash was such as to eliminate an air collision.

(3) It thus fell to the ground, apparently unaffected by external factors, only a few miles from the airport whence it had departed some hours earlier. Under the circumstances of the present case, "it seems reasonably clear that the accident probably would not have occurred without negligence by someone." (*Zentz v. Coca Cola Bottling Co., supra, 39 Cal.2d 436, 447.*) The evidence bearing on these circumstances is not only uncontradicted but of such a nature that no issue of fact is raised as to the existence of the first condition for the application of the doctrine of res ipsa loquitur. (*Roddiscraft, Inc. v. Skelton Logging Co., supra, 212 Cal.App.2d 784, 794.*) We conclude that the first condition is established as a matter of law.

(4) The doctrine's second condition, as traditionally formulated, is that the agency or instrumentality causing the accident must have been within the exclusive control or management of the defendant. The purpose of this requirement is to link the defendant with the probability, already established, that the accident was negligently caused. (*Zentz v. Coca Cola Bottling Co., supra, 39 Cal.2d 436, 443.*)

(5a) The facts of this case are such as to satisfy this condition, like the first, as a matter of law. Cheatham was the owner of the aircraft, and there is no dispute that he was at the controls when the plane took off on its final flight. Since neither of his passengers seems to have been a licensed pilot, there is no reason to suppose that anyone other than he operated the plane at any time before the crash. Moreover, Cheatham's ultimate responsibility for all decisions concerning the aircraft's operation was established by an applicable federal air regulation. (See *Lange v. Nelson-Ryan Flight Service, Inc. (1961) 259 Minn. 460 [108 N.W.2d 428, 432].*) These facts are sufficient to distinguish this case from those cited by defendant, in which no such exclusive control or responsibility existed. (*Olson v. Whitthorne & Swan (1928) 203 Cal. 206 [263 P. 518, 58 A.L.R. 129]*; *Gotcher v. Metcalf (1970) 6 Cal.App.3d 96 [85 Cal.Rptr. 566]*; *Cordova v. Ford (1966) 246 Cal.App.2d 180 [54 Cal.Rptr. 508].*)

Defendant argues, however, that plaintiffs have not negated the possibility that the crash was caused by something other than the manner in which the plane was operated. He states that such crashes commonly occur because of mechanical failures of one kind or another, and cites a considerable array of cases in which such failures were said to have occurred. The short answer is that the record is devoid of evidence of such kind of mechanical failure.

(5b) Furthermore, if such evidence had been produced, it would have no relevance to the second condition for the application of res ipsa loquitur, namely whether the airplane was within the exclusive control of Cheatham.

(6) With respect to the operation and maintenance of the aircraft, the control exercised by Cheatham as owner-pilot was complete. There thus can be no doubt that this element of the doctrine exists as a matter of law.

The third of the traditional conditions for the application of res ipsa loquitur is that the accident must not have been caused by any voluntary action or contribution on the part of the plaintiff.

(7) The purpose of this requirement, like that of control by the defendant is to establish that the defendant is the one probably responsible for the accident. (*Zentz v. Coca Cola Bottling Co., supra, 39 Cal.2d 436, 444.*) The plaintiff need not show that he was entirely inactive at the time of the accident in order to satisfy this requirement, so long as the evidence is such as to eliminate his conduct as a factor contributing to the occurrence. (*Shahinian v. McCormick (1963) 59 Cal.2d 554, 560.*)

Defendant contends that the trial court confused the existence of this third condition with the availability of the defenses of assumption of risk and contributory negligence. It is true that these are separate questions, since the burden of proof with respect to the first rests on the plaintiff as part of his general obligation to establish the defendant's negligence, while the burden of proof as to the latter rests on the defendant. (*Shahinian v. McCormick, supra, 59 Cal.2d 554, 560*; *Zentz v. Coca Cola Bottling Co., supra, 39 Cal.2d 436, 444.*)

(8) Quite apart from whether or not the trial court's remarks indicate that it confused the above two questions, the uncontradicted

evidence shows that the body of plaintiffs' decedent was found by the rescue party in one of the rear seats of the four-seater aircraft. From that position, it is difficult to imagine how he could have interfered physically with the operation of the aircraft in any way. (Cf. *Guerra v. Handlery Hotels, Inc. (1959) 53 Cal.2d 266, 271 [1 Cal.Rptr. 330, 347 P.2d 674].*) Moreover, as noted above, there is no dispute that Cheatham was the pilot in command of the aircraft, and it must be presumed that he made all decisions concerning its operation and preparation for flight. There is no basis for supposing that Newing exerted any influence with respect to the making of these decisions. Thus the evidence concerning the basic operation of the aircraft is such as to conclusively eliminate Newing's conduct as a potential cause of the accident.

A separate question in this respect, however, is said to arise from the evidence that the three men drank beer together on the day of the crash. Defendant argues that Newing's conduct in drinking with Cheatham may have contributed to the happening of the accident, and that plaintiffs have not carried their burden with respect to negating this possibility. For reasons which will be more fully discussed in connection with the defenses of contributory negligence and assumption of risk, the evidence concerning the beer drinking was too vague to support a finding that Newing contributed by means of it to the happening of the crash. Plaintiffs are not obligated to eliminate entirely speculative causal possibilities involving the conduct of their decedent. It is enough if they rebut those inferences of their decedent's responsibility which are reasonably supported by the evidence. Plaintiffs discharged this burden by introducing evidence from which it must be inferred that Newing did not interfere with Cheatham's operation or command of the aircraft.

(9) The evidence presented in the trial court, therefore, was such as to satisfy all three conditions for the applicability of res ipsa loquitur as a matter of law. Since the facts giving rise to the doctrine were undisputed, the inference of negligence arose as a matter of law (*Di Mare v. Cresci, supra, 58 Cal.2d 292, 300)*; to put it another way, the conclusion is compelled that there is a balance of probabilities pointing to the decedent's negligence. (See *Zentz v. Coca Cola Bottling Co., supra, 39 Cal.2d 436, 449*; Prosser, *Res Ipsa Loquitur in California* (1949) 37 Cal.L.Rev. 183, 194-195.) This gave rise to a presumption affecting the burden of producing evidence pursuant to *Evidence Code section 646*. It then became defendant's obligation to introduce sufficient evidence to sustain a finding either that the accident resulted from some cause other than Cheatham's negligence, or, else, that Cheatham exercised due care in all possible respects wherein he might have been negligent. (See Cal. Law Revision Com. comment to *Evid. Code, § 646*.) Defendant introduced no such evidence. He has at most argued that the crash *could* have resulted from causes other than the negligence of his decedent. Mere speculation of this sort is insufficient to discharge defendant's burden of explanation. (*Dierman v. Providence Hospital (1947) 31 Cal.2d 290, 295-296 [188 P.2d 12]*; *Roberts v. Trans World Airlines, supra, 225 Cal.App.2d 344, 354-355.*) Consequently, the trial court was correct in concluding that res ipsa loquitur established Cheatham's negligence as a matter of law.

Having thus determined that the negligence of Cheatham was established as a matter of law and having thereby resolved the first of the two questions posed at the beginning of this opinion, we now proceed to consider the second question, namely whether the defenses of contributory negligence and assumption of risk were inapplicable on the present record.

(10) The necessity for this is obvious; the fact that an inference of negligence is compelled as a matter of law does not mean that there was liability as a matter of law. (See *Di Mare v. Cresci, supra, 58 Cal.2d 292, 300.*) Indeed defendant argues in the alternative that even if there was no question of fact as to the application of res ipsa loquitur, such a question did arise as to the above defenses.

> As noted above, the question whether these defenses are available is separate from that concerning the third condition of res ipsa loquitur. Defendant's argument that the jury should have been instructed on the defenses is based upon the evidence, previously adverted to, that the three men drank beer together on the day of the crash. This is said to make the case analogous to those automobile guest cases which have held that a jury question exists concerning the defenses when the guest, injured in an accident caused by the intoxication of his driver host, participated in the latter's drinking activities or otherwise had reason to know of the driver's intoxication before accepting a ride with him. [Citations omitted.]

The proposed analogy, however, is inapposite. The evidence on the point shows only that Cheatham, Newing, and Bird drank some beer. It does not disclose how much they drank, or how it affected them. There is no indication that Cheatham became so obviously intoxicated as to put plaintiffs' decedent on notice as to his inability to operate the plane safely. [Citations omitted.] In *Mittelman v. Seifert, supra, 17 Cal.App.3d 51, 69, 79*, on the other hand, where there was significant evidence of pilot incapacity due to illness, fatigue, and consumption of alcohol and pharmaceuticals, the trial judge's refusal to instruct the jury on contributory negligence and assumption of risk was upheld on appeal.

(11) After having carefully reviewed the record, we fail to find any evidence sufficient to raise an issue of fact in respect to either of these two affirmative defenses. We are satisfied that the trial court properly concluded that plaintiffs' decedent as a matter of law neither was himself negligent nor assumed the risk of Cheatham's allegedly alcoholic condition. We conclude that the trial court properly determined that Cheatham was liable for Newing's death as a matter of law and properly granted plaintiffs' motion for a directed verdict on the issue of liability.

(12) We briefly dispose of defendant's remaining contention, which is that the trial court erred in preventing the witness Rudich from expressing an opinion regarding the adequacy of the investigation conducted by Rojo and the reliability of his conclusion as to the cause of the accident. If any error was committed in this respect, it was not prejudicial, since the clear implication of that portion of Rudich's testimony which was admitted was that Rojo's investigation and opinion were defective. This, however, does nothing to rebut the clear inference of negligence which, in the circumstances of this case, arose from the fact of the crash itself.

The judgment is affirmed.

LINDA WHITE et al v. INBOUND AVIATION et al.

COURT OF APPEAL OF CALIFORNIA, SIXTH APPELLATE
DISTRICT

82 Cal. Rptr. 2d 71

February, 1999

The industry standard in the aircraft rental business requires a pilot
to complete a "high altitude checkout" before being permitted to rent an
aircraft for a flight to a "high altitude" airport. Although defendant
Inbound Aviation had a policy incorporating just such a requirement, it
knowingly permitted a young inexperienced pilot who had not
completed a high altitude checkout to rent an airplane for a flight to the
South Lake Tahoe airport, a challenging and dangerous high altitude
airport. Due to his inexperience and lack of requisite knowledge and
skill, the pilot made a very basic error and crashed the aircraft while
attempting a takeoff from the South Lake Tahoe airport. The crash
killed the pilot and his two passengers. The parents of one of the
passengers sued defendant Inbound Aviation, the partners who owned
Inbound Aviation, the owner of the aircraft and the pilot. The jury
returned a verdict in favor of the parents. Defendants (other than the
pilot) appeal and claim that (1) the jury's verdict is not supported by the
evidence because there is no evidence that the pilot was not
"competent," (2) the jury instructions were confusing and prejudicially
erroneous, (3) the verdict against the owner of the aircraft was
erroneous because the evidence did not support it and it was based on
improperly given jury instructions and (4) the trial court erroneously
failed to limit the amount of damages assessed against the owner of the
aircraft for his vicarious liability. We modify and affirm the judgment.

FACTS

Defendant Inbound Aviation (hereafter Inbound) is a partnership
which, among other things, leases aircraft from owners and rents out
the aircraft to pilots. One of the aircraft leased by Inbound was a Piper
Archer owned by Jeffrey Marconet. Jeffrey Marconet was also an
Inbound employee who was the manager of the company's "day-to-
day" operations. John Rosselott was employed by Inbound as a flight
instructor. Inbound's policy was to require each individual who wished
to rent an aircraft to complete a "checkout" in the type of aircraft the
individual wished to rent. These checkouts were given by Inbound
flight instructors. An Inbound employee would review the individual's
logbook as part of the checkout procedure. The checkout included an
hour to an hour-and-a-half long "flight check" during which the
individual's skill at piloting the aircraft was evaluated and the
individual was informed by the flight instructor "what the airplane is
capable of and not capable of." The individual was required to pay for
aircraft rental and the flight instructor's time during the flight check.
Inbound kept a record of the successful completion of a checkout in a
file it maintained on each individual. This file also contained copies of
the individual's license and medical certificate. The completion of the
checkout would also be recorded in the individual's logbook.

The Federal Aviation Administration (FAA) imposes no special
requirements on private pilots with respect to high altitude airports.
Once a private pilot has obtained a license, this license may be retained

so long as the pilot demonstrates his or her general "proficiency" to a flight instructor at least once every two years. However, because airplanes do not perform as well at high altitudes, Inbound required an individual who wished to fly an aircraft to a "high altitude airport" to complete a "high altitude checkout." Most, but not all, businesses that rent aircraft require high altitude checkouts. The "good" ones have this requirement. Inbound defined "high altitude airport" as any airport over 4,000 feet. High altitude airports are "dangerous," and the South Lake Tahoe airport is particularly dangerous and has a history of a high "density of crashes." This is due to both the high altitude and the mountains that surround the South Lake Tahoe airport. At high altitudes, the aircraft's engine will produce less horsepower, its performance may be greatly degraded by high temperatures, the fuel-air mixture must be adjusted and mountain downdrafts can be much more dangerous.

During an Inbound high altitude checkout, the individual was informed about the differences between an aircraft's performance at sea level and its performance at high altitude. The individual was also given a high altitude flight check. This flight check included a flight to a high altitude airport. One purpose of the high altitude checkout procedure was to provide the individual with the requisite "skills" so that he or she "can make [his or her] own decisions" at a high altitude airport. These skills included takeoff and landing decisions such as whether or not to use the aircraft's flaps during these procedures. The point was to provide the individual with "actual hands-on experience" in high altitude conditions. The high altitude checkout procedure took about four to five hours. Inbound recorded an individual's completion of a high altitude checkout in Inbound's file on the individual and in the individual's logbook. Inbound employees were required to check an individual's file before releasing an aircraft to the individual. However, Inbound did not require its employees to verify that an individual had received a high altitude checkout before releasing an aircraft for a flight to a high altitude airport. Instead, Inbound relied on the individual to complete this requirement in compliance with Inbound's policy. Inbound informed each individual of the high altitude checkout requirement at the time of the initial checkout.

In March 1994, Charles Meier completed an Inbound checkout in a Piper Archer aircraft with Rosselott as his flight instructor. Although Meier's flying experience, as reflected in his logbook, included flights into and out of "high altitude" airports in Arizona, he had no experience flying into or out of any high altitude airport that was surrounded by mountains. Although Meier and Rosselott briefly discussed the use of flaps, Rosselott did not discuss with Meier whether it was appropriate to use flaps for high altitude takeoffs "because we weren't doing high altitude checkout." Rosselott told Meier that Inbound would require Meier to complete a high altitude checkout before Inbound would rent him an aircraft to fly to a high altitude airport. Rosselott perused Meier's logbook, which contained a complete record of Meier's flight experience, and noted that Meier was a "brand new pilot" with a total of about 75 hours of flying experience who had not flown for about 18 months since receiving his license. Meier had only 23 hours of "solo" flight experience, that is, without the presence of a flight instructor. The only airport listed in Meier's logbook with which Rosselott was familiar was the Prescott, Arizona airport. Rosselott thought that Meier "flew adequately" during the checkout with "average" takeoffs and landings which "showed a low level of skill." Meier appeared to have learned to "fly by rote" rather than to make judgment decisions. Nevertheless, Rosselott signed off on Meier's checkout and approved him for rental of a Piper Archer from Inbound.

Twice in the next two months, Meier rented a Piper Archer from Inbound and flew, on each occasion, for less than an hour. On July 2, 1994, Meier rented Marconet's Piper Archer from Inbound. He took two passengers and luggage with him in the aircraft. One of Meier's passengers was Mark White. Before Meier was permitted to fly the aircraft, Rosselott and two other Inbound employees learned that Meier was planning to fly to the South Lake Tahoe airport. Rosselott knew that he had not given Meier a high altitude checkout, but he did not check Meier's file to confirm whether Meier had completed a high altitude checkout with another flight instructor. In fact, Meier had not completed a high altitude checkout, and Inbound's file on Meier did not show that he had done so. Rosselott assumed that, since Meier was aware of the high altitude checkout requirement, Meier had complied with the requirement and completed a high altitude checkout. Jeffrey Marconet provided Meier with the keys to the aircraft.

When Meier attempted to take off from the South Lake Tahoe airport, the aircraft crashed. The crash was caused by Meier's "mismanagement of the aircraft" which caused the aircraft to stall. Proper "management" of the aircraft would have prevented the crash from occurring. Meier's takeoff procedure would have been appropriate at a sea level airport. However, he attempted to take off from a high altitude airport on a hot day with "25 degrees of flaps." The heat and altitude reduced the aircraft's power by more than 25 percent, and the use of flaps only exacerbated the power loss by creating additional drag. The "effect of flaps" and the fact that flaps "degrade climb performance" are part of "basic aerodynamics." It is "not a good idea" to use flaps at high altitude, and any reasonably competent pilot who had received a high altitude checkout would not have used flaps in a Piper Archer for a high altitude takeoff. Meier and his passengers, including Mark White, were killed in the crash.

PROCEDURAL BACKGROUND

Mark White's parents filed an action against Inbound, Gregory Marconet and Michael Lambert (the two partners who owned Inbound), Jeffrey Marconet and the estate of Charles Meier. They alleged that Inbound and Jeffrey Marconet had negligently entrusted the aircraft to Meier for a flight to a high altitude airport without ensuring that Meier had completed a "high altitude checkout" in advance of the flight. Defendants answered the complaint with a general denial. Jeffrey Marconet asserted as an affirmative defense that his liability as owner of the aircraft was limited by *Public Utilities Code section 21404.1*.

At trial, plaintiffs' expert testified that Meier's "competency" to make "the flight to Lake Tahoe" was "impossibly low." He believed that Meier was "desensitized" to the conditions that he should have anticipated at the South Lake Tahoe airport and lacked the "maturity of judgment" to deal with these conditions due to his inexperience. Although Meier had satisfied FAA requirements to obtain a pilot's license, plaintiffs' expert testified that Meier "was not competent" to fly an aircraft into and out of the South Lake Tahoe airport. This expert also expressed the opinion that a pilot could not be considered "proficient" or "competent" if the pilot had not flown in the last 90 days. At the close of plaintiffs' case-in-chief, defendants moved for nonsuit on the ground that there was no evidence of Meier's incompetence. The court denied this motion.

Defendants presented evidence that Meier had been taught about high altitude takeoffs and about the use of flaps when he was in training for his pilot's license. They also adduced evidence that Meier had flown without incident twice in May 1994 into and out of low altitude airports. Defendants also called an expert witness who testified that Meier's successful completion of Rosselott's March 1994 checkout established his competency to pilot a Piper Archer. This expert opined that Inbound's checkout procedures met the standard of care in the aircraft rental business. Defendants also presented evidence that Meier had taken some safety precautions prior to attempting the takeoff from the South Lake Tahoe airport. When Meier prepared to leave South Lake Tahoe, he requested that the aircraft be fueled only "to the tabs" in an apparent effort to keep the aircraft's weight as low as possible. Meier prepared a flight plan for his return flight. He was provided with a "handout" on the subject of "density altitude and take-off procedures at South Lake Tahoe" by a South Lake Tahoe airport employee. A South Lake Tahoe airport employee testified that there had been no major takeoff accidents at South Lake Tahoe airport for nearly four years prior to July 1994.

The jury returned unanimous special verdicts finding that (1) Meier had been negligent, (2) his negligence had caused Mark White's death, (3) Inbound had permitted Meier to use the aircraft when it knew or should have known that he was "not competent" to operate the aircraft, (4) Meier's incompetence had caused the accident, (5) 50 percent of the negligence that had caused Mark White's death was attributable to Inbound and the other 50 percent was attributable to Meier and (6) the total amount of damages was $ 890,000. The jury also made a unanimous special finding that Jeffrey Marconet had permitted Meier to use the aircraft when he knew or should have known that Meier was "not competent" to operate the aircraft. The court entered judgment on the jury's verdicts and finding. It ordered Jeffrey Marconet and Meier's estate to pay $ 445,000 in damages and Inbound, Lambert, Gregory Marconet and Jeffrey Marconet to pay damages of $ 445,000 to plaintiffs. Defendants' motion for a new trial was denied. Defendants (other than Meier's estate) filed a timely notice of appeal.

DISCUSSION

I. *Judgment Against Inbound*

A. *Sufficiency of the Evidence*

(1a) Defendants claim that there was no evidence that Meier was not "competent" within the meaning of that term as it is used in the elements of negligent entrustment.

(2) "Liability for negligent entrustment is determined by applying general principles of negligence, and ordinarily it is for the jury to determine whether the owner [or other entruster] has exercised the required degree of care." (*Allen v. Toledo (1980)* The seminal case on negligent entrustment is *Rocca v. Steinmetz* (1923) 61 Cal. App.. 102. "In its simplest form the question is whether the owner [or other

supplier] when he permits an incompetent or reckless person, whom he knows to be incompetent or reckless, to take and operate his car [or any other instrumentality], acts as an ordinarily prudent person would be expected to act under the circumstances." (61 Cal. App.. at p. 109.) California courts have long held that inexperience *alone* does not *necessarily* establish incompetency. [Citations omitted.] It is necessarily a question for the jury whether a prudent person, aware of the facts known to the supplier of the instrumentality, would have permitted the individual to operate the instrumentality.

(1b) Defendants argue that Meier was "competent" as a matter of law because he was "legally qualified" to pilot an aircraft by virtue of his possession of a pilot's license. They argued this point to the jury, and the jury rejected their claim that possession of a license necessarily established that Meier was "competent." The word "competent" is a fairly broad term which can have several different meanings. It is commonly understood to mean "having requisite or adequate ability or qualities" or "legally qualified or adequate." (Webster's New Collegiate Dict. (10th ed. 1993) pp. 234-235.) Similarly, the word "incompetent" is commonly understood to mean "inadequate to or unsuitable for a particular purpose," "lacking the qualities needed for effective action" or "not legally qualified." (Webster's New Collegiate Dict., *supra*, p. 588.) Defendants have seized on the narrowest of these alternative definitions. We do not believe that the general principles of negligence which govern the tort of negligent entrustment are so limited. If a supplier of a chattel is aware of facts which establish that an individual lacks the ability to safely use the chattel for a particular purpose, and the supplier nevertheless entrusts the chattel to that individual to use *for that purpose*, the supplier has acted imprudently and should be held accountable if harm arises from the individual's inadequacy.

(3) Defendants also challenge the sufficiency of the expert testimony presented at trial by plaintiffs. They claim that plaintiffs' expert improperly equated "competence" and "proficiency." While these two terms are not synonymous, plaintiffs' expert made it clear during his testimony that it was his opinion that Meier did not have the requisite flying ability to fly into and out of the South Lake Tahoe airport. Defendants did not object to this expert's testimony, and they utilized cross-examination to support their claim that lack of "proficiency" was an inappropriate basis for a finding of incompetence. The expert's testimony was sufficient to support a finding that Meier was not competent to fly into and out of the South Lake Tahoe airport.

In defendants' view, "[t]he concept of competence, in the negligent entrustment context, necessarily implies the *minimum* degree of skill required to operate the chattel." This view ignores the importance of the facts. If a supplier of an automobile is aware that a driver with minimal skill intends to utilize the vehicle for a *specific* purpose for which the driver lacks the requisite skill, it would be imprudent for the supplier to entrust the vehicle to this driver for this specific purpose. On the other hand, if the supplier lacks awareness of the purpose to which the driver intends to put the vehicle, the supplier would not be liable for negligent entrustment based on the driver's lack of skills other than those minimally necessary to safely drive the vehicle. The information available to the supplier about the individual and his or her purpose in obtaining the chattel determines whether the supplier acts imprudently in supplying the chattel.

The evidence produced at trial was sufficient to support the jury's liability verdict against Inbound. Inbound was aware that Meier was a brand new pilot with very little solo experience and no flying experience at any high altitude airport surrounded by mountains. Inbound's knowledge included the fact that Meier had only flown five times since receiving his pilot's license nearly two years earlier. It had also learned that Meier had a "low skill level" and seemed to have learned to fly "by rote." Inbound knew that Meier intended to fly the Piper Archer to the South Lake Tahoe airport. The South Lake Tahoe airport is known to be, at best, a challenging airport and, at worst, a dangerous airport. Because high altitude airports in California, many of which are surrounded by mountains, can challenge a pilot's skills, Inbound had an industry-standard high altitude checkout policy. This policy required an individual who wished to rent an aircraft to fly into and out of high altitude airports to complete an exercise which both taught the individual how to safely operate an aircraft at such airports and also tested the individual's skill in doing so under actual high altitude conditions at a high altitude airport.

If Meier had completed Inbound's high altitude checkout, he would have been taught the skills necessary to make proper takeoff and landing decisions at a high altitude airport, including whether to use flaps during such procedures. Notwithstanding its awareness of the dangers associated with high altitude airports and its industry-standard policy requiring a high altitude checkout to alleviate some of these dangers, Inbound knowingly permitted a pilot with questionable flying skills and judgment, minimal solo flying experience, little recent flying experience and no experience flying to any high altitude airport surrounded by mountains to fly the Piper Archer into and out of the South Lake Tahoe airport. On these facts, a jury certainly could have concluded that Meier was not competent to so use the aircraft entrusted to him by Inbound and that Inbound was aware of his incompetence. Since the crash was caused by a basic error which demonstrated Meier's lack of the knowledge and ability to utilize appropriate procedures for takeoff from a high altitude airport surrounded by mountains, Inbound's liability for negligent entrustment was supported by the evidence.

[Section regarding jury instructions being prejudicially erroneous omitted.].

II. *Judgment Against Jeffrey Marconet*

In their opening statement, plaintiffs pointed out that Jeffrey Marconet was both an Inbound employee and the owner of the aircraft. After the close of evidence, plaintiffs requested that the jury be asked to make a special finding as to Jeffrey Marconet's liability for negligent entrustment. Defendants asserted that Jeffrey Marconet's conduct in renting the aircraft to Meier was solely as an Inbound employee and therefore could not support personal liability for negligent entrustment. Defendants stipulated that, under Public Utilities Code section 21401.1, Jeffrey Marconet was vicariously liable as the owner of the aircraft for Meier's negligence, but that liability was limited to $ 15,000. Plaintiffs argued that the special finding was needed because it would permit the jury to find Jeffrey Marconet liable not simply as an owner but also as a "negligent entruster." Defendants offered to stipulate to a judgment of $ 15,000 against Jeffrey Marconet based on vicarious liability, but plaintiffs rejected the stipulation because they wished to seek a larger verdict against Jeffrey Marconet for negligent entrustment. The trial court stated that it would enter judgment in favor of plaintiffs for $ 15,000 if the jury returned a verdict finding Jeffrey Marconet vicariously liable as the owner of the aircraft.

At the instruction conference, plaintiffs argued that Jeffrey Marconet could be found liable in three different ways: (1) as Inbound's agent, (2) vicariously liable as owner of the aircraft and (3) personally liable for negligent entrustment "irrespective of whether Inbound is liable." Defendants did not challenge these assertions. The court noted that the jury could then allocate damages so that "you could wind up with Charles Meier with 30 percent, Inbound with 30 percent, and Jeffrey Marconet with 30 percent." The court asked plaintiffs if they wanted "damages allocated against Jeffrey Marconet?" Plaintiffs pointed out that, as plaintiffs, they did not want damages allocated at all. Plaintiffs asked defendants to stipulate that "if Inbound negligently entrusted the aircraft then Jeffrey Marconet also negligently entrusted the aircraft." Defendants declined to so stipulate. The court then proposed that the jury be asked to allocate damages among Meier, Inbound and Jeffrey Marconet. All counsel subsequently stipulated that the verdict form would include a special finding regarding Jeffrey Marconet's liability for negligent entrustment but the jury would not be asked to apportion any damages to Jeffrey Marconet.

Plaintiffs argued to the jury that "someone who controls the keys to an airplane has an obligation" and "is not supposed to give those keys to someone that he knows or should know is not competent to fly that aircraft." In response, defendants argued that Jeffrey Marconet "acted in a dual role here." "Partly he was registered owner of the airplane leased to Inbound Aviation and he was an employee of Inbound Aviation. There is one thing as far as Jeffrey Marconet's statutory liability as owner of the airplane that the judge has instructed you on and I will discuss with you. [P] But as to anything Jeffrey Marconet did in the course of acting as the manager of Inbound, that too, all gets lumped under the Inbound label."

A. *Sufficiency of the Evidence*

Defendant Jeffrey Marconet challenges the sufficiency of the evidence to establish that (1) he knew of Meier's destination when he entrusted the aircraft to Meier and (2) he had any control over the aircraft when he entrusted the aircraft to Meier.

(5) "'When a finding of fact is attacked on the ground that there is not any substantial evidence to sustain it, the power of an appellate court *begins* and *ends* with the determination as to whether there is any substantial evidence contradicted or uncontradicted which will support the finding of fact.'" [Citations omitted.] "

1. *Knowledge of Destination*

(6) Defendant Jeffrey Marconet argues that there was not substantial evidence that he was aware of Meier's destination. Plaintiffs' case was presented to the jury on the theory that defendants had been

negligent in knowingly entrusting the aircraft to Meier for a flight to the South Lake Tahoe airport. They did not assert that Meier was incompetent to fly to low altitude airports, but only that he was incompetent to fly into and out of the South Lake Tahoe airport. We find substantial evidence in the record to support a reasonable inference that Jeffrey Marconet was aware of Meier's destination when he entrusted the aircraft to him.

Jeffrey Marconet testified that he "[a]bsolutely" did not know at the time he surrendered the keys to the aircraft to Meier that Meier's destination was South Lake Tahoe. He claimed that, notwithstanding the fact that he personally handled the rental transaction with Meier and he personally released the aircraft to Meier, he had not inquired about Meier's destination, and no one had told him of Meier's destination prior to Meier's departure. The testimony at trial established that several other Inbound employees were aware that Meier intended to fly to South Lake Tahoe prior to Meier's departure. Although Jeffrey Marconet admitted that he had learned of Meier's destination from these employees, he insisted that he had not acquired this information until after Meier's death.

We believe that the jury could have reasonably inferred from this evidence that Jeffrey Marconet was in fact aware of Meier's destination prior to releasing the aircraft to him. Jeffrey Marconet's personal involvement in the transaction, his role as Inbound's manager and his insistent testimony of lack of awareness along with his demeanor at trial could have supported an inference by reasonable jurors that he was falsely denying knowledge of Meier's destination in an attempt to avoid responsibility. Obviously, it was not necessary for plaintiffs to obtain Jeffrey Marconet's admission of knowledge where their evidence was sufficient to support a reasonable inference of knowledge.

2. *Control Over Aircraft*

(7) Defendant Jeffrey Marconet argues that he could not be held liable for negligently entrusting the aircraft to Meier because Inbound, not he, "managed controlled and operated the aircraft" for rental purposes. The evidence at trial did indicate that Jeffrey Marconet had leased the aircraft to Inbound. The details of this transaction were not admitted into evidence at trial. Jeffrey Marconet admitted that he benefited from each rental transaction involving his aircraft. In the absence of evidence that Jeffrey Marconet *did not* retain some level of control over the aircraft, his personal release of the aircraft to Meier, combined with his admitted personal interest in renting the aircraft, could have supported a finding that he had the capacity to entrust the aircraft to others notwithstanding Inbound's lease.

He also claims that he could not be personally liable for entrusting the aircraft to Meier as he was acting solely as Inbound's employee when he did so. In light of his admitted personal interest in the rental of his aircraft, the jury could have reasonably inferred that he was not acting *solely* as Inbound's employee when he entrusted the aircraft to Meier. The jury could have concluded that he was acting in a dual capacity as both Inbound's employee *and* the aircraft's owner. Such an inference would support finding Jeffrey Marconet personally liable for negligent entrustment.

[Section on jury instructions omitted.]

C. Limit on Damages for Vicarious Liability

(9) Defendant Jeffrey Marconet also asks this court to modify the judgment to limit to $ 15,000 his liability for the damages attributed by the jury to Meier's negligence. He correctly points out that vicarious liability under *Public Utilities Code sections 21404* and *21404.1* is limited to $ 15,000. The trial court stated that it intended to so limit any judgment based on the vicarious liability verdict, but it did not do so. Plaintiffs concede that any judgment based on Jeffrey Marconet's vicarious liability must be limited to $ 15,000, but they argue that there is no portion of the damages to which this limitation may be applied because the jury was not asked to allocate any portion of the damages to Jeffrey Marconet's vicarious liability. We conclude that the judgment should be modified.

It is true that the jury was not asked to allocate damages as to Jeffrey Marconet. Ordinarily, a defendant who chooses not to request allocation of damages may not challenge the judgment on the ground that he should only be held liable for a portion of the damages. [citations omitted.] However, in this case, the instructions given by the trial court regarding allocation of damages establish that the damages allocated by the jury against Inbound included the damages attributable to *all* defendants found liable for negligent entrustment. The court gave the following instructions as to the special verdict form's interrogatory regarding allocation of damages. "Now, Question 5 is, assuming that 100 percent represents the total negligence which caused or contributed to the decedent's death, what percentage of this 100 percent is attributable to each defendant? And the defendants are Charles Meier and the other defendant Inbound Aviation. The reason the other defendants are not listed there--remember--there are other defendants-- but the reason they are not listed there is because counsel have agreed and stipulated *if any of them are negligent, then Inbound is negligent.* Simplifies your task." (Italics added.)

The court's instruction establishes that the damages allocated to Inbound included *any and all* damages that the jury attributed to Jeffrey Marconet's *negligent entrustment* of the aircraft to Meier. Hence, it is necessarily true that the damages apportioned by the jury to Meier's negligence were *not* attributable to Jeffrey Marconet's *negligent entrustment* of the aircraft to Meier. Thus, although Jeffrey Marconet is barred from challenging his liability for the whole portion of damages allocated to Inbound for the negligent entrustment liability of all defendants, the jury's verdict establishes that Jeffrey Marconet's liability for the damages allocated by the jury to Meier's negligence was attributable *solely* to his *vicarious liability* for Meier's negligence. Consequently, Jeffrey Marconet *is* entitled to limitation of his liability for this portion of the damages to the $ 15,000 amount authorized under *Public Utilities Code sections 21404* and *21404.1* for an owner's vicarious liability for a permissive user's negligence.

DISPOSITION

The judgment is hereby ordered modified in the following respect. Defendant Jeffrey Marconet's liability for the damages allocated to Meier's estate shall be limited to his $ 15,000 statutory vicarious liability under *Public Utilities Code sections 21404* and *21404.1*. The trial court is ordered to prepare and file an amended judgment reflecting this modification. This modified judgment is affirmed. Plaintiffs shall recover their appellate costs.

B. *Products Liability*

DONALD C. MACPHERSON V. BUICK MOTOR COMPANY

Court of Appeals of New York

111 N.E. 1050

March, 1916

The defendant is a manufacturer of automobiles. It sold an automobile to a retail dealer. The retail dealer resold to the plaintiff. While the plaintiff was in the car, it suddenly collapsed. He was thrown out and injured. One of the wheels was made of defective wood, and its spokes crumbled into fragments. The wheel was not made by the defendant; it was bought from another manufacturer. There is evidence, however, that its defects could have been discovered by reasonable inspection, and that inspection was omitted. There is no claim that the defendant knew of the defect and willfully concealed it. The case, in other words, is not brought within the rule of *Kuelling v. Lean Mfg. Co. (183 N. Y. 78)*. The charge is one, not of fraud, but of negligence. The question to be determined is whether the defendant owed a duty of care and vigilance to any one but the immediate purchaser.

The foundations of this branch of the law, at least in this state, were laid in *Thomas v. Winchester (6 N. Y. 397)*. A poison was falsely labeled. The sale was made to a druggist, who in turn sold to a customer. The customer recovered damages from the seller who affixed the label. "The defendant's negligence," it was said, "put human life in imminent danger." A poison falsely labeled is likely to injure any one who gets it. Because the danger is to be foreseen, there is a duty to avoid the injury. Cases were cited by way of illustration in which manufacturers were not subject to any duty irrespective of contract. The distinction was said to be that their conduct, though negligent, was not likely to result in injury to any one except the purchaser. We are not required to say whether the chance of injury was always as remote as the distinction assumes. Some of the illustrations might be rejected to-day. The *principle* of the distinction is for present purposes the important thing.

Thomas v. *Winchester* became quickly a landmark of the law. In the application of its principle there may at times have been uncertainty or even error. There has never in this state been doubt or disavowal of the principle itself. The chief cases are well known, yet to recall some of them will be helpful. *Loop v. Litchfield (42 N. Y. 351)* is the earliest. It was the case of a defect in a small balance wheel used on a circular saw. The manufacturer pointed out the defect to the buyer, who wished a cheap article and was ready to assume the risk. The risk can hardly have been an imminent one, for the wheel lasted five years before it broke. In the meanwhile the buyer had made a lease of the machinery. It was held that the manufacturer was not answerable to the lessee. *Loop* v. *Litchfield* was followed in *Losee v. Clute (51 N. Y. 494)*, the case of the explosion of a steam boiler. That decision has been criticised (Thompson on Negligence, 233; Shearman & Redfield on Negligence [6th ed.], § 117); but it must be confined to its special facts. It was put upon the ground that the risk of injury was too remote. The buyer in that case had not only accepted the boiler, but had tested it. The manufacturer knew that his own test was not the final one. The finality of the test has a bearing on the measure of diligence owing to persons other than the purchaser (Beven, Negligence [3d ed.], pp. 50, 51, 54; Wharton, Negligence [2d ed.], § 134).

These early cases suggest a narrow construction of the rule. Later cases, however, evince a more liberal spirit. First in importance is *Devlin v. Smith (89 N. Y. 470)*. The defendant, a contractor, built a scaffold for a painter. The painter's servants were injured. The contractor was held liable. He knew that the scaffold, if improperly constructed, was a most dangerous trap. He knew that it was to be used by the workmen. He was building it for that very purpose. Building it for their use, he owed them a duty, irrespective of his contract with their master, to build it with care.

From *Devlin* v. *Smith* we pass over intermediate cases and turn to the latest case in this court in which *Thomas* v. *Winchester* was followed. That case is *Statler v. Ray Mfg. Co. (195 N. Y. 478, 480)*. The defendant manufactured a large coffee urn. It was installed in a restaurant. When heated, the urn exploded and injured the plaintiff. We held that the manufacturer was liable. We said that the urn "was of such a character inherently that, when applied to the purposes for which it was designed, it was liable to become a source of great danger to many people if not carefully and properly constructed."

It may be that *Devlin* v. *Smith* and *Statler* v. *Ray Mfg. Co.* have extended the rule of *Thomas* v. *Winchester*. If so, this court is committed to the extension. The defendant argues that things imminently dangerous to life are poisons, explosives, deadly weapons -- things whose normal function it is to injure or destroy. But whatever the rule in *Thomas* v. *Winchester* may once have been, it has no longer that restricted meaning. A scaffold (*Devlin v. Smith, supra*) is not inherently a destructive instrument. It becomes destructive only if imperfectly constructed. A large coffee urn (*Statler v. Ray Mfg. Co., supra*) may have within itself, if negligently made, the potency of danger, yet no one thinks of it as an implement whose normal function is destruction. What is true of the coffee urn is equally true of bottles of aerated water (*Torgeson v. Schultz, 192 N. Y. 156*). We have mentioned only cases in this court. But the rule has received a like extension in our courts of intermediate appeal. In *Burke v. Ireland (26 App. Div. 487)*, in an opinion by Cullen, J., it was applied to a builder who constructed a defective building; in *Kahner v. Otis Elevator Co. (96 App. Div. 169)* to the manufacturer of an elevator; in *Davies v. Pelham Hod Elevating Co. (65 Hun, 573*; affirmed in this court without opinion, *146 N. Y. 363)* to a contractor who furnished a defective rope with knowledge of the purpose for which the rope was to be used. We are not required at this time either to approve or to disapprove the application of the rule that was made in these cases. It is enough that they help to characterize the trend of judicial thought.

Devlin v. *Smith* was decided in 1882. A year later a very similar case came before the Court of Appeal in England (*Heaven* v. *Pender*, L. R. [11 Q. B. D.] 503). We find in the opinion of Brett, M. R., afterwards Lord Esher (p. 510), the same conception of a duty, irrespective of contract, imposed upon the manufacturer by the law itself: "Whenever one person supplies goods, or machinery, or the like, for the purpose of their being used by another person under such circumstances that every one of ordinary sense would, if he thought, recognize at once that unless he used ordinary care and skill with regard to the condition of the thing supplied or the mode of supplying it, there will be danger of injury to the person or property of him for whose use the thing is supplied, and who is to use it, a duty arises to use ordinary care and skill as to the condition or manner of supplying such thing." He then points out that for a neglect of such ordinary care or skill whereby injury happens, the appropriate remedy is an action for negligence. The right to enforce this liability is not to be confined to the immediate buyer. The right, he says, extends to the persons or class of persons for whose use the thing is supplied. It is enough that the goods "would in all probability be used at once before a reasonable opportunity for discovering any defect which might exist," and that the thing supplied is of such a nature "that a neglect of ordinary care or skill as to its condition or the manner of supplying it would probably cause danger to the person or property of the person for whose use it was supplied, and who was about to use it." On the other hand, he would exclude a case "in which the goods are supplied under circumstances in which it would be a chance by whom they would be used or whether they would be used or not, or whether they would be used before there would probably be means of observing any defect," or where the goods are of such a nature that "a want of care or skill as to their condition or the manner of supplying them would not probably produce danger of injury to person or property." What was said by Lord Esher in that case did not command the full assent of his associates. His opinion has been criticised "as requiring every man to take affirmative precautions to protect his neighbors as well as to refrain from injuring them" (Bohlen, Affirmative Obligations in the Law of Torts, 44 Am. Law Reg. [N. S.] 341). It may not be an accurate exposition of the law of England. Perhaps it may need some qualification even in our own state. Like most attempts at comprehensive definition, it may involve errors of inclusion and of exclusion. But its tests and standards, at least in their underlying principles, with whatever qualification may be called for as they are applied to varying conditions, are the tests and standards of our law.

We hold, then, that the principle of *Thomas* v. *Winchester* is not limited to poisons, explosives, and things of like nature, to things which in their normal operation are implements of destruction. If the nature of a thing is such that it is reasonably certain to place life and limb in peril when negligently made, it is then a thing of danger. Its nature gives warning of the consequences to be expected. If to the element of danger there is added knowledge that the thing will be used by persons other than the purchaser, and used without new tests, then, irrespective of contract, the manufacturer of this thing of danger is under a duty to make it carefully. That is as far as we are required to go for the decision of this case. There must be knowledge of a danger, not merely possible, but probable. It is *possible* to use almost anything in a way that will make it dangerous if defective. That is not enough to charge the manufacturer with a duty independent of his contract. Whether a given thing is dangerous may be sometimes a question for the court and sometimes a question for the jury. There must also be knowledge that in the usual course of events the danger will be shared by others than the buyer. Such knowledge may often be inferred from the nature of the transaction. But it is possible that even knowledge of the danger and of the use will not always be enough. The proximity or remoteness of the

375

relation is a factor to be considered. We are dealing now with the liability of the manufacturer of the finished product, who puts it on the market to be used without inspection by his customers. If he is negligent, where danger is to be foreseen, a liability will follow. We are not required at this time to say that it is legitimate to go back of the manufacturer of the finished product and hold the manufacturers of the component parts. To make their negligence a cause of imminent danger, an independent cause must often intervene; the manufacturer of the finished product must also fail in *his* duty of inspection. It may be that in those circumstances the negligence of the earlier members of the series is too remote to constitute, as to the ultimate user, an actionable wrong (Beven on Negligence [3d ed.], 50, 51, 54; Wharton on Negligence [2d ed.], § 134; *Leeds v. N. Y. Tel. Co., 178 N. Y. 118; Sweet v. Perkins, 196 N. Y. 482; Hayes v. Hyde Park, 153 Mass. 514, 516).* We leave that question open. We shall have to deal with it when it arises. The difficulty which it suggests is not present in this case. There is here no break in the chain of cause and effect. In such circumstances, the presence of a known danger, attendant upon a known use, makes vigilance a duty. We have put aside the notion that the duty to safeguard life and limb, when the consequences of negligence may be foreseen, grows out of contract and nothing else. We have put the source of the obligation where it ought to be. We have put its source in the law.

From this survey of the decisions, there thus emerges a definition of the duty of a manufacturer which enables us to measure this defendant's liability. Beyond all question, the nature of an automobile gives warning of probable danger if its construction is defective. This automobile was designed to go fifty miles an hour. Unless its wheels were sound and strong, injury was almost certain. It was as much a thing of danger as a defective engine for a railroad. The defendant knew the danger. It knew also that the car would be used by persons other than the buyer. This was apparent from its size; there were seats for three persons. It was apparent also from the fact that the buyer was a dealer in cars, who bought to resell. The maker of this car supplied it for the use of purchasers from the dealer just as plainly as the contractor in *Devlin* v. *Smith* supplied the scaffold for use by the servants of the owner. The dealer was indeed the one person of whom it might be said with some approach to certainty that by him the car would not be used. Yet the defendant would have us say that he was the one person whom it was under a legal duty to protect. The law does not lead us to so inconsequent a conclusion. Precedents drawn from the days of travel by stage coach do not fit the conditions of travel to-day. The principle that the danger must be imminent does not change, but the things subject to the principle do change. They are whatever the needs of life in a developing civilization require them to be.

In reaching this conclusion, we do not ignore the decisions to the contrary in other jurisdictions. It was held in *Cadillac M. C. Co. v. Johnson (221 Fed. Rep. 801)* that an automobile is not within the rule of *Thomas* v. *Winchester.* There was, however, a vigorous dissent. Opposed to that decision is one of the Court of Appeals of Kentucky (*Olds Motor Works v. Shaffer, 145 Ky. 616).* The earlier cases are summarized by Judge Sanborn in *Huset v. J. I. Case Threshing Machine Co. (120 Fed. Rep. 865).* Some of them, at first sight inconsistent with our conclusion, may be reconciled upon the ground that the negligence was too remote, and that another cause had intervened. But even when they cannot be reconciled, the difference is rather in the application of the principle than in the principle itself. Judge Sanborn says, for example, that the contractor who builds a bridge, or the manufacturer who builds a car, cannot ordinarily foresee injury to other persons than the owner as the probable result (*120 Fed. Rep. 865, at p. 867*). We take a different view. We think that injury to others is to be foreseen not merely as a possible, but as an almost inevitable result. (See the trenchant criticism in Bohlen, *supra*, at p. 351). Indeed, Judge Sanborn concedes that his view is not to be reconciled with our decision in *Devlin* v. *Smith* (*supra*). The doctrine of that decision has now become the settled law of this state, and we have no desire to depart from it.

In England the limits of the rule are still unsettled. *Winterbottom* v. *Wright* (10 M. & W. 109) is often cited. The defendant undertook to provide a mail coach to carry the mail bags. The coach broke down from latent defects in its construction. The defendant, however, was not the manufacturer. The court held that he was not liable for injuries to a passenger. The case was decided on a demurrer to the declaration. Lord Esher points out in *Heaven* v. *Pender* (*supra, at p. 513*) that the form of the declaration was subject to criticism. It did not fairly suggest the existence of a duty aside from the special contract which was the plaintiff's main reliance. (See the criticism of *Winterbottom* v. *Wright*, in Bohlen, *supra*, at pp. 281, 283). At all events, in *Heaven* v. *Pender* (*supra*) the defendant, a dock owner, who put up a staging outside a ship, was held liable to the servants of the shipowner. In *Elliott* v. *Hall* (15 Q. B. D. 315) the defendant sent out a defective truck laden with goods which he had sold. The buyer's servants unloaded it, and were injured because of the defects. It was held that the defendant was under a duty "not to be guilty of negligence with regard to the state and condition of the truck." There seems to have been a return to the doctrine of *Winterbottom* v. *Wright* in *Earl* v. *Lubbock* (L. R. [1905] 1 K. B. 253). In that case, however, as in the earlier one, the defendant was not the manufacturer. He had merely made a contract to keep the van in repair. A later case (*White* v. *Steadman*, L. R. [1913], 3 K. B. 340, 348) emphasizes that element. A livery stable keeper who sent out a vicious horse was held liable not merely to his customer but also to another occupant of the carriage, and *Thomas* v. *Winchester* was cited and followed (*White* v. *Steadman*, *supra*, at pp. 348, 349). It was again cited and followed in *Dominion Natural Gas Co.* v. *Collins* (L. R. [1909] A. C. 640, 646). From these cases a consistent principle is with difficulty extracted. The English courts, however, agree with ours in holding that one who invites another to make use of an appliance is bound to the exercise of reasonable care (*Caledonian Ry. Co.* v. *Mulholland*, L. R. [1898] A. C. 216, 227; *Indermaur* v. *Dames*, L. R. [1 C. P.] 274). That at bottom is the underlying principle of *Devlin* v. *Smith*. The contractor who builds the scaffold invites the owner's workmen to use it. The manufacturer who sells the automobile to the retail dealer invites the dealer's customers to use it. The invitation is addressed in the one case to determinate persons and in the other to an indeterminate class, but in each case it is equally plain, and in each its consequences must be the same.

There is nothing anomalous in a rule which imposes upon A, who has contracted with B, a duty to C and D and others according as he knows or does not know that the subject-matter of the contract is intended for their use. We may find an analogy in the law which measures the liability of landlords. If A leases to B a tumbledown house he is not liable, in the absence of fraud, to B's guests who enter it and are injured. This is because B is then under the duty to repair it, the lessor has the right to suppose that he will fulfill that duty, and, if he omits to do so, his guests must look to him (Bohlen, *supra*, at p. 276). But if A leases a building to be used by the lessee at once as a place of public entertainment, the rule is different. There injury to persons other than the lessee is to be foreseen, and foresight of the conse quences involves the creation of a duty (*Junkermann v. Tilyou R. Co., 213 N. Y. 404*, and cases there cited).

In this view of the defendant's liability there is nothing inconsistent with the theory of liability on which the case was tried. It is true that the court told the jury that "an automobile is not an inherently dangerous vehicle." The meaning, however, is made plain by the context. The meaning is that danger is not to be expected when the vehicle is well constructed. The court left it to the jury to say whether the defendant ought to have foreseen that the car, if negligently constructed, would become "imminently dangerous." Subtle distinctions are drawn by the defendant between things inherently dangerous and things imminently dangerous, but the case does not turn upon these verbal niceties. If danger was to be expected as reasonably certain, there was a duty of vigilance, and this whether you call the danger inherent or imminent. In varying forms that thought was put before the jury. We do not say that the court would not have been justified in ruling as a matter of law that the car was a dangerous thing. If there was any error, it was none of which the defendant can complain.

We think the defendant was not absolved from a duty of inspection because it bought the wheels from a reputable manufacturer. It was not merely a dealer in automobiles. It was a manufacturer of automobiles. It was responsible for the finished product. It was not at liberty to put the finished product on the market without subjecting the component parts to ordinary and simple tests (*Richmond & Danville R. R. Co. v. Elliott, 149 U.S. 266, 272)*. Under the charge of the trial judge nothing more was required of it. The obligation to inspect must vary with the nature of the thing to be inspected. The more probable the danger, the greater the need of caution. There is little analogy between this case and *Carlson v. Phoenix Bridge Co. (132 N. Y. 273)*, where the defendant bought a tool for a servant's use. The making of tools was not the business in which the master was engaged. Reliance on the skill of the manufacturer was proper and almost inevitable. But that is not the defendant's situation. Both by its relation to the work and by the nature of its business, it is charged with a stricter duty.

Other rulings complained of have been considered, but no error has been found in them.

The judgment should be affirmed with costs.

DISSENT BY: BARTLETT

DISSENT

Willard Bartlett, Ch. J. (dissenting). The plaintiff was injured in consequence of the collapse of a wheel of an automobile manufactured by the defendant corporation which sold it to a firm of automobile dealers in Schenectady, who in turn sold the car to the plaintiff. The wheel was purchased by the Buick Motor Company, ready made, from the Imperial Wheel Company of Flint, Michigan, a reputable manufacturer of automobile wheels which had furnished the defendant with eighty thousand wheels, none of which had proved to be made of defective wood prior to the accident in the present case. The defendant relied upon the wheel manufacturer to make all necessary tests as to the strength of the material therein and made no such tests itself. The present suit is an action for negligence brought by the subvendee of the motor car against the manufacturer as the original vendor. The evidence warranted a finding by the jury that the wheel which collapsed was defective when it left the hands of the defendant. The automobile was being prudently operated at the time of the accident and was moving at a speed of only eight miles an hour. There was no allegation or proof of any actual knowledge of the defect on the part of the defendant or any suggestion that any element of fraud or deceit or misrepresentation entered into the sale.

The theory upon which the case was submitted to the jury by the learned judge who presided at the trial was that, although an automobile is not an inherently dangerous vehicle, it may become such if equipped with a weak wheel; and that if the motor car in question, when it was put upon the market was in itself inherently dangerous by reason of its being equipped with a weak wheel, the defendant was chargeable with a knowledge of the defect so far as it might be discovered by a reasonable inspection and the application of reasonable tests. This liability, it was further held, was not limited to the original vendee, but extended to a subvendee like the plaintiff, who was not a party to the original contract of sale.

I think that these rulings, which have been approved by the Appellate Division, extend the liability of the vendor of a manufactured article further than any case which has yet received the sanction of this court. It has heretofore been held in this state that the liability of the vendor of a manufactured article for negligence arising out of the existence of defects therein does not extend to strangers injured in consequence of such defects but is confined to the immediate vendee. The exceptions to this general rule which have thus far been recognized in New York are cases in which the article sold was of such a character that danger to life or limb was involved in the ordinary use thereof; in other words, where the article sold was inherently dangerous. As has already been pointed out, the learned trial judge instructed the jury that an automobile is not an inherently dangerous vehicle.

The late Chief Justice Cooley of Michigan, one of the most learned and accurate of American law writers, states the general rule thus: "The general rule is that a contractor, manufacturer, vendor or furnisher of an article is not liable to third parties who have no contractual relations with him for negligence in the construction, manufacture or sale of such article." (2 Cooley on Torts [3d ed.], 1486.)

The leading English authority in support of this rule, to which all the later cases on the same subject refer, is *Winterbottom* v. *Wright* (10 Meeson & Welsby, 109), which was an action by the driver of a stage coach against a contractor who had agreed with the postmaster-general to provide and keep the vehicle in repair for the purpose of conveying the royal mail over a prescribed route. The coach broke down and upset, injuring the driver, who sought to recover against the contractor

379

on account of its defective construction. The Court of Exchequer denied him any right of recovery on the ground that there was no privity of contract between the parties, the agreement having been made with the postmaster-general alone. "If the plaintiff can sue," said Lord Abinger, the Chief Baron, "every passenger or even any person passing along the road, who was injured by the upsetting of the coach, might bring a similar action. Unless we confine the operation of such contracts as this to the parties who enter into them, the most absurd and outrageous consequences, to which I can see no limit, would ensue."

The doctrine of that decision was recognized as the law of this state by the leading New York case of *Thomas v. Winchester (6 N. Y. 397, 408)*, which, however, involved an exception to the general rule. There the defendant, who was a dealer in medicines, sold to a druggist a quantity of belladonna, which is a deadly poison, negligently labeled as extract of dandelion. The druggist in good faith used the poison in filling a prescription calling for the harmless dandelion extract and the plaintiff for whom the prescription was put up was poisoned by the belladonna. This court held that the original vendor was liable for the injuries suffered by the patient. Chief Judge Ruggles, who delivered the opinion of the court, distinguished between an act of negligence imminently dangerous to the lives of others and one that is not so, saying: "If A. build a wagon and sell it to B., who sells it to C. and C. hires it to D., who in consequence of the gross negligence of A. in building the wagon is overturned and injured, D. cannot recover damages against A., the builder. A.'s obligation to build the wagon faithfully, arises solely out of his contract with B. The public have nothing to do with it. So, for the same reason, if a horse be defectively shod by a smith, and a person hiring the horse from the owner is thrown and injured in consequence of the smith's negligence in shoeing; the smith is not liable for the injury."

In *Torgeson v. Schultz (192 N. Y. 156, 159)* the defendant was the vendor of bottles of aerated water which were charged under high pressure and likely to explode unless used with precaution when exposed to sudden changes of temperature. The plaintiff, who was a servant of the purchaser, was injured by the explosion of one of these bottles. There was evidence tending to show that it had not been properly tested in order to insure users against such accidents. We held that the defendant corporation was liable notwithstanding the absence of any contract relation between it and the plaintiff "under the doctrine of *Thomas* v. *Winchester* (*supra*), and similar cases based upon the duty of the vendor of an article dangerous in its nature, or likely to become so in the course of the ordinary usage to be contemplated by the vendor, either to exercise due care to warn users of the danger or to take reasonable care to prevent the article sold from proving dangerous when subjected only to customary usage." The character of the exception to the general rule limiting liability for negligence to the original parties to the contract of sale, was still more clearly stated by Judge Hiscock, writing for the court in *Statler v. Ray Manufacturing Co. (195 N. Y. 478, 482)*, where he said that "in the case of an article of an inherently dangerous nature, a manufacturer may become liable for a negligent construction which, when added to the inherent character of the appliance, makes it imminently dangerous, and causes or contributes to a resulting injury not necessarily incident to the use of such an article if properly constructed, but naturally following from a defective construction." In that case the injuries were inflicted by the explosion of a battery of steam-driven coffee urns, constituting an appliance liable to become dangerous in the course of ordinary usage.

The case of *Devlin v. Smith (89 N. Y. 470)* is cited as an authority in conflict with the view that the liability of the manufacturer and vendor extends to third parties only when the article manufactured and sold is inherently dangerous. In that case the builder of a scaffold ninety feet high which was erected for the purpose of enabling painters to stand upon it, was held to be liable to the administratrix of a painter who fell therefrom and was killed, being at the time in the employ of the person for whom the scaffold was built. It is said that the scaffold if properly constructed was not inherently dangerous; and hence that this decision affirms the existence of liability in the case of an article not dangerous in itself but made so only in consequence of negligent construction. Whatever logical force there may be in this view it seems to me clear from the language of Judge Rapallo, who wrote the opinion of the court, that the scaffold was deemed to be an inherently dangerous structure; and that the case was decided as it was because the court entertained that view. Otherwise he would hardly have said, as he did, that the circumstances seemed to bring the case fairly within the principle of *Thomas* v. *Winchester*.

I do not see how we can uphold the judgment in the present case without overruling what has been so often said by this court and other courts of like authority in reference to the absence of any liability for negligence on the part of the original vendor of an ordinary carriage to any one except his immediate vendee. The absence of such liability was the very point actually decided in the English case of *Winterbottom* v. *Wright (supra)*, and the illustration quoted from the opinion of Chief Judge Ruggles in *Thomas* v. *Winchester (supra)* assumes that the law on the subject was so plain that the statement would be accepted almost as a matter of course. In the case at bar the defective wheel on an automobile moving only eight miles an hour was not any more dangerous to the occupants of the car than a similarly defective wheel would be to the occupants of a carriage drawn by a horse at the same speed; and yet unless the courts have been all wrong on this question up to the present time there would be no liability to strangers to the original sale in the case of the horse-drawn carriage.

The rule upon which, in my judgment, the determination of this case depends, and the recognized exceptions thereto, were discussed by Circuit Judge Sanborn of the United States Circuit Court of Appeals in the Eighth Circuit, in *Huset v. J. I. Case Threshing Machine Co. (120 Fed. Rep. 865)* in an opinion which reviews all the leading American and English decisions on the subject up to the time when it was rendered (1903). I have already discussed the leading New York cases, but as to the rest I feel that I can add nothing to the learning of that opinion or the cogency of its reasoning. I have examined the cases to which Judge Sanborn refers, but if I were to discuss them at length I should be forced merely to paraphrase his language, as a study of the authorities he cites has led me to the same conclusion; and the repetition of what has already been so well said would contribute nothing to the advantage of the bench, the bar or the individual litigants whose case is before us.

A few cases decided since his opinion was written, however, may be noticed. In *Earl* v. *Lubbock* (L. R. 1905 [1 K. B. Div.] 253) the Court of Appeal in 1904 considered and approved the propositions of law laid down by the Court of Exchequer in *Winterbottom* v. *Wright* (*supra*), declaring that the decision in that case, since the year 1842, had stood the test of repeated discussion. The master of the rolls approved the principles laid down by Lord Abinger as based upon sound reasoning; and all the members of the court agreed that his decision was a controlling authority which must be followed. That the Federal courts still adhere to the general rule, as I have stated it, appears by the decision of the Circuit Court of Appeals in the Second Circuit, in March, 1915, in the case of *Cadillac Motor Car Co. v. Johnson (221 Fed. Rep. 801)*. That case, like this, was an action by a subvendee against a manufacturer of automobiles for negligence in failing to discover that one of its wheels was defective, the court holding that such an action could not be maintained. It is true there was a dissenting opinion in that case, but it was based chiefly upon the proposition that rules applicable to stage coaches are archaic when applied to automobiles and that if the law did not afford a remedy to strangers to the contract the law should be changed. It this be true, the change should be effected by the legislature and not by the courts. A perusal of the opinion in that case and in the *Huset* case will disclose how uniformly the courts throughout this country have adhered to the rule and how consistently they have refused to broaden the scope of the exceptions. I think we should adhere to it in the case at bar and, therefore, I vote for a reversal of this judgment.

WILLIAM B. GREENMAN v. YUBA POWER PRODUCTS, INC.

Supreme Court of California

377 P.2d 897

January, 1963

Plaintiff brought this action for damages against the retailer and the manufacturer of a Shopsmith, a combination power tool that could be used as a saw, drill, and wood lathe. He saw a Shopsmith demonstrated by the retailer and studied a brochure prepared by the manufacturer. He decided he wanted a Shopsmith for his home workshop, and his wife bought and gave him one for Christmas in 1955. In 1957 he bought the necessary attachments to use the Shopsmith as a lathe for turning a large piece of wood he wished to make into a chalice. After he had worked on the piece of wood several times without difficulty, it suddenly flew out of the machine and struck him on the forehead, inflicting serious injuries. About 10 1/2 months later, he gave the retailer and the manufacturer written notice of claimed breaches of warranties and filed a complaint against them alleging such breaches and negligence.

After a trial before a jury, the court ruled that there was no evidence that the retailer was negligent or had breached any express warranty and that the manufacturer was not liable for the breach of any implied warranty. Accordingly, it submitted to the jury only the cause of action alleging breach of implied warranties against the retailer and the causes of action alleging negligence and breach of express warranties against the manufacturer. The jury returned a verdict for the retailer against plaintiff and for plaintiff against the manufacturer in the amount of $ 65,000. The trial court denied the manufacturer's motion for a new trial and entered judgment on the verdict. The manufacturer and plaintiff appeal. Plaintiff seeks a reversal of the part of the judgment in favor of the retailer, however, only in the event that the part of the judgment against the manufacturer is reversed.

Plaintiff introduced substantial evidence that his injuries were caused by defective design and construction of the Shopsmith. His expert witnesses testified that inadequate set screws were used to hold parts of the machine together so that normal vibration caused the tailstock of the lathe to move away from the piece of wood being turned permitting it to fly out of the lathe. They also testified that there were other more positive ways of fastening the parts of the machine together, the use of which would have prevented the accident. The jury could therefore reasonably have concluded that the manufacturer negligently constructed the Shopsmith. The jury could also reasonably have concluded that statements in the manufacturer's brochure were untrue, that they constituted express warranties, and that plaintiff's injuries were caused by their breach.

The manufacturer contends, however, that plaintiff did not give it notice of breach of warranty within a reasonable time and that therefore his cause of action for breach of warranty is barred by section 1769 of the Civil Code. Since it cannot be determined whether the verdict against it was based on the negligence or warranty cause of action or both, the manufacturer concludes that the error in presenting the warranty cause of action to the jury was prejudicial.

Section 1769 of the Civil Code provides: "In the absence of express or implied agreement of the parties, acceptance of the goods by the buyer shall not discharge the seller from liability in damages or other legal remedy for breach of any promise or warranty in the contract to sell or the sale. But, if, after acceptance of the goods, the buyer fails to give notice to the seller of the breach of any promise or warranty within a reasonable time after the buyer knows, or ought to know of such breach, the seller shall not be liable therefor."

(1) Like other provisions of the Uniform Sales Act (*Civ. Code, §§ 1721- 1800*), section 1769 deals with the rights of the parties to a contract of sale or a sale. It does not provide that notice must be given of the breach of a warranty that arises independently of a contract of sale between the parties. (2) Such warranties are not imposed by the sales act, but are the product of common-law decisions that have recognized them in a variety of situations. [citations omitted]. It is true that in many of these situations the court has invoked the sales act definitions of warranties (*Civ. Code, §§ 1732, 1735*) in defining the defendant's liability, but it has done so, not because the statutes so required, but because they provided appropriate standards for the court to adopt under the circumstances presented. (See *Clinkscales v. Carver, 22 Cal.2d 72, 75 [136 P.2d 777]*; *Dana v. Sutton Motor Sales, 56 Cal.2d 284, 287 [14 Cal.Rptr. 649, 363 P.2d 881].*)

(3) The notice requirement of section 1769, however, is not an appropriate one for the court to adopt in actions by injured consumers against manufacturers with whom they have not dealt. (*La Hue v. Coca-Cola Bottling, Inc., 50 Wn.2d 645 [314 P.2d 421, 422]*; *Chapman v. Brown, 198 F. Supp. 78, 85*, affd. *Brown v. Chapman, 304 F. 2d 149.*) (4) "As between the immediate parties to the sale [the notice requirement] is a sound commercial rule, designed to protect the seller against unduly delayed claims for damages. As applied to personal injuries, and notice to a remote seller, it becomes a booby-trap for the unwary. The injured consumer is seldom 'steeped in the business practice which justifies the rule,' [James, *Product Liability*, 34 Texas L. Rev. 44, 192, 197] and at least until he has had legal advice it will not occur to him to give notice to one with whom he has had no dealings." (Prosser, *Strict Liability to the Consumer*, 69 Yale L. J. 1099, 1130, footnotes omitted.) It is true that in *Jones v. Burgermeister Brewing Corp., 198 Cal.App.2d 198, 202-203 [18 Cal.Rptr. 311]*, *Perry v. Thrifty Drug Co., 186 Cal.App.2d 410, 411 [9 Cal.Rptr. 50]*, *Arata v. Tonegato, 152 Cal.App.2d 837, 841 [314 P.2d 130]*, and *Maecherlein v. Sealy Mattress Co., 145 Cal.App.2d 275, 278 [302 P.2d 331]*, the court assumed that notice of breach of warranty must be given in an action by a consumer against a manufacturer. Since in those cases, however, the court did not consider the question whether a distinction exists between a warranty based on a contract between the parties and one imposed on a manufacturer not in privity with the consumer, the decisions are not authority for rejecting the rule of the *La Hue* and *Chapman* cases, *supra*. (*Peterson v. Lamb Rubber Co., 54 Cal.2d 339, 343 [5 Cal.Rptr. 863, 353 P.2d 575]*; *People v. Banks, 53 Cal.2d 370, 389 [1 Cal.Rptr. 669, 348 P.2d 102].*) (5) We conclude, therefore, that even if plaintiff did not give timely notice of breach of warranty to the

manufacturer, his cause of action based on the representations contained in the brochure was not barred.

Moreover, to impose strict liability on the manufacturer under the circumstances of this case, it was not necessary for plaintiff to establish an express warranty as defined in *section 1732 of the Civil Code*. (6) A manufacturer is strictly liable in tort when an article he places on the market, knowing that it is to be used without inspection for defects, proves to have a defect that causes injury to a human being. Recognized first in the case of unwholesome food products, such liability has now been extended to a variety of other products that create as great or greater hazards if defective. [citations omitted].

(7) Although in these cases strict liability has usually been based on the theory of an express or implied warranty running from the manufacturer to the plaintiff, the abandonment of the requirement of a contract between them, the recognition that the liability is not assumed by agreement but imposed by law (see e.g., *Graham v. Bottenfield's, Inc., 176 Kan. 68 [269 P.2d 413, 418]*; *Rogers v. Toni Home Permanent Co., 167 Ohio St. 244 [147 N.E. 2d 612, 614, 75 A.L.R. 2d 103]*; *Decker & Sons v. Capps, 139 Tex. 609, 617 [164 S.W. 2d 828, 142 A.L.R. 1479]*), and the refusal to permit the manufacturer to define the scope of its own responsibility for defective products (*Henningsen v. Bloomfield Motors, Inc., 32 N.J. 358 [161 A. 2d 69, 84-96, 75 A.L.R. 2d 1]*; *General Motors Corp. v. Dodson, 47 Tenn.App. 438 [338 S.W. 2d 655, 658-661]*; *State Farm Mut. Auto Ins. Co. v. Anderson-Weber, Inc., 252 Iowa 1289 [110 N.W. 2d 449, 455-456]*; *Pabon v. Hackensack Auto Sales, Inc., 63 N.J. Super. 476 [164 A. 2d 773, 778]*; *Linn v. Radio Center Delicatessen, 169 Misc. 879 [6 N.Y.S. 2d 110, 112]*) make clear that the liability is not one governed by the law of contract warranties but by the law of strict liability in tort. (8) Accordingly, rules defining and governing warranties that were developed to meet the needs of commercial transactions cannot properly be invoked to govern the manufacturer's liability to those injured by its defective products unless those rules also serve the purposes for which such liability is imposed.

We need not recanvass the reasons for imposing strict liability on the manufacturer. They have been fully articulated in the cases cited above. (See also 2 Harper and James, Torts, §§ 28.15-28.16, pp. 1569-1574; Prosser, *Strict Liability to the Consumer*, 69 Yale L.J. 1099; *Escola v. Coca Cola Bottling Co., 24 Cal.2d 453, 461 [150 P.2d 436]*, concurring opinion.) (9) The purpose of such liability is to insure that the costs of injuries resulting from defective products are borne by the manufacturers that put such products on the market rather than by the injured persons who are powerless to protect themselves. Sales warranties serve this purpose fitfully at best. (See Prosser, *Strict Liability to the Consumer*, 69 Yale L.J. 1099, 1124-1134.) (10) In the present case, for example, plaintiff was able to plead and prove an express warranty only because he read and relied on the representations of the Shopsmith's ruggedness contained in the manufacturer's brochure. Implicit in the machine's presence on the market, however, was a representation that it would safely do the jobs for which it was built. Under these circumstances, it should not be controlling whether plaintiff selected the machine because of the statements in the brochure, or because of the machine's own appearance of excellence that belied the defect lurking beneath the surface, or because he merely assumed that it would safely do the jobs it was built to do. It should not be controlling whether the details of the sales from manufacturer to retailer and from retailer to plaintiff's wife were such that one or more of the implied warranties of the sales act arose. (*Civ. Code, § 1735.*) "The remedies of injured consumers ought not to be made to depend upon the intricacies of the law of sales." (*Ketterer v. Armour & Co., 200 F. 322, 323; Klein v. Duchess Sandwich Co., Ltd., 14 Cal.2d 272, 282 [93 P.2d 799].*) (11) To establish the manufacturer's liability it was sufficient that plaintiff proved that he was injured while using the Shopsmith in a way it was intended to be used as a result of a defect in design and manufacture of which plaintiff was not aware that made the Shopsmith unsafe for its intended use.

The manufacturer contends that the trial court erred in refusing to give three instructions requested by it. It appears from the record, however, that the substance of two of the requested instructions was adequately covered by the instructions given and that the third instruction was not supported by the evidence.

The judgment is affirmed.

ANNELIESE GOLDBERG V. KOLLSMAN INSTRUMENT CORPORATION ET AL.

Court of Appeals of New York

191 N.E.2d 81

May, 1963

We granted leave to appeal in order to take another step toward a complete solution of the problem partially cleared up in *Greenberg v. Lorenz (9 N Y 2d 195)* and *Randy Knitwear v. American Cyanamid Co. (11 N Y 2d 5)* (both decided after the making of the Special Term and Appellate Division orders here appealed from). The question now to be answered is: does a manufacturer's implied warranty of fitness of his product for its contemplated use run in favor of all its intended users, despite lack of privity of contract?

The suit is by an administratrix for damages for the death of her daughter-intestate as the result of injuries suffered in the crash near La Guardia Airport, New York City, of an airplane in which the daughter was a fare-paying passenger on a flight from Chicago to New York. American Airlines, Inc., owner and operator of the plane, is sued here for negligence (with present respondents Lockheed and Kollsman) but that cause of action is not the subject of this appeal. The two causes of action, from the dismissal of which for insufficiency plaintiff appeals to us, run against Kollsman Instrument Corporation, manufacturer or supplier of the plane's altimeter, and Lockheed Aircraft Corporation, maker of the plane itself. Kollsman and Lockheed are charged with breaching their respective implied warranties of merchantability and fitness. Those breaches, it is alleged, caused the fatal crash.

There is nothing in the complaint that says where the plane or its altimeter were manufactured or sold nor does the pleading inform us as to decedent's place of residence, although it is alleged that plaintiff's appointment as administratrix was by a New York court. Plaintiff argues that California law should apply on the "grouping of contracts" theory and it is clear (indeed in effect conceded by respondents) that California law allows recovery for a proven breach of implied warranties as to dangerous instrumentalities (see *Peterson v. Lamb Rubber Co., 54 Cal. 2d 339, 347*; *Greenman v. Yuba Power Prods., 59 Cal. 2d 67*). Special Term, however, said in its opinion in the present case that the governing law is that of New York State where the accident took place, citing *Poplar v. Bourjois, Inc. (298 N. Y. 62)* and that under New York law no claim for breach of implied warranty may be enforced by one not in privity with the warrantor. The Appellate Division, affirming, wrote no opinion. The Special Term opinion, as we have said above, was filed before our *Greenberg* and *Randy Knitwear* decisions (*supra*) and *Greenberg* and *Randy Knitwear* declared that in New York privity of contract is not always a requisite for breach of warranty recoveries. The *Randy Knitwear* opinion (*11 N Y 2d, p. 16*) at least suggested that all requirements of privity have been dispensed with in our State. That is the immediate, or at least the logical and necessary result of our decisions and, accordingly, it really makes no difference whether New York or California law be applied, since in this respect both States use the same rules.

The enormous literature on this subject and the historical development of the law of warranties to its present state need not be reviewed beyond the references in our *Greenberg* and *Randy Knitwear* opinions (*supra*). A breach of warranty, it is now clear, is not only a violation of the sales contract out of which the warranty arises but is a tortious wrong suable by a noncontracting party whose use of the warranted article is within the reasonable contemplation of the vendor or manufacturer. As to foodstuffs we definitively ruled in *Greenberg v. Lorenz (9 N Y 2d 195, supra)* that the persons thus protected and eligible to sue include the purchaser's family. We went no further in that case because the facts required no farther reach of the rule.

The concept that as to "things of danger" the manufacturer must answer to intended users for faulty design or manufacture is an old one in this State. The most famous decision is *MacPherson v. Buick Motor Co. (217 N. Y. 382)* holding the manufacturer liable in negligence to one who purchased a faulty Buick automobile from a dealer (see the recent and similar case of *Markel v. Spencer, 5 A D 2d 400*, affd. *5 N Y 2d 958*). But the *MacPherson* opinion cites much older cases such as *Devlin v. Smith (89 N. Y. 470* [1882]) where one who negligently built a scaffold for a contractor was adjudged liable to the contractor's injured employee. *MacPherson* and its successors dispelled the idea that a manufacturer was immune from liability in tort for violation of his duty to make his manufactures fit and safe. In MacPherson's day enforcement required a suit in negligence. Today, we know from *Greenberg* v. *Lorenz, Randy Knitwear v. American Cyanamid Co. (supra)* and many another decision in this and other States (see, for instance, *Henningsen v. Bloomfield Motors, 32 N. J. 358*, and *Thomas v. Leary, 15 A D 2d 438*) that, at least where an article is of such a character that when used for the purpose for which it is made it is likely to be a source of danger to several or many people if not properly designed and fashioned, the manufacturer as well as the vendor is liable, for breach of law-implied warranties, to the persons whose use is contemplated. The *MacPherson* holding was an "extension" of existing court-made liability law. In a sense, *Greenberg* v. *Lorenz and Randy Knitwear v. American Cyanamid Co. (supra)* were extensions in favor of noncontracting consumers. But it is no extension at all to include airplanes and the passengers for whose use they are built -- and, indeed, decisions are at hand which have upheld complaints, sounding in breach of warranty, against manufacturers of aircraft where passengers lost their lives when the planes crashed (see, e.g., *Conlon v. Republic Aviation Corp., 204 F. Supp. 865*; *Middleton v. United Aircraft Corp., 204 F. Supp. 856*; *Ewing v. Lockheed Aircraft Corp., 202 F. Supp. 216*; *Hinton v. Republic Aviation Corp., 180 F. Supp. 31*).

As we all know, a number of courts outside New York State have for the best of reasons dispensed with the privity requirement (see Jaeger, Privity of Warranty: Has the Tocsin Sounded?, 1 Duquesne U. L. Rev. 1). Very recently the Supreme Court of California (*Greenman v. Yuba Power Prods., 59 Cal. 2d 67* [Jan., 1963], *supra*) in a unanimous opinion imposed "strict tort liability" (surely a more accurate phrase) regardless of privity on a manufacturer in a case where a power tool threw a piece of wood at a user who was not the purchaser. The California court said that the purpose of such a holding is to see to it that the costs of injuries resulting from defective products are borne by the manufacturers who put the products on the market rather than by injured persons who are powerless to protect themselves and that implicit in putting such articles on the market are representations that they will safely do the job for which they were built. However, for the present at least we do not think it necessary so to extend this rule as to hold liable the manufacturer (defendant Kollsman) of a component part. Adequate protection is provided for the passengers by casting in liability the airplane manufacturer which put into the market the completed aircraft.

The judgment appealed from should be modified, without costs, so as to provide for the dismissal of the third (Kollsman) cause of action only and, as so modified, affirmed.

DISSENT BY: BURKE

DISSENT

Burke, J. (dissenting). We dissent.

If this were a case in which a manufacturer made express representations concerning the quality of its product calculated to promote its sale or use by persons in the plaintiff's position, our decision in *Randy Knitwear v. American Cyanamid Co. (11 N Y 2d 5)* would allow a recovery. If it were a case where a defendant sold a food or other household product to a member of a family, the warranty incident thereto would extend to all for whose consumption or use the product was obviously purchased. (*Greenberg v. Lorenz, 9 N Y 2d 195*; *Greenman v. Yuba Power Prods., 59 Cal. 2d 67.*) The conclusion reached by the majority might be correct even if the defective product were sold to an employer for the use of his employees. (*Thomas v. Leary, 15 A D 2d 438*; *Peterson v. Lamb Rubber Co., 54 Cal. 2d 339.*) This, however, is none of those cases. The conditions present in those cases are entirely different. There the manufacturer knew that the article he made was not to be inspected thereafter. Here Federal regulations provide for rigorous inspection and certification from the Federal Aviation Agency. There the risk of loss was a trap for the unwary. Here all are aware of the hazards attending air travel and accident and special insurance is readily available at moderate rates. Plaintiff is a purchaser of a service from an airline seeking to assert a warranty cause of action against Lockheed, the assembler of an airplane, and Kollsman, the manufacturer of an allegedly defective component part thereof. In such a situation we see no satisfactory basis on which to uphold against Lockheed a cause of action not grounded in negligence, while disallowing it against the manufacturer of an alleged defective part.

First, we do not find a cause of action stated under the implied warranty provisions of section 96 of the Personal Property Law. Plaintiff purchased no goods; she entered into a contract of carriage with American Airlines. By a long line of cases in this court, the most recent being *Kilberg v. Northeast Airlines (9 N Y 2d 34)*, it is settled that the measure of American Airlines' duty towards plaintiff was an undertaking of reasonably safe carriage. This duty is, of course, discharged by the use of due care. Crucial is the fact that this duty would be unaffected if American assembled its own planes, even if they contained a latent defect. Why, then, should plaintiff's rights be any greater simply because American chose to contract this work out instead of doing it itself? Absent some equity of direct reliance on the advertised representations of one of the manufacturers, which might invoke the reasoning of *Randy Knitwear v. American Cyanamid Co. (11 N Y 2d 5, supra)*, it is no concern of plaintiff how the person with whom she dealt, American, subdivided its responsibility of furnishing the machines and services in discharge of its undertaking of safe carriage.

Of course, plaintiff's right to due care cannot be diminished by American's delegating certain tasks to others. What would be actionable negligence if done by American is not less so because done by another; such a person may be sued by plaintiff, and so may American if the negligence was discoverable by it. By the same token, however, plaintiff's primary right to care from American (and, indeed, all whose actions foreseeably affect her) should not be enlarged to insurance protection simply because American chose to have a certain task performed by another. We note that the argument made in some cases based on the avoidance of a multiplicity of actions is inapplicable here. In such cases, the plaintiff himself is the recipient of a warranty incident to the sale of goods and if the defect is in the manufacture it is at least reasonable to suggest a procedure by which liability may be imposed by the person entitled to the recovery directly against the one who, through a chain of warranties, is ultimately liable. Here, however, plaintiff (or her family, etc.) was not sold the chattel which caused her injury and hence there is no warranty.

It is true we have extended the benefit of an implied warranty beyond the immediate purchaser to those who could be fairly called indirect vendees of the product. (*Greenberg v. Lorenz, 9 N Y 2d 195, supra.*) Without stressing the weakness of the analogy that plaintiff here is the indirect vendee of the airplane and its parts, or the effect of the interposition between plaintiff and defendants of a federally regulated service industry of dominant economic and legal significance, it must be recognized that the true grounds of decision in a case of this sort lie outside the purpose and policy of the Sales Act and must be evaluated accordingly. Most scholars who have considered this question acknowledge that the warranty rationale is at best a useful fiction. (See, e.g., Prosser, The Assault upon the Citadel [Strict Liability to the Consumer], 69 Yale L. J. 1099; James, Products Liability, 34 Tex. L. Rev. 192.) If a strict products or enterprise liability is to be imposed here, this court cannot escape the responsibility of justifying it. We cannot accept the implication of the majority that the difference between warranty and strict products liability is merely one of phrasing.

Inherent in the question of strict products or enterprise liability is the question of the proper enterprise on which to fasten it. Here the majority have imposed this burden on the assembler of the finished product, Lockheed. The principle of selection stated is that the injured passenger needs no more protection. We suggest that this approach to the identification of an appropriate defendant does not answer the question: Which enterprise should be selected if the selection is to be in accord with the rationale upon which the doctrine of strict products liability rests?

The purpose of such liability is not to regulate conduct with a view to eliminating accidents, but rather to remove the economic consequences of accidents from the victim who is unprepared to bear them and place the risk on the enterprise in the course of whose business they arise. The risk, it is said, becomes part of the cost of doing business and can be effectively distributed among the public through insurance or by a direct reflection in the price of the goods or service. As applied to this case we think the enterprise to which accidents such as the present are incident is the carriage of passengers by air -- American Airlines. The fact that this accident was due to a defective altimeter should be of no legal significance to plaintiff absent some fault (negligence) on the part of Kollsman or Lockheed. Here, the dominant enterprise and the one with which plaintiff did business and relied upon was the airline.

If the carrier which immediately profited from plaintiff's custom is the proper party on which to fasten whatever enterprise liability the social conscience demands, enterprises which supply the devices with which the carrier conducts its business should not be subject to an action based on this theory. This seems most persuasive where the business that deals directly with the public is not merely a conduit for the distribution of the manufacturer's consumer goods but assumes the responsibility of selecting and using those goods itself as a capital asset in the conduct of a service enterprise such as common carriage. In such a case the relationship between the assembler of these goods and the air traveller is minimal as compared to that obtaining between the traveller and the carrier. In a theory of liability based, not on the regulation of conduct, but on economic considerations of distributing the risk of accidents that occur through no one's neglect, the enterprise most strategically placed to perform this function -- the carrier, rather than the enterprise that supplies an assembled chattel thereto, is the logical subject of the liability, if liability there is to be.

Whatever conclusions may flow from the fact that the accident was caused by a defective altimeter should be merged in whatever responsibility the law may place on the airline with which plaintiff did business. To extend warranty law to allow plaintiff to select a defendant from a multiplicity of enterprises in a case such as this would not comport with the rationale of enterprise liability and would only have the effect of destroying whatever rights that exist among the potential defendants by virtue of agreement among themselves. If, on the other hand, plaintiff's maximum rights lie against the carrier, the rules of warranty can perform their real function of adjusting the rights of the parties to the agreements through which the airline acquired the chattel that caused the accident. If, as we maintain in this case, the true theory relied on by plaintiff is enterprise liability, then the rights of those from whom compensation is sought, no less than of those who seek it, "ought not to be made to depend upon the intricacies of the law of sales." (*Ketterer v. Armour & Co., 200 F. 322, 323.*)

We are therefore of the opinion that any claim in respect of an airplane accident that is grounded in strict enterprise liability should be fixed on the airline or none at all. Only in this way do we meet and resolve, one way or another, the anomaly presented by the reasoning of the majority, which, through reliance on warranty incident to sales, grants a recovery to a passenger injured through a nonnegligent failure of equipment but denies it to one injured through a nonnegligent failure of maintenance or operation.

Although no such claim is raised by the pleadings, as we stated earlier, it is clear that our cases limit the airline's duty to that of due care. (*McPadden v. New York Cent. R. R. Co., 44 N. Y. 478*; *Stierle v. Union Ry. Co., 156 N. Y. 70*; *Williams v. Long Is. R. R. Co., 294 N. Y.*

318; *Kilberg v. Northeast Airlines, 9 N Y 2d 34, supra.*) It is this rule, avowedly formed to deal with the problem of accidents, that must be re-evaluated by those who would support the theory of strict enterprise liability. A stricter rule is not without precedent in this court (*Alden v. New York Cent. R. R. Co., 26 N. Y. 102*, holding that the carrier "must be held accountable, in every event, to furnish a road-worthy coach; and that, if the event proved it not to have been so, he must suffer the consequences" [p. 104]; see, also, cases collected in *McLean v. Triboro Coach Corp., 302 N. Y. 49*). However, as long as our law holds a carrier chargeable only with negligence, what part of reason is it to hold to a greater duty an enterprise which supplied an assembled aircraft which was certified for commercial service by the Federal Aviation Agency?

Our reluctance to hold an air carrier to strict liability for the inevitable toll of injury incident to its enterprise is only the counsel of prudence. Aside from the responsibility imposed on us to be slow to cast aside well-established law in deference to a theory of social planning that is still much in dispute (Prosser, Torts [2d ed.], § 84; Patterson, The Apportionment of Business Risks through Legal Devices, 24 Colum. L. Rev. 335, 358; Pound, Introduction to the Philosophy of Law 100-104 [1954]), there remains the inquiry whether the facts fit the theory. It is easy, in a completely free economy, to envision the unimpeded distribution of risk by an enterprise on which it is imposed; but how well will such a scheme work in an industry which is closely regulated by Federal agencies? In consideration of international competition and other factors weighed by those responsible for rate regulation, how likely is it that rate scales will rise in reflection of increased liability? (See Pound, *supra*, pp. 102-103.) In turn, how likely is it that the additional risk will be effectively distributed as a cost of doing business? Such questions can be intelligently resolved only by analysis of facts and figures compiled after hearings in which all interested groups have an opportunity to present economic arguments. These matters, which are the factual cornerstones supporting the theory adopted by the majority, aside from our view that they apply it to the wrong enterprise, are classically within the special competence of the Legislature to ascertain. For a court to assume them in order to support a theory that displaces much of the law of negligence from its ancestral environment involves an omniscience not shared by us. For a court to apply them, not to the enterprise with which plaintiff dealt and relied upon, or to the enterprise which manufactured the alleged defective part, but to the assembler of the aircraft used by the carrier, involves a principle of selection which is purely arbitrary.

C. *Manufacturing and Design*

DORIS ELSWORTH et al. v. BEECH AIRCRAFT CORPORATION.

Supreme Court of California

691 P.2d 630

December, 1984

Section 669 of the Evidence Code sets forth the doctrine commonly called negligence per se. It provides that negligence of a person is presumed if he violated a statute or regulation of a public entity, if the injury resulted from an occurrence that the regulation was designed to prevent, and if the person injured was within the class for whose protection the regulation was adopted. This presumption may be rebutted by proof that the violator did what might reasonably be expected of a person of ordinary prudence, acting under similar circumstances, who desired to comply with the law.

Section 669 of the Evidence Code provides in relevant part:

"(a) The failure of a person to exercise due care is presumed if:

"(1) He violated a statute, ordinance, or regulation of a public entity;

"(2) The violation proximately caused death or injury to person or property;

"(3) The death or injury resulted from an occurrence of the nature which the statute, ordinance, or regulation was designed to prevent; and

"(4) The person suffering the death or the injury to his person or property was one of the class of persons for whose protection the statute, ordinance, or regulation was adopted.

"(b) This presumption may be rebutted by proof that:

"(1) The person violating the statute, ordinance, or regulation did what might reasonably be expected of a person of ordinary prudence, acting under similar circumstances, who desired to comply with the law; . . ."

The primary issue in this case is whether the doctrine may be applied to hold liable for defective design the manufacturer of an aircraft that allegedly violated safety standards promulgated by the Federal Aviation Agency (FAA), even though the agency had issued to the manufacturer a certificate declaring that the design of the airplane met all applicable safety standards.

In 1974 Edward O. Miro, an experienced pilot, took three prospective buyers on a demonstration flight in a Travel Air twin engine airplane manufactured by defendant Beech Aircraft Corporation (Beech). It was daylight, the weather was clear, and the winds were light. After takeoff, the airplane reached an altitude of 800 feet, made two right turns into the traffic pattern, then suddenly turned left out of the traffic pattern, fell over, and went into a spin. It recovered briefly, but fell again into a final flat spin and crashed seven minutes after takeoff. All aboard were killed.

When the Travel Air was found after the crash, it was discovered that Miro had turned off the left fuel selector, shut down the left engine, and feathered (i.e., streamlined in the direction of flight) the left propeller blades. The landing gear was in the "down" position, and the wing flaps were partially or all the way down. A thermostatic valve in the left engine was broken.

The wives and children of the three passengers filed wrongful death actions against Beech and Miro, and Miro's heirs filed an action against Beech. Miro's insurer settled with the heirs of the passengers, and the trial proceeded against Beech. The heirs of the passengers and of Miro (hereafter plaintiffs) sought recovery on several theories, including negligence per se, alleging that the Travel Air did not comply with various safety regulations adopted by the FAA.

At the trial, plaintiffs claimed that the crash was caused by the stall of the airplane with the left engine feathered, and an inadequate stall warning system. According to expert testimony produced by plaintiffs, the stall resulted in a nonrecoverable flat spin caused by the undue spinning tendency of the airplane. Plaintiffs' witness surmised that Miro had feathered the left engine propeller because a valve in the left engine had failed, causing the instrument that measured oil to show a low operating pressure. In these circumstances, the propeller had to be feathered quickly to prevent the engine from coming apart, and to avoid a fire.

A test pilot who tested a Travel Air in preparation for the trial testified on behalf of plaintiffs that, with only one engine operating, the stall characteristics of the Travel Air were dangerous because of an undue tendency of the airplane to spin. He testified also that the stall warning light was inadequate. It was his opinion that the Travel Air failed to comply with five specified safety regulations of the FAA.

Beech attributed the crash to pilot error. Its witnesses testified that Miro had failed to maintain sufficient speed to prevent the airplane from entering into a nonrecoverable stall.

The FAA had certified the design of the Travel Air as complying with all applicable safety regulations. The aircraft first received a type certificate in 1957, after Beech employees conducted various inspections and tests and submitted to the FAA details regarding the construction and design of the airplane. Beech did not conduct tests for the spinning characteristics of the Travel Air because Harold Hermes, then the regional chief of the FAA's flight test branch, interpreted the safety regulations as not requiring spin testing for twin engine aircraft. In 1958 a Travel Air crashed, and the Washington headquarters of the FAA ordered that the aircraft be tested for its spinning characteristics. The spin testing was performed by a Beech employee, accompanied by an FAA test pilot. Following the test, FAA officials, including the test pilot, recommended that the certification for the Travel Air be continued, finding that it complied with all applicable safety regulations. This recommendation was accepted by the agency.

At the conclusion of a four-month trial, the court read to the jury five FAA safety regulations that plaintiffs alleged Travel Air failed to meet, and instructed that the jury must find Beech negligent if they found that the regulations were violated and that the violations proximately caused decedents' injuries, unless Beech justified its failure to comply. (*BAJI No. 3.45* (6th ed. 1977).) After two weeks of deliberations, the jury returned a general verdict against Beech; two jurors voted in Beech's favor.

On this appeal from the ensuing judgment Beech claims that the court erred in instructing the jury on the doctrine of negligence per se, in admitting various items of evidence, and in refusing to grant Beech's motion for a new trial because of alleged jury misconduct.

Beech does not challenge the sufficiency of the evidence to support the verdict on any of the theories of recovery advanced by plaintiffs. Nor does it assert that the jury should have been prohibited from giving any consideration to the question of Beech's compliance with the FAA safety regulations. It concedes that satisfaction of the FAA standards would not constitute a complete defense and the jury could have found Beech liable for defective design of the Travel Air even if it had complied with the FAA regulations, because the jury could have determined that such compliance was insufficient to absolve Beech's duty as a manufacturer. (See *Wilson v. Piper Aircraft Corp. (1978) 282 Ore. 61 [577 P.2d 1322, 97 A.L.R.3d 606]*.)

(1a) Rather, Beech's claim is that the jury should have been compelled to give determinative effect to the FAA decision that the Travel Air complied with all applicable safety regulations, and that it was error to give the negligence per se instruction to the effect that Beech was guilty of negligence if the Travel Air did not meet the regulations. Beech urges that the effect of the instruction was to allow the jury to second-guess the FAA decision that the Travel Air complied with the regulations, thereby intruding into a field preempted by federal law.

The FAA is required by the Federal Aviation Act of 1958 to adopt minimum standards governing the design, construction and performance of aircraft. (49 U.S.C. § 1421 (a)(1).) It has issued detailed regulations setting forth safety standards and the requirements that must be met by an airplane as to both design and testing before a type certificate may be issued. (*14 C.F.R. § 21.1 et seq. (1984).*) The act authorizes the agency to delegate to any properly qualified person the examination, inspection and testing necessary to the issuance of a certificate. (49 U.S.C. § 1355 (a).) Pursuant to that authorization the agency has permitted manufacturers to perform the tests necessary to assure that the regulations are met, and that the aircraft complies with all certification requirements. (*14 C.F.R. §§ 21.21, 21.35.*)

An experienced manufacturer with employees qualified in the various aspects of airplane design may qualify for the "delegation option" program, which allows the manufacturer's employees to act on behalf of the FAA to assure that all the appropriate tests and inspections for certification are performed. This procedure avoids the necessity for FAA personnel to repeat the tests and inspections required for certification. The manufacturer notifies the FAA whether the aircraft complies with safety regulations. The function of the FAA is largely to police compliance with the regulations, although it may perform the testing of an aircraft with its own personnel. (*Id.*, § 21.33; *United States v. S.A. Empresa de Viacao Aerea Rio Grandense (1984) U.S.*) Beech was authorized by the FAA to act in accordance with the "delegation option" procedure.

(2) Under the doctrine of preemption, federal law prevails over state law if Congress has expressed an intent to occupy a given field in which federal law is supreme. But even if there is no such intent, state law is preempted if it conflicts with federal law so that it is impossible to comply with both, or if the state regulations stand as an obstacle to the accomplishment of the full purposes that Congress sought to achieve. (*Pac. Gas & Elec. v. Energy Resources Comm'n. (1983) 461 U.S. 190, 203-205.*) (3) Courts are reluctant to infer preemption, and it is the burden of the party claiming that Congress intended to preempt state law to prove it. (*Exxon Corp. v. Governor of Maryland (1978) 437 U.S. 117, 132*; *New York Dept. of Social Services v. Dublino (1973) 413 U.S. 405, 413.*)

(4) Applying these principles to the present case, we begin with the observation that there is nothing inherently inconsistent in the proposition that even if the federal government has entirely occupied the field of regulating an activity a state may simultaneously grant damages for violation of such regulations.

This precept was recognized in the recent decision in *Silkwood v. Kerr-McGee Corp. (1984) 464 U.S. 238*. The court there acknowledged the "tension between the conclusion that safety regulation is the exclusive concern of the federal law and the conclusion that a state may nevertheless award damages based on its own law of liability," but held that in the field of nuclear safety regulation "Congress intended to stand by both concepts and to tolerate whatever tension there was between them." (*Id. at p. 256.*)

In *Silkwood* the federal government had enacted regulations concerning the safety of nuclear power plants and the licensing of such plants. These regulations occupied the field of safety to the exclusion of state enactments on the subject. Nevertheless, the high court ruled that common law tort principles of Oklahoma law were applicable to hold the defendant employer liable to an employee for compensatory and punitive damages as the result of radiation at the defendant's plant. After a close analysis of the legislative background of federal laws relating to nuclear power, the court concluded that Congress had assumed persons injured by nuclear accidents were free to utilize state court remedies, and that "traditional principles of state tort law would apply with full force unless they were expressly supplanted." (*Id. at p. 25.*)

(1b) Here, there can be no question as to the intent of Congress to allow the states to apply their own laws in tort actions against aircraft manufacturers for the defective design of airplanes, in spite of the fact that federal law may have completely occupied the field of regulation of aircraft safety and certification. The Federal Aviation Act of 1958 expressly declares that its provisions are not intended to abridge remedies that a party may have under state law. (49 U.S.C. § 1506.) The doctrine of negligence per se is one of those remedies.

Since Congress has clearly allowed state tort remedies, the critical issues before us are not whether it has fully occupied the field of aircraft regulation, but whether there is an "irreconcilable conflict between the federal and state standards or whether the imposition of a state standard in a damages action would frustrate the objectives of the federal law." (*Silkwood, 464 U.S. at p. 256.*)

We can discern here no irreconcilable conflict between federal and state standards. Plaintiffs do not challenge the power of the FAA to adopt safety regulations or to certify aircraft as complying with those regulations. Nor do they seek to revoke the certification of the Travel Air. Even if the jury found that the Travel Air was defective on the basis of the negligence per se instruction, this would have no effect on the FAA's power to certify aircraft, or on the validity of its certification decisions. It is important to note that the negligence per se instruction plays a very limited role in the context of a state court's obligation to accord deference to the FAA's decisions regarding the safety of aircraft. In essence, it allows the jury to find defective an airplane design that the FAA has approved as safe. But a jury may make the same determination without the instruction because, as Beech concedes, it could find a manufacturer liable for defective design even if the airplane complies with every regulation. The negligence per se instruction therefore affects only the jury's *reason* for finding a design defect, rather than its power to find such a defect in the face of FAA certification.

In many respects this case is stronger for plaintiffs on the issue of conflict between federal and state law than *Silkwood*. There, the federal government had the authority to impose civil penalties against a licensee for violation of nuclear radiation standards. Nevertheless, the court held that a state tort remedy did not raise a conflict because it would not be physically impossible for defendant to pay both the federal fine and the state-imposed damages. (*Silkwood, supra, 464 U.S. at p. 257 [78 L.Ed.2d at p. 458, 104 S.Ct. at p. 626].*) We cannot say here that allowing the jury to find Beech guilty of negligence per se "[creates] a significant risk of prohibition of protected conduct, . . ." (*Sears, Roebuck & Co. v. Carpenters (1978) 436 U.S. 180, 207.*)

[several other of Apellee's arguments are omitted].

The judgment is affirmed.

RUTH C. BRAKE, v. BEECH AIRCRAFT CORPORATION

Court of Appeal of California, First Appellate District, Division Two

184 Cal. App. 3d 930

July, 1986

The 1976 crash of a twin-engine aircraft, a Beechcraft Baron 58, took the lives of William P. Brake and Donald E. McCarter. Their widows, as administrators of the estates, brought independent actions for wrongful death against the plane's manufacturer, Beech Aircraft Corporation, and the actions were consolidated for jury trial. Plaintiff widows (plaintiffs) appeal from a judgment entered on a special verdict in favor of defendant manufacturer (Beech) and from a subsequent order denying their motion to tax costs.

Background

The aircraft crashed in rugged high-desert terrain north of a ridge of the San Gabriel Mountains, near the town of Pearblossom in Los Angeles County, about one hour after a 9:05 a.m. takeoff from Hawthorne Municipal Airport. Eyewitnesses attracted by an "oscillating" engine sound saw the plane descend, with nose tilted downward, in a series of 13 to 15 tight circles to the right (pivoting on the right wing) just before impact.

Decedents both worked for Northrop Aircraft Corporation (Northrop), which owned the plane. McCarter, a certificated military jet fighter plane (F-5) instructor working in Saudi Arabia, had come to California for training toward a multiengine rating in order to fly such a plane in Saudi Arabia for Northrop. Not yet certified, but having logged 14 hours of "dual" time in the aircraft (i.e., with a copilot), McCarter, together with Brake, the manager of flight support operations for Northrop, took off on the morning of the accident for a "pilot check flight" -- an opportunity for Brake to evaluate McCarter's training progress. McCarter was in the pilot's and Brake in the copilot's seat. The plane was equipped with dual controls so that it could be flown from either position. Brake did not have an instructor's rating but had logged 225 hours in the plane and was an experienced commercial pilot.

It was undisputed at trial that the aircraft stalled and then entered into a fully developed "flat spin" from which it never recovered. The crucial question was why or how.

Plaintiffs attempted to prove negligent or defective design. To summarize, their evidence showed possible negligence or defect in the selection of the Baron 58's airfoils and its rudder configuration, which assertedly rendered the aircraft unusually susceptible to spins and difficult to control once a spin developed. They relied as well on claimed violations of federal aircrafts regulations governing standards for maneuverability, stall warnings and single-engine-out stall recovery. They further maintained that the aircraft's operating manual inadequately warned of stall/spin characteristics and recovery and that Beech inadequately tested the aircraft. Their factual theory of the accident was that the decedents were flying with reduced power in the left engine (probably to simulate single-engine-out conditions) when they inadvertently dipped below minimum control speed, stalled and rapidly entered the fatal spin.

Beech countered with evidence that the Baron 58 has the same airfoil and tail design found on other twin-engine aircraft, is FAA (Federal Aviation Agency) certified as complying with federal regulations, has adequate stall warnings, is not unduly prone to spin, recovers easily from "incipient" spins, and had a safety information booklet (distributed to owners before the accident and in response to an FAA communique) that specially warned of potential spin problems and instructed on recovery techniques.

Beech's theory was pilot negligence or error. The relative inexperience of both decedents with the Baron 58, their apparent use of asymmetric (simulated single-engine) power before the crash and the existence of strong turbulence in the San Gabriel Mountains that morning suggested the use of improper recovery techniques (perhaps those appropriate to the F-5 fighter) following a single-engine stall brought on or aggravated by winds. Examination of the wreckage showed the aircraft to have been trimmed for "blue line speed," indicating a safe single-engine speed and thus tending to rebut plaintiffs' theory of inadvertent loss of airspeed.

The jury returned a special verdict in favor of Beech, finding no negligence and no defect. Judgment on the verdict was entered on November 24, 1981, and Beech thereafter filed a memorandum for costs totaling over $ 107,000. Plaintiffs timely noticed motions for judgment notwithstanding the verdict, for new trial, and to tax costs. At a combined hearing, the superior court denied the motions for new trial and judgment notwithstanding the verdict and took the remaining motion under submission. By order of February 8, 1982, the court denied the motion to tax costs and allowed, as reasonable and necessary, $ 45,470.70 of the costs claimed.

Plaintiffs timely appeal from both the judgment and the order denying the motion to tax costs.

Appeal

(1) "Evidence of prior accidents is admissible to prove a defective condition, knowledge, or the cause of an accident, provided that the circumstances of the other accidents are similar and not too remote. " (*Elsworth v. Beech Aircraft Corp. (1984) 37 Cal.3d 540, 555*). Plaintiffs claim cumulative prejudice from several rulings denying the admission of other-accidents evidence.

(2) One ruling granted Beech's motion to exclude a computer-generated statistical analysis comparing accident rates for the Baron with rates for other aircraft, on a per-flight-hour basis. Statistician Brent Silver, an expert for plaintiffs, prepared the analysis from National Transportation Safety Board (NTSB) data on domestic aviation accidents. After hearing an extensive offer of proof through testimony by Silver, the court granted the motion on grounds that the proffered evidence was "hearsay upon hearsay, unreliable, speculative [and] conjectural." Plaintiffs have not presented arguments that surmount those problems. Error has not been shown. (Cf. *Luque v. McLean (1972) 8 Cal.3d 136, 147-148*).

(3) Plaintiffs also claim error in the exclusion of five accident report memoranda, produced by Beech during discovery, and three NTSB publications.

Taking first the Beech memoranda, plaintiffs failed to lay a foundation of similarity between the accidents discussed therein and the accident in this case. Descriptions of flight attitude, trim settings, engine power, loading, weather conditions, altitudes, feathering, etc., were widely varied. In addition, there are complex multiple hearsay problems in the documents. Plaintiffs cannot overcome these myriad problems by relying on similarity of airfoils or tail design. Similarly, there was no foundation laid to show similarity as to the accidents referred to in the NTSB documents. All of this evidence was presented for the first time at the close of plaintiffs' case, without calling witnesses.

Despite the lack of foundation to show similarity, however, those prior accidents involving stall/spins of Beech Baron 58's could have been admitted for the limited purpose of showing that Beech had notice of a dangerous condition. "For this purpose, ""all that is required . . . is that the previous injury should be such as to attract the defendant's attention to the dangerous situation. . . ."" [Citation.]" (*Elsworth v. Beech Aircraft Corp., supra, 37 Cal.3d 540, 555.*) Here, as in *Elsworth,* "[there] can be no question that the prior accidents should have alerted Beech to the faulty spinning characteristics of the [aircraft]. It was contrary to FAA regulations to spin . . . the Baron . . ., and Beech should therefore have been alerted to the fact that the spinning of the airplanes in the prior accidents was unintentional and may have been due to a defect in their design." (*Ibid.*, fn. omitted.)

Nevertheless, because Beech had requested that the evidence be excluded under *Evidence Code section 352* and because the court explained that its ruling was based in part on the risk of prejudice from undue consumption of time, we could not find exclusion of the evidence to be error unless an abuse of discretion appeared under all the circumstances. (*Simmons v.Southern Pac. Transportation Co. (1976.)*

Assuming, without deciding, that the court did abuse its discretion, however, we would not find reversible error on this record. (*Evid. Code, § 354; Cal. Const., art. VI, § 13; People v. Watson (1956) 46 Cal.2d 818, 836 [299 P.2d 243].*) The accidents would have been admissible only to show *knowledge* of a dangerous condition, not the existence of one, and it does not appear reasonably probable that the jury's verdict was predicated on doubt over the element of notice. Beech never disputed that it knew the Baron 58 would quickly develop a full spin if stalled and not promptly recovered. There was no conflict in the evidence -- all experts agreed that an unrecovered spin in the Baron 58 could be irreversible. The FAA materials were to the same effect, as was the placard on the plane itself. Beech's defense in this regard, rather, was that the plane was "docile" and easy to recover if proper techniques were employed and that its published materials adequately warned against the plane's spinning tendencies. In other words, the focus of the trial was on whether the plane's stall/spin characteristics constituted a dangerous condition, not whether Beech knew of them. By returning its special verdict of no negligence and no defect, the jury appears to have concluded that those characteristics were not unusually dangerous and that the efforts of Beech to warn against them were adequate.

[discussion of costs award omitted].

19   The assorted remaining arguments directed against the costs award are unsupported and meritless.

[appellee's collateral estoppel argument omitted].

Finding no prejudicial error at trial and no abuse of discretion or other error in the award of costs, we affirm both the judgment on special verdict and the order re motion to tax costs.

PIONEER SEED COMPANY (PTY) LIMITED v. CESSNA AIRCRAFT COMPANY

United States District Court for the Eastern District of Virginia, Alexandria Division

16 Av. Cas. (CCH) P17,941

August, 1981.

Findings of Fact and Conclusions of Law

1. Plaintiff is a corporation organized under the laws of South Africa, and its principal place of business is in that country. The defendant is a corporation organized under the laws of Kansas and has its principal place of business in that state. The amount in controversy exclusive of interest and costs is more than $ 10,000. The Court has jurisdiction on diversity grounds.

2. Plaintiff purchased a new Cessna 441 aircraft, serial number 0055, on June 7th, 1978 from South African Factors Limited who had purchased it from Commercial Air Services (PTY) Limited, a duly authorized South African Cessna dealer.

3. The subject aircraft was a high performance turbo-propeller executive jet manufactured by Cessna Aircraft Company in Wichita, Kansas.

4. Prior to purchasing the subject aircraft representatives from Pioneer went to Wichita, Kansas, to inspect a Cessna 441, and fully informed Cessna of the conditions that the aircraft would operate under and the uses to which it would be put.

5. Pioneer's regular pilot received training and instructions from Cessna in Wichita, Kansas. Pioneer is engaged in agricultural activities and purchased the aircraft as a working piece of equipment for its business.

6. Before a sale was consummated, Cessna represented to Pioneer that its aircraft had the capability to meet Pioneer's needs.

7. From the time Pioneer purchased the aircraft on June 7th, 1978, until the nosewheel collapsed on January 24th, 1979, it was regularly serviced and well maintained.

8. Pioneer did not make any alterations or modifications to the aircraft from the date of purchase to the date of failure that would relieve Cessna from its warranty obligations.

9. On January 24th, 1979, the aircraft had logged approximately 307 hours of flying time and was under the manufacturer's warranty (one year).

10. The pilot operating the subject aircraft when the nose gear collapsed was a well-qualified experienced professional pilot with approximately 8,000 pilot hours, roughly 300 of which were in the subject aircraft.

11. Hoopstad Airport, the place where the accident occurred, is listed on the South African airport directory as a grass-surfaced runway

with Published LCN figure of 8.0. Runways 14/32 were 4,800 feet in length and 98 feet in width.

12. The Cessna 441 at maximum weight had an LCN of 5.85 pounds. LCN is an airport weight classification.

13. Prior to the nose gear failure, the aircraft made a normal landing on runway 32, and after landing reversed course and taxied back on runway 14 to the runway threshold. At the runway threshold the aircraft started a left turn in the overrun area to a parking position to the right of the threshold of runway 32.

14. This procedure and this parking position was the normal practice used by Pioneer for both this aircraft and a Cessna 421 aircraft which Pioneer owned prior to purchasing the 441.

15. During the course of the turn the trunnion of the nose gear assembly suddenly failed, causing the nose gear to collapse. As a result of the collapse of the nose gear both propellers dug into the ground, both engines were badly shock-loaded, and major damage resulted.

16. As the aircraft could not be flown until new engines and nose gear were fitted, Pioneer constructed a hangar at the airport to protect it from the weather. Temporary repairs were completed late in May 1979, and the aircraft was flown to Rand Airport for completion of repairs by COMAIR, a Cessna repair facility and Cessna agent in South Africa.

17. Prior to the accident the subject aircraft was maintained under the Cessna progressive care program authorized by Cessna maintenance facilities.

18. The aircraft had never been subjected to hard landings, strains, or misuse, although the aircraft had on one prior occasion been pushed by hand from soft ground, and on another occasion it was taxied off the paved runway because of tire trouble and planks were inserted beneath the wheels in accordance with Cessna-approved procedure. Neither of these events damaged the nose gear trunnion.

19. The collapse of the nose gear was caused by the catastrophic failure of the nose gear trunnion, a component of the nose gear assembly.

20. The nose gear trunnion attached the nose gear to the aircraft structure by means of two lugs encased in a bearing which fitted into bearing retainers on either side of the nosewheel well. The nose gear collapse was the result of the failure of the left lug.

21. Metallurgical examination of the failed lug showed that it failed due to the presence of fatigue cracks originating in the bottom of the lug radius. The remaining cross-sectional area of the lug failed due to stresses that exceeded the strength of the remaining lug.

22. The fatigue cracks were caused by a steel washer Cessna placed over the lug during manufacture as a spacer, which etched a notch into the radius of the aluminum trunnion. The notch concentrated stress in the area of the notch, and the fatigue crack resulted. Fatigue cracks weaken the structure of metal and will cause eventual failure.

23. It was design error to use a steel washer as a shim or spacer. Knowledge that the steel washer would notch the lug radius and result

in fatigue cracks was within the state of the art when the subject aircraft was manufactured and sold.

24. Prior to the purchase of the subject aircraft Pioneer owned and operated a Cessna 421 in its business on the same airfield without problems. A 421 is a lighter aircraft but used the same nose gear assembly as that employed by Cessna when it switched to the heavier 441 model.

25. Cessna and its South African agents and distributors advised Pioneer that the Cessna 441 aircraft could operate anywhere the 421 could operate knowing that operations under certain South African field conditions imposed stress on nosewheel assemblies due to the nature of landing surfaces in South Africa and other airport factors. At the time of the sale of the subject aircraft Cessna knew that it was to be operated from grass and sod airfields and should have known that the Cessna 441 was not designed to operate from unimproved airports.

26. There were no restrictions in the pilot's handbook or any other aircraft document warning against operations from grass or sod airports.

27. The trunnion was of insufficient strength to support the Cessna 441 under South African field conditions.

28. The trunnion used by Cessna on the subject aircraft was designed in 1962 for the Cessna 411, an aircraft no longer in production, and an aircraft much lighter than the 441. The Cessna 441 and its jet engines generate far greater horsepower than the Cessna 411.

29. Cessna used the same trunnion on the Cessna 441 that it did on the 411 because it was cheaper to use a common part; that even though the nose gear trunnion designed by Cessna in 1962 was for use on a light plane, the trunnion had a design load capability that theoretically should have accommodated the Cessna 441; however, I find from the evidence that the variables of field conditions are such that the trunnion in use on non-improved surfaces would not perform its intended function on an aircraft as heavy as a Cessna 441.

30. The trunnion lug failed under normal operating conditions, and the evidence discloses that other Cessna 441 aircraft had experienced similar difficulties. At least two of the prior failures occurred as a result of the steel washer cutting into the radius of the lug.

31. The steel washer was required on all 441 aircraft. Washers were used to center the trunnion within the wheel well to correct faulty manufacturing. The requirement for the steel washer on the subject aircraft was a manufacturing defect.

32. By Service Information Letter PJ 79-23 of July 23rd, 1979, Cessna directed that a heavy-duty nose gear trunnion be installed on all Cessna 441 aircraft before returning them to service again. The heavy-duty trunnion was to be installed for increased strength and longevity.

33. The heavy-duty replacement trunnion leveled out the sharp lug radius from .040 inches to .120 inches and increased the lug diameter from 1.1875 inches to 1.3120 inches. It also provided a grease fitting for the lug bearing lubrication, and the steel washer or shim was eliminated.

34. Cessna was negligent in the manufacture of the aircraft in that it was foreseeable that: One, the steel washer on the trunnion lug would cause metal fatigue and ultimate failure of the lug; two, the sharp lug radius would concentrate stress; and, three, the lug diameter was insufficient for the weight and horsepower of the Cessna 441 aircraft. Use of a trunnion designed for the lighter Cessna 411 aircraft on the Cessna 441 was a design defect, as was the use of the steel washer on the trunnion lug.

35. At the time of the sale and delivery of the aircraft it was defective and unreasonably dangerous for the use for which it was sold, it being in substantially the same condition at the time of the accident as it was when it was sold.

36. Cessna knowingly misrepresented that the Cessna 441 as configured before the accident was fit for the uses and purposes that it knew Pioneer required in its normal business operations.

37. Cessna breached its expressed warranty that the Cessna 441 was fit for the aircraft operations conducted by Pioneer. Cessna also breached the implied warranty of fitness of the aircraft for its intended use.

PIONEER'S DAMAGE CLAIMS

The Court finds from the evidence of the various items of damages claimed by Pioneer that the following were established with sufficient certainty to enable the Court to award their recovery by Pioneer: Repair cost, $ 179,416; break-in fuel for new engines. $ 1,465; rental of other aircraft, $ 59,597, decreased by one third for operating expenses, or $ 39,732; one half of lost-time claim of $ 35,910, or $ 17,955. This results in a judgment award of $ 238,568.

In determining the law applicable to this case the Court has considered these three choices: The site of the accident; the forum state; and the place of manufacture and delivery.

I find from the evidence that the forum state has no relationship to the accident or sale, and was merely selected by the plaintiff as a location for processing the claim. At an earlier stage in the proceedings Cessna moved under forum non conveniens to transfer the action to Kansas for trial. This motion was denied for reasons fully stated in the record. I have no doubt that if the motion had been granted and the case transferred to Kansas, that a court in Kansas would have applied its own law since the manufacture, representations, and sale actually occurred in that state.

The cases seem to hold, and I so find, that in the commercial use of sophisticated equipment such as an aircraft, that the place of failure bears no reasonable relationship to the happening of an accident unless such defenses as contributory negligence, assumption of risk, misuse, and related defenses are raised. Since I do not find that any of these elements enter into a determination of the present case, there is no basis for applying any of South Africa's laws.

For the foregoing reasons an order will issue granting the plaintiff judgment in the amount of $ 238,568 with interest to run at the rate of 8% per annum from January 21st, 1981, the date this action was filed.

JOHN C. ALTSEIMER et al v. BELL HELICOPTER TEXTRON INC.

UNITED STATES DISTRICT COURT FOR THE EASTERN
DISTRICT OF CALIFORNIA

919 F. Supp. 340

March, 1996

Before the court is defendant Bell Helicopter Textron's motion for summary judgment on all the claims in plaintiffs' complaint.

BACKGROUND

On May 23, 1995, plaintiffs John Altseimer, Horizon Helicopters, Dennis Westerberg, and Sloane Westerberg filed this action for personal injuries, property damage, and economic losses allegedly arising out of a helicopter accident. Bell Helicopter Textron Inc. ("Bell") is the only named defendant. The complaint alleges that Bell designed, manufactured, assembled, tested, fabricated, produced, sold, or otherwise placed in the stream of commerce a defective helicopter and a defective 42 degree gearbox, one of the component parts of the helicopter. The complaint further alleges that Bell failed to provide proper warnings with respect to the negligent and defective design of the helicopter and the 42 degree gearbox.

Bell argues that it is entitled to summary judgment on the grounds that (1) the General Aviation Revitalization Act prohibits lawsuits against aircraft manufacturers arising out of the crash of an aircraft more that 18 years old, and (2) the destruction and rebuild of the "Bell" helicopter, on at least two occasions by unrelated entities, terminated any liability of Bell as manufacturer of the accident aircraft.

STANDARD OF REVIEW

Summary judgment is appropriate if the record, read in the light most favorable to the non-moving party, demonstrates no genuine issue of material fact. *Celotex Corp. v. Catrett, 477 U.S. 317, 322, 91 L. Ed. 2d 265, 106 S. Ct. 2548 (1986)*. Material facts are those necessary to the proof or defense of a claim, and are determined by reference to the substantive law. *See Anderson v. Liberty Lobby, 477 U.S. 242, 248, 91 L. Ed. 2d 202, 106 S. Ct. 2505 (1986)*. At the summary judgment stage the question before the court is whether there are genuine issues for trial. The court does not weigh evidence or assess credibility. *Id.*

DISCUSSION

The General Aviation Revitalization Act of 1994, Pub.L. 103-298, 108 Stat. 1552 *(49 U.S.C. § 40101* Note) (1994) ("GARA") is a statute of repose which prohibits all lawsuits against aircraft manufacturers arising out of accidents involving any general aviation aircraft or component part that is more than 18 years old. Section 2(a) of GARA, which sets forth the legislation's basic limitation on civil actions, provides:

(a) Except as provided in subsection (b), no civil action for damages for death or injury to persons or damage to property arising out of an accident involving a general aviation aircraft may be brought against the manufacturer of the aircraft or the manufacturer of any new component, system, subassembly, or other part of the aircraft, in its capacity as a manufacturer if the accident occurred --

> (1) After the applicable limitation period beginning on --

>> (A) The date of delivery of the aircraft to its first purchaser or lessee, if delivered directly from the manufacturer; or

>> (B) The date of first delivery of the aircraft to a person engaged in the business of selling or leasing such aircraft; or

> (2) With respect to any new component, system, subassembly, or other part which replaced another component, system, subassembly, or other part originally in, or which was added to, the aircraft, and which is alleged to have caused such death, injury, or damage, after the applicable limitation period beginning on the date of completion of the replacement or addition.

49 U.S.C. § 40101, Note Section 2(a)(1)-(2). *Section 3* defines the "limitation period" as 18 years, and section 2(d) provides that GARA supersedes any State law which permits civil actions such as those described in subsection (a) brought after the applicable 18 year limitation period.

Bell has provided undisputed evidence that the helicopter and 42 degree gearbox in question were more than 18 years old at the time of the crash. Parker Decl. PP 5-11. Bell has also produced undisputed evidence that the pinion gear, a component of the gear box, and purportedly the cause of the crash, was more than 18 years old at the time of the crash. *Id.* at P 10. Therefore, GARA effectively preempts plaintiffs' action. Although harsh, such a result is consistent with the purpose of GARA to:

> establish a Federal statute of repose to protect general aviation manufacturers from long-term liability in those instances where a particular aircraft has been in operation for a considerable number of years. A statute of repose is a legal recognition that, after an extended period of time, a product has demonstrated its safety and quality, and that it is not reasonable to hold a manufacturer legally responsible for an accident or injury occurring after that much time has elapsed.

140 Cong. Rec. H4998, H4999 (daily ed. July 27, 1994) (statement of Rep. Fish).

Plaintiffs argue that GARA should not be applied to this action because their claims accrued prior to the enactment of GARA. This contention is without merit. GARA was enacted on August 17, 1994, and plaintiffs did not file their complaint until May 23, 1995. Section 4 of GARA expressly states that "this act shall not apply with respect to civil actions commenced before the date of the enactment of this act." Both Federal and state law provide that a civil action "is commenced by filing a complaint with the court." *Fed. R. Civ. P. 3*; *see also Cal. Civ. Proc. Code § 350*. Since, plaintiffs' complaint was filed after the enactment of GARA, their claims are unambiguously subjected to GARA's preemptive provisions. Accordingly, Bell is entitled to summary judgment.

IT IS THEREFORE ORDERED that Bell's motion for summary judgment be, and the same is, hereby GRANTED.

VIII.   INTERNATIONAL LAW

A. *Jurisdiction*

LAKER AIRWAYS LIMITED v. PAN AMERICAN WORLD AIRWAYS.

UNITED STATES DISTRICT COURT FOR THE DISTRICT OF COLUMBIA

559 F. Supp. 1124

March , 1983

This is an antitrust action brought by Laker Airways against a number of American and foreign airlines. Presently before the Court is plaintiff's motion for a preliminary injunction. Because of the apparently unprecedented circumstances which gave rise to this application, it is appropriate to recite the background of the lawsuit in some detail.

I

On November 24, 1982, Laker Airways Limited (Laker) brought an action in this Court under the Sherman Act (*15 U.S.C. §§ 1* and *2*) and the Clayton Act (*15 U.S.C. § 15*) against Pan American World Airways, Inc. (Pan American), Trans World Airlines Inc. (TWA), McDonnell Douglas Corporation (McDonnell Douglas), McDonnell Douglas Finance Corporation (McDonnell Finance), British Airways Board (British Airways), Deutsche Lufthansa Aktiengesellschaft (Lufthansa), Swiss Air Transport Company Limited (Swissair), and British Caledonian Airways Limited (British Caledonian).   On February 15, 1983, a separate action [now consolidated with this one] containing essentially the same allegations as those recited in the November 1982 complaint, was brought by Laker against Sabena Belgian World Airlines (Sabena) and KLM Royal Dutch Airlines (KLM).

The complaints allege the following.

Since 1946 the fares for scheduled air transportation have been set by the International Air Transport Association (IATA), an association of the world's major airlines, at levels higher than would prevail in a competitive market.   Laker began charter flight operations between Great Britain and the United States in 1970, and, starting in June 1971, it also began to seek permission to operate low-cost "Skytrain" transatlantic service.   Resistance from the IATA airlines delayed implementation of the scheduled service until September 1977, but eventually Laker was able to provide every week over forty scheduled flights at low fares, in addition to extensive charter service between the United States and Great Britain.   Prior to the advent of Laker's Skytrain service from London to New York, which cost $115, the IATA-fixed economy fare on the same route was almost three times as much, or $313.

The complaints further allege that, in response to Laker's low-fare service, the IATA airlines agreed on a predatory scheme to destroy both Laker's transatlantic charters and its Skytrain service. In execution of that scheme, some of the IATA airlines offered their services on the New York-London route at below cost, expecting to drive Laker out of business, and expecting further that, once Laker was gone, they could and would raise their fares again to their previous high levels or above. In short, the complaint alleges a classic antitrust conspiracy.

Plaintiff further claims that although the conspiracy did not bear fruit at first, by 1981 Laker was so weakened by defendants' predatory activities and by a substantial drop in the dollar value of the pound sterling that it could not afford to reduce its fares further so as to compete with the fares adopted by defendants on some of Laker's routes. In October 1981, Pan American, TWA, and British Airways, seeking to end Laker's low-fare competition once and for all, decided to offer their own attractive, high-cost services at Laker's low prices on all of Laker's routes. Subsequently, in the winter of 1981-82, the IATA met in Switzerland and in Florida to agree on a program to set new and higher fares for the spring and summer of 1982, but to fix the fares of IATA members at Laker's level as long as Laker was in business.

According to the complaint, the defendants also interfered with Laker's financing. By Christmas 1981, Laker had reached an agreement with its lenders for the financial support made necessary by its weakened condition. The IATA members thereupon successfully pressured Laker's lenders to deny Laker that financing, and on February 5, 1982, succumbing to this pressure, Laker was forced into liquidation.

It was in response to these alleged activities that Laker filed the instant actions in this Court.

II

The first lawsuit proceeded in its normal course from November 24, 1982 to January 21, 1983. On that date, with no challenge to jurisdiction having been raised in this Court by any of the defendants, British Airways filed a declaratory judgment action against Laker filed in the Queen's Bench Division of the High Court of Justice in England seeking a declaration of non-liability to Laker and a permanent injunction preventing Laker from continuing with its suit against British Airways in the United States. At the time of the filing of its complaint, British Airways also applied for and was immediately granted an injunction against interference with the conduct of the British court proceedings. Within hours, British Caledonian, Lufthansa, and Swissair filed similar writs against Laker in the British court, and they likewise applied for, and were granted the identical injunction against Laker's seeking a counterinjunction.

Mr. Justice Parker of the Queen's Bench Division set a hearing for March 21, 1983, at which it is to be determined whether Laker should be permanently enjoined from proceeding with its lawsuit in this Court against both British airlines on the basis that Great Britain is the more appropriate forum.

However, subsequently, by an order dated March 2, 1983, the British court all but decided this question at least with respect to British Airways and British Caledonian. That order, issued without a hearing and without any notice to plaintiff or to this Court, enjoins Laker from "taking any further steps in Civil Action 82-3362 [in this Court]" against the two British defendants. The March 2 order, if valid, would preclude plaintiff from filing applications or motions in this Court, oppositions to motions filed by the defendants, and any other pleadings or papers. It can hardly be said that an order which, for example, directs a party not to file further papers in this Court, as did the order of the British court of March 2, is anything other than a direct interference with the proceedings in this Court. The orders secured by the defendant airlines on January 21, 1983, have a like effect

The British court has indicated that it will decide at a later date the appropriateness of a permanent injunction at Lufthansa's and Swissair's urging, and that it will also hold trials on the merits of the claims that the airlines are not liable to Laker. In passing on these claims, the court apparently intends to decide issues of American antitrust law as well as of British law.

The papers filed in the British court, which have been forwarded to this Court by various parties indicate two bases for the extraordinary action of the British tribunal: (1) Laker is incorporated in Britain and for that reason it may and in these circumstances should be restrained from suing in the United States courts, and (2) because of the way the American legal system is structured, it is unlikely that the defendants can receive justice here.

III

The Court must decide whether to issue a preliminary injunction against the four American defendants and Sabena and KLM. The Court will consider first the question whether it is likely that plaintiff will prevail on the merits of its permanent injunction request, and thereafter (in Part VI) it addresses the relative balance of injuries and the public interest.

First. If the British court is proceeding on the assumption that, because Laker is a British corporation, it may not, under American law, sue in the courts of the United States to vindicate rights under the American antitrust laws, it would be mistaken. See *Pfizer Inc. v. India, 434 U.S. 308, 54 L. Ed. 2d 563, 98 S. Ct. 584 (1978)*. As the Supreme Court there said:

> The fact that Congress' foremost concern in passing the antitrust laws was the protection of Americans does not mean that it intended to deny foreigners a remedy when they are injured by antitrust violations. Treble-damages suits by foreigners who have been victimized by antitrust violations clearly may contribute to the protection of American consumers.

434 U.S. at 314.

Second. Except in unusual, very narrow circumstances, there is no basis -- at least not in a free country -- for precluding a citizen by an injunction-type order from suing in the courts of another nation. A number of courts have repeated in dicta the proposition that a court "has the power to enjoin a party over whom it has personal jurisdiction from pursuing litigation before a foreign tribunal." See, *e.g., Western Electric Co. v. Milgo Electronic Corp., 450 F. Supp. 835, 837 (S.D.*

Fla. 1978). The power is rarely exercised, however, for "restraining a party from pursuing an action in a court of foreign jurisdiction involves delicate questions of comity and therefore 'requires that such action be taken only with care and great restraint.' *Canadian Filters (Harwich) Ltd. v. Lear-Siegler, Inc., 412 F.2d 577, 578 (1st Cir. 1969)."* *Compagnie dex Bauxites de Guinea v. Insurance Company of North America, supra, 651 F.2d at 887 n.10 (3rd Cir. 1981).* Indeed, when one examines the reported instances in which this power has actually been used, one finds that the fact situations are quite different from those involved in the instant cases.

> [case discussions where that power is distinguished are omitted].

Third. In addition to the circumstance that the American precedents would not support issuance of an injunction on the facts presented to Mr. Justice Parker, there is the perhaps even more significant fact that there are so few instances where any court, either in the United States or the United Kingdom, has asserted the power to enjoin its citizens from suing in the courts of another nation. The minimum lesson one can draw from this paucity of precedent is that, if a court has the authority to prevent a national from suing elsewhere, it may exercise this power only in the most extraordinary circumstances.

Yet there is nothing extraordinary about the suits brought in this Court by Laker. They are the garden-variety type of antitrust suit, involving what is claimed to be a combination of American corporations and foreign corporations doing substantial business in the United States which allegedly committed anticompetitive acts. In this age of multinational corporations, ever closer trade relations among the nations, instant communications, and air carriers closely binding the continents together, it is not at all unusual that activities of the kind here alleged should be claimed to have occurred in some instances. In short, there is nothing either unusual or vexatious about the lawsuits brought in this Court.

Thus, if these lawsuits may be singled out for the extraordinary remedy of an injunction requiring a national to cease prosecuting this action, then a great many other lawsuits on both sides of the Atlantic, in the field of antitrust law as in many other fields, would qualify for similar treatment. To put it another way, any decision which accepted the proposition that the court of the plaintiff's nationality may interfere with and effectively halt proceedings abroad in circumstances such as those involved here would set a far-reaching and dangerous precedent.

American companies operate, directly or through subsidiaries, in many counties all over the world, sometimes on a massive scale. Under the rationale which underlies the lawsuit in Great Britain, and which has at least provisionally been accepted by the British tribunal, American courts could legitimately interject themselves, by means of injunctions, between those American corporations and the foreign courts, and the courts of nations other than the United States and the United Kingdom could, and no doubt would, do likewise. The consequences to international trade and to amicable relations between nations that would result from this kind of interference are difficult to overestimate.

Fourth.   As concerns defendants' contention that the American courts are unable to do justice, the theory appears essentially to be that the discovery process established by American law is too expensive. Debates have been going on for some time in the American legal profession as to whether pretrial discovery is, on balance, beneficial because it removes the element of surprise from litigation and contributes to fairer trials and fairer settlements by revealing evidence that might otherwise not be available, or whether it is detrimental because of its cost.   Whatever may be the answer to that question, it is hardly the proper province of a foreign court to prohibit the conduct of litigation here because it does not agree with the way in which the United States Congress and the American courts, including the Supreme Court, have dealt with this particular procedural problem.

Again, if that were a proper standard in the British courts, it would also be appropriate for the American courts and the courts of other nations to take like factors into account in determining whether they should interfere with litigation abroad.   There are few nations which measure up to the elaborate safeguards guaranteeing fairness that one finds in the United States Constitution and laws.   Under the rationale upon which the British proceedings involving Laker and the other airlines are thus predicated, injunctions against foreign proceedings involving American citizens or corporations could become commonplace in the courts of this country whenever a United States court regarded the foreign country's procedures as inadequate.

What is perhaps even more surprising than the denigration of American law by British courts is that very large and reputable American law firms which routinely proceed under, and whose clients daily benefit from, the American discovery rules, would send their English solicitors into a foreign court to seek to enjoin proceedings in the United States on the ground that American courts cannot, under American legal procedure, be expected to do justice. The argument based on the expense of litigation in this country is especially strange when it is advanced on behalf of many of the largest airlines in the world represented by these vast and, no doubt, expensive law firms against a plaintiff which is insolvent.

Fifth.   While two of the defendants are British, four of the other corporations are American and four are carriers chartered in continental Europe.   It is difficult to visualize on what basis a British court could legitimately take jurisdiction -- let alone displace the jurisdiction of a United States tribunal -- where the complaint alleges violations of American law by American corporations and by foreign corporations which provide air service between the United States and Rotterdam, Brussels, Frankfurt, and other cities of continental Europe. The arguments of the European defendants distill down to the proposition that continental Europe is closer to Britain than to the United States. This is hardly a distinction that may be thought to make a difference in an era of multinational corporations and instant communications, especially when it is the parties' business to   provide frequent commercial air service between Europe and America.

Sixth.   This Court does not know what evidence of antitrust violations will be adduced at trial.   As noted, the complaint alleges a conspiracy involving both the American and the foreign carriers to

413

violate the American antitrust laws with respect to their operations between Europe and the United States. Nevertheless, it would not be surprising if the effective elimination from the lawsuit of several of the defendants could cripple plaintiff's lawsuit. Furthermore, if that elimination through the action of the British court were to succeed, a precedent would be set that would be likely to undermine the effectiveness of the antitrust laws whenever multinational or foreign corporations are part of the anticompetitive scheme: a court somewhere in the world could surely always be found to issue orders similar to those sought from the British court in these cases to abort an ongoing antitrust action in this country.

IV

The defendants argue with considerable emphasis that the British court has an interest in deciding whether a British plaintiff may prosecute a lawsuit in a foreign court. Assuming that such an interest exists -- as discussed *supra*, at least in the United States and in Great Britain any power based on such an interest is exercised only in very narrow circumstances -- it cannot displace the Court's authority and duty to entertain and decide the instant lawsuits.

These actions were brought under a positive command of a crucial American statute that represents a very strong public policy. Indeed, the Sherman Act has frequently been called the charter of economic freedom and its role has been compared to that which the *Bill of Rights* plays with respect to personal freedoms. See *United States v. Topco Associates, Inc., 405 U.S. 596, 610, 31 L. Ed. 2d 515, 92 S. Ct. 1126 (1972)*. The duty of this Court to entertain the present actions is buttressed by the constitutional mandate which guarantees to all those residing or doing business in the United States, such as Laker, due process and the equal protection of the laws. See, *e.g., Plyler v. Doe, 457 U.S. 202, 72 L. Ed. 2d 786, 796, 102 S. Ct. 2382 (1982)*; quoting *Yick Wo v. Hopkins, 118 U.S. 356, 369, 30 L. Ed. 220, 6 S. Ct. 1064 (1886)*. See also, *Russian Volunteer Fleet v. United States, 282 U.S. 481, 489, 75 L. Ed. 473, 51 S. Ct. 229 (1930)*.

In the end, then, what is involved in this unfortunate controversy is the question whether greater weight ought to be accorded in cases of conflicting claims of jurisdiction to the nationality of the plaintiff or to the substantive law and the substantive public policies of the nation in whose courts the plaintiff brings the action. That question, moreover, must here be decided in the context of a factual situation where all the defendants were and still are substantially engaged in doing business in the United States; where certain of the acts allegedly committed in furtherance of the illegal conspiracy occurred in the United States; where only in the United States can all the defendants surely be reached; and where, if the British court enjoins the plaintiff with respect even to some of the defendants, it may be impossible to prove the conspiracy against any of them.

But these are matters to be explored more fully at other stages -- perhaps on the motion for partial summary judgment on the *forum non conveniens* issue. The immediate question is whether this Court shall have the opportunity to decide whether it is an appropriate forum or whether a British court will assume that function. See Transcript of proceedings, January 27, 1983, where counsel for defendants stated (at pp. 16-17) that "the point of forum non conveniens . . . [is an issue which] we want . . . decided by the English court and not by the American court." This Court is aware of no precedent, and none has been cited by any party, holding that a *forum non conveniens* claim is to be decided by the tribunal to which a defendant wishes to have an action transferred rather than by the court in which the action is pending.

V

The conflict here is far from being a dry, abstractly legal dispute between jurisdictions or courts -- that is the least of it. Plaintiff has represented that in 1981 one in seven passengers flying between the United States and the United Kingdom was using low-fare Laker; today, by contrast, travellers using scheduled airlines must pay the fare set by the IATA. According to the complaint, this result was brought about because several of the most powerful airlines of the western world banded together to commit violations of the American antitrust laws, engaging in activities which had the effect of driving Laker out of business and of injuring American consumers, among others, by making it impossible for them to continue to benefit from low airfares over the North Atlantic route.

If the allegations of the complaint are true, but if United States courts are nevertheless prevented by the actions of a foreign tribunal from deciding these cases under American law, transatlantic airfares are likely to be kept artificially inflated by the alleged cartel on a permanent basis. Such a development would every year cost many thousands of American travellers hundreds of dollars each, and it would significantly injure American tourism and other businesses which depend upon or make substantial use of commercial air transport between the United States and Europe.

Now that lawsuits are pending which are designed to determine whether the charges of law violations have merit, the defendant airlines have taken steps which, whatever the intention, would have the effect of aborting these actions so that they could never be decided. Clearly, this Court has an obligation to see to it that the cases before it are disposed of in accordance with law, and it intends to discharge that obligation.

It is to be hoped that the court in Great Britain will ultimately decide that it has no basis for interjecting itself into ongoing foreign lawsuits, or that those who sought or have indicated their intention to seek an injunction in the British court will, upon reflection, proceed by way of normal litigation procedures here. In any event, for the reasons stated, should these injunction cases be required to go forward, it is likely that plaintiff will prevail on the merits of its request for a permanent injunction. See note 20 *supra*.

VI

What remains to be considered is the balance of injuries and the public interest.

It is clear that, if this Court does not issue an injunction to preclude the defendants from joining British Airways, British Caledonian, Swissair and Lufthansa in their actions in the British court, at least some of them, or more likely all of them, will do just that. KLM and

Sabena have acknowledged their desire to join the British suits; the American defendants disavow any present intention to sue in the British courts but state that they may wish to "participate" in the proceedings there. Given the advantages to antitrust defendants of having the merits of antitrust claims adjudicated in the United Kingdom rather than in the United States (see *infra*), there is a strong likelihood that all defendants would move in the British courts as soon as they would be legally free to do so.

Defendants argue that even if this forecast is accurate, plaintiff would still not be injured because the British court may decide that Britain is not the only proper forum for Laker's claims and may decline to issue a permanent injunction restraining the proceedings here. If the British court does proceed to the merits of the allegations, they continue, it may be expected to grant just relief, either under the United States antitrust laws or the British conspiracy laws. These predictions can only be characterized as a mirage.

It is quite clear that no British tribunal could or would proceed to enforce the Sherman Act. *15 U.S.C. § 15* lays venue only "in any district court of the United States." *Cf. General Investment Co. v. Lake Shore & Michigan Southern Ry. Co., 260 U.S. 261, 287, 67 L. Ed. 244, 43 S. Ct. 106 (1922)* (state court may not hear claim brought under antitrust laws; right to sue to be "exercised only in a 'court of the United States'"). The problems that would be involved in trying to prove American antitrust law for purposes of application by a foreign court are reason enough for a foreign court to decline to hear such a case.

Moreover, given the hostility of the British courts to the American antitrust laws, see *infra*, it would be wholly unrealistic to assume that a British court would enforce the Sherman Act even if it had legal power to do so.

Confining Laker to British law is equally inadequate. The House of Lords has ruled twice, once in 1891 and again in 1982, that under British law it is not unlawful for a corporation to monopolize commerce by offering exceptional terms resulting in losses so as to drive competitors out of business, with the expectation that the losses will be recouped later once the competitor has been eliminated. These decisions further hold that the crux of an unlawful conspiracy is an intent to injure the plaintiff, and that an agreement or combination which has as its purpose the protection of the interests of the defendants, whatever they may be, is not unlawful. See *Lonhro Ltd. v. Shell Petroleum Co. Ltd.*, [1982] A.C. 173, 189 (1981); *Mogul Steamship Co., Ltd. v. McGregor, Gow & Co.*, [1982] A.C. 25, 35-6, 40 (1891). In these critical respects, British law is thus totally different from American law, and it is plain that to relegate Laker to British law as applied by the British courts would only be to ensure that those courts would issue the declaration of non-liability that the airlines which are already before the Queen's Bench are presently seeking.

Such a result is quite consistent with the way in which British law, both parliamentary and judge-made, regards antitrust principles in general. The Protection of Trading Interests Act of 1980 directs British courts not to enforce treble damage awards against British firms, and this same act's "clawback" provision allows non-United States firms doing business in the United Kingdom to sue there to recover two-thirds of treble damage awards levied against them in the United States. British courts have long bemoaned what they regard as the wrongful extraterritorial reach of the American antitrust laws. See, *e.g., British Nylon Spinners Ltd v. Imperial Chemical Industries Ltd.*, [1953] 1 Ch. 19 (Court of Appeal, 1952).

In short, the situation is not that British law might be slightly less favorable to plaintiff than American law, and that therefore Laker cannot be deemed to be truly injured if it is left to its remedies in the British courts. See note 59 *infra*. Rather, it may be expected that, if this Court should fail to issue an injunction and thus allow those defendants which are still before this Court to join with their alleged coconspirators before the Queen's Bench Division, the British court may very well (1) enjoin Laker from pursuing its remedies against any of the defendants in this Court, and (2) enter a judgment on the merits that the defendants here (plaintiffs there) are not liable to Laker for the acts averred in the complaints. The Court finds that, for these reasons, plaintiff would be irreparably injured if the Court does not issue an injunction.

The defendants argue that they will suffer irreparable injury if an injunction is granted. Sabena states that if "forced to defend itself against Laker's claims in the United States, it will be exposed to the risk of enormous potential liability, the possible use of 'escalating settlement' tactics by the plaintiffs, substantial litigation expense, and a significant disruption of its affairs." Memorandum at 15. It observes that "all of these undesirable consequences can be avoided if the British courts determine that Laker may not lawfully pursue its claims against Sabena in the United States. None of them can be recouped if Sabena is prevented from obtaining such a ruling." KLM makes a similar argument.

A court of the United States can have little sympathy with such a position. If Sabena and KLM are concerned about the prospect of United States antitrust liability they should not do business here. On the other hand, if they feel strongly that they are immune from the antitrust laws for some reason, or that this Court should decline to exercise its subject matter jurisdiction in this case, they may legitimately be expected to follow the established American procedures and file appropriate motions to that effect. Their proper remedy is not to assume the existence of a "right" to go into the courts of a third country so as to circumvent American substantive and procedural law.

The irreparable injury claimed by the American defendants consists of their being prevented "from protecting their rights by participating, or even providing evidence, in the ongoing English proceedings whose outcome may well reflect on the American defendant's own potential liability, if any, under English law." This injury is purely speculative at this point. Moreover, as noted *infra* (note 63), the Court will entertain a proposal by the American defendants to modify the order.

For the foregoing reasons, the Court finds that the injury to Laker from a denial of the injunction far outweighs the injury to defendants resulting from its issuance. Considerations of the public interest also favor the plaintiff. Laker alleges that numerous American consumers were injured by the defendants' predatory acts that led to its demise and with it the alternative of low-cost, no frills transatlantic air service. The public interest clearly favors a full airing of these claims in the manner envisioned by the Sherman Act.

VII

The Court exceedingly regrets that it must issue an injunction in this case. However, it is worth emphasizing that this Court had no part in precipitating the current dispute. The lawsuit pending before it was proceeding in its normal course, when the British court, without appropriate regard to principles of comity, proceeded to interfere with that action. At that juncture, this Court's options were severely limited. It could either issue its own injunction to prevent at least the remaining defendants -- those from the United States and some of those from the European continent -- from seeking shelter from United States law in a British court, or it could acquiesce in silence in the effort to have a foreign tribunal decide on this Court's jurisdiction and to see the plaintiff's Sherman Act rights dissipated. With regret, the Court has no choice but to follow the former course.

For the reasons stated, a preliminary injunction was issued restraining the defendants from taking any action in a foreign forum that would impair or interfere with the jurisdiction of this Court in these cases or the freedom of plaintiff to prosecute these actions.

LAKER AIRWAYS LIMITED v. PAN AMERICAN WORLD AIRWAYS.

UNITED STATES DISTRICT COURT FOR THE SOUTHERN DISTRICT OF NEW YORK

607 F. Supp. 324

March, 1985

By separate motions argued together and fully submitted on March 12, 1985, Midland Bank plc ("Midland") and Samuel Montagu & Co. Ltd. ("Montagu") moved for orders pursuant to *Rule 45(b), F.R.Civ.P.* quashing deposition subpoenas *duces tecum*, which were served respectively in this district on the Midland Bank's New York branch office, and upon Montagu's New York Representative Office, or agency, also in this district, by plaintiff.

The subpoenas seek information and documents from movant non-party witnesses in the above entitled action, which is now pending in the United States District Court for the District of Columbia, under docket number 82-3362.

We describe briefly the underlying action. It is a private civil action seeking treble damages for federal antitrust violations alleged to have resulted in injury to Laker Airways Limited ("Laker") at one time a well-known British passenger airline of which Sir Freddie Laker was the founder and chief executive officer. On February 5, 1982, Laker ceased doing business due to insolvency, and on February 17, 1982 an individual residing in the United Kingdom was appointed Liquidator.

The action filed November 24, 1982 and thereafter consolidated with companion cases thereafter filed, alleges that plaintiff, described as a "foreign corporation in liquidation," exists under the laws of the Island of Jersey in the Channel Islands having its principal office in London, England. Plaintiff is represented to this Court to be insolvent allegedly as a result of the tortious and conspiratorial misconduct of various defendant American, British, Swiss, German, Dutch and Belgian airlines, the British Airways Board, an American aircraft manufacturer, and its finance subsidiary.

The thrust of the two-pronged complaint is, first, that "the airline defendants agreed to a predatory scheme to destroy Trans Atlantic Charters and Laker's scheduled Skytrain [passenger] service by offering, among other things, high cost service, at prices below the costs of those services." (Complaint para. 18). After alleging other wrongful competition, which need not concern us here, the complaint also alleged as a second factual basis, that "Laker realized in May of 1981 that it might be unable to meet its aircraft loan repayment requirements in January 1982 and explained the situation to its lenders." (Complaint para. 24). In para. 30, the Complaint alleges that "by Christmas Eve 1981 Laker was advised that all of the lenders had agreed to provide the necessary finance" to reschedule Laker's debts. It is then alleged that certain named airline defendants "pressured Laker's lenders" to deny Laker the necessary finance so as to force Laker out of business, that the lender defendants continued to mislead Laker into

419

believing that the financing was being provided as agreed, that Laker relied on this misrepresentation to its detriment and did not seek other sources of financing.

The non-party witnesses Midland and Montagu are not sued in the District of Columbia at this time. Implicit, however, is the suggestion that they are among the "lenders" believed by plaintiff to have colluded with Laker's competitors to deny financing to Laker.

Movants have not been sued because a court in the United Kingdom enjoined such action by the Laker Liquidator, a person subject to its jurisdiction. A motion is pending to vacate that injunction in light of a decision subsequently rendered by the House of Lords in a related case, *British Airways v. Laker Airways*, decided July 19, 1984, 3 W.L.R. 416. It is highly likely that the injunction will be vacated in the due course of time, and thereafter movants will be named as additional parties defendant in the District Court of the District of Columbia. *See generally Laker Airways v. Sabena, Belgian World Airlines, 235 U.S. App. D.C. 207, 731 F.2d 909 (D.C. Cir. 1984)*. At present they are no more than non-party witnesses, entitled to have their pending motion adjudicated in accordance with the present state of the litigation. Should either or both movants become parties defendant in the future, then any necessary pre-trial discovery may be obtained directly through the exercise of the powers of the district court in which the above entitled action is pending.

These subpoenas presently before this Court are extremely broad and burdensome as drafted. Although apparently intended only to elicit evidence for purposes of trial to demonstrate such pressuring or collusion with regard to Midland and Montagu in their capacity as potential lenders to Laker, the demands extend as well to all papers relating to Sir Freddie Laker personally. A Midland subsidiary has provided banking services to Sir Freddie Laker for, we are told, in excess of 30 years, generating a lot of paper. Midland, for its part, and Montagu deny that they were pressured, and attribute the failure to make the loan to the continuous deterioration of the airline industry generally, and Laker in particular in the latter part of 1981.

This Court concludes that the subpoenas must be vacated for a number of reasons. Foremost among them is the fact that all of Midland's activities in connection with this matter took place solely in the United Kingdom, and Midland's New York branch office had no involvement whatsoever with Laker. This point is not disputed at the hearing. The fact is that the New York branch of Midland did not open until April 1983, long after the alleged antitrust violations sued on in the District of Columbia. Similarly Montagu does not have a branch office in this District; it has a "representative office" which conducts no banking operations in New York. Here again there are no files or documents in the New York Representative Office of Montagu concerning Laker and no person at that office has any knowledge of the matters concerning Laker. That office also was not opened in New York until long after the events complained of by Laker in the District of Columbia action. Essentially then the deposition subpoenas *duces tecum* seek to require Midland and Montagu, by officers having custody in the United Kingdom to produce in New York for use in the District of Columbia litigation, documents and records regularly maintained at their home offices in London. This is inappropriate. *See generally Ings v. Ferguson, 282 F.2d 149 (2d Cir. 1960)*; *First

National City Bank of New York v. Internal Revenue Service, 271 F.2d 616 (2d Cir. 1959); *Cates v. LTV Aerospace Corp., 480 F.2d 620 (5th Cir. 1973)*; and *Elder-Beerman Stores Corp. v. Federated Dept. Stores, Inc., 45 F.R.D. 515 (S.D.N.Y. 1968)* (by then District Judge Mansfield), which continue to reflect the law applicable to non-parties.

As a second reason to vacate, this Court finds that the service of the subpoenas in New York is a transparent attempt to circumvent the Hague Convention on the Taking of Evidence Abroad in Civil or Commercial Matters, codified at *28 U.S.C. § 1871* (hereinafter the "Hague Convention"), which sets forth agreed international procedures for seeking evidence in this Court from non-parties abroad.

The failure to use the Hague Convention is more than a mere technicality. The extraterritorial jurisdiction asserted over foreign interests by the American antitrust laws has long been a sore point with many foreign governments, including that of the United Kingdom. The English Protection of Trading Interests Act of 1980. ("PTIA") authorizes and empowers the Secretary of State for Trade and Industry to interpose the official power of the British Government so as to prevent persons conducting business in the United Kingdom from complying with foreign judicial or regulatory provisions designated by the Secretary of State as intrusive upon the sovereignty of that nation.

With respect to the District of Columbia *Laker* action, the Secretary has already issued one directive that "no person or persons in the United Kingdom shall comply, or cause or permit compliance, whether by themselves, their officers, servants or agents, with any requirement to produce or furnish to the district court any commercial document in the United Kingdom or any commercial information . . . ." That the entire *Laker* litigation situation is a matter of sensitive international interest also is emphasized by the determination of the Department of Justice of the United States, announced November 20, 1984 to refrain from initiating civil or criminal antitrust action with respect to the refinancing aspect of the collapse of Laker, and the publicly announced determination on November 19, 1984 by the President that the grand jury investigating Laker antitrust violations in the District of Columbia since June 1983 should terminate its inquiry for "foreign policy reasons."

Implicit in the concerns expressed by the British Government is the notion that the British bureaucracy had the power to consider and investigate all tariffs on international routes flying in and out of the United Kingdom with respect to which the predatory pricing was allegedly conducted, with the power to disapprove such fares, but did not exercise its power, accordingly the allegations against "predatory pricing" in the American antitrust suit brought by Laker, challenge indirectly the validity and indeed the honesty of decisions of the British Government with respect to tariff decisions made in exercise of the sovereignty of the British Government. The power of the British Government to regulate such matters, presumably in the interests of its own nationals, is clearly recognized by international treaty and agreements. The validity of the antitrust claims being made in the District of Columbia are of course of no direct concern to this Court. However, the very real problems presented by the PTIA are cited to demonstrate that the attempt to effect the subpoena duces tecum in this District is in effect an end run, not only around the Hague Convention, but also an end run on the PTIA. In effect, this Court is being asked to

421

aid the plaintiff in the District of Columbia in obtaining an order from this Court which would cause the Midland branch in New York and the Montagu agency to compel their principals in London to violate British law by disgorging in London and transferring to their New York offices, documents which plaintiff would like to see, none of which are now or ever were located in New York. This is clearly an improper abuse of the subpoena power of this Court, and should not be permitted.

In reaching the foregoing conclusion we need not consider whether the Hague Convention is always the exclusive method of discovery against a non-party, nor do we consider the case where the discovery is sought from a party plaintiff, *cf. Coface v. Phillips Petroleum Co.*, 81 Civ. 4463-JFK (S.D.N.Y. December 11, 1984), or even from a defendant.

Both motions are granted, and the subpoenas are each vacated. No costs.

So Ordered.

AIR FRANCE v. SAKS

SUPREME COURT OF THE UNITED STATES

470 U.S. 392

March, 1995

JUSTICE O'CONNOR delivered the opinion of the Court.

Article 17 of the Warsaw Convention makes air carriers liable for injuries sustained by a passenger "if the accident which caused the damage so sustained took place on board the aircraft or in the course of any of the operations of embarking or disembarking." We granted certiorari, *469 U.S. 815 (1984)*, to resolve a conflict among the Courts of Appeals as to the proper definition of the word "accident" as used in this international air carriage treaty.

I

On November 16, 1980, respondent Valerie Saks boarded an Air France jetliner in Paris for a 12-hour flight to Los Angeles. The flight went smoothly in all respects until, as the aircraft descended to Los Angeles, Saks felt severe pressure and pain in her left ear. The pain continued after the plane landed, but Saks disembarked without informing any Air France crew member or employee of her ailment. Five days later, Saks consulted a doctor who concluded that she had become permanently deaf in her left ear.

Saks filed suit against Air France in California state court, alleging that her hearing loss was caused by negligent maintenance and operation of the jetliner's pressurization system. App. 2. The case was removed to the United States District Court for the Central District of California. After extensive discovery, Air France moved for summary judgment on the ground that respondent could not prove that her injury was caused by an "accident" within the meaning of the Warsaw Convention. The term "accident," according to Air France, means an "abnormal, unusual or unexpected occurrence aboard the aircraft." *Id.,* at 9. All the available evidence, including the postflight reports, pilot's affidavit, and passenger testimony, indicated that the aircraft's pressurization system had operated in the usual manner. Accordingly, the airline contended that the suit should be dismissed because the only alleged cause of respondent's injury -- normal operation of a pressurization system -- could not qualify as an "accident." In her opposition to the summary judgment motion, Saks acknowledged that "[the] sole question of law presented . . . by the parties is whether a loss of hearing proximately caused by normal operation of the aircraft's pressurization system is an 'accident' within the meaning of Article 17 of the Warsaw Convention . . . ." *Id.,* at 30. She argued that "accident" should be defined as a "hazard of air travel," and that her injury had indeed been caused by such a hazard.

Relying on precedent which defines the term "accident" in Article 17 as an "unusual or unexpected" happening, see *DeMarines v. KLM Royal Dutch Airlines, 580 F.2d 1193, 1196 (CA3 1978)*, the District

Court granted summary judgment to Air France. See also *Warshaw v. Trans World Airlines, Inc., 442 F.Supp. 400, 412-413 (ED Pa. 1977)* (normal cabin pressure changes are not "accidents" within the meaning of Article 17). A divided panel of the Court of Appeals for the Ninth Circuit reversed. *724 F.2d 1383 (1984)*. The appellate court reviewed the history of the Warsaw Convention and its modification by the 1966 Montreal Agreement, a private agreement among airlines that has been approved by the United States Government. Agreement Relating to Liability Limitations of the Warsaw Convention and the Hague Protocol, Agreement CAB 18900, *31 Fed. Reg. 7302 (1966)*, note following 49 U. S. C. App. § 1502. The court concluded that the language, history, and policy of the Warsaw Convention and the Montreal Agreement impose absolute liability on airlines for injuries proximately caused by the risks inherent in air travel. The court found a definition of "accident" consistent with this history and policy in Annex 13 to the Convention on International Civil Aviation, Dec. 7, 1944, 61 Stat. 1180, T. I. A. S. No. 1591, 15 U. N. T. S. 295; conformed to in *49 CFR § 830.2 (1984)*: "an occurrence associated with the operation of an aircraft which takes place between the time any person boards the aircraft with the intention of flight and all such persons have disembarked . . . ." *724 F.2d, at 1385*. Normal cabin pressure changes qualify as an "accident" under this definition. A dissent agreed with the District Court that "accident" should be defined as an unusual or unexpected occurrence. *Id., at 1388* (Wallace, J.). We disagree with the definition of "accident" adopted by the Court of Appeals, and we reverse.

II

Air France is liable to a passenger under the terms of the Warsaw Convention only if the passenger proves that an "accident" was the cause of her injury. *MacDonald v. Air Canada, 439 F.2d 1402 (CA1 1971);Mathias v. Pan Am World Airways, Inc., 53 F.R.D. 447 (WD Pa. 1971)*. See 1 C. Shawcross & K. Beaumont, Air Law para. VII(147) (4th ed. 1984); D. Goedhuis, National Airlegislations and the Warsaw Convention 199 (1937). The narrow issue presented is whether respondent can meet this burden by showing that her injury was caused by the normal operation of the aircraft's pressurization system. The proper answer turns on interpretation of a clause in an international treaty to which the United States is a party. "[Treaties] are construed more liberally than private agreements, and to ascertain their meaning we may look beyond the written words to the history of the treaty, the negotiations, and the practical construction adopted by the parties." *Choctaw Nation of Indians v. United States, 318 U.S. 423, 431-432 (1943)*. The analysis must begin, however, with the text of the treaty and the context in which the written words are used. See *Maximov v. United States, 373 U.S. 49, 53-54 (1963)*.

A

Article 17 of the Warsaw Convention establishes the liability of international air carriers for harm to passengers. Article 18 contains parallel provisions regarding liability for damage to baggage. The governing text of the Convention is in the French language, and we accordingly set forth the French text of the relevant part of Articles 17 and 18 in the margin. The official American translation of this portion of the text, which was before the Senate when it ratified the Convention in 1934, reads as follows:

"Article 17

"The carrier shall be liable for damage sustained in the event of the death or wounding of a passenger or any other bodily injury suffered by a passenger, *if the accident which caused the damage* so sustained took place on board the aircraft or in the course of any of the operations of embarking or disembarking.

"Article 18

"(1) The carrier shall be liable for damage sustained in the event of the destruction or loss of, or of damage to, any checked baggage or any goods, *if the occurrence which caused the damage* so sustained took place during the transportation by air." 49 Stat. 3018-3019.

Two significant features of these provisions stand out in both the French and the English texts. First, Article 17 imposes liability for injuries to passengers caused by an "accident," whereas Article 18 imposes liability for destruction or loss of baggage caused by an "occurrence." This difference in the parallel language of Articles 17 and 18 implies that the drafters of the Convention understood the word "accident" to mean something different than the word "occurrence," for they otherwise logically would have used the same word in each article. See Goedhuis, *supra*, at 200-201; M. Milde, The Problems of Liabilities in International Carriage by Air 62 (Caroline Univ. 1963). The language of the Convention accordingly renders suspect the opinion of the Court of Appeals that "accident" means "occurrence."

Second, the text of Article 17 refers to an accident *which caused* the passenger's injury, and not to an accident which *is* the passenger's injury. In light of the many senses in which the word "accident" can be used, this distinction is significant. As Lord Lindley observed in 1903:

"The word 'accident' is not a technical legal term with a clearly defined meaning. Speaking generally, but with reference to legal liabilities, an accident means any unintended and unexpected occurrence which produces hurt or loss. But it is often used to denote any unintended and unexpected loss or hurt apart from its cause; and if the cause is not known the loss or hurt itself would certainly be called an accident. The word 'accident' is also often used to denote both the cause and the effect, no attempt being made to discriminate between them." *Fenton* v. *J. Thorley & Co.*, [1903] A. C. 443, 453.

In Article 17, the drafters of the Warsaw Convention apparently did make an attempt to discriminate between "the cause and the effect"; they specified that air carriers would be liable if an accident *caused* the passenger's injury. The text of the Convention thus implies that, however we define "accident," it is the *cause* of the injury that must satisfy the definition rather than the occurrence of the injury alone. American jurisprudence has long recognized this distinction between an accident that is the *cause* of an injury and an injury that is itself an accident. See *Landress v. Phoenix Mutual Life Ins. Co., 291 U.S. 491 (1934)*.

While the text of the Convention gives these two clues to the meaning of "accident," it does not define the term. Nor is the context in which the term is used illuminating. See Note, Warsaw Convention -- Air Carrier Liability for Passenger Injuries Sustained Within a Terminal, 45 Ford. L. Rev. 369, 388 (1976) ("The language of Article 17 is stark and undefined"). To determine the meaning of the term "accident" in Article 17 we must consider its French legal meaning. See *Reed v. Wiser, 555 F.2d 1079* (CA2), cert. denied, *434 U.S. 922 (1977)*; *Block v. Compagnie Nationale Air France, 386 F.2d 323 (CA5 1967)*, cert. denied, *392 U.S. 905 (1968)*. This is true not because "we are forever chained to French law" by the Convention, see *Rosman v. Trans World Airlines, Inc., 34 N. Y. 2d 385, 394, 314 N. E. 2d 848, 853 (1974)*, but because it is our responsibility to give the specific words of the treaty a meaning consistent with the shared expectations of the contracting parties. *Reed, supra, at 1090*; *Day v. Trans World Airlines, Inc., 528 F.2d 31 (CA2 1975)*, cert. denied, *429 U.S. 890 (1976)*. We look to the French legal meaning for guidance as to these expectations because the Warsaw Convention was drafted in French by continental jurists. See Lowenfeld & Mendelsohn, The United States and the Warsaw Convention, 80 Harv. L. Rev. 497, 498-500 (1967).

A survey of French cases and dictionaries indicates that the French legal meaning of the term "accident" differs little from the meaning of the term in Great Britain, Germany, or the United States. Thus, while the word "accident" is often used to refer to the *event* of a person's injury, it is also sometimes used to describe a *cause* of injury, and when the word is used in this latter sense, it is usually defined as a fortuitous, unexpected, unusual, or unintended event. See 1 Grand Larousse de La Langue Francaise 29 (1971) (defining "accident" as "Evenement fortuit et facheux, causant des dommages corporels ou materiels"); *Air France v. Haddad, Judgment of June 19, 1979*, Cour d'appel de Paris, Premiere Chambre Civile, 1979 Revue Francaise de Droit Aerien 327, 328, appeal rejected, *Judgment of February 16, 1982*, Cour de Cassation, 1982 Bull. Civ. I 63. This parallels British and American jurisprudence. See *Fenton* v. *J. Thorley & Co., supra*; *Landress v. Phoenix Mutual Life Ins. Co., supra*; *Koehring Co.* v. *American Automobile Ins. Co., 353 F.2d 993 (CA7 1965)*. The text of the Convention consequently suggests that the passenger's injury must be caused by an unexpected or unusual event.

B

This interpretation of Article 17 is consistent with the negotiating history of the Convention, the conduct of the parties to the Convention, and the weight of precedent in foreign and American courts. In interpreting a treaty it is proper, of course, to refer to the records of its drafting and negotiation. *Choctaw Nation of Indians v. United States, 318 U.S., at 431*. In part because the "travaux preparatoires" of the Warsaw Convention are published and generally available to litigants, courts frequently refer to these materials to resolve ambiguities in the text. See *Trans World Airlines, Inc.* v. *Franklin Mint Corp., 466 U.S. 243, 259 (1984)*; *Maugnie v. Companie Nationale Air France, 549 F.2d 1256 (CA9 1977)*; *Fothergill* v. *Monarch Airlines, Ltd.*, [1980] 2 All E. R. 696 (H. L.).

The treaty that became the Warsaw Convention was first drafted at an international conference in Paris in 1925. The protocol resulting from the Paris Conference contained an article specifying: "The carrier is liable for accidents, losses, breakdowns, and delays. It is not liable if it can prove that it has taken reasonable measures designed to pre-empt damage . . . ." The protocol drafted at Paris was revised several times by a committee of experts on air law, and then submitted to a second international conference that convened in Warsaw in 1929. The draft submitted to the conference stated:

"The carrier shall be liable for damage sustained during carriage:

"(a) in the case of death, wounding, or any other bodily injury suffered by a traveler;

"(b) in the case of destruction, loss, or damage to goods or baggage;

"(c) in the case of delay suffered by a traveler, goods, or baggage." International Conference on Air Law Affecting Air Questions, Minutes, Second International Conference on Private Aeronautical Law, October 4-12, 1929, Warsaw 264-265 (R. Horner & D. Legrez trans. 1975).

Article 22 of this draft, like the original Paris draft, permitted the carrier to avoid liability by proving it had taken reasonable measures to avoid the damage. *Id., at 265*. None of the early drafts required that an accident *cause* the passenger's injury.

At Warsaw, delegates from several nations objected to the application of identical liability rules to both passenger injuries and damage to baggage, and the German delegation proposed separate liability rules for passengers and baggage. *Id., at 36*. The need for separate rules arose primarily because delegates thought that liability for baggage should commence upon delivery to the carrier, whereas liability for passengers should commence when the passengers later embark upon the aircraft. *Id., at 72-74* (statements of French, Swiss, and Italian delegates). The Reporter on the Preliminary Draft of the Convention argued it would be too difficult to draft language specifying this distinction, and that such a distinction would be unnecessary because "Article 22 establishes a very mitigated system of liability for the carrier, and from the moment that the carrier has taken the reasonable measures, he does not answer for the risks, nor for the accidents [occurring] to people by the fault of third parties, nor for accidents [occurring] for any other cause." *Id., at 77-78* (statement of Reporter De Vos). The delegates were unpersuaded, and a majority voted to have a drafting committee rework the liability provisions for passengers and baggage. *Id., at 83*.

A few days later, the drafting committee proposed the liability provisions that became Articles 17 and 18 of the Convention. Article 20(1) of the final draft contains the "necessary measures" language which the Reporter believed would shield the carrier from liability for "the accidents [occurring] to people by the fault of third parties" and for "accidents [occurring] for any other cause." Nevertheless, the redrafted Article 17 also required as a prerequisite to liability that an accident *cause* the passenger's injury, whereas the redrafted Article 18 required only that an occurrence cause the damage to baggage. Although Article 17 and Article 18 as redrafted were approved with little discussion, the President of the drafting committee observed that "given that there are *entirely different* liability cases: death or wounding, disappearance of goods, delay, we have deemed that it would be better to begin by setting out *the causes* of liability for persons, then for goods and baggage, and finally liability in the case of delay." *Id.*, at 205 (statement of Delegate Giannini) (emphasis added). This comment at least implies that the addition of language of causation to Articles 17 and 18 had a broader purpose than specification of the time at which liability commenced. It further suggests that the causes of liability for persons were intended to be different from the causes of liability for baggage. The records of the negotiation of the Convention accordingly support what is evident from its text: A passenger's injury must be caused by an accident, and an accident must mean something different than an "occurrence" on the plane. Like the text of the Convention, however, the records of its negotiation offer no precise definition of "accident."

Reference to the conduct of the parties to the Convention and the subsequent interpretations of the signatories helps clarify the meaning of the term. At a Guatemala City International Conference on Air Law in 1971, representatives of many of the Warsaw signatories approved an amendment to Article 17 which would impose liability on the carrier for an "event which caused the death or injury" rather than for an "accident which caused" the passenger's injury, but would exempt the carrier from liability if the death or injury resulted "solely from the state of health of the passenger." International Civil Aviation Organization, 2 Documents of the International Conference on Air Law, Guatemala City, ICAO Doc. 9040-LC/167-2, p. 189 (1972). The Guatemala City Protocol of 1971 and the Montreal Protocols Nos. 3 and 4 of 1975 include this amendment, see S. Exec. Rep. No. 98-1 (1983), but have yet to be ratified by the Senate, and therefore do not govern the disposition of this case. The statements of the delegates at Guatemala City indicate that they viewed the switch from "accident" to "event" as expanding the scope of carrier liability to passengers. The Swedish Delegate, for example, in referring to the choice between the words "accident" and "event," emphasized that the word "accident" is too narrow because a carrier might be found liable for "other acts which could not be considered as accidents." See International Civil Aviation Organization, 1 Minutes of the International Conference on Air Law, ICAO Doc. 9040-LC/167-1, p. 34 (1972). See also Mankiewicz, Warsaw Convention: The 1971 Protocol of Guatemala City, 20 Am. J. Comp. L. 335, 337 (1972) (noting that changes in Article 17 were intended to establish "strict liability").

In determining precisely what causes can be considered accidents, we "find the opinions of our sister signatories to be entitled to considerable weight." *Benjamins v. British European Airways, 572 F.2d 913, 919 (CA2 1978)*, cert. denied, *439 U.S. 1114 (1979)*. While few decisions are precisely on point, we note that, in *Air France* v. *Haddad, Judgment of June 19, 1979*, Cour d'appel de Paris, Premiere Chambre Civile, 1979 Revue Francaise de Droit Aerien, at 328, a French court observed that the term "accident" in Article 17 of the Warsaw Convention embraces causes of injuries that are fortuitous or unpredictable. European legal scholars have generally construed the word "accident" in Article 17 to require that the passenger's injury be caused by a sudden or unexpected event other than the normal operation of the plane. See, *e. g.*, O. Riese & J. Lacour, Precis de Droit Aerien 264 (1951) (noting that Swiss and German law require that the damage be caused by an accident, and arguing that an accident should be construed as an event which is sudden and independent of the will of the carrier); 1 C. Shawcross & K. Beaumont, Air Law para. VII(148) (4th ed. 1984) (noting that the Court of Appeals for the Third Circuit's definition of accident accords with some English definitions and "might well commend itself to an English court"). These observations are in accord with American decisions which, while interpreting the term "accident" broadly, *Maugnie v. Compagnie Nationale Air France, 549 F.2d, at 1259,* nevertheless refuse to extend the term to cover routine travel procedures that produce an injury due to the peculiar internal condition of a passenger. See, *e. g., Abramson v. Japan Airlines Co., 739 F.2d 130 (CA3 1984)* (sitting in airline seat during normal flight which aggravated hernia not an "accident"), cert. pending, No. 84-939; *MacDonald v. Air Canada, 439 F.2d 1402 (CA5 1971)* (fainting while waiting in the terminal for one's baggage not shown to be caused by an "accident"); *Scherer v. Pan American World Airways, Inc., 54 App. Div. 2d 636, 387 N. Y. S. 2d 580 (1976)* (sitting in airline seat during normal flight which aggravated thrombophlebitis not an "accident").

III

We conclude that liability under Article 17 of the Warsaw Convention arises only if a passenger's injury is caused by an unexpected or unusual event or happening that is external to the passenger. This definition should be flexibly applied after assessment of all the circumstances surrounding a passenger's injuries. *Maugnie, supra, at 1262.* For example, lower courts in this country have interpreted Article 17 broadly enough to encompass torts committed by terrorists or fellow passengers. See *Evangelinos v. Trans World Airlines, Inc., 550 F.2d 152 (CA3 1977)* (en banc) (terrorist attack); *Day v. Trans World Airlines, Inc., 528 F.2d 31 (CA2 1975)* (en banc) (same), cert. denied, *429 U.S. 890 (1976)*; *Krystal v. British Overseas Airways Corp., 403 F.Supp. 1322 (CD Cal. 1975)* (hijacking); *Oliver v. Scandinavian Airlines System,* 17 CCH Av. Cas. 18,283 (Md. 1983) (drunken passenger falls and injures fellow passenger). In cases where there is contradictory evidence, it is for the trier of fact to decide whether an "accident" as here defined caused the passenger's injury. See *DeMarines v. KLM Royal Dutch Airlines, 580 F.2d 1193 (CA3 1978)* (contradictory evidence on whether pressurization was normal). See also *Weintraub v. Capitol International Airways, Inc.,* 16 CCH Av. Cas. 18,058 (N. Y. Sup. Ct., 1st Dept., 1981) (plaintiff's testimony that "sudden dive" led to pressure change causing hearing loss indicates injury was caused by an "accident"). But when the injury indisputably results from the passenger's own internal reaction to the usual, normal, and expected operation of the aircraft, it has not been caused by an accident, and Article 17 of the Warsaw Convention cannot apply. The judgment of the Court of Appeals in this case must accordingly be reversed.

We recognize that any standard requiring courts to distinguish causes that are "accidents" from causes that are "occurrences " requires drawing a line, and we realize that "reasonable [people] may differ widely as to the place where the line should fall." *Schlesinger v. Wisconsin, 270 U.S. 230, 241 (1926)* (Holmes, J., dissenting). We draw this line today only because the language of Articles 17 and 18 requires it, and not because of any desire to plunge into the "Serbonian bog" that accompanies attempts to distinguish between causes that are accidents and injuries that are accidents. See *Landress v. Phoenix Mutual Life Ins. Co., 291 U.S., at 499* (Cardozo, J., dissenting). Any injury is the product of a chain of causes, and we require only that the passenger be able to prove that some link in the chain was an unusual or unexpected event external to the passenger. Until Article 17 of the Warsaw Convention is changed by the signatories, it cannot be stretched to impose carrier liability for injuries that are not caused by accidents. It remains "[our] duty . . . to enforce the . . . treaties of the United States, whatever they might be, and . . . the Warsaw Convention remains the supreme law of the land." *Reed, 555 F.2d, at 1093.*

Our duty to enforce the "accident" requirement of Article 17 cannot be circumvented by reference to the Montreal Agreement of 1966. It is true that in most American cases the Montreal Agreement expands carrier liability by requiring airlines to waive their right under Article 20(1) of the Warsaw Convention to defend claims on the grounds that they took all necessary measures to avoid the passenger's injury or that it was impossible to take such measures. Because these "due care" defenses are waived by the Montreal Agreement, the Court of Appeals and some commentators have characterized the Agreement as imposing "absolute" liability on air carriers. See Lowenfeld & Mendelsohn, 80 Harv. L. Rev., at 599. As this case demonstrates, the characterization is not entirely accurate. It is true that one purpose of the Montreal Agreement was to speed settlement and facilitate passenger recovery, but the parties to the Montreal Agreement promoted that purpose by specific provision for waiver of the Article 20(1) defenses. They did not waive other provisions in the Convention that operate to qualify liability, such as the contributory negligence defense of Article 21 or the "accident" requirement of Article 17. See *Warshaw, 442 F.Supp., at 408.* Under the Warsaw Convention as modified by the Montreal Agreement, liability can accordingly be viewed as "absolute" only in the sense that an airline cannot defend a claim on the ground that it took all necessary measures to avoid the injury. The "accident" requirement of Article 17 is distinct from the defenses in Article 20(1), both because it is located in a separate article and because it involves an inquiry into the nature of the event which *caused* the injury rather than the care taken by the airline to avert the injury. While these inquiries may on occasion be similar, we decline to employ that similarity to repeal a treaty provision that the Montreal Agreement on its face left unaltered.

Nor can we escape our duty to enforce Article 17 by reference to the equation of "accident" with "occurrence" in Annex 13 to the Convention on International Civil Aviation. The definition in Annex 13 and the corresponding Convention expressly apply to aircraft accident *investigations*, and not to principles of liability to passengers under the Warsaw Convention. See B. Cheng, The Law of International Air Transport 106-165 (1962).

Finally, respondent suggests an independent ground supporting the Court of Appeals' reversal of the summary judgment against her. She argues that her original complaint alleged a state cause of action for negligence independent of the liability provisions of the Warsaw Convention, and that her state negligence action can go forward if the Warsaw liability rules do not apply. Expressing no view on the merits of this contention, we note that it is unclear from the record whether the issue was raised in the Court of Appeals. We leave the disposition of this claim to the Court of Appeals in the first instance. See *Hoover v. Ronwin, 466 U.S. 558, 574, n. 25 (1984).*

The judgment of the Court of Appeals is reversed, and the case is remanded for further proceedings consistent with this opinion.

It is so ordered.

EL AL ISRAEL AIRLINES, LTD. v. TSUI YUAN TSENG

SUPREME COURT OF THE UNITED STATES

525 U.S. 155

January, 1999

Plaintiff-respondent Tsui Yuan Tseng was subjected to an intrusive security search at John F. Kennedy International Airport in New York before she boarded an El Al Israel Airlines May 22, 1993 flight to Tel Aviv. Tseng seeks tort damages from El Al for this occurrence. The episode-in-suit, both parties now submit, does not qualify as an "accident" within the meaning of the treaty popularly known as the Warsaw Convention, which governs air carrier liability for "all international transportation." Tseng alleges psychic or psychosomatic injuries, but no "bodily injury," as that term is used in the Convention. Her case presents a question of the Convention's exclusivity: When the Convention allows no recovery for the episode-in-suit, does it correspondingly preclude the passenger from maintaining an action for damages under another source of law, in this case, New York tort law?

The exclusivity question before us has been settled prospectively in a Warsaw Convention protocol (Montreal Protocol No. 4) recently ratified by the Senate. In accord with the protocol, Tseng concedes, a passenger whose injury is not compensable under the Convention (because it entails no "bodily injury" or was not the result of an "accident") will have no recourse to an alternate remedy. We conclude that the protocol, to which the United States has now subscribed, clarifies, but does not change, the Convention's exclusivity domain. We therefore hold that recovery for a personal injury suffered "on board [an] aircraft or in the course of any of the operations of embarking or disembarking," Art. 17, 49 Stat. 3018, if not allowed under the Convention, is not available at all.

The Court of Appeals for the Second Circuit ruled otherwise. In that court's view, a plaintiff who did not qualify for relief under the Convention could seek relief under local law for an injury sustained in the course of international air travel. *122 F.3d 99 (1997)*. We granted certiorari, *523 U.S. 1117 (1998)*, and now reverse the Second Circuit's judgment. Recourse to local law, we are persuaded, would undermine the uniform regulation of international air carrier liability that the Warsaw Convention was designed to foster.

I.

We have twice reserved decision on the Convention's exclusivity. In *Air France v. Saks, 470 U.S. 392, 84 L. Ed. 2d 289, 105 S. Ct. 1338 (1985)*, we concluded that a passenger's injury was not caused by an "accident" for which the airline could be held accountable under the Convention, but expressed no view whether that passenger could maintain "a state cause of action for negligence." *Id. at 408*. In *Eastern Airlines, Inc. v. Floyd, 499 U.S. 530, 113 L. Ed. 2d 569, 111 S. Ct. 1489 (1991)*, we held that mental or psychic injuries unaccompanied by physical injuries are not compensable under Article 17 of the

Convention, but declined to reach the question whether the Convention "provides the exclusive cause of action for injuries sustained during international air transportation." *Id., at 553.* We resolve in this case the question on which we earlier reserved judgment.

At the outset, we highlight key provisions of the treaty we are interpreting. Chapter I of the Warsaw Convention, entitled "SCOPE -- DEFINITIONS," declares in Article 1(1) that the "Convention shall apply to all international transportation of persons, baggage, or goods performed by aircraft for hire." 49 Stat. 3014. Chapter III, entitled "LIABILITY OF THE CARRIER," defines in Articles 17, 18, and 19 the three kinds of liability for which the Convention provides. Article 17 establishes the conditions of liability for personal injury to passengers:

"The carrier shall be liable for damage sustained in the event of the death or wounding of a passenger or any other bodily injury suffered by a passenger, if the accident which caused the damage so sustained took place on board the aircraft or in the course of any of the operations of embarking or disembarking." 49 Stat. 3018.

Article 18 establishes the conditions of liability for damage to baggage or goods. Id. at 3019. Article 19 establishes the conditions of liability for damage caused by delay. *Ibid.* Article 24, referring back to Articles 17, 18, and 19, instructs:

(1) In the cases covered by articles 18 and 19 any action for damages, however founded, can only be brought subject to the conditions and limits set out in this convention.

"(2) In the cases covered by article 17 the provisions of the preceding paragraph shall also apply, without prejudice to the questions as to who are the persons who have the right to bring suit and what are their respective rights." *Id.,* at 3020.

II

With the key treaty provisions as the backdrop, we next describe the episode-in-suit. On May 22, 1993, Tsui Yuan Tseng arrived at John F. Kennedy International Airport (hereinafter JFK) to board an El Al Israel Airlines flight to Tel Aviv. In conformity with standard El Al preboarding procedures, a security guard questioned Tseng about her destination and travel plans. The guard considered Tseng's responses "illogical," and ranked her as a "high risk" passenger. Tseng was taken to a private security room where her baggage and person were searched for explosives and detonating devices. She was told to remove her shoes, jacket, and sweater, and to lower her blue jeans to midhip. A female security guard then searched Tseng's body outside her clothes by hand and with an electronic security wand.

After the search, which lasted 15 minutes, El Al personnel decided that Tseng did not pose a security threat and allowed her to board the flight. Tseng later testified that she "was really sick and very upset" during the flight, that she was "emotionally traumatized and disturbed" during her month-long trip in Israel, and that, upon her return, she underwent medical and psychiatric treatment for the lingering effects of the body search. *122 F.3d 99, 101 (CA2 1997)* (internal quotation marks omitted).

Tseng filed suit against El Al in 1994 in a New York state court of first instance. Her complaint alleged a state law personal injury claim based on the May 22, 1993 episode at JFK. Tseng's pleading charged, *inter alia*, assault and false imprisonment, but alleged no bodily injury. El Al removed the case to federal court.

The District Court, after a bench trial, dismissed Tseng's personal injury claim. See *919 F. Supp. 155 (SDNY 1996)*. That claim, the court concluded, was governed by Article 17 of the Warsaw Convention, which creates a cause of action for personal injuries suffered as a result of an "accident . . . in the course of any of the operations of embarking or disembarking," 49 Stat. 3018. See *919 F. Supp. at 157-158*. Tseng's claim was not compensable under Article 17, the District Court stated, because Tseng "sustained no bodily injury" as a result of the search, *id., at 158*, and the Convention does not permit "recovery for psychic or psychosomatic injury unaccompanied by bodily injury," *ibid.* (citing *Floyd, 499 U.S. at 552*). The District Court further concluded that Tseng could not pursue her claim, alternately, under New York tort law; as that court read the Convention, Article 24 shields the carrier from liability for personal injuries not compensable under Article 17. See *919 F. Supp. at 158*.

The Court of Appeals reversed in relevant part. See *122 F.3d 99 (CA2 1997)*. The Second Circuit concluded first that no "accident" within Article 17's compass had occurred; in the Court of Appeals' view, the Convention drafters did not "aim to impose close to absolute liability" for an individual's "personal reaction" to "routine operating procedures," measures that, although "inconvenient and embarrassing," are the "price passengers pay for . . . airline safety." *Id., at 103-104*. An "accident" under Article 17 is "an unexpected or unusual event or happening that is external to the passenger." *Saks, 470 U.S. at 405*. That definition, we have cautioned, should "be flexibly applied after assessment of all the circumstances surrounding a passenger's injuries." In some tension with that reasoning, the Second Circuit next concluded that the Convention does not shield the very same "routine operating procedures" from assessment under the diverse laws of signatory nations (and, in the case of the United States, States within one Nation) governing assault and false imprisonment. See *id., at 104*.

Article 24 of the Convention, the Court of Appeals said, "clearly states that resort to local law is precluded only where the incident is 'covered' by Article 17, meaning where there has been an accident, either on the plane or in the course of embarking or disembarking, which led to death, wounding or other bodily injury." *Id., at 104-105*. The court found support in the drafting history of the Convention, which it construed to "indicate that national law was intended to provide the passenger's remedy where the Convention did not expressly apply." *Id., at 105*. The Second Circuit also rejected the argument that allowance of state-law claims when the Convention does not permit recovery would contravene the treaty's goal of uniformity. The court read our decision in *Zicherman v. Korean Air Lines Co., 516 U.S. 217, 133 L. Ed. 2d 596, 116 S. Ct. 629 (1996)*, to "instruct specifically that the Convention expresses no compelling interest in uniformity that would warrant . . . supplanting an otherwise applicable body of law." *122 F.3d at 107*.

III

We accept it as given that El Al's search of Tseng was not an "accident" within the meaning of Article 17, for the parties do not place that Court of Appeals conclusion at issue. See *supra*, at 7, n. 9. We also accept, again only for purposes of this decision, that El Al's actions did not constitute "wilful misconduct"; accordingly, we confront no issue under Article 25 of the Convention, see *supra*, at 5, n. 7. The parties do not dispute that the episode-in-suit occurred in international transportation in the course of embarking.

Our inquiry begins with the text of Article 24, which prescribes the exclusivity of the Convention's provisions for air carrier liability. "It is our responsibility to give the specific words of the treaty a meaning consistent with the shared expectations of the contracting parties." *Saks, 470 U.S. at 399*. "Because a treaty ratified by the United States is not only the law of this land, see U.S. Const., Art. II, § 2, but also an agreement among sovereign powers, we have traditionally considered as aids to its interpretation the negotiating and drafting history (*travaux preparatoires*) and the postratification understanding of the contracting parties." *Zicherman, 516 U.S. at 226*.

Article 24 provides that "cases covered by article 17" -- or in the governing French text, "les cas prevus a l'article 17" -- may "only be brought subject to the conditions and limits set out in the Convention." 49 Stat. 3020. That prescription is not a model of the clear drafter's art. We recognize that the words lend themselves to divergent interpretation.

In Tseng's view, and in the view of the Court of Appeals, "les cas prevus a l'article 17" means those cases in which a passenger could actually maintain a claim for relief under Article 17. So read, Article 24 would permit any passenger whose personal injury suit did not satisfy the liability conditions of Article 17 to pursue the claim under local law.

In El Al's view, on the other hand, and in the view of the United States as *amicus curiae*, "les cas prevus a l'article 17" refers generically to all personal injury cases stemming from occurrences on board an aircraft or in embarking or disembarking, and simply distinguishes that class of cases (Article 17 cases) from cases involving damaged luggage or goods, or delay (which Articles 18 and 19 address). So read, Article 24 would preclude a passenger from asserting any air transit personal injury claims under local law, including claims that failed to satisfy Article 17's liability conditions, notably, because the injury did not result from an "accident," see *Saks, 470 U.S. at 405*, or because the "accident" did not result in physical injury or physical manifestation of injury, see *Floyd, 499 U.S. at 552*.

Respect is ordinarily due the reasonable views of the Executive Branch concerning the meaning of an international treaty. See *Sumitomo Shoji America, Inc. v. Avagliano, 457 U.S. 176, 184-185, 72 L. Ed. 2d 765, 102 S. Ct. 2374 (1982)* ("Although not conclusive, the meaning attributed to treaty provisions by the Government agencies charged with their negotiation and enforcement is entitled to great weight."). We conclude that the Government's construction of Article 24 is most faithful to the Convention's text, purpose, and overall structure.

A

The cardinal purpose of the Warsaw Convention, we have observed, is to "achieve uniformity of rules governing claims arising from international air transportation." *Floyd, 499 U.S. at 552*; see *Zicherman, 516 U.S. at 230*. The Convention signatories, in the treaty's preamble, specifically "recognized the advantage of regulating in a uniform manner the conditions of . . . the liability of the carrier." 49 Stat. 3014. To provide the desired uniformity, Chapter III of the Convention sets out an array of liability rules which, the treaty declares, "apply to all international transportation of persons, baggage, or goods performed by aircraft." *Ibid.* In that Chapter, the Convention describes and defines the three areas of air carrier liability (personal injuries in Article 17, baggage or goods loss, destruction, or damage in Article 18, and damage occasioned by delay in Article 19), the conditions exempting air carriers from liability (Article 20), the monetary limits of liability (Article 22), and the circumstances in which air carriers may not limit liability (Articles 23 and 25). See *supra,* at 3-4, and n. 7. Given the Convention's comprehensive scheme of liability rules and its textual emphasis on uniformity, we would be hard put to conclude that the delegates at Warsaw meant to subject air carriers to the distinct, nonuniform liability rules of the individual signatory nations.

The Court of Appeals looked to our precedent for guidance on this point, but it misperceived our meaning. It misread our decision in *Zicherman* to say that the Warsaw Convention expresses no compelling interest in uniformity that would warrant preempting an otherwise applicable body of law, here New York tort law. See *122 F.3d at 107*; *supra*, at 8. *Zicherman* acknowledges that the Convention centrally endeavors "to foster uniformity in the law of international air travel." *516 U.S. at 230*. It further recognizes that the Convention addresses the question whether there is airline liability *vel non.* See *id., at 231*. The *Zicherman* case itself involved auxiliary issues: who may seek recovery in lieu of passengers, and for what harms they may be compensated. See *id., at 221, 227*. Looking to the Convention's text, negotiating and drafting history, contracting states' postratification understanding of the Convention, and scholarly commentary, the Court in *Zicherman* determined that Warsaw drafters intended to resolve *whether there is liability*, but to leave to domestic law (the local law identified by the forum under its choice of law rules or approaches) determination of the compensatory damages available to the suitor. See *id., at 231*.

A complementary purpose of the Convention is to accommodate or balance the interests of passengers seeking recovery for personal injuries, and the interests of air carriers seeking to limit potential liability. Before the Warsaw accord, injured passengers could file suits for damages, subject only to the limitations of the forum's laws, including the forum's choice of law regime. This exposure inhibited the growth of the then-fledgling international airline industry. See *Floyd, 499 U.S. at 546*; Lowenfeld & Mendelsohn, The United States and the Warsaw Convention, 80 Harv. L. Rev. 497, 499-500 (1967). Many international air carriers at that time endeavored to require passengers, as a condition of air travel, to relieve or reduce the carrier's liability in case of injury. See Second International Conference on Private Aeronautical Law, October 4-12, 1929, Warsaw, Minutes 47 (R. Horner & D. Legrez transls. 1975) (hereinafter Minutes). The Convention drafters designed Articles 17, 22, and 24 of the Convention as a compromise between the interests of air carriers and their customers worldwide. In Article 17 of the Convention, carriers are denied the contractual prerogative to exclude or limit their liability for personal injury. In Articles 22 and 24, passengers are limited in the amount of damages they may recover, and are restricted in the claims they may pursue by the conditions and limits set out in the Convention.

Construing the Convention, as did the Court of Appeals, to allow passengers to pursue claims under local law when the Convention does not permit recovery could produce several anomalies. Carriers might be exposed to unlimited liability under diverse legal regimes, but would be prevented, under the treaty, from contracting out of such liability. Passengers injured physically in an emergency landing might be subject to the liability caps of the Convention, while those merely traumatized in the same mishap would be free to sue outside of the Convention for potentially unlimited damages. The Court of Appeals' construction of the Convention would encourage artful pleading by plaintiffs seeking to opt out of the Convention's liability scheme when local law promised recovery in excess of that prescribed by the treaty. See *Potter v. Delta Air Lines, Inc., 98 F.3d 881, 886 (CA5 1996)*. Such a reading would scarcely advance the predictability that adherence to the treaty has achieved worldwide.

The Second Circuit feared that if Article 17 were read to exclude relief outside the Convention for Tseng, then a passenger injured by a malfunctioning escalator in the airline's terminal would have no recourse against the airline, even if the airline recklessly disregarded its duty to keep the escalator in proper repair. See *122 F.3d at 107*. As the United States pointed out in its *amicus curiae* submission, however, the Convention addresses and concerns, only and exclusively, the airline's liability for passenger injuries occurring "on board the aircraft or in the course of any of the operations of embarking or disembarking." Art. 17, 49 Stat. 3018; see Brief for United States as *Amicus Curiae* 16. "The Convention's preemptive effect on local law extends no further than the Convention's own substantive scope." Brief for United States as *Amicus Curiae* 16. A carrier, therefore, "is indisputably subject to liability under local law for injuries arising outside of that scope: *e.g.*, for passenger injuries occurring before 'any of the operations of embarking or disembarking.'" *Ibid.* (quoting Article 17).

Tseng raises a different concern. She argues that air carriers will escape liability for their intentional torts if passengers are not permitted to pursue personal injury claims outside of the terms of the Convention. See Brief for Respondent 15-16. But we have already cautioned that the definition of "accident" under Article 17 is an "unusual event . . . *external to the passenger*," and that "this definition should be flexibly applied." *Saks, 470 U.S. at 405* (emphasis added). In *Saks*, the Court concluded that no "accident" occurred because the injury there -- a hearing loss -- "indisputably resulted from *the passenger's own internal reaction* to the usual, normal, and expected operation of the aircraft." *Id., at 406* (emphasis added). As we earlier noted, see *supra*, at 7, n. 9, Tseng and El Al chose not to pursue in this Court the question whether an "accident" occurred, for an affirmative answer would still leave Tseng unable to recover under the treaty; she sustained no "bodily injury" and could not gain compensation under Article 17 for her solely psychic or psychosomatic injuries.

B

[a discussion of the drafting history of the Montreal Convention is omitted].

C

Montreal Protocol No. 4, ratified by the Senate on September 28, 1998, amends Article 24 to read, in relevant part: "In the carriage of passengers and baggage, any action for damages, however founded, can only be brought subject to the conditions and limits set out in this Convention . . . ." Both parties agree that, under the amended Article 24, the Convention's preemptive effect is clear: The treaty precludes passengers from bringing actions under local law when they cannot establish air carrier liability under the treaty. Revised Article 24, El Al urges and we agree, merely clarifies, it does not alter, the Convention's rule of exclusivity.

Supporting the position that revised Article 24 provides for preemption not earlier established, Tseng urges that federal preemption of state law is disfavored generally, and particularly when matters of health and safety are at stake. See Brief for Respondent 31-33. See also *post*, at 5 ("[A] treaty, like an Act of Congress, should not be construed to preempt state law unless its intent to do so is clear.") (Stevens, J., dissenting). Tseng overlooks in this regard that the nation-state, not subdivisions within one nation, is the focus of the Convention and the perspective of our treaty partners. Our home-centered preemption analysis, therefore, should not be applied, mechanically, in construing our international obligations.

Decisions of the courts of other Convention signatories corroborate our understanding of the Convention's preemptive effect. In *Sidhu*, the British House of Lords considered and decided the very question we now face concerning the Convention's exclusivity when a passenger alleges psychological damages, but no physical injury, resulting from an occurrence that is not an "accident" under Article 17. See 1 All E.R. at 201, 207. Reviewing the text, structure, and drafting history of the Convention, the Lords concluded that the Convention was designed to "ensure that, in all questions relating to the carrier's liability, it is the provisions of the Convention which apply and that the passenger does not have access to any other remedies, whether under the common law or otherwise, which may be available within the particular country where he chooses to raise his action." *Ibid.* Courts of other nations bound by the Convention have also recognized the treaty's encompassing preemptive effect. The "opinions of our sister signatories," we have observed, are "entitled to considerable weight." *Saks, 470 U.S. at 404* (internal quotation marks omitted). The text, drafting history, and underlying purpose of the Convention, in sum, counsel us to adhere to a view of the treaty's exclusivity shared by our treaty partners.

For the reasons stated, we hold that the Warsaw Convention precludes a passenger from maintaining an action for personal injury damages under local law when her claim does not satisfy the conditions for liability under the Convention. Accordingly, we reverse the judgment of the Second Circuit.

It is so ordered. [dissent by Justice Stevens omitted].

RUBINA HUSAIN v. OLYMPIC AIRWAYS.

UNITED STATES DISTRICT COURT FOR THE NORTHERN
DISTRICT OF CALIFORNIA

116 F. Supp. 2d 1121

August, 2000

On an international passenger flight January 1998, Dr. Abid M. Hanson a non-smoker in who suffered from asthma, inhaled a significant amount of second-hand smoke and died in the company of his wife and three children. Dr. Hanson was not seated in the "smoking" section of the airplane on which he died, but in a seat three rows ahead. Considerable ambient smoke was present at this location. Had Olympic Airways' flight crew responded appropriately to the repeated requests to move Dr. Hanson from this area, he might be alive today.

Plaintiffs Rubina, Hannah, Sarah and Isaac Husainbring this wrongful death action under the liability provisions of the Warsaw Convention. The parties agree that the Warsaw Convention presents plaintiffs' exclusive remedy. Therefore, to determine liability in this case, the Court must decide whether plaintiffs' claim satisfies the requirements of that treaty. Specifically, the Court must decide: (1) whether an "accident" occurred aboard Olympic Airways Flight 417 on January 4, 1998; (2) whether that accident caused the death of Abid Hanson; (3) whether the crew's in-flight actions constituted "willful misconduct"; and (4) to what extent, if any, Dr. Hanson's own negligence contributed to his death.

Plaintiffs filed this suit in state court on December 24, 1998, and defendant removed the case to this Court on March 23, 1999. The Court heard testimony and received evidence in this case on May 30, May 31, and June 1, 2000. After receiving the parties' post-trial briefs, the Court heard final arguments on July 20, 2000. Supplemental letter briefs were submitted shortly thereafter. This memorandum and order shall constitute the Court's findings of fact and conclusions of law in this matter.

FACTUAL BACKGROUND

I. Dr. Hanson's Medical History

Dr. Abid Hanson was 52 years old in January 1998. For more than two decades prior to his death, Dr. Hanson suffered from asthma. Although Dr. Hanson did not receive regular treatment for his condition, he carried a Proventil/Albuterol inhaler on his person most of the time to assist his breathing. According to the testimony of Dr. Hanson's wife, Ms. Rubina Husain, Dr. Hanson used his inhaler more and more frequently as he aged. Perhaps as a result of his asthmatic condition, Dr. Hanson was particularly sensitive to second-hand cigarette smoke, and he generally tried to avoid smoke-filled areas. Prior to January 4, 1998, Dr. Hanson had never been affected by cigarette smoke during domestic or international air travel.

439

In addition to his asthma, Dr. Hanson suffered from multiple food allergies. The evidence is somewhat unclear regarding the extent of Dr. Hanson's allergies, or even the particular foods to which he was allergic. A blood test prior to his death indicated that Dr. Hanson was allergic to grapes, yeast and tomatoes. However, Dr. Hanson frequently ate tomato-based dishes at home without incident.

In the two years preceding Dr. Hanson's death, he suffered two notable medical emergencies of unknown origin. In each instance, the incident may have been precipitated by Dr. Hanson's asthma or by an allergic reaction to certain foods. The most serious incident occurred during a family vacation in Las Vegas in December 1996. One evening, Dr. Hanson and his wife spent approximately ten minutes in a smoky restaurant, shared some cheese pizza and a piece of quiche, and returned to their hotel room. Shortly thereafter, Dr. Hanson began to have trouble breathing. As his breathing difficulties worsened, Dr. Hanson began to turn blue. Ms. Husain performed CPR until the paramedics arrived, at which point Dr. Hanson was administered a shot of epinepherine, a form of adrenaline. After resuscitating Dr. Hanson, the paramedics moved him to the hospital, where he was held overnight. The next morning, Dr. Hanson checked himself out of the hospital against medical advice.

The precise cause of Dr. Hanson's near-fatal experience in Las Vegas is not entirely clear. Although the dry Nevada air or the smoke of the restaurant may have triggered the attack, it was more likely caused by a reaction to certain foods. After reviewing Dr. Hanson's medical records, Dr. Stephen Wasserman, defendant's expert witness, described Dr. Hanson's troubles in Las Vegas as anaphylaxis caused by a severe allergic reaction to food. Plaintiffs' expert, Dr. Jeffrey Golden, agreed, characterizing the episode as "bona fide food-related anaphylaxis."

After the incident in Las Vegas, Dr. Hanson purchased an emergency carrying case containing epinepherine to treat any future attacks. Shortly thereafter, Dr. Hanson experienced a second medical crisis in the summer of 1997, at the home of a friend in Alameda, California. On the evening in question, Dr. Hanson had eaten dinner and then taken a walk outside. Upon Dr. Hanson's return, Ms. Husain noticed that he was having trouble breathing. Fearing that her husband was suffering an asthma attack, Ms. Husain called the paramedics. When they arrived, the paramedics administered oxygen and observed Dr. Hanson for about ten minutes, but did not take him to the hospital. No epinepherine was administered on that occasion.

The cause of Dr. Hanson's breathing problems in Alameda are unknown. Although defendant posits that this second incident was food-related, there is no evidence to support that hypothesis. Equally likely is that the cold dry air which Dr. Hanson breathed during his walk triggered an asthmatic reaction. In either case, the incident in Alameda reveals little about the cause of Dr. Hanson's death aboard Flight 417 six months later.

II. Dr. Hanson's Death

In late 1997, Dr. Hanson, his wife, Rubina Husain, and their three children ("the Husains") traveled from San Francisco to Athens and

Cairo for a family vacation. They were accompanied on their trip by family friends, Dr. Umesh Sabharwal, his wife and their children.

Prior to arriving at the airport, the Husains were unaware that Olympic Airways ("Olympic") permitted passengers to smoke cigarettes on international flights. Upon learning for the first time at the New York airport that their flight would include a smoking section, the Husains requested non-smoking seats. On the 12-hour flight from New York to Athens, the Husains were seated toward the middle or front of the aircraft. On the connecting flight to Cairo, the Husains were again seated away from the smoking section of the cabin. No ambient smoke was present at either location. Dr. Hanson experienced no problems breathing on either flight.

The Husain family spent 12 days in Egypt, and embarked on their return trip to the United States on January 4, 1998. According to the testimony of Ms. Husain, the family arrived at the airport early on the day of the return flight because they wanted to ensure that they would be seated in the non-smoking section. After receiving the family's seat assignments, Ms. Husain returned briefly to the counter and showed the check-in agent a letter signed by Dr. Hanson's brother, also a medical doctor, explaining that Dr. Hanson had a history of asthma. After showing the letter to the agent, Ms. Husain asked the agent to ensure that the family would be seated in the non-smoking section of the plane.

The first leg of the family's return trip was uneventful, but Dr. Hanson began to experience some breathing trouble during a layover in the Athens airport. The layover in Athens lasted approximately three to four hours, and the large room in which the family was seated was filled with cigarette smoke. During the delay, Dr. Hanson used his inhaler more frequently than usual. Because he was bothered by the pervasive smoke, Dr. Hanson attempted to move into the restricted but slightly less smoky area of the first class lounge, but airport officials asked that he move back to the main room.

After the delay, the Husains and the Sabharwals boarded Olympic Airways Flight 417. It was at this time that the Husains first realized that they had been assigned seats at the rear of the airplane cabin, only a few rows in front of the smoking section. The airplane, a Boeing 747, contained a total of 426 passenger seats in 56 rows. Rows one through 13 were designated as business class seats, and rows 14 through 56 were designated as economy class seats. In the economy class, rows 14 through 50 were designated as non-smoking seats. The economy class smoking section began at row 51 and extended to the rear of the cabin. The Husains were seated in row 48 in seats A through E. The Sabharwals were seated nearby. Dr. Husain was seated in seat 48E, just three rows in front of the smoking section. No partition separated the smoking from the non-smoking section.

When the Husains arrived at their seats, Ms. Husain noticed Maria Leptourgou, an Olympic flight attendant, circulating in the cabin and advising passengers to sit down for takeoff. Ms. Husain approached Ms. Leptourgou and told her that her husband could not sit in a smoking area. Ms. Husain said to Ms. Leptourgou, "You have to move him." The flight attendant paid little attention to Ms. Husain's request, telling her to "have a seat."

Once the plane was fully boarded, but prior to takeoff, Ms. Husain again approached Ms. Leptourgou and asked the flight attendant to move her husband now that all the passengers on the plane were seated. This time Ms. Husain explained that her husband was "allergic to smoke." At trial, Ms. Husain described her pre-takeoff requests to the flight attendant as "adamant." Ms. Leptourgou replied that she could not transfer Dr. Hanson to another seat because the plane was "totally full." The flight attendant also told Ms. Husain that she was too busy at the moment to assist the Husains.

The Husains remained in their assigned seats during takeoff, and the first several minutes of the flight passed without incident. Shortly after takeoff, however, the captain turned off the "no smoking" signs, and passengers in the rows behind the Husains began to light cigarettes. From this point on, according to the testimony of Sarah Husain, passengers in rows 51 through 56 were smoking continuously. In addition to those seated in rows 51 through 56, a number of passengers from other rows stood temporarily in the aisles behind the Husains, smoking and socializing. As a result, smoke was both pervasive and constant.

As soon as the smoking began, the Husains were surrounded by ambient smoke which had floated forward into their row. When the smoke began to linger in row 48, Dr. Hanson gestured to his wife and complained that the smoke was "like a chimney." Ms. Husain then stood up and contacted Ms. Leptourgou for a third time. This time, Ms. Husain told the flight attendant, "You have to move my husband from here." Again, Ms. Leptourgou curtly refused, stating that the plane was full. Ms. Leptourgou indicated to Ms. Husain that Dr. Hanson could switch seats with another passenger, but that, in order to do so, Ms. Husain would have to walk through the cabin and ask other passengers herself. She could not enlist the assistance of the flight crew in changing her husband's seat. Ms. Husain, becoming more desperate and more adamant, told the flight attendant that her husband *had* to move, even if the only available seat were in the cockpit or the first class area of the cabin. The flight attendant, however, was equally resolute. She offered no assistance. Finally, Ms. Husain, seeing no hope for accommodation, returned to her seat.

Unbeknownst to the Husains, Flight 417 was actually not full. In fact, the flight contained eleven empty passenger seats. The cabin had a capacity of 426 seats, 44 of which were located in business class and 382 of which were located in economy class. Four of these seats, located in a row immediately behind the smoking section, were designated as "crew rest" seats. Only 411 passengers traveled on Flight 417 on January 4. Therefore, the flight had eleven unoccupied seats, not including those designated for crew rest. Two of those empty seats were located in the business class section of the cabin.

In addition to the unoccupied seats, Flight 417 carried 28 "non-revenue passengers." Non-revenue passengers include employees and relatives of employees of Olympic Airways and other airlines. Of these 28 passengers, eleven were seated in the cabin's smoking sections. Of the remaining 17 non-revenue passengers, two were seated in rows one and two in business class and 15 were seated in rows 15 through 36 in economy class.

As the flight progressed, ambient smoke continued to circulate in the area of row 48. Approximately two hours into the flight, the crew served a meal. The evidence before the Court establishes that Dr. Hanson ordered a meal and that he ate some portion of it. He also shared some of his food with his daughter, Sarah, and with a woman seated to his right. According to Sarah, Dr. Hanson "wasn't really eating that much" of his meal.

Immediately after the meal service, smoking increased noticeably in the rows behind the Husains. Around this time, Dr. Hanson became unusually quiet. At some point shortly after the meal, Dr. Hanson asked his wife for a new inhaler, indicating that the one he had been using had emptied. Ms. Husain retrieved a full inhaler from the overhead bin. Dr. Hanson turned around several times to look at the smoke in the rows behind him. He then told Sarah that the smoke was bothering his allergies, and decided to move toward the front of the cabin to breathe fresher air.

Sarah notified her mother of Dr. Hanson's discomfort, and Ms. Husain followed him to the front of the aircraft. Dr. Hanson walked forward a number of rows, stopping in the galley area between rows 19 and 20, well into the non-smoking area. When Ms. Husain reached him, he was leaning against a chair near the galley area. Dr. Hanson gestured to Ms. Husain to get the epinepherine that he carried in his emergency kit, which Ms. Husain had stored in a carry-on bag. Ms. Husain rushed to the rear of the plane to retrieve the epinepherine, then returned to the galley area and administered a shot to her husband in a pre-measured syringe. She then ran to the rear of the cabin to wake Dr. Sabharwal.

Within seconds, Dr. Sabharwal, who, by chance, was an allergy specialist, arrived at the front of the plane to assist. Noticing that Dr. Hanson was in respiratory distress, Dr. Sabharwal pulled him onto the floor, gave him another shot of epinepherine (.20 ccs), and began to administer CPR. At this point, Dr. Hanson's pulse was barely palpable. Dr. Sabharwal noticed that, while Dr. Hanson's lower airways were obstructed, his upper airway was not. For this reason, he was able to push some air into Dr. Hanson's lungs during the administration of CPR. During the treatment, Dr. Sabharwal also gave Dr. Hanson a shot of Bricanyl, which had been retrieved from the Husains' emergency kit.

At some point during this period, Ms. Husain requested that one of the flight attendants provide an oxygen canister and mask for her husband. According to Ms. Husain's testimony, two flight attendants attempted to open the oxygen canister, but were unable to do so. Ms. Husain summoned Sarah, who was walking toward the front of the aircraft, and asked her to retrieve Dr. Hanson's oxygen canister with its nasal canula from the family's emergency kit. Sarah relayed this message to her brother, Isaac, who brought the oxygen to Ms. Husain.

As they attempted to resuscitate Dr. Hanson, Dr. Sabharwal and Ms. Husain administered oxygen through a nasal canula. In addition, oxygen may have been administered through Olympic's canister with an attached mask. However, because Dr. Hanson was not able to breathe spontaneously, Dr. Sabharwal determined that the oxygen was not useful. About five minutes after Dr. Sabharwal arrived on the scene, the Olympic flight crew brought him a medical kit. By this point, however, Dr. Sabharwal believed that only a fully-equipped medical crash kit could save Dr. Hanson's life.

As time passed, a few other passengers arrived in the galley to assist Dr. Sabharwal, but no one was able to save Dr. Hanson. At approximately 4:40 p.m. Greenwich Mean Time, Dr. Sabharwal announced that Dr. Hanson had died.

During the entire incident, the airplane's captain never turned on the "no smoking" sign or otherwise requested that the passengers in the rear of the plane stop smoking.

III. The Medical Causes of Dr. Hanson's Death

For religious reasons, no autopsy was performed on Dr. Hanson's body after his death, and the direct cause of his fatal attack is a matter of some dispute. Plaintiffs argue that Dr. Hanson's death was caused by a severe asthma attack brought on by inhalation of cigarette smoke. Defendant, on the other hand, argues that Dr. Hanson died as a result of anaphylaxis caused by an allergic reaction to food, or that he died as a result of some other unknown medical problem. As discussed below, the Court finds that plaintiff has established by a preponderance of the evidence that smoke ingestion during the first two hours of Flight 417 was a primary cause of Dr. Hanson's death.

Anaphylaxis is an allergic emergency which may be caused by an allergy to external material. Symptoms of anaphylaxis include skin discoloration, obstruction of the upper airway, disturbance in the intestinal tract, drop in blood pressure, shock or rapid, ineffective heartbeat. An asthmatic attack, on the other hand, is a reversible narrowing of the airway caused by air pollutants or other irritants, such as cigarette smoke.

The symptoms of asthma and anaphylaxis overlap significantly. Indeed, some severe asthma attacks may be characterized as anaphylactic reactions. In this case, the course of events with respect to the timing of the meal, Dr. Hanson's smoke inhalation, and the onset of his reaction support theories labeling the cause of death as both anaphylaxis and asthma. Both anaphylaxis and asthma attacks produce the same symptoms in the lower airway. Either can result in death. Epinepherine can be used to treat both anaphylaxis and asthma, but it is not necessarily efficacious in either case. The fact that Dr. Hanson received two or more injections of epinepherine during the flight and that the drug had no effect does not assist the Court in arriving at a cause of death.

Although anaphylaxis and asthma are sometimes difficult to differentiate, the Court finds that smoke played a significant causal role in Dr. Hanson's death. As both Dr. Golden and Dr. Wasserman acknowledged, cigarette smoke can act as an irritant. Moreover, the greater an individual's exposure to smoke, both in terms of time and intensity, the greater the irritant effect. As Dr. Golden explained in his testimony before the Court, the presence of an irritant can cause bronchospasm, constricting an individual's airways.

The Court finds significant the testimony of the Husain family and Dr. Sabharwal regarding Dr. Hanson's behavior in the Athens airport. During the hours-long delay in Athens, Dr. Hanson used his inhaler frequently and was increasingly bothered by the prevalent smoke. To escape the effects of the smoke, Dr. Hanson illicitly entered the first class lounge, where the air quality was slightly better. Dr. Hanson's problems in Athens indicate his sensitivity to smoke on the day in question.

Once the family was airborne toward New York on Flight 417, but prior to the in-flight meal service, Dr. Hanson again complained about the smoke. During the first hours of the flight, Dr. Hanson used his inhaler to remedy the effects of the smoky air while aboard the plane. The Court cannot credit defendant's suggestion that Dr. Hanson's breathing problems prior to the meal were causally unrelated to his later asphyxiation. The evidence before the Court suggests exactly the opposite conclusion. Dr. Hanson explicitly complained that smoke was affecting his breathing just hours before his death, complained to his wife about the level of cigarette smoke on the plane, and relied extensively on his inhaler for support during the hours leading to his fatal attack. To conclude, as defendant urges, that the smoke on Flight 417 did not trigger Dr. Hanson's death is to ignore the chain of events leading up to his attack.

Defendant introduced evidence at trial to establish that Dr. Hanson may have died as a result of an anaphylactic reaction to yeast, tomatoes or grapes in the in-flight meal. This contention is belied by several facts in the record. First, there is no evidence that Dr. Hanson ate any grapes, tomatoes or bread-based products on the flight. In fact, the only credible evidence regarding Dr. Hanson's food intake was the testimony of his daughter, Sarah. According to Sarah, Dr. Hanson received a meal on the flight, but did not eat the whole thing, and in fact shared it with both of his neighbors. No witnesses testified that they observed Dr. Hanson eating any of the foods to which he was allergic while seated in row 48. Without further evidence of Dr. Hanson's sensitivities and his food intake aboard the flight, the Court cannot conclude that his death was caused by a reaction to the food.

Further, Dr. Hanson's death lacked certain symptoms that frequently appear in cases of anaphylaxis. Anaphylaxis caused by oral injection of an allergen commonly causes swelling in the upper airway. In this case, Dr. Sabharwal observed that Dr. Hanson's upper airway was not obstructed. Anaphylaxis frequently, but not always, causes discoloration, redness and hives on a victim's chest and neck. Dr. Sabharwal noticed none of those symptoms in this case.

Moreover, the testimony of Dr. Sabharwal; the only doctor who actually treated Dr. Hanson during his trauma, supports the Court's conclusion. While Dr. Sabharwal testified that he could not definitively diagnose the cause of Dr. Hanson's death, he did offer a differential diagnosis, assessing the likely causes of death in order of their probability. Dr. Sabharwal opined that, in light of Dr. Hanson's asthma and the obstruction of Dr. Hanson's airways, he most likely died as a result of status asthmaticus, or "totally uncontrolled asthma." The second most likely cause of death, according to Dr. Sabharwal, was anaphylaxis, and the third was "cardiac problems." Failing each of these potential causes, Dr. Sabharwal concluded that Dr. Hanson's death may have been precipitated by unknown causes.

Dr. Golden's testimony further supports the Court's factual findings regarding the cause of Dr. Hanson's death. Dr. Golden testified that, in the absence of food, the only possible cause of death in this case would be an asthmatic reaction. Because Dr. Hanson may have eaten some of his meal, Dr. Golden concluded that it is difficult to distinguish whether Dr. Hanson's condition was anaphylaxis or asthma. However, Dr. Golden was able to conclude that smoke was a significant contributing factor in Dr. Hanson's death, regardless of whether he ate a meal on Flight 417.

Dr. Wasserman, defendant's expert witness in this case, attributed Dr. Hanson's death to asphyxiation or heart failure brought on by a reaction to an allergen, possibly tomatoes or yeast. Even Dr. Wasserman acknowledged, however, that cigarette smoke may have contributed to Dr. Hanson's death, although he was unable to determine the extent of that contribution.

In conclusion, the Court finds that Dr. Hanson's death was the result of respiratory distress which was caused by an exacerbation of his asthmatic condition due to the prolonged and extensive exposure to second-hand smoke on Olympic's Flight 417.

DISCUSSION

I. Applicable Law: The Warsaw Convention

This case is governed by the provisions of the Warsaw Convention ("the Convention"). The Convention is a comprehensive international treaty governing the liability of carriers in "all international transportation of persons, baggage or goods." *49 U.S.C. § 40105*. The purposes of the Convention were to achieve uniformity and to limit the liability of air carriers. See *El Al Israel Airlines v. Tseng, 525 U.S. 155, 119 S. Ct. 662, 671-72, 142 L. Ed. 2d 576 (1999)*; *Carey v. United Airlines, Inc., 77 F. Supp. 2d 1165, 1169 (D. Or. 1999)*. The parties agree that, because Dr. Hanson's death occurred during international travel, the Convention provides plaintiffs' exclusive remedy. See *Tseng, 119 S. Ct. at 668*. ("Recovery for a personal injury suffered 'on board [an] aircraft or in the course of any of the operations of embarking or disembarking,' if not available under the Convention, is not available at all.").

The Convention provides for strict liability for carriers in certain situations, and precludes liability altogether in others. Article 17 of the Convention explains that a carrier "shall be liable" for death or bodily injuries of passengers sustained during flight as the result of an "accident." Articles 20 and 22 limit a carrier's liability under Article 17 to $ 75,000 per passenger. However, under Article 25, the $ 75,000 limitation does not apply if the carrier has committed "wilful misconduct." See generally *Hermano v. United Airlines, 1999 U.S. Dist. LEXIS 19808, 1999 WL 1269187* (N.D. Cal. Dec 21, 1999).

II. The "Accident" Requirement

Article 17 of the Convention provides that

> The carrier shall be liable for damages sustained in the event of the death or wounding of a passenger or any other bodily injury suffered by a passenger, if the accident which caused the damage so sustained took place on board the aircraft during the course of any of the operations of embarking and disembarking.

49 U.S.C. § 40105. The Supreme Court has interpreted this language to require the occurrence of an "accident" for a carrier to be held liable under the Convention. See *Air France v. Saks, 470 U.S. 392, 396, 84 L. Ed. 2d 289, 105 S. Ct. 1338 (1985).*

In Saks, the Supreme Court defined "accident" as "an unexpected or unusual event or happening that is external to the passenger." *Saks, 470 U.S. at 405.* The Court noted that "accident," as that term is used in the Convention, has a narrower definition than the term "occurrence." *Id. at 398.* This inquiry is an objective one, and does not focus on the perspective of the person experiencing the injury. See *Gotz v. Delta Airlines, Inc., 12 F. Supp. 2d 199, 201 (D. Mass. 1998).* Further, "when the injury indisputably results from the passenger's own internal reaction to the usual, normal, and expected operation of the aircraft, it has not been caused by an accident." *Saks, 470 U.S. at 406.* It is the cause of the injury, not merely the occurrence of the injury, that must qualify as an accident. See *id. at 399; Gotz, 12 F. Supp. 2d at 201.*

Despite these limitations, the Court emphasized that its definition "should be flexibly applied after assessment of all the circumstances surrounding a passenger's injuries." *470 U.S. at 405.* Other courts have also concluded that the term "accident" should be "interpreted broadly." See *Carey, 77 F. Supp. 2d at 1170.*

The Supreme Court has also explained that, while the "accident" must cause the passenger's injury, it need not be the *sole* causal factor. *Saks, 470 U.S. at 405.* Rather, because "any injury is the product of a chain of causes," a plaintiff under the Convention need only "prove that some link in the chain was an unusual or unexpected event external to the passenger." *Id. at 406.*

In this case, plaintiffs posit three specific occurrences aboard Flight 417 that might be construed as "accidents" contributing to Dr. Hanson's death: (1) Ms. Leptourgou's three refusals to move Dr. Hanson to another seat; (2) the flight crew's inability to provide a usable oxygen canister in a timely manner; and (3) and the captain's failure to turn on the "no smoking" sign during Dr. Hanson's attack. As discussed below, the Court concludes that only the first of these occurrences was an "accident" which caused Dr. Hanson's death.

A. Refusal to Move Dr. Hanson

Plaintiffs first argue that Ms. Leptourgou's refusal to transfer Dr. Hanson to another row and her failure to follow company procedure was an "unusual" or "unexpected" event. The Court agrees.

The negligent failure of the flight crew to appropriately serve the needs of an ailing passenger can be considered an "accident" under the Convention. See *Fishman v. Delta Air Lines, Inc., 132 F.3d 138, 142 (2d Cir. 1998)* (flight attendant negligently spilled scalding water on passenger while attempting to attend to passenger's earache). A claim "does allege an accident if it arises from some inappropriate or unintended happenstance in the operation of the aircraft or airline. Thus, an injury resulting from routine procedures in the operation of an aircraft or airline can be an 'accident' if those procedures or operations are carried out in an unreasonable manner." *Id. at 143;* see also *Schneider v. Swiss Air Transport Company Ltd., 686 F. Supp. 15 (D. Me. 1988)* (finding possible accident where flight attendant refused to assist passenger by asking other passengers sitting in front of her to raise their seats); *Langadinos v. American Airlines, Inc., 199 F.3d 68, 71 (1st Cir. 1999)* (finding possible accident where flight attendant imprudently served alcohol to a passenger whose behavior was already "erratic" and "aggressive"); *Carey, 77 F. Supp. 2d at 1171* (flight attendant's "acts of preventing plaintiff and his children from changing seats, engaging in heated, argumentative exchanges with plaintiff, informing him that he could be arrested if he did not stay in his seat and if his children did not stay in their seats, and publicly humiliating him, meet the definition of 'accident' as articulated in Saks.").

Defendant argues that no unusual event occurred during the Husains' flight. According to defendant, ambient smoke is an expected and usual aspect of international flying. See *Warshaw v. Trans World Airlines, Inc., 442 F. Supp. 400 (E.D. Pa. 1977)* (routine repressurization of cabin was not an accident, even though it caused plaintiff to lose his hearing); *Saks, 470 U.S. at 394* (routine cabin pressurization during landing is not an accident); *Gotz, 12 F. Supp. 2d 199* (injury to passenger during attempt to stow baggage in overhead compartment was not accident, because crew "worked perfectly").

The Court does not dispute that smoke in the cabin may be an expected aspect of international travel. Indeed, it is clear from the record that the Husains knew before boarding that the January 4 flight would have a smoking section. However, defendant's argument misses the mark. The smoke in the cabin was not the "unusual" or "unexpected" event which caused Dr. Hanson's death, although, as detailed above, the smoke undoubtedly had a significant place in the causal chain. Rather, the unusual and unexpected event on which plaintiffs base their claim was the failure of the flight attendant to adequately respond to Ms. Husain's transfer requests. Indeed, in both Warshaw and Gotz, in which the courts found that injuries not attributable to unusual aircraft operations were not actionable under the Convention, the courts specifically mentioned that the injured passengers *had failed to request assistance from the flight crew.* In this case, the opposite is true. With increasing urgency, Ms. Husain three times requested the crew's assistance prior to her husband's death, and her request was thrice denied.

Under no reasonable interpretation of the facts can one conclude that Ms. Leptourgou's failure to assist Dr. Hanson was expected or usual. The Court has heard extensive testimony on the standard of care for flight attendants in situations such as this, and concludes that Ms. Leptourgou acted in an unexpected and unusual manner in several respects.

First, the recognized standard of care for flight attendants during international air travel demands that a flight attendant make efforts to accommodate a passenger who indicates that he or she needs to be moved for medical reasons. In this case, despite Ms. Leptourgou's repeated statements that the flight was full, eleven seats stood unoccupied. The Court can conceive of no acceptable reason for Ms. Leptourgou's refusal to assist Dr. Hanson after Ms. Husain's second and third requests. Moreover, according to Diane Fairechild, a flight attendant with 21 years of experience in international travel, even if the flight had no empty seats in the economy section, the crew should have transferred Dr. Hanson to an empty seat in the business class section of the cabin. Notably, Ms. Husain's suggestion to this effect during her third plea for a seat change went unheeded by Ms. Leptourgou.

Ms. Xourgia, now a chief cabin attendant working for Olympic, testified that, if she were in Ms. Leptourgou's position at the time of Ms. Husain's third request (i.e., after takeoff, when smoking had commenced in row 51), she would have transferred Dr. Hanson "immediately." Ms. Fairechild, testified that, according to recognized industry standard of care, Ms. Leptourgou "should have absolutely responded" to Ms. Husain's requests.

Second, even if the flight were entirely full, the flight attendant should have attempted to move Dr. Hanson. Ms. Fairechild testified that, when faced with a medical request like Ms. Husain's during a full flight, the crew will often attempt to entice other passengers to switch their seats. In this case, a seat transfer would not have been difficult to effectuate, considering that 17 passengers seated in the cabin's non-smoking section were "non-revenue" passengers. The evidence reveals that such a transfer would be appropriate under the controlling standard of care. Even Theocharis Fotiades, the chief cabin attendant on Flight 417, explained that Ms. Leptourgou should "definitely" have attempted to find another seat for Dr. Hanson when Ms. Husain made her requests.

Third, not only did Ms. Leptourgou's failure to act violate the accepted industry standard of care, it also violated Olympic Airways' policy. As Mr. Fotiades testified at trial, Olympic crew members generally make efforts to move passengers who become ill during flights if moving those passengers will assist in their recovery. Mr. Fotiades explained that this policy applies when a passenger must be moved because of smoke-related illness. Further, according to Mr. Fotiades, Olympic flight attendants are familiar with this policy. Ms. Leptourgou, however, entirely ignored it. Such behavior cannot be considered either expected or usual.

Fourth, even if Ms. Leptourgou did not personally assist Dr. Hanson to find a new seat, Olympic policy required that she, at least, alert the chief cabin attendant ("CCA") of Ms. Husain's medical requests. Ms. Xourgia testified that as a flight attendant in Ms. Leptourgou's position, she would have immediately contacted the CCA when Ms. Husain requested a seat change prior to takeoff. Although no written policy was placed into evidence by the parties, Ms. Xourgia testified that written Olympic policies require that when a passenger indicates that he needs to be moved for a medical reason, the flight attendant must report that request to the CCA.

In this case, Ms. Leptourgou did not contact the chief cabin attendant to alert him to Dr. Hanson's medical condition or Ms. Husain's requests. In fact, according to the evidence before the Court, Ms. Leptourgou did not contact any other members of the flight crew concerning Ms. Husain's three requests. Nor did she ask another member of the crew whether or not the flight was full. Mr. Fotiades, the chief cabin attendant, did not learn about Ms. Husain's requests for a seat change until after Dr. Hanson had died. Had he learned of the requests earlier in the flight, Mr. Fotiades testified that he would have made further inquiries and attempted to move Dr. Hanson to another seat.

Finally, because of Ms. Husain's precautionary actions in both the New York and the Cairo airports, Ms. Leptourgou's failure to assist Dr. Hanson is even more unexpected and unusual than in the typical case of a passenger transfer request. At the New York airport where the Husains first learned that Olympic permitted smoking on its flights, Ms. Husain informed the check-in agent that her husband was "susceptible to smoke" and could not "be in any smoke." As a result of this initial conversation, the Husains had reason to expect that Olympic was aware of Dr. Hanson's sensitivity to smoke. This expectation was further bolstered by Ms. Husain's conversation with the check-in agent at the Cairo airport prior to the family's return trip. After the Husains were given their tickets in Cairo, Ms. Husain returned to the counter to ensure that her husband had been given a seat in the non-smoking sections of the two return flights. At that time, Ms. Husain showed the agent a letter from Dr. Hanson's brother explaining that Dr. Hanson had a history of asthma. Again, one would expect that, as a result of this conversation, Olympic was aware of Dr. Hanson's medical needs. In light of this fact, Olympic's subsequent failure to move Dr. Hanson after three requests is even more unusual and unexpected.

Moreover, Dr. Hanson's expectation that Ms. Husain's requests would be accommodated was even more reasonable in light of the normal operating procedures of international carriers. Diane Fairechild testified that medical information and special requests like Ms. Husain's are normally inputted in a "special information log," which is given to the airplane's CCA prior to takeoff. The log serves to inform the CCA of the special needs of the passengers. In this case, despite Ms. Husain's warnings to Olympic check-in agents regarding her husband's condition, nothing to that effect appeared in Olympic's special information log. A passenger in Dr. Hanson's position should expect that medical needs expressed to an agent prior to check-in will be considered once the flight has been boarded. In Dr. Hanson's case, that reasonable expectation was not met.

In sum, Ms. Leptourgou's behavior was far from usual or expected. She violated the industry standard of care, she misrepresented to Ms. Husain that the flight was full, and she acted in contravention of accepted Olympic Airways policy. This aberrant behavior was both unexpected and unusual.

In the face of this evidence, defendant analogizes to a number of published cases in which the Convention's "accident" requirement was narrowly applied. For instance, defendant relies on *Margrave v. British Airways, 643 F. Supp. 510 (S.D.N.Y. 1986)*, in which the district court noted that sitting in "a very cramped position" during a flight delay is neither unusual nor unexpected. The plaintiff in Margrave sat in her seat for approximately five hours while her plane waited for takeoff. Because "normal travel procedures" were followed by the crew, the court concluded that no "accident" had occurred. *Id. at 512*. Defendant argues that, under Margrave, sitting in an assigned seat cannot be considered an "accident," even if remaining seated causes injury to the passenger. However, Margrave is distinguishable from the instant case. In Margrave, the plaintiff never told a flight attendant about her discomfort. *Id. at 511*. In contrast, here the unusual event was not Dr. Hanson's seat location, but the flight attendant's refusal to accommodate his needs despite three requests.

Defendant also cites a number of cases in which the crew's failure to assist an ailing passenger was held to not constitute an "accident." For instance, in *Krys v. Lufthansa German Airlines, 119 F.3d 1515 (11th Cir. 1997)*; the Eleventh Circuit held that an airplane crew's negligent decision to continue a flight to its scheduled destination despite a passenger's in-flight heart attack was not an actionable "accident" under Article 17. See also *McDowell v. Continental Airlines, 54 F. Supp. 2d 1313, 1320 (S.D. Fla. 1999)* (reluctantly following Krys); *Fischer v. Northwest Airlines, Inc., 623 F. Supp. 1064, 1065 (N.D. Ill. 1985)* (refusal to aid passenger with heart attack was not "accident"). But see *Seguritan v. Northwest Airlines, Inc., 86 A.D.2d 658, 446 N.Y.S.2d 397, 398-99 (N.Y. App. Div. 1982)* ("The 'accident' is not the heart attack suffered by the decedent. Rather, it is the alleged aggravation of decedent's condition by the negligent failure of defendant's employees to render her medical assistance.").

The seminal case in this line of "failure to assist" decisions is *Abramson v. Japan Airlines Co., Ltd., 739 F.2d 130 (3d Cir. 1984)*. In Abramson, the plaintiff was suffering from a preexisting paraesophagael hiatal hernia when he boarded the flight. The plaintiff's condition worsened during the flight, and he asked the flight attendant if he could lie down in empty seats so that he could apply a useful "self help" remedy which included massaging his stomach and occasionally inducing vomiting. *Id. at 131*. The court found that no accident had occurred because the aggravation of the passenger's injury was not an unusual or unexpected occurrence. *Id. at 132*. The court noted that "in the absence of proof of abnormal external factors, aggravation of a pre-existing injury during the course of a routine and normal flight should not be considered an 'accident' within the meaning of Article 17." *Id. at 133*.

Each of these cases, including Abramson, is distinguishable from the one at bar. Unlike Dr. Hanson, the passengers in each of the cited cases suffered an injury as a result of entirely "internal" forces. While the inaction of the crew may have aggravated the passengers' injuries, it did not precipitate the injuries as such. Here, on the other hand, the flight attendant's failure to transfer Dr. Hanson--or her failure to at least follow the proper procedures--*precipitated* Dr. Hanson's injury and death. See *Fishman, 132 F.3d at 141-142* (distinguishing Abramson and Fischer on similar grounds).

Additionally, none of the cases cited by defendant arose from a crew member's blatant disregard of industry standards and airline policies. As described above, the testimony in this case indicates that Ms. Leptourgou's actions were anything but usual. When a passenger boards an airplane, he or she should be able to expect that the flight crew will comply with accepted procedures and rules. A failure to do so is unexpected.

Finally, to the extent that any of defendant's cited cases are not distinguishable from the instant case, the Court finds that they are both unconvincing and non-binding in this Circuit. The Court finds little merit in the notion that a flight crew has no legal obligation to care for its ill or endangered passengers. The practical effect of cases like Abramson is to dissolve the airlines' duty of care and to "create[] an incentive to airlines engaged in international travel not only not to exercise the highest degree of care but to completely refuse to treat" or assist passengers with medical problems. *McDowell, 54 F. Supp. 2d at*

451

1320. In the absence of binding authority, the Court declines to adopt such a rule.

The Court concludes that when a flight attendant's acts create a foreseeable risk of injury to passengers, an "accident" has occurred. See *Langadinos v. American Airlines, Inc., 199 F.3d 68, 71*. In this case, Ms. Leptourgou's failure to respond appropriately to Ms. Husain's requests and her failure to comply with the applicable standards of care were both "unexpected" and "unusual." See *Tsevas v. Delta Air Lines, Inc., 1997 U.S. Dist. LEXIS 19539, 1997 WL 767278* (N.D. Ill. Dec. 1, 1997) (flight attendant's failure to move passenger upon request in order to keep her away from a second passenger's lewd behavior was an "accident" under Article 17). Therefore, Ms. Leptourgou's behavior is actionable under the Warsaw Convention.

Having concluded that Ms. Leptourgou's failure or refusal to assist Dr. Hanson constituted an "accident," the Court must next consider whether that "accident" caused Dr. Hanson's death. As discussed above, the coincidental occurrence of both an accident and an injury aboard an international flight does not necessarily support a cause of action under the Convention. To prevail, plaintiffs must establish that the accident *caused* the injury. *Gotz, 12 F. Supp. 2d at 201*. In Saks, the Supreme Court recognized that "any injury is the product of a chain of causes." *Saks, 470 U.S. at 406*. To establish liability, a plaintiff need only "prove that some link in the chain was an unusual or unexpected event external to passenger." Id. Courts have traditionally applied regular proximate cause analysis to determine carrier liability under the Convention. See *Margrave, 643 F. Supp. at 512*.

In light of this standard, the Court finds that Olympic's failure to move Dr. Hanson caused Dr. Hanson's death. As discussed above, Dr. Hanson's death was caused, at least in significant part, by smoke inhalation which triggered a severe asthmatic reaction. Dr. Hanson was seated in row 48, only three rows in front of the designated smoking section. Four witnesses at this trial were seated in Dr. Hanson's vicinity on Flight 417, and all four noted that the ambient smoke was noticeably thick in row 48. At several points in the flight, Dr. Hanson indicated his discomfort with the seating arrangement. As noted above, Ms. Leptourgou or another member of the Olympic crew could have moved Dr. Hanson to any of the eleven empty seats on the plane or to one of the 17 non-smoking seats occupied by non-revenue passengers. If Ms. Leptourgou had moved Dr. Hanson out of the vicinity of the smoking section, he would not have died aboard Flight 417. Therefore, the Court must conclude that Dr. Hanson's death was caused by an accident, triggering liability under the Warsaw Convention.

B. Administration of Oxygen

In addition to Ms. Leptourgou's failure to move Dr. Hanson to another seat, plaintiffs argue that two other "accidents" occurred aboard Flight 417 which caused Dr. Hanson's death. First, plaintiffs assert that defendant's failure to effectively administer oxygen to Dr. Hanson through a face mask should be considered an "accident" under the Convention. According to plaintiffs, Dr. Hanson may not have died if the flight crew had properly prepared and supplied oxygen during Dr. Hanson's fatal attack.

To resolve this question, the Court must engage in a three-step inquiry. First, the Court must decide whether, as a purely legal matter, the failure to properly administer oxygen can be considered an accident. Second, the Court must decide as a factual matter whether the acts of the flight crew in this case constituted an unexpected or unusual event. If so, the Court must finally determine whether the flight crew's acts caused Dr. Hanson's death.

Turning first to the legal issue, the Court is aware of two published cases which address the question of whether an airline may be held liable under the Convention for the failure to properly administer oxygen. In *Tandon v. United Airlines, 926 F. Supp. 366 (S.D.N.Y. 1996)*, the plaintiff suffered a heart attack during an international flight. When a doctor attempted to administer oxygen from the airplane's on-board canister, he discovered that the canister had expired two month's earlier, and that it contained insufficient oxygen supply. *Id. at 368.* The plaintiff did not receive proper care, and died aboard the flight. The district court found that, because no unusual or unexpected event external to the plaintiff had *triggered* the plaintiff's heart attack, the later failure of the defendant to save her did not constitute an accident. *Id. at 369.*

The Court declines to follow the rule enunciated in Tandon. The Court cannot agree with the Tandon court that an expired oxygen container or a negligently maintained medical kit can somehow be considered an "expected" or "usual" aspect of international flight. Rather, the Court adopts the reasoning of the district court in *McDowell v. Continental Airlines, 54 F. Supp. 2d 1313 (S.D. Fla. 1999).* In McDowell, the court noted that improper maintenance of a carrier's on-board medical equipment can be considered an "accident." *54 F. Supp. 2d at 1318.* In determining whether an accident had occurred, the court considered the carrier's level of care in maintaining the medical kit and the carrier's compliance or non-compliance with federal regulations and industry standards. *Id. at 1318.* Although the court in McDowell concluded that the plaintiff had failed to establish facts showing negligent maintenance of the on-board medical kit, the court's discussion is instructive. Therefore, the Court holds that the failure to properly maintain or administer oxygen to an ailing passenger aboard an international flight may be considered an accident.

The Court must next apply this legal conclusion to the facts of this case. As described above, the testimony on this subject is contradictory at best. Both Dr. Sabharwal and Ms. Husain testified that the Olympic crew members were unable to provide bottled oxygen with an attached mask, while members of the crew testified that they did, in fact, provide an oxygen mask and canister, and that the apparatus functioned properly. Mr. Fotiades was particularly adamant in his testimony that he observed Dr. Hanson breathing oxygen through an Olympic-supplied mask at some point during the incident.

In light of this conflicting testimony, the Court finds that the evidence on the question of the oxygen administration is inconclusive. While the flight crew may have had some trouble preparing the oxygen when first asked by Ms. Husain, it is far from clear that the Olympic oxygen canister and mask were not used on Dr. Hanson or that the delay during the flight crew's troubles lasted more than a few moments. The Court notes that the time period between Ms. Husain's first request for oxygen and Dr.Hanson's death was approximately ten minutes.

During a significant portion of that time, Dr. Sabharwal and Ms. Husain were administering CPR, making the availability of oxygen irrelevant. In the flurry of intense activity that preceded Dr. Hanson's death, it is possible that both Ms. Husain and Dr. Sabharwal failed to notice that Olympic's oxygen tank was in use.

Additionally, even if the flight crew did have some trouble preparing the oxygen canister, the Court cannot find that an accident necessarily occurred. In the heat of the moment, a certain amount of fumbling is normal and expected, even by experienced flight attendants. Plaintiffs have not established that the flight crew's problems providing an oxygen canister lasted for a significant period of time.

In sum, the Court finds that plaintiffs have failed to meet their burden of establishing that the flight crew's behavior in preparing the oxygen was unusual or unexpected. Therefore, the Court concludes that the flight crew's acts during Dr. Hanson's fatal attack did not constitute an accident.

Further, even if the acts of the flight crew could be described as an "accident," the Court finds as a matter of fact that any failure to properly administer oxygen did not cause Dr. Hanson's death. Even if the flight crew did commit an error, the Court cannot conclude that this error provided a link in the causal chain that resulted in Dr. Hanson's death. See *Saks, 470 U.S. at 406.* In reaching this conclusion, the Court is cognizant of the testimony of Dr. Zarir G. Marawala, who explained that a nasal canula is typically less effective than a mask when a patient is experiencing respiratory distress. According to Dr. Marawala, a person in such a condition is more likely to attempt to breathe through his mouth.

While this may be true as a general proposition, the Court finds that the use of a mask would not have been useful in this case. By the time Ms. Husain and the Olympic crew attempted to administer oxygen to Dr. Hanson, his condition had progressed beyond salvation. According to the testimony of Dr. Wasserman, the administration of oxygen by way of a mask or a nasal canula is generally useless when a patient is experiencing airway obstruction. After reviewing the entire record, Dr. Wasserman concluded that any error in the administration of oxygen and CPR to Dr. Hanson did not cause his death. Rather, by the time Dr. Hanson was seated in row 19, properly-administered oxygen, even through a mask, would not have prevented Dr. Hanson's death. Dr. Golden's testimony also supports this conclusion. According to Dr. Golden, when a patient's airways are constricted, an oxygen mask is no more effective than a nasal canula.

On the basis of this testimony, the Court concludes that, even if the flight crew's delay in providing oxygen to Dr. Hanson constituted an "accident" under the terms of the Convention, that "accident" did not cause Dr. Hanson's death.

C. Failure to Ignite "No Smoking" Sign

Plaintiffs also argue that a separate "accident" occurred when the flight crew failed to request that the smoking passengers extinguish their cigarettes. Plaintiffs argue that the captain should have ignited the sign to ensure that no passengers would smoke in the vicinity of Dr. Hanson during his attack. According to plaintiffs, the failure of the

454

captain and the flight crew to request that other passengers stop smoking while Dr. Hanson received oxygen constituted an "unusual" or "unexpected" event.

The Court rejects this argument for three reasons. First, according to the testimony of Olympic Airways captain Demetrios Karayannis, it is not standard procedure to ignite the "no smoking" whenever a passenger is experiencing medical problems. Viewed in light of this testimony regarding the standard of care, the Court cannot credit plaintiffs' argument.

Second, the Court finds nothing in the record to suggest that any passengers were smoking in the vicinity of Dr. Hanson while he received oxygen. Indeed, the smoking section of the airplane began in row 51, but, by the time the crew was aware of Dr. Hanson's distress, he was seated 31 rows away in row 19. Therefore, the flight crew's failure to turn on the "no smoking" sign did not constitute an unexpected or unusual event.

Finally, as discussed above, by the time the administration of Dr. Hanson's oxygen began, his condition had already become irreversibly fatal. Whatever minimal level of ambient smoke may have reached row 19 during the incident, it certainly had no effect on Dr. Hanson's treatment, and did not cause his death.

III. Willful Misconduct

As discussed in section IIA above, Ms. Leptourgou's failure to move Dr. Hanson to another seat was an "accident," creating liability under the Warsaw Convention Carrier liability under the Convention is normally limited to $ 75,000 per passenger. However, that limitation on damages does not apply if the defendant airline committed willful misconduct in causing the accident. See *Koirala v. Thai Airways Int'l, 126 F.3d 1205, 1209 (9th Cir. 1997).* Article 25, the Convention's "willful misconduct" provision, does not create a distinct cause of action separate from Article 17, the Convention's "accident" provision. See *McDowell, 54 F. Supp. 2d at 1320.* Rather, Article 25 simply modifies the potential recovery of a passenger who has established the occurrence of both an "accident" and "willful misconduct." Id. In other words, if no "accident" occurred on the flight, the Court cannot find that defendant is separately liable for the "willful misconduct" of the crew. In this case, because the Court has concluded that an "accident" caused Dr. Hanson's death, the Court must next determine whether the behavior of the flight crew constituted "willful misconduct."

The Ninth Circuit has defined "willful misconduct" as "the intentional performance of an act with knowledge that the ... act will probably result in injury or damage or the intentional performance of an act in such a manner as to imply reckless disregard of the probable consequences." *Koirala, 126 F.3d at 1209.* See also Hermano, 1999 WL 1269187 at 5 (citing *Piamba Cortes v. American Airlines, Inc., 177 F.3d 1272, 1290 (11th Cir. 1999))* (to establish willful misconduct, plaintiff must show that defendant acted with "intent to cause damage" or "'recklessly and with knowledge' that damage would probably result."). In a case published earlier this year, the Fourth Circuit considered whether "willful misconduct" requires subjective or objective recklessness. See *Bayer Corp. v. British Airways, PLC, 210 F.3d 236 (4th Cir. 2000).* The court concluded that the former standard was more appropriate, noting that "on a mens rea spectrum from negligence to intent, article 25's standard is very close to the intent end." *Id. at 238*. Rather than establishing that the actor "should have known" of an obvious risk, the plaintiff in a case brought under the Warsaw Convention must, at a minimum, prove that the actor "must have known" of the risk in order to establish willful misconduct. *Id. at 239* (quoting *Piamba, 177 F.3d at 1291*). The plaintiff bears a "heavy burden" in proving willful misconduct. Id.; see also *Saba v. Compagnie Nationale Air France, 316 U.S. App. D.C. 303, 78 F.3d 664, 668 (D.C. Cir. 1996)* (requiring plaintiff to show actor's subjective state of mind in order to prove "willful misconduct"); *Piamba Cortes, 177 F.3d at 1291*. Although the Ninth Circuit has not explicitly decided whether Article 25 requires an element of subjective knowledge, the Koirala court held that "conscious and reckless disregard" of the crew's duties constituted willful misconduct under the Convention. *Koirala, 126 F.3d at 1212*. For the purposes of this decision, the Court will assume that the Article 25 requires a finding of subjective recklessness.

The Court must note, however, that Ms. Leptourgou's subjective state of mind "may be established solely by inferences taken from circumstantial evidence; the inferences thus act as 'a legitimate substitution for intent to do the proscribed act because, if shown, it is a proxy for that forbidden intent." *Piamba Cortes, 177 F.3d at 1286* (quoting *Saba, 78 F.3d at 668*). In fact, it is possible to infer subjective recklessness based on "the very fact that the risk was obvious." *177 F.3d at 1291* (quoting *Farmer v. Brennan, 511 U.S. 825, 842, 128 L. Ed. 2d 811, 114 S. Ct. 1970 (1994)*).

In this case, the Court finds that the flight attendant's failure to move Dr. Hanson or to report Ms. Husain's request to the CCA was "willful misconduct." The Court concludes that, at the time of her third refusal to assist Dr. Hanson, Ms. Leptourgou *must have known* that the cabin was not full, that Dr. Hanson had a medical problem and a special susceptibility to smoke, and that her failure to move him would aggravate his condition and cause him probable injury. The Court reaches this conclusion only after a careful examination of the testimony and the circumstances of Ms. Leptourgou's repeated refusals to help the Husains.

A number of considerations support the Court's conclusion. First, the Court finds that, at the time of the accident, Ms. Leptourgou was aware of the industry standard of care described in section 11, supra. Mr. Fotiades testified at trial that the flight attendants working under his supervision were aware of the appropriate responses to seat transfer requests. Second, the Court finds that Ms. Leptourgou was aware of Olympic's specific policy requiring that a flight attendant inform the CCA when a passenger requests a seat transfer for medical reasons. Ms. Xourgia testified that Olympic flight attendants receive formal training on this policy. Third, the Court finds that Ms. Leptourgou must have known that Flight 417 was not "totally full," as she informed Ms. Husain. The evidence shows that Ms. Leptourgou passed through the cabin prior to takeoff to ensure that all passengers were seated. During this walk-through, Ms. Leptourgou must have seen several empty seats. In the face of this inference, defendant has submitted no evidence whatsoever to suggest that Ms. Leptourgou did not know or might not have known that the plane contained empty seats.

From this understanding, the Court next turns to the crucial testimony of Ms. Husain. Because Ms. Leptourgou was not available to testify in this trial, Ms. Husain's memory of her conversations with the flight attendant are entirely uncontested. The Court finds Ms. Husain's testimony on this topic highly credible.

The testimony of Ms. Husain makes one thing clear: Ms. Husain was not merely a typical passenger complaining about an inconvenient seat assignment. Ms. Husain made three requests to be moved. Nothing in the record indicates that any other passenger requested any such assistance more than once. Additionally, each of Ms. Husain's requests was more emphatic and desperate than the last. Once the passengers seated behind Dr. Hanson had begun to smoke, Ms. Husain's pleas reached a level of unmistakable urgency and seriousness. According to her testimony, Ms. Husain literally *begged* Ms. Leptourgou to move her husband. She told the flight attendant, "I don't care if the plane is full. Sit him on the carpet, sit him in first class, but don't sit him here." The Court finds that Ms. Husain communicated her husband's problem to the flight attendant so emphatically that Ms. Leptourgou must have recognized the danger. Further, Ms. Husain indicated to Ms. Leptourgou several times that she wanted only her husband moved, not the rest of the family. The fact that Ms. Husain was willing to sit apart from her husband during the entire ten-hour flight should have indicated to the flight attendant that the situation was serious enough to merit further consideration. After hearing the testimony of Ms. Husain, the Court concludes that Ms. Leptourgou cannot have failed to recognize that Dr. Hanson's problem was a medical one and that sitting near the smoking section was likely to cause him injury.

Moreover, the evidence suggests that Ms. Leptourgou *did* in fact recognize the seriousness of Ms. Husain's request, even though she failed to respond appropriately. The fact that Ms. Leptourgou gave Ms. Husain permission to act on her own to find another seat indicates that she understood the seriousness of Ms. Husain's entreaties. Clearly, Ms. Leptourgou understood that Dr. Hanson's problem was serious enough to merit a seat transfer of some type. Her subsequent failure to assist Ms. Husain or to follow standard procedures by contacting the CCA is inexplicable. The Court can only conclude that by refusing to perform her duties, Ms. Leptourgou deliberately closed her eyes to the probable consequences of her acts. This was willful misconduct.

Defendant has suggested that, because Ms. Leptourgou could not have known that Dr. Hanson would die as a result of his allergy, she could not have recognized the risks inherent in her actions. While the Court agrees that Ms. Leptourgou did not know that Dr. Hanson would die if not moved, this fact alone does not preclude a finding of willful misconduct. Plaintiffs must show only that Ms. Leptourgou was aware that her refusal to assist Dr. Husain was likely to cause an injury to him; they need not establish that Ms. Leptourgou was aware of the exact injury that her act was likely to cause. See *Saba, 78 F.3d at 668.* In other words, Ms. Leptourgou need not have known, and in all likelihood did not know, that Dr. Hanson might die as a result of her refusal to assist him. However, for the reasons discussed above, she did know--she *must have known*--that her acts in violation of recognized policy were likely to cause him injury.

Defendant has also suggested that Ms. Husain should have been even more explicit than she was in making her pleas to Ms.

Leptourgou. No doubt she could have used precise medical terms rather than stating that her husband was "allergic" to smoke. Arguably, she could have explained that her husband had suffered two serious medical incidents in the previous year that required the assistance of the paramedics. Perhaps these more explicit explanations would have propelled the flight attendant to take the appropriate action. However, the Court rejects this argument for two reasons. First, as explained above, Ms. Husain's pleas, while factually bare, were sufficiently straightforward to alert Ms. Leptourgou of the impending danger and the need to move Dr. Hanson to another seat. Ms. Husain's use of the term "allergic to smoke" notified Ms. Leptourgou that Dr. Hanson's problems were medical in nature, even though her words may have been medically imprecise. Further, the emotional urgency of Ms. Husain's requests, which was conveyed in her testimony before this Court, informed Ms. Leptourgou of the potential seriousness of Dr. Hanson's medical problems. Although Ms. Husain did not use the word "asthma" or describe the incident in Las Vegas, Ms. Leptourgou must have known the gravity of Dr. Hanson's condition.

Second, the Court declines to place the unreasonable burden on airplane passengers to provide a detailed explanation of their medical history in order to receive the mandatory and expected acceptable level of service. When aboard a commercial airplane, passengers can be anxious and inarticulate. Airline regulations, both written and unwritten, recognize that passengers are not always able to completely articulate their needs. For this very reason, airlines create policies and procedures, such as Olympic Airways' requirement that a flight attendant must inform the chief cabin attendant upon learning of a passenger's medical needs. At a minimum, compliance with such procedures leads to a more accurate exchange of information between the passenger and the crew. Ms. Leptourgou knew that Dr. Hanson had a susceptibility to smoke, knew that his wife feared serious injuries if he remained in row 48, knew that the flight was not entirely full, and knew that Olympic regulations required her to contact the CCA and/or to make an effort to move Dr. Hanson. In spite of all this knowledge, she did nothing.

Ms. Fairechild, a 21-year veteran of commercial airline service, testified to the egregiousness of Ms. Leptourgou's behavior, noting that she was "shocked" by Ms. Leptourgou's failure to act and labeling it "criminal." After reviewing the record, Ms. Fairechild testified that "I've never seen anybody treated like this on an international flight, so it's not--it's not airline service as far as I experienced or I would expect." In light of all this evidence, the Court must conclude that Ms. Leptourgou's behavior constituted willful misconduct, as that term has been interpreted under the Warsaw Convention. See *Koirala, 126 F.3d at 1211* (finding inference of willful misconduct based on expert testimony that "the flight crew's actions in this case were 'completely substandard of any scheduled airlines in the world.'").

IV. Comparative Negligence

The Court must next turn to the difficult question of comparative negligence. While the Warsaw Convention creates a strict liability standard for injuries caused by accidents during international travel, that liability is not absolute. Article 21 of the Convention provides:

If the carrier proves that the damage was caused by or contributed to by the negligence of the injured person the court may, in accordance with the provisions of its own law, exonerate the carrier wholly or partly from his liability.

Both parties agree that the Court should apply California's comparative negligence standard in this case rather than a traditional contributory negligence standard. Accord *Eichler v. Lufthansa German Airlines, 794 F. Supp. 127, 130 (S.D.N.Y. 1992)* (applying federal common law comparative negligence standard); *Bradfield v. Transworld Airlines, Inc., 88 Cal. App. 3d 681, 685, 152 Cal. Rptr. 172 (1979)* (applying state law comparative negligence standard).

A recent unpublished district court opinion from New York perhaps best describes the Convention's rule regarding comparative negligence. See *Eichler v. Lufthansa German Airlines, 1994 U.S. Dist. LEXIS 762, 1994 WL 30464 (S.D.N.Y. Jan 28, 1994).* The Eichler court noted the apparent incongruity of the Convention's no-fault standard of liability under Article 17 and its consideration of contributory negligence under Article 21. Analogizing to the arena of strict products liability, the court concluded that Article 21's standard is best described as a "comparative causation" standard rather than a "comparative fault" standard. In other words, although the predicate for triggering Article 21 is negligence, "the basis for apportioning liability is the *comparative responsibility or causation* of the parties." Id. at 5 (emphasis added). The Court adopts this well-reasoned interpretation of the Convention.

Accordingly, the Court must consider two questions. First, the Court must determine whether Dr. Hanson acted negligently during Flight 417. If the Court answers that question in the affirmative, it must next consider the comparative causation of Ms. Leptourgou's refusal to assist Dr. Hanson and Dr. Hanson's own negligent failure to act.

A. Dr. Hanson's Negligence

Defendant suggests that Dr. Hanson was negligent in two ways. First, defendant contends that Dr. Hanson's failure to request to speak with Ms. Leptourgou's supervisor was unreasonable. Second, defendant asserts that Dr. Hanson's failure to make any attempt to find another passenger who was willing to switch seats with him was also negligent. The Court will address these two arguments in turn.

1. Failure to Seek Assistance of Supervisor

First, defendant suggests that Dr. Hanson and Ms. Husain should not have merely accepted Ms. Leptourgou's refusal to move Dr. Hanson. Rather, they should have requested to speak with Ms. Leptourgou's supervisor. The Court disagrees. Imposing such a duty would place an unreasonable burden on a passenger, penalizing her for obeying the instructions of a flight attendant. Moreover, it is not realistic to expect Ms. Husain to understand the flight crew hierarchy aboard commercial aircraft. Indeed, as Ms. Husain testified at trial, she did not know at the time of the incident that Ms. Leptourgou even had a supervisor. A reasonable passenger in Ms. Husain's position would have reached precisely the conclusion that Ms. Husain herself reached after listening to the flight attendant's final rebuff: her husband could either remain in his assigned seat or take it upon himself to exchange seats with another passenger. The Court cannot fault either Dr. Hanson or Ms. Husain for failing to realize that the aircraft also carried a CCA to supervise the flight attendants.

2. Failure to Attempt to Move Independently

Defendant's second argument is far more persuasive. The Court finds that Dr. Hanson was negligent in failing to attempt to transfer his seat after Ms. Husain's third interaction with Ms. Leptourgou. As described above, after Ms. Husain's third request to move her husband, the flight attendant responded that the plane was full and that she could not move Dr. Hanson. She then told Ms. Husain, "You have to go ask people yourself"

Without question, Ms. Leptourgou's instruction to Ms. Husain was inappropriate in light of Olympic's policies. However, once the flight attendant granted Dr. Hanson and Ms. Husain permission to find a seat on their own, that option was available to them. Dr. Hanson, after apparently weighing the potential risk to himself against the inconvenience, discomfort and probability of success of personally requesting a seat transfer from other passengers, chose not to act. The Court finds that this decision was unreasonable under the circumstances.

Dr. Hanson was in a unique position to understand precisely how serious his condition was. He knew his medical history. He was aware of his near-fatal attack in Las Vegas and his breathing troubles in Alameda. As a doctor, he probably understood his condition and the risks associated with it. He alone knew exactly how the ambient smoke was affecting his body during the hours leading up to his death. In other words, like Ms. Leptourgou, Dr. Hanson must have known that he would probably be injured if he remained in row 48. Ms. Leptourgou presented him with an option to escape the potential injury that inhaling the smoke-filled air would cause: he could walk toward the front of the cabin and approach other passengers to ask them to switch seats with him. In light of what Dr. Hanson knew and what he should have known, the Court concludes that he should have accepted Ms. Leptourgou's option, as unappealing as it may have appeared. The failure to do so constituted negligence.

B. Comparative Causation

While Dr. Hanson's failure to act was negligent, that negligence does not necessarily eradicate the effects of Ms. Leptourgou's wrongdoing. Dr. Hanson does not bear the full responsibility for the events that transpired after the meal service. *Either* Dr. Hanson *or* Ms. Leptourgou could have taken action to move Dr. Hanson to the front of the plane. Both should have taken such action. Neither can point to the other as being solely responsible for Dr. Hanson's death. The Court must therefore determine how each actor's wrongful or negligent decisions contributed to the tragedy that followed.

At first glance, it may appear that Dr. Hanson's failure to act played the larger role in causing his death. As discussed above, he had intimate knowledge of both the extent of his sensitivity to smoke and the effect of the ambient smoke on his ability to function during the flight. Further, it was Dr. Hanson who made the ultimate decision not to attempt to move. Viewing the facts from this perspective, whatever

Ms. Leptourgou's culpability, Dr. Hanson should bear the greater responsibility for causing his own death.

After careful consideration of the evidence, the Court concludes that this "first glance" position is incorrect for two reasons. First, while Dr. Hanson should have attempted to switch seats with another passenger, there is no guarantee at all that his actions would have resulted in his finding a new seat farther from the smoking section. Nothing in the record indicates that other passengers would have been willing (or are typically willing) to switch seats at the request of a fellow passenger with an assigned seat in close proximity to the airplane's smoking section. Further, it is far from clear that Dr. Hanson would have discovered the availability of the eleven unoccupied seats during his proposed sojourn to the front of the cabin. The evidence before the Court establishes that, to the average observer, the plane appeared to be full. The open seats were likely scattered throughout the cabin, and were difficult to see with an unfamiliar eye. Dr. Hanson may not have discovered an empty seat or found another passenger willing to swap seats.

On the other hand, if Ms. Leptourgou had acted properly, it is highly unlikely that Dr. Hanson would have remained in row 48. It is far more likely that, had Ms. Leptourgou followed the appropriate procedures, the CCA would have been able to move Dr. Hanson into one of the empty non-smoking seats. Further, the CCA also had unique knowledge as to which passengers were "non-revenue" passengers who could be easily asked to move. Therefore, in terms of likely outcomes, Ms. Leptourgou's failure to act was of greater consequence than Dr. Hanson's.

Second, although Ms. Leptourgou gave Dr. Hanson and Ms. Husain her permission to search for another seat, the fact remains that the flight attendant was in a far better position to effectuate a change. Ms. Leptourgou had knowledge of the flight crew hierarchy and had access to the CCA and his additional knowledge and influence. She also had the ability to find Dr. Hanson an open seat without any significant effort. Further, as a trained flight attendant, she had both experience and expertise in making requests such as the one she suggested that Ms. Husain make on her own. None of this can be said for Dr. Hanson himself. In other words, Ms. Leptourgou, had she merely responded to Ms. Husain's pleas in an appropriate manner, could have achieved a seat transfer with far less effort than Dr. Hanson acting alone.

When a passenger enters a commercial flight, he surrenders a certain level of freedom--freedom of movement, of expression and of choice--in return for a promise of safety and comfort. Passengers agree to abide by a set of rules; they are expected to behave in a certain way in order to avoid communal danger. As an element of this unwritten compact, passengers bestow upon the airline and the flight crew nearly absolute authority to control and manipulate the mobile environment for the benefit of all those aboard. Courts have recognized this authority in both civil and criminal contexts See, e.g., *49 U.S.C. § 44902*; *14 C.F.R. § 91.11*. Passengers grant a certain level of power to the airlines, but with that power comes responsibility. The flight crew has the unique ability to provide comfort and safety during air travel, which passengers have the right to expect. See *McDowell, 54 F. Supp. 2d at 1319* ("It is recognized in most jurisdictions that airlines owe a

461

heightened duty of care to their passengers."); *Williams v. Trans World Airlines, 509 F.2d 942, 946 n.8 (2d Cir. 1975)* ("It has generally been held ... that commercial airlines ... owe their passengers the duty of utmost care for their safety.").

In this case, as a result of his position as an airline passenger, Dr. Hanson's ability to make decisions about his fate and to act on those decisions was diminished. By entering the controlled environment of the airplane, Dr. Hanson had authorized the flight crew to act on his behalf to protect his safety. In return, he implicitly agreed to obey the commands of the flight crew--to remain in his assigned seat until permitted to move, to sit when told to do so, and not to disrupt the cabin environment. Therefore, while Dr. Hanson himself may have been in the best position to recognize the danger that row 48 presented to him, he was in the worst position to actually do something about it.

For these reasons, the Court cannot find that Dr. Hanson's negligence played a more significant causal role in his death than did Ms. Leptourgou's wrongdoing. By the same token, because of Dr. Hanson's unique knowledge of the danger, the Court cannot conclude that he played no role in causing his death. In the end, the Court concludes that the failures of both parties contributed equally to the tragedy that followed. Therefore, the Court finds that Dr. Hanson was comparatively liable for his death at a rate of 50%.

V. Damages

Having determined that defendant is liable under the Warsaw Convention, that defendant's liability is not limited to $ 75,000, and that defendant was contributorily negligent in causing his own death, the Court must next determine the total amount of damages suffered by plaintiffs as a result of Olympic's misconduct. The evidence before the Court supports an award of damages commensurate with the pecuniary loss to Dr. Hanson's surviving family. The parties have not established in their briefs or their arguments to the Court that damages in excess of that amount are legally appropriate in this case.

To determine the amount of pecuniary damages, the Court received a report and heard testimony from C. Daniel Vencill, Ph.D., who examined Dr. Hanson's financial health for the purposes of determining damages in this case. Dr. Vencill's testimony was uncontradicted, and his conclusions went largely unchallenged by defendant. Defendant's post-trial brief and argument do not attack the validity of Dr. Vencill's methodology or his calculations.

Dr. Hanson's earning history shows an average taxable income of $ 140,052.12 over the six-year period prior to his death. He intended to work until at least age 65 in order to provide for his family and finance his children's college education. Based on Dr. Vencill's uncontroverted testimony, assuming a 5.5% discount rate and a 2% growth rate, and deducting at a rate of 31% for personal consumption, the Court concludes that the total amount of pecuniary loss to plaintiffs as a result of Dr. Hanson's death was $ 1,400,000.00.

This finding is supported by Dr. Vencill's calculations, as presented in his written and oral testimony to the Court. In reaching this conclusion, the Court is guided by Dr. Vencill's testimony that the most accurate calculation of Dr. Hanson's income is reached by modifying Dr. Hanson's taxable income to account for cash flow. Additionally, the

Court finds Dr. Vencill's calculations based on Dr. Hanson's six-year earnings more reliable than the calculations based on Dr. Hanson's 1997 earnings alone. Finally, although Dr. Vencill posited at trial that a higher figure of approximately $ 1.5 to $ 1.6 million was appropriate, the Court accepts the $ 1.4 million figure because it more accurately reflects the total amount of non-market work performed by Dr. Hanson in his home prior to his death.

As noted above, the Court finds that Dr. Hanson was comparatively negligent at a rate of 50% in causing his death. Therefore, plaintiffs may recover only 50% of their $ 1,400,000.00 in economic losses. The Court awards plaintiffs $ 700,000.00 in total damages.

CONCLUSION

For the foregoing reasons, the Court hereby finds that an accident occurred aboard Olympic Airways Flight 417 on January 4, 1998, and that the accident caused the death of Dr. Abid Hanson. The Court further finds that Olympic Airways committed willful misconduct in failing to react to Ms. Rubina Husain's requests for a seat transfer for her husband. Finally, the Court finds that Dr. Hanson himself was contributorily negligent in causing his death, and that his negligence contributed to his death at a rate of 50%. Accordingly, the Court hereby awards plaintiffs $ 700,000.00 in damages.

IT IS SO ORDERED.

IX   CRIMINAL LAW

A. *Crimes specific to Aviation*

LAWRENCE B. HAVELOCK v. UNITED STATES OF AMERICA

UNITED STATES COURT OF APPEALS FOR THE TENTH
CIRCUIT

427 F.2d 987

June, 1970

HILL, Circuit Judge:

Havelock appeals his conviction under *18 U.S.C. § 32* for wilfully
setting fire to an airplane while in flight and being operated in interstate
commerce. A jury trial was waived and, after hearing the evidence and
recording its findings, the trial court found the accused guilty as
charged.   Appellant now argues that prejudicial testimony and
prejudicial exhibits were erroneously admitted into evidence and that,
excluding that evidence, the remaining proof was insufficient to
convict.

When reviewing the transcript and exhibits to determine a
sufficiency question, this Court has repeatedly held that the evidence is
viewed in the light most favorable to the government. Furthermore, we
do not weigh conflicting evidence or consider the credibility of
witnesses. To determine the sufficiency of the evidence, we look to see
if there is direct and circumstantial evidence, along with all reasonably
drawn inferences, from which guilt may be ascertained beyond a
reasonable doubt.

It is uncontested that a fire occurred in the middle aft restroom
during a Los Angeles to Denver flight on November 19, 1968, just a
few minutes prior to landing in Denver. It is likewise undisputed that
the fire did not result from any aircraft malfunction but was started
either intentionally or accidentally. Two government expert witnesses
testified that in their opinion the fire was incendiary, as opposed to
accidental. Their testimony is convincing and is, in terms, not
contradicted by appellant's expert. At most, the latter submitted that it
could have been caused by a careless smoker. When viewed in a
posture favorable to the prosecution, the evidence sufficiently infers a
fire of incendiary origin.

As in most cases of wilfull burning of another's property, because
of the nature of the crime, direct evidence is seldom available to prove
the accused's participation.   The same is true of this case and,
consequently, circumstantial evidence, plus reasonable inferences, must
be relied on to establish the identity and willfulness of the guilty
person.

Appellant used the lavatory facilities three times during a period of
one hour and ten minutes, each time for the ostensible purpose of
shaving. On the initial trip he attempted to use his own razor but was
unable to complete the task because the flight was too rough. Flight

personnel and passengers testified that the flight was smooth and without turbulence until just outside Denver -- long after the first shaving attempt. On the second trip appellant used a borrowed razor but apparently was unsuccessful since he later returned for a third attempt at a "better shave."

On the last journey to the lavatory, he was observed as nervous and almost overly polite. At this time he allowed other passengers to take his turn in all but the middle restroom. When it was empty, he entered and remained in it for about ten minutes, during which time the "fasten seat belt" sign was on and the aircraft was descending to Denver. As he exited, he was seen wearing yellow rubber gloves. Another passenger testified that upon returning to his seat, Havelock either stuffed a yellow object into his pocket or in between the seats. He was, without contradiction, the last person in the middle aft restroom. A few minutes later the door burst open and the fire was discovered.

Havelock asked another passenger what had happened and he answered that he did not know but that something must have blown up and there was a fire. Appellant then queried "Is there any wires on fire?" As smoke filled the cabin the passengers, including Havelock, were asked to move to the foreward part of the airplane. During the commotion and attempt to extinguish the fire, appellant was observed near seat 14-C where the yellow gloves containing pieces of matchbook covers were later found. He was also located near seat 11-C where other matching pieces of the matchbook covers were found in an ash tray. In the opinion of the head of the Denver Fire Department Arson Squad, "Undoubtedly a match has to be applied to something to leave this type of debris and damage to the floor itself."

We think the inferences here point directly at Havelock as the guilty party. The fire was incendiary in nature. Appellant was the last person in the lavatory prior to the fire, and he occupied the room for about ten minutes. It stretched the credulity of the trier of fact, and has the same effect on this Court, to say that if appellant did not set the fire, he could have overlooked an incendiary device that was placed on the floor of the lavatory prior to his occupancy. His demeanor during the entire flight, and particularly that just prior and subsequent to the fire; the statements made to other passengers; the admittedly bizarre behavior in wearing yellow gloves and the attempt to secrete them; and the crucial fact that appellant was the last visitor to the destroyed lavatory prior to the ignition of an incendiary fire, all convinces us that guilt was properly assessed by the trial court. Even though the proof was not as weighty as direct evidence, it was not so insufficient to require reversal; it is not equally consistent with innocence as with guilt. The inferences drawn were reasonable and sufficiently clear to support appellant's conviction.

We now turn to the allegedly prejudicial testimony and exhibits. Basically, the testimony is that of a Los Angeles hotel security guard relating events in a hotel six days prior to the aircraft fire. Gas odors had been reported and, upon investigation, appellant's room appeared to be the source. Upon gaining entry into the room, the guard detected a strong odor of gasoline and obvious traces of the fuel on the commode and sink top. In addition, a Pan Am flight bag containing a one gallon gasoline can was partially concealed under the bedspread. Appellant was then asked to leave the hotel.

After his arrest in Denver, among appellant's effects was found a Pan Am flight ticket from Los Angeles to Honolulu scheduled to depart November 13, 1968. In addition he had taken out a $60,000 insurance policy with his wife as beneficiary. The Honolulu flight was never taken.

Proof of these events was tendered along with the ticket and insurance policy near the conclusion of the government's evidence and was offered to prove design, scheme and intent. The objection posed is that this evidence was irrelevant and prejudicial to appellant's case.

Wigmore draws a refined distinction between the admissibility of similar acts which evidence intent and those which evidence scheme or design. Although the general rule is that independent criminal acts may not be used to prove the charged act, we have held on numerous occasions that such evidence may be admissible on issues of intent, motive, scheme or plan. When similar acts are introduced to prove intent, the act itself is assumed to be done and the object is to negative inadvertence or accident. In *Fish v. United States, 215 F. 544 (1st Cir. 1914)*, the main case relied on by appellant, the defendant had been charged with burning a yacht with intent to prejudice the insurer. Because of the proof on the fire's cause, the only doubtful question was whether the defendant set the fire. The prosecution introduced evidence of two previous incidents where another yacht and a car of appellant's were burned. The court held this evidence inadmissible to negative any idea that the fire may have been accidental; that question simply was not before the jury. However, the court was not without question on its ruling, and proceeded to consider the alternatives.

In the case at bar, the evidence may be sufficiently clear on the incendiary nature of the fire to ultimately reduce the question to one of identity, not cause. Dealing only in the abstract, and momentarily ignoring practicalities, once the cause was established, the evidence as to intent became unnecessary because the fire, being incendiary, definitionally required wilfulness. That being the state of proof, the use of the hotel incident to show inadvertence or accident may have been unnecessary, but not prejudicial. Again recognizing practicalities although wilfulness could be inferred once it was established that the fire was incendiary, intent remained an unresolved issue until that time. It would be awkward to refuse evidence bearing on an element of the crime because, through hindsight, we are able to say that it proved unnecessary in the end.

The generally applied rule is that when a case is tried by a court without a jury, it is presumed, absent an affirmative showing to the contrary, that only material and competent evidence is considered. This presumption of correctness has not been rebutted by appellant. The argument on the prejudicial effect of the hotel incident is no more than a mere conclusory statement that because the evidence was admitted, the entire trial was tainted. This does not measure up to the standard of proving prejudicial error upon which reversal may be predicated.

Even if the evidence as to the accused's intent was irrelevant, as suggested by appellant, it was not prejudicial error to have accepted it. Not every error occurring during a trial requires reversal; only errors which affect substantial rights are prejudicial. The standard for determining prejudicial error is set forth in *Kotteakos v. United States, 328 U.S. 750, 765, 90 L. Ed. 1557, 66 S. Ct. 1239 (1946)*: "But if one cannot say, with fair assurance, after pondering all that happened without stripping that erroneous action from the whole, that the judgment was not substantially swayed by the error, it is impossible to conclude that substantial rights were not affected. The inquiry cannot be merely whether there was enough to support the result, apart from the phase affected by the error. It is rather, even so, whether the error itself had substantial influence. If so, or if one is left in grave doubt, the conviction cannot stand."

Following the evidence and arguments, the court made a lengthy statement which served as a basis for the findings and conclusions. After determining the existence of a fire, its incendiary origin, and that appellant was responsible for setting it, the court commented on the wilfulness of the act. "Now it must be determined as to whether or not the act was wilful. Well, the usual definition that we give to this word in legal terms is that the act is intentional and with an awareness of what one is doing. Having found that the fire was of incendiary origin, it must necessarily follow, of course, that the person who set it did it intentionally, because otherwise it wouldn't be an incendiary act."

We say with fair assurance that if the evidence was properly admitted for the one purpose but inadmissible for the other, it did not substantially sway the judgment. The trial court recognized in the foregoing statement what we have heretofore pointed out -- that having found the fire to be incendiary as opposed to accidental, no added evidence needed to be considered to prove the elements of *18 U.S.C. § 32*. That was the crux of his decision and we are left with no grave doubts that if the evidence on intent was irrelevant, it did not have a prejudicial influence on the judgment.

The government also tendered the evidence to prove scheme or design. When introduced for this purpose, the similar acts are admissible to show a design or system from which the setting of the fire charged may be inferred, provided the other acts have common features indicating a common plan. The prior acts must be similar in results and there must be "such a concurrence of common features that the various acts are naturally to be explained as caused by a general plan of which they are the individual manifestations."

Applying these rules to this evidence requires the conclusion that the evidence was not erroneously admitted. All of the facts and circumstances surrounding the incident at the hotel manifest sufficient common features to be of probative value in inferring the commission of the charged act. It would, in effect, be turning away from the obvious similarities and inferences and totally disregarding experience to refuse this testimony. The gasoline in the restroom of the hotel, the Pan Am flight ticket, and the Pan Am flight bag containing a partially filled gasoline can hidden under a bedspread, suggest too much to be labeled as irrelevant in this case. The sum of the hotel evidence illustrates sufficient fundamental features of a scheme which culminated in the fire aboard the airplane to be admissible at the trial.

The judgment is AFFIRMED.

UNITED STATES OF AMERICA, v. ZVONKO BUSIC et al.

UNITED STATES COURT OF APPEALS FOR THE SECOND CIRCUIT

549 F.2d 252

January, 1977

KAUFMAN, Chief Judge:

Prominent among the injuries inflicted upon the American colonists by King George III, according to the signers of the Declaration of Independence, was the despised practice of "transporting us beyond Seas to be tried for pretended offences." This revulsion for adjudication of criminal charges in a remote region, before a jury drawn from a hostile or insouciant citizenry, was responsible for the codification of both Article III, section 2 and the *Sixth Amendment to the Constitution*. Today, when our vast country can be traversed in a matter of hours, these provisions stand as bulwarks against prosecutorial overreaching in forcing the defendant to answer accusations in a spatially distant and unfriendly environment. But two centuries have wrought changes in our society that have increased both the range of crimes that federal courts confront and the factors underlying the selection of the proper situs of trial. The instant case presents to us five alleged "skyjackers," a variety of malefactor of which the Founders never would have dreamed, and requires us to determine whether it is impermissible to try them in the Eastern District of New York, which embraces the busy airport at which they boarded the airplane they are charged with hijacking and is part of the major metropolitan area in which they reside and effected significant steps toward the ultimate commission of their crime. We believe that trial in that District is proper under the Air Piracy Act, and accords with the relevant constitutional policy. Accordingly, we reverse the order of the district court that dismissed on the basis of improper venue the substantive counts of the indictment, and remand the case for trial.

I. FACTS

To the limited end of presenting the legal issue for this appeal, the parties have stipulated to the validity of a factual statement drawn from various Government affidavits introduced before the district court. While we must accept the truth of these assertions for this purpose, we wish emphatically to stress that our opinion should not be construed as an expression of views on the merits of the prosecution.

Zvonko and Julienne Busic, Peter Matanic, Frane Pesut and Mark Vlasic were indicted for the September 10, 1976 hijacking of TWA Flight 355, which was scheduled to fly from LaGuardia Airport in New York City to Chicago. During the preceding several days, pursuant to a carefully devised plan, appellee Zvonko Busic had supplied false names when purchasing five tickets for the flight at various locations in New York City, including LaGuardia Airport. Prior to embarkation he placed a powerful explosive device in a Grand Central Station locker and discarded the key in the Hudson River. The appellees boarded the aircraft with a previously prepared typewritten hijack note and several cast iron pots, which escaped confiscation by security personnel because of an ingenious ruse. By wrapping them with gift paper and ribbons, the appellees convinced the operators of the airport's metal detection devices that the pots were presents for acquaintances. In addition, prior to boarding the appellees had prepared several imitation dynamite sticks by wrapping a quantity of putty in black tape commonly used by electricians. They also had filled their luggage with political pamphlets which they intended to scatter widely by throwing them out of the aircraft as it flew over several European cities.

These were the largely unknown background facts as they existed when the flight crew closed the doors of TWA Flight 355. Shortly thereafter, but before the airplane left the ground, a passenger attempted to use a lavatory in the rear of the cabin. Prior to reaching his destination, however, he confronted Vlasic, who was blocking the aisle. Drawing the passenger's attention to a large leather bag at his feet, Vlasic uttered the following command: "Stop, do not use the lavatory, there are three bombs in this bag. This is a hijack, return to your seat." The passenger complied.

The import of Vlasic's statement was clear and correct. Scant moments later, at an undetermined point beyond the boundaries of the Eastern District of New York, Zvonko Busic handed a note to a flight attendant for transmittal to the pilot. It read:

> 1. This airplane is hijacked.
>
> 2. We are in possession of five gelignite bombs, four of which are set up in cast iron pans, giving them the same kind of force as a giant grenade.
>
> 3. In addition, we have left the same kind of bomb in a locker across from the Commodore Hotel on 42nd Street. To find the locker, take the subway entrance by the Bowery Savings Bank. After passing through the token booth, there are three windows belonging to the bank. To the left of these windows are the lockers. The number of the locker is 5713.
>
> 4. Further instructions are contained in a letter inside this locker. The bomb can only be activated by pressing the switch to which it is attached, but caution is suggested.
>
> 5. The appropriate authorities should be notified from the plane immediately.
>
> 6. The plane will ultimately be heading in the direction of London, England.

Two to six minutes later, when the aircraft was in the vicinity of Buffalo, New York, the pilot received the message. By this time Busic, who had transformed the iron pots into imitation bombs in the lavatory, appeared in the cockpit and opened his jacket to reveal a "dynamite vest," which he threatened to detonate if his demands were not met. The pilot, pursuant to the hijacker's orders, flew the airplane first to Montreal and then to Gander, Newfoundland where 33 hostages were released prior to a transatlantic voyage. The hijackers eventually surrendered in Paris.

Authorities in New York, meanwhile, descended upon the locker in Grand Central Station referred to in the hijacking message and which contained the authentic explosive device planted by Busic as well as a list of demands. Following the instructions concerning publication set forth in the note, the New York Times, Washington Post, Chicago Tribune, Los Angeles Times and International Herald Tribune proceeded to afford prominent coverage in their morning editions to a Croatian "Appeal to the American People." Tragically, New York City police officer Brian Murray was killed while attempting to defuse the Grand Central bomb. Upon his return to New York, Zvonko Busic is alleged to have said: "We are proud of what we did. Don't be surprised if you hear about other attacks in the future. We are defending a just cause, yet we are with handcuffs on our wrists."

II. PROCEEDINGS BELOW

The grand jury charged the two Busics, Matanic, Pesut and Vlasic with two counts of air piracy, which are identical except that the first also alleges that the commission of the offense resulted in the death of officer Murray, 49 U.S.C. § 1472(i)(2), and conspiracy, *18 U.S.C. § 371*:

> Aircraft piracy
>
> > (i)(1) Whoever commits or attempts to commit aircraft piracy, as herein defined, shall be punished -
> >
> > (A) by imprisonment for not less than 20 years; or
> >
> > (B) if the death of another person results from the commission or attempted commission of the offense, by death or by imprisonment for life.
> >
> > (2) As used in this subsection, the term "aircraft piracy" means any seizure or exercise of control, by force or violence or threat of force or violence, or by any other form of intimidation, and with wrongful intent, of an aircraft within the special aircraft jurisdiction of the United States.
> >
> > (3) An attempt to commit aircraft piracy shall be within the special aircraft jurisdiction of the United States even though the aircraft is not in flight at the time of such attempt if the aircraft would have been within the special aircraft jurisdiction of the United States had the offense of aircraft piracy been completed.
>
> 49 U.S.C. § 1472.
> An aircraft is "in flight"
>
> > . . . from the moment when all external doors are closed following embarkation until the moment when one such door is opened for

disembarkation or in the case of a forced landing, until the competent authorities take over the responsibility for the aircraft and for the persons and property aboard.

49 U.S.C. § 1301(34).

The appellees moved to dismiss the substantive counts of the indictment because, they argued, venue was improper in the Eastern District. Judge Bartels granted the motion on November 22, 1976 and the Government appealed.

Judge Bartels was aware, as he stated in his opinion, that "none of the defendants and none of the witnesses will have anything more than a fortuitous connection with any district over which the plane flew other than the Eastern District of New York and its surrounding metropolitan area." Moreover, he realized that "the most logical place for air piracy cases to be tried would be in the district where defendants boarded the aircraft." He stressed that the appellees "conspired, prepared to commit the offense, had the intent to commit the crime and boarded the plane in this district." Nevertheless, he said they had not seized and exercised actual control over the aircraft before it had entered the airspace of the Western District of New York. And he reasoned that although 49 U.S.C. § 1473(a) authorized the laying of venue in, *inter alia*, any district where the offense of air piracy had "begun," the acts here had not reached that stage "where the preparations have progressed to the first steps toward the commission of the crime, such as the first contact with the aircraft personnel notifying them of the intention to hijack" prior to the airplane's passing the boundaries of the Eastern District. Thus he concluded that under the relevant statutory provision venue clearly was improper in Brooklyn. We disagree and believe that the appellees plainly are triable in the place where the crime had "begun," the Eastern District of New York.

III. DISCUSSION

The Constitution and 49 U.S.C. § 1473(a) establish the parameters for our consideration of the instant appeal. Article III, section 2 provides that trials "shall be held in the State where the said Crimes shall have been committed; but when not committed within any State, the Trial shall be at such Place or Places as the Congress may by Law have directed." The *Sixth Amendment*, adopted after the Judiciary Act of 1789 divided the states into federal judicial districts, speaks similarly: "In all criminal prosecutions, the accused shall enjoy the right to a speedy and public trial, by an impartial jury of the State and district wherein the crime shall have been committed, which district shall have been previously ascertained by law. . . ." In cases of air piracy, Congress by special statute has determined that

Whenever the offense is begun in one jurisdiction and completed in another, or committed in more than one jurisdiction, it may be dealt with, inquired of, tried, determined, and punished in any jurisdiction in which such offense was begun, continued, or completed, in the same manner as if the offense had been actually or wholly committed therein. 49 U.S.C. § 1473(a).

The appellees contend that the facts presented here make § 1473(a) susceptible to only one narrow constitutional reading, which would advance the moment of beginning so near the point of consummation of the crime that the words might as well be read as synonymous and without any significant statutory difference. They argue that the essence of the crime of air piracy, according to the language in the Act, is the intentional and forcible "seizure or exercise of control" of an aircraft. Thus the offense charged here cannot be committed until there is a transfer of control from pilot to hijacker. This, they say, did not occur until the airplane was flying over Buffalo. Moreover, they claim that the requisite transfer of control had not "begun" until Busic gave his threatening note to a member of the flight crew who then transmitted it to the captain. This event transpired, they argue, after the aircraft left the Eastern District and thus, the appellees are not triable there since all of their conduct prior to the precise moment when the hijack note was passed constituted "mere preparation" rather than a "beginning" of the crime.

We do not think that this tortured and hyperconstricted reading of the statute is warranted. Congress responded to a national epidemic of hijackings by making air piracy a federal crime. A major benefit of this action, according to the Report of the House Committee on Interstate and Foreign Commerce, was the expected alleviation of the insuperable difficulties that law enforcement officials encountered in determining the exact state and county in which the seizure of an aircraft occurred. Recent airborne crimes had dramatically underscored gaps in existing laws that provided suspects with a haven from prosecution. 1961 U.S. Code Cong. & Adm. News 2563-2566. Any rational construction of § 1473(a) must account for Congress's special concern to permit a just and convenient locus for prosecution of this most unique crime which can begin and continue to be committed over several states in this high speed jet travel age in a matter of minutes. Accordingly, it appears - and the appellees do not seriously dispute - that Congress intended the Government to enjoy the broadest possible choice of venue within constitutional bounds.

The facts of this case bear eloquent testimony to the fact that the crime of hijacking had begun in the Eastern District of New York. Essential to the success of the appellees' scheme was their ability to board the aircraft with the cast iron pots and imitation dynamite sticks. Their goal was accomplished through an ingeniously conceived stratagem designed to circumvent the suspicion of airport security personnel. Busic purchased tickets for the flight at LaGuardia and elsewhere through the use of fictitious names. He planted a bomb in a locker at Grand Central Terminal with a list of demands. The appellees also filled their luggage with Croatian freedom pamphlets for ultimate distribution in European cities. Once aboard the airplane, and before it left the ground, Vlasic obstructed access to the lavatory (into which Busic went to construct his imitation explosive devices) and announced, "This is a hijack." In short, every one of the appellees' acts prior to the actual transmittal of the typewritten note was unambiguously corroborative of their unequivocal intention to hijack Flight 355. Since the substantive crime was consummated, the appellees clearly could not have been prosecuted for "attempted" air piracy. Nevertheless, an analysis of the appellees' conduct in terms of whether they would have been guilty of an inchoate crime had their plans failed to materialize provides some insight into whether commission of the actual offense had begun. The considerations, however, are not analogous. Judicial inquiry into whether a defendant is chargeable with an attempt is necessarily predictive and focuses on the point when the accused's conduct has progressed sufficiently to minimize the risk of an unfair conviction. See *U.S. v. Stallworth, 543 F.2d 1038 (2d Cir. 1976)*. For purposes of determining proper venue, on the other hand, we are merely called upon to ascertain in which jurisdiction it is just to try a defendant for an offense that by hypothesis has been carried to fruition. The terminology of the law of attempt is therefore useful, but the basic considerations inapplicable. Where, as in the instant case, the accused's purposeful conduct bespeaks so eloquently the beginning of a crime, it is neither necessary nor appropriate to speculate whether he properly could have been convicted of an attempt.

Under these circumstances it is obvious to us that 49 U.S.C. § 1473(a) serves its purpose well and intelligently by permitting prosecution in the Eastern District of New York.

It is equally clear to us that this result does not violate any constitutional rights of the appellees. Although Article III, section 2 concerns venue (place of trial) and the *Sixth Amendment* vicinage (residence of petit jurors), both can be traced to the ancient historical fact that at one time jurors decided cases on the basis of personal knowledge, see 3 Blackstone, Commentaries 359-60; 1 Coke On Littleton 125 (1853), and were drawn from the vicinity of the crime. See Blume, *The Place of Trial of Criminal Cases*, 43 Mich. L.Rev. 59, 60-63; Comment, 115 U. Pa. L. Rev. 399, 405-07 (1967). An even more significant source of these constitutional standards, however, can be discerned in the vigorous reaction of the American colonists evoked by Parliament's provision that trials of individuals accused of treason in Massachusetts be conducted in England. The Virginia Resolves responded to that edict by declaring: "thereby the inestimable Privilege of being tried by a Jury from the Vicinage, as well as the Liberty of summoning and producing Witnesses on such Trial, will be taken away from the Party accused." Journals of the House of Burgesses of Virginia, 1766-1769, at 214 (Kennedy ed. 1906). "For, how truly deplorable must be the Case of a wretched American, who, having incurred the Displeasure of any one in Power, is dragged from his native Home, and his dearest domestic Connections, thrown into Prison, not to await his Trial before a Court, Jury, or Judges, from a Knowledge of whom he is encouraged to hope for speedy Justice; but to exchange his Imprisonment in his own Country, for Fetters amongst Strangers? Conveyed to a distant Land, where no Friend, no Relation, will alleviate his Distresses, or minister to his Necessities; and where no Witness can be found to testify his Innocence; shunned by the reputable and honest, and consigned to the Society and Converse of the wretched and the abandoned; he can only pray that he may soon end his Misery with his life." Journals of the House of Burgesses of Virginia, 1766-1769, at 216 (Kennedy ed. 1906)..

The Framers' mandate for trial in the vicinity of the crime was meant to be a safeguard against the injustice and hardship involved when the accused was prosecuted in a place remote from his home and acquaintances. Indeed, the appellees in this case urge us to enforce this privilege, and cite to us Justice Frankfurter's oft-repeated language in *United States v. Johnson, 323 U.S. 273, 276, 89 L. Ed. 236, 65 S. Ct. 249 (1944)*:

> If an enactment of Congress equally permits the underlying spirit of the constitutional concern for trial in the vicinage to be respected rather than to be disrespected, construction should go in the direction of constitutional policy even though not commanded by it.

Of course, the appellees would have us hold that the "vicinage" contemplated by the Founders and Justice Frankfurter forbade the Government, in this instance, from proceeding in the Eastern District and mandated that it prosecute in Buffalo, a city whose only contact with this case is the mere fortuity of being five miles below the speeding jet airplane that the appellees had just hijacked. We cannot perceive any justification in the Constitution for such a result.

We do not believe that the appellees' blind insistence that the dictionary meaning of the term "seizure" mechanically govern our interpretation of "begun" is warranted. Congress did not direct its statute to an abstract world of Platonic forms, but to the real world of action. We are compelled, therefore, to reject the appellees' attempt, by their crabbed construction of the term "begun," to fasten upon the federal Air Piracy Act the precise over-technicality that Congress explicitly wished to avoid. The many purposeful and unambiguous acts of the appellees in the Eastern District clearly support our determination that the crime of hijacking had begun there within the intent of Congress. It is incomprehensible to us that courts must conduct a potentially fruitless search to determine exactly where a crime is committed when the alleged perpetrators are traveling at 600 m.p.h. In the case before us the note was passed in New Jersey or Pennsylvania, but Busic first confronted the pilot in western New York State. If the steward had tripped, Busic may not have reached his destination until the aircraft passed over Ohio, or was speeding over the middle of Lake Erie. And since the appellees concede that the Government could indict and try them at any point over which the jet flew after leaving the Buffalo airspace, we are hard pressed to accept the validity of the argument that constitutional restrictions on prosecutorial discretion preclude trying this case in the Eastern District of New York, which Judge Bartels correctly recognized as the sensible one, but instead permit prosecution in other districts over which the aircraft chanced to fly after seizure, no matter how fortuitous the contact.

Finally, we believe that the extensive case law under *18 U.S.C. § 3237(a)*, the venue provision for so-called continuous crimes after which 49 U.S.C. § 1473(a) was modeled, supports, to the extent that it is relevant, the result we have reached. Generally applicable to mobile offenses other than air piracy, *section 3237* requires an initial judicial inquiry into whether a particular crime involves a single act or movement. If the court determines, after considering the nature of the offense and the legislative and constitutional policies, *see United States v. Anderson, 328 U.S. 699, 90 L. Ed. 1529, 66 S. Ct. 1213 (1946)*, that it requires only a single act, then the prosecution must proceed in the district where the crime was committed *in toto*; if the crime, however, involves a continuous course of conduct, the offense may be tried wherever it was "begun, continued or completed." Since the appellees concede, as they must, that hijacking is by its very nature a continuous crime, the many cases that limit prosecution to the solitary district in which the offense was "committed," and abjure conducting the trial where mere preparatory acts took place, are clearly distinguishable. See *Travis v. United States, 364 U.S. 631, 5 L. Ed. 2d 340, 81 S. Ct. 358 (1961)* (non-Communist affidavit "on file" in Washington, D.C.); *United States v. Bozza, 365 F.2d 206 (2d Cir. 1966)* ("receiving" stolen government property); *United States v. Walden, 464 F.2d 1015 (4th Cir. 1972)*, cert. denied, *409 U.S. 867, 93 S. Ct. 165, 34 L. Ed. 2d 116 and 410 U.S. 969, 93 S. Ct. 1436, 35 L. Ed. 2d 705 (1973)* (illegal "entry" of bank); *United States v. Sweig, 316 F. Supp. 1148 (S.D.N.Y. 1970)* (illegally "acting" as agent of private person to defraud United States).

The proper focus of our inquiry, rather, is upon cases such as *United States v. Cashin, 281 F.2d 669 (2d Cir. 1960)* in which this court realized that the crime of use of the mails to facilitate a fraudulent scheme in violation of the Securities Act was begun in Alabama where "most of the acts necessary to [the] execution" of the crime occurred, although the alleged mailing took place in New York. *Id. at 674. See also United States v. Gross, 276 F.2d 816* (2d Cir.), cert. denied, *363 U.S. 831, 4 L. Ed. 2d 1525, 80 S. Ct. 1602 (1960)*. The principle that is gleaned from these cases is that when the nature of the offense defies the notion that it was committed in a single district Congress may, within constitutional norms, fix venue wherever sufficient purposeful acts occurred. *See United States v. Cores, 356 U.S. 405, 2 L. Ed. 2d 873, 78 S. Ct. 875 (1958); Armour Packing Co. v. United States, 209 U.S. 56, 52 L. Ed. 681, 28 S. Ct. 428 (1908)*. In the case before us involving hijacking, a crime which Congress considered sufficiently unique to require its own special venue provision, we conclude that the appellees' alleged acts in the Eastern District of New York easily surpassed this behavioral threshold.

Because of our disposition of this appeal, we need not consider the Government's other ground justifying venue in the Eastern District - that the appellees were "arrested or . . . first brought" there.

The order of the district court is reversed and the case remanded for trial.

UNITED STATES OF AMERICA v. JIMMY HICKS et al.

UNITED STATES COURT OF APPEALS FOR THE FIFTH
CIRCUIT

980 F.2d 963

December, 1992

KING, Circuit Judge:

Appellants, passengers aboard a commercial airline flight from
Jamaica to Houston, were convicted of "intimidating" members of the
flight crew "so as to interfere with" the performance of their duties, in
violation of 49 U.S.C. § 1472(j). Appellants raise a number of claims
on appeal, most notably a *first amendment* challenge to § 1472(j). After
carefully considering all their claims, we affirm.

I.

Appellants Jimmy Hicks and Latonya Moore, who were traveling
companions, boarded Continental Airlines Flight 1919 in Montego
Bay, Jamaica on July 23, 1991. The flight, carrying approximately 145
passengers, was bound for Houston. Hicks carried on board a
"boombox," a portable stereo system consisting of an AM-FM radio, a
tape player, and speakers. Immediately after boarding and taking a seat,
Hicks discovered that his seat was malfunctioning, which prevented
him from sitting next to Moore. Hicks subsequently requested that
Melissa Bott, the aircraft's flight service manager, find alternative
seating for them. Bott responded that she could do so only after
everyone with pre-assigned seating had claimed their seats. Hicks
expressed his displeasure with Bott's response by using the expletive
"shit." Rather than following Bott's instructions, Hicks immediately
proceeded to procure alternative seating by offering another passenger
free drinks in exchange for his seat. Also, during this time, Bott
observed Hicks remove a newspaper from another passenger's lap. The
passenger -- a total stranger to Hicks -- protested that he had not yet
finished reading the paper. Hicks angrily threw the paper back at the
other passenger. Bott said that she was "alarmed" by Hicks' extreme
arrogance.

Shortly thereafter, still prior to take-off, Moore turned on the radio
component of the boombox. Bott testified that the radio was playing
"loudly." Bott immediately approached Moore and informed her that
Federal Aviation Administration (FAA) regulations prohibited the
playing of radios on board aircraft because radio-playing interferes with
the proper functioning of a plane's navigational equipment. Moore
agreed to turn the radio off -- but only for the time being, as later events
would prove. Following take-off, one of the flight attendants, Eileen
DuBois, heard loud music playing on the aircraft; she noticed that
Hicks and Moore once again were playing their boombox. After
DuBois approached Hicks, he claimed that he was playing an audio
tape rather than the radio. DuBois informed him that Continental policy
required that passengers may only listen to tape players through
headphones. Hicks angrily refused to turn off the machine, claiming
that all of the passengers seated within listening range desired to hear
his tape. Hicks' claim was in fact somewhat unfounded. Rather than

476

confronting Hicks any further, DuBois believed that the wisest course was to inform her superior, Melissa Bott, of Hicks' refusal to use headphones. Bott subsequently entered the cockpit to apprise the captain of the situation.

The captain instructed Bott to order Hicks and Moore to discontinue use of the boombox. The captain stated that he believed that the playing of the radio was the cause of the malfunctioning of aircraft's navigational equipment during the plane's ascension to cruising altitude. Prior to Bott's entry into the cockpit, the captain and his first and second officers had attempted in vain to determine why the navigational equipment had failed, including running internal tests on the equipment, contacting a nearby American Airlines aircraft to inquire if it was experiencing similar difficulties, and contacting the airport in Jamaica to see if the malfunctioning was the result of a problem in the air traffic control tower. By the time Bott informed him of appellants' radio-playing, the captain had already concluded that the source of the problem was within the aircraft, although not equipment-related. Bott's report about the boombox strongly suggested that Hicks and Moore had continued to play the radio after being instructed not to do so.

Before Bott returned to the portion of the aircraft occupied by Hicks and Moore, another flight attendant, Carol McWilliams, approached them after other passengers complained about the boombox. McWilliams informed Hicks that he must not play the radio -- as it would interfere with the plane's navigational equipment -- and that if he played a tape he must use headphones. Hicks responded that McWilliams was "the third bitch" who had complained about the boombox. He also angrily ordered her to serve him a drink. At that point, Moore interjected that all of the passengers around them wished to hear the boombox. Like DuBois before her, McWilliams realized that Hicks and Moore were too obstinate to reason with; the flight attendant thus went to the front of the aircraft to inform Bott. As McWilliams walked up the aisle, she met Bott, who was coming from the cockpit. McWilliams informed Bott of Hicks and Moore's continued non-compliance.

Bott again approached Hicks and Moore. She requested that they should turn the boombox over to her for the remainder of the flight. Hicks responded that the "f---ing radio was going to stay on" and that he would not relinquish it to anyone. In a confrontational manner, he then passed it to Moore and stated "if you want the radio, you need to get it from her." Moore also refused to give up the boombox and cursed at Bott. Moore firmly stated that "the radio is going to stay on," and ordered Ms. Bott to get her "ass[] back there and do [her] job to get them something to eat and drink." She also ordered the flight attendants to "quit bothering" them. At this point, Appellant Canty, who was seated nearby but who was not a traveling companion of Hicks and Moore, intervened and began to curse at Bott and McWilliams. No member of the flight crew had heretofore directed any comment to Canty. Bott stated that she asked appellants not to use profanity, as young children were seated nearby. Bott also stated that she began to feel "frightened" by appellants' increasingly angry obstinacy, although all the while she maintained her composure.

Bott returned to the cockpit to inform the captain of the latest developments in the escalating disturbance. At that point, the captain instructed his second officer to attempt to retrieve the boombox. In the meantime, McWilliams had another encounter with Hicks and Moore, although this time Canty again vocalized his own angry sentiments to the flight attendant. McWilliams directed appellants' attention to a Continental Airlines flight magazine wherein the proscription on radio playing and the requirement that a tape player could be played only with headphones were clearly set forth. Canty angrily responded that McWilliams should "get out of [his] face." Shortly thereafter, the second officer, Jim McKelvain, arrived and informed Hicks and Moore that their radio had interfered with the aircraft's navigational equipment. He asked them to relinquish the boombox. Hicks told the second officer "to get f---ed" and that Hicks would rather pay a fine than cooperate. The second officer described Hicks as totally "uncooperative," even after being told that he was violating federal law. As he had done when confronted with Bott's demand to turn over the boombox, Hicks proceeded to pass it to Moore. Moore refused to hand it over to the second officer, even after the officer stated that rather than confiscating it, he would merely place it in the overhead compartment located above Hicks and Moore.

Hicks then instructed the second officer to get his "mother- f---ing ass to the cockpit" and fly the plane. The second officer returned to the cockpit and informed the captain of his belief that physical force would be required to retrieve the boombox. Meanwhile, Bott was making a last ditch effort to explain to Hicks and Moore that they were violating federal law. Moore stated that she did not care and that she was going to keep the boombox in her possession. Hicks stated that all of the passengers around him wished to hear the radio and that he did not care about a "f---ing" fine; in fact, he claimed, he would "buy the f---ing airplane." According to Bott, Hicks' countenance was extremely menacing. Furthermore, Canty "kept turning around and saying things the whole time I kept trying to talk to Miss Moore or Mr. Hicks." Among other things, Canty angrily stated "f--- you bitch" to Bott and told her to leave Hicks, Moore, and Canty alone. Bott also stated that the volume of the boombox was intentionally increased. Without identifying particular passengers, Bott also stated that "at that point everyone around them . . . were laughing" and that someone began to videotape Bott with a portable camera.

Bott and McWilliams testified that, because of the disturbance, for a significant amount of time numerous members of the flight crew were unable to perform their regular duties aboard the aircraft. Bott, McWilliams, and Dubois also stated that they were very much intimidated by Hicks, Moore, and Canty. At one point during her efforts to retrieve the boombox, Bott testified, she felt the need visually to locate fire extinguishers to use in her defense in the event that she was physically assaulted by any or all of the three passengers. Bott also stated that numerous passengers seated around the disturbance had expressed their fear "that a riot . . . might break out."

Realizing that further efforts to retrieve the boombox would be futile -- short of physical force -- the captain diverted the aircraft's course to Cancun, Mexico, where an unscheduled landing occurred. The captain stated that he was unwilling to order the crew members to attempt to retrieve the boombox by physical force. He was also unwilling to risk the possibility that further radio playing would again interfere with the aircraft's navigational equipment. Upon landing, Mexican authorities removed several passengers from the plane, including Hicks, Moore, and Canty. Canty initially refused to deplane. It is undisputed that, throughout the flight, none of the appellants committed assault or battery or verbally threatened any Continental flight crew member with physical harm. Rather, according to the testimony of the various members of the Continental flight crew, intimidation resulted solely from appellants' verbal and non-verbal expressive activity -- consisting primarily of appellants' repeated angry and profane remarks, although also including menacing stares, the refusal by Hicks and Moore to relinquish the boombox, and the intentional increase in the boombox's volume by Hicks and Moore. Bott also cited Hicks and Moore's repeated passing of the boombox between themselves after being asked to relinquish it. The Government argues that such intimidating expression, which occupied the attention of numerous members of the flight crew for a significant amount of time and ultimately caused the plane to be diverted to Cancun, is the gravamen of appellants' § 1472(j) violation.

On September 4, 1991, a jury found Hicks, Moore, and Canty guilty of violating 49 U.S.C. § 1472(j). That provision reads, in pertinent part, as follows:Whoever, while aboard an aircraft within the special aircraft jurisdiction of the United States, assaults, intimidates, or threatens any flight crew member or flight attendant (including any steward or stewardess of such aircraft), so as to interfere with the performance by such member of his duties, shall be fined not more than $ 10,000 or imprisoned not more than twenty years, or both. Sentencing occurred in the following November. Hicks was sentenced to fourteen months imprisonment to be followed by three years of supervised release. Moore was sentenced to eight months imprisonment to be followed by three years of supervised release. Canty was sentenced to four months imprisonment to be followed by three years of supervised release. All three appellants were also each ordered to pay restitution in the amount of $ 1,871.35 to Continental Airlines, as well as a special assessment of $ 50.00.

II.

A. The *first amendment* challenge

Appellants Hicks and Moore claim that their convictions under 49 U.S.C. § 1472 (j) are in violation of the free speech clause of the *first amendment to the United States Constitution*. Appellants specifically claim that the statute's operative term "intimidate" is overbroad because a person using profanity, which is not specifically [proscribed by] the statute, [but] which is constitutionally protected, could be accused of violating the statute. . . . That is, the [statutes's use of the] word "intimidate" cannot be limited to core criminal conduct but becomes an enforceable ordinance generally prohibiting [profane] speech, which is constitutionally protected. . . . By including . . . the term "intimidate" the statute fails to properly exclude[profane] speech which [is] protected by the *First Amendment* but which may also cause intimidation.

Although this passage from Hicks and Moore's briefs appears to be challenging the statute solely on overbreadth grounds, in reply briefs appellants respond that their "overbreadth challenge is both to the face of the statute, and *as applied* to the facts in this case" (emphasis added).

The Government argues that not only is § 1472(j) not overbroad, but also that "profanity [such as that spoken by appellants] used . . . to intimidate is proscribable speech. . . . It is similar to fighting words and obscenity." The Government proceeds to note, though, that § 1472(j) "proscribes intimidation of crew members that interferes with their duties, not profanity. It is not a content regulation of speech. . . To the extent that it proscribes profanity used to intimidate crew members aboard an aircraft in flight, that proscription is permissible," as merely an "incidental" restriction on speech. At oral argument, however, the Government repeated its argument that profanity in general is not protected speech and, for that reason, appellants have no basis for challenging the statute on *first amendment* grounds.

We agree with the Government that § 1472 (j) does not violate the *first amendment*, although we do not rely on the totality of the Government's reasoning to reach this result. In addressing this claim, we are required to address both parts of appellants' two-pronged challenge -- that the statute is both overbroad and in violation of the *first amendment as applied* to the facts of the instant case.

i) The overbreadth challenge

Appellants have made a spirited attempt to invalidate § 1472(j) on overbreadth grounds; however, as is evident from the above-quoted passage from their briefs, they have misconceived the overbreadth doctrine, at least as it applies to the instant case. Appellants argue that the term "intimidate" is overbroad in that it effectively criminalizes a form of speech -- simple profanity or vulgarity -- that may well intimidate, but should nevertheless be afforded protection under the *first amendment*. We agree with appellants that the profanity generally is protected by the *first amendment*. However, the statute that appellants are challenging does not criminalize profanity *per se*, but instead criminalizes any speech or conduct, which may incidentally include profanity, that intimidates an airline's flight crew so as to interfere with the performance of their duties. *See infra* Part II.A.ii While such an argument at first blush appears to be an overbreadth challenge, appellants are in fact only making a substantive challenge to § 1472(j) as it applies to intimidating profanity or vulgarity such as that used by appellants. Appellants have not argued that "intimidate" is overbroad in that it may also chill *other* types of protected expression besides profanity.

Appellants fail to realize that the rationale of the overbreadth doctrine is to protect the expressive rights of *third parties* who are not before the court. An overbreadth challenge is not appropriate if the *first amendment* rights asserted by a party attacking a statute are essentially coterminous with the expressive rights of third parties. *See Brockett v. Spokane Arcades, Inc., 472 U.S. 491, 504, 86 L. Ed. 2d 394, 105 S. Ct. 2794 (1985)* (Courts need not entertain an overbreadth challenge "where the parties challenging the statute are those who desire to engage in protected speech that the overbroad statute purports to punish . . . . There is then no want of a proper party to challenge the statute, no concern that the attack on the statute will be unduly delayed or protected speech discouraged."); *Members of the City Council of the City of Los Angeles v. Taxpayers for Vincent, 466 U.S. 789, 801-02, 80*

L. Ed. 2d 772, 104 S. Ct. 2118 (1984) ("[Appellees] have . . . failed to identify any significant difference between their claim that the ordinance is invalid on overbreadth grounds and their claim that it is unconstitutional when applied to their political signs."); *International Society for Krishna Consciousness of New Orleans, Inc. v. City of Baton Rouge, 876 F.2d 494, 499-500 (5th Cir. 1989)* (citing *Vincent*); L. Tribe, *Constitutional Law*, § 12-27, at 1022-24 & n.7.

Even if appellants had argued that § 1472(j) is overbroad because it chills expression other than profanity or vulgarity, we do not believe that such an overbreadth challenge would be viable. The only type of protected speech besides profanity that would have the potential to intimidate a reasonable person would be non-profane invective. We note that profanity should be distinguished from two somewhat related, but distinguishable, species of non-protected speech -- "fighting words" and obscenity. *See Chaplinsky v. New Hampshire, 315 U.S. 568, 86 L. Ed. 1031, 62 S. Ct. 766 (1942)* (fighting words not protected); *Miller v. California, 413 U.S. 15, 37 L. Ed. 2d 419, 93 S. Ct. 2607 (1973)* (obscenity not protected). With reference to remarks made in the instant case, we believe that none rose to the level of "fighting words" or obscenity. For instance, we can hypothesize a scenario in which an intoxicated airline passenger becomes angry at a member of the flight crew because of the crew member's refusal to serve alcohol to the passenger. The passenger could hurl non-profane invective at the crew member, which -- depending on the tenor of the invective -- could intimidate the crew member so as to interfere with the performance of his duties. A similar hypothetical was actually mentioned by the sponsor of 49 U.S.C. § 1472(j) in the United States Senate. *See* remarks of Senator Engle, 107 Cong. Rec. 17170 (August 28, 1961) (hypothesizing scenario of "a drunk quarrelling with a stewardess over whether or not he could keep his bottle").

Even assuming, without deciding, that § 1472(j) could not constitutionally criminalize such angry non-profane invective, we observe that the statute's potential to criminalize such speech is too insubstantial to permit an overbreadth challenge. "It is clear . . . that the mere fact that one can conceive of some impermissible applications of a statute is not sufficient to render it susceptible to an overbreadth challenge." *Vincent, 466 U.S. at 800.* Rather, a party challenging a statute on overbreadth grounds must demonstrate that there is a "substantial" potential that the overbroad statute will chill third parties' speech. *See Broadrick v. Oklahoma, 413 U.S. 601, 615, 37 L. Ed. 2d 830, 93 S. Ct. 2908 (1973).* Unlike the party who successfully challenged a somewhat similar statute invalidated on overbreadth grounds by this court and later by the Supreme Court in *City of Houston v. Hill, 482 U.S. 451, 96 L. Ed. 2d 398, 107 S. Ct. 2502 (1987), aff'g, 789 F.2d 1103 (5th Cir. 1986)* (en banc), appellants have not offered any proof that there is a realistic and substantial danger that § 1472(j) will be used to chill constitutionally protected speech. In *Hill*, the plaintiff actually documented numerous prior instances where the challenged statute had been used to chill constitutionally protected speech. *See 789 F.2d at 1113-14* (Appendix to majority opinion.) Appellants have offered no such data. Our own research of reported cases has revealed that § 1472(j) has resulted in relatively few convictions. Of those convictions discussed in reported decisions, the type of activity prosecuted invariably has not been protected by the *first amendment.* *See* Annotation, Construction and Application of § 902(i-l) of Federal Aviation Act of 1958, as Amended (49 U.S.C. § 1472(i-l), Punishing Aircraft Piracy, Interference with Flight Crew Members, and Other Crimes Abroad Aircraft in Flight, 10 A.L.R. Fed. 844 (& Supp.) (discussing cases); Annotation, Validity, Construction, and Application of Provisions of Federal Aviation Act Punishing Air Piracy and Certain Acts Aboard Aircraft in Flight, or Boarding Aircraft, 109 A.L.R. Fed. 488, § 17B (discussing cases). In every reported case in which a § 1472(j) conviction has occurred, the defendant has not simply engaged in "pure speech," whether profane language or non-profane invective, but has also directly threatened, assaulted, or battered a member of the flight crew. *See, e.g., United States v. Tabacca, 924 F.2d 906 (9th Cir. 1991); United States v. Hall, 691 F.2d 48 (1st Cir. 1982); United States v. Meeker, 527 F.2d 12 (9th Cir. 1975); Mims v. United States, 332 F.2d 944 (10th Cir. 1964).*We believe that § 1472(j) does not pose a "substantial" threat of overbreadth.

ii) The as-applied challenge

There is still a need to review appellants' *first amendment* challenge to § 1472(j) as applied to the facts of the instant case. As an initial matter, we must address the Government's threshold contention that profanity is not constitutionally protected speech. This argument is meritless. The Supreme Court has long held that, as a general rule, simple profanity or vulgarity -- not rising to the level of "fighting words" or obscenity -- is constitutionally protected speech. By "profanity" or "vulgarity," we refer to words that, while not obscene, nevertheless are considered generally offensive by contemporary community standards. *Cf. FCC v. Pacifica Foundation*, 438 U.S. at 741 (discussing humorist George Carlin's "Filthy Words" monologue as qualifying as "indecent" or "profane" language). We note that such words usually refer to "offensive sexual or excretory speech." *Id.* at 743. We also believe that certain other language, at least when used in certain contexts, qualifies as profanity. For instance, with reference to the instant case, we believe that Appellant Canty's angry reference to Ms. Bott as a "bitch" and Appellant Moore's angry admonition that Ms. Bott should get her "ass" to the plane's kitchen qualified as profane. *See, e.g., Lewis v. City of New Orleans, 415 U.S. 130, 39 L. Ed. 2d 214, 94 S. Ct. 970 (1972); Gooding v. Wilson, 405 U.S. 518, 31 L. Ed. 2d 408, 92 S. Ct. 1103 (1972); Cohen v. California, 403 U.S. 15, 29 L. Ed. 2d 284, 91 S. Ct. 1780 (1971); see generally* Tribe, *supra,* § 12-10, at 849-56.

Although we disagree with the Government's broad contention about the constitutional status of profanity, we do recognize that general rules do have their exceptions. As the Supreme Court has repeatedly held, *first amendment* protections are not absolute, even in cases involving "pure speech." *See, e.g., Elrod v. Burns, 427 U.S. 347, 360, 49 L. Ed. 2d 547, 96 S. Ct. 2673 (1976)* ("the proscription on encroachment of *First Amendment* protections is not an absolute"). In the instant case, we believe appellants' use of angry profanity and vulgarities may be constitutionally criminalized. We note at the outset of our *first amendment* analysis that the Supreme Court has traditionally bifurcated its review of statutes challenged on *first amendment* grounds between cases involving a content-based regulation of speech and cases involving a content-neutral "time, place, or manner" restriction. *See generally* Tribe, *supra*, § 12-2, at 789-794. The Court has applied significantly greater scrutiny to content-based regulation, requiring a "compelling" governmental interest to justify the curtailment of speech based on its content and also requiring that the statute be "'narrowly drawn to achieve that end.'" *Simon & Schuster, Inc. v. Members of New York Crime Victims Bd., 116 L. Ed. 2d 476, 112 S. Ct. 501, 509 (1992)*. Conversely, the Supreme Court has been somewhat more deferential to legislative efforts to regulate time, place, and manner of expression -- requiring only a "substantial" governmental interest and "narrow tailoring," so long as such regulations are content-neutral. *See Ward v. Rock Against Racism, 491 U.S. 781, 791-92, 796, 105 L. Ed. 2d 661, 109 S. Ct. 2746 (1989)* ("reasonable" regulations on time, place, or manner "only if they are 'justified without reference to the content of the speech'" and if they are "'narrowly tailored to serve a substantial governmental interest'") (citations omitted).

Rather than discriminating against protected profanity or vulgarity, the statute reasonably regulates the time, place, and manner of speech, irrespective of its particular content. The content of passengers' speech is thus regulated only in an incidental fashion. Only intimidating speech in a quite limited context is proscribed. *See CISPES v. Federal Bureau of Investigation, 770 F.2d 468 (5th Cir. 1985)*. In other contexts, profanity -- even if intimidating -- would not go unprotected. *See, e.g., Nash v. State of Texas, 632 F. Supp. 951, 972-76 (E.D. Tex. 1986)* (intimidating language in context of labor strikes is protected by *first amendment*).

Nevertheless, even if we were to accept appellants' argument that § 1472(j) does discriminate against profane or vulgar language, and thus apply the more stringent analysis required in cases involving a content-based regulation, we would still hold that the statute is constitutional. Assuring the utmost in airline safety is the clear purpose behind § 1472(j). *See United States v. Meeker, 527 F.2d 12, 14 (9th cir. 1975)* ("The goal which Congress sought in this provision . . . was to deter [acts] which, if committed on the terrain below, might be considered relatively minor, but when perpetrated on an aircraft in flight would endanger the lives of many.") In view of the special context of air travel -- pressurized vessels routinely carrying hundreds of passengers and traveling at speeds of up to 600 miles per hour and 40,000 feet above the ground -- we cannot gainsay that there is a compelling governmental interest in § 1472(j). Congress did not unnecessarily infringe passenger's *first amendment* liberties to use intimidating profanity. The potential for disaster being so great, even the more mundane duties of flight attendants which implicate safety cannot be taken for granted. Moreover, we note that in the instant case, it was not only flight attendants, but also a member of the cockpit crew whose duties were interfered with by appellants.

We also believe that the statute is narrowly tailored. It does not cast a sweeping net at amorphous categories of speech. *See, e.g., Gooding v. Wilson, 405 U.S. 518, 523, 31 L. Ed. 2d 408, 92 S. Ct. 1103 (1972)* (invalidating statute that proscribed "opprobrious" or "abusive" language). Rather, the statute requires a passenger to "assault[], intimate[], or threaten[] . . . so as to interfere" with a crew member's duties. 49 U.S.C. § 1472(j). "Intimidate," the operative term in the instant case, is a word that is not simply associated with a type of speech, but includes conduct as well. We note that at least Appellants Hicks and Moore engaged not merely in intimidating speech, but also intimidating conduct. The parties, however, had limited their arguments to the speech elements of appellants' intimidation. In fact, it encompasses only a relatively narrow range of speech, which frequently will be a concomitant of intimidating conduct, as in the instant case. Moreover, only intimidating acts or words that actually interfere with a crew member's duties are penalized. Usually only extreme or repeated intimidation -- such as that in the instant case -- will actually have the effect of interfering with a crew member's duties.

We hold that § 1472(j) is constitutional as applied to appellants in the instant case.

B. Vagueness

Appellants have raised a related challenge to the statute as being unconstitutionally vague. This argument is also without merit. We observe that the instant case is not an appropriate one in which to raise a void-for-vagueness challenge. "In a facial challenge to the . . . vagueness of a law[], a court's first task is to determine whether the enactment reaches a substantial amount of constitutionally protected conduct." *Village of Hoffman Estates v. Flipside, 455 U.S. 489, 494-95, 71 L. Ed. 2d 362, 102 S. Ct. 1186 (1982)*. If the statute does not proscribe a "substantial" amount of constitutionally protected conduct, a party may raise a void-for-vagueness challenge only if "the enactment is impermissibly vague in *all* of its applications." *Id. at 495* (emphasis added). As we discussed in connection with appellants' overbreadth challenge, the statute does not reach a "substantial" amount of constitutionally protected conduct. Thus, because § 1472(j) obviously is not impermissibly vague in *all* its applications, appellants' void-for-vagueness challenge must fail. Furthermore, we note that "one to whose conduct a statute clearly applies may not successfully challenge it for vagueness." *Id. at 495 n.7*. There is no question that appellants' conduct violated § 1472(j). Nevertheless, we note that the Ninth Circuit, in a void-for-vagueness challenge in which the court actually reached the merits, has upheld § 1472(j). *See United States v. Tabacca, 924 F.2d 906, 913 (9th Cir. 1991)*.

[discussion about evidence and jury charges omitted]

III.

For the foregoing reasons, we AFFIRM all three appellants' convictions under 49 U.S.C. § 1472(j).

UNITED STATES OF AMERICA v. TODD KEVIN WALLACE

UNITED STATES COURT OF APPEALS FOR THE NINTH CIRCUIT

800 F.2d 1509

September, 1986

W. D. BROWNING, District Judge:

Todd Kevin Wallace appeals from a jury verdict convicting him of violating *18 U.S.C. § 2314*, by transporting stolen goods having a value in excess of five thousand dollars in interstate commerce, and convicting him of violating 49 U.S.C. § 1472(*l*), by boarding an airplane while concealing a dangerous weapon. We affirm both convictions.

[the issues of speedy trial, fraud, and jury trial are omitted].

III

The final issues raised on appeal concern Wallace's conviction pursuant to 49 U.S.C. § 1472(*l*) for boarding a plane with a concealed dangerous weapon. 49 U.S.C. § 1472(*l*) provides, in pertinent part, that whoever "while aboard, or while attempting to board [any aircraft in, or intended for operation in air transportation or intrastate air transportation] has on or about his person or his property a concealed deadly or dangerous weapon, which is, or could be, accessible to such person in flight; . . . .Shall be fined not more than $10,000 or imprisoned not more than one year, or both."

Wallace initially contends that the trial judge erred in determining that the question of whether an electronic taser or stun gun is a dangerous weapon is an issue of law to be resolved by the court. If, however, an instrument is designed for the purpose of producing death or great bodily harm, the question of whether the instrument is an inherently dangerous weapon may be determined as a matter of law. *See United States v. Dishman, 486 F.2d 727, 732 (9th Cir. 1973).* Moreover, an instrument that has been designed to produce death or great bodily harm may be held to be an inherently dangerous weapon as a matter of law if the instrument is ready to be used to produce bodily harm or may be quickly adapted to produce bodily harm. *Id.* Accordingly, we hold that the trial court correctly found that the question of whether a stun gun is a dangerous weapon may be determined as a matter of law.

Wallace further contends that the trial court erred when it found that a stun gun is a dangerous weapon proscribed under 49 U.S.C. § 1472(*l*). Wallace urges that the statutory prohibition against deadly or dangerous weapons only prohibits weapons that are likely to produce death or great bodily harm and does not apply to a weapon such as a stun gun that incapacitates its victims temporarily and does not inflict serious permanent harm.

Wallace's position is without merit. First, evidence was introduced at trial indicating that stun guns may cause permanent injury to eyes and that a single stun gun may incapacitate twenty to forty people at a time. *Cf. United States v. Brown, 376 F. Supp. 451, 459 (W.D. Mo.), rev'd on other grounds, 508 F.2d 427 (8th Cir. 1974)* (relying on similar evidence to find that tear gas is a dangerous weapon under 49 U.S.C. § 1472(*l*)). Moreover, the potential for devastating injury that is present during even a temporary incapacitation of key personnel aboard an aircraft in flight requires courts applying the statutory prohibition against a deadly or dangerous weapon to consider both the transitory and permanent nature of the weapon's effect. *See* H.Rep. No. 958, 87th Cong., 1st Sess. 10, *reprinted in* 1961 U.S. Code Cong. & Ad. News 2563, 2570. Finally, a stun gun may be found to be a dangerous weapon because display of the gun is likely to provoke fear in the surrounding passengers creating "an immediate danger that a violent response will ensue." *McLaughlin v. United States, 476 U.S. 16, 106 S. Ct. 1677, 1678, 90 L. Ed. 2d 15 (1986)* (interpreting the statutory requirement of a dangerous weapon in *18 U.S.C. § 2113(d)*).

Wallace's final contention on appeal is that the trial court erred in excluding evidence indicating that Wallace did not intend to conceal the stun gun as he boarded the plane. Wallace claims that he sought to introduce evidence at trial that he boarded a plane the day before the arrest with a stun gun and that the security officers inspected the gun and allowed him to board with it. Accordingly, Wallace reasons that he could not have been attempting to conceal the stun gun on the day he was arrested, because he had no reason to believe that he would be prohibited from taking the weapon on board the aircraft.

Wallace's assertion that he sought to introduce this evidence is contradicted by his statement that the parties stipulated to the existence of all elements necessary for a conviction under 49 U.S.C. § 1472 (*l*), with the one exception concerning the question of whether a stun gun is a dangerous weapon within the meaning of the statute. Brief for Appellant at 7. Accordingly, the Government opposes Wallace's attempt to raise the question of his intent to conceal the weapon on appeal because the record does not show any effort to introduce evidence on non-concealment at trial. *See United States v. Whitten, 706 F.2d 1000, 1012 (9th Cir. 1983), cert. denied, 465 U.S. 1100, 80 L. Ed. 2d 125, 104 S. Ct. 1593 (1984)* (holding that errors not raised before the trial court will not generally be considered on appeal).

Assuming, however, that this issue is properly raised on appeal, Wallace's good faith belief that it was not illegal to carry a stun gun onto the aircraft is not an adequate ground for reversal. *See United States v. Flum, 518 F.2d 39, 45 (8th Cir.), cert. denied, 423 U.S. 1018, 96 S. Ct. 454, 46 L. Ed. 2d 390 (1975)* (holding that it is the fact of concealment, and not the intent to conceal, that is prohibited under 49 U.S.C. § 1472(*l*)). The Government presented a submissible case when it established that Wallace boarded the aircraft with a dangerous weapon about his person that was hidden from view. *Id.*

AFFIRMED.

UNITED STATES OF AMERICA v. JORGE A. PULIDO-
BAQUERIZO

UNITED STATES COURT OF APPEALS FOR THE NINTH
CIRCUIT

800 F.2d 899

September, 1986

J. BLAINE ANDERSON, Circuit Judge:

The government seeks to overturn the district court's granting of Jorge A. Pulido-Baquerizo's (Pulido) motion to suppress evidence seized and statements made in the course of an airport search. The suppression of both the evidence and the statements centers upon the extent to which a passenger impliedly consents to a visual inspection and limited hand search of carry-on luggage for the detection of weapons or explosives as a condition to airline travel. In light of the gravity of the dangers involved in airline terrorism and the traveling public's awareness of minimally intrusive airplane boarding inspections, we find the district court erred in granting the motion to suppress. Accordingly, we reverse.

I.

FACTS

On September 30, 1985, at approximately 8:00 a.m., appellee Pulido attempted to board an airplane at Terminal 3 of the Los Angeles International Airport. Pulido approached the pre-boarding inspection checkpoint and placed two briefcases onto the x-ray machine's conveyor belt. The security agent operating the machine, Willie Collins, noticed a "dark object with what looked to be lines in it" in one of the briefcases. Suspecting the object might be a bomb, Collins turned to a second agent, Jessie Gonzalez, and asked if she could determine what the object was. She could not. Paul McCurn, the agents' supervisor who was stationed nearby, was summoned to see if he could identify the object. He was also unable to identify the object, but privately believed he saw wires which indicated a bomb or explosive device.

At this point, Pulido was asked what was in the briefcase. He answered, "clothes." The case was run through the x-ray machine a second time. Since none of the agents could identify the object, McCurn removed the briefcase to a nearby inspection table and conducted a visual inspection and hand search. The search disclosed 2138 grams of cocaine. Pulido was indicted for possession of cocaine with intent to distribute in violation of *21 U.S.C. § 841(a)(1)*.

At the pretrial suppression hearing, Pulido moved to suppress evidence obtained by the search and the inculpatory statements he made in the course of the search. The district court found Pulido did not give express consent to search his briefcase, legal justification did not exist on the basis of implied consent, and that Pulido was not free to leave during the agent's questioning. On these grounds the motion to suppress was granted.

487

II.

THE SEARCH

The government argues that by placing his briefcase on the x-ray machine's conveyor belt, Pulido impliedly consented to the subsequent visual inspection and hand search. The issue of implied consent presents a question of mixed law and fact which we review *de novo*. *See United States v. McConney, 728 F.2d 1195, 1199-1204 (9th Cir.)* (en banc), *cert. denied, 469 U.S. 824, 105 S. Ct. 101, 83 L. Ed. 2d 46 (1984)*. It is clear the search, conducted without a warrant, was *per se* unreasonable under the probable cause requirement of the *fourth amendment* and unlawful unless conducted pursuant to Pulido's consent, express or implied. *See Schneckloth v. Bustamonte, 412 U.S. 218, 219, 93 S. Ct. 2041, 36 L. Ed. 2d 854 (1973)*.

In *United States v. Davis, 482 F.2d 893, 912-914 (9th Cir. 1973)*, we indicated that a pre-boarding search is not unlawful if there is implied consent, the search is reasonable, and the prospective airplane boarder has the right to leave without being subject to a search. In delineating these requirements, we stated:

> [A] screening of passengers and of the articles that will be accessible to them in flight does not exceed constitutional limitations provided that the screening process is no more extensive nor intensive than necessary, in the light of current technology, to detect the presence of weapons or explosives, that it is confined in good faith to that purpose, and that potential passengers may avoid the search by electing not to fly.

Davis, 482 F.2d at 913 (footnote omitted). Having approached the question in light of the circumstances surrounding today's airport checkpoints, we hold that those passengers placing luggage on an x-ray machine's conveyor belt for airplane travel at a secured boarding area impliedly consent to a visual inspection and limited hand search of their luggage if the x-ray scan is inconclusive in determining whether the luggage contains weapons or other dangerous objects.

Under the *fourth amendment*, only unreasonable searches and seizures are prohibited. The determination of reasonableness requires a balancing of an individual's right to be free of intrusive searches with society's interest in safe air travel. "What is reasonable depends upon all of the circumstances surrounding the search or seizure and the nature of the search or seizure itself." *United States v. Montoya De Hernandez, 473 U.S. 531, 105 S. Ct. 3304, 3308, 87 L. Ed. 2d 381, 388 (1985)*.

The governmental interest in detecting the weapons employed in airline terrorism is great. Airplane skyjacking and bombings at airports have proliferated since our decision in *Davis*. Additionally, firearms and explosives can be small and easily concealed. Their detection is difficult if limited to an inconclusive x-ray scan. The scan and subsequent search involves only a slight privacy intrusion as long as the scope of the search is limited to the detection of weapons, explosives, or any other dangerous devices, and is conducted in a manner which produces negligible social stigma. Given these circumstances, a visual inspection and limited hand search of luggage which is used for the purpose of detecting weapons or explosives, and not in order to uncover other types of contraband, is a privacy intrusion we believe free society is willing to tolerate. Our approach is consistent with that of other circuits where the purpose of the search is to detect skyjack weaponry. *See United States v. Herzbrun, 723 F.2d 773, 776 (11th Cir. 1984)* (automatic consent to a hand search); *United States v. Wehrli, 637 F.2d 408, 409-10 (5th Cir.), cert. denied, 452 U.S. 942, 101 S. Ct. 3089, 69 L. Ed. 2d 958 (1981)* (implied consent where x-ray inconclusive); *United States v. DeAngelo, 584 F.2d 46, 47-48 (4th Cir. 1978), cert. denied, 440 U.S. 935, 99 S. Ct. 1278, 59 L. Ed. 2d 493 (1979)* (implied consent); *United States v. Williams, 516 F.2d 11, 12 (2d Cir. 1975)* (per curiam) (implied consent).

Pulido argues that under *Davis* his statements show he preferred to leave rather than submit to the search. However, *Davis* does not specifically hold that consent to an additional search could be withdrawn after an inconclusive x-ray scan if the passenger agreed not to board the plane. While *Davis* implies a passenger may withhold such consent by electing not to fly, *Davis* did not determine at what point in the boarding process a passenger may decide not to fly and thereby withdraw his implied consent. In *United States v. Homburg, 546 F.2d 1350 (9th Cir. 1976), cert. denied, 431 U.S. 940, 97 S. Ct. 2654, 53 L. Ed. 2d 258 (1977)*, in dicta we refused to adopt a general doctrine of implied consent in the context of airport luggage searches, stating that "such a view runs contrary to *Davis.*" *Homburg at 1352*. However, three years later, in *United States v. Henry, 615 F.2d 1223, 1228 (9th Cir. 1980)*, we noted that the precise issue of whether implied consent to a subsequent search existed by the mere fact of placing luggage on the x-ray machine remained undecided. "We express no opinion as to whether submission to the x-ray scan constitutes consent to physical inspection if requested." *Henry at 1229 n.7* (citing *United States v. DeAngelo, 584 F.2d 46 (4th Cir. 1978), cert. denied, 440 U.S. 935, 99 S. Ct. 1278, 59 L. Ed. 2d 493 (1979))*.

The requirement in *Davis* of allowing passengers to avoid the search by electing not to fly does not extend to a passenger who has already submitted his luggage for an x-ray scan. *Davis* requires notice, not actual knowledge, of the need to submit luggage for inspection. It was met here by evidence showing signs at the airport advised passengers of the luggage inspection. *See Henry at 1231*. Moreover, to accept Pulido's argument would circumvent the purpose of conducting pre-boarding searches. *See DeAngelo at 48*. A rule allowing a passenger to leave without a search after an inconclusive x-ray scan would encourage airline terrorism by providing a secure exit where detection was threatened. Also, an airport screening agent has a duty to ferret out firearms and explosive devices carried by passengers. *See Wehrli at 410*. This duty could not be fulfilled if the agent was prohibited from conducting a visual inspection and limited hand search after an inconclusive x-ray scan. *Id*. Thus, if a potential passenger chooses to avoid a search, he must elect not to fly before placing his baggage on the x-ray machine's conveyor belt. *See DeAngelo at 47-48*.

489

III.

THE STATEMENTS

Between the time Mr. McCurn was summoned and the subsequent hand search, Pulido made inculpatory statements to the effect that his briefcase contained cocaine. The district court suppressed the statements. In this, the district court's oral findings make it unclear whether the statements were suppressed on the basis that they were the fruit of the search or because they were the product of custodial questioning. Pulido, however, concedes he was not in custody at the time of the search. We therefore approach the question of the admissibility of the statements on the ground that they were the fruit of the search. In light of our holding that the search of Pulido's briefcase was not unreasonable, it follows that the inculpatory statements were not the product of an unconstitutional search requiring them to be suppressed.

REVERSED.

UNITED STATES OF AMERICA v. JOHN DOE, a/k/a GERONIMO
PIZARRO-CALDERON

UNITED STATES COURT OF APPEALS FOR THE FIRST
CIRCUIT

61 F.3d 107

August, 1995

CYR, *Circuit Judge.* Appellant Geronimo Pizarro-Calderon
("Pizarro") contends that the district court erred in refusing to suppress
six block-like articles packaged in opaque beige and brown tape which
ultimately led to his conviction for possessing cocaine with intent to
distribute in violation of *21 U.S.C. § 841(a)(1) (1993)*. We reverse.

I

BACKGROUND

The district court adopted the findings recommended by the
magistrate judge who conducted the suppression hearing. On January 8,
1993, Security Officer Gladys Martinez del Valle ("Martinez") was
screening passengers and monitoring their carry-on luggage for
weapons and explosives at a security checkpoint in the Isla Verde
Airport terminal. *See* 14 C.F.R. § 107.20 (1995) (Federal Aeronautics
Administration ("FAA") regulation mandating screening requirements
for carry-on luggage), § 107.21 (banning unauthorized possession of
any "explosive, incendiary, or deadly or dangerous weapons" beyond
airport checkpoints). Prominent signs forewarned passengers, in
English and Spanish, that their persons and carry-on luggage were
subject to screening and search for weapons and explosives. Security
screeners normally use x-ray machines to scan all carry-on luggage;
metal detectors and hand scanners to screen passengers.

While tending the x-ray monitor, Martinez noticed a carry-on bag
containing an unidentifiable dark object. She had been trained to regard
such dense, nonreflective objects as possible camouflage for weapons
or explosives. Upon questioning by Martinez, appellant Pizarro stated
that the carry-on bag belonged to him, and the nonreflective objects
inside were gift boxes containing "figurines." Concerned that the
figurines reflected no distinguishable silhouette on the x-ray monitor,
Martinez asked Pizarro to open the carry-on bag. When Pizarro "sort of
hesitated," United States Department of Agriculture Inspector Jose
Mercado, working beside Martinez, directed Pizarro to open the carry-
on bag, then summoned a local law enforcement officer, Juan Aviles, to
the security checkpoint.

Pizarro opened the carry-on bag in the presence of Martinez,
Officer Aviles, and Inspector Mercado, revealing a box wrapped in
Christmas paper. The box contained a layer of sanitary napkins, a layer
of dark blue paper and, finally, six blocks wrapped in opaque beige and
brown tape. A nineteen-year veteran of the Puerto Rico Police, Officer
Aviles immediately suspected that the concealed blocks contained
cocaine. Whereupon he seized the carry-on bag and its contents, then
arrested and handcuffed Pizarro.

After placing Pizarro in an airport police-station cell, Aviles contacted the United States Drug Enforcement Administration ("DEA"). Shortly thereafter, DEA agents tested the blocks by piercing their opaque wrappings; the contents tested positive for cocaine. In due course, Pizarro was indicted for possessing six kilograms of cocaine with intent to distribute, in violation of *21 U.S.C. § 841(a)(1), (b)(1)(A)*.

Pizarro moved to suppress the test results and the cocaine, on the ground that the warrantless searches of the carry-on bag and the containers inside it (i.e., the Christmas box and the blocks enclosed in intact, opaque wrapping) violated the *Fourth Amendment to the United States Constitution*. The government successfully defended the challenged DEA testing as a mere continuation of the administrative search aimed at ensuring airline security. *See United States v. Pizarro-Calderon, 829 F. Supp. 511, 515 (D.P.R. 1993)*. Following a jury trial, Pizarro was convicted and sentenced.

II

DISCUSSION

The government must demonstrate that the warrantless DEA testing of the enclosed blocks either entailed no *Fourth Amendment* search or came within some recognized exception to the warrant requirement. *See, e.g., United States v. Doward, 41 F.3d 789, 791 (1st Cir. 1994)*. The government contends that the carry-on bag initially was opened and searched at the airport security checkpoint pursuant to a lawful administrative search for weapons and explosives. *See, e.g., United States v. Skipwith, 482 F.2d 1272, 1277-78 (5th Cir. 1973)* (holding that inadvertent discovery of evidence of criminal activity in course of lawful security search for weapons at airport checkpoint does not violate *Fourth Amendment*). Further, it argues, once Pizarro's carry-on bag and the Christmas gift box lawfully had been opened for security purposes, it was proper to seize and open the packaged blocks thereby exposed to Aviles' "plain view." *See Coolidge v. New Hampshire, 403 U.S. 443, 466, 29 L. Ed. 2d 564, 91 S. Ct. 2022 (1971)*.

Pizarro protests on both counts. First, he says, carry-on luggage screenings must be confined to ferreting out threats to airline security (i.e., weapons and explosives used in air piracy), whereas the customary presence of Officer Aviles at the security checkpoint permitted an inference that security concerns were a mere subterfuge for intercepting contraband posing no threat to airline security. Second, even assuming probable cause to seize the suspicious blocks, a search warrant was required before the intact, opaque packaging enclosing the blocks could be pierced to test for cocaine.

A. *The Searches and Seizure at the Security Checkpoint*

Pizarro argues that the warrantless search of the carry-on bag violated his *Fourth Amendment* rights, *ab initio*, since the customary presence of Aviles at the checkpoint subverted an otherwise lawful airline security screening into a warrantless general search for contraband (viz., cocaine) unrelated to airline security. The district court found that

> the search was conducted by a security agent at the airport, and that the local police officer was summoned to the site of the search only *after* the initial X-ray scan did not rule out the presence of either weapons or explosives in defendant's luggage, requiring the presence of additional security.

Pizarro-Calderon, 829 F. Supp. at 514 (emphasis added).

Routine security searches at airport checkpoints pass constitutional muster because the compelling public interest in curbing air piracy generally outweighs their limited intrusiveness. *See, e.g., United States v. Pulido-Baquerizo, 800 F.2d 899, 902 (9th Cir. 1986); cf. United States v. Ferrer, 999 F.2d 7, 9 (1st Cir. 1993)* (upholding warrantless search of checked luggage on alternate ground of "abandonment," but faulting government's "falling-domino approach, by which each intrusion diminishes privacy expectations enough to permit further infringements"). Consequently, *all* carry-on luggage can be subjected to initial x-ray screening for weapons and explosives without offending the *Fourth Amendment*. In the event the initial x-ray screening is inconclusive as to the presence of weapons or explosives, the luggage may be hand-searched as reasonably required to rule out their presence. *Pulido-Baquerizo, 800 F.2d at 902.*

Other contraband inadvertently discovered during a routine checkpoint search for weapons and explosives may be seized and introduced in evidence at trial even though unrelated to airline security. *See, e.g., Skipwith, 482 F.2d at 1277-78.* On the other hand, lawful airline security searches of carry-on luggage may not be enlarged or tailored systemically to detect contraband (*e.g.,* narcotics) unrelated to airline security. *See, e.g., United States v. $ 124,570 U.S. Currency, 873 F.2d 1240, 1243-45 (9th Cir. 1989)* (upholding suppression of contraband unrelated to airline security where screeners were rewarded monetarily by law enforcement authorities for detecting such contraband in carry-on luggage).

As we conclude that the government failed to demonstrate that the *subsequent* warrantless search of the packaged blocks by the DEA satisfied the *Fourth Amendment* warrant requirement, *see infra* Section II.B, for present purposes we simply assume *arguendo* that the carry-on bag and the Christmas box were subjected to lawful airport administrative searches.

B. *The Subsequent DEA Searches of the Seized Blocks*

The district court upheld the warrantless penetration of the opaque packaging enclosing the seized blocks on the ground that the DEA tests were "not . . . searches *per se*" but merely "more thorough examinations of the objects which had already been lawfully seized." *Pizarro-Calderon, 829 F. Supp. at 515.* We cannot agree.

The uncontroverted evidence reveals that until the DEA agents conducted their field tests, the opaque packaging enclosing the six blocks remained intact, precluding any "plain view" of their contents such as might permit a warrantless search in the absence of exigent circumstances. *See, e.g., United States v. Miller, 769 F.2d 554, 558 (9th Cir. 1985)* (poking finger through plastic bag containing white powder, or cutting into opaque fiberglass container inside plastic bag, constitutes "search" requiring warrant, where both "containers were originally packed inside suitcase"). Thus, regardless whether the packaged blocks could have been subjected to lawful warrantless search *at the security checkpoint*, the question with which we are presented is whether a warrant was required before the packaging enclosing the blocks could be pierced once the blocks had been seized and *removed from the security checkpoint*. The government neither cites, nor have we found, any case upholding a warrantless administrative search for contraband unrelated to airline security concerns, absent exigent circumstances, consent, a finding of "virtual certainty," or some other recognized exception to the warrant requirement.

Although probable cause, as well as exigent circumstances, may support the warrantless *seizure* of an enclosed opaque container, *see Texas v. Brown, 460 U.S. 730, 743, 75 L. Ed. 2d 502, 103 S. Ct. 1535 (1983)* (involving validity of warrantless *seizure* of tied-off balloon containing drugs), the *same* probable-cause showing is not necessarily sufficient to justify its subsequent warrantless *search. Id. at 749-51* (Stevens, J., concurring); *United States v. Chadwick, 433 U.S. 1, 13-14 n.8, 53 L. Ed. 2d 538, 97 S. Ct. 2476 (1977)*; *Miller, 769 F.2d at 558*; *cf. United States v. Jacobsen, 466 U.S. 109, 114, 80 L. Ed. 2d 85, 104 S. Ct. 1652 (1984)* (upholding seizure to prevent loss or destruction of contraband, but noting that "*Fourth Amendment* requires that [the police] obtain a warrant before examining contents of such a package"). These discrete treatments stem from the recognition that seizure temporarily deprives the defendant of a *possessory* interest only, whereas a search entails an intrusion upon *privacy* interests as well. *See generally Segura v. United States, 468 U.S. 796, 806, 82 L. Ed. 2d 599, 104 S. Ct. 3380 (1984)*. Normally, therefore, once an exigency ends, as by an arrest or the seizure and custodial retention of a container by the police, a *neutral judicial officer* must authorize any subsequent search on a showing of probable cause. *United States v. Soule, 908 F.2d 1032, 1040 (1st Cir. 1990)* (citing *Shadwick v. City of Tampa, 407 U.S. 345, 350, 32 L. Ed. 2d 783, 92 S. Ct. 2119 (1972)*).

Although the government was required to show that any warrantless search was valid under an exception to the warrant requirement, *see Doward, 41 F.3d at 791; United States v. Rutkowski, 877 F.2d 139, 141 (1st Cir. 1989)*, it has not attempted to demonstrate that the warrantless piercing of the packaged blocks was either an integral part of the security-checkpoint search or came within any other exception to the warrant requirement. The government instead simply concludes, as did the district court, *see Pizarro-Calderon, 829 F. Supp. at 515*, and without argumentation or citation to authority, that the warrantless piercing of the packaged blocks at the police station was simply an extension of the hand-search initiated at the checkpoint. *But see supra* note 5. Moreover, the government does not pretend that the DEA agents pierced the packaged blocks for any purpose other than to test for illicit drugs. Thus, although we may affirm the denial of a suppression motion on any ground supported by the record, *see, e.g., Soule, 908 F.2d at 1036 n. 7*, the legal theories relied on by the government have led to a dearth of record evidence   not to mention argumentation to support such an exercise of discretion.

494

The litigation strategy adopted by the government seems especially remarkable considering the portentous district court opinion previously entered in the *companion* case, *United States v. Figueroa-Cruz, 822 F. Supp. 853 (D.P.R. 1993)*; *see supra* note 2, wherein the government elected not to appeal from an order suppressing virtually identical evidence seized from the person next in line to Pizarro at the security checkpoint. In the companion case, the district court suppressed the cocaine Figueroa was carrying in *Christmas gift packages* inside his luggage because Aviles had permitted the DEA to conduct the *initial* search at the airport police station without first obtaining a warrant. Aviles testified that he arrested Figueroa based on probable cause to believe that the gift boxes, exposed to view during the security-checkpoint search of his carry-on bag, were so similar to Pizarro's gift box that it was likely that they too contained blocks of cocaine.

The government's attempt to distinguish the two cases misses the mark. The carry-on bags, the gift boxes, and the blocks enclosed in opaque packaging *all* were discrete closed containers. Even assuming the warrantless checkpoint searches conducted on the carry-on bags and the gift boxes were lawful, the government nevertheless failed to establish that the subsequent warrantless DEA penetration of the previously unopened blocks enclosed in opaque packaging came within any recognized exception to the warrant requirement. Consequently, their warrantless search at the police station after any exigency had ceased violated the *Fourth amendment*.

III

CONCLUSION

As the government failed to shoulder its burden, by demonstrating either that its warrantless searches of the opaque packaged blocks were permissible under the *Fourth Amendment*, or that the admission of the tainted evidence was harmless beyond a reasonable doubt, *see United States v. Modarressi, 886 F.2d 6, 8 (1st Cir. 1989)*, appellant's conviction must be reversed.

The district court judgment is reversed.

UNITED STATES OF AMERICA v. DANIEL KUUALOHA AUKAI

UNITED STATES COURT OF APPEALS FOR THE NINTH CIRCUIT

497 F.3d 955

August, 2007

BEA, Circuit Judge:

More than 700 million passengers board commercial aircraft in the United States each year. The Transportation Security Administration ("TSA") is given the task of ensuring their safety, the safety of airline and airport personnel and, as the events of September 11, 2001, demonstrate, the safety of the general public from risks arising from commercial airplane flights. To do so, the TSA conducts airport screening searches of all passengers entering the secured area of the airport. We have previously held such airport screening searches are constitutionally reasonable administrative searches. Today we clarify that the reasonableness of such searches does not depend, in whole or in part, upon the consent of the passenger being searched.

I.

A.

On February 1, 2003, Daniel Kuualoha Aukai arrived at the Honolulu International Airport intending to take a Hawaiian Airlines flight from Honolulu, Hawaii, to Kona, Hawaii. He proceeded to check in at the ticket counter but did not produce a government-issued picture identification. Accordingly, the ticket agent wrote the phrase "No ID" on Aukai's boarding pass.

Aukai then proceeded to the security checkpoint, at which signs were posted advising prospective passengers that they and their carry-on baggage were subject to search. He entered the security checkpoint at approximately 9:00 a.m., placed his shoes and a few other items into a plastic bin, and voluntarily walked through the metal detector or magnetometer. The parties agree that the magnetometer did not signal the presence of metal as Aukai walked through it. Nor did his belongings trigger an alarm or otherwise raise suspicion as they passed through the x-ray machine. After walking through the magnetometer, Aukai presented his boarding pass to TSA Officer Corrine Motonaga.

Pursuant to TSA procedures, a passenger who presents a boarding pass on which "No ID" has been written is subject to secondary screening even if he has passed through the initial screening without triggering an alarm or otherwise raising suspicion. As it was performed here, secondary screening consists of a TSA officer passing a handheld magnetometer, known as a "wand," near and around the passenger's body. If the wand detects metal, it sounds an alarm. The TSA officer then discerns the cause of the alarm, using techniques such as feeling the outside of the passenger's clothes in the area that caused the alarm and, if that area is near a pocket, directing the passenger to empty his pocket.

Because Aukai's boarding pass had the "No ID" notation, Motonaga directed Aukai to a nearby, roped-off area for secondary screening. Aukai initially complied but complained that he was in a hurry to catch his flight which, according to the boarding pass, was scheduled to leave at 9:05 a.m., just a few minutes later. Although Aukai went to the roped-off area as directed, he did not stay there. When Motonaga noticed that Aukai had left the area and was gathering his belongings from the plastic bin, she instructed Aukai that he was not allowed to retrieve his property and that he had to stay in the roped-off area.

Aukai then appealed to TSA Officer Andrew Misajon, who was to perform the secondary screening, explaining again that he was in a hurry to catch his flight. Misajon nonetheless had Aukai sit in a chair and proceeded to use the wand to detect metal objects. At some point, Misajon had Aukai stand, and when Misajon passed the wand across the front of Aukai's body, the wand alarm was triggered at Aukai's front right pants pocket. Misajon asked Aukai if he had anything in his pocket, and Aukai responded that he did not. Misajon passed the wand over the pocket a second time; again the wand alarm was triggered. Misajon again inquired whether Aukai had anything in his pocket; again Aukai said he did not. Misajon then felt the outside of Aukai's pocket and concluded that something was inside the pocket. Misajon could also see the outline of an unknown object in Aukai's pocket. At some point during this screening process, Aukai informed Misajon that he no longer wished to board a plane and wanted to leave the airport.

At this point, TSA Supervisor Joseph Vizcarra approached Misajon and asked whether he needed assistance. Misajon related the events and Vizcarra asked Misajon to pass the wand over Aukai's pocket again. When the wand alarm again was triggered, Vizcarra directed Aukai to empty his pocket. Aukai again protested that he had nothing in his pocket. Using the back of his hand, Vizcarra touched the outside of Aukai's pocket and felt something in the pocket. He again directed Aukai to empty his pocket. This time Aukai reached into his pocket and removed either his keys or change, but a bulge was still visible in his pocket. Vizcarra directed Aukai to remove all contents from his pocket. After claiming at first that there was nothing more, Aukai finally removed an object wrapped in some form of tissue paper and placed it on a tray in front of him.

Suspecting that the object might be a weapon, Vizcarra summoned a nearby law enforcement officer. Vizcarra then unwrapped the object and discovered a glass pipe used to smoke methamphetamine. The law enforcement officer escorted Aukai to a small office near the security checkpoint. Aukai was placed under arrest and was searched incident to his arrest. During the search, the police discovered in Aukai's front pants pockets several transparent bags containing a white crystal substance. Aukai eventually was taken into federal custody, where he was advised of and waived his *Miranda* rights, and then gave a statement in which he inculpated himself in the possession of methamphetamine.

B.

Aukai was indicted for knowingly and intentionally possessing, with the intent to distribute, 50 grams or more of methamphetamine in violation of *21 U.S.C. § 841(a)* and *841(b)(1)(A)(viii)*. Aukai filed a motion to suppress the evidence found incident to his arrest at the airport and the statement he later made, which the district court denied.

Aukai then pleaded guilty pursuant to a written plea agreement that preserved his right to appeal the denial of his suppression motion. The district court sentenced Aukai to a term of imprisonment of 70 months and a term of supervised release of 5 years. Aukai timely appealed.

II.

We review de novo the district court's legal basis for denying a motion to suppress, but review the district court's findings of fact for clear error. *United States v. Marquez, 410 F.3d 612, 615 (9th Cir. 2005)* (as amended).

III.

The *Fourth Amendment* requires the government to respect "[t]he right of the people to be secure in their persons . . . and effects, against unreasonable searches and seizures." *U.S. Const. amend. IV.* "A search or seizure is ordinarily unreasonable in the absence of individualized suspicion of wrongdoing. While such suspicion is not an 'irreducible' component of reasonableness, [the Supreme Court has] recognized only limited circumstances in which the usual rule does not apply." *City of Indianapolis v. Edmond, 531 U.S. 32, 37, 121 S. Ct. 447, 148 L. Ed. 2d 333 (2000)* (citations omitted). However, "where the risk to public safety is substantial and real, blanket suspicionless searches calibrated to the risk may rank as 'reasonable'--for example, searches now routine at airports and at entrances to courts and other official buildings." *Chandler v. Miller, 520 U.S. 305, 323, 117 S. Ct. 1295, 137 L. Ed. 2d 513 (1997)* (holding Georgia's requirement that candidates for state office pass a drug test did not fit within this exception) (citing *Nat'l Treasury Employees Union v. Von Raab, 489 U.S. 656, 674-76, 109 S. Ct. 1384, 103 L. Ed. 2d 685 & n.3 (1989)* (upholding warrantless drug testing of employees applying for promotion to positions involving drug interdiction)). Thus, "where a *Fourth Amendment* intrusion serves special governmental needs, beyond the normal need for law enforcement, it is necessary to balance the individual's privacy expectations against the Government's interests to determine whether it is impractical to require a warrant or some level of individualized suspicion in the particular context." *Von Raab, 489 U.S. at 665-66.*

Under this rationale the Supreme Court has repeatedly upheld the constitutionality of so-called "administrative searches." In *New York v. Burger, 482 U.S. 691, 107 S. Ct. 2636, 96 L. Ed. 2d 601 (1987)*, the Supreme Court upheld the warrantless search of a junkyard's records, permits, and vehicles. The Supreme Court reasoned: "Because the owner or operator of commercial premises in a 'closely regulated' industry has a reduced expectation of privacy, the warrant and probable-cause requirements, which fulfill the traditional *Fourth Amendment* standard of reasonableness for a government search have lessened application . . . ." *Id. at 702* (internal citation omitted). Thus, New York's interest in regulating the junkyard industry, in light of the rise of motor-theft and comprehensive motor vehicle insurance premiums, served as a "special need" allowing inspection without a warrant. *Id. at 708-09; see also id. at 702.* The regulatory statute also provided a "constitutionally adequate substitute for a warrant" because the statute informed junkyard operators that inspections would be made on a regular basis and limited the discretion of inspecting officers. *Id. at 711.*

In *Michigan Department of State Police v. Sitz, 496 U.S. 444, 110 S. Ct. 2481, 110 L. Ed. 2d 412 (1990)*, Sitz challenged the constitutionality of suspicionless sobriety checkpoints conducted on Michigan's highways, contending that the program violated the *Fourth Amendment's* protection against unreasonable seizures. *Id. at 447-48.* The Supreme Court upheld the sobriety checkpoints because "the balance of the State's interest in preventing drunken driving, the extent to which [the sobriety checkpoints] can reasonably be said to advance that interest, and the degree of intrusion upon individual motorists who are briefly stopped, weighs in favor of" finding the sobriety checkpoints constitutionally reasonable. *Id. at 455.*

Significantly, the Supreme Court has held that the constitutionality of administrative searches is not dependent upon consent. In *United States v. Biswell, 406 U.S. 311, 92 S. Ct. 1593, 32 L. Ed. 2d 87 (1972)*, the Supreme Court upheld the warrantless search of a pawn shop owner's gun storeroom. The search was authorized by a federal gun control statute. The Court held that, "[i]n the context of a regulatory inspection system of business premises that is carefully limited in time, place, and scope, the legality of the search depends not on consent but on the authority of a valid statute." *Id. at 315.* Thus, "[w]hen a [gun] dealer chooses to engage in this pervasively regulated business and to accept a federal license, he does so with the knowledge that his business records, firearms, and ammunition will be subject to effective inspection." *Id. at 316..*

We have held that airport screening searches, like the one at issue here, are constitutionally reasonable administrative searches because they are "conducted as part of a general regulatory scheme in furtherance of an administrative purpose, namely, to prevent the carrying of weapons or explosives aboard aircraft, and thereby to prevent hijackings." *United States v. Davis, 482 F.2d 893, 908 (9th Cir. 1973); see also United States v. Hartwell, 436 F.3d 174, 178 (3d Cir.), cert. denied, 127 S. Ct. 111, 166 L. Ed. 2d 255 (2006);Marquez, 410 F.3d at 616.* Our case law, however, has erroneously suggested that the reasonableness of airport screening searches is dependent upon consent, either ongoing consent or irrevocable implied consent.

The constitutionality of an airport screening search, however, does not depend on consent, *see Biswell, 406 U.S. at 315*, and requiring that a potential passenger be allowed to revoke consent to an ongoing airport security search makes little sense in a post-9/11 world. Such a rule would afford terrorists multiple opportunities to attempt to penetrate airport security by "electing not to fly" on the cusp of detection until a vulnerable portal is found. This rule would also allow terrorists a low-cost method of detecting systematic vulnerabilities in airport security, knowledge that could be extremely valuable in planning future attacks. Likewise, given that consent is not required, it makes little sense to predicate the reasonableness of an administrative airport screening search on an irrevocable implied consent theory. Rather, where an airport screening search is otherwise reasonable and conducted pursuant to statutory authority, *49 U.S.C. § 44901*, all that is required is the passenger's election to attempt entry into the secured area of an airport. *See Biswell, 406 U.S. at 315; 49 C.F.R. § 1540.107.* Under current TSA regulations and procedures, that election occurs when a prospective passenger walks through the magnetometer or places items on the conveyor belt of the x-ray machine. The record

499

establishes that Aukai elected to attempt entry into the posted secured area of Honolulu International Airport when he walked through the magnetometer, thereby subjecting himself to the airport screening process.

To the extent our cases have predicated the reasonableness of an airport screening search upon either ongoing consent or irrevocable implied consent, they are overruled.

IV.

Although the constitutionality of airport screening searches is not dependent on consent, the scope of such searches is not limitless. A particular airport security screening search is constitutionally reasonable provided that it "is no more extensive nor intensive than necessary, in the light of current technology, to detect the presence of weapons or explosives [ ] [and] that it is confined in good faith to that purpose." *Davis, 482 F.2d at 913*. We conclude that the airport screening search of Aukai satisfied these requirements.

The search procedures used in this case were neither more extensive nor more intensive than necessary under the circumstances to rule out the presence of weapons or explosives. After passing through a magnetometer, Aukai was directed to secondary screening because his boarding pass was marked "No ID." Aukai then underwent a standard "wanding procedure." When the wand alarm sounded as the wand passed over Aukai's front right pants pocket, TSA Officer Misajon did not reach into Aukai's pocket or feel the outside of Aukai's pocket. Rather, Misajon asked Aukai if he had something in his pocket. When Aukai denied that there was anything in his pocket, Misajon repeated the wanding procedure. Only after the wand alarm again sounded and Aukai again denied having anything in his pocket did Misajon employ a more intrusive search procedure by feeling the outside of Aukai's pocket and determining that there was something in there.

At that point, TSA Supervisor Vizcarra became involved. Vizcarra asked Misajon to pass the wand over Aukai's pocket again. When the wand alarm again sounded, Vizcarra directed Aukai to empty his pocket. Aukai again protested that he had nothing in his pocket. Using the back of his hand, Vizcarra touched the outside of Aukai's pocket and felt something inside. Vizcarra again directed Aukai to empty his pocket. This time Aukai reached into his pocket and removed either his keys or change, but a bulge was still visible in his pocket. Vizcarra directed Aukai to remove all contents from his pocket. After first claiming there was nothing more, Aukai removed an object wrapped in some form of tissue paper and placed it on a tray in front of him. Suspecting that the item might be a weapon, Vizcarra unwrapped the item, discovering drug paraphernalia.

Like the Third Circuit, we find these search procedures to be minimally intrusive. *See Hartwell, 436 F.3d at 180* (holding similar search procedures to be "minimally intrusive," explaining that the procedures are "well-tailored to protect personal privacy, escalating in invasiveness only after a lower level of screening disclosed a reason to conduct a more probing search").

The duration of the detention associated with this airport screening search was also reasonable. Witnesses testified that Aukai entered the checkpoint area at approximately 9:00 a.m. and that the entire search at issue--starting from when Aukai walked through the checkpoint until the TSA's efforts to rule out the presence of a weapon resulted in the discovery of drug paraphernalia--took no more than 18 minutes. Although longer than detentions approved in other cases, *see, e.g., Sitz, 496 U.S. at 448* (average delay of 25 seconds); *United States v. Martinez-Fuerte, 428 U.S. 543, 546-47, 96 S. Ct. 3074, 49 L. Ed. 2d 1116 (1976)* (average detention of 3-5 minutes), the length of Aukai's detention was reasonable, especially in light of Aukai's conduct, because it was not prolonged beyond the time reasonably required to rule out the presence of weapons or explosives. *See Illinois v. Caballes, 543 U.S. 405, 407, 125 S. Ct. 834, 160 L. Ed. 2d 842 (2005)* (stating that a seizure can become unlawful if it is "prolonged beyond the time reasonably required to complete [its] mission").

Accordingly, we hold that the airport screening search of Aukai was a constitutionally reasonable administrative search.

AFFIRMED.

CONCUR BY: Susan P. Graber

GRABER, Circuit Judge, with whom HAWKINS and WARDLAW, Circuit Judges, join, specially concurring:

I concur in the result and nearly all of the reasoning in the majority opinion. I write separately, however, because I cannot join the majority's irrelevant and distracting references to 9/11 and terrorists. Daniel Aukai is no terrorist and yet, whether in 1997 or 2007, the search that law enforcement personnel conducted of his person falls squarely within the confines of a reasonable administrative search.

The majority holds, and I agree, that once a passenger enters the secured area of an airport, the constitutionality of a screening search does not depend on consent. That legal conclusion rests firmly on Supreme Court precedent and on the government's interest in ensuring the safety of passengers, airline personnel, and the general public. For decades, nefarious individuals have tried to use commercial aircraft to further a personal or political agenda at the expense of those on board and on the ground. And the threat continues to exist that individuals, whether members of an organized group or not, may attempt to do the same. In my view, references to a "post-9/11 world," maj. op. at 9657, do not advance the analysis. Nor is there any legal significance to whether or not an individual is a terrorist. *See* maj. op. at 9657-59. By relying on those factors, the majority unnecessarily makes its solid holding dependent on the existence of the current terrorist threat, inviting future litigants to retest the viability of that holding.

UNITED STATES OF AMERICA v. DAJER CUEVAS-REYES, and
ELUID GOMEZ-GARCIA.

Criminal No. 2007-66

UNITED STATES DISTRICT COURT FOR THE DISTRICT OF
THE VIRGIN ISLANDS, DIVISION OF ST. THOMAS AND ST.
JOHN

February, 2008

MEMORANDUM OPINION

(February 25, 2008)

Before the Court is the motion of Eliud Gomez-Garcia ("Gomez-Garcia"), joined by Dajer Cuevas-Reyes ("Cuevas-Reyes") (together, the "Defendants"), to suppress all evidence obtained as a result of the search and seizure of an airplane on November 20, 2007. Additionally, Gomez-Garcia moves to suppress any statements he made to the officers after his arrest. A suppression hearing was conducted in this matter on January 31, 2008. At the conclusion of the hearing, the Court denied the motion to suppress. This Memorandum Opinion memorializes the Court's January 31, 2008, ruling.

I. FACTS

On November 20, 2007, Customs and Border Patrol Officer Williams Santiago was patrolling the Cyril E. King airport in St. Thomas, U.S. Virgin Islands. On that day, Officer Santiago was investigating a tip that people would be transporting illegal aliens to and from St. Thomas on small private aircraft. Pursuant to the tip, Officer Santiago was instructed to patrol the north runway.

While conducting surveillance, Officer Santiago saw people boarding a small privately owned airplane on the north runway. The plane's engines were running, and after the last person boarded it began to taxi down the runway for takeoff. Officer Santiago called the air traffic control tower and asked that the tower deny takeoff so he could perform an "enforcement boarding." At the suppression hearing, Officer Santiago explained that an "enforcement boarding" involved the Customs and Border Patrol officers boarding an aircraft to ensure that it had an accurate passenger manifest declaring the identities and nationalities of all the passengers on board.

After takeoff was denied, the plane returned to the place where it was originally idling. Officer Santiago approached the airplane and asked the pilot, Gomez-Garcia, to step out of the aircraft, Gomez-Garcia complied. Officer Santiago asked Gomez-Garcia to state his name, destination, and asked for a passenger declaration. Gomez-Garcia responded that they were headed to Santo Domingo, Dominican Republic, and that they did not have a passenger declaration. Officer Santiago then asked the five passengers of the airplane to get out of the plane. The passengers included Cuevas-Reyes, as well as four females.

Officer Santiago asked one of the female passengers where she was from. The passenger admitted that she was from Santo Domingo and was present in the U.S. Virgin Islands illegally. The other three women also indicated that they were citizens of the Dominican Republic, and were unlawfully present in the U.S. Virgin Islands. Thereafter, all six people were transported to the Customs and Border Patrol facility at the airport.

At the Customs and Border Patrol facility, Gomez-Garcia told the officers that he wanted a Spanish interpreter. Gomez-Garcia was advised of his rights in Spanish. The interpreter then asked Gomez-Garcia in Spanish whether he understood the *Miranda* warnings, and Gomez-Garcia responded in the affirmative. The officers also gave Gomez-Garcia an explanation of rights form in Spanish, which he was allowed to read twice. Gomez-Garcia verbally confirmed in Spanish that he understood the explanation of rights form, and then signed the form. Thereafter, Gomez-Garcia gave a statement to the officers.

A criminal complaint was filed against the Defendants on November 21, 2007, charging them with unlawfully harboring and transporting illegal aliens. The complaint was followed by an indictment, which was returned by the grand jury on December 6, 2007.

II. ANALYSIS

A. Evidence

The Defendants argue that the stop of the aircraft on November 20, 2007, and their subsequent arrests, occurred in violation of their rights under the *Fourth Amendment*. They claim that any evidence obtained as a result of the search and seizure of the airplane should be suppressed as the fruit of the poisonous tree.

The *Fourth Amendment* protects citizens "against unreasonable searches and seizures." *U.S. Const., amend. IV*. "What is reasonable depends upon all of the circumstances surrounding the search or seizure and the nature of the search or seizure itself." *United States v. Montoya de Hernandez, 473 U.S. 531, 537, 105 S.Ct. 3304, 87 L.Ed.2d 381 (1985)*. There is a presumptive requirement that searches or seizures be carried out pursuant to a warrant. *See Katz v. United States, 389 U.S. 347, 357, 88 S.Ct. 507, 19 L.Ed.2d 576 (1967)* ("[S]earches conducted outside the judicial process, without prior approval by judge or magistrate, are *per se* unreasonable under the *Fourth Amendment* -- subject only to a few specifically established and well-delineated exceptions.") (internal citations omitted)).

In some instances, warrantless searches or seizures will be considered reasonable if based on probable cause. *See Hill v. California, 401 U.S. 797, 804, 91 S.Ct. 1106, 28 L.Ed.2d 484 (1971)* ("[S]ufficient probability, not certainty, is the touchstone of reasonableness under the *Fourth Amendment...* ."). For example, the police may search a vehicle without a warrant if they have probable cause to do so. *Ornelas v. United States, 517 U.S. 690, 693, 116 S.Ct. 1657, 134 L.Ed 2d 911 (1996)*. The police may also lawfully arrest a suspect without a warrant if the officer has probable cause to believe the suspect has committed a felony and the arrest does not occur in the suspect's home. *See Maryland v. Pringle, 540 U.S. 366, 373-74, 124 S.Ct. 795, 157 L.Ed.2d 769 (2003)* (upholding a warrant-less arrest where the police had probable cause to believe the defendant had committed a felony after they found cocaine within his reach).

Probable cause exists where the totality of the circumstances known to the officers at the time supported a fair probability that the suspect had committed or was committing a crime. *See Ornelas, 517 U.S. at 696; Beck v. Ohio, 379 U.S. 89, 91, 85 S.Ct. 223, 13 L.Ed.2d 142 (1964); Brinegar v. United States, 338 U.S. 160, 175-76, 69 S.Ct. 1302, 93 L.Ed. 1879 (1949)*. Whether probable cause exists is an objective inquiry. *See Whren v. United States, 517 U.S. 806, 813, 116 S.Ct. 1769, 135 L.Ed.2d 89 (1996)* ("Subjective intentions play no role in ordinary, probable-cause *Fourth Amendment* analysis.").

Even without probable cause, an officer may "stop and briefly detain a person for investigative purposes if the officer has a reasonable suspicion supported by articulable facts that criminal activity 'may be afoot.'" *United States v. Sokolow, 490 U.S. 1, 7, 109 S.Ct. 1581, 104 L.Ed.2d 1 (1989)* (quoting *Terry v. Ohio, 392 U.S. 1, 30, 88 S.Ct. 1868, 20 L.Ed.2d 889 (1968))*. Similarly, an officer may stop a moving vehicle to investigate a reasonable and articulable suspicion that its occupants were involved in criminal activity. *Ornelas, 517 U.S. at 693; United States v. Hensley, 469 U.S. 221, 226-27, 105 S.Ct. 675, 83 L.Ed.2d 604 (1985)*.

Reasonable suspicion has been characterized as "a particularized and objective basis for suspecting the person stopped of criminal activity." *Ornelas, 517 U.S. at 695* (quotations omitted). Courts must look to the totality of the circumstances of each case to determine whether reasonable suspicion exists. *United States v. Arvizu, 534 U.S. 266, 273-74, 122 S.Ct. 744, 151 L.Ed.2d 740 (2002)*. Law enforcement officers may use their own training and experience "to make inferences ... and deductions about the cumulative information available to them that might well elude an untrained person." *Id.* (citations and quotations omitted). Reasonable suspicion may not, however, be based on an officer's hunch alone. *Id. at 274*. The likelihood of criminal activity required for reasonable suspicion is lower than that required for probable cause. *Id.* Additionally, "[a] determination that reasonable suspicion exists ... need not rule out the possibility of innocent conduct." *Id. at 277*.

Here, Officer Santiago was investigating a tip that similar aircraft would be unlawfully transporting illegal aliens using the north runway of the Cyril E. King airport in St. Thomas. Officer Santiago then observed a small, twin-engine aircraft fitting the description of the aircraft described in the tip, on the same runway as indicated in the tip. Additionally, the plane's engines were running, and Officer Santiago concluded that the plane was preparing for takeoff. Based on the totality of the circumstances, Officer Santiago had reasonable suspicion to make the initial stop of the airplane. *See United States v. Sharpe, 470 U.S. 675, 682 n.3, 105 S.Ct. 1568, 84 L.Ed.2d 605 (1985)* (finding reasonable suspicion based on an officer's observation that a truck had a camper shell similar to those often used to transport drugs that was driving with a car and evading police); *see also Arvizu, 534 U.S. at 274* (explaining that the degree of certainty required to establish reasonable suspicion is less than that required for probable cause). Because there was objectively reasonable suspicion to stop the aircraft, the initial stop of all of its occupants was also lawful. *See, e.g., Maryland v. Wilson, 519 U.S. 408, 414, 117 S.Ct. 882, 137 L.Ed.2d 41 (1997)* (holding that officers could not only stop passengers but order them out of the vehicle during a lawful stop without violating their *Fourth Amendment* rights).

Accordingly, Officer Santiago could properly stop the aircraft to confirm or dispel his suspicion that it was engaged in criminal activity.

Immediately upon asking the passengers of the aircraft basic questions such as their names and destinations, all four of the female passengers told Officer Santiago that they were illegally in the U.S. Virgin Islands and were traveling to Santo Domingo. The admissions of the women combined with the totality of the circumstances described above gave Officer Santiago probable cause to search and seize the aircraft, and to arrest Gomez-Garcia and Cuevas-Reyes. *See, e.g., United States v. Laville, 480 F.3d 187, 48 V.I. 1012 (3d Cir. 2007)* (holding that probable cause existed to arrest the defendant for alien smuggling offenses where, while investigating a tip that a boat had run aground in the harbor and illegal aliens were coming ashore, the officer saw such a boat in the harbor, and a group of persons sitting nearby on the boardwalk identified themselves as Cubans who had come off the boat, amongst other facts). Accordingly, any evidence seized as a result of searching the airplane was obtained as a result of a lawful search.

B. Statements

Gomez-Garcia also argues that the statements he made to the agents at the Customs and Border Patrol office after his arrest should be suppressed.

Statements obtained during the custodial interrogation of a defendant who has not been read his *Miranda* rights are inadmissible at trial. *See Miranda v. Arizona, 384 U.S. 436, 479, 86 S.Ct. 1602, 16 L.Ed.2d 694 (1966)*. Two elements must be present for *Miranda* to apply. First, the defendant must have been in police custody at the time the statements were made. *See, e.g., Yarborough v. Alvarado, 541 U.S. 652, 662-63, 124 S. Ct. 2140, 158 L. Ed. 2d 938 (2004)* (holding that custody for *Miranda* purposes is determined by examining the totality of the circumstances surrounding interrogation and determining whether a reasonable person would have felt free to terminate the interrogation and leave). A defendant who is under arrest is clearly in custody. *See Orozco v. Texas, 394 U.S. 324, 329, 89 S.Ct. 1095, 22 L.Ed.2d 311 (1969)* ("Once arrest occurs, the application of *Miranda*, is automatic."). Second, the police must have interrogated the defendant, which includes not only direct questioning, but any words or actions that the police should know are reasonably likely to elicit an incriminating response. *Rhode Island v. Innis, 446 U.S. 291, 301-02, 100 S.Ct. 1682, 64 L.Ed.2d 297 (1980)*.

A defendant who has been advised of his *Miranda* rights may waive them, as long as such waiver is knowing, intelligent, and voluntary under the totality of the circumstances. *See Moran v. Burbine, 475 U.S. 412, 422-23, 106 S.Ct. 1135, 89 L.Ed.2d 410 (1986)*. "The prosecution bears the burden of proving, at least by a preponderance of the evidence, the *Miranda* waiver ... . " *Missouri v. Seibert, 542 U.S. 600, 609, 124 S.Ct. 2601, 159 L.Ed.2d 643 (2004)* (citation omitted). "The voluntariness of a waiver of [the *Fifth Amendment*] privilege has always depended on the absence of police overreaching, not on 'free choice' in any broader sense of the word." *Colorado v. Connelly, 479 U.S. 157, 170, 107 S.Ct. 515, 93 L.Ed.2d 473 (1986)* (reasoning that the *Fifth Amendment* is solely concerned with protection from governmental coercion). Either physical or psychological coercion by law enforcement may render a *Miranda* waiver involuntary. *Miller v. Fenton, 796 F.2d 598, 604 (3d Cir. 1986)*.

Here, Gomez-Garcia was clearly in police custody when he made a statement to the agents. The agents were therefore required to advise Gomez-Garcia of his rights to remain silent and to counsel before subjecting him to interrogation. The evidence in this case shows that Gomez-Garcia was read his rights in his native language of Spanish, after specifically requesting a Spanish interpreter. He also verbally confirmed that he understood his rights, and waived his rights in writing. There is nothing in the record to suggest that the warnings given to Gomez-Garcia were defective in any way. Nor is there any evidence showing that Gomez-Garcia was subjected to repeated or prolonged questioning at the time he waived his rights, or when he made his statements.

Given the totality of the circumstances, the Court finds that Gomez-Garcia knowingly, intelligently, and voluntarily waived his *Miranda* rights. *See, e.g., Moran, 475 U.S. at 422-23* (validating the defendant's waiver of his *Miranda* rights because such waiver was uncoerced, the defendant knew he could remain silent and request a lawyer, and he was aware of the government's intention to use his statements against him); *Miller, 796 F.2d at 611-12* (holding that a defendant's confession was voluntary, despite police interrogation tactics aimed at winning the defendant's trust and making him feel more comfortable about confession); *United States v. Lux, 905 F.2d 1379, 1382 (10th Cir. 1990)* (finding the defendant's statements voluntary, notwithstanding the fact that the detective lied to the defendant about her codefendant's statement, leaned over and hit his fist on the table, and accused the defendant of lying).

III. CONCLUSION

For the foregoing reasons, the Court will deny the Defendants' motion to suppress in its entirety. An appropriate order follows.

ORDER

Before the Court is the motion of Eliud Gomez-Garcia ("Gomez-Garcia"), joined by Dajer Cuevas-Reyes ("Cuevas-Reyes") (together, the "Defendants"), to suppress all evidence obtained as a result of the search and seizure of an airplane on November 20, 2007. Additionally, Gomez-Garcia moves to suppress the statements he made to the officers after his arrest. For the reasons stated in the Memorandum Opinion of even date, it is hereby

ORDERED that the motion to suppress is DENIED in its entirety.

CPSIA information can be obtained
at www.ICGtesting.com
Printed in the USA
LVHW051409180620
658396LV00001B/1

9 780757 560002